William Burgh

An Inquiry into the Belief of the Christians of the first three centuries

Respecting the one Godhead of the Father, Son and Holy Ghost

William Burgh

An Inquiry into the belief of the Christians of the first three centuries
Respecting the one Godhead of the Father, Son and Holy Ghost

ISBN/EAN: 9783337284213

Printed in Europe, USA, Canada, Australia, Japan

Cover: Foto ©Lupo / pixelio.de

More available books at **www.hansebooks.com**

AN INQUIRY

INTO THE

BELIEF of the CHRISTIANS

OF THE

FIRST THREE CENTURIES,

RESPECTING THE

ONE GODHEAD

OF THE

FATHER, SON, and HOLY GHOST.

BEING A

SEQUEL

TO A

SCRIPTURAL CONFUTATION

OF THE

Rev. Mr. LINDSEY's late APOLOGY.

By WILLIAM BURGH, Esq.

QUANQUAM APUD BONOS JUDICES SATIS HABEANT FIRMITATIS
VEL TESTIMONIA SINE ARGUMENTIS, VEL ARGUMENTA SINE
TESTIMONIIS; NOS TAMEN NON CONTENTI ALTERUTRO SU-
MUS, CUM SUPPETAT NOBIS UTRUMQUE, NE CUI PERVERSE
INGENUOSO AUT NON INTELLIGENDI AUT CONTRA DISSE-
RENDI LOCUM RELINQUAMUS.   LACTANTIUS.

YORK:
Printed by A. WARD, for the AUTHOR, and sold by
W. NICOLL, in St. Paul's Church-Yard, London.
MDCCLXXVIII.

Advertisement.

THE intention of the following work is to confute a claim laid by Unitarians to the prescriptive concurrence of all the Christians of the first three centuries, in those tenets which they now entertain themselves.———To this end the doctrines professed by every several Christian who flourished within that period, and who has transmitted an account of his belief to us, are, in a faithful translation, stated from his own writings: And in the margin throughout, in order not only to vouch for my fidelity, but to assist in the correction of any errour into which I may have unconsciously lapsed, the original language of the writer, from whom the extracts are made, is annexed; or if this has not come to my hands, such antient versions as have obtained credit are quoted; not, however, without some note of discrimination by which the reader is apprized that the language is in the instance not original.

To each century a chapter is assigned; and thus the writers of the primitive Church, arranged in a chronological series, appear in due succession before the reader, and each is in his own language heard, not only to make profeſſion of that faith which he in reality embraced, but many, by aſſertions directly oppoſed to ſuch ſyſtems as might have coincided with, or borne a ſimilitude to, modern Unitarianiſm, to enter, as it were, their ſolemn proteſtation againſt the doctrines which they in reality abjured. The reading alſo which they received, and the ſenſe in which they accepted, the declarations of the holy Scripture are occaſionally ſtated; and in this point of enquiry their authority is nothing leſs than concluſive.

I am not conſcious of having omitted to enquire into the ſentiments of any Chriſtian writer; and as a corroboratory proof of the doctrines they were generally underſtood to teach or to avow, I have ſubjoined to the whole, in a ſeparate chapter, ſuch obſervations as were made upon the religious tenets of the early Church, by thoſe Heathen or Jewiſh authors, who have in any particular manner adverted to them.

The reader ſhould be here apprized of what he will find frequently urged in the Body of the work: The members of the primitive Church are not produced in evidence

dence of the Godhead of the Father, Son, and Holy Ghost; to so large an inference their uninspired assertions are not considered as by any means adequate. They are only called upon to authenticate that verdict which they, to whom the evidence of the Scripture was first referred, originally returned upon it, but which has been lately misrepresented to the world, in order to obtain a judgement, not bearing any reference to the relinquished evidence itself, but grounded upon an absolute falsification of the primary verdict. When, therefore, it is known to the reader, that an appeal has been thus made from the word of God to the sense in which it was received by the early Church, he will probably deem the present enquiry into that sense, not only important, but even necessary, in order to rescue the indolent and *unlearned* from the consequences of these fallacious assertions concerning the primitive faith; and should his own good sense cause him to acquiesce in the Scriptures alone, he cannot be displeased to see that men, who had no other source to draw from than the pure and uncorrupted word, and who were therefore uninfluenced by those prejudices, which are unfairly objected by Unitarians

to

to the members of an established Church, concurred with himself in judgement upon every article of the Christian Religion that has here come under our investigation.

As I have proceeded rather to shew the tenets of each Father separately, than to draw together the sentiments of all to each particular point, the argument must appear less accumulated than it might otherwise have been rendered. To remedy this necessary defect I have, for the most part, annexed references to similar passages, by which they may be turned to with ease; and by an Index, in the nature of a Concordance, have, in the end, brought together all the concurrent assertions of antiquity which, in the tenour of the work, are placed at a distance from one another. In the conduct of this Index, as I know not of any names by which the Articles of our Faith are so generally called, that alphabetical order could have assisted enquiry, I have assumed that order in which they have been already arranged in the Creed ascribed to St. Athanasius, which is of easy access, and is universally known to the members of the Church of England.—It is a common practice with Unitarians to
elude

elude the force of an expreffion which they cannot fubvert, by depreciating its value, and affirming that "if inftead of the terms ufed, fuch and fuch other words had been fubftituted, the meaning of the paffage had then indeed been clearly againft themfelves; but that as the cafe now ftands, there is room for a doubt whether the author intended to glorify our Saviour, &c." In order, to facilitate the overthrow of all objections of this nature, I have annexed another Index, referring to the original language of antiquity, by the means of which the reader may, with greater eafe, advert to the feveral paffages, in which the early writers have not only ufed the expreffions objected to in a fenfe that refufes the reftrictions contended for, but in which they have actually employed that very language to which the Unitarian has himfelf allowed the neceffity of yielding, provided only it were feen to be the language of the primitive ages.

If the bulk of thofe enormous tomes, whence the following pages have been extracted, be taken under confideration, the fize of the prefent volume, which is in a manner their offspring, will not require
any

any other apology. I muſt, however, acknowledge that it very greatly exceeds my own original idea. When I commenced the work, I intended no more than to lay a few confutatory aſſertions before the public; and thus, by the deduction of a part, to deſtroy a propoſition which was univerſal, and which could, therefore, not be true, if it were ſeen to comprehend a falſehood. The aſcertainment of the ſenſe in which ſome diſputed texts of Scripture had been accepted by men, to the greater part of whom the language in which they are written was native, came alſo within the compaſs of my deſign. But as I proceeded in the execution of this ſcheme, there were many perſons occupied in projecting farther employment for me, and the diligent adverſaries of our religion ſupplied new ſubjects for confutation. A book, ſuch as mine is, like the architecture of a fortification which the enemy neceſſitates, not the builder conceives, muſt derive its form and extent from the caprice of its opponent, rather than the preconcerted plan of its writer; the mode of attack preſcribes and aſcertains the mode of defence.—In few words, finding myſelf poſſeſſed of means effectually to ſubvert the moſt ſpecious aſſertions of the Unitarian,

tarian, and still able to oppose some explicit declaration of antiquity against whatever he might urge in behalf of his unbelief, I did not chuse to leave even the shadow of an argument undispelled; and under this encouragement, at length determined to relinquish the narrow limits I had originally prescribed to myself, and pursue the steps of the adversary, let them conduct me whithersoever they would.—This resolution, together with my former assurance, that at the time of publishing the Scriptural Confutation of Mr. Lindsey's Apology I was an entire stranger to the fathers, may likewise account for the length of the interval between my former and the present publication; besides which, there is nothing in the writers from whom I have collected the materials of this work so very alluring as should engage me in an uninterrupted perusal of their unclassical pages. The fact is, I have frequently been repulsed by fatigue and disgust, and the work has, by consequence, been frequently suspended.

Let not this exception, however, be understood to extend beyond their style; for although they did not possess the graces of diction, their matter is for the moſt part profound, and well worthy of purſuit; their learning is extenſive, their judgement ſolid, their reaſoning acute and concluſive, and their integrity unblemiſhed. I ſpeak of them in ſuch general terms as may beſt comprehend them all; for it were foreign from my ſubject to diſcriminate among their ſeveral characters, and aſſign to each the peculiar points by which he ſtands diſtinguiſhed from the reſt.

It is preſumed, that if the ſame articles, and the ſame arguments to maintain them, be found to recur under ſeveral heads, I may yet be allowed to ſtand exempt from a charge of tautology; an irrefragable proof that the Fathers all concur in doctrine, can hardly be conſidered as a defect in a book written expreſsly with a view to prove the concurrence of the Fathers.

I have not, by any means, ſought to lay before the world a chaſtiſed compoſition; to convince, not to amuſe, has been my ſole endeavour; my ſole object in an arduous and laborious undertaking, the advantage of my reader; and my end, I ſhall conſider as happily attained to, if I
ſhall

shall decide the judgement of even a single hesitating Christian. With this declaration it were inconsistent to apologize for any defects of style, or even such aukward expressions as may have escaped my pen, and subsequent correction, but do not disturb the sense of the passage in which they occur; for such, and every literary fault of a similar nature, I accordingly refuse to make any apology whatsoever; and with all due contempt for that malevolence of criticism which I have already experienced, and perfectly indifferent to the frivolous censures of such as will neither hear me for my cause, nor have respect to my cause that they may hear, I address myself only to the candid reader, who, respecting the great end alone, will, I humbly confide, extend a ready pardon to all defects which do not obstruct the general question. Of him indeed I seek for indulgence to this endeavour to maintain the princples of the Christian Religion; to him, with submission and with great truth, I address the plea and supplication of the Poet,

Da veniam scriptis, quorum non gloria nobis
 Caussa, sed utilitas, officiumque fuit.

ERRATA.

Page 32, line 9 of the note, *for* benedicts *read* benedictus.
P. 48, l. 1 of the note, *for* eft *read* es.
P. 72, l. 1 of the note, *for* fpiritatis *read* fpiritalis.
P. 83, l. 1 of the fecond nore, *for* κοινυμιν *read* κοινωνωμιν.
P. 83, l. 1 of ditto, *for* γνωριζονlες *read* γνωριζονlες.
P. 84, l. 21 of the note, *for* conflicatione *read* conflictatione.
P. 87, l. 1 of the laft note, *for* ἵ *read* ἃ.
P. 92, l. 5 of the note, *for* παϑὰ *read* πάϑας.
P. 121, l. 3 of the note, *for* hominum *read* hominem.
P. 124, l. 14, to confefs *dele* to.
P. 140, l. 1 of the laft note, *for* alià *read* alia.
P. 166, l. 1 of the third note, *for* πῷ *read* τῷ.
P. 176, l. 5 ditto, *for* only begotten *read* connatural.
P. 180, l. 19, of the 3d note, *for* acknowlege *read* acknowledges.
P. 187, l. 2 of the note, *for* fcripturam *read* fcripturarum.
P. 190, l. 2 of the fecond note, *for* honoraffent r. adoraffent.
P. 251, l. laft of the note, *for* 285 *read* 385.
P. 358, l. 2 of the 4th note, *for* παρειληφότες r. παρειληφότις.
P. 369, l. 2 of the 2d note, *for* της *read* τῇ.
P. 384, l. laft of the note, *for* de âvere *read* de verâ.

I have not obferved any other miftakes which the eye of a reader cannot at once correct.—The difficulty of fuperintending the typography of Greek accents muft be admitted as an excufe for any errours that may have happened with refpect to them.—It is hoped there are not many, and of thefe that none are of confequence.

An ENQUIRY, &c.

INTRODUCTION.

AS there are but few who are capable of diſtinguiſhing between the degrees of teſtimony, or of ſeeing in what meaſure different arguments have a right to claim their aſſent; as there are indeed but few who are capable of even learning to make the proper diſtinction, an endeavour to teach it would be a work of very limited utility. My ſubject is of too general import to admit of a diſcuſſion that cannot be generally entered into; in the maſs of mankind whatever has the appearance of argument will find its adherents. There is ſcarcely a ſophiſm can be broached but ſome capacity will be found mean enough to find conviction in it, or if prejudice influence, we depoſe our better judgment, we place our will on the throne of our underſtanding, and give the conduct of our lives to it.

As therefore an extended or unclouded intellect is not conferred on every man, and yet as every individual is intruſted with an immortal ſoul, the eternal felicity or miſery of which is placed in his power, and is to be decided on by him in this life, I conceive that I ſhall do a more beneficial ſervice to mankind by deſcending to a confutation of each particular aſſertion, by which they might be led into deſtructive errour, than if I were to furniſh a key for fallacy in the abſtract, that could only be applied in the inſtance by ſkilful hands.

A   Under

Under the influence of this idea I appear now upon very different ground from that on which I formerly met Mr. Lindfey; and, after having drawn ample conviction to my own mind from that fource whence alone it flows with purity, I have for the fake of thofe, on whom my former labours may not have wrought the effect I looked for, bowed myfelf to a meer toil (for fuch truly I have found it.) The Scriptures had afforded to me all that was neceffary to eftablifh my belief, Mr. Lindfey has fought to eftablifh his upon another foundation. For their fatisfaction who may concur with him in thinking that farther authority is requifite, I mean, in the fubfequent fheets, to produce that authority to which he has appealed.

In the courfe of his work this gentleman has made the following affertion, "If the matter is to be put to the vote as it were, it is abfolutely neceffary that the lefs learned fhould be told what upon enquiry will be found undeniably true, viz. THAT THE FATHERS OF THE FIRST THREE CENTURIES, AND CONSEQUENTLY ALL CHRISTIAN PEOPLE FOR UPWARD OF THREE HUNDRED YEARS AFTER CHRIST TILL THE COUNCIL OF NICE, WERE GENERALLY UNITARIANS." Apology, p. 23. See alfo Scriptural Confutation, p. 193.

Though I cannot conceive that the fact, if proved, ought to influence the fentiments of any chriftian before whom God has been pleafed to lay the evidence of his religion, yet as I faw one gentleman capable of a perfuafion that he ought to attend to the opinion of others rather than form a judgement upon that evidence for himfelf, I feared that perfons of the fame way of thinking might confider the bold affurance, " that the immediate fucceffours of the apoftles were all Unitarians,"

tarians," as an argument of too high importance; and thence conceive that the example of men fo early inftructed in the doctrines of Chriftianity ought to be purfued without hefitation or farther enquiry.

As I had not the fmalleft doubt of Mr. Lindfey's veracity, and was confident that he had delivered the truth to the beft of his information and apprehenfion, I muft acknowledge that I was exceedingly furprized to find that the fcriptures which, upon the moft diligent fearch, had afforded to me fuch evidence of the Trinity as I could not controvert, fhould have borne to the early Fathers of the Church the very reverfe teftimony. I confidered myfelf in the light of their brother juror, and that the evidence which had been delivered to them was now before me, and therefore was exceedingly at a lofs to account for the different fentiments we had formed, and the different verdicts we were difpofed to pronounce upon it.

There is however a deference due to the judgement of men whofe abilities have lifted them into the efteem of mankind, and who have turned thofe abilities to the inveftigation of the fubject into which we are defirous of enquiring ourfelves. Though mere antiquity cannot confer value on a work, yet furely to have paffed down to us through many ages, and to have received a plaudit from each, is a letter of recommendation which our modefty is called upon to refpect. In this light I confidered the Fathers, as men no otherwife inftructed than myfelf, but who might have formed a clearer judgement upon the fame information; I hoped therefore that I fhould find the reafons affigned by them, upon which they inferred conclufions, fo different from thofe which appeared to my underftanding, and that if I had fallen into an erroneous interpretation of the

A 2   fcripscriptures, I should learn where my error lay, and be enabled by their arguments to rectify it. To this purpose, immediately after I had published "A Scriptural Confutation of Mr. Lindsey's Doctrines," I conceived it my duty to consult the venerable Fathers of our Church, and that with the most candid disposition towards them. Under this idea I sate down to their vast volumes; but judge of my surprize when I found that, instead of being Unitarians, there was not one among the Fathers of the first three centuries who has not (so far as the brevity of his work would admit, or the subject he treated of afforded occasion) declared his belief in the godhead of our Saviour; and that very far the majority of them were explicit adorers of the Trinity: For, though the word Trinity has not come down to us as of an earlier date than the middle of the second century, when it was used by Theophilus bishop of Antioch, yet the following extracts, from the still earlier preachers of christianity, will prove that they were just as much aware of the doctrine as he was; and although I think the date of a name of no consequence I will even go farther, and say, that it seems to have been a term in common use when Theophilus employed it; for the cotemporary and immediately subsequent Christians, who do not seem, from their writings, ever to have looked toward him, use it with the most current familiarity.

I mean to confine myself to the Fathers of the first three centuries only, for it is from their example that Mr. Lindsey would persuade us to Unitarianism: To the less learned he has addressed an assertion concerning them; to the less learned I open out what they have written; and desire no credit but where I prove. In a subject so important nothing should be admitted upon trust. But when I have proved my point, I must

must call upon those, who now consider the tenets of the primitive Christians as of any weight in argument, and esteem themselves well warranted, by their practice, to deny the Godhead of the Son and of the Holy Ghost, not then first to degrade their authority when they appear to be on the opposite side of the question; but with candour submit to the force, which they had themselves conferred upon the argument, so long as they conceived its strength to be turned against their adversaries. For my own part I make no appeal from the Scriptures to any other testimony; on them alone I rest my cause. I only desire those, who have not abided by their depositions, but cited the Fathers to give evidence, to abide by the evidence they give, though it should be found to make altogether against them.

There are some few writers, besides the Fathers, who may be reckoned among the CHRISTIAN PEOPLE of the first three hundred years after Christ, to whom Mr. Lindsey's assertion extends; I shall produce some of these to give an account of their own belief, and refer it then to my reader's determination, how justly, and even how honestly this gentleman has declared the Fathers, and all christian people, antecedent to the council of Nice, to have been Unitarians.

I would have it observed that I draw very little from the dubious writings of any of the authors from which the following extracts are taken; whenever I do, I apprize my reader of it. But if, after all, Mr. Lindsey should choose to contest the authenticity of any work that I make use of, I shall not take upon me to establish it. If it be not genuine, nor of the first three centuries, it is a nullity, and consequently can make no more for his position than for mine; and if his affirmation, that the Fathers of the first three centuries
were

were Unitarians, has been made without a poffibility of being proved, from a defect of writers, it is a good ground of denial to fay that it wants the only proof upon which it could have been fupported: If he therefore fhall choofe to conteft the authority of thofe works which I make ufe of, I am ready to refign them to him; but in return to demand that he will refign his bold affertion to me, or forgive the liberty, which I muft take upon his refufal, of flatly denying the truth of it.

CHAP. I.

The Sentiments of the Fathers of the First Century.

BESIDES the canonical writers, who are the authentick witnesses of the Trinity, and whose testimony I have already produced, the Fathers of the first century are only three in number, and these three are all mentioned with high honour in the New Testament—their names are CLEMENS ROMANUS, BARNABAS, and HERMAS.

Of ST. CLEMENT we are told by St. Paul that his name was written in the Book of Life, and that he was his fellow labourer, Philippians iv. 3. He suffered martyrdom under Trajan, A. D. 100, for, after a long confinement in the mines, he was at length thrown into the sea with an anchor hung round his neck.

There has come down to our time but one very short work of his, an epistle to the Corinthians, the object of which is to allay disagreements and contentions which seem to have arisen among them on the subject of the resurrection; and to recommend humility and concord. He adheres closely to these points, and is so intent on establishing their morality, that he is doctrinal but in a very small degree. Many other writings have been ascribed to him, but of this alone he is the unquestioned author. A second epistle to the same people has been doubted, but in the opinion of many judicious men without good reason.

These

These two epistles have been translated by Archbishop Wake, who vindicates the authenticity of the second. In the first epistle to the Corinthians, having quoted the entire fifty-third chapter of Isaiah and applied it to our Saviour Jesus Christ, he dissuades them from envy and contention, and desires them to be of a more humble disposition, for that Christ is theirs who are humble, and that HE had set them an example which they ought to follow, and then proceeds to use the following words, which afford a good comment upon Philippians ii. 6, 7, 8. " The scepter of the majesty of God, our Lord Jesus Christ, came not in the noisy pomp of vain glory and splendid station, although he was able to have assumed them, but he came in lowliness of mind." " Beloved, you see what the example, that has been afforded to us, is; for, if the Lord thus humbled himself, how should we do who have come under the yoke of his grace *?" In another part of the same epistle he says, " let us venerate the Lord Jesus Christ whose blood was given for us †;" and he commences his second epistle, the authority of which has been already stated, " Brethren, we should so think of Jesus Christ as of God ‡."

As

---

* " Τὸ σκῆπτρον τῆς μεγαλωσύνης τȣ̃ Θεȣ̃, ὁ κύριος ἡμῶν Χριϛὸς Ἰησȣ̃ς, ἐκ ἦλθεν ἐν κόμπῳ ἀλαζονείας, ἐδὲ ὑπερηφανίας, καίπερ δυνάμενος, ἀλλὰ ταπεινοφρονῶν." " Ὁρᾶτε, ἄνδρες ἀγαπητοὶ, τίς ὁ ὑπογραμμός ὁ δεδομένος ἡμῖν· εἰ γὰρ ὁ κύριος ȣ̃τως ἐταπεινοφρόνησε, τί ποιήσωμεν ἡμεῖς, οἱ ὑπὸ τὸν ζυγὸν τῆς χάριτος αὐτȣ̃ ἐλθόντες."

† " Τὸν κύριον Ἰησȣ̃ν Χριϛὸν, ȣ̃ τὸ αἷμα ὑπὲρ ἡμῶν ἐδόθη, ἐντραπῶμεν."

‡ " Ἀδελφοὶ, ȣ̃τως δεῖ ἡμᾶς φρονεῖν περὶ Ἰησȣ̃ Χριϛȣ̃ ὡς περὶ Θεȣ̃."

As I have said that the first of the above extracts from St. Clement serves to illustrate Philippians ii. 6, 7, 8, I shall take occasion to vindicate the translation of that passage which is given in our Bible, and of setting aside the version which the author of *Familiar Illustrations of certain Passages of Scripture* would substitute for it. In our Bible it stands thus, " Who being in the form of God, thought it not robbery to be equal with God: but made himself of no reputation, and took upon him the form of a servant, and was made in the likeness of men: and being found in fashion as a man, he humbled himself and became obedient unto death, even the death of the cross." And thus in the original, " ὅς ἐν μορφῇ Θεοῦ ὑπάρχων, ουχ ἁρπαγμὸν ἡγήσατο τὸ εἶναι ἴσα Θεῳ. 'Αλλ' ἑαυτὸν ἐκένωσε, μορφὴν δούλου λαβών, ἐν ὁμοιώματι ἀνθρώπων γενόμενος. Καὶ, &c. &c." And to this the author under consideration has affixed the following translation, " Who being in the form of God, did not think that being equal to God was a thing to be seized (i. e. by him) but made himself of no reputation." This, he asserts, is preferable to our common version, because he says, " this makes the whole passage just and coherent as a recommendation of humility; and also hints a fine contrast between the conduct of Christ, whom St. Paul elsewhere calls *the second Adam*, and the first who is also said to have been * made in *the likeness of God*; but aspiring to be as God fell. Whereas Christ, who had more of the likeness or *form of God*, on account of his extraordinary powers, not grasping at any thing higher but humbling himself, was exalted." " Indeed the word BUT, which introduces the next verse, evidently leads us to expect some contrast between what goes before and after

B   ter

---

* This is said of Adam, but not of Christ. *To be*, and *to be made*, differ very widely, even as far as God and his creature.

ter it, which is very ſtriking in the manner in which I tranſlate this text, but is altogether loſt in our common verſion, *for he made himſelf equal to God* BUT *humbled himſelf*, is not even ſenſe." *Familiar Illuſtrations.*

Before I examine the value of this reaſoning, I deſire my reader to refer this writer's tranſlation to the Greek original, and decide for himſelf whether the word Ἁρπαγμός, which ſignifies the " act of ſeizing," can be ſtrained to the ſenſe which he has aſſigned to it, or be put, by any poſſible figure, for " the thing ſeized" or " to be ſeized upon." Ἡγέομαι alſo ſignifies to eſtimate the quality or nature of the ſubject under conſideration; and according to this interpretation of the words our tranſlation is made. The ſubject under conſideration is τὸ εἶναι ἴσα Θεῷ, to be equal with God; and this Chriſt ἡγήσατο eſteemed or thought to be, ἐχ ἁρπαγμόν, not a robbery, or ſeizure of that which was not his own. And hence we may conclude that to be equal with God was his own.

To ſhew that a verſion is not true to the original, I ſhould conceive a very ſufficient reaſon for ſetting it aſide. I ſhall neverthelefs annex a ſhort comment on this author's arguments already ſtated.

He ſays that his tranſlation " hints a fine contraſt between the conduct of Chriſt, whom St. Paul *elſewhere* calls the ſecond Adam, and the firſt," &c. as above. Elſewhere indeed; for in the paſſage before us, there is not even the moſt diſtant reference to the paternal character of Chriſt, which he aſſumed in the fleſh, that we might inherit from him, as our ſecond Adam, what we had forfeited by the lapſe of the firſt progenitour of mankind; but on the contrary, the conduct of Chriſt, here ſpoken of, was antecedent to his

having

having been made in the likeness of men; antecedent to his having descended from the glory which he had with the Father before the world was; it was even while he was yet in the form of God: And consequently the apostle never intended in this place to hint any contrast, or other species of comparison whatsoever, between the conduct of him, who was not yet our second Adam, and that of the first, who never sustained any other character but that of a man.

The whole passage I grant, nay I contend for it, is a recommendation of humility after the example of Christ, and so considered, is just and coherent in our very literal translation.

" Indeed," says this writer, " the word BUT, which introduces the next verse, *(But made himself of no reputation, &c.)* evidently leads us to expect some contrast between what goes before and after it, which is very striking in the manner in which I translate this text, but is altogether lost in our common version. For *he made himself equal to God* BUT *humbled himself*, is not even sense." And what then? I allow it to be stark nonsense. But is it the language of the apostle? is it even a paraphrase of his assertion? No; nor does it bear the most remote similitude to a passage, which does not state that Christ *made* himself equal to God, but that he possessed that equality, without the mention of any agency; that BEING in the form of God he was able to maintain his equality as of right, not robbery; BUT (and here the contrast between what goes before and after this word is so very obvious, that it might justify the use of a term yet more evidently leading us to expect it) notwithstanding this dignity, such was his humility, that he descended from it, to take upon him an inferiour nature, to unite himself with a

crea-

creature, and to BE MADE Man. That even here on earth he fought not worldly fplendour (and was this a thing not to be feized by him? was this too above his claim?) but taking upon him an humble ftation, came in the form of a fervant. That even fo meek and lowly of fpirit was he, that he humbled himfelf ftill lower, and became obedient to an ignominious death. If then, " ye know the grace of our Lord Jefus Chrift, that though he was rich, yet for your fakes he became poor, that ye through his poverty might be rich," 2 Corinthians viii. 9, it will appear that the context may be ftated thus, " Let this mind be in you which was in Chrift Jefus; who being in the form of God, and juftifiable in adhering to his equality, and not chargeable with any injury to you, though he had not bowed himfelf down for your redemption, which was an act of his love, not of your right, yet

	BUT	
He maintained not his dignity		took upon him your nature, and for your fakes ftooped to be made man.
And even as man he fought not to exalt himfelf over his brethren		took upon him the form of a fervant and miniftered to you, ever extending his beneficial affiftance to fuch as fought it of him.
As he was without fin, he might have exempted himfelf from farther forrows, and as he had power he might		it was for your redemption he came, to this his fuffering was neceffary, he therefore made no refiftance, but yielded

might have fruſtrated the efforts of human ſtrength to afflict him BUT yielded himſelf without reluctance to a death of ignominy, deſpiſing the ſhame, as hereby you are ranſomed from the power of death.

Wherefore be ye like minded, and even as Chriſt looked not upon his own things, but looking upon yours, aſſumed the humility of your nature, ſo do ye, look every man not upon his own, but upon the things of others, having, in lowlineſs of mind, the ſame love, being of one accord and of one mind."

But to return to St. CLEMENT. He calls Jeſus Chriſt " the defender and helper of our weakneſs;" * declares that " by him the eyes of our hearts are opened, and that, as, beneath the vernal ſun returning in ſucceſſion to the torpid gloom of winter, the vegetable, which had lien in a lifeleſs ſtate, renews its bloom, ſo by his agency our feeble intellect, which had heretofore been wrapt in ſterile darkneſs, is invigorated, and puts forth its verdure beneath his marvellous light." † After having quoted the 2d verſe of the 32d Pſalm, " Bleſſed is the man unto whom the Lord imputeth not iniquity, and in whoſe ſpirit there is no guile," he makes the following ſhort comment from himſelf: " Now this bleſſing is fulfilled in thoſe who are choſen by God, through Jeſus Chriſt our Lord, to whom be glory for ever and ever, Amen." ‡ With this doxology, which is

* Τὸν προςάτην κὶ βοηθὸν τῆς ἀσθενείας ἡμῶν.

† Διὰ τέτου ἠνεώχθησαι ἡμῶν οἱ ὀφθαλμοὶ τῆς καρδίας· διὰ τέτου ἡ ἀσύνετ@ κὶ ἐσκοτισμένη διάνοια ἡμῶν ἀναθάλλει εἰς τὸ θαυμαςὸν αὐτῦ φῶς. The metaphor here neceſſitates a paraphraſe.

‡ Οὗτ@ ὁ μακαρισμὸς ἐγένετο ἐπὶ τῆς ἐκλελεγμένης ὑπο τῦ Θεῦ, διὰ Ἰησῦ Χριςῦ τῦ κυρίυ ἡμῶν, ᾧ ἡ δόξα εἰς τὸς αἰῶνας τῶν αἰώνων, Αμην.

is three times repeated in his fhort work, I fhall conclude my extracts from this early Father; juft remarking, that confidering the brevity of an epiftle written purely with a view to the morals of the Corinthians, to whom it is directed, it is extraordinary that fo much occurs to afcertain the faith of the author, who muft evidently appear not to have been an Unitarian.

St. BARNABAS was no lefs a man than the affociate of St. Paul, as is largely recorded of him in the Acts. He was a Jew of Cyprus, where he is faid to have been ftoned to death, under the Emperour Claudius, about the year 50; but this is very doubtful, the 16th chap. of his epiftle general, the only work of his that has come down to our days, argues that he furvived the deftruction of the temple. *

Though "he was a good man, and full of the Holy Ghoft and of faith," Acts xi. 24, his epiftle has neverthelefs been refufed a place in the canon; even its authenticity has been called in queftion, but fo far as I can fee without good reafon; for Clemens Alexandrinus, Tertullian, and Origen, who are all within Mr. Lindfey's defcription, make mention of it, and afcribe it to him. But let us fay that it is not his, it is yet a work antecedent to thefe Fathers, and therefore within the firft three centuries, and fo far has been adopted by their approbation, that the doctrines contained in it may in a great meafure be imputed to them, which equally anfwers my purpofe.

I do not from myfelf maintain that the plurals of the Old Teftament afford any proof of the Trinity, and

---

* Only part of 'his has defcended in the original Greek; but the fenfe of the whole has been tranfmitted by means of an antient Latin verfion. Archbifhop Wake has tranflated it into Englifh.

and yet the following paſſage from St. Barnabas, who was himſelf a Jew, and conſequently competent to give the meaning of a Hebrew expreſſion, affords ſome argument that they do. I only quote it to ſhew the ſenſe in which he took them, and thence to demonſtrate that he was not an Unitarian.

" That man ſhall juſtly periſh, who having knowledge of the way of truth, neverthelefs refrains not from the way of darkneſs. And for this end our Lord was content to ſuffer for our ſouls, even though he be the Lord of the whole earth, to whom *(God)* ſaid before the appointment of time, " let US make man in OUR image after OUR likeneſs," Geneſis i. 26. Seeing then that he ſuffered by men, learn how he was content to do ſo. The prophets having received from him the gift of phrophecy ſpake before concerning him. But he, that he might aboliſh death and make known the reſurrection from the dead, was content to appear in the fleſh, that he might perform the promiſe given to our fathers, becauſe he ought to perform it.". " For had he not come in the fleſh, how could men have been able to look upon him that they might be ſaved? Who looking only upon the finite ſun, which ſhall hereafter ceaſe to exiſt, and which is but the work of his hands, cannot endure to keep their eyes ſtedfaſtly fixed againſt his rays. Wherefore the Son of God came in the fleſh for this cauſe, that he might completely fill up the meaſure of their iniquity who have perſecuted his prophets unto death. For the ſame reaſon alſo he ſuffered, for ſaith God *." Here part
of

---

* Juſte periet homo habens viam veritatis, ſcientiam, et ſe a via tenebroſa non cohtinet adhuc. Et ad hoc dominus ſuſtinuit pati pro anima noſtrâ, cum ſit orbis terrarum dominus, cui dixit die ante conſtitutionem ſæculi, " *faciamus hominem ad imaginem & ſimilitudinem noſtram,*" quomodo ergo
ſuſtinuit

of the 53d chap. of Isaiah is quoted as the saying of God, whereas it was but just before said that the prophets spake as the gift of prophecy had been imparted to them by Christ, whose prophets they were.

Let it only be remembered that I am not now proving the Godhead of our Saviour by the testimony of the Fathers. I only produce what they say, in evidence of what they believed themselves; to that and that alone it is adequate. This short extract is therefore sufficient to my purpose, for it fully proves that St. Barnabas was not an Unitarian. If Mr. Lindsey or any of his adherents think not, let them adopt it as their own sentiment, and try how far it is consistent with those which they have heretofore entertained and promulgated.

ST. HERMAS is saluted by Paul in his epistle to the Romans xvi. 14, and there called one of the brethren. Little more is known of him; the manner and even the time of his death is uncertain.

A work of his, intitled *the Shepherd*, has been preserved, which, considering the contents of it, is very extraordinary. It consists of the most fanciful visions,

---

sustinuit cum ab hominibus hoc pateretur, discite. Prophetæ, ab ipso habentes donum, in illum prophetaverunt: ille autem ut vacuam faceret mortem, et de mortuis resurrectionem ostenderet, quia in carne oportebat eum adparere, sustinuit, ut promissum parentibus redderet." " Ἐι γὰρ μὴ ἦλθεν ἐν σαρκὶ, πῶς ἂν ἐσώθησαν ἄνθρωποι οἱ βλέποντες αὐτὸν; ὅτι τὸν μέλλοντα μὴ εἶναι ἥλιον, ἔργον χειρῶν αὐτῶ ὑπάρχοντα, βλέποντες ἐχ ἰσχύοσιν εἰς ἀκτῖνας αὐτῶ ἀντοφθαλμῆσαι. Οὐκοῦν ὁ υἱὸς τοῦ Θεοῦ εἰς τοῦτο ἦλθεν ἐν σαρκὶ, ἵνα τὸ τέλειον τῶν ἁμαρτιῶν κεφαλαιώσῃ τοῖς διώξασιν ἐν θανάτῳ τοῖς προφήτας αὐτῶ. Οὐκοῦν εἰς τοῦτο ὑπέμεινε· λέγει γὰρ ὁ Θεὸς," &c.

sions, which he has written in three books. He seems to have been a man of much more piety than genius, and it is surely to this circumstance that the applause which Irenæus and Origen have bestowed upon his writings is to be ascribed. This work has also been translated by Archbishop Wake, who vindicates its authenticity. For this I am little concerned. It was certainly written before Irenæus, and consequently before the middle of the second century, which is all that I desire.

He declares that "the Son of God is indeed more antient than any creature, insomuch that he was in council with the Father upon the subject of creation*." " The name of the Son of God is great and without bounds, and the whole world is supported by it †." He tells us that " the right hand of holiness belongs to as many as shall suffer for the name of God ‡." And again in the same work, speaking of the Son of God to such as had suffered death for his name, and who ought therefore to honour him, having been esteemed worthy to bear his name, he says, " Had ye not suffered for his name's sake, ye had been dead unto the Lord; wherefore I speak these things unto you who deliberate whether ye shall confess or deny him, confess that ye have the Lord for your God, lest at any time denying him ye may be delivered over unto bonds ||." For he had

* Filius quidem Dei omni creaturâ antiquior est, ita ut in consilio patri suo adfuerit ad condendam creaturam. Lib. 3. similitudo 9. cap. 12.

† Nomen filii Dei magnum et immensum est, et totus ab eo sustentatur orbis. Lib. 3. sim. 9. cap. 14.

‡ Illorum sunt dextræ partes sanctitatis, quisquis patietur propter nomen Dei. Lib. 1. visio 3. cap. 2.

|| Nisi passi essetis hujus nominis causâ, propter peccata certè vestra mortui eratis Deo. Hæc igitur vobis dico, quicumque deliberatis de confessione

had juft before laid it down, "that they who are fear-ful and doubtful and have deliberated with themfelves whether they fhould confefs or deny Chrift have yet fuf-fered *." Whereas they who have been firm in the faith, " and whofoever have fuffered for the name of the Lord are had in honour with God, and all their offences are blotted out, becaufe they have fuffered death for the name of the Son †."

The Shepherd of Hermas contains many more paffa-ges to the fame purpofe, which anfwer my end and prove the writer not to have been an Unitarian. This is all that I feek to prove, and all that his ftrange work feems good for. But St. Hermas has always been ranked with the Apoftolick Fathers, and therefore I cite him. From each of thefe I have now made ex-tracts, and fhewed beyond a contradiction that not one of them was of that religion which Mr. Lindfey la-bours to propagate. For not a fyllable of that doctrine which I have produced from them, has the leaft con-fiftency with the doctrine which he profeffes. I put it to him to anfwer whether he is ready to fubfcribe thefe tenets, and if not, I demand St. Clement, St. Barna-bas, and St. Hermas; in fhort, I demand the whole firft century to be confidered as an exception from his defperate pofition, and to be handed over to my fide of the queftion.

aut de abnegatione. Confiteamini igitur vos habere dominum deum, ne forte negantes, tradamini in vincula. Lib. 3. fim. 9. cap. 28.

* Qui vero timidi et dubii fuerunt, et deliberaverunt in corde fuo utrum faterentur an negarent, et paffi funt. Ibidem.

† Quicumque propter nomen domini paffi funt, honorati apud deum ha-bentur; et omnia eorum deleta funt delicta, quia propter nomen Filii mor-tem obierunt. Ibidem.

CHAP.

CHAP. II.

The Sentiments of the Fathers of the Second Century, together with those of some other Christian People.

THE Fathers of the second century were more numerous, and some of them infinitely more voluminous than their predecessors in the former age. Their names were IGNATIUS, POLYCARP, JUSTIN MARTYR, IRENÆUS, THEOPHILUS of Antioch, and CLEMENT of Alexandria. There were besides these some other Christian writers who are not reckoned among the Fathers of the Church, whose names I shall produce when I come to make extracts from their writings. Ignatius and Polycarp deserve to be distinguished from the rest on account of their greater affinity to the apostles. They were both instructed by them in the doctrines of christianity, and particularly by St. John, whose disciples they had been. They had both lived in the first century, but as they survived it, and that their works which have come down to us were written in the second, I have thought the second better entitled to the honour of their names.

ST. IGNATIUS, the disciple of St. John, was appointed Bishop of Antioch, in Syria, by St. Paul, and approved of by St. Peter; his authority therefore seems to me of a higher nature than that of any other writer, who was not an inspired witness of the Godhead of our Redeemer. He steadily adhered to the doctrines which he had received from the Apostles, and in consequence of his firmness suffered martyrdom in the year 107, under Trajan, by whose command he was

dragged

dragged from Antioch to Rome, and there thrown to wild beasts, to be devoured *for the entertainment of the people*. I shall have occasion presently to speak of his sufferings and his constancy under them, so shall drop the subject for the present, and dwell no more upon it than is necessary to the proof of my own point. The invention of some zealous fabulist, that St. Ignatius had been the individual child whom our Saviour set in the midst of his disciples, and pointed out as an example of innocency, Matth. xviii. 2, 3, 4, though probably groundless, is a proof of the high veneration in which succeeding ages held the memory of this valuable man.

Seven epistles written by him have come to our hands. By the diligence of Archbishop Usher, Isaac Vossius, and Cotelier, these have been purged from the interpolations and inaccuracies of their several transcribers, and I should hope, in consequence of their labours, are possessed by us now in their original purity. Of one of them addressed to Polycarp, bishop of Smyrna, some doubt has been entertained. The remaining six are granted to be authentick. Archbishop Wake has translated them all into English. They are directed to the Smyrnæans, Ephesians, Magnesians, Trallians, Philadelphians, and the Romans. And, what is very well deserving of notice, Eusebius informs us that he wrote these *seven* epistles not only after he had received sentence of death, but while he was actually on his journey to Rome to undergoe it.

He begins his epistle to the Smyrnæans thus, " I glorify Jesus Christ the God who hath thus filled you with wisdom *." And in the same work the following

* Δοξάζω Ἰησῦν Χριςὸν τὸν Θεὸν ὕτως ὑμᾶς σοφίσαντα.

ing paſſage alſo occurs, " All theſe things (Jeſus Chriſt) ſuffered for us that we might be ſaved, and he did truly ſuffer, as alſo he did truly raiſe up himſelf *." He farther calls our Redeemer " God clothed in fleſh †." And in anſwer to an objection made to his having raiſed his true human body, he anſwers, " After his reſurrection he did eat and drink with them as a man in the fleſh, although in ſpirit he was one with the Father ‡." " For I know that after his reſurrection he was in the fleſh, and I believe that he is in it §." He tells them alſo " Ye have done well in having received Philo and Rheus and Agathopus as the deacons of Chriſt God ‖."

Writing to Polycarp, biſhop of Smyrna, the ſame venerable Father admoniſhes him to " conſider the times and expect him who is above all time, eternal, inviſible, yet for our ſakes made viſible, impalpable, impaſſive, yet for us made ſubject to ſufferings, and in every way undergoing them with patience for our ſake **;" and concludes with ſaying, " I pray that you

* Ταῦτα γὰρ πάντα ἔπαθεν (Ἰησοῦς Χριστὸς) δι' ἡμᾶς ἵνα σωθῶμεν· καὶ ἀληθῶς ἔπαθεν, ὡς καὶ ἀληθῶς ἀνέστησεν ἑαυτὸν.

† Σαρκοφόρον Θεὸν. Edit. Uſher. & Cotelier.

‡ Μετὰ δὲ τὴν ἀνάστασιν συνέφαγεν αὐτοῖς, καὶ συνέπιεν ὡς σαρκικὸς, καίπερ πνευματικῶς ἡνωμένος τῷ πατρί.

§ Ἐγὼ γὰρ καὶ μετὰ τὴν ἀνάστασιν ἐν σαρκὶ αὐτὸν οἶδα, καὶ πιστεύω ὄντα.

‖ Φίλωνα, καὶ Ῥέον, καὶ Ἀγαθόπον, καλῶς ἐποιήσατε ὑποδεξάμενοι, ὡς διακόνους Χριστοῦ Θεοῦ.

** Τοὺς καιροὺς καταμάνθανε· τὸν ὑπέρκαιρον προσδόκα, τὸν ἄχρονον, τὸν ἀόρατον, τὸν δι' ἡμᾶς ὁρατὸν, τὸν ἀψηλάφητον, τὸν ἀπαθῆ, τὸν δι' ἡμᾶς παθητὸν, τὸν κατὰ πάντα τρόπον δι' ἡμῶν ὑπομείναντα.

you may be in every respect confirmed in your God Jesus Christ *."

He addresses himself to the church of Ephesus, which is chosen, he says, " according to the will of the Father and Jesus Christ our God †." And in the course of his epistle informs them, that " there is one physician both fleshly and spiritual, created and not created, God in true immortal life," (or rather as Wake translates it from a corrected reading to which all the editours give the preference, " God in man, true life in death,") " both of Mary and of God, first made subject to sufferings and then impassive *Jesus Christ our Lord* ‡." To the same purpose he tells them that " our God Jesus Christ was, according to the dispensation of God, conceived in the womb of Mary, of the seed of David, by the Holy Ghost §."

As a consequence he points out that " Ignorance was taken away, the old kingdom was abolished, God appearing manifest in the nature of man to the renewal of

* Ἐῤῥῶσθαι ὑμᾶς διὰ παντὸς ἐν Θεῷ ὑμῶν Ἰησοῦ Χριστῷ εὔχομαι.

† Ἐν θελήματι τοῦ Πατρὸς καὶ Ἰησοῦ Χριστοῦ τοῦ Θεοῦ ἡμῶν.

‡ Εἷς ἰατρός ἐστιν σαρκικός τε καὶ πνευματικὸς, γεννητὸς καὶ ἀγέννητος, ἐν σαρκὶ γενόμενος, Θεὸς ἐν ἀθανάτῳ ζωῇ ἀληθινῇ (vel forte rectius, ἐν ἀνθρώπῳ Θεὸς, ἐν θανάτῳ ζωῆ ἀληθινή) καὶ ἐκ Μαρίας καὶ ἐκ Θεοῦ, πρῶτον παθητὸς, καὶ τότε ἀπαθής, (Ἰησοῦς Χριστὸς ὁ Κύριος ἡμῶν.)

§ Ὁ γὰρ Θεὸς ἡμῶν Ἰησοῦς ὁ Χριστὸς ἐκυοφορήθη ὑπὸ Μαρίας, κατ᾽ οἰκονομίαν Θεοῦ, ἐκ σπέρματος μὲν Δαβίδ, πνεύματος δὲ ἁγίου.

of eternal life ‖." He demands therefore " why are we not all wife who have received the knowledge of God who is Jefus Chrift ? *" declares " it is meet and right that you fhould in every way glorify Jefus Chrift who hath glorified you ‡;" and finally charges them faying " gather yourfelves together in the love of Jefus Chrift, who according to the flefh is of the race of David, the Son of Man, and the Son of God §."

As this paffage bears a ftrong affinity to Romans ix. 5, I fhall here take occafion to vindicate that text from fome of the extraordinary efforts which have been made by Unitarians to overcome, or efcape from, its force. The commencement of their procefs is always a charge of inaccuracy againft our tranflation of the Bible; if they be unable to make this good by the moft violent wrefting of the original, the charge is carried over to the tranfcribers, who are even accufed of defign and wilful alteration; but if again they fail here, and that a general concurrence of manufcripts, and frequent quotations by writers ftill more antient, authenticate the text as it has come down to us, the next ftep is obvious; a plurality of perfons in the one Godhead is the confequence of the eftablifhed reading, and this is an abfurdity with which their well-informed reafon can never be brought to concur. This their reafon

working

‖ Ἄγνοια καθηρεῖτο, παλαιὰ βασιλεία διεφθείρετο, Θεῶ ἀνθρωπίνως φανερουμένω εἰς καινότητα ἀϊδίω ζωῆς.

* Διατί δὲ ὁ πάντες φρόνιμοι γινόμεθα λαβόντες Θεῶ γνῶσιν, ὅ ἐστιν Ἰησοῦς Χριστός.

‡ Πρέπον ὂν ἐστιν κατὰ πάντα τρόπον δοξάζειν Ἰησοῦν Χριστὸν τὸν δοξάσαντα ὑμᾶς.

§ Πάντες ἐν χάριτι συντρέχεσθε ἐν Ἰησοῦ Χριστῷ τῷ κατὰ σάρκα ἐκ γένους Δαβίδ, τῶ υἱῷ ἀνθρώπου καὶ υἱῷ Θεοῦ.

working upon premises of its own making is pronounced competent to the knowledge of a God, with whose nature a Trinity is altogether inconsistent; the Deism of their own imagination is acquiesced in, and revelation rejected by wholesale—the utter extirpation of christianity is visibly the consequence, and I must go so much farther as to say that it is visibly the object. But let it be observed, that their very rejection of the Bible is a proof of my point. They reject it only because it teaches the trinal unity of God. They appeal to their reason because they do not find deism the religion of the scriptures. However, as I hope that the majority of my countrymen are of opinion that the word of their Maker is their best guide to the knowledge of him, and that the relation which subsists between God and his creatures is better referred to the appointment of him from whom they have derived being, than reserved to the appointment of their own derived and narrowly limited faculties, I shall think myself well employed in an attempt to rescue his holy word, our only guide in these disquisitions, from perversion.

With respect therefore to the text under consideration, the two first steps have been already taken; our translation has been quarrelled with; and the original Greek has been disputed. As I have already said that their rejection of the Bible on this ground is an argument in my behalf, and a proof that Unitarians find the doctrine of the Trinity in Unity contained in it, I will now endeavour to reduce them to this last necessity. There are however some among them on whom I should hope that the establishment of a strong assertion, made by an inspired writer, would work another effect, and persuade them to believe the fact itself which he has asserted. The author of *Familiar Illustrations*, already quoted, has called himself *a lover of*

the

the Gospel: Such I doubt not he is, and that he will act in conformity with this title, and therefore I expect that, if what I write should ever come under his observation, he will either, upon feeling it, acknowledge conviction; or, if he shall still continue to think me in an errour, he will at the least consider me as engaged in the pursuit of truth; that if I freely combat his arguments, he will not look upon me as waging hostilities, but as amicably divesting the truth of that veil which has hid her from his own eyes, and with which he has endeavoured to seclude her from the observation of other men. I here assume my own question, to yield it were a larger concession than I am confident he would desire.

And yet these hopes of candour are far from being extensive. Experience has convinced me that there is nothing less amiable in the sight of some men than truth herself, nor more obnoxious than an honest and disinterested effort to produce her beauties to the general eye. To the copious obloquy, however, with which I have been personally treated by men whose own practice might have taught them my right to support an opinion, I shall not advert: I consider it merely as a judgement pronounced by themselves upon the weakness of their cause*, and yield them my free forgiveness. My temper, I trust in God, is not vindictive; but if it were, my utmost vengeance would be amply wreaked by those occasional quotations from the arguments of my opponents, which the conduct of this work will make it necessary for me to state; of these the present case requires that I should immediately produce one to the observation of my reader.

* Remarks on a late publication, intitled, A Scriptural Confutation, &c. In an Address to the Author. By a Member of the Church of Christ.

The words of St. Paul are, as tranflated in our Bible, " Whofe are the Fathers and of whom as concerning the flefh Chrift came, who is over all God bleffed for ever, Amen, Romans ix. 5." In the original Greek they are Ὧν οἱ Πατέρες, κ̀ ἐξ ὧν ὁ Χριςὸς, τὸ κατὰ σάρκα, ὁ ὢν ἐπὶ πάντων Θεὸς ἐυλογητὸς εἰς τὸς αἰῶνας. Ἀμήν. This the author of Familiar Illuftrations render thus, " *Whofe are the Fathers, and of whom as concerning the flefh Chrift came. God who is over all be bleffed for ever. Amen:*" And gives as a reafon that " it is very common in Jewifh writings to add a doxology after barely mentioning the name of God." But furely this is very inapplicable here; for the name of God does not precede it in the whole chapter, but is firft made ufe of in the fuppofed doxology itfelf, which is therefore not added after the mention of his name, unlefs the writer make a conceffion and admit that Chrift, whofe name is immediately followed by the doxology, is God, who is glorified in it. He thinks himfelf at liberty to point the paffage differently from the accepted reading, and to divide it into two fentences, the firft ending at σάρκα; but the participle ὢν ftands in the way, unites the parts of the text, and will not admit of fuch a punctuation. This *my Remarker* has alfo obferved * ; but is extremely angry with me for not having adopted another divifion of it from Mr. Locke, who refers ὁ ὢν ἐπὶ πάντων, " who is over all" to the name of Chrift, puts his full point there, and converts the remainder of the verfe into a doxology. But with a happy inconfiftency, in the maintenance of which alone he is 'confiftent, after venting his rage at my abfurdity in not having adopted this propofal of Mr. Locke, he immediately tells me that he thinks it ought not to be adopted

* Were peculiar phrafeology of weight againft authority, John i. 18— John iii. 13—viii. 47—Rev. i. 5—v. 5, &c. might exempt the ὢν in this paffage from the charge—to thefe add and refer to the next note, Rom. i. 25, in which the Apoftle has indicatively faid τὸν κτίσαντα, ὅς ἐςὶν ἐυλογητὸς εἰς τὸς αἰῶνας. Ἀμήν.

adopted himself. Indeed I should conceive not too, for, if Christ be over all, it is no great addition to the possessor of omnipotence, to say that he is God blessed for ever; and the very sense would here shew the futility of the effort to divide the text *. But the Remarker would perhaps have held fast here, if he had not been able to supply two other reasons for setting aside the usual acceptation of this passage from his own common place-book. And surely my reader will think he would have done more wisely in abiding by the name of Mr. Locke, than letting go the only stay he had, and catching at two such resources as have let him plunge fairly down.

It is said in St. Paul's Epistle to the Hebrews, chap. i. ver. 2, δἰ ὁ καὶ τὑς αἰῶνας ἐποίησε, which our version has rendered "by whom (Christ) he made the worlds." St. Matthew also tells us that the disciples desired to learn of our Saviour "what shall be the sign of thy coming, and *of the end of the world*," or as it stands in the original συντελείας τῦ αἰῶνος, Matt. xxiv. 3. The former of these passages our Remarker has translated "by whom he *disposed the ages*, the different periods of the world with respect to God's moral government, of which the Christian is to be the last;" the latter he turns "*the end of the age*," and from these two passages thus interpreted he proceeds to explain the

words

---

* The final word of the passage being *Amen*, seems to have suggested the idea of a doxology. But it should be remembered that the same word follows a declaration made by our Saviour himself, who says to St. John, "I am he that liveth and was dead; and behold I am alive for evermore. Amen." Rev. i. 18. If there be any doxology in either case it must consist in that one term alone. After either making or receiving such a communication of spiritual things, the Apostles might without any impropriety express their own assent to the eternal Godhead of their Lord, by annexing that term by which we still continue to express concurrence, and immediately follow the assertion with uttering as from themselves "Amen."

words εἰς τὲς αἰῶνας, *(for ever)* at the clofe of the paffage in queftion, and concludes that Chrift " is over all God to be bleffed *fo long as the ages fhall continue.*"

Now let us, for a moment only, admit of this curious idea, and fee what are the confequences of it. The Lord's Prayer concludes with afcribing to God the power and the glory *for ever and ever*, and the original Greek of this is εἰς τὲς αἰῶνας, Matth. vi. 13, which being expreffed in the very fame language, muft precifely mean the very fame duration of time through which, in the paffage before us, Chrift is pronounced to be *God to be bleffed*. I will draw the neceffary inference myfelf, either therefore the Godhead of the Father is *limited* to the term of the ages, which is a blafphemy of the deepeft dye, or an irrefragable argument lent to me in fupport of my tenet, that the Lord's Prayer is addreffed to Jefus Chrift. For either εἰς τὲς αἰῶνας means an * indeterminable eternity, or it is not applicable to God the Father; but if it be applicable to God the Father, and therefore mean an indeterminable eternity, the application of it to Jefus Chrift is a proof that he is over all God bleffed *for ever*.

Though my Remarker has not been able to fee this conclufion, yet he was aware that his bufinefs was not finifhed while the text remained undifturbed in the original Greek, and therefore he moves on, from the childifh mifinterpretations which I have ftated, to the fecond ftep of the procefs, and declares " a fufpicion has

---

* My Remarker, who has found *a fubordinate God* and *a fupreme God*, has reduced me to the neceffity of ufing this fpecies of jargon, of which he is the fole inventour, and in the fole poffeffion of which I fhould rejoice to leave him. But as there are with him degrees in the infinite majefty of God, he has here found out degrees in his eternal exiftence—fo that we muft afcribe to this clear and penetrating genius the device of *fubject fupremacy, finite infinity*, and *determinable eternity*.

has arifen, that a fmall tranfpofition has happened" in the Greek; and, with great candour of difpofition, charges the tranfcribers of the antient manufcripts with being carelefs and knavifh, with having taken advantage of all the arts of fraud, and all the terrours of force, in fhort, of having entered into a plot to deform and pollute the facred writings; for how elfe, forfooth, could it have happened that every manufcript in the world agrees with the accepted reading of our Greek Teftament? and when all this is faid, the fmall tranfpofition contended for is, that the words ο ων επι παντων (without accents) fhould be changed into ων ο επι παντων; which ων he would afpirate, and fo change the fenfe of the whole paffage.

Perhaps he will fay that the fame tranfpofition has been made by all the Fathers, or that they found it made in manufcripts antecedent to their time. If fo, Mr. Lindfey's affertion muft fall to the ground, and the Fathers be admitted not only to have been believers, but crafty promoters of a belief in a Trinity of perfons in the one Godhead; or to have derived the belief from a faction of tranfcribers formed in days yet earlier than their own. But as I fuppofe this will not be infifted on, and that the genuine reading of the text before us muft be decided by authority, I fhall produce that authority upon which its authenticity is inconteftibly eftablifhed.

The Remarker acknowledges himfelf that the reading is general, and the only one of the manufcripts: and furely fuch a circumftance would have allayed the fufpicions of an honeft enquirer, and precluded all conjecture in a candid mind. But he acknowledges that this text feems to fay fomething for Athanafianifm:

at

at all events, therefore, the word of God muſt be ſuperſeded.

I am obliged here to make a ſmall infringement upon the method I had preſcribed to myſelf, and to quote from ſome of the Fathers before I have reached them in their chronological order. But as they have applied or tranſlated this text, it will appear, from their manner of applying or tranſlating it, how they found it written in the original.

Of IRENÆUS I ſhall have occaſion to ſpeak more at large preſently; it is enough now to ſay that he lived in the ſecond century. Had the original Greek in which he wrote deſcended to our days, to exhibit the verſe alone, would have been ſufficient to aſcertain how he read the paſſage under conſideration. The antient Latin verſion of his work, which is preſerved, ſhews us to a certainty how he applied it, and therefore I ſhall give the whole context.

Speaking of the generation of Jeſus Chriſt he ſays, " that he is called *God with us*, left by any means we ſhould conceive that he was only a man. For the word was made fleſh, not by the will of the fleſh, nor by the will of man, but by the will of God. Nor ſhould we indeed ſurmiſe Jeſus to have been another, but know him to be one and the ſame God. And this Paul has interpreted him to be (in the four firſt verſes of the firſt chapter to the Romans, which he quotes) and again, writing to the Romans, he ſays concerning Jeſus, *whoſe are the Fathers and of whom as concerning the fleſh Chriſt came*, WHO IS *over all God bleſſed for ever* *."

TER-

---

* Et quoniam hic eſt Emanuel, (quod interpretatum eſt, nobiſcum Deus) ne fortè tantùm eum hominem putaremus. Non enim ex voluntate carnis, neque

TERTULLIAN, whose name belongs to the third century, and whose faith shall be enquired into under that head, wrote in Latin, and has given us a translation of the text in question, which evidently demonstrates that it stood in the Greek, in his day, exactly as it does now in ours *. And CYPRIAN, A. D, 248, in his second book against the Jews, produces this text in proof of the Godhead of Christ †.

NOVATIAN, a man of great learning, though not reckoned among the Fathers, has given us a version of this text also. He wrote in the year 240, and, as I shall not have occasion to speak of him again, I shall now dismiss his subject, and by a quotation from his treatise on the Trinity, in which the verse occurs, put it beyond all controversy that he was not an Unitarian.

" But if, when it belongs to God alone to know the secrets of the heart, Christ looks into the secrets of the heart: But if, when it belongs to God alone to forgive sins, the same Christ forgives sins: But if, when it is not the possible act of any man to come from heaven,

neque ex voluntate viri, sed ex voluntate Dei, verbum caro factum est: neque alium quidem Jesum suspicemur fuisse, sed unum et eundem Deum sciremus esse: hoc ipsum interpretatus est Paulus. Et iterum ad Romanos scribens de Israel, dicit, *quorum Patres, et ex quibus Christus secundum carnem,* QUI EST DEUS *super omnes benedictus in secula.*" Irenæus adversus Hæreses, Lib. iii. cap. 18. p. 203.

* Ex quibus Christus QUI EST DEUS super omnia benedictus in ævum omne. *Tertull. adv. Praxean. p.* 1020.
Christum autem et ipsum Deum cognominavit (Paulus); quorum Patres et ex quibus Christus secundum carnem, QUI EST *super* omnia Deus benedictus in ævum. *Ejusdem, p.* 1021.

† Quorum Patres, ex quibus Christus secundum carnem QUI EST super omnia Deus benedictus in sæcula.
Cypriani adversus Judæos, lib. 2. *cap.* 6. *p.* 35.

heaven, Christ in his advent descended from heaven: But if, when no man can utter these words, I and my Father are one, Christ alone, from a consciousness of his Godhead, proclaimed them: But if, lastly, the apostle Thomas, when supplied with all the circumstances and evidences of the Godhead of Christ, answering, said unto Christ, my Lord and my God: But if the apostle Paul too, in his epistles, says, *whose are the Father's, and of whom, as concerning the flesh, Christ came,* WHO IS *over all God blessed for ever:* But if the same Paul publishes himself to have been constituted an apostle, not of men, neither by man, but by Jesus Christ: But if the same Paul contend for it, that he did not learn the gospel from men, neither receive it by man, but by Jesus Christ: Christ is worthily God." " And yet the Heretick still hesitates to acknowledge Christ to be God, whom he sees proved to be God by the evidence of so many circumstances and declarations *."

Thus then I have rescued this poor text from the sophistical efforts which have been made to suppress it, and

---

* Quòd si cum nullius sit nisi Dei cordis nosse secreta, Christus secreta conspicit cordis: Quòd si, cum nullius sit nisi Dei peccata dimittere, idem Christus peccata dimittit: quòd si, cum nullius sit hominis de cœlo venire, de cœlo veniendo descendit: quòd si, cum nullius hominis hæc vox esse possit, Ego & Pater unum sumus, hanc vocem de conscientiâ divinitatis Christus solus edicit: quòd si postremò omnibus divinitatis Christi probationibus et rebus instructus Apostolus Thomas, respondens Christo, Dominus meus et Deus meus dicit: Quòd si, et Apostolus Paulus, *quorum,* inquit, *Patres, et ex quibus Christus secundum carnem,* QUI EST *super omnia Deus benedictus in sæcula,* in suis literis scribit: Quòd si, idem se Apostolum non ab hominibus, aut per hominem sed per Jesum Christum constitutum esse depromit: Quòd si, idem Evangelium non se ab hominibus didicisse aut per hominem, sed per Jesum Christum accepisse contendit: MERITO DEUS EST CHRISTUS." " Et tamen adhuc dubitat hæreticus Christum dicere esse Deum, quem Deum tot et rebus animadvertit et vocibus adprobatum."

Novatiani de Trinitate lib. p. 1242.

and by the authority of the earliest writers of the church, incontestibly proved the Greek to be genuine as we have received it. The antient transcribers must therefore stand acquitted of the charge of knavery preferred against them; and I should think it but fair also that they should be presented with a copy of their indictment.

I have shewed that the proposed construction of the Greek makes against the hypothesis of the propounder. This may deter *him* from insisting upon it. For the rest of my readers they will probably reject it because it is nonsense.

But I have shewed also that our translation, concurring with the Greek as it was originally written, and as it was understood by the Fathers, is made according to the genuine meaning of the apostle: and therefore desire that the same favour shall now be extended to the translators, that I had before demanded for the transcribers.

But this text is found to say something for Athanasianism. And what then? The modest and humble reader of the word of his Creator will attend to it, and believe; he knows that it is from God alone that he can learn the things which belong to God. But my Remarker marching more boldly on, arrives at once at what I have already laid down to be the great end of all Unitarian process, and declares that his reason informs him that this proposition (namely, that the Son and the Holy Ghost are, with the Father, one God) is false, by a much clearer evidence than she affords him of the existence of any revelation whatever. And surely that she should act by him in this peculiar manner is not at all to be wondered at, when we consi-

E   der

der the peculiar nature of this Remarker's reason, which he has himself let us into, for he tells us that she is the *first vehicle of human information* from God to men, that she is *the communication of truths*, and the *first source of knowledge* planted by God in the mind of man. He might as well have called his eye the source of light, (and yet I doubt it is not a very brilliant one) or his journey's end the post-horse that had carried him to it. But such is the definition of reason given to us by the Remarker, and when I have set it before my reader he will probably be satisfied, without enquiring into the superstructure which he has raised upon such a foundation. I am only glad that a man of such reasoning faculties has thrown aside the mask, and declared that he will, upon a competition between this sort of reason, which he has, and the word of God, depend upon this reason, and renounce revelation: for such is the amount of his menaces in the 9th page of his Remarks. I am as sensible as this man that my system, if true, is the most astonishing that ever was presented to the human mind. But I do not therefore think it incredible—from nothing, nothing comes, is an axiom of which perhaps this Remarker's reason has been the vehicle. And yet from this sterile nothing has God called forth all matter; from this unfruitful nothing his word has ushered an universe into existence. A position that may possibly be found as much to oppose *the vehicle of the Remarker's knowledge*, as that on account of which he is in such haste to fling away all revelation. Unless he maintain the doctrines of eternal worlds or eternal matter, he must allow his axiom does neither extend to nor controul the operations of God. And whence has he been supplied with axioms to which the inscrutable and incomprehensible nature of God must of such absolute necessity exactly conform? He shall here give his

own

own anſwer that *it is no matter. For wherever reaſon finds the clear perception it has of the agreement or diſagreement of its own ideas, it finds certainty, and ſo far it may be ſafely truſted. But the certainty ariſes not from the nature of the object under contemplation, but from the clear perception it has of the agreement or diſagreement of its own ideas* *. So that the plain Engliſh of this paſſage, if it will bear plain Engliſh, is briefly this, that a truth which does not agree with a falſe preconception, muſt be ſet aſide without any reſpect whatſoever being paid to its agreement with its own archetype, its adequacy ſhall avail it nothing if it diſagree with an idea which is inadequate. And inadequate muſt every human conception be to the extent of any one of the divine perfections. How then ſhall we poſſeſs a juſt idea of the great almighty aggregate of all? We may determine, it is true, that whoever is not infinitely wiſe, juſt, and true, is not ſupreme God; but what idea have we of the exerciſe of infinite wiſdom, infinite juſtice, or even of infinite truth, which we ſhould rely upon as a criterion of our Creator, and according to the agreement or incongruity with which we ſhould pronounce on the ſupreme Godhead? I have ſaid before, that infinite wiſdom may do that which to us does not ſeem wiſe, becauſe we do not comprehend it; and, for the ſame reaſon, that infinite juſtice may

E 2  to

---

* That I may not be thought to miſrepreſent the Remarker, I ſhall ſtate his exact words here, whence it may be ſeen that I have only ſubſtituted the things referred to for the pronouns referring to them. He is ſpeaking of reaſon, which he ſays is infallible in its deciſions ſo far as it has *clear, diſtinct, and adequate conceptions* of God, which the Remarker would inſinuate that he has himſelf; and then he proceeds to ſay, " The certainty ariſes not from the nature of the object under contemplation, but from the clear perception it has of the agreement or diſagreement of its own ideas. Wherever it finds *that* it finds certainty, and ſo far may be ſafely truſted." *Remarks.* p. 5. This is the very depth of Nonſenſe. My Remarker has attempted to parody me, but pointed out his own wretched miſapprehenſion as my language, which is a very diſhoneſt proceeding. I take ſuch conduct, however, as an acknowledgement that as I really ſtand he cannot reach me. *Rem.* p. 64.

do that which to us does not seem just; I now add that infinite truth may pronounce those things to agree which may appear to us at variance; and that when it speaks concerning the nature of God, it may, and probably will, reveal somewhat at variance with our ideas, formed only upon a finite and limited scale; and pronounce that concerning him who has never had room in our *vehicle of knowledge*, which is not possessed in common with those ideas which really occupy it. My Remarker pronounces that I have taught a doctrine so incredible, that were an angel from heaven to teach the like, and work innumerable miracles, yet reason would reject his evidence, because it would feel an irresistible conviction that what he taught was false. Upon what ground reason would find this irresistible conviction I cannot comprehend, unless we agree in the Remarker's definition; but as my reason is rather a receptacle than a vehicle, or source of knowledge or information, I should yield my belief to an angel of God, who corroborated his testimony by supernatural power, when he imparted his knowledge on a subject of which I had certainly never before entertained *an adequate* idea, and this, though it might stand opposed to any preconception I had before entertained, for I know very well that however infallible reason may be where she has adequate ideas, such ideas of God I have not; and therefore I am ready to receive such intelligence as one better informed can give me, and to resign any prepossession that might before have taken hold of me. *My* reason is not *the communication of truths*; it is the recipient of such a communication when made. It is, as it were, the scale-beam which decides the weight of evidence, and marks the prevalence of preponderating truth.

If all which reason cannot reach is to be rejected, reason must resign her own function, of which it is a
con-

confiderable part to diftinguifh what is cognizable by her and what is not; and, before fhe proceed to decide upon a queftion, to decide upon her own competency, and determine whether the queftion be properly before her or not. But all things, fay the advocates of Unitarianifm, are properly before her, and fhe may peremptorily pronounce a negative on that propofition, the truth of which fhe does not fee into, and that too intuitively. This is the utmoft extent of Arian argument. We differ only in refpect to what fort of premifes are to come before reafon, what teftimony is to be examined into. They pretend a perfect innate acquaintance with the nature of God, and affert that it is not poffible for that nature to differ from their idea of it. The Church of England fays the nature of God is altogether incomprehenfible to man, and that our notions of it are to be obtained by middle terms, the teftimony of which it looks into. Thefe it pronounces to be the revelation of God himfelf, from which we are contented to derive our knowledge of him, and according to which we believe, from a conviction that here alone we can learn any thing concerning " the deep things of God, which God hath revealed unto us by his fpirit which fearcheth all things," 1 Cor. ii. 10. Hence we affirm the divinity of our Saviour, becaufe we find it there affirmed, for we acknowledge our own incompetency to fee to the contrary and fo to deny it. In brief, the Bible, and not God, is the proper object of a Chriftian man's difcuffion; the Bible, and not God, is before our reafon; the one is laid open to our infpection and enquiry; the other, how withdrawn from both!

I wifh to be ferviceable to fuch of my fellow creatures as, from the meannefs of their natural endowments, are incapable of entering into enquiries of this nature

for

for themfelves. To this end I have undertaken the prefent publication, and after what I had already done I hoped to have found a collection of fuch paffages as declare the faith of the primitive Chriftians, fully fufficient to remove doubts grounded on an opinion that they were Unitarians. To this I had intended to have confined myfelf, but the publication which has come under my notice fince the commencement of the prefent work, has fhewed me that I had not ftooped quite low enough to comprehend every degree of mental imbecillity. There may be more, I hope but very few more, men whofe talents do not exceed thofe of my Remarker; for their fake I have bowed myfelf ftill lower, and made this digreffion, for the length of which I hope this reafon will be received as a fufficient apology. I fhall ftretch it but little farther, and then return with pleafure to the venerable Martyr whom we have fo long wandered from. I choofe to finifh with the Remarker on this general topick at once, that we may get rid of his interruptions in the fubfequent parts of the work.

This man has told his reader (and there may be a reader like the writer) that " I have delivered a doctrine calculated folely for the meridian of Rome, that if we admit it we throw the gates of our Church open to receive tranfubftantiation, and all the concomitant abominations of idolatrous worfhip," p. 4. Every reader of common fenfe, who has honoured my Scriptural Confutation with a perufal, knows to the contrary of this affertion. My doctrine is, that admitting God to have fpoken, we fhould believe him, and rely upon his revelation. That being utterly unable to look into the poffible relations of God or man, our reafon cannot compare the two natures, and confequently cannot pronounce the impoffibility of an union

between

between them *. Now what fimilitude does this bear to the Remarker's charge againſt me? how does it follow hence that tranſubſtantiation is to be received? Are the objects and their ſeveral relations alike before the tribunal of reaſon? No, there ſubſiſts this eſſential difference between them, that in the one caſe, which I have already ſtated, we have no perception of the relative qualities of God and of man, and conſequently our reaſon muſt act only upon the revelation made by God, who can and does comprehend them both. Whereas in the other caſe the objects are in every part referable, being ſubmitted to our ſenſes; upon their teſtimony reaſon is competent to pronounce a judgement, and accordingly ſhe puts a direct negative upon that relation to which our aſſent is required, ſhe perceives the diſagreement between bread and fleſh, and alſo between wine and blood, and at once denies that either of theſe is the other. Can ſhe thus decide upon the nature of God, or even upon the nature of man, that God ſhall be precluded by her decree from uniting with man? If he has ſaid that he has done ſo, our modeſty might inculcate belief, for our reaſon, whatever our preſumption may, will never ſuggeſt that he has not.

Such aſſertions as are made in the holy Scriptures concerning the objects which are ſubmitted to our comprehenſion, and which we find not literally true concerning them, we may venture to pronounce ſpoken figuratively; ſuch as are made concerning incomprehenſible objects we muſt take literally. When our Saviour, for inſtance, tells us that he is bread, that he is wine, that he is water, that he is a ſhepherd, a gate, a door, &c. &c. we know enough of bread, of wine, of water, &c. to make us perfectly certain that he is not, ſtrictly

---

* See Scriptural Confutation, p. 15, &c.

strictly speaking, any one of these; the predicate is such as cannot be literally declared of the subject. Whereas when he tells us that he and the Father are one, we do not know any thing of either of them, we do not comprehend their respective natures, to enable us to see the truth or falsehood of this upon any other ground than the credit of the speaker, and consequently we cannot contradict it. It is also the more to be relied upon as strictly true for that reason, for our Lord would probably not have spoken figuratively of matters, into which we could never look in order to develope the figure, and find the literal truth that lay concealed within it.

But how does my doctrine of reason restrain the liberty of thinking? I deny that that imagination of the brain, which is formed upon other principles than those which I have stated, is the result of thought; it is the offspring of errour. Thinking (not thinking wrong, to which I will not allow the name, and which, however it may in reality be, I presume is not professedly the thing contended for) is proceeding from premises well understood to just conclusions resulting from them: It is the mind's looking about itself and observing upon the objects of its sense, not upon objects of which it has no sense whatever. No reasonable man sits listening to catch the music of the spheres, though, were they rendered audible, the ear is the sense they would strike upon. No reasonable man stands gazing up into heaven in hope of enjoying the beatific vision, though, were the bright effluence of our Maker's glory made perceptible to human sense, the eye is the organ through which we should receive it. In like manner no reasonable man casts abroad the eye of his mind in search of objects which he knows are not submitted to mental vision, though, were God to become com-

prehensible

prehenſible by us, it is with our mental eye we ſhould behold him. But I am told that we may have a partial view of the nature of God, and aſked whether becauſe "reaſon cannot comprehend the infinite and incomprehenſible nature of God *," whether becauſe it cannot do all, it follows that it can do nothing†? To which I anſwer, that it does follow as in every other caſe, that from a partial view of the ſubject we never can be ſupplied with *clear*, *diſtinct*, *or adequate conceptions* of the whole, and therefore that we never can deny an aſſertion concerning the properties of the whole, only becauſe we do not ſee how they are the properties of a part; nay, though we were to ſee that they were not the properties of the part which we had a view of. But with regard to the infinite God, in every attribute infinite, how much of him has our reaſon comprehended, that we ſhould dare to ſet our peep into his nature in competition with the infinite reality, or declare ‡ that he is not a God of truth, if he give a ſubſequent declaration of his will, which does not agree with our previous ideas of him? which is there moſt of him within or without our mind? I aſk this upon a ſuppoſition that we have had an intimation of his nature, and a courſe of conduct adapted to it, previous to the promulgation of his revealed will. A mariner afflicted by a calenture, may with equal juſtice complain that he is withheld from expatiating in the fantaſtick ſcenes which are figured to his eye by a diſtempered imagination, as my opponent, that he is reſtrained from thinking upon premiſes which his own imagination, and not their reality, has pictured to him. Give to each the liberty to purſue their courſes and an equal fate ſhall betide them. They both relinquiſh their firm footing, they both plunge into an unfathomable ocean, alike they flounder, and alike the mariner and our Thinker are

F

* Scriptural Confutation. † Remarks, p. 4. ‡ Ibidem.

are swallowed up and lost in unmeasurable depths. A Man, who at crofs-roads has enquired of his way, may with equal justice complain that he cannot reach his journey's end by any other than the one true direction, and say I have treated him ill in having pointed out only one road to him. Let him however try the others for himself. What is the consequence? let him go on; so far shall he be from approaching his place of destination, that every step he moves forward but carries him so much farther from it. Go on and talk, I cannot help you; but as for thinking, go think if you can upon the truths of holy writ on other principles than those which are stated;—go and form conclusions upon no premises *.

Once

---

* Natural Religion at the utmost can only assure us that Nature has had a Creator; and if it be said that his unity, nay his attributes, are also clear from the same premises, 1 do not mean to controvert it. Farther than this it is impossible for us to conclude. This is, but a partial view of what revelation has more fully delivered, and never can be put into opposition with what is there declared. As to our reason being a communication of truth and a *revelation* itself, to which the Scripture, if it testify a Trinity in the Unity of God, is a contradiction, it is an absurdity to assert it. If *a first revelation, from God, of his nature* may be substituted for the word *reason*, which, I allow, is an universal gift to mankind, we have then an innate idea not only complex, but the archetype of which is infinite in every component quality. Are we then ushered into life without one simple idea, and yet furnished with not only a compound one, but with a compound idea adequate to an assemblage of every infinite attribute? Natural Religion can only mean a belief in a God inferred from his works. And what does such a religion say in contradiction to Christianity as we receive it? Does it follow from their same premises, which argue to the existence of a God, that the Divine shall not unite with the human nature, and that Jesus Christ is not one with the Father God? The only previous persuasion with which we are to come to the Scriptures is, that there is a God, with infinite and good attributes; the exercise of these we are unable to judge of; we admit that he has spoken, and in his word alone we can learn how he has exercised them; but we find this conduct inconceivable, (inconsistent it cannot be) it is yet all we can judge of him from; and that it is such a conduct as man does not comprehend, is with me an argument that it befits a Being I do not comprehend; and a certain proof that it is not a human fiction, for man would apply to God such a conduct as man would see applicable.

Once more I urge my defire to ferve the meaneft of my fellow creatures, as an excufe for taking up fo much of my readers time in fetting afide abfurdity, which none, but men of talents fimilar to thofe of my Remarker, will think it was neceffary to have beftowed a word upon. He had from a confcioufnefs of his inability to fubvert the received reading of Romans ix. 5, and confequently of removing our tranflation, proceeded to the rejection of revelation at large. In vindication of this procefs he has endeavoured to intimate that he was defirous of forming a little fyftem, upon which the Bible ought to be thrown away. This I conjecture only, becaufe of a few terms which occur up and down his book, fuch as *reafon*, which he fays is *a vehicle of information*; and *ideas of God*, which he fays are *adequate*; and *certainty* refulting not from the *adequacy* of the *idea* to God, but a *perception* of its *agreement* or *difagreement* with itfelf, or fome other of *reafon's own ideas*. Larger bodies I know would pafs through fuch a web without perhaps obferving that any obftacle had been drawn acrofs their way, but as I wifh to fave fmaller animals from fticking in the thin-fpun film, I have thought it better upon the whole to fweep it quite away. I hope therefore that I have now left my reader not only in poffeffion of his Bible, but in a temper to retain it, though he fhould find it to teach doctrines which my Remarker cannot accede to; and that I have fufficiently proved the authenticity of the text to demand his acquiefcence in the Godhead and Manhood of our Redeemer, fince we are indifputably told, that of the Jews as concerning the flefh Chrift came, and that he is over all God bleffed for ever.———

Had the following words occurred in all the editions of St. Ignatius's epiftle to the Ephefians, I fhould have produced them before. Archbifhop Ufher has given them in the 33d page of his, but Cotelier has inserted them only in what he calls, and probably with justice, the interpolated epistles of Ignatius. What a man of Archbishop Usher's qualifications could admit into the text deserves however some degree of attention. "But we have also a Physician the Lord our God Jesus the Christ, before ages the only begotten Son and Word, but afterwards Man also of the Virgin Mary." For "the word was made flesh," John i. 14. Incorporeal in a body; exempt from sufferings in a body obnoxious to them; immortal in a mortal body; life in corruption*." This passage is of the same import as one quoted in p. 22 above, which see.———

Writing to the Magnesians the same Father tells them, "there is one Jesus Christ than whom nothing is better †." "Who was with the Father before all ages and in the end was made manifest ‡." He recommends concord and order to them, "Be ye subject to the Bishop and one to another as Jesus Christ is to the Father, as concerning the flesh, and the Apostles to Christ, and to the Father, and to the Spirit §." And

in

---

* Ἔχομεν ἰατρὸν καὶ τὸν Κύριον ἡμῶν Θεὸν Ἰησοῦν τὸν Χριστόν, τὸν πρὸ αἰώνων υἱὸν μονογενῆ καὶ λόγον, ὕστερον δὲ καὶ ἄνθρωπον ἐκ Μαρίας τῆς παρθένου· ὁ λόγος γὰρ σὰρξ ἐγένετο· ὁ ἀσώματος ἐν σώματι, ὁ ἀπαθὴς ἐν παθητῷ σώματι, ὁ ἀθάνατος ἐν θνητῷ σώματι, ἡ ζωὴ ἐν φθορᾷ.

† Εἷς ἐστιν Ἰησοῦς Χριστὸς οὗ ἄμεινον οὐδὲν ἐστιν.

‡ Ὃς πρὸ αἰώνων παρὰ πατρὶ ἦν, καὶ ἐν τέλει ἐφάνη.

§ Ὑποτάγητε τῷ ἐπισκόπῳ καὶ ἀλλήλοις, ὡς Ἰησοῦς Χριστὸς τῷ πατρὶ κατὰ σάρκα, καὶ οἱ ἀπόστολοι τῷ Χριστῷ, καὶ τῷ πατρὶ, καὶ τῷ πνεύματι.

in the conclusion he takes his leave of them saying, "Be ye strengthened in concord, possessing the inseperable spirit of God, who is Jesus Christ *."———

To the Trallians he gives a caution against Heresy, "Stand therefore on your guard against such (as maintain Heresies) and success shall await you if you be not puffed up, and that you adhere inseperably to our God Jesus Christ †."———

But in his epistle to the Romans he speaks so directly and so frequently to this point that he seems to bend his whole force against Unitarianism, and to bear his testimony to the Godhead of our Redeemer with encreasing fervour, as he approached nearer to the martyrdom, that he was appointed to suffer for his name, and which he certainly considered as the most joyful event. He was under sentence of death, and on his way to execution, when he wrote before him to the Church at Rome, to solicit their acquiescence in his death,

---

* Ἔῤῥωσθε ἐν ὁμονοίᾳ, Θεῶ κεκλημένοι ἀδιάκριτον Πνεῦμα, ὅς ἐστιν Ἰησοῦς Χριστός. Let it be remembered here, that I have removed the first comma in the sentence from coming after Θεῶ, where it appears in all the editions, and placed it after ὁμονοίᾳ. The sense is good either way, but the masculine pronoun ὅς, seems to require such a position of the words as shall mark its reference to Θεῶ, with which I am of opinion it agrees. If any meer grammarian shall think it refers to Πνεῦμα, he is at liberty to restore the old pointing. Let him however recollect, that it makes no difference in the doctrine, whether we say that Jesus Christ be God or be that Spirit. "Now the Lord is that Spirit," says St. Paul, 2 Corinthians iii. 17; and whether this be spoken of the Father, or Son, I care not; for if the Father, the assertion of Ignatius makes the Godhead of the Son and Father to agree; if the Son, the assertion is found to agree with St. Paul's doctrine;—and the Spirit is personified.

† Φυλάτ[τ]εσθε ἐν τοῖς τοιούτοις, τοῦτο δὲ ἔσται ὑμῖν μὴ φυσιουμένοις καὶ ἔσιν ἀχωρίστοις Θεοῦ Ἰησοῦ Χριστοῦ.

death, that they would not interfere through an unreasonable good will in his behalf, and so take from him the opportunity of testifying his faith and confidence in Christ, but that they would suffer him to be devoured, be his torment never so extreme, that he may obtain his reward from him. He addresses himself to the church beloved and illuminated through the will of him who willeth all things that are " according to faith and the love of Jesus Christ our God and Saviour *." He salutes them, and prays that they may have joy " in our Lord God Jesus Christ †." He tells them that " our God Jesus Christ now that he is in the Father doth the more appear ‡." He desires their prayers, saying, " pray unto the Lord for me;" or as Wake turns it after an antient Greek manuscript, and after the old Latin version, " pray unto Christ for me §." Fearful lest they to whom he wrote should seek to preserve his life, which he earnestly wishes to lay down, as he says himself, " that I may enjoy Jesus Christ ‖." This stedfast Martyr beseeches them to let him become " the Freeman of Christ **." And again entreats them saying, " suffer me to l y hold on or to enter into pure light, where being come I shall indeed be

---

* Καΐα πίςιν και αγάπην Ίησε Χριςε τε Θεε και Σωτηρος ημων. The expression here is exactly similar to 2 Peter i. 1.

† Ἐν τῷ Κυρίῳ ἡμῶν Ἰησε Χριςῷ Θεῷ ἡμῶν.

‡ Ὁ Θεὸς ἡμῶν Ἰησες Χριςὸς ἐν Πατρὶ ὤν μᾶλλον φαίνεται.

§ Λιτανεύσατε τὸν Κύριον ὑπὲρ ἐμε. vel ut in mss. λιτανεύσατε τῷ Χριςῷ ὑπὲρ ἐμε.

‖ Ἴνα Ἰησε Χριςε ἐπιτύχω.

** Ἀπελεύθερος γενήσομαι Ἰησε Χριςε.

be the fervant of God *." He then breaks out into the following earneft requeft, "Permit me to be an imitatour of the fufferings of my God †." Are thefe equivocal terms? was Ignatius now an Unitarian? and yet the fecond century had commenced before this truely Chriftian man bore his laft teftimony to the divinity of our Lord. Archbifhop Wake is of opinion that he did not fuffer till the year 116, though the date of his martyrdom is more ufually placed in the year 107.

The RELATION OF THE MARTYRDOM OF ST. IGNATIUS has been written by men who accompanied him from Antioch to Rome, and who had been witneffes of his condemnation and death. The old Latin interpretation of it has been given by Archbifhop Ufher. From this I make my extracts, as Wake from this made his tranflation. There is a Greek copy, which is evidently corrupt. Cotelier has given an edition of it. He has likewife republifhed the old Latin verfion from Ufher.

When this venerable and conftant fpirited man ftood before Trajan at Antioch, to receive condemnation for being a Chriftian, he confeffed the charge boldly; and in a dialogue with the Emperour explained himfelf very fully upon it. He was furnamed THEOPHORUS (i. e. a Bearer of God) and alluding to the interpretation of this furname he replied to Trajan, who had opprobioufly called him "*Devil*," "no man fhould call Theophorus Devil," "for having within me Chrift the heavenly King, I diffolve the devices of the Devil."

To

* Ἀφίλε μὴ καθαρὸν φῶς λαμβάνειν· ἐκεῖ παραγινόμενος ἄνθρωπος Θεῦ ἔσομαι.

† Ἐάσέλέ με μιμηλὴν εἶναι. πάθης τῦ Θεῦ μῦ.

To the succeeding question of Trajan "and who is Theophorus?" he answered by thus translating the name, "he who has Christ in his breast." That Trajan understood him as declaring Christ to be God, the question which he put to him on receiving this answer will evince. "And do not we then seem to thee to have the Gods in our breast, who fight on our side against our enemies?" Ignatius having then declared that "they were evil spirits whom the Heathen esteemed to be Gods; that there is but one God, who made heaven and earth, and the sea, and all that are in them;" adds " and one Lord Jesus Christ his only begotten Son, whose favour may I enjoy." On which Trajan exclaimed, " his favour, you say, who was crucified under Pontius Pilate?" To which the Martyr subjoined, " who crucified sin with the inventour of it, and has put all the power and malice of the Devil under their feet, who bear him in their hearts." On this Trajan put his final interrogatory, " dost thou then carry Christ within thee?" and received an answer from Ignatius which must put his belief in our Lord's divinity beyond all farther controversy, for he says, " I do; for it is written I will dwell in them and walk in them *." Now where is this written? and by whom is it spoken? St. Paul shall tell us, " Ye are the temple

---

* *Traj.* Quis est tu, Cacodæmon? *Ignat.* Nullus THEOPHORUM vocat Cacodæmonem—Christum enim habens supercœlestem Regem, dissolvo horum insidias. *Traj.* Et quis est Theophorus? *Ignat.* Qui Christum habet in pectore. *Traj.* Et nos non tibi videmur habere Deos in pectore, quos habemus auxiliatores contra hostes? (Vel ut alias interpretatur " habere secundum intellectum Deos, quibus utimur compugnatoribus adversus adversarios?") *Ignat.* Dæmonia gentium Deos appellas; errans. unus enim est Deus, qui fecit cœlum et terram et mare et omnia quæ in ipsis; et unus Jesus Christus filius ipsius unigenitus, cujus amicitiâ fruar. *Traj.* Crucifixum dicis sub Pontio Pilato? *Ignat.* Crucifigentem peccatum, cum ipsius inventore; et omnem condemnantem dæmoniacam malitiam sub pedibus eorum qui ipsum in corde ferunt. *Traj.* Tu igitur in teipso Christum circumfers? *Ignat.* Etiam. scriptum est enim. " Inhabitabo in ipsis et inambulabo."

ple of the living God; AS GOD HATH SAID, I will dwell in them, and walk in them," 2 Corinthians vi. 16. Leviticus xxvi. 12. So that Christ dwelt within Ignatius, according to a promise made by God that he would do so. The Emperour then proceeded to give judgement, that he should be carried bound to Rome, there to be devoured by wild beasts, " having confessed that he bears about within himself him that was crucified *." And upon hearing this sentence the undaunted man cried out with joy, " I thank thee ô Lord, that thou hast vouchsafed to honour me with a perfect love towards thee, and hast made me to be put in iron bonds with thine apostle Paul †." We have already seen him in his progress to Rome writing to all the Churches, those epistles from which I have already drawn tho few extracts that are given above, with a mind perfectly disengaged from anxiety on the approach of a violent death. We are now to behold him undergo it, and the very last action which is recorded of him, is, that immediately before he was delivered to the beasts, " all the Brethren at Rome kneeling down with him, *he prayed to the Son of God* in behalf of the churches, that he would put a stop to the persecution, and encrease the love of the Brethren towards each other ‡." The historians of the death of this Martyr conclude their account of it with an assignment of their reason for giving it, viz. That the anniversary may be set apart to commemorate it, " that being assembled according to the time of his martyrdom we may communicate with the combatant.

G and

* *Trajanus sententiavit*, Ignatium præcipimus in seipso dicentem circumferre crucifixum, vinctum duci, &c.

† Gratias ago tibi, domine, quia me perfectâ ad te charitate honorare dignatus es, cum Apostolo tuo Paulo vinculis collocari ferreis.

‡ Cum genuflexione omnium Fratrum, deprecans Filium Dei pro Ecclesiis, pro persecutionis quietatione, pro Fratrum adinvicem Charitate, &c.

and valiant Martyr of Chrift, who trod under-foot the Devil, and bare down his fnares even unto the end, in his venerable and holy memory glorifying our Lord Jefus Chrift: *through whom and with whom* all glory and power be to the Father, with *the Holy Ghoft*, in the Holy Church for ever and ever. Amen *." This account I have already faid was written by men who accompanied St. Ignatius from Antioch to Rome, and had been themfelves witneffes both to his trial and his death; they have given us a picture of his laft moments, which were fpent in prayer to Chrift (and we do not hear that this Martyr faw Chrift when he called upon him †) fo that his practice concurred with the doctrines he delivered.—The writers of his martyrdom were themfelves Chriftians alfo in no later than the beginning of the fecond century, and the concluding doxology, together with the concurrence which they declare the brethren to have teftified with Ignatius, with whom they kneeled down and called upon Chrift, afford inconteftible proof that there were many Chriftians of that early age who were not Unitarians, and I believe that notwithftanding there were fome herefies exifting even then, the proof that any of the Church were of Mr. Lindfey's way of thinking, is more than he can make out, however boldly he may have afferted it.

St. Polycarp was likewife the difciple of St. John, and by him appointed Bifhop of Smyrna, over which Church he prefided at the time when " the firft and the laft which was dead and is alive" bore
teftimony

---

* Ut fecundùm tempus Martyrii congregati, communicemus athletæ et virili Chrifti Martyri, qui conculcavit diabolum, et hujus infidias in finem proftravit; glorificantes, in ipfius venerabili et fanctâ memoriâ, dominum noftrum, Jefum Chriftum. per quem, et cum quo, Patri gloria et potentia, cum fpiritu fancto, in fanctâ ecclefiâ in fecula feculorum. Amen.

† See Apology, p. 129.

testimony to the purity of its religion, saying, " I know thy works, and tribulation, and poverty, *but thou art rich*," Revelation ii. 8, 9. It is to be hoped that he has received from our Redeemer " a crown of life," as he has been found " faithful unto death," for with unshaken constancy he underwent the infliction of the severest torments for the sake of the name of Jesus Christ, in whose divinity we shall presently see him professing his belief, and, rather than relinquish it, yielding up his life at a stake. It is not decided whether he suffered under Antoninus Pius, in the year 147, or M. Aurelius, in the year 167. I rather conceive the former myself, for though it be certain that he lived to a very great age, it comes more within the limits of probability, that he survived Ignatius only forty than sixty years. They had been cotemporaries and received the doctrines of Christianity from St. John together, and when Ignatius was put to death they were both advanced in years. For the same reason I think the martyrdom of Ignatius more likely to have been inflicted in the year 116 than 107, for, these two dates being allowed of, the survivourship of Polycarp is reduced from sixty to no more than thirty-one years; which is yet a great difference in the ages of two old men.

St. Polycarp has left behind him one short epistle to the Philippians. Archbishop Wake has translated it into English. We have likewise a version of it by Doctor Cave annexed to his history of this Martyr's life.

As he writes to the Philippians he seems to refer to the epistle which St. Paul had formerly addressed to the same people, for after a benediction and prayer that " mercy and peace may be abundantly granted to them

them by God Almighty and the Lord Jefus Chrift *," he fpeaks of our Lord in terms fimilar to thofe of the Apoftle, *Philippians* ii. 10, as of him " to whom all things heavenly and earthly are fubject, whom every breath worfhippeth, who cometh the judge of the quick and the dead, whofe blood God fhall require of thofe who believe not on him" or " who are difobedient unto him †." " For," he farther fays, " we are all before the eyes of the Lord and God, and we muft all ftand before the judgement feat of Chrift, and each render an account for himfelf, let us therefore humbly ferve him with fear and all reverence ‡." Paul " knowing the terrour of the Lord" has ufed the fame argument as a motive to the prefervation of a good confcience; and knowing alfo that " it is written, every tongue fhall confefs to God," urges the judgement feat of Chrift, before which we fhall all ftand, every man to give an account of himfelf to God, as a reafon for deferring to judge one another," fee Romans xiv. 10, 11, 12, and 2 Corinthians v. 10, 11. Having in another place of the fame epiftle quoted 1 Peter ii. 24, in which our Saviour is faid to have borne our fins in his own body on the tree, and to have healed us by his ftripes, St. Polycarp proceeds in his own perfon to fay, " but he fuffered all things for us that we might live in him, let us therefore imitate his patience, and if we

suffer

* Ἔλεος ὑμῖν καὶ εἰρήνη παρὰ Θεῦ παντοκράτορος καὶ Κυρίε Ἰησῦ Χριστῦ τῦ Σωτῆρος ἡμῶν πληθυνθείη.

† Ὧ ὑπετάγη τὰ πάντα ἐπουράνια καὶ ἐπίγεια, ᾦ πᾶσα πνοὴ λατρεύει, ὃς ἔρχεται κριτὴς ζώντων καὶ νεκρῶν· ὃ τὸ αἷμα ἐκζητήσει ὁ Θεὸς ἀπὸ τῶν ἀπειθούντων αὐτῷ.

‡ Ἀπέναντι γὰρ τῶν τῦ Κυρίυ καὶ Θεῦ ἐσμεν ὀφθαλμῶν, καὶ πάντας δεῖ παραστῆναι τῷ βήματι τῦ Χριστῦ, καὶ ἕκαστον ὑπὲρ ἑαυτῦ λόγον δῦναι· ὅπως οὖν δουλεύσωμεν αὐτῷ μετὰ φόβου καὶ πάσης εὐλαβείας.

suffer for his name let us glorify him *." He then exhorts them to follow the example of patience which was set them by Ignatius, by Paul, and the rest of the Apostles and Martyrs, " being confident that all these have not run in vain but in faith and righteousness, and are gone to the place which was due to them from the Lord, with whom also they suffered †."

From these few extracts taken from the only short work of Polycarp, we may clearly see what was the faith of this holy man, to whom he preferred worship, to whom he ascribed glory and reverence, and from whom he expected the promised reward of his patience, even from our Lord Jesus Christ, who had promised him a crown of life if he were found faithful unto death, Rev. ii. 10. And faithful unto death we shall find that he was from the history of his martyrdom delivered by persons present at his sufferings. For in an EPISTLE FROM THE CHURCH AT SMYRNA directed to the Church of God at Philadelphia, on which it calls down " the multiplication of peace and love from God the Father and the Lord Jesus Christ ‡," we learn that he was burned to death at Smyrna in the presence of his own church. This epistle has been published by Archbishop Usher, and from his edition, in Valesius's

---

* Ἀλλὰ δι' ἡμᾶς, ἵνα ζήσωμεν ἐν αὐτῷ, πάντα ὑπέμεινε. Μιμηταὶ ἐν γενώμεθα τῆς ὑπομονῆς αὐτοῦ· καὶ ἐάν πάσχωμεν διὰ τὸ ὄνομα αὐτοῦ, δοξάζομεν αὐτόν.

† Πεπεισμένους ὅτι οὗτοι πάντες ἐκ εἰς κενὸν ἔδραμον· ἀλλ' ἐν πίστει καὶ δικαιοσύνῃ· καὶ εἰς τὸν ὀφειλόμενον αὐτοῖς τόπον εἰσι παρὰ τῷ Κυρίῳ, ᾧ καὶ συνέπαθον.

‡ Ἔλεος, εἰρήνη, καὶ ἀγάπη Θεοῦ Πατρὸς, καὶ Κυρίου ἡμῶν Ἰησοῦ Χριστοῦ πληθυνθείη.

fius's notes upon Eufebius, who has only given a part of it in his hiftory. Archbifhop Wake has tranflated this epiftle alfo into Englifh.

The writers in the courfe of their relation, fpeaking of the holy Martyrs of Chrift who had fuffered at Smyrna, fay, that not fo much as a figh or groan efcaped them, " for being fupported by the grace of Chrift they defpifed all the torments of the world *; and concerning Polycarp himfelf they declare, that when the Proconful would with promifes of liberty have perfuaded him to " reproach Chrift †," he gave for anfwer, " eighty and fix years have I now ferved Chrift, and he hath never done me the leaft injury, how then can I blafpheme my Saviour and my King ‡ ?" Even at the moment when he was tied to the ftake and the executioner about to light the fire, he expreffed his gratitude to God for bringing him into the number of his Martyrs, " for this and for all things elfe I praife thee, I blefs thee, I glorify thee, through the eternal High Prieft Jefus Chrift thy beloved Son, through whom, to thee, with him in the Holy Ghoft be glory both now and to all fucceeding ages. Amen §." Thefe were the laft words of this ftedfaft

man,

* Προσέχονίες τῇ τῶ Χριςῶ χάριλι, τῶν κοσμικῶν καλεφρόνυν βασάνων.

† Λοιδόρησον τὸν Χριςὸν.

‡ Ὀγδοήκονία καὶ ἓξ ἔιη δυλεύω αυτῷ καὶ ἐδεν με ἠδίκησε. καὶ πῶς δύναμαι βλασφημῆσαι τὸν βασιλέα μῶ, τον σωσανία μι.

§ Διὰ τῶτο, καὶ περὶ πάνων Ϲὲ αἰνῶ, Ϲὲ εὐλογῶ, Ϲὲ δοξάζω, διὰ τῶ αἰωνίε αρχιερέως Ἰησῶ Χριςῶ, τῶ ἀγαπηλῶ Ϲῶ παιδός· δι' ἆ Ϲοι Ϲὺν αυτῷ ἐν πνεύμαλι ἁγιῷ δόξα καὶ νῦν, καὶ ἲις τὲς μέλλονίας αἰῶνας. Ἀμήν. Archbifhop Wake has tranflated this paffage,

from

man, who suffered about the middle of the second century; and though I do not defire to make even this difciple of our Lord's immediate witneffes a witnefs himfelf, from whom we fhould derive any acquaintance with the nature of our Lord, yet his words may teftify thus much to a certainty, that he did himfelf believe the divinity not only of our Saviour but alfo of the Holy Ghoft, for he here dies with a doxology to the whole Trinity as explicit as any that has been ufed fince his day.

But let us fay that the writers of this epiftle are not to be credited in their relation of St. Polycarp's death, it amounts equally to a confutation of Mr. Lindfey's affertion, for they were themfelves cotemporary with their Bifhop; and fuppofing that Polycarp had never uttered fuch words, the Church of Smyrna, which has afcribed them to him, has undoubtedly expreffed its own tenets, and they were a very early body of Chriftian men, who were therefore not Unitarians.

But the hiftorians of this Martyrdom proceed to give a ftill clofer teftimony of their own belief in Chrift, for they tell us, that Nicetas urged the Governour not to fuffer the Smyrnæans to take away the bones of Polycarp, " left," fays he, " forfaking him that was crucified, they fhould begin to worfhip this Polycarp; and this he faid at the fuggeftion and inftance of the Jews, who alfo watched us that we fhould not take any part of him out of the fire; not knowing that neither is it poffible for us to forfake Chrift, who fuffered

---

from a copy which I have not, as follows: " For this and for all things elfe I praife thee, I blefs thee, I glorify thee, with the eternal and heavenly Jefus Chrift, thy beloved Son, with whom, to thee, and the Holy Ghoft, be glory, both now and to all fucceeding ages. Amen."

fered for the falvation of all fuch as fhall be faved throughout the whole world, the righteous for the ungodly; nor worfhip any other befides him, for him indeed who is the Son of God we do adore; but for the Martyrs we worthily love them as the difciples and imitatours of our Lord, and on account of their exceeding great devotion towards their King and Mafter *." Farther on the writer's defire that the epiftle when read may be fent unto the Brethren that are at a diftance, " that they alfo may glorify the Lord who maketh fuch choice of his own fervants, and is able to bring all of us by his grace and help to his eternal kingdom, through his only begotten Son Jefus Chrift, to whom be glory, and honour, and power, and majefty for ever and ever. Amen †." But as this doxology may be fuppofed (however perverfely ‡) to refer to

the

* Μὴ, φησὶν, ἀφέντες τὸν ἐςαυρομένον, τῦτον ἄρξωνίαι ςέβειν· καὶ ταῦτα εἶπον ὑποβαλόνίων καὶ ἐνισχυσάνίων Ἰυδάιων, οἳ γὰρ ἐτήρησαν μελλόνίων ἡμῶν ἐκ τῦ πυρὸς αὐτὸν λαμβάνειν· ἀγνοῦνίες ὅτι ὅτε τὸν Χριςὸν ποτὲ καταλιπεῖν δυνησόμεθα, τὸν ὑπὲρ τῆς τῦ παντὸς κόσμε τῶν σωζομένων Σωτηρίας παθόντα, ὅτε ἕτερόν τινα ςέβειν· τῦτον μὲν γὰρ υἱὸν ὄντα τῦ Θεῦ προσκυνῦμεν, τές δὲ μάρτυρας, ὡς μαθητὰς τῦ Κυρίυ καὶ μιμητὰς, ἀγαπῶμεν ἀξίως ἕνεκα ἐυνοίας ἀνυπερβλήτυ τῆς εἰς τὸν ἴδιον βασιλέα καὶ διδάσκαλον.

† Ἵνα καὶ ἐκεῖνοι δοξάζωσι τὸν Κυρίον τὸν ἐκλογὰς ποιῦντα ἀπὸ τῶν ἰδίων δέλων: τῷ δυναμένῳ πάντας ἡμᾶς εἰσαγαγεῖν ἐν τῇ αὐτῦ χάριτι, καὶ δωρεᾷ, εἰς τὴν αἰώνιον αὐτῦ βασιλείαν, διὰ παιδὸς αὐτῦ τῦ μονογενῦς Ἰησῦ Χριςῦ, ᾧ ἡ δόξα, τιμή, κράτ⊙, μεγαλωσύνη εἰς αἰῶνας. Ἀμήν.

‡ I expect the doxology quoted from St. Clement, p. 13 above, will come under the fame mifinterpretation. St. Clement has, befides the epiftle which has defcended to our time, written feveral others which were extant in the days of Eufebius, who quotes Gaius, faying, that " by Clement and feveral others Chrift is declared to be God," Cambridge edition, 1720, book 5, chap. 28. p. 252. Gaius was himfelf a writer in the beginning of

the

the name of God preceding his incarnate name Jefus Chrift, the following paffage, from the fame epiftle, may ferve to remove fuch a fuggeftion, and obviate any Unitarian inferences that might be drawn from it, for when the writers are giving the date of Polycarp's martyrdom, they fay " he was taken by Herod, Philip the Trallian being High-Prieft; Stratius Quadratus Proconful; but our Saviour Chrift reigning for evermore, to whom be honour, glory, majefty, and an eternal throne from generation to generation. Amen *;" and then conclude their epiftle, praying for all happinefs to the Brethren, " by living according to the rule of the gofpel of Jefus Chrift, with whom glory be to God the Father and the Holy Ghoft, for the falvation of his chofen faints †."

Though, for the greater uniformity, I have produced the names of Ignatius and Polycarp in the fecond century,

the third century, and I fhall hereafter bring a larger teftimony than this, that *be* was not an Unitarian. But with refpect to St. Clement, from whom however I have fupplied fome ftrong paffages, fuppofing that not one of them be allowed to me, I anfwer in the words of Bifhop Bull on the fame fubject, " Mihi fanè perridiculi femper vifi funt, qui cum epiftolam aliquam veteris Scriptoris, aut breviufculum tractatum (unicum illud & forte induhitatum authoris (ωζόμενοι) legunt, in eoque fentiunt dogma aliquod chriftianæ fidei vel omnino intactum, vel non fatis liquido explicatum efie (authore fcilicet, re exigente, in aliud intento) continuô fcriptorem ipfum, nefcio cujus hærefis fufpectum habent. Sed nobis fufficit quod ipfe Clemens in epiftolâ fuâ nufquam (Photio ipfo favente) Chriftum Dominum blafphemet."

* Συνελήφθη ὑπο Ἡρώδε, ἐπι ἀρχιερέως Φιλίππε Τραλλιανε, ἀνθυπατεύοντος Στρατίε Κοδράτε, βασιλεύοντος δὲ εἰς τὰς αἰῶνας Ἰησε Χριςε, ᾧ ἡ δόξα, τιμή, μηγαλωσύνη, θρονος αἰώνιος ἀπο γενεᾶς εἰς γενεάν. Ἀμήν.

† Ἐρρῶσθαι ὑμᾶς εὐχόμεθα, ἀδελφοὶ, ςοιχῶντες τῷ, κατα τὸ εὐαγγέλιον, λόγῳ Ἰησε Χριςε, μεθ᾽ ε δόξα τῷ Θεῷ, καὶ Πατρὶ, καὶ ἁγιῳ Πνεύματι, ἐπι Σωτηρια τῃ τῶν ἁγιῶν ἐκλεκτῶν.

tury, I do not confider the firſt age of the Church to have cloſed till theſe venerable men were withdrawn from her. They had been the diſciples of our Lord's immediate witneſſes, and we may therefore ſuppoſe preſerved the purity of our religion untainted. Their precept and their practice I have now laid before my reader; I have ſhewed them active in propagating the true belief, and pouring out their blood to teſtify that this belief is in the Godhead of our Saviour; I have produced their frequent recommendations to worſhip and rely upon Chriſt; and I have exhibited them both in their laſt moments, teſtifying their own reliance on him; in expectation of their reward from him, committing their ſpirits into the hands of their Redeemer; and even expiring with a doxology to the Father, the Son, and the Holy Ghoſt. But this is not all, "the flocks of God, which he had purchaſed with his own blood" and committed to the care of theſe faithful ſhepherds, have been preſented to the reader's view, and have made it very apparent with what food they had been nouriſhed by them. Theſe alſo we find repeatedly glorifying the three Perſons in one Godhead. Shall we now ſay that a Trinity was the invention of a ſubſequent age? that a belief in the Godhead of Chriſt was a late corruption of the Goſpel, and with Paul of Samoſata, who, like Mr. Lindſey, *amended* the Liturgy of his time, pronounce the worſhip of our Lord an innovation, and "aboliſh the Pſalms ſung to Jeſus Chriſt as novel and the productions of modern men?" Let Paul himſelf confute the aſſertion ſo far as the queſtion now agitating is concerned, for if he had ſuch a worſhip to aboliſh, it muſt have ſubſiſted in the ſecond century, and therefore it was not an innovation after the cloſe of the third; but I ſhall reſerve the particular detail of Paul's condemnation for its proper place, I now only allude to it, in order to ſhew that

Chriſt

Chrift was the fubject of facred hymns during the time of the firft Chriftians, and to confirm the more particular teftimony of Pliny, the minifter of Trajan, and cotemporary of thefe Apoftolic Fathers, who declares of the Chriftians that it was their cuftom " to fing refponfive hymns to Chrift as to God *."

Had Herefy gone abroad and calumniated the truth, we fhould hardly have found her affertours more explicit in maintaining the divinity of our Saviour than thefe early difciples of the Gofpel have been. It is true that fome corrupted doctrines had been broached even in the days of the Apoftles themfelves, as from their writings we may collect; in thofe of their immediate fucceffours the number encreafed, but they had not yet obtained confequence enough to provoke a controverfy, in which men fetting themfelves againft errour are always more direct to the point miftaken, and more exprefs in eftablifhing the particular truth from which the deviation had been made. They endeavour to give it ftrength to maintain its ground againft the affault which has been made upon it. The fame fun which warms the bloffom into fweetnefs, vivifies the canker that confumes its beauty. Time, the reputed parent of truth, gives birth likewife to many an errour which would fupplant her. And hence we may very eafily account for the encreafing particularity with which the advocates of truth defend her; wherever the enemy appears they prefent themfelves, and wherever a breach has been attempted they fly to occupy the fcene and repel the attack. It is a difingenuous fallacy to fay that every new expreffion for an old doctrine, is itfelf a new doctrine; or that a more explicit affertion of an antient tenet, is the introduction of a new tenet. I am bold to fay there is no man who, having found himfelf

* Carmenque Chrifto quafi Deo canere fecum invicem.
Plin. Lib. 10. Epift. 97.

himself mifapprehended upon the firft delivery of his fentiments, would not, upon a call to explain himfelf, give other terms to a repetition of his opinion, and this too without making the fmalleft alteration in it. In the fame manner, mifapprehended or wilfully mifreprefented, Chriftianity required the explanation of its adherents to vindicate it, and they have repeated in other words thofe tenets which had been mifapprehended as at firft delivered. As errour fpread, it became neceffary, in order to obftruct its progrefs, to fend abroad the truth in as concife terms as it could be fummed into. Hence creeds were framed, and hence, as the feparate tenets of our religion met with oppofition, thofe tenets were more largely avowed, and added from time to time to thofe profeffions of faith by which, as we make them in the congregation, we affure one another that we are members of one and the fame communion, and not of the communion of thofe who deny thefe truths. Is the body of the Church to dangle after every diffenter? and if not, is it not neceffary to give a marked expreffion to the doctrines which it retains, though diffented from? In thefe doctrines the diftinction lies, and our adherence fhould be rendered obvious by terms too perfpicuous to admit of being wrefted. General terms will do well where all concur, but where variance fubfifts, a language that fhall difcriminate profeffions becomes indifpenfably requifite. And I cannot agree with Mr. Lindfey in thinking that the latter claufe of our doxology (*viz. As it was in the beginning is now*, &c.) had either "an unchriftian or uncharitable origin, becaufe it was added by St. Jerom, left crafty heretics might ftill have gone on with their blafphemy in underftanding the Son of God not to have exifted always with the Father, but to have had a beginning of exiftence," fee Apol. p. 119. I cannot conceive a better reafon for the addition; and I think

alfo

also that a denial of the procedure of the Holy Ghost from the Son was a full justification of those who added *and the Son* to the clause in the Nicene Creed, which now says that he " proceedeth from the Father *and the Son.*" He does proceed from the Son, and what matter when it was first professed in a creed; it was without doubt judiciously inserted whenever the fact, which it affirms, came first to be denied. There is scarce a common-place sentiment existing on which volumes have not been written, the original simplicity of the thought is still however unimpaired. Heterodox tenets have called men to abet the doctrines of the holy Scriptures, and in the performance of this duty they have indeed swelled to volumes of enormous magnitude; there is nothing so plain on which we may not enlarge; and can they be blamed who have made the word of God their subject, especially when they saw that there was nothing so plain which might not be mistaken, and which errour might not pervert? The original simplicity of the Gospel is still however unimpaired, and with the properties of a right line continues a test of all that can be spoken concerning the nature of our Creator and Redeemer; to this whatever doctrines are written must finally be referred, to this they must be brought as to a standard, and by their conformity with, or deviation from, this, we must determine upon their rectitude or perversion; the circumstance that induced them is out of the question, whether it be the confutation of a new doctrine which makes us large and particular in the vindication of the old, or the natural warmth of conviction which animates our utterance of an interesting persuasion.—We find, however, that without the stimulus of controversy, the Apostolic Fathers have all declared their firm belief in the divinity of our Lord Jesus Christ; and though I will not go so far upon these grounds as to say that therefore he is one with the Father God, I will

yet

yet infer the conclusion which necessarily results, therefore the Apostolick Fathers, and consequently all Christian people of their age, were not Unitarians. Many writers have ascribed inspiration to these reverend men: If any reader concur in this sentiment, he must deduce a larger inference than I have ventured to draw from their assertions. Though I cannot go so far, I must however say that the tenets of the Instructor are in a great measure deducible from those of the Disciple, and therefore that the works of the Apostolick Fathers may very well serve to illustrate the writings of the Apostles themselves, whose disciples or associates they had been. *

Were there any reason to acquiesce in the writings ascribed to Dionysius the Areopagite, I should have investigated the faith of this immediate convert to the preaching of St. Paul, Acts xvii. 34, before I had entered upon an enquiry into the doctrines of the subsequent Fathers of the Church, who did not derive their Christianity directly from the Apostles, but were instructed in it by their disciples, or by the study of the holy Scriptures as they were now sent out into all the world. From a state of the sentiments, however, of a writer who flourished so early as the middle of the second century, and in the year 177, presented an apology for the Christians to M. Aurelius Antoninus, the tenets originally embraced by the Church of Athens may be very reasonably collected, those entertained in the time of our author himself irrefragably proved.

Thus then writes ATHENAGORAS, the Christian Philosopher at Athens, in his " Ambassy for the Christians,"

* Archbishop Wake, by a translation sufficiently faithful, has made all their genuine remains, together with the martyrdom of the two last, accessible to the English reader.

ftians," which, with another little tract on the refurrection, are all the remains of this author now extant.

The Son of God is his subject, of whom he affirms that "by him and through him were all things made, the Father and the Son being one, the Son being in the Father, and the Father in the Son, in the unity and power of the Spirit *." He then proceeds more largely to declare his belief in the divinity of the Holy Ghost, and having professed it, sums up the whole doctrine he had been delivering, and opposes it to the calumny of the Gentiles against the Christians, saying, " who is he then that will not hesitate to believe when he hears us called Men without a God, who preach the Father to be God, the Son to be God, and the Holy Ghost, who manifest their power in unity and their distinction in order? †" and again he says, that the Christians set but little value on a life of sensuality, that they look to a future state, and therefore make it their business " to know God and his word, what is the unity of the Son with the Father, what the community of the Father with the Son, what is the Spirit, what is the Unity," or to borrow an expression from Mr. Lindsey, " the Oneness of these who are so many, and what is the distinction of these who are

---

* Πρὸς αὐτῶ γὰρ καὶ δι᾽ αὐτῶ πάντα ἐγένετο, ἑνὸς ὄντος τῶ Πατρὸς καὶ τῶ Υἱῶ· ὄντος δὲ τῶ Υἱῶ ἐν Πατρὶ, καὶ Πατρὸς ἐν Υἱῶ, ἐνότητι καὶ δυνάμει Πνεύματος." Πρεσβεία πέρι Χριστιανῶν, p. 38, Oxford edit. 16mo, 1682.

† Τίς ἂν ἐκ ἂν ἀπορήσαι, λέγοντας Θεὸν Πατέρα, καὶ Υἱὸν Θεὸν, καὶ Πνεῦμα ἅγιον: δεικνύντας αὐτῶν καὶ τὴν ἐν τῇ ἑνώσει δύναμιν καὶ τὴν ἐν τῇ τάξει διαίρεσιν, ἀκούσας ἀθέους καλυμένους. P. 41.

are one, the Spirit, the Son, the Father *." He farther endeavours to make the unity of the Father and his " inseparable Son †" intelligible to the Emperours M. Aurelius Antoninus, and his son and partner in government L. Aurelius Commodus, by exemplifying it in the unity of their empire ‡.

An

---

* Θεὸν καὶ τὸν παρ' αὐτᾶ λογὸν ἔιδεναι, τίς ἡ τᾶ παιδὸς πρὸς τὸν Παλέρα ἑνότης, τίς ἡ τᾶ Παλρὸς πρὸς τὸν Ὑιὸν κοινωνία, τί τὸ Πνεῦμα, τίς ἡ τῶν τοσύτων ἕνωσις, καὶ διάιρεσις ἑνεμένων, τᾶ Πνεύματ⊙, τᾶ Παιδὸς, τᾶ Παλρ⊙. P. 49.

† Υἱῷ ἀμερίσῳ. P. 70.

‡ Ausonius, who wrote just fifty years after the council of Nice, in a poem entitled *Versus Paschalis*, makes a most horribly blasphemous address to Valentinianus, Gratianus, and Valens. His subject is the Resurrection, &c. After having recited his belief in the Trinity, having called Christ " the Word, and God, Verbum, Deumque," declared him " equal to the Father, Patri parem ;" and having professed " his faith in a Trinity, in the Unity of God, his firm hope of salvation from embracing this number and adding virtues to his faith,

   Trina fides, Auctore uno; spes certa salutis
   Hunc numerum junctis virtutibus amplectenti,"

he compliments Valentinianus with the paternal Character; and in conjunction with his son and brother Gratianus and Valens, whom he had taken into partnership of empire, he pronounces them all together a Trinity in Unity. The application is very different, but the thought is the same with that of the pious Athenagoras.

Besides this, some remarkable expressions occur in the poems of Ausonius; he lived in the fourth century, and therefore I shall throw them into the note. In a poem entitled *Gryphus* he says,

Tres Deus unus. V. 88. - | The one God is three.

In another, stiled *Ephemeris*, he allots the first hours of the day to prayer,

Deus precandus est mihi,	God is to be invoked by me, and
Ac Filius summi Dei,	the Son of the most high God,
Majestas uniusmodi,	their Majesty in conjunction with
Sociata sacro Spiritu.	the Holy Ghost being equal, or
	of one nature.

And

An attempt to illuſtrate the myſtery of godlineſs, by which we learn that God was made manifeſt in the fleſh, and know that our crucified Saviour is one with the Father, the God who purchaſed us with his own blood, 1 Timothy iii. 16, and Acts xx. 28, muſt for ever fail of rendering it comprehenſible by us. The Fathers have neverthelefs frequently attempted to bring parallels from objects we are acquainted with, in order to introduce us in ſome degree to the knowledge of a matter which cannot have its parallel in created nature. If therefore, in the courſe of this work, I ſhall produce any of their efforts to elucidate the Trinity, or the eternal generation or procedure of the Son or Spirit, I ſhall do it not with a view of elucidating the ſubject myſelf, or ſhewing that they entertained any more adequate idea of it than we poſſeſs, but of proving to a certainty that they firmly believed in it. For they would not have taken pains to form, or endeavoured to communicate adequate ideas of a doctrine which they did not believe. It is not the wiſdom or the ſagacity of the Fathers that I am about to exhibit, but their faith. That they did not ſee the limits of their own faculties, nor conſider that the ſubject of their reſearches is placed beyond their utmoſt extent, is no reaſon for ſaying that they did not believe what they made ineffectual efforts to explain; they muſt have believed it in order to prompt the endeavour. The coëvality of the ſun and his brightneſs which, though generated from him, is yet a

fine

And then proceeding to the prayer itſelf he addreſſes it to Chriſt, whom he calls upon by the titles of
    Salvator, Deus, ac Dominus, Mens, Gloria, Verbum.
  Filius, ex Vero Verus, de Lumine Lumen. Ver. 81.
Saviour, God and Lord, Mind, Glory, Word, Son, very *God* of very *God*, Light of Light.
  ' Though Auſonius wrote after the council of Nice, we find a ſingular concurrence between his language and that of the Antenicene Athenagoras, whoſe words or ſentiments were certainly not borrowed from the deciſions of that great Synod.

sine quâ non of his existence; of a springing fountain and its effluent stream; and such-like examples are brought very frequently to illustrate the coëternity of God and his inherent wisdom; the coëternity and unity of the Father and the Son; and we shall in the following passage, the last which I mean to bring in evidence of its author's belief, find Athenagoras endeavouring by an example to set the unity and procedure of the Holy Ghost before our understanding, for he says, " we profess God and the Son his word and the Holy Ghost, and that the Father, the Son, and the *Holy Ghost* are truly one as concerning power; that the Son is the Mind, the Word, the Wisdom of the Father; and the Holy Ghost a proceeding Effluence as Light is from fire *."

St. Paul himself preached Christ at Athens, where we see that he was still considered to be the God which the Apostle had declared him. *Acts* xvii. *see also Scriptural Conf. p.* 94. I think therefore that from these few extracts taken from *the ambassy of Athenagoras*, I may fairly hope for my readers concurrence in this conclusion, that neither this ambassadour nor the Athenian Christians, whose sentiments he was employed to represent to the Emperour, were Unitarians.

Unitarians so seldom make affirmative propositions, that it must appear to them a very extraordinary instance of generosity in me not to put them to the proof of their own assertions, and sit down as they usually do themselves in the indolent possession of a negative. Perhaps they affirmed for once, in hopes that nothing but

---

* Θεὸν Φαμὶν, καὶ Ὑιὸν τὸν λογὸν αὐτῦ, καὶ Πνεῦμα ἅγιον, ἑνόμενα μὲν κατὰ δύναμιν τὸν Πατέρα, τὸν Ὑιὸν, τὸ Πνεῦμα. ὅτι νῦς, λόγος, σοφία, Ὑιὸς τῦ Πατρὸς, καὶ ἀπόρροια ὡς φῶς ἀπὸ πυρὸς τὸ Πνεῦμα. P. 110.

but an unsupported denial would be given. It may be bold to undertake the proof of a negative, they may call it illogical, and I grant it would have been more easy to have called on them to make good what they had affirmed. The testimony, however, on which alone it could have been supported, is as open to my enquiry as to theirs, and I was referred to an enquiry in order to ascertain its *undeniable truth*. This I have accordingly proceeded to make, and how far I have found the assertion deniable or undeniable I now proceed to shew. Though the great truths of religion by no means depend upon what opinions any set of men have entertained of them, it is of importance to take away every prop on which errour may even hope to support herself. I had before endeavoured to merge her in the waters of the sacred fountain, where in the end she must drown; but in order to cut off every hope of recovery, every respite, and to prevent her power to lift her pernicious head again, I now tear away from the bank every bough, every reed at which she might catch and delay her own extirpation. I had already shewn that the word of God altogether opposed the Deism of the Unitarians; the Fathers have been implored to protect the tenet, they too refuse their succour; and when in the end I shall have made this fully appear, I shall appear myself to have argued to somewhat more than a meer negative; a negative pregnant with an affirmation, to whose delivery I shall leave the judgement of my reader to act the midwife.

The earliest of the Fathers who drew their belief from the holy Scriptures without any personal knowledge of their inspired writers, is JUSTIN MARTYR. He was a Samaritan, the Son of a Gentile, who had been fent by Flavius Vefpafianus, with other colonifts, into the city antiently called Sichem, but from that Emperour's prenomen afterwards denominated Flavia.

The adjunct to this eminent man's name, which he has always borne fince his fufferings, points out that he preferred the forfeit of his life to the furrender of his Chriftianity. He did fo, for at the inftance of Crefcens, a Philofopher at Rome, he was brought to bear the laft teftimony to the fincerity of his faith, and on the alternative being propofed to him, declared that he defired nothing more earneftly than to endure torments for the fake of Jefus Chrift, as he might thence hope to obtain falvation, and to appear with fuller confidence before the dreadful tribunal of our Lord and Saviour. He was accordingly firft whipped with fcourges, and afterwards, upon his perfeverance, beheaded at Rome A. D. 164, under M. Aurelius Antoninus; an Emperour who tarnifhed the brightnefs of a virtuous name by fprinkling it over with a lamentable effufion of Chriftian blood.

There fubfifts fo fingular a contraft between the conduct of this ingenuous man and that of our modern Unitarians, that I cannot avoid a fhort digreffion in order to mark it to my reader.

Though a native of Samaria, he was not only brought up in ignorance of the Jewifh Law, but even of the language of the country in which he was born. His father, who was a Gentile, had inftructed him in the tenets he embraced himfelf, and accordingly we find that the fon had, at an early period of his life, become a very great proficient in the philofophy of the Gentiles. He earneftly wifhed to acquire a knowledge of the truth, and with an impartiality fitted to fuch a

purfuit

pursuit sought for her, not by an attachment to the dogmas of any one master; but by a diligent enquiry into the tenets of all, and in the end we find him declare himself dissatisfied with his researches; that neither the Peripateticks nor Stoicks, the followers of Pythagoras nor of Plato, had rendered him any satisfactory account of the Supreme Being, of the nature or destination of the human soul.

The object of his pursuit was high, and as his ardour was suitable, it is not to be conceived that he should relinquish it upon this disappointment; a speculative habit, acquired by much reading, had qualified him for perseverance, and he determined to try whether his own suggestions on the subject might not prove more successful than those of men whose opinions he had already condemned. Solitude was more favourable to such an enquiry as he was now engaged in, than the haunts of men; he accordingly sought for retirement, and withdrawing from the converse of the world, in an agreeable narrative, presents himself to our view taking a lonely walk on the sea-shore, working on his own ideas towards the discovery of the nature of God.

While thus philosophically employed, he informs us himself, that one day he was accosted by an unknown old man *, of a venerable and benevolent countenance, to whom,

---

* Whatever occurs in the antient writers of history of a speculative nature, we find to be an inference from a fact stated, without any seeming view to the deduction, but to the unadulterated representation of which the historian appears to have religiously attended. Whatever occurs in the modern writers of history of a narrative nature, we find to be an inference from a system previously assumed, without any seeming view to the truth of the facts recorded, but to the establishment of which the historian appears, through every species of misrepresentation, to have zealously directed

whom, in the courſe of a converſation, he communicated the occaſion of his ſolitude, and the little ſatisfaction he found himſelf able to obtain concerning the object of his difquiſition. That, on this complaint, the old man referred his inquiſitive mind to the prophets, as a better and ſurer guide to the true knowledge and underſtanding of God, than the writings among which he had heretofore looked for it. That on this recommendation he accordingly turned to the ſtudy of the ſacred Scriptures, and, acquieſcing in the great truths revealed therein, adhered to them as the only means by which God can be known to man. He pronounces on this occaſion his ſupreme contempt of all the Gentile ſchools; but

ed his force. The late Mr. Hume, for inſtance, converted the hiſtory of this nation into a defence of the Stuart principles of government: To this end he has adduced facts only as arguments, has warped the train of events from their real courſe of ſucceſſion, and, in order to render them ſubſervient to his predetermined concluſion, has beſtowed on each that falſe colouring which may give it, in ſome degree, the appearance of a caſe in point. A ſimilar plan has been ſince purſued; and as the ſubverſion of freedom was the evident purpoſe of Mr. Hume in writing *the hiſtory of England*, ſo, I fear, we may with too much juſtice affirm the ſubverſion of Chriſtianity to be the object of Mr. Gibbon in writing *the hiſtory of the decline and fall of the Roman Empire*. As a narrative founded on the authority of antient writers muſt have defeated his end, it is curious to obſerve the ſubtlety and variety of thoſe artifices with which this gentleman has endeavoured to work away their credit, and thus to obtain a favourable reception for his own ſubſtituted conjectures as a ſuperior ground of hiſtory. To one alone I ſhall now advert, becauſe it has been directed againſt the veracity of that father who is immediately under my conſideration. It is briefly this: When an antient, and particularly a Chriſtian writer makes an aſſertion, the admiſſion of which might be found inconſiſtent with Mr. Gibbon's hypotheſis, he feigns a poſition which may ſhake the faith of his reader, and, aſcribing this to the author from whoſe pen it never flowed, defcants on his credulity, and inculcates the neceſſity of ſtanding on our guard againſt the danger of too implicit confidence in one at the leaſt liable to impoſition, and whoſe authority is therefore not ſufficient to remove the perplexities thus introduced into the ſceptical mind. I have laid this charge generally, becauſe I ſhall hereafter bring farther proofs of its truth, at preſent let us exemplify it in our hiſtorian's warning againſt the credibility of Juſtin.

" Juſtin

but of the word of God declares, " this alone I found to be a steady and profitable philosophy.". *

Such is the account of this worthy man's converfion to Chriftianity, and fuch the mazes in which he wandered before he found his feet fixed on certain ground. We at length, however, fee him ftationed on a rock, and thankful to heaven for having placed him there. It was not the purfuit, but the fubftantial attainment of truth with which his mind could be fatisfied.—Let us now turn to the oppofite character fo eminently exhibited in our own day.

Inftructed from early infancy in the doctrine of one God, the Father and Maker of all things earthly and heavenly; of our own fall, and reftoration by the death of a body affumed by the eternal Son, that through his blood, fhed as a facrifice for us, we might receive the atonement; of the affiftance of the Holy Ghoft

proceed-

" Juftin Martyr," he affirms, " had fought divine knowledge in the fchools of Zeno, of Ariftotle, of Pythagoras, and of Plato, before he fortunately was accofted by the old man, *or rather the angel*, who turned his attention to the ftudy of the Jewifh prophets." Gibbon's Hift. of Decl. and Fall of the Rom. Emp. p. 514.

Now I would have my reader underftand, that for this interpretation of the old man's character and converfion into an angel, Juftin has not afforded the flighteft authority, but " the ftory is prettily told in Juftin's dialogue. Tillemont, who relates it after him, is fure that the old man was a difguifed angel." *Gibbon. note on the above paffage.* But is Mr. Gibbon fure, that he thus adopts the conjectures of Tillemont into the text? It is true the conjecture is modern, while the teftimony of the martyr himfelf labours under the defect of antiquity; yet ftill I afk, does the hiftorian adopt it as his own opinion, that it was an angel rather than an old man that accofted Juftin; or does he not rather, for the convenient ruin of Juftin's credit, thus infinuate, that he is authorized to make the affertion by the teftimony of the martyr himfelf?

* Ταύτην μόνην εὕρισκον φιλοσοφίαν ἀσφαλῆ τε καὶ σύμφορον. Juftin. Martyr. Dial. cum Tryphone Judæo, p. 225. edit. Par. 1630. folio.

proceeding from the Father and the Son*, fuggefting and abetting our good purpofes of faithful obedience to the will of God, and taught to hope that our fruitful faith in the one Godhead of thefe three perfons is to be rewarded with eternal felicity; and not only fo inftructed, but, when of competent years, furnifhed with the infallible teftimony of God's own word that thefe things are fo, we commence our life at that point to which Juftin Martyr at length arrived after an intricate and tedious procefs. We are as it were the natives of a country towards which he bent his courfe, and where he rejoiced to abide. Why then do not we find the fame fatisfaction at home that a foreigner declares he has experienced among us ? It is certain however that fome do not enjoy it, their reftlefs fpirits, unfitted to the terra firma of truth, launch out again into the uncertain and deceitful depths of philofophy from which he rejoiced to efcape. He proceeded from philofophy to chriftianity; they endeavour to meafure back his fteps from chriftianity to philofophy, and of this the utmoft pride, to which I doubt but few among them fhall attain, is an affent to Deifm. And even here what are the grounds of affent, and what the affent granted? The one at the very utmoft can afcend no higher than probability; the other, by a neceffary confequence, cannot exceed belief. And what more than belief does Chriftianity demand; and are its grounds of probability inferiour to thofe on which a philofophic religion is contended for?

It is not knowledge that is required of us, and confequently there does not fubfift any neceffity for a mathematical demonftration, in which the conclufion is
drawn

---

* Quæ poteft effe magis fpiritatis oratio quam quæ a Chrifto nobis data eft, a quo nobis et Spiritus Sanctus miffus eft ? Cyprian. de Oratione Dominica, lib. p. 139.

drawn from premises intuitively certain, or premises which have by inference already deduced their certainty from such as are so. As every defect in these is necessarily derived to the conclusion, from the ascertainment of these alone, the conclusion can be rendered certain, or knowledge may with justice be predicated of the conclusion. Suppose a geometrical controversy, and that here the disputants were, without proof, and upon mere presumption, to admit the equality of the three angles of a right-lined triangle with two right angles, as the ground-work of enquiry, and proceeding thenceforward to deduce every consequent inference. Should any difference arise between them, concerning the grounds of their process, could either call the other to the proof of what had been before conceded, or could knowledge have been the object sought for when the concession was made? Axioms were precluded, and therefore probability alone could attend upon the nicest deductions: but this defect of certainty 'would arise, not from false or doubtful argumentation, but from a neglect to ascertain the first position admitted as a principle; for had this been done, the conclusion, if justly inferred, must also have been necessarily certain. Thus, with regard to Christianity, we may deduce from the Bible what is certainly true, provided the Bible be certainly true; but the certainty of revelation is not capable of a mathematical demonstration, so that we are forced to rest here; arguments for its high probability are therefore all that can be brought, and consequently no more can be adduced to our religion: But the Bible being once admitted, all appeal to antecedent revelation, as Reason has been stupidly denominated, is precluded. Were the Bible certain, then were the Trinity certain: but it is only probable, herein then lies the defect of certainty in the inference; and therefore our faith alone is all that can be afforded to it; it

K   is is indeed all that is required, and all to which merit can in any fenfe be afcribed; for knowledge has no counterpoife to call for the interpofition of the will, without fome act of which, and that too conducted by the grace of the Almighty, it is impoffible for us to deferve, or rather to claim the imputation of that merit which has fuperfeded the tranfmitted fin of our firft Father. Faith ftands at an equal diftance from knowledge as from infidelity, it coëxifts not with either. Infidelity, which is its direct contradictory, of courfe implies that faith has not obtained exiftence, while in knowledge it is terminated and fwallowed up, as hope is in fruition. And do we then complain that we have not that knowledge which muft fuperfede the rewards gracioufly annexed to our attefted obedience of an injunction to believe, while it is evident that too full a proof would as effectually deftroy our faith as the moft infufficient and defective intimation?

So congenial with the human mind is truth, that final conclufions are not even popularly admitted unlefs they follow juftly, or with ftrong appearances of juftice from their premifes. Only fteal thefe away from the examination of the intellect, and ftamp upon them the authority of axioms, and the very Papift, from the conceffion of pontifical infallibility, proceeds to reafon juftly. He has, I grant it, fixed upon a falfehood as the bafis of his doctrines, but having conferred eftablifhment upon it, he wifely refers himfelf hither for the eftablifhment of whatever is attefted by it. If the Pope cannot err, and that he fays " bread is flefh and blood," the Pope has not erred in the affertion, and therefore it is incontrovertibly certain that bread is flefh and blood; the inference of neceffity follows, and wants nothing of abfolute certainty but the removal of defect from the premifes; but thefe have been originally conceded, and

confeconsequently all appeal to a higher source of argument is rescinded. Now, with respect to the question at present under enquiry, the scriptures have been allowed; by their attestation all parties agree to be determined, and therefore tho' I were henceforward to admit that from end to end the scriptures of God are but the promulgation of falsehood, yet they have been previously rendered the dernier resort, and "the suffrage of reason may" NOT "be taken," even though on other grounds "she should" be found competent to "decide with mathematical and intuitive certainty that the Athanasian doctrine is not true." Remarks, p. 76. No other premises are before her now than those upon which the point in issue has been already placed, and therefore reason, so long as she retains her integrity and proper character, will refuse to hear any alien testimony, and will give judgment only upon the premises by which the parties had originally agreed to be decided. I grant this appeal to an extrajudicial sort of Reason amounts to a rejection of the scripture evidence relative to the litigated point, but it comes too late to be admitted; it comes subsequent to the deposition of the witness, and from that party whose cause has been subverted by it. The appeal itself therefore argues a concession that the doctrine of Unitarianism is not tenable on the grounds of scripture; and what shall now be said of a cause which relies, for its only maintenance, upon the rejection of that testimony which is borne by the voice of the unerring Truth himself? *

It

* With respect to one of the books received into the canon, I shall here state and then animadvert upon the declaration of Mr. Gibbon, who, in note 152 upon the 15th chapter of his History of the Decline and Fall of the Roman Empire, affirms that "the Alogians disputed the genuineness of the Apocalypse, because the Church of Thyatira was not yet founded. Epiphanius, who allows the fact, extricates himself from the difficulty by ingeniously supposing that St. John wrote in the spirit of prophecy."

Now,

It is not, however, my intention to call into comparison the different arguments that may be adduced in favour of a religion derived from philosophic premises, and

Now, though I admit that the Alogians disputed the genuineness of the Apocalypse, I deny that it was because the Church of Thyatira was not yet founded; for consistently with such a reason for rejecting this work, they could hardly have ascribed it to the pen of Cerinthus, who, being the contemporary of St. John, must have preceded the foundation of that Church, at least as long as the Apostle. Their objection, on this ground, was to the truth of the contents of the book, and the veracity of a writer who could absurdly address himself to a body not yet instituted. The objection, I grant, is nonsense, it is nevertheless the true objection of the Alogians.

Such, and such alone, is the difficulty in which Epiphanius is involved: and now let us see how he extricates himself; is it, because he was unable to contradict the assertion, by a general allowance of the fact, such as may warrant us to say, upon his authority, that the Church of Thyatira was not yet founded, and then by an ingenious supposition that St. John therefore wrote in the spirit of prophecy? No, this too I flatly deny.— The fact, as stated by the Alogians themselves, he does allow, but it is only that he may assume it as an argument *ad hominem*, and thence infer to the divine authority and consequent truth of a book which the author must in that case have necessarily written in the spirit of prophecy; for if, says he, the Church of Thyatira were not yet founded, how could St. John have possibly addressed it otherwise than by the means of prophetic inspiration. Thus, from their own position, he derives the refutation of their general inference, which I do not see that he could very conveniently have effected by any other mode of argument than an allowance of the fact; an allowance made, not because he acquiesced in the assertion, or found any difficulty in proving the direct contrary, but for the purpose of fastening upon themselves the very premises from which their own ruin must inevitably proceed. Epiphanii Hæref. 51, Sect. 33 tom. i. p. 455, Edit. Coloniæ, 1682, fol.

But whence does Mr. Gibbon infer, that the Church of Thyatira was not yet founded. We are told by Justin Martyr, who refers to the 21st chapter, that the Apostle John was the author of the Apocalypse Ἰωάννης ἕις τῶν ἀποστόλων τῷ Χριστῷ, ἐν ἀποκαλύψει γενομένῃ αὐτῷ χίλια ἔτη, &c. *Dial. cum Tryph. p.* 308. And we have the authority of this book, (against which I believe no fair man of sense will suffer the Alogian puerilities stated here, or any inference drawn from them to stand in competition) as the firm ground of an asseveration, that the Church of Thyatira had been founded when St. John wrote the second chapter of the Apocalypse. See also Acts xvi. 14.

and a religion founded on the fcriptures; be it enough to fay that the votaries of the former (as not being poffefled of any other) have given their voice againft the fufficiency of their own grounds of belief, and afforded an *a priori* argument in favour of revelation: For declaring the difficulty attendant upon the acquifition, the abfolute impoffibility that obftructed the communication of divine knowledge *, fome of the wifeft among them have pronounced it, upon thofe conclufions with which they were the beft fatisfied, but in which they never refted as final, to be an expectation no way derogatory from the God of their apprehenfions, that he fhould make himfelf known in order to rectify the errours and refolve the doubts of a Being on whom he had beftowed faculties for inveftigation, and a zeal for the difcovery of truth, without having at the fame time imparted a light fufficient to conduct his enquiry.

At length, in correfpondence with this humble hope, the infinite Luminary has been pleafed to fhed a ray upon the darknefs of mankind, and we accordingly find the confiftent difciple of a generous and inquifitive philofophy, whofe heart, by cultivation, had, like the fun's orb in Milton, been previoufly
——— made porous to receive
And drink the liquid light ———
with joy repair to the fountain, and imbibe that true light which lighteth every man that cometh into the world; whilft, on the other hand, we have the misfortune to behold fpirits, that we might reafonably have conceived native to the light, chafed into extravagant and erring flight by the hallowed fplendours of our dayftar, when the bird of dawning fings, they ftart, and with

---

* Plato has exprefsly acknowledged this; " to find the Father and Creator of the univerfe," he fays, " is a toil, to divulge him an impoffibility.
Τὸν μὲν Πατέρα κὶ δημιεργὸν τᾶδε τῦ παντὸς εὑρεῖν τὸ ἔργον, κὶ εὑρόντα εἰς πάντας ἀδύναλον λέγειν.

with the confident apoftle, relying only on their own internal ftrength (would I might add with him alfo relenting) perfift, even while the cock crows, in denying the falvation of God which he hath prepared before the face of all people, a light to lighten the Gentiles. The ineffectual fire of that mere glow-worm, *their* luminous reafon*, they muffle up, and thus fecuring its mimic luftre from the touch of heaven's genuine beam, hurry into darknefs, hence demonftrably more congenial with their minds, and diligently fortify themfelves againft the radiance of the Gofpel.

But Juftin Martyr is our prefent fubject, to him, therefore, let us now return, and fo far as the example of a man eminently diftinguifhed by his zeal for truth may perfuade to a return from errour, let us, without farther preface, ftate the doctrines for which he relinquifhed the vague conjectures of an uncertain philofophy.

Befides fome tracts of lefs eminence, this venerable father has left behind him two Apologies for the chriftians, and a Dialogue with Trypho the Jew. In the former he endeavours to mitigate the feverity of Roman perfecution carried on againft the followers of the Gofpel; and to this purpofe, touching but incidentally upon their tenets, he lays himfelf out with particularity to vindicate their morals, and to prove that they were not only inoffenfive but virtuous citizens: But in the latter, as I fhall have occafion to fhew hereafter, he enters more fully into the doctrines of chriftianity.

I fhall follow the order in which his writings have been publifhed in the Paris edition, folio, 1636, and therefore fhall begin with what is there entituled his Firft Apology, though in reality it is the fecond which he

* To " the light of reafon," however, when figuratively fpoken, I have no more objection than to " the vifual ray," by which Mr. Pope has exprefled the act or power of feeing.

he prefented. The former one, now called the fecond, was preferred to M. Aurelius Antoninus in the year 162—that which paffes as the firft was fubmitted to the fenate of Rome in the year of our Lord 164: but to how little effect, the martyrdom of the apologift himfelf, which was inflicted the fame year, bears a melancholy teftimony.

To the fenate of Rome he declares in behalf of the chriftians " the word of the unbegotten and unfpeakable God, which is with God we adore, and love, becaufe that, for our fake, he was made man, becoming a partaker of our paffions that he might effect our cure *."

To M. Aurelius Antoninus he fays, " We are named atheifts, and we confefs that, with refpect to thofe (dæmons) which are efteemed to be gods, atheifts we are; but not with refpect to the moft true God, the Father of righteoufnefs and temperance, and every other virtue, who is without alloy of evil; but him; and the Son who has come from him and given this inftruction to us, and to the hoft of good angels that follow him, and are made like unto him; and the prophetick Spirit, we worfhip and adore, honouring them in word and in truth †." In perfect conformity with which, he

fays

* Τόν γὰρ ἀπὸ ἀγενήτε καὶ ἀρρήτε Θεῦ λόγον μετὰ τόν Θεὸν προσκυνῶμεν, καὶ ἀγαπῶμεν, ἐπειδὴ καὶ δἰ ἡμᾶς ἀνθρωπος γέγονεν, ὅπως καὶ τῶν παθῶν τῶν ἡμετέρων συμμέτοχος γενόμενΘ-, καὶ ἰασιν ποιήσηται. Apologia 1ma, p. 51.

† Ἐνθένδε καὶ ἄθεοι κεκλήμεθα, καὶ ὁμολογῶμεν τῶν τοιύτων νομιζομένων Θεῶν ἄθεοι εἶναι, ἀλλ᾽ ὐχὶ τῦ ἀληθεστάτυ, καὶ Παῖρὸς δικαιοσύνης καὶ σωφροσύνης, καὶ τῶν ἄλλων ἀρητῶν, ἀνεπιμίκτυ τε κακίας Θεῦ. Ἀλλ᾽ ἐκεῖνον τε: καὶ τόν παρ᾽ αὐτῦ Ὑιόν ἐλθόντα, καὶ διδάξαντα ἡμᾶς ταῦτα, καὶ τόν τῶν ἄλλων ἐπομενων καὶ ἐξομοιυμένων ἀγαθῶν ἀγγέλων ϛρατὸν: Πνεῦμά τε τό προφη-
τικόν

says again in the same Apology, " We worship God alone ‖ :" and farther on he declares that, " having learned, and holding the Son of the most high God to be in the second place, and the prophetick Spirit in the third rank, we will demonstrate to you that we honour them according to the word of God *."

He testifies that it was " Christ who, under the appearance of fire, spoke with Moses from the bush †;" and says that the Jews, in thinking it was the Father who spoke from the bush, and not the Son of God, are chargeable with ignorance, both of the Father and the Son, according to Matth. xi. 27. " For they who say that the Son is the Father are convicted of not knowing the Father, and also of not knowing that the universal Father hath a Son, who, being the word, the first begotten of God, is himself God also ‡." We may remember that it was he who spoke from the bush to Moses, that declared his name to be I AM THAT I AM, Exodus iii. 14; and therefore, without any great violence, may admit that our Lord referred to this
former

ἱκὸν σεβόμεθα καὶ προσκυνῶμεν, λόγῳ καὶ ἀληθείᾳ τιμῶντες. Apologia 2da, p. 56.

‖ Θεὸν μὲν μόνον προσκυνῶμεν. Ibid. p. 64.

* Ὑιὸν αὐτῦ τῦ ὄντως Θεῦ μαθόντες, καὶ ἐν δευτέρᾳ χώρᾳ ἔχοντες, Πνεῦμα τε προφητικὸν ἐν τρίτῃ τάξει, ὅτι μετὰ λόγου τιμῶμεν, ἀποδείξομεν. Apologia 2da, p. 60.

† Ἐν ἰδίᾳ πυρὸς ἐκ βάτυ προσωμίλησεν αὐτῷ ὁ ἡμέτερος Χριςὸς. Ibid. p. 95.

‡ Οἱ γὰρ τὸν Ὑιὸν Πατέρα φάσκοντες εἶναι, ἐλέγχονται μήτε τὸν Πατέρα ἐπισταμένοι, μήθ' ὅτι ἔςιν Ὑιὸς τῷ Πάτερι τῶν ὅλων γινώσκοντες, ὃς καὶ λόγος πρωτότοκος ὢν τῦ Θεῦ καὶ Θεός ὕπαρχει. Ibid. p. 96.

former declaration, when he fays again, " Before Abraham was I AM," John viii. 15 : but he who fpoke from the fire farther denominates himfelf " the Lord God of your fathers, the God of Abraham, the God of Ifaac, and the God of Jacob," Exod. iii. 15. Whether Juftin Martyr be right or not in faying that it is Chrift who appeared and fpoke with Mofes from the burning bufh, is not the matter in debate, but whether he who was one of the fathers of the fecond century has faid it? and if he has, which from the quotation and reference may appear, it is put beyond all further controverfy that Juftin Martyr believed Chrift to be God.

But in his dialogue with Trypho the Jew, though it is impoffible for him to be more explicit than in the extracts already made, we find this writer much more copious. He meets his opponent upon the ground of his own fcriptures, (the Old Teftament) from which he propofes to prove that the omnipotence of God, and the afflictions of a meah man, are foretold of Chrift; and thence to infer, that the fufferings of the affumed nature afford no argument againft the divinity of our Lord, as the concurrence of both were neceffary to a completion of thofe prophecies, to the truth of which the Jews themfelves acceded.

That Chrift is God he firft undertakes to demonftrate,—and then to fhew that the lowlinefs and fufferings of our Saviour do not preclude Jefus from being the Chrift.

Having quoted from Mofes and the prophets a vaft multitude of paffages, (amongft which are Deut. x. 16, 17. Ifa. liv. to v. 3.—lxiii.—lxv. 1, 2, 3, &c. &c.) every one of which he declares bears reference to our
Saviour,

Saviour, he censures Trypho for the Jewish misapplication of them, and shews that it is altogether impossible to make them bear the sense which the Jews ascribed to them. You, for instance, he says, apply the 72d Psalm to King Solomon, " while the language of the Psalm itself fully demonstrates that it is referable only to the eternal King, that is, to Christ; for, as I make it appear from all the scriptures, Christ is therein proclaimed a King, and a Priest, and God, and Lord, and an Angel, and a Man, and a Captain of hosts, and a *(corner)* Stone, and an Infant born; first made obnoxious to sufferings, thence ascending up into heaven, and again returning with glory, and possessing an eternal kingdom *."

The

---

* Τῶν λόγων τῦ Ψαλμῦ διαρρήδην κηρυσσόντων εἰς τὸν αἰώνιον βασιλία, τυτέςιν, εἰς τὸν Χριςὸν, εἰρῆσθαι· ὁ γάρ Χριςὸς βασιλεὺς, καὶ Ἱερεὺς, καὶ Θεὸς, καὶ Κύρι©·, καὶ Ἄγ[ελ©·, καὶ Ἄνθρωπ©·. καὶ Ἀρχιςρατήγ©·, καὶ Λίθ©·, καὶ Παιδίον γενώμενον, καὶ Παθητὸς γενόμεν©· πρῶτον, εἶτα εἰς ὐρανὸν ἀνερχομέν©·, καὶ πάλιν παραγινόμεν©· μετὰ δόξης, καὶ αἰώνιον τὴν βασιλείαν ἔχων κεκήρυκται, ὡς ἀπὸ πασῶν τῶν γραφῶν ἀποδείκνυμι. Dinlogus cum Tryphone Judeo, p. 251.

As the proofs of our Saviour's Godhead, being an article of the Christian faith in the Ante-nicene ages of the church, are all that I am concerned in producing, it seems necessary to shew that this was not confounded with other tenets which we do not now embrace in the church of England; and to this purpose I shall here refer to the authority upon which J. Martyr has conferred these titles upon our Lord: that he is a King, he proves by the 2d, 72d, and 99th Psalms; a Priest, from the 110th, and from Zach. vi. 13; a Captain of hosts, from Josh. v. 14, where he says that the man who appeared to, and spoke with Joshua in the character of Captain of the host of the Lord " was God, that is, Christ." See J. M. p. 284. He proves him a *(corner)* Stone from the 118th Psalm, v. 22, and Isa. xxviii. 16; and an Angel from Exod. iii. 2, in which the God of Abraham, of Isaac, and of Jacob is called the *Angel of the Lord* who spoke to Moses in the burning bush; and this God he has already called Christ. On this appellation the following passage may also throw some light, and demonstrate the sense in which the

Martyr

The father then recites the whole Pfalm in order to fhew that it is not applicable to Solomon, but to Chrift; for that however magnificent Solomon might have been, kings have never fallen down to worfhip him.

He then boafts of the conftancy of the Chriftian, and afferts that they preferred torments and death to the guilt of idolatry; on which Trypho takes him up, and declares that he had heard of fome who faid they profeffed Chrift, and were called Chriftians, who, neverthelefs, eat meats facrificed to idols: but to this the Martyr replies, that Chrift had himfelf foretold fchifm and falfe difciples; that he knew himfelf there were many who taught Chrift, and alfo the God of Abraham, *(which is added here as a fort of recrimination upon the Jew)* and yet blafphemed the Maker of all things; " that with fuch we hold no communion, knowing them to be without God, without religion, without righteoufnefs, without law; and who, inftead of worfhipping Jefus, confefs him only in name *."

Trypho next calls on him to prove that Jefus is the Chrift, which he declines doing till he fhall firft fhew from the prophecies " that the Chrift is God, and the Lord of hofts †." To this purpofe he recites the

24th

Martyr underftood the word Angel when applied to God; for he fays himfelf in his fecond Apology, Ἀγ[ελ]Θ- δὲ καλεῖται, αὐτὸς γὰρ ἀπαγ[ελλει ὅσα δεῖ γνωσθῆναι, p. 95, which may be thus literally turned, " he is called a *Revealer*, becaufe he *reveals* fuch things as are neceffary to be known."—Revealer bearing here the fame fignification as Angel.

* Ὧν ἀδενὶ κοινῶμεν, οἱ γνωρίζοντες ἀθέες, καὶ ἀσεβεῖς, καὶ ἀδίκες, καὶ ἀνόμες αὐτὰς ἱπάρχοντες, καὶ ἀντὶ τᾶ τὸν Ἰησᾶν σέβειν, ὀνόματι μόνον ὁμολογεῖν. P. 253.

† Ὅτι καὶ Θεὸς καὶ Κύριος τῶν δυνάμεων ὁ Χριςός. P. 254.

24th Pſalm, and ſays that they are fools ‡ who apply it, not to Chriſt, but to Solomon: he conſiders the Pſalm as a dialogue, and makes the Princes of heaven, when commanded to open the gates for Chriſt upon his aſcenſion, to doubt concerning the dignity of one whom they had looked down upon, and ſeen in earth, without beauty or honour, and ſo to demand, "who is this King of glory?" "and to them the Holy Ghoſt makes anſwer, either from the perſon of the Father, or from his own perſon, the Lord of hoſts, he is the King of glory, &c. *."

On

‡ Ἀνόητοι εἰσι. p. 254.

* Καὶ ἀποκρίνεται αὐτοῖς τὸ Πνεῦμα τὸ ἅγιον, ἢ ἀπο προσώπου τοῦ Πατρὸς, ἢ απο τοῦ ἰδίου, Κύριος τῶν δυνάμεων, &c, &c. P. 255.

This manner of interpreting the 24th Pſalm is not peculiar to Juſtin Martyr; J. FIRMICUS MATERNUS, in the year 342, preſented to the Emperours Conſtantius and Conſtans a Treatiſe on the Errours of the Gentile Religions, in which the following remarkable paſſage occurs. I conſign it to a note only, becauſe the author is of the fourth century. His work is, however, not without authority; for he is the earlieſt writer after the council of Nice; and as he has addreſſed it, not to Conſtantinus, but to Conſtantius, he muſt ſtand exempted from the charge of writing under any influence but that of ſincere conviction. I ſhall make no ſort of apology for the length of the paſſage cited. "Ecce terra contremuit, & fundamentorum ſuorum ſtabilitate concuſſâ præſentis CHRISTI NUMEN agnovit. Ante præfinitum tempus præcipitat diem mundi rotata vertigo; & ſol, non completo diurnarum horarum ſpacio, properato curſu vergit in noctem. Ecce veli faſtigia ſumma finduntur, & obſcurioribus tenebris orbem terrarum caligo noctis abſcondit. Omnia elementa, Chriſto pugnante, turbata ſunt, tunc ſcilicet, cum primum contra mortis tyrannidem humanum corpus armavit. Per triduum iſtâ conflictatione pugnatum eſt, quamdiu mors, ſuperatis malitiæ ſuæ viribus, frangeretur." Here this author rebukes the impatience of man, who cannot endure our Saviour's three days abſence, and ſays that David foretold it in the 44th Pſalm, which he quotes, and then proceeds to deſcribe his reſurrection, calling him by a no leſs ſignificant name than "CHRIST THE ALMIGHTY GOD." "Ecce poſt triduum lucidior ſolito dies oritur, & reddita ſoli præteriti luminis gratia. OMNIPOTENS DEUS CHRISTUS ſplendidioribus ſolis radiis adoratur. Exultat

SALU-

On this paſſage I muſt collaterally remark, that the three perſons of the Trinity are accurately diſtinguiſhed in it. Our Saviour is the ſubject ſpoken of as diſtinct from the Father and the Holy Ghoſt; and a doubt is ſuggeſted, whether the Holy Ghoſt ſpoke from his own perſon, or the perſon of the Father? which are evidently diſcriminated by the doubt; for if they be not diſtinct, why ſhould the doubt be entertained?

" God

SALUTARE NUMEN, et triumphales currus ejus juſtorum ac fanctorum turba comitatur. Tunc elato gaudio clamat elata mortalitas. *Ubi eſt, mors, aculeus tuus?* Tunc præcurrens SALUTARE NUMEN aperiri ſibi cœleſtes januas præcipit. Aperite, aperite, & immortalia clauſtra convellite. CHRISTUS DEUS, calcatâ morte, ad cœlum hominem quem ſuſceperat revocat. Hoc a venerando propheta ſanctâ voce præcanitur, et ex ore prophetico vox jubentis auditur, ait enim Spiritus ſanctus, ut nobis potentiam Chriſti jubentis oſtenderet: *tollite portas, principes, veſtras, & extollite portæ æternales, & introibit Rex gloriæ.* Hoc angelis neſcientibus imperatur, neque enim ſcire potuerunt, quando verbum Dei deſcendit ad terram, ideo & ipſi ſollicitâ interrogatione reſpondent: *Quis eſt Rex gloriæ?* quibus quærentibus PERSPICUA CHRISTUS NUMINIS SUI MAJESTATE reſpondit: *Dominus fortis & potens, Dominus potens in prælio.*" J. Firm. Maternus de Errore Profanarum Religionum, p. 48. Edit. Ludg. Bat. 1672. cum Minucii Felicis Octavio.

The ſame author ſays that the ſin of Adam could only be compenſated for by ſuch a propitiation as Chriſt became for us. " That therefore the word of God united himſelf with the human body, that he might emancipate mankind and conquer death." Verbum Dei humano ſe miſcuit corpori, ut hominem liberaret, ut mortem vinceret. p. 51. And again he ſays, " that thus human nature, by man and God in union, ſhould come from the merit of obedience to a reign of immortality." Et ſic humanum genus, per hominem pariter & Deum æquatâ ſocietatis comparatione conjunctum, ad immortalitatis imperium obedientiæ merito perveniret. Ibidem. He cloſes his work with an admonition to the Emperours: " Let your merciful diſpoſition look ever up to heaven; from God let it ever wait for help; let it implore the adorable Godhead of Chriſt; and for the world's, and your own ſalvation, offer to the God of ſalvation ſpiritual ſacrifices." Clementia veſtre cœlum ſemper aſpiciat, a Deo ſemper expectet auxilium, Chriſti venerandum Numen imploret, & pro ſalute orbis terrarum & veſtrâ, ſalutari Deo ſpirituales offerat victimas. p. 64.

" God is gone up with a fhout, the Lord with the found of a trumpet. Sing praifes to God, fing praifes: fing praifes unto our king, fing praifes. For God is the king of all the earth." " The Lord reigneth, let the people tremble; he fitteth between the cherubims, let the earth be moved. Mofes and Aaron among his priefts; they called upon the Lord, and he anfwered them. He fpake unto them in the cloudy pillar. Exalt ye the Lord our God, and worfhip at his footftool, for he is holy." Thefe are the words of David in the 47th and 99th Pfalms, and Juftin Martyr applies them both to Chrift, declaring that he is the God fpoken of in them *. This application provokes the refentment of Trypho, who fays he muft decline all farther communication with one who can thus blafphemoufly endeavour to perfuade him that this crucified Man had fpoke with Mofes and Aaron from the pillar of the cloud; " that in a fubfequent time he was made man, and hanged upon a crofs; that he afcended up into heaven, is again to appear on earth, and that he is an object of worfhip" †. And in another part of the dialogue, in the very fame fpirit of modern Unitarianifm, the Jew declares: "What you fay, that this Chrift is God from all eternity, and yet that, being made man, he underwent a human birth, and that he was man without being the Son of a man, appears to me, not only a paradox, but to be actual folly ‡". As St.

* Εἰς τὸν Χριςόν ἕτως ἔιρηται, ἀνέβη ὁ Θεός ἐν ἀλαλαγμῷ, &c. P. 256.

† Εἶτα ἄνθρωπον γενόμενον, ϛαυρωθῆναι, καὶ ἀναβεβηκέναι εἰς τὸν ἀρανὸν, καὶ πάλιν παραγίνεσθαι ἐπὶ τῆς γῆς, καὶ προσκυνητὸν ἔιναι. P. 256.

‡ Τὸ γὰρ λέγειν σε, προϋπάρχειν Θεὸν ὄντα πρὸ αἰώνων τῦτον τὸν Χριςον, εἶτα καὶ γεννηθῆναι ἄνθρωπον γενόμενον ὑπομεῖναι, καὶ

St. Paul had before declared the gospel a stumbling block to the Jews, so to this Jew the Martyr replies: "I know that this revelation seems a paradox, and particularly to those of your race who have never been disposed to understand the things which are of God, nor to do them, but, as God himself proclaims against you, only those things which are taught by your own Rabbis †." "I know that, as the word of God hath spoken, this great wisdom of God, the almighty Creator of the universe, is hid from you ‡".

Without dwelling on the Martyr's application of the 18th chapter of Genesis to the three Persons in the one Godhead, numerically three, but in mind one *, I shall pass on to his assertion, that the account which wisdom gives of her own generation in the 8th chapter of Proverbs, is properly the language of Christ: and "the discourse of wisdom shall bear me witness, that he who is God, begotten of the Father of the universe, is the word, and the wisdom, and the power, and the glory of him who begot him §". St. Paul has, in his first epistle to the Corinthians, chap. i. 24, called "Christ the Power of God, and the Wisdom of God," which may well authorize this father's interpretation of wisdom's magnificent claims, which he has ushered in with an assertion that the Son is generated from the Father as one flame is from another; the original blaze com-

καὶ ὅτι ἐκ ἀνθρώπου ἐξ ἀνθρώπου, ὃ μόνον παράδοξον δοκεῖ μοι εἶναι, ἀλλα καὶ μῶρον. P. 267.

† Ibidem. ‡ P. 256.

* Ἀριθμῷ λέγω, αλλα ὃ γνώμῃ.

§ Μαρτυρήσει δὲ μοι ὃ λόγος τῆς σοφίας, αὐτὸς ὢν ὅτος ὃ Θεὸς ἄπο τȣ Πατρὸς τῶν ὅλων γεννηθεὶς, καὶ λόγος, καὶ σοφία, καὶ δύναμις, καὶ δόξα τȣ γεννήσαντος ὑπάρχων. P. 284.

communicating of its own fubftance without fuffering diminution, even though it has kindled a blaze equal to itfelf †.

This early writer alfo confirms St. Barnabas's pofition, that the Hebrew Plurals bear reference to the perfons in the one Godhead; for with him he afferts that the following paffages, "Let us make man in OUR image," Gen. i. 26; and "Adam has become as one of US, Gen. iii. 22, are addreffed by the Father to the Son. See p. 15.

He recites the 45th Pfalm, and, applying it to our Lord, fays " that he is herein teftified by the Creator of this world, and that the words of the Pfalm eloquently fignify that he is the adorable God and Chrift ‡;" and now recapitulating the feveral paffages which he had adduced in proof of his pofition, and adding to them the 19th Pfalm, he defires the Jew " to refleƈt upon the neceffity that God fhould defcend from heaven and be made man among men; and that he fhall come again; whom they who have pierced him fhall look upon and bewail *;" which being an allufion to the declaration of God by the mouth of Zechariah

† Καὶ ὁποῖον ἐστι πυρὸς ὁρῶμεν ἀλλὸ γινόμενον, ἐκ ἐλαττωμένω ἐκείνω ἐξ οὗ ἡ ἀνάψις γέγονεν, ἀλλὰ τῶ αὐτῶ μενοντ@·, καὶ τὸ ἐξ αὐτῶ ἀναφθεν, καὶ ἄλλο ὂν φαίνεται, ἐκ ἐλαττῶσαν ἐκεῖνο ἐξ οὗ ἀνήφθη. P. 284.

‡ Ὅτι γεν καὶ προσκυνητός ἐστι καὶ Θεὸς καὶ Χριστὸς ὑπὸ τῦ ταῦτα ποιήσαντ@· μαρτυρύμεν@·, καὶ οἱ λόγοι ἕτοι διαρρήδην ζημαίνυσι. P. 287.

* Ἀναμνήσθητε, ἵνα καὶ Θεὸν ἄνωθεν προελθόντα, καὶ ἄνθρωποι εν ἀνθρώποις γενόμενον γνωρίσητε· καὶ πάλιν ἐκεῖνον παραγινόμενον, ὃν ὀψᾶν μέλλετε καὶ κόπτεσθαι οἱ ἐκκεντήσαντες αὐτόν. P. 289.

Zechariah xii. 10, he makes a tranſition to thoſe prophecies which predict ſorrows, and humiliation, and death, to the ſame Being whom they likewiſe announced to be the almighty God: but the impatient Unitarian ſtops him and ſays, " You have taken in hand to demonſtrate a fact which is incredible, and almoſt impoſſible, that God has ſubmitted to be born, and to be made man †:" to which our author gives an anſwer that may be very properly addreſſed to our modern Judaizers: " If indeed I had undertaken to prove this fact by arguments merely human, and the ſuggeſtions of men, I ought not to obtain your aſſent to it; but if, repeatedly urging the ſcriptures which ſpeak to this purpoſe, I require your acknowledgement of what they ſet forth, I muſt declare that your hearts are hardened againſt the knowledge of the mind and the will of God ‡."

The Jew is notwithſtanding reduced at laſt to make a conceſſion, and admit that the numerous ſcriptures of the Old Teſtament, which foretell both the dignity and the humility of our Lord, are referable to the Chriſt; on which our author expreſſes his wonder that he ſhould ſtill deny Jeſus to be that Chriſt, only becauſe of his humble ſtate and ſufferings, ſince theſe things were evidently a part of the Meſſiah's predicted character; and therefore ſo far from being a ground of objection to his being the perſon, that they afforded proof that Jeſus was actually the Chriſt. The teachers among the Jews, he ſays, " of neceſſity acknowledge that theſe ſcriptures which I produce, and which explicitly demonſtrate that the Chriſt ſhould ſuffer, and be the God

† Ἄπιςον γὰρ καὶ ἀδύναλον σχηδὸν πρᾶγμα ἐπιχειρεις ἀποδεικνύναι, ὅτι Θεὸς ὑπεμεινε γενηθῆναι, καὶ ἄνθρωπ©· γενίσθαι. P. 292.

‡ Ibidem.

God of our adoration, are spoken with reference to the Christ; and yet they dare to deny that this Jesus is that Christ, even while they confess that the Christ is to come, and to suffer, and to reign, and to be the God of our worship; which is surely ridiculous and senseless" in them, as all these things meet in that Jesus whom they deny, and characterise him according to their own expectations ‡. " David has proclaimed the Christ to have come forth from the womb according to the council of the Father, and demonstrated him to be God strong, and to be worshipped *". As such the venerable Martyr declares that he prefers his own supplications to him; and, speaking of our Saviour's crucifixion, and the promises of God made to those who confide in him, proceeds to assure Trypho that, with charity very different from the persecuting tenets of the Jews, " we pray that you may obtain compassion from Christ; that you may be also made partakers of these promised benefits;" for he taught us to pray even for our enemies §.

Of

‡ Ἃς δὲ ἂν λέγωμεν αὐτοῖς γραφὰς, αἳ διαρρήδην τὸν Χριςὸν καὶ παθητὸν, καὶ προσκυνητὸν καὶ Θεὸν ἀποδεικνύωσι, τάυτας εἰς Χριςὸν μὲν εἰρῆσθαι ἀναγκαζόμενοι ξυντίθενται, τῦτον δὲ μὴ εἶναι τὸν Χριςὸν τολμῶσι λέγειν. Ἐλεύσεσθαι δὲ καὶ παθεῖν, καὶ βασιλεύσαι, καὶ προσκυνητὸν γενέσθαι Θεὸν ὁμολογῦσι· ὅπερ γελοῖον καὶ ἀνόητον. P. 294.

* Καὶ Δαβὶδ ἐκ γαςρὸς γεννηθήσεσθαι αὐτὸν κατὰ τὴν τῦ Πατρὸς βυλὴν ἐκήρυξε, καὶ Θεὸν ἰσχυρὸν καὶ προσκυνητὸν, Χριςὸν ὄντα ἐδήλωσε. P. 302.

§ Καὶ πρὸς τύτοις πᾶσι εὐχόμεθα ὑπερ ὑμῖν ἵνα ἐλεηθῆτε ὑπὸ τῦ Χριςῦ. P. 323. St. Ignatius, in his Epistle to the Smyrnæans, has delivered the same precept, and desires them to pray for their enemies, if by any means they may come to repentance, which is indeed difficult; " but of this Jesus Christ, who is our true life, has the power." Τύτυ δὲ ἔχει ἐξυσίαν Ἰησῦς Χριςὸς τὸ ἀληθινὸν ἡμῶν ζῆν: to whom therefore should they address their supplications but to him who has the power to grant them?

Of the numerous types which Juſtin interprets of our Lord, I ſhall preſent only two to my reader: their juſtice I am not concerned to vindicate. Be it remembered I am only ſtating the mind of Juſtin Martyr. He pronounces Joſhua, the ſucceſſour of Moſes, to be a type of our Saviour; and ſays, that as the one diſtributed the land of Canaan to the children of Iſrael, ſo ſhall the other diſtribute a good land to his followers, but that in one particular their gifts differ. " Joſhua gave to the children of Iſrael a temporary inheritance, inaſmuch as he was not Chriſt, who is God, neither the Son of God, but *Jeſus Chriſt* will, after an holy reſurrection, give to us an eternal poſſeſſion †:" and the circumſtances of Joſhua the prieſt who returned with Ezra from Babylon, and with Zerubbabel, promoted the building of the ſecond temple, (ſee Ezra iii. 2, 9; he ſays are " a type of thoſe things which were afterwards to be done by our Prieſt, and God, and Chriſt the Son of the Father of the univerſe *."

The Martyr quotes then the firſt chapter of Malachi, in which God refuſes to accept the ſacrifices of the Jews, but declares that incenſe ſhall be offered to his name, *a pure offering*, and that his name ſhall be great among the Gentiles. That is, ſays the Jew, it ſhall be magnified by the Hebrews who are in captivity among

† Ὁ μὲν γὰρ προσκαιρὸν ἔδωκεν ἀυτοῖς τὴν κληρονομίαν, ἅτε ἆ Χριςὸς ὁ Θεὸς ὤν, ἒδε Ὑιὸς Θεῦ· ὁ δὲ μεῖὰ τὴν ἁγιαν ἀνάςασιν, ἀιώνιον ἡμῖν τὴν κατάσχησιν δώσει. P. 340.

* Ἐρχομαι νῦν ἀποδεῖξαι ἀποκήρυξιν ἐῖναι ἴων ὑπὸ ἴα ἡμείερε ἱερέως, καὶ Θεῦ, καὶ Χριςῦ υἱῦ ἴα παῖρὸς ἴων ὁλῶν γίνεσθαι μελλόνίων. p. 344. The conformity of our Lord to theſe two men ſeems to conſiſt chiefly in the circumſtance of name, for they are both called JESUS in the ſeptuagint verſion of the Old Teſtament.

among the Gentiles, and not by the Gentiles themfelves; but this interpretation of the fcripture the Chriftian rejects, and declares that it bears reference to the facrament of the bread and cup, which was inftituted by Jefus Chrift; and then proceeds: "I fay that the prayers and thankfgivings of fuch as are worthy, are the only perfect and acceptable facrifices to God: thefe alone the Chriftians have learned to make, and thefe too in commemoration of their nourifhment both dry and moift, *(meaning the body and blood of Chrift commemorated in the facramental elements of bread and wine)* in which memory is had of the fufferings which God underwent, through him who is God; whofe name the high priefts and teachers of your people have diligently laboured to have profaned and blafphemed throughout the whole earth *."

It would be an unneceffary tafk to purfue this author's train of argument throughout, or to bring to view every proof of our Saviour's Godhead that he produces in oppofition to the Jew who denied it. Let it be ftill remembered that I am not now engaged in bringing evidence of the tenet itfelf, but in proving that our Lord's divinity was the tenet of the Antenicene fathers. That Juftin Martyr held it, I have already produced fo copious a teftimony, that I fhall now finifh my extracts from him with his own inference upon a recapitulation of the feveral fcriptures

he

---

* Ὅτι μὲν ὂν καὶ εὐχαὶ καὶ εὐχαριϛίαι ὑπο τῶν ἀξίων γινόμενοι, τέλειαι μόναι καὶ εὐάρεϛοι εἰσι τῷ Θεῷ θυσίαι, καὶ αὐτὸς φημί· ταῦτα γὰρ μόνα καὶ Χριϛιανοὶ παρέλαβον ποιεῖν, καὶ ἐπ' ἀναμνήσει δὲ τῆς τροφῆς αὐτῶν ξηρᾶς τε καὶ ὑγρᾶς, ἐν ᾗ καὶ τῦ πάθυς, ὃ πέπονθε δι' αὐτὸ ὁ Θεὸς τῦ Θεῦ, μέμνηται, ὧ τὸ ὄνομα βεβηλωθῆναι καλὰ πᾶσαν τὴν γῆν, καὶ βλασφημεῖσθαι οἱ ἀρχιερεῖς τε λαοῦ ὑμῶν καὶ διδάσκαλοι εἰργάσανλο. P. 345.

he had cited: "from which," he fays, "I would have you to know that this fame crucified Perfon is explicitly declared to be both God and man, and that his crucifixion and death are revealed in them *." "That he is both the Chrift and the adorable God †;" "that the Holy Ghoft has called him God ‡; and that, by what has been already laid down, it is abundantly demonftrated that Chrift, the Son of God, is Lord and God §."—It may afford fome fatisfaction to my reader to learn the event of this Dialogue. The Jew did not altogether adopt the fentiments of the Chriftian, but acknowledged, with fome candour, that there was more argument in behalf of his pofition than he could have conceived, and expreffes a ftrong defire to fearch the fcriptures along with him, affuring himfelf, from their prefent difcuffion, that fuch an exercife would be attended with great profit.

From the whole, it is now incontrovertibly certain that Juftin Martyr was not an Unitarian; and yet Mr. Lindfey has drawn from this author a paffage, which he fets before his reader, as an argument that chriftianity is not neceffary to falvation; for that the virtuous predeceffours of our incarnate Lord were faved without

out

---

* Ἐξ ὧν διαρῥήδην ὅτ☉ ἀυῖ☉ ὁ ςαυρωθεὶς, ὅτι Θεὸς, καὶ ἄνθρωπ☉, καὶ ςαυρέμεν☉, καὶ ἀποθνήσκων κεκηρυγμέν☉ ἀπο- δείκνυῖαι, ἰιδέναι ὑμᾶς βύλομαι. P. 297.

† Καὶ Χριςὸς καὶ Θεὸς προσκυνηῖὸς. P. 355.

‡ Ὅτι δὲ καὶ Θεὸν τὸν Χριςὸν καλεῖ (τὸ πνεῦμα τὸ ἅγιον) ἐν πολλοῖς ἀποδέδεικῖαι. P. 354.

§ Καὶ ὅτι Κύρι☉ ὢν ὁ Χριςὸς καὶ Θεὸς Θεῦ Ὑιὸς ὑπάρχων ἀποδέδεικῖαι ἐν πολλοῖς τοῖς εἰρημένοις. P. 357.

out his incarnation and sufferings for their redemption. The translation which Mr. Lindsey gives of this passage, in the 18th page of his Apology, is as follows: "They that have formerly lived (and they that now live) AGREEABLY TO REASON are Christians, and in a secure and quiet state *." Had he proceeded only to the next sentence, he might have added the explanation which the venerable Martyr himself annexes to this assertion; for he there tells us " that it was for this very purpose of their redemption, and that of all men, that our Saviour took flesh, died upon a cross, arose from the dead, and ascended into heaven †."

But, to the understanding of an author, we are not always to take words according to their general acceptation, but in that sense in which the author himself has accepted them. And with regard to the word (λόγῳ), which Mr. Lindsey has translated *reason*, we find that Justin Martyr has used it, in several passages similar in meaning to that under contemplation, in the sense of the WORD, which was God, according to St. John i. 1, and which was manifested in the flesh as Man also. And as we find it so understood in the very same Apology, in which the passage above occurs, we must conclude that, in this passage also, it means our Lord and Saviour Jesus Christ, according to whom, by his assistance from heaven, they who are in a secure and quiet state lived; and not as Mr. Lindsey turns

---

* Ὁι δὲ ΜΕΤΑ᾽ ΛΟΓΟΥ βιωσανῆες, καὶ βιῶνῆες, Χριςιανοὶ, καὶ ἄφοβοι, καὶ ἀτάραχοι ὑπάρχυσι. Apol. i. p. 83.

† Δἰ ἣν δὲ αἰτίαν διὰ παρθένε ἀνθρώπῳ ἀπεκυήθη, καὶ Ἰησες ἐφωνομάθη, καὶ ςαυρωθεὶς ἀποθανὼν ἀνέςη, καὶ ἀνελήλυθεν εἰς ὑρανὸν. Ibid.

turns it, "agreeably to reason," importing an exclusion of our Lord's divine help. I repeatedly urge it, that I am not concerned to maintain any of the tenets of the fathers, but to prove that their tenets were averse from those of the Unitarians; to which end it is but just to explain their assertions in one place by such as they have themselves made in others. To the present purpose, therefore, let me now show that Socrates is said, by Justin Martyr, to have stood up against idolatry and dæmon worship by the true WORD *; and it is then immediately declared of him that "these things were not reproved BY THE WORD, thro' Socrates, in the Greeks alone, but also among the Barbarians, BY THE WORD HIMSELF taking the form, and becoming Man, and being called Jesus Christ †," in whom, he proceeds, we also believing, reprove these things. Whether Socrates, and other wise and virtuous men, by divine inspiration and assistance, believed in Christ, is another question; but that Justin Martyr believed they did, and, therefore, that, according to this belief, he is to be interpreted as having said that they are in a secure and quiet state, who have lived (not *agreeably to reason*, as Mr. Lindsey translates it, but) *agreeably to the dictate of the Word, which was God*, is put out of all doubt; and, by consequence, the authority of this venerable man taken away from Mr. Lindsey, and proved to stand even in full opposition to the very doctrine which he was called in to support. Suppose it, however, true of the worthy predecessors of our Saviour in the flesh, that, according to Mr.
Lindsey's

* Ἀληθεῖ λόγῳ.

† Οὐ γὰρ μόνον Ἕλλησι διὰ Σωκράτες ὑπὸ λόγε ἠλέγχθη ταῦτα, ἀλλὰ καὶ ἐν βαρβάροις, ὑπ᾽ ΑΥΤΟΥ ΤΟΥ ΛΟΓΟΥ μορφωθέντος, καὶ ἀνθρώπε γενομένε, καὶ Ἰησᾶ Χριστᾶ κληθέντος.— Apol. i. p. 56.

Lindfey's tranflation, they are happy now in confequence of having lived ("*agreeably to reafon*"); to what can the doctrine lead? Can any among us become predeceffours to our Lord? or does it argue to apoftacy? Can it be inferred that, becaufe the difcharge of a duty is not required of thofe on whom it was never impofed, the neglect or defertion of that duty is juftifiable in thofe who have been called upon to difcharge it? I hope there is no man fo utterly loft to virtue as to maintain the affertion.

There is yet another paffage, of which Mr. Lindfey's erroneous tranflation makes it neceffary for me to take fome notice; but in this I fhall be very brief, as I have it in my power to refer my reader to the writings of two very learned men, whofe fellow-labourer in the caufe of true chriftianity I am happy in confidering myfelf. I mean the Reverend Mr. Bingham, who has publifhed "A Vindication of the Doctrine and Liturgy of the Church of England," and the Reverend Dr. Randolph, who has likewife very ably exerted himfelf in "A Vindication of the Worfhip of the Son and Holy Ghoft;" both of which excellent works are written in confutation of Mr. Lindfey's tenets.

The paffage referred to is taken from the 267th page of Juftin Martyr's Dialogue with Trypho the Jew, and quoted by Mr. Lindfey in the 160th page of his Apology. In his tranflation of it, the apologift has converted an addrefs to the perfons prefent into a declaration that there were many Chriftians, with whom our author lived in amity, who denied the divinity of our Lord. "*O my friends,*" fays the Martyr, "there are fome of our generation who confefs that he is the Chrift, who yet maintain that he is a man, born of human parentage, with whom I by no means agree."

agree *." But the apologist (I sincerely hope, through errour only) has put into the place of this assertion one altogether foreign from the meaning of the original; for he makes his author declare, "*there are some friends of mine amongst us* (CHRISTIANS) who profess him to be the Christ, but affirm him to be a Man born of men, with whom, however, I do not agree." The original Greek at the bottom of this page, will demonstrate the injustice of this version, and make it sufficiently clear that the application of *Christians* is a meer interpolation. This passage immediately follows that already quoted in the 87th page, in which God himself proclaims the obstinacy of the unbelieving Jews; and the very declaration, that the sentiments of such persons differ from his own in a point so essential, might help to evince the absurdity of bestowing

* Ἢδὲ μὲν τοι, ὦ Τρύφων, εἶπον, ἐκ ἀπόλλυται τὸ τοιοῦτον εἶναι Χριςὸν τῷ Θεῷ, ἐὰν ἀποδεῖξαι μὴ δύναμαι ὅτι καὶ προϋπῆρχεν Ὑιὸς τῷ ποιητῇ τῶν ὅλων Θεὸς ὤν, καὶ γεγένηται ἄνθρωπ۞ διὰ τῆς παρθένε: ἀλλά, ἐκ πάντ۞ ἀποδεικνυμένη ὅτι ἐτ۞ ὁ Χριςὸς ὁ τῷ Θεῷ, ὅςις ἐτ۞ ἔςαι, ἐὰν δὲ μὴ ἀποδείκνυω ὅτι προϋπῆρχε καὶ γεννηθῆναι ἄνθρωπ۞ ὁμοιοπαθὴς ἡμῖν, ζάρκα ἔχων, κατὰ τὴν τῷ Πατρὸς βελὴν, ὑπέμεινεν, ἐν τέτῳ πεπλανῆσθαι με μόνον λέγειν δίκαιον, ἀλλὰ μὴ ἀρνεῖςθαι ὅτι ἐτ۞ ἐςιν ὁ Χριςὸς, ἐὰν φαίνηται ὡς ἄνθρωπ۞ ἐξ ἀνθρώπων γεννηθείς, καὶ ἐκλογῇ γενόμεν۞ εἰς τὸν Χριςὸν εἶναι ἀποδεικνύηται. ΚΑΙ ΓΑΡ ΕΙΣΙ ΤΙΝΕΣ, Ὦ ΦΙΛΟΙ, ἔλεγον, ἀπὸ τοῦ ἡμετέρα γένες ὁμολογοῦντες αὐτὸν Χριςὸν εἶναι, ἄνθρωπον δὲ ἐξ ἀνθρώπων γενόμενον ἀποφαινόμενοι: οἷς ἐ ζυνθιθεμαι, ἐδὲ ἂν πλεῖςοι ταῦτα μοι δοξάσαντες εἴποιεν, ἐπειδὴ ἐκ ἀνθρωπείοις διδάγμασι κεκελεύσμεθα ὑπ᾽ αὐτῷ τῷ Χριςῷ πείθεσθαι, ἀλλὰ τοῖς διὰ τῶν μακαρίων προφητῶν κηρυχθεῖσι, καὶ δἰ αὐτῷ διδαχθεῖσι. P. 267.

I have here transcribed the entire passage from Justin Martyr, the more easily to demonstrate Mr. Lindsey's defective version of a part of it; so his translation is as little agreeable to the context as the particular languag of the original. For a further discussion of this passage, see Mr. Bingham's Vind. Doct. and Lit. p. 23, and Dr. Randolph's Vind. of the Worship of the Son and Holy Ghost, p. 133.

flowing such a title upon them. But how shall he boast of a friendship with men, whose principles and communion he has already so emphatically disavowed? Shall he now be supposed to denominate those his friends whom he has already pronounced to be "without God, without religion, without righteousness, without law, and who, instead of worshipping Jesus, confess him only in name?" Not such was this Martyr's confession of Jesus; he had a God, a religion, and a law, and he accordingly preferred his adoration to his Saviour and Redeemer, whose Godhead he has so explicitly asserted throughout his entire controversy with the Jew, that it is an indisputable fact that Justin Martyr was not an Unitarian.

TATIAN was the cotemporary and disciple of Justin Martyr. The immoderate austerity of his life and doctrine incurred the censure of the church, from which, however, he did not essentially differ in mere matters of faith.

He has written an oration against the Greeks, the end of which is to curb the pride of superiority to what they called Barbarians. Some of the tenets of christianity, however foreign from his subject, he has nevertheless found an occasion of professing.

St. Paul, urging a future judgement as an argument for a good life, tells the Corinthians that " we must all appear before the judgement seat of Christ; and that, knowing therefore the terrour of the Lord, he would persuade men." 2 Cor. v. 10, 11. If, therefore, there be any justice in the following assertion of Tatian's, Jesus Christ is one with the Father, God. " Man may be respected as man, but God alone is to
be

be feared *." But this early Chriftian has borne a more direct teftimony to his own faith, which muft put it out of controverfy that he was not an Unitarian; for, in the name of all the Chriftians, he fays, "We fpeak not foolifhly, ô Greeks, nor do we utter trifles when we declare to you that God was born in the form of a man †".

IRENÆUS, by birth a Greek, and the difciple of Polycarp, was appointed bifhop of Lyons in the year 179, upon the martyrdom of his predeceffour Pothinus. He was himfelf called upon to bear a fimilar teftimony to the fincerity of his faith; for, about the year 202, he was beheaded at Lyons, under an order from the Emperour Severus.

There is only one of his numerous volumes extant. It is "A Refutation of Herefies," in five books. He probably wrote it in Greek; but the original, excepting part of the firft book, is loft. The remainder of the work is preferved by a Latin verfion, which is very antient, but fo exceedingly barbarous, that it requires the utmoft attention to develope the author's meaning. This, in all human probability, has been tranfmitted to us very faithfully; and, poffeffing this, we may eafily difpenfe with thofe graces of ftyle and language which the tranflator of Dr. Mofheim's Ecclefiaftical Hiftory conceives to have reigned through the original.

---

* The Greek of St. Paul for the terrour of the Lord is, φόϐον κυρίȣ of Tatian's affertion, τὸν μὲν γὰρ, ἀνθρώπον ἀνθρωπίνως τιμητέον: φοϐητέον δὲ μόνον τὸν Θεόν. P. 144. Edit. Parif. Fol. 1636, cum Juft. Mart. Oper.

* Ου γαρ μωραίνομεν, ἄνδρες Ἕλληνες, ȣδὲ λήρȣς ἀπαγγέλλομεν, Θεὸν ἐν ἀνθρώπȣ μορφῇ γεγονέναι καταγγέλλοντες. P. 155.

I more lament that perspicuity which probably was possessed by the original, but has altogether vanished in the translation.

Besides the barbarity of his style, this author is encumbered with another difficulty, the barbarity of his subject; for the heresies which he undertakes to refute, are some of them of so fantastic, and even so monstrous a nature, that they rather seem to have been the dreams of madmen, than the suggestions of a serious understanding. They so evidently carried the seeds of their own decay within them, that Irenæus appears to have undertaken an unnecessary and superfluous work in attacking them. So far as I can accomplish it, I will keep these heresies out of my reader's view. This " God-denying heresy," as Eusebius calls the tenet of Paul of Samosata and Artemon, which is now again revived, is all that I am engaged to controvert; and such declarations of his own faith as this venerable father has delivered to the world on this head, I shall produce in proof that Irenæus was not an Unitarian. It is not, however, possible to exclude these heretics altogether. Among others, which are better forgotten, they held tenets similar to those now embraced; and so far as our author's refutation affects these only, I am obliged to bring them forward.

Like our modern Unitarians, they divided from God " the Word, which was God;" but not being able to combat the apostolical testimony of the Godhead of the Word, they had recourse to a similar solution with a certain polytheistical writer, who contends that there is a supreme God, and another God. To this purpose they devised a strange genealogy for the Word, which they separated from God; thus, rather than admit a personal distinction, dividing the Godhead itself.

But

But our venerable author, condefcending to their abſurdity, and anſwering the fool according to his folly, argues from the illimitable extent of God, that no effluence can go forth from him that can be divided from him; and thence concludes, that, as he is all mind uncompounded, in all parts alike, whole and equal; all thought, all mind, the Word being an expreſſion of the mind, is inſeparable from the indiviſible mind, and that, in the utterance, it cannot go out of that circumference which the boundleſs God forms around it; and, therefore, that being the ſame with the mind, which is God, the Word itſelf is God, and that it is ever one with the Father, from whom it is inſeparable. " But if they ſay that intellect is thus divided from intellect, they cut into parts, and parcel out the intellect of God. But whither, and whence is it ſent forth? Whatever is ſent forth, is caſt upon ſome recipient beyond the projectile; but what is there beyond the intellect of God, upon which, according to them, it ſhould be caſt forth from him? What ſpace is there to receive and comprehend the mind of God? But if, to uſe their own example of a ray from the ſun, they would ſhew that, in like manner as the air is more antient than the ray, and of capacity to receive it when projected, there ſubſiſts any ſubject, upon which the intellect of God ſhall be caſt forth, capable of containing it, and of greater antiquity, it will become neceſſary for them *(to purſue the illuſtration)* to ſay, that as the ſun, which we ſee to be limited, ſheds his rays to a diſtance from himſelf, ſo the progenitour ſheds a ray out of, and far beyond himſelf: but what is there out of, what is there beyond God, into which he ſhall beam a radiance that ſhall be diſtinct from himſelf? But if then they admit that the mind of God is not projected beyond the Father, but ſtill continues within him, then the Word, which *(according*

cording to the Gnostics whom he contends with) is the effluence again from this emitted mind, is circumscribed within the Father, and being in the bowels of the Father, *is* exempt from sufferings *. " This writer farther combats these extraordinary tenets, saying, " God is all mind, God is all Word, what he thinks, that he speaks, and what he speaks, that he thinks; for thought is his word, and the Word is mind, and Mind is the Father himself, who comprehends all things. He, therefore, who speaks of the mind of God, and ascribes to mind a proper distinct procedure or generation, pronounces God a compound, as if there was one thing God, and another thing the principal mind. In like manner, ascribing to the Word a third descent from the Father, his ignorance of the greatness of God appears, inasmuch as that he separates the Word from God, tho' the prophet has said, " Who shall declare his generation? Isa. liii. 8. " If any shall, therefore, say to us, how then is the Son generated of the Father? we answer him that, whether he will call it procedure, or generation, or expression, or utterance, or disclosure,

---

* Si autem de sensû sensum dicant emissum, præcidunt sensum Dei et partiuntur. Quo autem & unde emissus est? quod enim ab aliquo emittitur in aliquod subjectum emittitur. Quid autem subjacebat quàm sensus Dei, in quô emissum dicunt eum? quantus autem & erat locus ut susciperet & caperet Dei sensum? Si autem quemamodum a sole radium dicunt, sicut subjacet aër hic susceptor, & antiquior erit quam ipse radius, & illic ostendant subjacens aliquid in quô emissus est sensus Dei, capabile ejus & antiquius: post opportebit, quemamodum solem minorem esse, quem omnia videmus longè a semetipso emittentem radios, sic & propatorem dicere extrà longè & a semetipso emisisse radium; quidnam autem extrà aut longè sentiri a Deo potest in quod radium emisit? Si autem non emissum extra Patrem illum dicent, sed in ipso Patre, is qui ab eo Logos erit intrà Patrem, & impassibiles *(aliæ scilicet præter Logon, emissiones Logi, de quibus hic disserere prorsûs abs re)* omnes similiter perseverabunt, cum sint in paternis visceribus.—Irenæi adversus Heræses, lib. ii. cap xvij. p. 114. Edit. Gallasii, Genevæ, 1570, folio.

sure, or by any other denomination, no man, neither the angels, nor the archangels, nor the principalities, nor the powers, nor any other knows his unspeakable generation besides the Father alone, who begot him, and the Son who was born †." The necessity under which Irenæus lay of using the language of the Heretics, with whom he contended, occasions an obscurity in these passages, which, however, does not affect the question in debate; for, notwitstanding their obscurity, they still sufficiently prove the only truth that I here contend for, namely, that Irenæus believed in the divinity of Christ; for here we see the inexplicable generation, and yet the inseparable unity of the Son with the Father as God, asserted by him in the most explicit manner; and we are farther warned not to argue from human imbecility to a restraint on Omnipotence, nor judge of an infinite and incomprehensible God by analogies which cannot subsist.

Appofite to this last assertion, having declared that he alone is God " who, by himself, that is, by his word and his wifdom, created the heaven and earth," this writer farther says, that " they know him to whom
the

† Deus autem totus existens Mens, & totus existens Logos, quod cogitat hoc et loquitur, et quod loquitur hoc et cogitat. Cogitatio enim ejus Logos, et Logos mens, et omnia concludens mens, ipse est Pater. Qui ergo dicit mentem Dei, et prolationem propriam menti donat, compositum eum pronunciat, tanquam aliud quiddam fit Deus, aliud autem principalis mens existens. Similiter autem rursus et de Logo, tertiam prolationem ei â Patre donans, unde et ignorat magnitudinem ejus: porro et longè Logon â Deo feperavit, et propheta quidem ait de eo, *generationem ejus quis ennarravit?* Si quis itaque nobis dixerit, quomodo ergo Filius prolatus â Patre est? dicimus ei, quia prolationem istam, five generationem, five nuncupationem, five adapertionem, aut quomodolibet quis nomine vocaverit, generationem ejus inenarrabilem existentem nemo novit, neque angeli, neque archangeli, neque principes, neque potestates, nisi solus qui generavit Pater et qui natus est Filius. Lib. ii. cap. xlviii. p. 149.

the Son has revealed him, the Son eternally cöexiftent with the Father *;" and he thus afferts the union of God and man in the perfon of Jefus Chrift, " who, from his moft exalted love to his creature, fubmitted to be born as a man of a virgin, thus in himfelf uniting man and God, and fuffering under Pontius Pilate, and arifing from the dead, and being openly received up into glory, will come again the Saviour of all who are faved, and Judge of all who are judged ‡" Here Jefus Chrift is pronounced the Creator, as it is for the love he bore to his own work that he is faid to have taken manhood upon him; and, confonant with this declaration, the fame author fays that " the Word of God is the Father of mankind *." To him, therefore, as one with the Father, fuch as concur in believing this article of Irenæus's faith muft naturally prefer the Lord's prayer; " for, when we fay, our Father which art in heaven, in calling him Father we name him our God; for this appellation acknowledges both his goodnefs and power; and in the Father the Son alfo is invoked; for he fays himfelf, " I and the Father are one †."

In another part of his work, Irenæus tells us that " Simon Magus was by many glorified as God; that he

* " Qui fecit per femetipfum, hoc eft, per Verbum et per Sapientiam fuam cœlum et tèrram." " Cognofcunt enim eum hi quibus revelaverit Filius, femper autem coexiftens Filius Patri." Lib. ii. cap. lv. p. 157.

‡ Qui, propter eminentiffimam erga figmentum fuum delectionem, eam quæ effet ex virgine, generationem fuftinuit, ipfe per fe hominem adunans Deo, et paffus fub Pontio Pilato, et refurgens, et in claritate receptus in gloria, venturus Salvator eorum qui falvantur, et Judex eorum qui judicantur. Lib. iii. cap. iv. p. 172.

* Pater autem generis humani Verbum Dei eft. Lib. iv. cap. li. p.287.

† Dicendo autem Patrem, Deum cognominamus; appellatio ifta et pietatis et poteftatis eft. Item in Patre Filius invocatur; Ego enim inquit et Pater unum fumus.—Tertulliani Lib. de Oratione, cap. ii.

he taught them that he was the same who appeared among the Jews as the Son; but, in Samaria, descended as the Father, and came also into other nations as the Holy Ghost; but that he was the most sublime virtue, that is he who is Father over all ‡." We see here the three Persons enumerated, and it is of no importance to object that it is by Simon they are named. He allows Jesus Christ to have been God the Son; the Holy Ghost, whom he had learned at his own baptism when he believed, (see Acts viii. 10. &c.) he declares to be God, who visited the Gentiles; and in this he is strictly right, for it is by his assistance sent to the apostles that Christ was witnessed to the Gentiles, and that we now believe; the Person of the Father he reserves to himself, calling his own Samaritan nativity the descent of the Father into Samaria. To each of these three Persons he unquestionably ascribes the name and dignity of God; so that, even in the apostolic days, we here find an acknowledgement that the Father is God, the Son is God, and the Holy Ghost is God: an acknowledgement too on which I place much reliance; for, upon the doctrines disseminated by the apostles, and which were now very generally received, he grounded his own extravagant blasphemy; he assumed to himself the Godhead, which was admitted; and though he has come under the scourge of Irenæus for most blasphemously arrogating to himself the *great power of God*, yet does this very assumption, horrible as it is, bear an important testimony that the Father, the Son, and the Holy Ghost were at that time generally believed to be, God.

Justin

‡ Hic igitur (Sc. Simon Magus) a multis quasi Deus glorificatus est, et docuit semetipsum esse qui inter Judæos quidem quasi Filius adparuerit, in Samariâ autem quasi Pater descenderit, et in reliquis vero gentibus quasi Spiritus Sanctus adventaverit. Esse autem se sublimissimam virtutem, hoc est, eum qui sit super omnia Pater. Irenæi, lib. i. cap. xx. p. 75.

Juftin Martyr has, in his Dialogue with Trypho, afked the Jews, " Think ye that any other is held forth in the fcriptures as the object of worfhip, and Lord and God, befides the Creator of the univerfe and Chrift, who is by fo many fcriptures revealed to you to have been made man †?" And to this queftion, the following affertion of Irenæus affords a full and fatiffactory anfwer: " Neither the Lord, nor the Holy Ghoft, nor the apoftles would have definitively and abfolutely denominated him God, who was not God, nor given this name to any, unlefs he were the true God; neither, from their own perfons, would they have called any Lord but God, who beareth dominion over all things, the Father, and the Son who hath received the dominion from the Father. As the fcripture fays, " The Lord faid unto my Lord, fit thou on my right hand until I make thine enemies thy footftool," Pfa. cx. 1, which fhews the Father, who gave him the heathen for an inheritance, and put all his enemies under him, here fpeaking to the Son. Seeing then that the Father is truly Lord, and that the Son is truly Lord, the Holy Ghoft has properly fignified them by the appellation of Lord." " But the fcripture alfo faith, Thy throne, O God, is for ever and ever; a fceptre of righteoufnefs is the fceptre of thy kingdom; thou haft loved righteoufnefs, and hated iniquity; therefore God, even thy God, hath anointed thee. Pfa. xlv. 6, 7. The Holy Ghoft has here fignified both by the appellation of God, him who is anointed,
the

† Μὴ τὶ ἄλλον τινὰ προσκυνητὸν, καὶ κύριον, καὶ Θεὸν λεγομένον ἐν ταῖς γραφαῖς νοεῖτε ἔιναι, πλὴν τῦ τῦτο πεποιηκότ@- τὸ πᾶν, καὶ τῦ Χριςῦ, ὅς διὰ τῶν τοσέτων γραφῶν ἀπεδείχθη ὑμῖν ἄνθρωπ@- γενομέν@-. Dialogus cum Tryphone Judæo, p. 295.

the Son, and him who anointeth him, the Father *." He quotes many other paſſages of holy writ to the ſame purpoſe, and then declares that, "when ſcripture names any gods which are not Gods, it does not do ſo without qualification, but with ſome addition or interpretation, by which they are ſhewn not to be Gods †." As examples, he cites Exod. vii. 1. Pſalm xcvi. 5. Iſaiah xlii. 17.— xliv. 9, and, among many other texts, 1 Cor. viii. 4, 5, 6; "for tho' there be that are called gods, whether in heaven or in earth, (as there be gods many and lords many) but to us there is but one God, the Father, of whom are all things, and we in him, *(in illo)* and one Lord Jeſus Chriſt, by whom are all things, and we by him." And upon this paſſage the father makes the following ſhort comment, that " St. Paul has ſeparated or diſtinguiſhed thoſe who are called gods, but are not ſuch, from the one God, the Father, of whom are all things, and in his own perſon has moſt firmly confeſſed the one Lord Jeſus Chriſt ‡." And, in the words

---

* Neque igitur Dominus, neque Spiritus Sanctus, neque apoſtoli eum qui non eſſet Deus definitivè et abſolutè Deum nominaſſent aliquando niſi eſſet verus Deus, neque Dominum apellaſſent aliquem ex ſuâ perſonâ niſi qui dominatur omnium Deum, Patrem, et Filium ejus qui dominium accepit a Patre ſuo omnis conditionis: quemadmodum habet illud " dixit Dominus Domino meo, &c." Pſa. cx. 1. Matth. xxii. 44. Patrem enim cum Filio colloquutum oſtendit qui et dedit ei hæreditatem gentium, et ſubjecit ei omnes inimicos. Verè, igitur, cum Pater ſit Dominus, et Filius verè ſit Dominus, meritò Spiritus Sanctus Domini appellatione ſignificavit eos." " Similiter habet illud " ſedes tua, Deus, in eternum, &c." Pſa. xlv. 6, 7. Heb. i. 8. Utroſque enim Dei appellatione ſignificavit Spiritus, et eum qui ungitur, Filium, et eum qui ungit, id eſt Patrem. Lib. iii. cap. vi. p. 174.

† Cum autem eos qui non ſunt, deos nominat, non in totum ſcriptura oſtendit illos Deos, ſed cum aliquo additamento et ſignificatione, per quam oſtenduntur non eſſe Dii. Ibidem.

‡ Seperavit eos qui dicuntur quidem, non ſunt autem dii, ab uno Deo Patre ex quo omnia, et unum Dominum Jeſum Chriſtum ex ſuâ perſonâ firmiſſime confeſſus eſt. P. 176.

words of ORIGEN, let me proceed to say that "I wonder how any who read what the apoſtle Paul has ſaid "that there is one God, the Father, of whom are all things, and one Lord Jeſus Chriſt, by whom are all things," ſhould yet deny that they ought to confeſs the Son of God to be God, leſt they ſhould ſeem to acknowledge two Gods. How will they diſpoſe of this paſſage of the apoſtle, in which Chriſt is openly declared to be God over all? Rom. ix. 5. *(See alſo p. 26, above).* But they who hold theſe opinions do not conſider, that as he has not termed the Lord Jeſus Chriſt the one Lord in ſuch excluſive manner, that God the Father ſhall hence be pronounced not Lord; ſo alſo he has not denominated God the Father God in ſuch excluſive manner as that the Son ſhall not hence be believed to be God; for that ſcripture is true which ſays, " Be ye ſure that the Lord he is God," Pſa. c. 3; for they are both one God, becauſe there is no other commencement of the Son's Godhead than the Father; but of that paternal fountain (as wiſdom ſaith) the Son is the pureſt emanation. Chriſt is therefore God over all. What all? doubtleſs over principalities, and powers, and virtues, and over every name that is named, not only in this, but in every future age. But he who is above all, has no ſuperior above him; for he is not beneath, or after the Father, but of the Father. But, concerning the Holy Ghoſt alſo, the wiſdom of God has given us information, when he ſays, " For the Spirit of the Lord filleth the world, and that which containeth all things hath knowledge of the voice." *(Wiſdom of Solomon, chap. i. 7).* If therefore the Son of God be declared over all; if the Holy Ghoſt be ſaid to contain all things; and if the Father be God, of whom are all things, the nature and one ſubſtance of a Trinity,

which

which is over all, is clearly demonstrated *." I have
the more willingly digressed into a comment on this
passage in St. Paul's Epistle to the Corinthians, because
that a moiety of the first part of the 6th verse has been
produced in evidence of the Father's exclusive Godhead, and even made the motto of a work levelled at
the divinity of our Redeemer. It is true that such an
argument is a just epitome of that system which is
pursued to this blasphemous end: half sentences are
torn away from their context, and their weight then
turned against the very purposes for which they were
dictated by the Spirit. I think myself fortunate in
being able to bring this sensible remark of an antient
Christian into direct opposition to the stratagems of a
modern apostate, on whom I call to withdraw the denomination under which he publishes, and no longer
to boast himself " a Member of the church of Christ,"

in

* Et miror quomodo quidam, legentes quod idem apostolus in aliis dicit
unus Deus Pater ex quo omnia, et unus Dominus Jesus Christus per quem
omnia, negent Filium Dei Deum debere profiteri, ne duos Deos dicere videantur. Et quid de hoc loco apostoli facient, in quo apertè Christus super omnia Deus esse perscribitur? Rom. ix. 5. Sed non advertunt, qui
hæc ita sentiunt, quòd sicut Dominum Jesum Christum non ita unum
esse Dominum dixit, ut ex hoc Deus Pater non Dominus dicatur, ita et
Deum Patrem non dixit ita esse unum Deum, ut Deus Filius non credatur. Vera est enim scriptura quæ dicit " scitote quoniam Dominus ipse
est Deus." Psa. c. 3. Unus enim uterque Deus, quia non est aliud Filio
divinitatis initium quàm Pater, sed ipsius paterni fontis (sicut sapientia
dicit) purissima est emanatio Filius. Est ergo Christus super omnia
Deus. Quæ omnia? sine dubio super principatus, et potestates, et virtutes, et omne nomen quod nominatur non solùm in hoc sæculo sed etiam
in futuro. Qui autem super omnes est super se neminem habet. Non
enim post Patrem ipse, sed de Patre.—Hoc autem (id est sapientia Dei)
etiam de Sancto Spiritu intelligi dedit ubi dicit, " Spiritus Domini reple-
vit orbem terrarum et qui continet omnes scientiam habet vocis." Si ergo
Filius Dei super omnes dicitur; et Spiritus Sanctus continere omnia me-
moratur; Deus autem Pater est ex quo omnia; evidenter ostenditur natura
Trinitatis et substantia una quæ est super omnia. Origenis Opera, tom ii.
p. 376. In Epistolam ad Romanos, lib. vii. cap. ix.

in contiguity with a paſſage half-quoted, for the purpoſe of denying and excluding the Head and Inſtitutor of " that church which God, that is the Son himſelf, through himſelf, has aſſembled together."

Irenæus, ſtill purſuing the ſame argument, that none are called gods who are not Gods, without ſome terms of exception, ſays, " that none of the ſons of Adam is called god, without ſome qualifying term, as the Lord is called, we have demonſtrated from the ſcriptures; and to all, who have attained to but a moiety of the truth, it is obvious, that he alone of all mankind is denominated God, and Lord, and the eternal King, and the Only-begotten, and the incarnate Word, both by the prophets, and apoſtles, and the Holy Ghoſt himſelf. And theſe things the ſcriptures would not have teſtified of him, had he been but a Man as all other men are; but the holy ſcriptures teſtify both theſe things of him, that, different from all other men, he alone had in himſelf a glorious generation from the moſt high Father, and that he alſo accompliſhed a glorious birth of a virgin; that he was a Man without beauty, obnoxious to ſufferings, riding on an aſs's colt, drinking vinegar and gall, deſpiſed of the people, and bowing down even to the death; that he was the Lord holy, the wonderful Counſellor, beautiful in form, God mighty, coming in the clouds, the Judge of all men. All theſe things have the ſcriptures prophecied concerning him. For as he was man that he might undergo temptations, ſo was he the Word that he might receive glory; the Word acquieſcing that he might be liable to temptation, and diſhonour, and crucifixion, and death; but the Man being taken into the Word becauſe of his victory, his ſuffering, his reſurrection and aſſump-

* Hi autem ſunt eccleſia; hæc enim eſt ſynagoga Dei, quam Deus, hoc eſt Filius ipſe, per ſemet ipſum collegit. Lib. iii. cap. vi. p. 175.

assumption *." "But St. John," says our venerable author, "has cut off all controversy from us by saying, "He was in the world, and the world was made by him, and the world knew him not. He came unto his own, and his own received him not." Yet, according to Marcion, and such as are like to him, the world was not made by him, neither did he come to his own, but to another's †." But " there is one Word of God, by which are all things, by whom all things were made; for the Word of God is truly the Maker of the world; and he is our Lord who, in the latter times, was made Man ‡." And therefore Christ himself,

---

* Quoniam enim nemo in totum ex filiis Adæ deus appellatur, fecundum ut Dominus nominatur, ex scripturis demonstravimus; quoniam ipse proprie præter omnes qui fuerunt tunc homines, Deus, et Dominus, et Rex æternus, et Unigenitus, et Verbum incarnatum prædicatum, et a prophetis, et apostolis, et ab ipso Spiritu, adest videre omnibus qui vel modicum de veritate attigerint. Hæc autem non testificarentur scripturæ de eô, si similiter ut omnes homines homo tantûm fuisset. Sed quoniam præclaram, præter omnes, habuit in se eam quæ est ab altissimo Patre genituram, præclarâ autem functus est et eâ quæ est ex virgine generatione, utraque scripturæ divinæ de eo testificantur, et quoniam Homo indecorus, et passibilis, et super pullum asinæ ascendens, aceto et felle potatur, et spernebatur in populo, et usque ad mortem descendit; et quoniam Dominus sanctus, et mirabilis Consiliarius, et decorus specie, et Deus fortis, super nubes veniens universorum Judex. Omnia de eo scripturæ prophetabant. Sicut enim Homo erat ut tentaretur, sic et Verbum ut glorificaretur; requiescente quidem Verbo, ut posset tentari, et inhonorari, et crucifigi, et mori; absorpto autem Homine, in eo quòd vincit, et sustinet, et resurgit, et assumitur. Lib. iii. cap. xxi. p. 212.

† Abstulit autem a nobis dissensiones omnes ipse Joannes, dicens, "In hoc mundo erat, et mundus per eum factus est, et mundus eum non cognovit. In sua propria venit, et sui eum non receperunt." Secundum autem Marcionem, et eos qui similes sunt ei, neque mundus per eum factus est, neque in sua venit sed in aliena. Lib. iii. cap. xi. p. 184.

‡ Unum Verbum Dei per quod omnia, per quem omnia facta sunt. Mundi enim Factor verè Verbum Dei est. Hic autem est Dominus noster, qui in novissimis temporibus Homo factus est. Lib. v. cap. xvi. p. 340.

self, with the Father, is the God of the living, who spoke with Moses, and was made manifest to the fathers *." And now " do thou, O God, who, thro' the multitude of thy mercy, hast dealt graciously by us, that we should know thee who hast made the heaven and earth, and rulest over all; who, with our Lord Jesus Christ, rulest in the power of the Holy Ghost, and art the only true God, besides whom there is no God; grant to every one that readeth this scripture to know thee, that thou art the only God, and to be confirmed in thee, and to turn away from every heretical, godless, and impious tenet †."

St. Ignatius, as I have already stated, p. 21, says " that our Saviour truly raised up himself from the dead;" and with him Irenæus agrees; for he asserts that, " being invisible, he took manhood upon himself and became visible; being incomprehensible, he became comprehensible; that, being exempt from sufferings, he became obnoxious to them; and that, being

---

* Ipse igitur Christus, cum Patre, vivorum est Deus, qui et locutus est Moysi, qui et patribus manifestus est. Lib. iv. cap. xi. p. 239.

† Deus, qui per multitudinem misericordiæ tuæ, & bene sensisti in nobis, ut te cognoscamus qui fecisti cœlum, & terram, & dominaris omnium, qui es solus & verus Deus, super quem alius Deus non est, præter Dominum nostrum Jesum Christum, dominatione quoque dominaris Spiritûs Sancti, da omni legenti hanc scripturam cognoscere te quia solus Deus es, & confirmari in te, & absistere ab omni hæreticâ, & quæ est sine Deo, & impiâ sententiâ. Lib. lii. cap. vi. p. 176.

If any person object to the translation of this prayer as not being literal, let him just consider that a version made exactly according to the letter would place the Son above the Father, which, I am confident, was not the intention of the author, though his miserable translator has substituted it for him. The words of the Latin version will bear the sense I have ascribed to them; and as this is consistent with the general doctrine of his book, I have not the smallest doubt that it is the true one.

ing the Word, he became Man ‡;" " that he suffered in our stead, and arose for our sake §." " And to this purpose our Lord, in these latter times, came to us, not so as he might have come, but so as we might be able to behold him; for he might have come to us in his own unspeakable glory, but we should be unable to endure the majesty of his glory *:" " for he is the Word of God, the Only-begotten of the Father, Jesus Christ our God †."

That Irenæus considered, and, from habit, felt the words God, Lord, and Christ to be perfectly synonimous, the two following quotations will evince; and from the first of them we may also deduce this certain conclusion, that our Lord was the object of a Christian's worship in the second century.

St. Paul, warning the Thessalonians of future defection, to take place when the Man of sin shall be revealed, describes this Son of perdition as " sitting in the temple of God, shewing himself that HE IS GOD."
2 Thess.

---

‡ Hominem ergo in semetipso recapitulatus est invisibilis, & visibilis factus, & incomprehensibilis, factus comprehensibilis, & impassibilis, passibilis, & Verbum Homo. Lib. iii. cap. xviii. p. 205.

§ Ipse est Jesus Christus Dominus noster qui passus est pro nobis, & surrexit propter nos. Ibidem, p. 204.

* Et propter hoc Dominus noster, in novissimis temporibus venit ad nos, non quomodo ipse poterat, sed quomodo illum nos videre poteramus. Ipse enim in sua inenarrabili gloria ad nos venire poterat, sed nos magnitudinem gloriæ suæ portare non poteramus. Lib. iv. cap. lxxiv. p. 3c9.
Compare this with the assertion of St. BARNABAS, (page 15 above); refer it also to what has been said on Philippians ii. 6, 7, 8, in the 9th page, under the head of CLEMENS ROMANUS.

† Ipse enim Verbum Dei, ipse Unigenitus a Patre, Christus Jesus Deus noster. Lib. iii. cap. xviii. p. 206.

2 Theff. ii. 4.; but Irenæus, referring to this paffage, defcribes the Son of perdition as "fitting in the temple of God, that they who are feduced by him may ADORE HIM AS CHRIST *."

"CHRIST died for our fins," fays St. Paul; and, without changing the antecedent, goes on to fay that "*he* rofe again the third day; that *he* was feen of Cephas, then of the twelve, after that of five hundred brethren at once, and, laft of all, *he* was feen of me alfo." 1 Cor. xv. 3, &c. Here the Perfons who had feen CHRIST after his refurrection are enumerated by St. Paul, for the purpofe of proving their teftimony equally competent with his own. But Irenæus, for the fame purpofe, produces this paffage, and thus proceeds, " that Paul, in his epiftle to the Corinthians, when he had named all who had feen GOD after his refurrection, has inferred: " Therefore, whether it were I, or they, fo we preached, and fo ye believed." 1 Cor. xv. 9; thus confeffing the agreement in doctrine of all thofe who faw GOD after his refurrection †."

It may not be amifs to remark here, that, of thofe Hereticks with whom Irenæus contended, fome rejected the writings of St. Paul, while by others thefe alone were received; and that fome there were who chofe only certain paffages out of the fcriptures, to which

---

* In templo Dei fedente, ut ficut CHRISTUM adorent illum qui feducuntur ab illo. Lib. v. cap. xxiii. p. 352.

† Et rurfus in Epiftolâ quæ eft ad Corinthios, cum prædixiffet omnes qui DEUM poft refurrectionem viderunt, intulit, " Sive autem ego, five illi, fic annunciamus & fic credidiftis." Unam & eandem prædicationem confitens omnium eorum qui DEUM viderunt poft refurrectionem a mortuis. Lib. iii. cap. xiii. p. 197.

which they would allow the authority of divine infpiration. With equal candour do thofe moderns proceed, who are daily calling into queftion the authenticity of fuch texts of the facred writings as teftify our Saviour's Godhead. They declare themfelves ready and willing to fubfcribe the New Teftament, provided no farther fubfcription be required: but I afk them now, what is that New Teftament which they are thus prepared to admit of as the rule of their faith? Is it the Englifh tranflation which we ufe? That is impoffible; for the obnoxious texts are all contained in it; they have already declared that *it is falfe*, and that "*that which was only a lye, originally, is metamorphofed into abfurdity.*" Is it the Complutenfian edition? That too is impoffible. "*Here is a manifeft interpolation;*" for herein " we perceive the love OF GOD, becaufe he laid down his life for us." 1 John iii. 16 *. is it yet

the

---

* The words in Italicks are quoted from Unitarian productions.

Some of the manufcripts of St. John's firft epiftle omit "of God", and read only, " hereby perceive we love, becaufe he laid down his life for us:" Ἐν τούτῳ ἐγνώκαμεν τὴν ἀγάπην, ὅτι ἐκεῖνος ὑπὲρ ἡμῶν τὴν ψυχὴν αὐτοῦ ἔθηκε. While others, of as good authority, have the words τῦ Θεῦ after ἀγάπην, affording the fenfe which our Englifh tranflation has adopted. Whether thefe words are admitted into, or excluded from the text, is a matter of lefs importance than Unitarians, who contend fo ftrenuoufly for their exclufion, feem to think. For if the poffeffour of " *the love*" be not expreffed, *the love of God* is the general fubject which St. John is urging as an example, and, confequently, "*of God*" muft be here underftood. The form of the expreffion requires that a poffeffour be at leaft underftood; for it is not " hereby perceive we love" in the abftract (ἀγάπην), as they ftate it, but " hereby perceive we *the* love," (τὴν ἀγάπην). And, after thus particularizing the love, it is even neceffary to indicate the love of whom; and this, as I have already ftated, is fufficiently done without expreffing the poffeffour, for the love OF GOD is the general fubject. " If we love one another, God dwelleth in us." 1 John iv. 12. " Beloved, let us love one another, for love is of God, and every one that loveth is born of God, and knoweth God; he that loveth not, knoweth not God; for God is love." 1 John iv. 8.

The

the elaborate edition of Dr. Mill? I doubt, not; for in this appears " *that nonsensical proposition,*" " *that impious*

The very next verse to this recounts the goodness of God in sending his only begotten Son into the world to become a propitiation for our sins, that we might live through him: and, in terms exactly similar to those in question, the apostle tells us that, " in this was manifested THE LOVE OF GOD towards us." 1 John iv.—viii. Ἐν τούτῳ ἐφανερώθη ἡ ἀγάπη τοῦ Θεοῦ ἐν ἡμῖν. 1 John iv. 8. In short, not to multiply examples, the whole end and purpose of the apostle, in writing this short epistle, is to urge THE LOVE OF GOD as an example and motive to brotherly love; and the very passage under consideration closes with a question concerning the uncompassionate: " How dwelleth the love of GOD in him?" Where incontrovertibly the same love that is used as an argument to benevolence in the commencement of the sentence, and is there said to be perceived by such as lay down their lives for the brethren, is denied to dwell in such as, on the contrary, shut up their bowels of compassion from them.

But perhaps that critical Acumen, which has discovered two Gods, a Θεός and an ὁ Θεός, *a vicegerent God, and a supreme God,* in the scriptures *, (in which these terms are found almost as often as the word Trinity) may, upon a new exertion of itself, discriminate also between ἀγάπη and ἡ ἀγάπη, and so prove to a demonstration that the article precedes ἀγάπη in the passage before us for the sake of energy. But " God is love," says the apostle: and if, in any instance, this word should be emphatically distinguished, one would imagine it then most necessary when it is predicated of God himself; notwithstanding which, it stands here unattended by its satellite article, and we are in plain terms told ὁ Θεὸς ἀγάπη ἐστίν.

Out of one hundred and twenty manuscripts consulted by Wetstein, says this Polytheist, the word Θεοῦ was found but in one: but, in a note, he has been most graciously pleased to inform us that St. John's epistles were not contained in the one hundred and twenty manuscripts. I cannot therefore sufficiently testify my surprize that this text was not contained in them all. Pray, in how many of these manuscripts did St John's epistles appear? When we are told the number of these, we shall be better able to judge of the authority of one, which may bear a larger proportion to the truth when tardily told, than to one hundred and twenty fallaciously advanced into the text, and conspicuously obtruded upon the eye.

But he proceeds: " Of printed editions of any repute, it is only to be found in the Complutensian and Genevan; and, of versions, the modern English

---

* See *Remarks on Script. Confut.* p. 70 and 94.

impious forgery," " which belies the Holy Ghost." " He has foisted into the sacred writings one whole text, which deforms

English only has it." The fraudulence of this assertion I shall presently demonstrate, but, in the mean time, will shew that the author is himself conscious of it; for, in the very next sentence, waving the advantage that might accrue to his cause, if he could maintain the position, he declares, " But there is no occasion to appeal to manuscripts, editions, or versions to reprobate the word. It is impossible St. John should have wrote ἐκεῖνος, referred to an antecedent immediately preceding;" and as a reason for this impossibility, he farther proceeds to say that " there is a use of the Greek pronoun ἐκεῖνος very frequent in all authors when they mean to mark out a person with particular emphasis without naming him." Remarks on Script. Conf. p. 94. Thus do we see the beloved disciple and witness of our Lord tied down to transcribe only the suggestions of this man's understanding, and interdicted the use of any language but such as he shall prescribe; but the evangelist must be set at liberty from the narrow circumscription, or admitted very frequently to have performed more than miracles, even impossibilities; for in no less than twenty-two instances have I found him using ἐκεῖνος, not referred to an antecedent, which, for the advantage of energy and perspicuity, is emphatically nameless, but referred to an antecedent immediately preceding. A few of these shall be laid before my reader, and will probably suffice to set aside this silly rule. For the English I refer to the chapter and verse in our Bible.

Οἶδα ὅτι Μεσσίας ἔρχεται, ὁ λεγόμενος Χριστός. Ὅταν ἔλθῃ ἐκεῖνος ἀναγγελεῖ ἡμῖν πάντα. John iv. 26.

Ὁ ποιήσας με ὑγιῆ, ἐκεῖνός μοι εἶπεν. John v. 11.

Ὁ ἀναβαίνων ἀλλαχόθεν, ἐκεῖνος κλέπτης ἐστὶ καὶ λῃστής. John x. 1.

Ὁ λόγος ὃν ἐλάλησα, ἐκεῖνος κρινεῖ αὐτόν. John xii. 48.

Ἦλθον οὖν οἱ ὑπηρέται πρὸς τοὺς ἀρχιερεῖς καὶ Φαρισαίους, καὶ εἶπον αὐτοῖς ἐκεῖνοι. John vii. 45.

Ἔρχεται οὖν πρὸς Σίμωνα Πέτρον, καὶ λέγει αὐτῷ ἐκεῖνος. John xiii. 16.

Ὅταν δὲ ἔλθῃ ἐκεῖνος, τὸ Πνεῦμα τῆς ἀληθείας, &c. John xvi. 13.

deforms and pollutes them in spite of demonstrative evidence." Is it the Alexandrian manuscript? May not anti-

As I have already said that the expression of these words is of no great importance to the main question, because, if not expressed, they are certainly implied; and that, as "love is of God," the words τὴν ἀγάπην, if he article be used only for eminence, must signify "the love of God," I am the less anxious to establish the reading: and I should drop the subject here, were it not essential to the reader's ease in forming his own judgement, that he should know, and so stand guarded against such unwarrantable arts as have been used to inveigle him into errour.

Editions and versions can go but a little way towards deciding a question of this kind; but where a new species of logic is introduced, and a general negative positively affirmed, it may be worth while to shew how little reliance is to be placed upon the assertions of such writers, and how very cautiously we should admit their attestations where we have it not in our power to examine.

"Of versions," this man says, "the *modern* English only has it."

In York Minster Library there is a very antient English translation of the New Testament It is a manuscript, the age of which I find no rule precisely to ascertain. The Saxon character of *th* is used throughout, and the language is at least as old as that of Chaucer. By whom it was made I care not, but suspect it to be Wycliffe's version, and to have been written during his own life. The character, the Saxon termination of plurals and participles, and the spelling, which does not use so many redundant letters as were introduced about a century and a half after his time, justify this conjecture, into the truth of which I have now neither leisure nor opportunity to examine.—The controverted text, however, is thus translated in this certainly *not modern* English version.

"In this thing we hav knowe the charite of God : for he puttide his lyf for us : and we owen to putte oure lyves for oure brithren. He that hath the catel *(quære* chattel*)* of this world and seeth that his brother hath need, and closith hise entrailis fro him : how dwellith the charite of God in him ?"

The obscurity in which this manuscript has heretofore lien might be admitted as an amply sufficient apology for not having known it, if that very ignorance were not made use of as an argument. This man, if we may believe him, (and when he attests his ignorance I do believe him) certainly did not know of any version which contained the text thus, except the modern English. Had he modestly said so, he should have received the information I now give him without a rebuke; but this best witness of an *alibi* did not know that *there is such a version*, and therefore, he concludes, *there is not such a version.*—But farther:

Le Clerc turns it *de Dieu*.

The vulgate version acknowledges τοῦ Θεοῦ.

Arias

antiquity plead for the admiſſion of this venerable record? No, no: that Chriſt is over all God bleſſed for ever, Rom. ix. 5, is atteſted in it; and that aſſertion, which " *St. Paul could never make, becauſe the thing is abſolutely impoſſible,*" is yet produced here; and the authority of this apoſtle brought to evince that Chriſt, being in the form of God, thought it not robbery to be equal with God, but made himſelf of no reputation. And no matter whether the ground of this queſtion be in ſcripture or not, it muſt be anſwered before the authority of the Alexandrian manuſcript is allowed of, " *if Chriſt were the ſupreme God, by what means did he ceaſe to be*

Arias Mortanus, in the 15th century, turns it charitatem Dei.

And N°. 38, in the Harleian collection, which is the edition of Nicholas de Lyra, printed at Rome ſo early as the year 1472, contains this verſe thus tranſlated, " In hôc cognovimus charitatem DEI, quum ille animam ſuam pro nobis poſuit, & nos debemus pro fratribus ponere,"

Who is to decide upon *the repute* of editions? Plantin exhibits, and Scaliger acknowledges the words τῦ Θεῦ. To me this ſeems ſufficient to ſet aſide the excluſive aſſertion of the Polytheiſt, that none but the Complutenſian and Genevan editions contain it. But if the Complutenſian ſtood alone, its authority is ſuch, that all the ſucceeding editions cannot preponderate againſt it; for, being the firſt ever publiſhed, it had only manuſcripts to follow; of theſe a great number were collected and collated together, and of their contents this valuable book bears an ample teſtimony.

In the public library of Complutum (which is *Alcala* in Spain) there is contained a manuſcript, ſent thither from Rhodes, in which Dr. Mill acknowledges theſe words are read. He ſays this manuſcript is of venerable antiquity *(venerandæ vetuſtatis)*. *A ſuſpicion ariſes* that this is not the manuſcript in which Wetſtein found the words τὴν ἀγάπην τῦ Θεῦ, and if not, here is a ſecond manuſcript which contains them. I need add no more to falſify the affirmative negation of my Remarker. "Sophiſtry may expoſe its own weakneſs, but enquiry is neceſſary to the detection of falſehood." This I have gone into for my reader's eaſe, and the reſult I have ſtated as a warning againſt the ſnares that are ſpread for him. If he find this note tedious, let him remember that he would have found the diſcuſſion of the paſſage much more ſo. I therefore hope he will conſider the far greater trouble which I have taken off of his hands as my ſufficient apology for what unavoidably remains to him in the peruſal of a few diminutive pages, which I here ſubmit to his candour.

be so?" The means by which the omnipotent operates shall never be acknowledged till he explains them, and so this manuscript cannot be subscribed; but this is the only reading of all the manuscripts; these therefore are not to be acknowledged; all the editions adopt it; every version is made accordingly. In short, whatever little variety may appear among the manuscripts, editions, or versions, in some of these obnoxious texts they all concur; there is not one of them but in some of these particulars lays this predicted stumbling block in the way of the Jew and the Unitarian. What then is to be done, is the New Testament to be subscribed? It cannot be, nor, tho' proposed, was it ever seriously intended. The scriptures, as transmitted to us, must be rejected all together; for no Unitarian, unless (for the sake of a bishoprick or archdeaconry) he be capable of subscribing to the thirty-nine articles, while he writes against the propriety of such an act, can set his hand to such *absurdities, forgeries, and falsehoods* as they contain in their present form. They must be new-modelled: suspicions may arise that transpositions may have happened; corrections must be admittted; and before subscription to the gospel can be rendered proper, the gospel must be new made by Unitarians, and rendered proper for subscription. I propose a brief question to men of this denomination: What subsisting scriptures are you ready conscientiously to subscribe?

It is predicted of our Saviour, that " a virgin shall conceive and bear a Son, and shall call his name Emanuel: butter and honey shall he eat, &c." Isa. vii. 14, 15; on which Irenæus proceeds to remark, "that both these circumstances are stated of him, lest, from an assertion that he shall eat butter and honey, we should understand him to be barely man; and lest, on the other hand, from the name of Emanuel, we

should

should surmise that he was God without flesh:" "and thus the Spirit has diligently signified his birth, that it was of a virgin, and his substance, that he is God *." " That he is Man, and that he is God; that as Man he may have a feeling of our infirmities; and as God, have mercy upon them, and forgive us our debts which we owe to God our Maker †." " To this end God was made Man, and the Lord himself shall be our salvation ‡." " Destroying sin, he extended salvation to his own work; for the Lord is most tender, and merciful, and loving to mankind; he therefore attached and united Man to God; for if Man had not overcome the enemy of Man, the enemy had not been fairly overcome. And again: unless God had extended salvation, we had not firmly possessed it; and unless Man had been joined to our God, Man could not have been made a partaker of incorruption; for it was necessary for a Mediator between God and men, that, by a participation and fellowship with both, he should reconcile both, and cause that God should receive man, and that man should dedicate himself to God §." " The breath of

---

* Diligenter igitur significavit Spiritus Sanctus, per ea quæ dicta sunt, generationem ejus quæ ex virgine, & substantiam quoniam Deus, uti non per hoc quod manducat butyrum & mel nudè solummodò eum hominum intelligeremus, neque rursus per nomen Emanuel, sine carne eum Deum suspicaremur. Lib. iii. cap. xxvi. p. 217.

† Quomodo Homo & quomodo Deus: & quomodo Homo compassus est nobis, tanquam Deus misereatur nostri, & remittat nobis debita nostra quæ factori nostro debemus Deo. Lib. v. cap. xv. p. 338.

‡ Deus igitur Homo factus est, & ipse Dominus salvabit nos. Lib. iii. cap. xxiii. p. 215.

§ Salutem donavit plasmati suo, destruens peccatum; est enim piissimus & miserecors Dominus, & amans humanum genus, hærere itaque fecit & adunivit hominem Deo. Si enim Homo non vicisset inimicum Hominis,

of life, which was from God, being united to the clay, of which he was formed, animated man, and held forth a rational animal. Thus, in the end, the word of the Father and Spirit of God being united to the old substance of Adam's veſſel, forms a living and perfect Man, taking on him the perfection of paternal character, to the end that, as we all die in the animal breath, which we derive from Adam, ſo we ſhall all be made alive by the ſpiritual life," which has been given to the Man Jeſus Chriſt, from whom we are henceforward to derive a new inheritance in thoſe things which we loſt in Adam †. "Vain, therefore, are ſuch as do not receive into their faithleſs minds the union of God and Man, but, perſiſting in the old leaven, are unwilling to underſtand that the Holy Ghoſt came upon Mary, and the power of the Higheſt overſhadowed her; wherefore that which was conceived is holy, and the Son of the moſt high God, the Father of the univerſe, who effected his incarnation, and ſhewed an example of a new generation, that, inaſmuch as by

the

---

nis, non juſtè victus eſſet inimicus. Rurſus autem, niſi Deus donaſſet ſalutem, non firmiter haberemus eam. Et niſi Homo conjunctus fuiſſet Deo noſtro, non potuiſſet particeps fieri incorruptibilitatis. Oportuerat enim Mediatorem Dei & hominum per ſuam ad utroſque domeſticitatem, & ad amicitiam & concordiam utroſque reducere, & facere ut Deus aſſumeret hominem, & homo ſe dederet Deo. Lib. iii. cap. xx. p. 211.

† Ea quæ fuit a Deo inſpiratio vitæ, unita plaſmati animavit hominem & animal rationabile oſtendit: ſic in fine verbum Patris & Spiritus Dei, adunitus antiquæ ſubſtantiæ plaſmationis Adæ, viventem & perfectum hominem, capientem perfectum Patrem, ut quemadmodum in animali omnes mortui ſumus, ſic in ſpiritali vivificemur. Lib. v. cap. iii. p. 318.

Tertullian ſays, "His fleſh being formed in the womb of a virgin, he was born a Man mixt with God." Naſcitur Homo Deo miſtus. Tertul. Apolog. adv. Gent. p. 62. Edit. Plantin. 1583. fol. Cyprian has uſed a ſimilar expreſſion; and the teſtimony of their predeceſſours has been largely ſtated as to this point already.

the former generation, we inherited death, so by this generation we might inherit life *." How unfortunately, therefore, has Mr. Lindsey selected Irenæus as an example that the early fathers were ignorant of the two natures in Christ! Apology, p. 205.

Can we now hesitate to pronounce, upon the faith of Irenæus, that he believed " the Son of God to be God †," and to be one with the Father, God ‡? and can we entertain a doubt that he believed also in the Holy Ghost, as personally distinguishable from the Father and the Son, though with them one in Godhead, when he tells us " that man was fashioned after the image and likeness of the uncreated God, the Father willing his creation, the Son ministering and forming him, the Holy Ghost nourishing and encreasing him § ?" And when he farther declares " that the church disseminated through the whole world, even to the ends of the earth; received from the apostles and their disciples a belief in one God, the Father almighty, Maker of heaven and earth, the sea, and all that

---

* Vani autem et Ebionœi, ynitionem Dei & Hominis perfidam non recipientes in suam animam, sed veteri generationis perseverantes fermento, neque intelligere volentes quoniam Spiritus advenit in Mariam & virtus Altissimi adumbravit eam: quapropter & quod generatum est sanctum est, & Filius altissimi Dei Patris omnium; qui operatus est incarnationem ejus & novam ostendit generationem: uti quemadmodum per priorem generationem mortem hæreditavimus, sic per generationem hanc hæreditaremus vitam. Lib. v. cap. ii. p. 316.

† Filius Dei qui Deus est. Lib. iii. cap. xxiii. p. 215.

‡ Vide supra, p. 112.

§ Plasmatus homo secundum imaginem & similitudinem constituitur infecti Dei, Patre quidem bene sentiente, Filio vero ministrante & formante, Spiritu vero nutriente & augente. Lib. iv. cap. lxxv. p. 310.

in them is; and in one Jesus Christ, who hath taken flesh for our salvation; and in the Holy Ghost, who, by the prophets, revealed the dispensation, and the advent, and the birth by a virgin, and the sufferings, and the resurrection from the dead, and the assumption into heaven of the flesh of the beloved Christ Jesus our Lord; and his return or advent from heaven in the glory of the Father, to gather together in one all things, and to raise up all flesh of all mankind, that, according to the good pleasure of the invisible Father, every knee of things in heaven, and things in earth, and things under the earth, should bow to Christ Jesus our Lord, and God, and Saviour, and King, and every tongue to confess to him; that in all things he will judge righteously, and that he will send into eternal fire the irreligious, the unrighteous, the lawless, and the blasphemer; but to the righteous and the holy, to such as have kept his commandments, and have continued in his love, whether from the beginning, or from having turned to him with repentance, he will, of his grace, grant life incorruptible, and invest them with eternal glory ‡."

With

‡ Ἡ μὲν γὰρ ἐκκλησία, καίπερ καθ' ὅλης τῆς οἰκουμένης ἕως πρώτων τῆς γῆς διεσπαρμένη, παρὰ δὲ τῶν ἀποστόλων, καὶ τῶν ἐκείνων μαθητῶν παραλαβοῦσα τήν, εἰς ἕνα Θεὸν Πατέρα παντοκράτορα, τόν πεποιηκότα τὸν οὐρανόν, καὶ τὴν γῆν, καὶ τὰς θαλάσσας, καὶ πάντα τὰ ἐν αὐτοῖς, πίστιν. Καὶ εἰς ἕνα Χριστὸν Ἰησοῦν τὸν υἱὸν τοῦ Θεοῦ, τὸν σαρκωθέντα ὑπερ τῆς ἡμετέρας σωτηρίας. Καὶ εἰς πνεῦμα ἅγιον, τὸ διὰ τῶν προφητῶν κεκηρυχὸς τὰς οἰκονομίας, καὶ τὰς ἐλεύσεις, καὶ τὴν ἐκ παρθένου γέννησιν, καὶ τὸ πάθος, καὶ τὴν ἔγερσιν ἐκ νεκρῶν, καὶ τὴν ἔνσαρκον εἰς τοὺς οὐρανοὺς ἀνάληψιν τοῦ ἠγαπημένου Χριστοῦ Ἰησοῦ τοῦ κυρίου ἡμῶν, καὶ τὴν ἐκ τῶν οὐρανῶν, ἐν τῇ δόξῃ τοῦ Πατρὸς, παρουσίαν αὐτοῦ ἐπὶ τὸ ἀνακεφαλαιώσασθαι τὰ πάντα, καὶ ἀναστῆσαι

With this early creed I shall conclude my extracts from the venerable Irenæus, whose entire work must be perused by a reader desirous of examining into every assertion, which he has made to the same purpose. The few which I have produced are amply sufficient to warrant an inference that Irenæus was not an Unitarian.—What modern Unitarian concurs with the doctrines here exhibited?

The second century still subsists, the church has not yet survived the apostles many years, when, lo! the dreaded name of Trinity grates harshly on the ears of Ebion, Marcion, Artemon, and Paul of Samosata; nor does it sound more harmoniously in those of their modern disciples, who treat with the utmost resentment the memory of THEOPHILUS BISHOP OF ANTIOCH, who first pronounced it, or who is at least the earliest writer in whose works this term is preserved to us. Mr. Lindsey, who appears to possess by far the best heart of the whole fraternity, is content with saying, "that it was first used by Theophilus, a Gentile convert, Bishop of Antioch, but in no great conformity with what it is made to signify at present." Apol. p. 12.

The

ςῆσαι πᾶσαν σάρκα πάσης ἀνθρωπότητ⟨ος⟩, ἵνα Χριςῷ Ἰησῦ τῷ κυρίῳ ἡμῶν, καὶ Θεῷ, καὶ σωτῆρι. καὶ βασιλεῖ, κατὰ τὴν εὐδοκίαν τῦ Πατρὸς τῦ ἀοράτυ, πᾶν γόνυ κάμψῃ ἐπουρανίων, καὶ ἐπιγείων, καὶ καταχθονίων, καὶ πᾶσα γλῶσσα ἐξομολογήσηται αὐτῷ: καὶ κρίσιν δικαίαν ἐν τοῖς πᾶσι ποιήσηται, καὶ τὺς ἀσεβεῖς, καὶ ἀδίκυς, καὶ ἀνόμυς, καὶ βλασφήμυς τῶν ἀνθρώπων εἰς τὸ αἰώνιον πῦρ πέμψῃ, τοῖς δὲ δικαίοις, καὶ ὁσίοις, καὶ τὰς ἐντολὰς αὐτῦ τετηρηκόσι, καὶ ἐν τῇ ἀγάπῃ αὐτῦ διαμεμενηκόσι, τοῖς ἀπ᾽ ἀρχῆς, τοῖς δὲ ἐκ μετανοίας, ζωὴν χαρισάμεν⟨ος⟩ ἀφθαρσίαν δωρήσηται, καὶ δόξαν αἰωνίαν περιποιήσῃ. Lib. i. cap. ii. p. 34.

The origin of Theophilus is unknown: that he was a Gentile convert, is true; but by what means brought over to chriftianity, unlefs by ftudying the fcriptures, is uncertain. In the year 169 he was appointed Bifhop of Antioch, where he prefided thirteen years, and then died, it is to be prefumed, a natural death, as there fubfifts no record of his having fuffered martyrdom.

There is extant but one fhort work of this father, written in a diffufive, but not inelegant ftile: it confifts of three books, and carries internal evidence of having been compofed only as an introduction to a much larger account of the doctrines of chriftianity.

Our author directs it to his friend Autolycus, who ftill continued in the belief of the heathen gods, and appears, from the tenor of Theophilus's difcourfe, to have grounded his belief in them upon the antiquity of their religion, and alfo to have vilified chriftianity, not only on account of its novelty, but its irreconcileablenefs with the Greek philofophy; and particularly with the doctrines of Plato, which he feems to have adopted and maintained.

The converfion of this friend is the purpofe of the writer, who had been a convert himfelf. Having therefore once entertained the fame opinions, he was well acquainted with the grounds of Autolycus's diflike to chriftianity, and accordingly oppofes himfelf to the tenets of his friend with a good deal of addrefs. He decries the abfurdity of heathen worfhip, and fhews that the gods of the Greeks were either the work of men's hands, or at the beft but men born in, and therefore fubfequent to the formation of, the world; whereas his God was the creator of it, therefore exifting before it, and by confequence the infpirer of any hiftory

of

of the creation, to which no man could otherwife bear teftimony. He then proceeds to declare, that God did infpire fuch a hiftory, from which it appears that he revealed himfelf to the firft-made man; and thence takes occafion to fhew that chriftianity commenced with the firft revelation, and was therefore of higher antiquity than heathenifm. He advances a little way in the recital of God's difpenfations towards man, but in fuch a manner as makes it evident that he is laying a groundwork for a much larger communication than he dare to make at once, knowing well the prejudices which he had to combat with. He gets a little upon the philofophic ground of his competitor, and borrows as many conceffions as a man profeffedly an advocate of the Greek philofophy muft neceffarily make. He fhews that the wifeft of the philofophers themfelves wifhed for a revelation from God, in order to difpel the ignorance which they acknowledged, again avers that fuch a revelation had been given; and then proceeds to compare the doctrines contained in it with thofe inculcated by philofophy, which, upon a comparifon, he declares to be exceedingly contemptible. He begins his proofs of chriftianity with the firft book of Mofes, through which he proceeds in a direct line to the fecond, and fo on through a confiderable part of the Pentateuch, in fuch a manner as fairly authorizes a conclufion that he had intended, in a regular feries, to have gone through the facred writings, and produced all the fcriptural proofs of chriftianity.

But this opinion receives much confirmation from the following circumftance: Throughout an entire work, written purely with a view to the converfion of an heathen to the truths of chriftianity, the name of Chrift does not once occur. Is it likely then that the author has brought his whole argument to an end,

when

when he has not yet so much as named the great object of it? Of the WORD indeed he speaks, expressly calls him God, and refers his friend to St. John's gospel for farther information; and, for the more easy transition to an account of the incarnation of God, he declares it was the WORD which walked in the garden, and pronounced sentence of death upon our fallen forefather. Whence he infers the possibility of local presence to him who is infinite. It is therefore indisputable that when the WORD is spoken of in the passage which I shall presently lay before my reader, it is to be interpreted of our Lord and Saviour Jesus Christ.

Concerning the Holy Ghost, he speaks of him as God who spoke by the prophets, whom he terms " the Bearers of the Spirit *;" but that he may the more easily take his philosophic friend along with him, he conforms to his prejudices, and sometimes, as in the passage referred to by Mr. Lindsey, calls the Spirit the Wisdom of God. This passage therefore, thus considered, (and after a diligent perusal of the original work, I am certain that this is the right manner of considering it) will be found to bear a meaning altogether conformable with that sense in which the present time accepts the word Trinity.

It is of no consequence why Theophilus considers the three first days of creation, before the sun and moon were ordained, to have been typical of the Trinity; but that proposition, in which this tremendous word was

first

---

* Πνευμαΐοφοροί. Theoph. ad Autol. lib. ii. p. 101. Parif. Edit. cum Juft. Mart. Operib. Folio, 1636.

Ὑπὸ Πνεύματ^Ὸ· ἁγίυ διδασκόμεθα, τῶ λαλήσαν^Ὸ· ἐν τοῖς ἁγίοις προφήταις καὶ τὰ πάντα προκαταγ[ιλον]^Ὸ·. Lib. ii. p. 110.

first pronounced, afferts that "they are types of the TRINITY of God, and his Word, and his Wisdom *."

The Word he declares to have been from all eternity in the bowels of God, and born before all things; to have been the Creatour of all things that were made by him, and that by him he made all things †. And in language which may affift in the explanation of St. John's affertion, that Chrift is " the beginning of the creation of God," Rev. iii. 14, this father fays that " the Word is called the Beginning, becaufe he commences, and rules all things that were made by him ‡." And again: " In the beginning God made the heaven, that is, the heaven was made by him who is the beginning §."

In the Acts of the Apoftles St. Peter is recorded to have addreffed the Jews, faying, " ye have killed the *Prince* of Life," Acts iii. 15. The word tranflated *Prince* in the text, is, in the margin of our Bible, acknowledged to fignify *Author*, which I conceive from the laft quotation to be the preferable term ; for it is a

deri-

* Τύποι εἰσι τῆς ΤΡΙΑ'ΔΟΣ τᾶ Θεᾶ, καὶ τᾶ λόγε αὐτᾶ, καὶ τῆς σοφίας αὐτᾶ. Theophili lib. ad Autolycum, lib. ii. p. 94. Edit. Parif. 1636, Fol. unâ cum Juftini Martyris Operibus.

† Ἔχων ἐν ὁ Θεὸς τὸν ἑαυτᾶ λογὸν ἐνδιάθετον ἐν τοῖς ἰδίοις σπλάγχοις, ἐγέννησεν αὐτὸν μετὰ τῆς ἑαυτᾶ σοφίας ἐξερευξάμενος πρὸ τῶν ὅλων. Τᾶτον τὸν λόγον ἐσχεν ὑπηργὸν τῶν ὑπ' αὐτᾶ γεγενημένων, καὶ δι' αὐτᾶ πάντα πεποίηκεν. Theoph. ad Aut. lib. ii. p. 88.

‡ Οὐτὸς λέγεται ἀρχὴ, ὅτι ἄρχει καὶ κυριεύει πάντων τῶν δι' αὐτᾶ δεδημιυργημένων. Ibidem.

§ Ἐν ἀρχῇ ἐποίησεν ὁ Θεὸς τὸν ἄρανον. Τᾶτις, διὰ τῆς ἀρχῆς γεγενῆσθαι τὸν ἄρανον. Ejufd. lib. p. 92.

R

derivative from that word which is by Theophilus in- terpreted Beginning, or Incipient. Cleanthes in his hymn to Jupiter, in language extremely fimilar to that of St. Peter, invokes his God by the title of " Prince or Author of Nature;" but as a reafon for afcribing this title to him, he proceeds, " for from thee we are," &c. *. Such a reafon reftrains the fenfe of the word to that particular meaning which it accounts for, and therefore in this paffage I fhould rather conclude Ju- piter addreffed as Author than Prince of Nature. The apoftle, it is true, has not limited the fenfe of this term in the text in which he ufes it, but it is the very fame as that ufed by Cleanthes; the manner of applying it is alfo the fame, and, befides this, life may with great propriety be faid to have had an Author, whereas it is rather a bold expreffion to denominate it a Princi- pality. Therefore, on the whole, I fhould think the marginal tranflation of this affertion of St. Peter better adopted, " YE HAVE KILLED THE AUTHOR of LIFE."

If Jefus Chrift then be the *Author of Life*, according to St. Peter, the words of St. John, " this is the true God and eternal Life," 1 John v. 20, are certainly ap- plicable to him. But the whole paffage, of which this affertion makes a part, being " And we know that the Son of God is come, and hath given us an underftand- ing that we may know him that is true, and we are in him that is true, *even* in his Son Jefus Chrift. *This is the true God and eternal Life;*" the author of familiar illuf-

---

* Ζευς, ΦΎΣΕΩΣ ᾿ΑΡΧΗΓΕ ******.
᾿Εκ σοῦ γὰρ γένΘ- ἐσμὲν, ἠχῶ μίμημα λαχόντες
Μοῦνον, ὅσα ζώει τε καὶ ἕρπει θνήτ᾽ ἐπὶ γαῖαν. Cleanthis Hymnus ad Jovem.
Τὸν δὲ ᾿ΑΡΧΗΓΟ῀Ν ΤΗ῀Σ ΖΩΗ῀Σ ἀπεκτείνατε. Actorum, cap. iii. ver. 15.

illustrations of certain passages of scripture, says, that "this last clause is manifestly explanatory of the title *him that is true*, or *the true one*, in the preceding clauses, of whom he hath given us an understanding, or with whom he has made us acquainted." This doctrine has been abetted by another writer*, who says that "the word *even* is an interpolation, and the translation of the Greek preposition ἐν ambiguous, and that "we ought to read verbatim, we are *in* him that is true, 'EN τῶ ὑιῶ αὐτῶ, by or *through*, that is, by the ministry of his Son Jesus Christ." "This" he says "is in a thousand places the meaning of the preposition ἐν."—Be it so; and yet if there were any other term signifying *by* or *through* to be found in the whole extensive compass of the Greek language, St. John would most assuredly have preferred the use of it here to the repetition of a word that has been but that moment employed in a different sense.

Ἐσμεν 'EN τῶ ἀληθινῶ, 'EN τῶ ὑιῶ αὐτῶ Ἰησοῦ Χριστῷ. Οὗτός ἐστιν ὁ ἀληθινὸς Θεὸς καὶ ζωὴ αἰώνιος. Such are the words of the original: and now, why we ought in this case to take this one and the same word in two distinct senses, making it in one instance signify *in*, and in the other contiguous assertion *by* or *through*; why we ought to read *verbatim*, "we are *in* him that is true, *by* or *through* the ministry of his Son Jesus Christ," any more than we ought to read *verbatim*, "we are, *by* or *through* the ministry of him that is true, *in* his Son Jesus Christ," unless for the purpose of maintaining a presumed hypothesis, I acknowledge myself too blind to see. But if, as the case indisputably stands, the same word in both these instances signify the same thing, then "his Son Jesus Christ" is put into ap-

* See Remarks on Script. Confut. p. 71.

position with " him that is true," and the connecting term *even* has been properly supplied by the tranflators, not as an interpolation, which it has been fo uncandidly called, but as an expletive required by the idiom of our language, in order to mark that appofition; in fhort, as neceffary to the only adequate Englifh phrafe, into which it was poffible to render the original Greek. —But the procefs is, this is a truth, therefore the fcriptures teach it.—But the fcriptures do not teach it; then wreft them, cries the Unitarian.—But they are too ftrong to be bent to the purpofes of your fect; then utterly reject them, cries the Unitarian, henceforward be the appeal to our own infallible reafon, on which there is an hand-writing, that we need no Daniel, with the Spirit of God, to interpret for us; beyond what is here explained we defire, we will admit no explanation, and God is ignorant beyond what we know.

With regard to the declaration already ftated, that the claufe, " *This is the true God,*" is explanatory of the preceding claufes, I fhould conceive that the original Greek, if confulted, will be found to confute it. I will not take upon me to affert that it was *impoffible* for St. John to have written the pronoun ὅυτος with reference to any other antecedent than that which immediately precedes it; but in the prefent inftance, I think it extremely improbable that he wrote it with reference to any other antecedent but the name of our Lord Jefus Chrift, which does immediately precede it; for, on the mention of his name, the pronoun is changed apparently with a view of diftinguifhing the Son from the Father. The fentence runs ἐν τῷ υἱῷ ΑΥΤΟΥ, (that is, *of the Father*) and the name of our Lord put into appofition with υἱῷ, immediately follows ('Ιησοῦ Χριστῷ), upon which the apoftle, inftead of taking up

ΑΥ-

ἈΥΤΟ῁Σ, which might have referred to the Father, whom he had already fignified by it, proceeds, ὉΥΤΟ῁Σ ἐςιν ὁ ἀληθινὸς Θεὸς, making ufe of a pronoun which I am firmly perfuaded refers to the name which is immediately antecedent. In this country, let us fpeak of ever fo many perfons, we have but the one pronoun *he* to refer to each of them. This very frequently occafions confufion, and renders it difficult to decide which is the antecedent intended by it; but the more copious language of the Greeks poffeffed many pronouns of this fignification, by the due difpofition of which they were enabled to maintain the diftinction among their refpective antecedents, without coming under a neceffity of recurring to the names referred to by them. It is not therefore in order to controvert our tranflation that I appeal to the original Greek, I apply to it only for an explanation of a paffage, the fenfe of which our lefs extenfive language has not been able fo fully and diftinguifhingly to exprefs.

But the author of the interpretation juft confidered proceeds, and declares the verfe before us to be " an allufion to the words of Chrift addreffed to the Father, and recorded by this very apoftle. " *This is life eternal, that they may know thee the only true God, and Jefus Chrift whom thou haft fent,*" John xvii. 3; and then afferts, that unlefs his explanation of 1 John v. 20, be admitted, " thefe two texts flatly contradict one another; for how can the Father be the only true God if the Son be God alfo?" However averfe this gentleman may be to the tenets of our church, he cannot be a ftranger to them; he muft know that had he extended his queftion fo as to make it comprehend the Holy Ghoft alfo, we are yet furnifhed by that creed, which has given fuch offence to Unitarians, with a direct anfwer, " the Father is God, the Son is God, and the Holy

Holy Ghoſt is God, and yet they are not three Gods, but one God *." Thus we reconcile the Godhead of
each

* Were I to quote immediately from Athanaſius, I ſhould certainly fail to engage the attention of Unitarians, who will perhaps pay more reſpect to a citation at ſecond-hand from this obnoxious writer, particularly when they learn that it has been made by Mr. Lindſey himſelf, who tells us that "'St. Athanaſius, writing againſt the Arians, owns that, on account of the doctrine of the Trinity, the Heathens of that time charged them with holding many Gods themſelves." Apology, p. 91.

Since, therefore, the objection was made on account of the doctrine of the *Trinity*, it is evident that the *many* Gods objected to the early Chriſtians amounted exactly to *three*. This charge, therefore, it is that Athanaſius (if Athanaſius be indeed the Author) would refute in that profeſſion of his faith which I have quoted above; and the great particularity which prevails throughout this creed was, at the time of its compoſition, abſolutely neceſſary in order to obviate Gentile calumny and heretical miſconſtruction. In almoſt every propoſition the author ſtates the premiſes from which we are to infer, he then pronounces a negative upon the inference of the Greek or the Unitarian, to which he immediately oppoſes that truth which the apoſtles, the fathers, who had been his predeceſſours, and the whole ſubſiſting church, in concurrence with his own excellent underſtanding, had deduced from them. Does not an air of controverſy prevail through the whole compoſition? Is it not evidently held forth as a ſhield to protect the true faith from the aſſaults of Arius? Nay, the very objections and evaſive ſubtilties of thoſe who endeavoured to corrupt Chriſtianity are almoſt as obvious, from the negatives put upon them throughout this declaration of a Chriſtian's faith, as the truth is from the affirmatives with which he ſuſtains her cauſe.—In proof that the Holy Ghoſt was not worſhipped in the primitive church, Mr. Lindſey declares that "the antient fathers, when they mention the objections of the Heathens on this ſubject, (viz. of Chriſtians holding more Gods than one) do not ſpeak of them as levelled againſt the notion of *three Gods*, but of *two* only; whereas, if the notion of the divinity of the Holy Ghoſt had been then faſhionable, they would have made the ſame objection as is now made by Jews and Mahommedans; not againſt *two* Gods, but againſt *three*." P. 146. In the firſt place, I cannot avoid obſerving that this remark acknowledges the divinity of Jeſus Chriſt to have been faſhionable, as one of the two Gods objected to; and gives us reaſon to think that, if the charge had extended to three Gods, Mr. Lindſey would admit worſhip to have been paid to the Holy Ghoſt as the third. In order, therefore, to induce his admiſſion of the Holy Ghoſt as God, I would recommend to this gentleman firſt to reperuſe his own aſſertion concerning St. Athanaſius, which I have tranſcribed above; he will

there

each with the uninfringed Unity of the Godhead; for finding it revealed that each of these three persons is

there find that more than *two* Gods were objected; let him then consult Tertullian, and learn that " they object the doctrine of two or *three* Gods to us." Itaque duos aut tres jam jactitant a nobis prædicari. Tertul. adv. Praxean, cap. iii. Some grounds for this objection he may also find in the 44, 50, 54, 57, 63, 66, 79, 80, 84, 108, 112, 124, pages of this Enquiry, from which it will appear that the worship of the Holy Ghost was quite fashionable with all the fathers as yet quoted. But, to use the language of Tertullian concerning the Hereticks of his time, " they conceive the number and disposition of the Trinity to be a division of the Unity; whereas the Unity, *(which implies the combination of a number)* deriving out of itself a Trinity, is not subverted, but abetted by it." Numerum & dispositionem Trinitatis divisionem præsumunt Unitatis, quando Unitas ex semetipsâ derivans Trinitatem non destruatur ab illâ sed administretur. Adv. Prax. cap iii.

Concerning that clause in the Nicene, or rather Constantinopolitan creed, which now says that the Holy Ghost proceedeth from the Father and the Son, Mr. Lindsey quotes from Bishop Pearson an assurance that, not having constituted a part of the original formulary, the words " *and the Son*" were added by Pope Nicholas the First. *(See Apol. Note,* p. 146.) I grant the fact; but what would Mr. Lindsey infer from it? that as he has made the doctrine of the Trinity subsequent to the name of it, so this doctrine had its commencement when first professed in a creed? If this be the point insinuated, a declaration made in the fourth century shall defeat the purpose. Pope Nicholas the First, against whom the charge of inventing new articles of faith seems brought, presided at Rome, A. D. 868, whereas Aurelius Prudentius Clemens, a poet of no mean reputation, had, near five hundred years before the date of his pontificate, preferred the following address to the Trinity in Unity:

Ades, Pater supreme,	Be present, O supreme Father,
Quem nemo vidit unquam,	whom no man hath seen at any time,
Patrisque sermo, Christe,	O thou Word of the Father, Christ,
Et Spiritus benigne;	and thou O merciful Spirit; O thou
O Trinitatis hujus	one Power, one Light of this Trinity,
Vis una, Lumen unum,	eternal God of God; O God sent
Deus ex Deo perennis,	forth *from both*.
Deus *ex utroque* missus.	

Here the procedure of the Holy Ghost from both the Father and the Son is as explicitly set forth as in the article added to the Constantinopolitan creed by Pope Nicholas, which is sufficient to establish the antiquity of this tenet

is God, and finding it alfo revealed that there is but one God, we do not fay that there are therefore three Gods; but confiding in the word of the fpirit of truth that each affertion is true, we have recourfe to this folution, that there is a Trinity in Unity. We do not polytheiftically fay there are therefore two, or three Gods; but on the contrary, that there is but one God. It is not becaufe we comprehend the modus of this trinal Unity that we fpeak thus, but becaufe we have been gracioufly informed of it by the unerring teftimony of our Creatour. This we do not impioufly reject, but knowing our own infufficiency to enquire beyond what he has been pleafed to reveal, in his word we

tenet in the Church. Its truth is another queftion; and this the frequent promifes of our Lord, that the Holy Ghoft fhould go forth, both from the Father and from himfelf, that he fhould take of his and fhew it, &c. have fo frequently attefted, that a farther enquiry into the fubject is unneceffary.

I have chofen the Words of Prudentius, becaufe they are fo direct, rather than thofe of any more antient writer, whofe language might not fo exactly concur with that of our Creed. I might produce many affertions from the earlier fathers to the fame purpofe, but more diffufively written; and there is no occafion for farther proof that Nicholas was not the inventor of this tenet.

Prudentius frequently denominates Chriftians *Chrifticolas*, or the worfhippers of Chrift, to whom he addreffes his waking thoughts thus:

Tu, Chrifte, fomnum disjice,   Do thou, O Chrift, difpell fleep,
Tu rumpe noctis vincula,   burft afunder the chains of darknefs,
Tu folve peccatum vetus,   do away the old offence, and pour in-
Novumque lumen ingere.   to me a new light.

"To thofe who love and worfhip Chrift, he fays that the fpontaneous gifts of nature afford fufficient."

" Hæc opulentia Chrifticolis
Servit & omnia fuppeditat."

And, after a frugal meal, he acknowledges and afcribes our exiftence and well-being to the reign of Trinal mercy.

Denique quod fumus & agimus
Trina fupernè regat pietas.

we lay the foundation of that faith which we humbly dedicate to him. We do not divide the fubftance while we avoid confufion of perfon. And that moft excellent man, the late Dr. Leland, though a Diffenter from the difcipline of our church, fo far concurs in her doctrine as to declare that we do not hold a Trinity inconfiftent with the Unity of God.—But antiquity fhall enter into the queftion. Primate Ufher has quoted Gregorius Nazianzenus, faying on the verfe which fuggefted it, "that the Son and Holy Ghoft are not excluded by it from the Godhead, but only the multitude of falfe gods *." On which he proceeds to fay from himfelf, " nor certainly will any man of a competent underftanding accept thefe words of St. John xvii. 3, in any other fenfe than as if he had faid, this is life eternal, that they may know thee to be the only true God, and Jefus Chrift whom thou haft fent to be in like manner the only true God; for of neceffity he muft be acknowledged the *only* God who is the *true* God. Since Metaphyficians teach us that this *one* and *true* have a primary place in the firft *Being*, and Theologifts inftruct us, that in the attributes of the divine effence the particle *only* does not exclude any of the perfons fubfifting in that one and undivided nature, but only creatures, and idols, and whatever is different from that infinite effence †." And that it does not exclude our Lord Jefus Chrift, Clement of Alexandria bears teftimony, for to him in diftinction not from the Father,

S or

---

* Non excludi a Divinitate Filium & Spiritum Sanctum fed tantùm deorum falforum multitudinem.

† Neque certè quis rectè fapiens aliter verba illa Johannis xvii. 3. acceperit, quam fi dictum fuiffet, " Hæc eft vita æterna ut cognofcant te effe folum verum Deum; & Jefum Chriftum, quem mififti, folum itidem effe verum Deum." Qui enim verus Deus eft, ut folus Deus agnofcatur, neceffe eft: quum in primo *ente* illud *unum* & *verum* primarium habere locum Metaphyfici; & in divinæ effentiæ attributis particulam illam
folam.

or the Holy Ghoſt, but from Mammon and his train of attendant pleaſures, he aſcribes the title of the *only* God, and aſſerts that the ſervants of Mammon cannot know God. " For from the beginning there is *one alone* who is an enemy to all luſts, even the merciful Lord, who alſo became Man for our ſake ‡;" which latter circumſtance, this Father knowing that we cannot ſerve God and Mammon, urges as a motive to us to ſerve him in preference to Mammon. But " if indeed Chriſt were only Man, why did he impoſe upon us ſuch a rule of faith as that he ſhould ſay, " this is life eternal, that they may know thee the only true God, and Jeſus Chriſt whom thou haſt ſent? If he were unwilling to be underſtood to be himſelf God, nay unleſs he intended to be conſidered as God, why did he add " and Jeſus Chriſt whom thou haſt ſent?" Had he intended to be thought not God, he would have added, " and *the Man* Jeſus Chriſt whom thou haſt ſent;" but he has not annexed this appellation, neither has Chriſt revealed himſelf to us to be only a Man, but has conjoined himſelf with God, that by the conjunction he may be underſtood to be, as he really is, God. According therefore to this preſcript, we are to believe in one Lord, the true God, and conſequently on him whom he ſent, Jeſus Chriſt, who, as we have ſaid, would not without a purpoſe have joined himſelf with the Father, nor unleſs he deſired to be believed God himſelf alſo. Had he not deſired to be thought God, he would have diſtinguiſhed himſelf from

---

ſolum, perſonarum nullam in unâ & indiviſâ illâ Naturâ ſubſiſtentium, ſed creaturas tantum, & idola, & quicqꞌ id ab illâ infinitâ Eſſentiâ eſt diverſum excludere, nos doceant Theologi. *Comment. in Epiſt. ad Philipp. Edit. ſuæ Ignat. & Polycarp. Epiſt. præfix.* p. 88.

‡ Ἑις μὲν ἓν μόνος, ὁ ἀνεπιθύμητος ἐξ ἀρχῆς, ὁ κύριος ὁ φιλάνθρωπος, ὁ καὶ δι' ἡμᾶς ἄνθρωπος. Clement. Alex. Stromat. lib. vii. p. 216.

from him. Had he known himself to be but Man, he would have ranked himself among men; and had he not known himself to be God, he would not have joined himself with God. But because none doubts that he was a Man, he is silent here on the subject of his Manhood; but he joins himself with God that he may prescribe a rule and formulary of belief in his Godhead *." That Christ was therefore believed by the primitive church to be *the only true God*, set forth in both these texts, I have produced the testimony of the early fathers to prove; that he was also considered to be " the eternal Life," let the still earlier fathers attest. Ignatius, in a passage already quoted, (p. 90.) declares that *Christ, who is our true Life*, has the power to grant repentance unto life. But let me prove more than the faith of antiquity here, let me prove the fact itself, " When Christ, who is our Life, shall appear," says God by the mouth of Paul, Colos. iii. 4; but from himself let us hear, and let us accede to the attestation, that " I am the Resurrection and the Life," John xi. 25.

The

---

* Si Homo tantummodo Christus, quare credendi nobis talem regulam posuit, quo diceret hæc est vita æterna, ut sciant te unum & verum Deum, & quem misisti Jesum Christum, si noluisset se etiam Deum intelligi? cur addidit & quem misisti Jesum Christum nisi quoniam & Deum accipi voluit? quoniam, si se Deum nollet intelligi, addidisset & quem misisti *Hominem* Jesum Christum; nunc autem neque addidit, nec se hominem nobis tantummodo Christus tradidit, sed Deo junxit, ut & Deum per hanc conjunctionem, sicut est, intelligi vellet. Est ergo credendum, secundum præscriptam regulam, in Dominum unum verum Deum, & in eum quem misit Jesum Christum consequenter, qui se nequaquam Patri, ut diximus, junxisset, nisi Deum quoque intelligi vellet: separasset enim ab eo, si Deum intelligi se noluisset: inter homines enim tantummodo se collocasset, si hominem se esse tantummodo sciret; nec cum Deo junxisset, si se non & Deum nosset. Nunc & de Homine tacet, quoniam Hominem illum nemo dubitat; & Deo se jungit merito, ut credituris Divinitatis suæ formulam poneret. Novitiani lib. de Trinitate, cap. 24.

The Trinity spoken of by Theophilus, consisting of GOD, and his WORD, and his WISDOM, I have already shewed that the second Person of that Trinity, which we believe, is intended by the WORD, which Theophilus has placed in the very same rank; but that the WISDOM, which occupies the third place in his, is the same as the Holy Ghost, to whom we (with Athenagoras, Justin Martyr, (*see p.* 80.) and the other fathers already quoted) ascribe the third rank in our Trinity, remains yet to be proved. To this purpose I shall extract but a single passage, in which the author, repeating his first position, makes use of the *Spirit* where he had before named the *Wisdom*. "By his Word and his Wisdom he founded the universe; for by his Word and his Spirit the heavens were established †." Finding now such a concurrence between this father's tenets and those of his predecessours, why are we to doubt that he used the Word in conformity with their descriptions of the subject? But inasmuch as we agree with them all, why are we to suppose that he used it in any other sense but that in which we accept the word Trinity? "It is the perfection of science to know the Father, the Son, and the Holy Ghost," says Origen *. Can any doubt here that Origen meant the Trinity? and yet this passage no more proves his belief in the Trinity than that quoted from Theophilus does the conformity of that father's sentiments with ours; not so much indeed, for Theophilus has not only enumerated God, the Word, and the Wisdom, but has brought them under the one denomination

† Ὁ Θεὸς, διὰ τῦ λόγυ, καὶ τῆς σοφίας, ἐποιήσε τὰ πάντα. Τῷ γὰρ λόγῳ αὐτῦ ἐςεριώθησαν οἱ ὐρανοὶ καὶ τῷ πνεύματι αὐτῦ. Theoph. ad Autol. lib. i. p. 74.

* Quæ est aliâ perfectio scientiæ nisi agnovisse Patrem & Filium & Spiritum Sanctum? Origen in Num. cap. xviii. homil. v.

nation of a *Trinity*, which is more than Origen has done in this inftance. And had time fwallowed up the enormous volumes of Origen, as it has deftroyed the works of Theophilus, we fhould have been left without fuch an explanation as occurs in another place, where he makes this fimilar affertion, that " it is the principal office of fcience to know the Trinity, and that the knowledge of *his* creature is in the fecond place ‡." Had the former of thefe two extracts only come

‡ Principale munus fcientiæ cognofcere Trinitatem, fecundo vero in loco cognofcere creaturam ejus. Origen. in Cant. Cant. hom. ii.

This doctrine is frequently inculcated by Origen, who maintains that it is found in many paffages of fcripture, where I freely confefs that I do not find it; but the tenets of the fathers of the firft three centuries being the fubject, I am not engaged to juftify the arguments from which they deduced them, but only to fhew what tenets they did infer and embrace. The following paffage being to my prefent purpofe, I fhall pruduce it, though I do not fee the juftice of the author's reafoning. On the words, "Drink waters from the fountain of your wells," he thus comments, "Let us fee now to what wells it is that he afcribes this one fountain. I think that the knowledge of the unbegotten Father may be underftood to be one well, that the knowledge of the only-begotten Son fhould be underftood of another well; for the Son is another from the Father, for the Son is not the Father, as he himfelf fays in the gofpel, "There is another who beareth witnefs of me, even the Father." And again. I think that the third well may feem to be the knowledge of the Holy Ghoft, for he is another from the Father and the Son, as it is fpoken of him in the gofpel, " He fhall fend you another comforter, even the Spirit of Truth." It is therefore this diftinction of the three Perfons, the Father, the Son, and the Holy Ghoft, which is applicable to the plural number of *wells*. But of thefe wells there fubfifts but *one* fountain, for the fubftance and nature of the Trinity is but *one*; and thus the diftinction of the holy fcripture, which fays, *from the fountain of your wells*, will be found no idle one. But the myftic fentence has curioufly intimated, that what is fpoken plurally fhould agree to the perfons, but that what is fpoken fingularly fhould agree to the fubftance.

" Bibe aquas de puteorum tuorum fonte." Videamus ergo quorum puteorum unum dixerit fontem. Ego puto quòd fcientia ingeniti Patris unus poffit intelligi puteus; fed et unigeniti Filii ejus agnitio alius puteus intelligi debeat; alius enim a Patre Filius & non idem Filius qui et Pater, ficut ipfe in evangeliis dicit *alius eft qui & teftimonium de me dicit Pater*.

Et

come down to us, I make no doubt we should now be told that Origen, though indeed he had enumerated the three Persons, did not entertain any idea of a Trinity; the latter, however, has snatched it from controversy; and, upon a comparison of both, it is now to be collected that he most certainly believed in this doctrine. But Theophilus has, in one view, placed before us the same three Persons, whom we acknowledge to be in the Unity of the Godhead, together with that denomination by which we still continue to express their personal distinction. And why we are now to conceive that Theophilus of Antioch did not use the word Trinity in exact " conformity with what it is made to signify at present," I must leave it with Theophilus of Essex-street to shew, for I am myself unable to perceive the disagreement. Does Mr. Lindsey accede to the Trinity of Theophilus? If not, he must admit that this Father is an exception to his general position; but if he concur, the bosom of our lenient church is open to receive the returning penitent; and, from my heart, I shall congratulate both true Christianity and this conscientious Man upon their mutual reconciliation: a reconciliation which must in this case take effect; for the few extracts which I have laid before my reader afford conclusive evidence that Theophilus of Antioch was not only not an Unitarian, but, on the contrary, altogether concurrent in such tenets as are at this

---

Et rursus tertium puto videri puteum posse cognitionem Spiritûs Sancti, alius enim & ipse est a Patre & Filio sicut & de ipso in evangelio dicitur, *mittet vobis alium paracletum Spiritum Veritatis.* Est ergo hæc trium distinctio Personarum in Patre & Filio & Spiritu Sancto quæ ad luralem puteorum numerum revocatur. Sed horum puteorum unus est fons, una enim substantia est & natura Trinitatis. Et hoc modo non otiosa invenietur scripturæ sanctæ distinctio quæ dicit *de puteorum tuorum fonte.* Sed observanter mystica signavit eloquia ut quod pluraliter dictum est personis, singulariter substantiæ conveniret. Origen, in Numer. cap. xxi, hom. xii.

this day profeffed by thofe of the communion of our eftablifhed church.

CLEMENS ALEXANDRINUS, or CLEMENT OF ALEXANDRIA, brings up the rear of this century, and proves that true Chriftianity had not undergone any change from the time of Ignatius who commenced it. This father was by birth an Athenian, but having, at Alexandria, prefided over a fchool for the inftruction of catechumens, (that is, ftudents in the gofpel not yet received into the church by baptifm) he took his denomination from this feat of his refidence. He was a man of the moft extenfive learning, as his writings largely fhew. His Chriftianity he derived from the fcriptures, in which he was exceedingly converfant, and alfo from the immediate difciples of the apoftles. Eufebius fpeaks of him as being Prefbyter of Alexandria in the year 195. His life, the end of which is unrecorded, extended into the third century; but the works from whence I quote were compofed in the fecond, which fufficiently authorizes his being brought forward under that head.

He was a very voluminous writer, but there have defcended to our time only three of his publications; they are entitled An Exhortation to the Greeks, The Pedagogue and Stromata, or Mifcellanies. Some others have been afcribed to him, but being of doubtful authority, are excluded from my confideration.

Where the fubject of the author's argument does not affect my pofition, I fhall keep it out of fight. The errours which he combats with, whether Gentile or Heretical, are not within my province; I am only concerned

cerned to difplay the truths which he would eftablifh in their room.

In his exhortation to the Greeks, he fays, "Now has appeared to men this Word, who alone is both God and Man, the caufe of all good to us, by whom, being inftructed to live well, we are conducted to eternal life †."

In the 9th page of this work I undertook the defence of our tranflation of the 6th, 7th, and 8th verfes of the 2d chapter of St. Paul's Epiftle to the Philippians, and, as I humbly conceive, there refcued that remarkable paffage from fuch mifinterpretation as fubfifted when I printed the comment referred to. It is with regret I am now obliged to return to the fame fubject; but as the priefts of infidelity multiply their diligence in fupport of her finking caufe, I fhall not decline the controverfy: it becomes a duty to engage in the behalf of truth, and not to fuffer even the infignificance of an opponent to be his protection. My Remarker muft therefore come forward once more, and once more the public muft be implored to pardon his appearance thus obtruded upon them. I fhould only combat the arguments he makes ufe of, (if I may fo call the fuggeftions of *his* underftanding) and fuffer the man to ftand withdrawn from notice, were it not exceedingly contributary to his confutation to quote him with precifion.

In his advertifement he declares that "*it is a nonfenfical propofition that Jefus Chrift is one with the Father God,*"

† Νῦν δὴ ἐπιφάνη ἀνθρώποις αὐτὸς ἔτω ὁ λόγω: ὁ μόνω ἄμφω, Θεός τε καὶ ἀνθρώπω: ἁπάντων ἡμῖν αἴτιω ἀγαθῶν: παρ' ὃ τὸ εὖ ζῆν ἐκδιδασκόμενοι εἰς ἀΐδιον ζωὴν παραπεμπόμεθα. P. 7. Edit. Florent. ex Bibliothecà Medicéà a Petro Victorio, fol. 1550.

God," p. 7; and in the epiftle which contains the Remarks, fays "*that fhe* (reafon) *informs me that this propofition is falfe, by a much clearer evidence than fhe affords me of the exiftence of any revelation whatever. Shall I therefore renounce the clearer, and be guided by the darker evidence? No; I will not do that.*" p. 9. Having thus metamorphofed reafon into a revelation, he afferts that from her he has received information that there are not three Perfons in the one Godhead. And then making God refponfible for whatever the writer thinks he has thus fpoken, he pronounces that, "*if he be a God of truth, therefore he cannot contradict himfelf, nor, by a fubfequent difcovery of his will, confound thofe truths which were received from him by a former communication.*" p. 4. I have already dwelt fufficiently on the exceeding weaknefs of converting reafon, which is the recipient of information, into a communication of truths, *(fee p. 33, above)* fo fhall proceed directly to our author's comment on this paffage of St. Paul's Epiftle to the Philippians ii. 6, 7, 8, in which he modeftly declares that, as our tranflation ftates the fact, "*the thing is abfolutely impoffible, and St. Paul could never fay it,*" p. 89; and in the fame fpirit again fays that, "*the difficulty lying in the word* ἁρπαγμον, *which is generally fuppofed to fignify actively,* ipfa actio rapiendi, *the very act of feizing, if the word be taken in this fenfe, all the foregoing abfurdities will follow; and therefore St. Paul certainly meant it not in this fenfe.*" p. 91. Such argument, I truft, can have but little influence upon the thinking part of mankind, who will rather enquire into the meaning of the apoftle's infpired language, and infer from what he has faid, than conceive him only an Amanuenfis to the crude conceptions of half-reafoning men; who will argue, from what he has uttered, to their own belief, not from their own belief to what he ought to utter; and will rather conclude

T that,

that, if St. Paul has spoken the word in the controverted sense, the consequence is not absurdity; but, if incomprehensible, a mystery, and a fact concerning the incomprehensible nature of a Being, placed beyond the reach of human enquiry, unless so far as it may have pleased his infinite wisdom to make it known to us by revelation. That he may be a God of truth, whose subsequent discovery of his will shall altogether supersede the preconceptions of men, however they may have presumed upon their unquestionable certainty, however erroneously they may have even conceived them the dictate of a previous revelation. From amongst the ruins of this Remarker's shattered syllogisms there is yet to be gathered a concession, to which I shall hold him; for tho' he has most blasphemously reviled, yet has he admitted the consequence, provided the premises can be established. Upon their establishment, therefore, even he must concur in the necessary inference that Jesus Christ is one with the Father, God *.

The

* " We begin our researches into theology with the assumption of a certain set of religious tenets, and employ the most valuable hours of our existence in collecting arguments in their favour, and in vain endeavours to explain them, while every text of scripture is in its turn perverted from its obvious meaning in order to support them.

How much more reasonable previously to investigate, with patience and critical attention, the sense of each particular text or passage, in the natural order of the writer, and to defer the formation of opinion until, like a principle of sound philosophy, suggested by a numerous train of experiments, it forces itself with accumulated evidence on the yielding mind."—Such is the language of Mr. Jebb: and his illustration, which I do not clearly understand, alone passed by, the passage contains a melancholy truth, and a sensible remark upon it. I cannot therefore sufficiently testify my surprise, that my Remarker's train of reasoning should appear to Mr. Jebb to be irresistible. If analyzation be what this gentleman would recommend, I cannot understand how so gross a synthesis as that stated above can carry conviction with it to his mind. Am I to believe that Mr. Jebb has not assumed a certain set of religious tenets, when he can approve of such inverted argumentation: *this tenet alone is true*, ergo *the apostle has maintained this tenet?* Is it a principle of sound philosophy, that

the

The great difficulty lying in the word ἁρπαγμον, as signifying *the very act of seizing*, this writer propofes two modes of removing it.

The firſt is much the fame with that already refuted in the 9th page, for the Remarker fuppofes the word equivalent to ἁρπαγμα, in which cafe he fays the meaning would have been clear: Non, ut prædam, arripuit, non prædam fibi duxit; *he confidered it not as a thing which he had a right to feize and hold faſt as his own*; and in this very fenfe it is probable that the apoſtle ufed ἁρπαγμον." p. 92. And in this acceptation of the text he farther fays, " It will prove as ſtrongly as poſſible againſt the Athanafian Trinity."—What it will prove in this cafe is perfectly immaterial, until fome reafon be aſſigned for tranſlating the word into a fenfe which it cannot bear. It is not only not probable that the apoſtle ufed ἁρπαγμον for ἁρπαγμα, but it is abfolutely not poſſible. By this new method of criticifm, any one propofition that can be formed may be brought in proof of any one fact that ſtands in need of witneſſes; for if the words of which it is compofed have a direct contrary tendency, it is only to fay they were written in the fenfe of any other words that will anfwer

the premifes are falfe unlefs the hypothefis be true, and by inverfion the premifes follow from the hypothefis? I ſhrewdly apprehend that this mode of experimental religion, which Mr. Jebb recommends, is no other than a trial to be made upon the experiments themfelves, which are to be judged of by the prefuppofed refult, not the refult deduced from the experiments; and fuch an experiment, as in any way oppofes the fyſtem it was intended to fupport, muſt be pronounced to have failed, or to have been injudiciouſly made. The fyſtem is erected into the criterion, nor is the formation of opinion thus deferred: but fcripture, confulted with a religion ready made, is altered, nay, flatly contradicted where it oppofes, and only admitted true where it can be wreſted to the maintenance of that religion.—The explanation of facred myſtery is furely not objected to our church with juſtice; it is only the Unitarian who withholds belief where he cannot explain.

fwer the purpofe, and the bufinefs is done at once. St. Paul might as well have written ἁρπαγμον for any other word in the Greek, or even in the Englifh language, as for ἁρπαγμα *. Ἁρπαγμὸ- as certainly fignifies *the act of feizing* as our Englifh word robbery does, and can no more be put for *the thing feized*. The licence of poetry is far exceeded here by the loofe licentioufnefs of this Remarker's criticifm.

I fhall prefently demonftrate that the early fathers of the church had no conception of fuch an abufe of language; but that, upon the authority of this paffage concurring with many others, and coinciding with the general tenour of the holy fcriptures, they believed exactly thofe truths which are at this day received among us.

The Remarker's fecond method of removing the difficulty attendant upon Unitarianifm from the accepted

inter-

* Wetftein, the laborious editour of the New Teftament, has fufficiently proved the truth of this affertion. His unexampled diligence to fubvert the fenfe univerfally put upon this paffage, muft have fucceeded if fuccefs were poffible; but he has failed moft egregioufly, and in effect become a powerful advocate of the accepted interpretation. Dr. Harwood alfo, the *liberal* tranflator of the word of God, has contributed his involuntary aid to the eftablifhment of our *literal* and *fervile* verfion; but, rather than acknowledge the force of the only argument he has adduced, he makes Plutarch, in his Treatife on Education, advife that young perfons be reftrained from committing *acquifition*. This is a perfectly new fpecies of crime: but as every crime is properly an action, I fhould rather conclude that, when Plutarch defires that young perfons be reftrained from perpetrating ἁρπαγμον, he means by this term *the act of making acquifitions by violence*.—What the acquifition or act in this cafe is, the reader may find by confulting Dr. Harwood on this verfe.

The word ἁρπασμα being indifferently ufed for ἁρπαγμα, analogy requires that ἁρπαγμὸς be underftood to fignify the fame as ἁρπασμὸς; and the meaning of this term Plutarch has afcertained in faying, ἢ γὰρ φιλικὸν προοίμιον ἐυωχίας, ὑφαίρεσις, καὶ ἉΡΠΑΣΜΟ'Σ, καὶ χειρῶν ἅμιλλα. Sympof. ii. fub fin. Does it not here fignify an act? Yes; *the very act of feizing*.

interpretation of ἁρπαγμον, is "a suspicion that this word may possibly be a passive adjective of that sort of signification which adjectives in *bilis* and participles in *dus* have among the Latins, and in this case the meaning of the passage would be indisputably determined to the same effect as has been just set down. Theocritus, idyll. xxiv. verse vii. has said ἐγερσίμον ἵππον, *a wakeable sleep*. I suppose therefore ἁρπαγμον to be formed as a passive adjective from ἁρπαζω by the same kind of analogy as ἐγερσίμ☉- is from ἐγείρω." p. 92. In a subsequent publication, entitled "Addenda" to his Remarks, this writer has endeavoured to strengthen his suspicion by saying, "The conjecture that ἁρπαγμ☉- may possibly be a passive adjective seems to receive farther confirmation from a passage in Xenophon's Cyropœdia, lib. vi. where we read that Cyrus, having invented a carriage of a new construction, to be drawn by eight yoke of oxen, for the purpose of conveying towers, πεῖραν ἐλαμβάνε τῦ ἀγωγίμυ, *made a trial how far the drawing of it was practicable.*" p. 11.

In the first place, all this conjectural distress manifests that the suspector is not himself satisfied with his former efforts to elude this text, and that he does not consider himself to be extricated by them from the close-drawn trammels in which it binds him, and in which he exhibits such awkward writhings; for the conjecture itself, in order to set it aside, it might suffice to say it is void of all authority; but as this does not appear an argument of any weight with a well-determined Unitarian, I will not drop it here. The utter ignorance of the Greek language which the Remarker has betrayed shall first be exhibited, and the consequence of his conjecture, if admitted, shall be laid before my reader, who cannot impute this promise of success to vanity, having already seen the shadow I am going to engage.

Although

Although ἄγω, duco, veho, *to draw*, be the radix of ἀγωγίμον, vehi practicabilis, which (if I may be allowed the liberty taken by my Remarker of forming a word) I would tranflate *drawable*; yet it is not from ἄγω that this adjective is immediately derived, the fubftantive ἀγωγη, vectura, *conveyance*, or *the act of drawing*, intervenes, and from this it is that ἀγωγιμ⊙ is formed. In like manner, between the radix ἰγείρω, expergifcor, *to awake*, and the adjective ἰγιρσίμ⊙, expergifcibilis, *wakeable*, the fubftantive ἰγιρσις, excitatio, *the act of awaking*, ftands interpofed, and from this it is that ἰγιρσίμ⊙ is immediately derived. But to ἁρπαζω, rapio, *to rob*, the fubftantive ἁρπαγμ⊙, ipfa actio rapiendi, *robbery*, or *the act of feizing*, bears the very fame relation that ἀγωγη does to ἄγω, that ἰγιρσις does to ἰγείρω, that ἀγιρμ⊙, congregatio, *the act of affembling together*, bears to ἀγειρω, congrego, *to affemble together*; and laftly, not to multiply examples, that ἀγμ⊙, fractio, *the act of breaking*, bears to its radical verb ἄγω, frango, *to break*.

This man of erudition has alfo brought a paffage from Longinus to maintain his conjecture, but what it has to fay to the queftion I own I do not fee. The word φώριον, being ufed as *a prey*, he has urged as an example of a fimilar kind; but φώριον does ufually fignify *a prey*, and therefore the term is not abufed by Longinus's application of it. Befides this, it is neither an adjective nor a derivative from any verb, but, on the contrary, a fubftantive, drawing its original from a noun, φώρ, *a thief*.

But let it now be for one moment granted that ἁρπαγμ⊙ fignifies, as conjectured, *robable*, *feizable, of practicable feizure*, or *to be come at by robbery*, which is the precife meaning of fuch a paffive adjective as the

Re-

Remarker would form here; let us then stand on our guard against the juggle with which, in a translation of his own, he cunningly slips the *impropriety* of seizing the Godhead into the place of the *impracticability* which he had contended and endeavoured to argue for, and let us thence proceed to weigh the boasted merit of this proposed interpretation: the meaning will then be, " that Christ, not thinking the sceptre of heaven a seizable thing, not esteeming it a matter of practicable acquisition, but pondering the difficulties attendant upon an attempt to rob God of it, on consideration took another thought; and since he could not effect the possession of omnipotence and an eternal throne, but found that he might be crucified without obstruction, he therefore chose to undergo this most ignominious of deaths as the feazable or practicable side of an alternative." This is incontrovertibly the true interpretation, if the conjecture be admitted; state it in closer terms and no change appears; " who being in the form of God, thought it not practicable to seize equality with God, or thought not to be equal with God a matter to be come at by robbery, but made himself of no reputation, and took upon him the form of a servant." Contract it yet farther, " not being able to fill himself he emptied himself." Thro' every change the same amazing absurdity is conspicuous. Impracticability must for ever defeat attempt, and so far argue inability in him who either has made, or by this consideration is restrained from making it. In human affairs, it would be a most extraordinary mode of proceeding for a man to throw away his own property, meerly because his neighbour's house is impregnable, and he cannot rob him. It is too absurd to be seriously argued with, and might be easily run to ridicule if the importance of the subject did not forbid it: the mere absurdity to which it argues, tolerably painted, would afford it largely. What a pee-

vish

with Being does such an interpretation make of our great example of humility! In what a blasphemy does it terminate!

I know not what future sense may be fastened upon this word ἁρπαγμον, but for my own part can only see one meaning which the original Greek can bear; in this the translatours of our English Bible have accepted it; and as from every other mode of interpretation absurdity so very gross results, I sincerely hope for my reader's concurrence in this conclusion, that, since being in the form of God, Christ thought it not ROBBERY to be equal with God; Jesus Christ, who of right possesses that equality, is therefore one with the Father and the Holy Ghost that God, who is but one, and who giveth not his glory to another.

I have not yet done, apology can but protract, so I proceed to obviate an objection, not yet indeed applied to this passage, but which having been raised against another that contains a similar expression, I apprehend will be resorted to as the last refuge of defeated Unitarianism. Let me therefore be beforehand with them, and by anticipation take away the grounds of subsequent controversy.

An unsupported assertion having been made on John v. 18, that the words Ἴσον ἑαυτὸν ποιῶν τῷ Θεῷ, which we translate "making himself equal with God," should not be so turned, but rendered "making himself like to God," my apprehension is, that this mode of translation may, if admitted, be carried over to the text in controversy, and the words τὸ εἶναι ἴσα Θεῷ be declared to signify only "to be like to God." It is true that equality always implies similitude, so far as the objects compared are equal; but similitude does not in

like

like manner imply equality; and hence, in both of these passages, our translation is justly made by the word "equal," which signifies like in degree only. The labourers who had wrought the whole day complain that the lord of the vineyard had given as much to those who had laboured but an hour as to them who had borne the heat of the day, saying, Καὶ ἴσας ἡμῖν αὐτοὺς ἐποίησας, "Thou hast made them equal to us," Matth. xx. 12. In the Acts xi. 17, God is said to have given τὴν ἴσην δωρεὰν, "an equal gift to them as to us."—" Sinners also lend to sinners, ἵνα ἀπολάβωσι τὰ ἴσα, that they may receive an equivalent," Luke vi. 34.—Concerning the new Jerusalem, St. John says that τὸ μῆκος, καὶ τὸ πλάτος, καὶ τὸ ὕψος αὐτῆς ἴσα ἐςι, "the length, and the breadth, and the height of it are equal," Revel. xxi. 16.—Now every one of these instances, being concerned in measurement, prove to a demonstration that absolute equality is the likeness intended by the word ἴσα; and in a verse or two after that last quoted, St. John has evinced that this is the only kind of similitude which he means to signify by it; for when he has another sort to specify, he says that " the city was like unto clear glass," not by ἴσα, which would have implied equality, but by ὁμοία ὑαλῷ καθαρῷ, Rev. xxi. 18, ὁμοία being the proper word to express mere resemblance.

But if at any time it shall be contended for, that this new construction of ἴσα is to be adopted in the passage under consideration, it must be esteemed a concession that the accepted meaning of the word ἁρπαγμὸν is not to be overturned; the very effort acknowledges it to signify *robbery* still; for surely it would be a most singular assertion to say that he who was in the form of God did not esteem it practicable to be like him; this could be no great "robbery" in "the express

U   image

image of his perfon." And therefore, whenever Unitarians fhall deem it more expedient to leave Chrift only in poffeffion of a likenefs to, than a full equality with God, it muft be confidered as an acknowledgement made by themfelves, that the object of Chrift's thought, while yet in the form of God, (whatever it was) was evidently his right and property.

I know I fhall be thought too timid in thus foreboding objections not yet brought, but I have good reafon for this caution; the interpretation has already reached a fimilar paffage, and is therefore, I conclude, at no great diftance from this. When the Jews fought to kill Chrift for "making himfelf equal with God," Ἴσον ἑαυτὸν ποιῶν τῷ Θεῷ, John v. 18, they efteemed it a robbery in him: in this, as in every other tenet, the modern Unitarian concurs with the Jew. So long as τὸ εἶναι ἴσα Θεῷ is admitted to fignify "to be equal with God," the word ἁρπαγμον muft be wrefted to any fenfe but its genuine one; but, leaving this term in poffeffion of its literal meaning, then τὸ εἶναι ἴσα Θεῷ (whatever it fignify) is certainly the fubject which Chrift did not confider as a robbery. But, "to be equal with God," fay the Jew and Unitarian, or, as they both ftate it, "to have made himfelf equal with God," is certainly a moft flagitious robbery in one whofe Godhead muft not be admitted upon any terms. Is it not therefore now to be apprehended that, upon the eftablifhment of the accepted fignification of ἁρπαγμον, which I truft I have eftablifhed, the fubject τὸ εἶναι ἴσα Θεῷ muft next be dragged to the torture, and undergo the feverity of Unitarian criticifm? And is not that warning voice of fervice to mankind, which either obviates, or inftructs in the means of obviating, fuch meafures as are likely to be taken for the fubverfion of the Chriftian faith?

After

[155]

After the proofs already brought, that the words under confideration fignify "to be equal with God," it may be deemed fuperfluous to adduce the farther authority of claffic authors to afcertain their meaning: but Homer has made Apollo chide the prefumption of Diomedes, who, making himfelf "equal to a God," Δαίμονι ἴσ⊕, encountered Æneas while under his divine protection, faying to him, that he fhould reftrain his ardour, and "not conceive himfelf a match for, or equal to the Gods," μηδὲ Θεοῖσιν ἴσ' ἔθελε φρονέειν; and Sappho has commenced her well-known Ode with a declaration that the happy fubject of it to her "appears equal with the Gods."

Φαίνεται μοι 'κῆνος ἴσ⊕ Θεοῖσι.

The ftrict meaning of which words Catullus has preferved in his Latin tranflation of this exquifite little Poem.
"Ille mi par effe Deo videtur *."

Having now defeated the difingenuous efforts that have been made ufe of to deftroy the authority of this text; having inconteftibly proved that each particle of it is rightly tranflated, firft that the fubject is "*to be equal with God*," and fecondly that of this it is rightly predicated that Chrift thought it not a "*robbery*," I fhall

pro-

---

* I have poffibly detained my reader too long on conjectures and fufpicions, the abfurdity of which his own eye may have at once detected; but as this paffage has undergone "a numerous train of experiments," I chofe to exhibit it as a fine example of the new procefs in religious alchemy. There is fcarce a fyllable of it which has not been tormented in the Unitarian crucible. It feems however to be of a very fixed nature, and not readily fufible under the hands of our modern Van Helmonts, which is rather extraordinary, as the imagination of my Remarker has afforded fo very hot a furnace, which Mr. Jebb has fince been pleafed to provide with a reverberator.

proceed next to establish the whole together by the authority of the early fathers of the church.

And first the venerable Clement, whose Athenian birth, in all human probability, made him an equally competent judge of the Greek language with my Remarker, has quoted this passage; but, not having mentioned our Lord Jesus Christ, whose name, contained in a preceding verse, is the antecedent of WHO, with which this passage and his quotation commence, he has substituted such a nominative case to the verb ἐκένωσεν (*made himself of no reputation*) as to a certainty proves how he understood the apostle, and whom he conceived to be the subject of his infpired assertion. "The Lord himself it was who spoke by Isaiah, he it was who spoke by Elijah, he it was who spoke by the mouth of the prophets; but if you will not believe the prophets, the Lord himself shall speak to you, who, being in the form of God, thought it not robbery to be equal with God: but the tenderly merciful GOD, desirous of man's salvation, made himself of no reputation *."

Of

---

* Αὐτὸς ἐν Ἡσαΐα ὁ κύριος λαλῶν, αὐτὸς ἐν Ἠλίᾳ, ἐν στόμασι προφητῶν αὐτὸς. Σὺ δὲ, ἀλλ' εἰ προφήταις μὴ πιστεύεις, αὐτὸς σοι λαλήσει ὁ κύριος, ὃς ἐν Μορφῇ Θεοῦ ὑπάρχων οὐχ ἁρπαγμὸν ἡγήσατο τὸ εἶναι ἴσα Θεῷ, ἐκένωσεν δὲ ἑαυτὸν ὁ φιλοικτίρμων Θεὸς, σῶσαι τὸν ἄνθρωπον γλιχόμενος. Exhortatio ad Græcos, sive Προτρεπτικὸς Λόγος, p. 8.

My Remarker, zealous for his own two Gods, may say here that "the tenderly merciful God" is not the supreme God, but the other vicegerent God, in whose form he was; but he has already displayed his argumentative talents on a similar subject, and on John i. 1, 2, 3, has exhibited a fine specimen of his abilities; for the Word, which is there declared to have been in the beginning, to be with God, and to be God, he substitutes the name of Jesus Christ, and proceeds then to annex the epithet *supreme* to both the God with whom Jesus Christ was, and who he is, and so concludes that he has argued to an absurdity. Now the fact

is,

Of TERTULLIAN's words, which appear below, I
shall give in the text that version which is contained in
the

is, that the name of God stands in both assertions without any epithet to
distinguish it in one from what it means in the other; and a brief mathematical rule may let this acute critic see that, by adding one and the
same epithet to it in both places, he has not himself created any distinction; for if, to or from equals, we add or deduct equals, we constitute or
leave the sums or remainders equal: take away therefore the word supreme from each, and leave them as they stood before without it, as no
difference is made between them now from what subsisted when preceded
by this addition, the whole absurdity must be laid to the charge of St.
John; but as *the thing is absolutely impossible*, we shall probably hear next
that *St. John could never say it*; and Mr. Jebb may once more receive
"irresistible conviction into his yielding mind," in consequence of the
well-conducted experiment.

The Polytheist having maintained his thesis, "that there are two
Gods," with an assertion that they are distinguished in scripture by the
annexation or omission of the article ὁ, whereby "supremacy is opposed
to subordination," is desired to inform the public which of the Gods it is
whom "no man hath seen at any time, Θεὸν ὐδεὶς ἑώρακε πώποτε,"
John i. 18; from which of the Gods it was that "Jesus knew he was
come," ὅτι ἀπὸ Θεῦ ἐξῆλθε, John xiii. 3; of which of the Gods "we
are called, and are the sons," and to whom, on his appearance, we shall be
like," ἵνα τέκνα Θεῦ κληθῶμεν· νῦν τέκνα Θεῦ ἐσμεν, 1 John iii. 1, 2?
If, from the omission of the article, he answer the vicegerent, subordinate second God, I must e'en say that there can be no great impropriety
in us, who are his sons, calling him "our Father," nor can the paternal
character, with relation to us, exclude him from being the object of our
worship under that appellation.—But if he answer, the supreme, upper
God, I apprehend he must relinquish his rule.—The Polytheist is farther
desired to inform the public which of the Gods it is "who hath purchased
the church with his blood," τὴν ἐκκλησίαν ΤΟΥ Θεῦ, ἣν περιεποι-
ήσατο διὰ τῦ ἰδίυ αἵματος, Acts xx. 28, that church "which is the
church of the living God," ἐκκλησίαν Θεῦ ζῶντος, 1 Tim. iii. 15.
If the upper God be meant here, I doubt the Polytheist "will make but
an aukward figure with his bleeding God:" he thinks so himself, and
has accordingly contended for the rejection of the words τῦ Θεῦ, but
surely τῦ would have been enough to omit, in order to reduce this passage to the system contended for; for, if I understand this man aright,
Christ is not even his own Θεὸς, καὶ ἄνθρωπος, but the carnal man
Jesus Christ is his Θεὸς, or subordinate God, whose blood was easily
shed. I have little doubt that, to this end, he will wrest the following
assertion of Ignatius, who speaks of the blood of God, and which I produce

the old manufcript already mentioned (p. 118): who, "whanne he was in the forme of God demyde not raveyn that himfilf were even to God: but he lowede himfilf *."

CYPRIAN has alfo quoted this paffage, and in no refpect differs from Tertullian.—Novatian has likewife ufed the very fame words in his verfion of it †. Ori-

---

duce as a means of eftablifhing the received reading of the text: Μιμηταὶ ὄντες Θεῦ, ἀναζωπυρήσαντες ἘΝ 'ΑΙΜΑΤΙ ΘΕΟΎ τὸ συγ-
γενικὸν ἔργον τελείως ἀπηρτίσατε, Epift. ad Ephef. The article, it is true, is not ufed here; but Ignatius being fo unhappy as to live before the Polytheift taught Greek, did not know any thing of the new diftinction, and, from mere ignorance, has fo confounded with Θεὸς the ὁ Θεὸς, that he muft come under correction for defiring to be μιμητὴν παθῦς τῦ Θεῦ. Of the fufferings of what God does this difciple of St. John defire to be an imitator? Of that God, ΤΟΎ Θεῦ, who in thofe fufferings bled. And Jefus Chrift, both God and Man, is fpoken of in the text before us in that character which can give the greateft energy to the apoftle's charge; for though the blood ftreamed from his human body, as that body was affumed by God himfelf, in order to render one Man a due facrifice and propitiation for all men, the Being who fuffered is here denominated by that name which was beft calculated to enforce the precept.—A common news-paper, now lying before me, fuggefts a vulgar illuftration of this fubject; for I there read that a veffel, having fifty hands on board, was caft away, and every foul perifhed; whereas, literally told, the waters came not over a fingle foul, but every hand perifhed.——The union of God and man in Chrift was a fubject fo familiar to the thoughts of the apoftles, that, as occafion influenced, they fpoke of him by either appellation: we fay either body or foul of a creature compounded of both, without guarding againft mifapprehenfion, or annexing that hereby we mean a man: the Chrift bleeds, God bleeds; a man is drowned, a foul has perifhed. We never entertain a doubt that, by the name of foul or hand, we fhall be underftood to mean a man.— The apoftle never entertained a doubt that, by the name of God or Man, he fhould be underftood by faithful Chriftians to mean the Chrift.—But Chrift crucified is the predicted ftumbling block.

* Non rapinam exiftimavit effe fe æqualem Deo. Tertul. adv. Praxean. cap. vii.——Non rapinam exiftimavit pariari Deo. Ejufdem adv. Marcionem, lib. v. cap. xx.

† Non rapinam arbitratus eft effe fe æqualem Deo. Cypriani Teftimoniorum Lib. cap. xxxix; et rurfus in Libro adverfus Judæos, cap. xiii.

Origen, in his answer to Celsus, says that "the nature of God is altogether incorruptible, simple, uncompounded, and indivisible; that the Word which descended to man was *in the form of God*, and, through his great love for mankind, *made himself of no reputation*, that he might be comprehended by men, and yet without inducing any change of good into evil; that he who, through the Word, which is God, and which was in him, became Physician to the diseases of our souls, received not any infection from the ills he remedied: but if the Word, the immortal God, seem to Celsus to be changed and transubstantiated by having assumed a mortal body and a human soul, let him learn that the Word is still in substance the Word, and that the Word suffers none of those things which the body and the soul suffer; that, condescending to man, who is unable to look upon the light and splendour of the Godhead, he became flesh, speaking in a body, till he who received or heard him thus, being by little and little sublimed by the word, should be enabled to behold him in his original form ‡." The father immediately,

‡ Καταβεβηκὸς εἰς ἀνθρώπους ἐν μορφῇ Θεῦ ὑπάρχει καὶ διὰ φιλανθρωπίαν ἑαυτὸν ἐκένωσεν, ἵνα χωρηθῆναι ὑπ' αὐτῶν δυνηθῇ. Οὐ δήπου δ' ἐξ ἀγαθοῦ εἰς κακὸν γέγονεν αὐτῷ μεταβολή—ὁ δὲ τραύματα τῶν ψυχῶν ἡμῶν θεραπεύων διὰ τὸν ἐν αὐτῷ λόγον Θεῦ, αὐτὸς πάσης κακίας ἀπαράδεκτος ἦν. Εἰ δὲ καὶ σῶμα θνητὸν καὶ ψυχὴν ἀνθρωπίνην ἀναλαβὼν Ὁ ΑΘΑΝΑΤΟΣ ΘΕΟ'Σ ΛΟΓΟΣ, δοκεῖ τῷ Κέλσῳ ἀλλάττεσθαι καὶ μεταπλάττεσθαι: μανθανέτω ὅτι ὁ λόγος τῇ οὐσίᾳ μένων λόγος, οὐδὲν μὲν πάσχει ὧν πάσχει τὸ σῶμα ἢ ἡ ψυχή. Συγκαταβαίνων δ' ἐσθ' ὅτε τῷ μὴ δυναμένῳ αὐτοῦ τὰς μαρμαρυγὰς καὶ τὴν λαμπρότητα τῆς θειότητος βλέπειν, οἱονεὶ σὰρξ γίνεται, σωματικῶς λαλούμενος, ἕως ὁ τοιοῦτος αὐτὸν παραδεξάμενος, κατὰ βραχὺ ὑπὸ τοῦ λόγου μετεωριζόμενος δυνηθῇ αὐτοῦ καὶ τὴν προηγουμένην μορφὴν θεάσασθαι. Origenis contra Celsum, lib. iv. p. 169. Edit. Cantab. Spencer, 1658, 4to.

diately, after speaking of our Lord's transfiguration on the Mount, calls him "our God §," and declares Jesus, by the union of God and man, to be at once "mortal and immortal ‖," and "to be compounded in his nature of the Word, which is God, and the Soul of Jesus," between which he defires that the diftinction shall always be maintained *; and this union he fays that Celfus would not probably deride or detract from if he underftood the fcriptures, for that there he might learn the immortality of the human foul, which is united with flefh, and thence argue to at leaft a poffibility of uniting incorruptibility to corruption †. That the Word received no pollution from having taken mortal flefh, he fhews from a continuance of the fame illuftration, for that even the human foul is uncontaminated, and remains immortal notwithftanding its union with the body; and that the Word did not fuffer any degradation, he proves from the fcriptures, wherein it is often declared that he returned to the fame dignity from which he had voluntarily defcended. The words of St. Paul, he fays, are fufficient to prove the fact, on which he quotes the paffage under confideration

§ Μεταμορφώθη ὁ Θεὸς ἡμῶν. Origenis contra Celfum, lib. iv. p. 169. Edit. Cantab. Spencer. 1658, 4to.

‖ Θνητὸν καὶ ἀθάνατον. Ibidem.

* Πρὸς τοῦτο λέγοιτ' ἄν, ποῖ μὲν περὶ τῆς τοῦ Θείου ΛΟΓΟΥ φύσεως ΟΝΤΟΣ ΘΕΟΥ, πῆ δὲ περὶ τῆς Ἰησοῦ ψυχῆς. Lib. iv. ejufd. p. 171.

† Οὐδαμῶς ἐν ὁ Κέλσος οἶδε τὸ βέλημα τῶν ἡμετέρων γραμμάτων.—Εἰ δὲ ἦν ἐννοήσας τί ἀκολουθεῖ ψυχῇ ἐν αἰωνίῳ ἐσομένῃ ζωῇ, καὶ τί χρὴ φρονεῖν περὶ τῆς ἐσίας αὐτῆς, καὶ περὶ τῶν ἀρχῶν αὐτῆς. Οὐκ ἂν ἔτι διέσυρε τὸν ἀθάνατον εἰς θνητὸν ἐρχόμενον σῶμα. Ibidem.

[161]

tion from the 5th to the 9th verses inclusive ‡. On our Lord's ascension, we know from the first chapter of St. Paul's Epistle to the Hebrews how he was received, how restored (as it were) to the throne of God, which is for ever and ever, and to his own sceptre of righteousness: and, in the passage before us, we find an ordinance that every knee, of things in heaven and things in earth, shall bow to him. Can we then suppose that Origen understood the word ἁρπαγμον in any other sense than that of *robbery?* Could Origen have considered equality with the Father as transcending the claims of that Being whom he has, in an express comment on the passage, termed the immortal God, whose salutation, under that name and appointment to the dominion of the universe, he declares to be but a restoration to original glory? Origen most assuredly thought it not robbery in the Word to be equal with God.

I am not aware of any future misinterpretation, and so have not only warded off the wily and weak attacks
which

‡ Ἐι δὲ ἐπι τῆς Ἰησοῦ ψυχῆς λαμβάνει τις τὴν μεταβολὴν αὐτῆς εἰς σωμα ἐλθούσης. Πευσόμεθα πῶς λέγει μεταβολὴν; ἐι μὲν γὰρ τῆς οὐσίας, ὃ δίδολαι, ὃ μόνον ἐπ' ἐκείνης, ἀλλ' ὀυδὲ περὶ ἄλλης λογικῆς ψυχῆς — μηδεὶς τῶν πρότερον θεραπεύειν ἐπαγγειλαμένων τοσοῦτον ἐδύναλο, ὅσον αὐτὴ ἐπεδείξαλο δι' ὧν πεποίηκε, καὶ ἱκεσίως εἰς τὰς ἀνθρωπίνας χῆρας ὑπὲρ τοῦ γένους ἡμῶν καλαβᾶσα. Ταῦλα δὲ ἐπιστάμενος ὁ Θεῖος λόγος, πολλὰ πολλαχοῦ λέγει τῶν γραφῶν. Ἀρκεῖ δ' ἐπὶ τοῦ παρόνλος μίαν παραθέσθαι Παύλου λέξιν οὕτως ἔχουσαν. Τοῦτο φρονείσθω ἐν ἡμῖν, &c. Originis contra Celsum, lib. iv. p. 172. Edit. Cantab. Spencer. 1658, 4to.

This passage may serve to answer the horribly blasphemous question of my Remarker, proposed in the 15th page of his Addenda: "What became of the universe, and its complicated machinery, while the supreme God, he who could not die, was dead?" The supreme God assumed a body that was mortal, and this prepared body was our propitiation, having died for our offences.

X

which have been made upon this paſſage, but, by eſtabliſhing the true and genuine meaning, hope that I have given it ſtrength to contend for itſelf hereafter. Self-preſervation calls on the whole Unitarian band to maintain the war againſt it, ſo I do not expect them to deſiſt from their endeavours to overturn it. If, however, any, from conviction that they have engaged in the cauſe of errour, ſhall abandon her banners, to ſuch, the venerable father, whoſe faith is the preſent ſubject of enquiry, gives an aſſurance that they ſhall be received on turning from their evil ways, that no difficulty is an impediment to thoſe who ſeek God; for that he who loves the Poſſeſſour of all things, can want but few; and "Chriſt is every where a Saviour *." He calls upon them to pour out their whole hearts before him, for that he has compaſſion on thoſe who bewail their offences; and therefore, " O man, believe on him who is Man and God; O man, believe on him who ſuffered; ye ſervants, put your truſt in him who liveth, the God of your worſhip, and who was dead; O, all men, truſt in him who alone is the God of all men; believe, and receive ſalvation as your reward †." " Receive light, that you may perfectly know him to be both God and Man ‡."

He

* Ὁ Χριςὸς ἐςι παν]αχε σωτηρι⊙. Clement. Exhort. ad. Græcos, p. 37.

† Ἐκχέι]ε ἐνώπιον αὐτᾶ πάσας τὰς καρδίας ὑμῶν πρὸς τὰς καιρὰς τῆς πονηρίας, λεγει, ἐλεεῖ, καὶ δικαιοσύνης πληρῶι. Πίςευσον ἄνθρωπε ἀνθρώπῳ καὶ Θεῷ, πίςευσον ἄνθρωπε τῷ παθόν]ι, καὶ τῷ προσκυνεμένῳ Θεῷ ζῶν]ι, πιςεύσα]ε οἱ δᾶλοι, τῷ νεκρῷ, πάν]ες ἀνθρώποι πιςεύσα]ε μονῷ τῷ πάν]ων ἀνθρώπων Θεῷ, πιςεύσα]ε καὶ μισθὸν λάβε]ε σωτηριαν. Ibidem.

‡ Ἀπόλαβε σὺ τὸ φῶς, ὀφρ' ἐν γινώσκοις ἠμεν Θεὸν ἠδὲ καὶ ἄνδρα. Ibidem, p. 39.

He invites the incredulous "to taste and see that Christ is God; faith will introduce to this knowledge; experience will teach it; the scripture, which says, " come ye children, hearken unto me, I will teach you the fear of the Lord," will instruct in it §." He recommends it to the Greeks to have faith, and not bring all things into doubt, of which faith is the only evidence; and says, " You make it a question whether worship is to be offered up, or obedience yielded to him who is the wise God and Christ *." And here I will annex the words of St. Chrysostom as a commentary on this passage: " If any shall object to you that you worship him who was crucified, say, with a chearful voice and an elated countenance, I both do worship him, and shall unceasingly adore him: if then he shall laugh, do thou weep at his madness †."

---

§ Γεύσεσθε καὶ ἴδετε ὅτι Χριςὸς ὁ Θεὸς, ἡ πίςις εἰσάξει, ἡ πεῖρα διδάξει, ἡ γραφὴ παιδαγωγήσει, " δεῦτε, ὦ τέκνα," λεγέσα, " ἀκέσατε μȣ, φόϐον κυρίȣ διδάξω ὑμᾶς." Pſ. xxxiv. p. 32.

Here it should be remarked that Clement, having had the 34th Psalm in his eye, as appears from the quotation, probably took the form of the whole sentence from the Psalmist, who, according to the Septuagint version, which the father used, has said in the 8th verse, " Oh! taste and see, ὅτι Χρηςὸς ὁ κύρι⊙-, that the Lord is gracious or good." This I do not think it even politick to conceal, for I am confident it would be objected to me as uncandid. I should myself have deemed the text of Clement corrupted, from Χρηςὸς to Χριςὸς, had this been the only change made; but Θεὸς being substituted for κύριος, it is carried so much farther, that I cannot now admit that it is. Allusions of this kind are very much in the spirit of the Author, who frequently expresses his sentiment in the language of the scripture with such change as is necessary to appropriate it to his own idea.

* Ἐι θεοσεϐήτεον, ζητεῖτε, καὶ εἰ τῷ σοφῷ τέτῳ δὴ τῷ Θεῷ καὶ τῷ Χριςῷ καταϰολȣθητέον. Clement. Exhort. ad Græcos, p. 35.

† Ἂν τοίνυν εἴπη σοι τις, τὸν ἐςαυρωμένον προσκυνεῖς; εἶπε, φαιδρᾷ τῇ φωνῇ, γεγηθότι τῷ προσώπῳ, καὶ προσκυνῶ, καὶ ȣ παυ-

In his Tract entitled the Pædagogue, divided into three books, this father has so very frequently asserted his belief in the divinity of our Redeemer, that a close pursuit of such passages as contain the professions of his faith would not only be prolix but unnecessary; I shall therefore select only a few; these also I shall lay before my reader without much regard to the order in which they appear in a work written in a stile and manner so desultory, that the author seems to have utterly disregarded order himself. In this, as in his Stromata, there is contained an immense profusion of miscellaneous learning; and though they appear without arrangement, or obvious tendency, the many noble passages that occur throughout his works make it impossible to peruse them without advantage. The classick, as well as the theological reader, must receive much information from the writings of Clement of Alexandria.

He supposes the human mind under the tuition of a Pædagogue, on whom also he confers the character of a mental physician; for such a conductor and physician, he says, we require to lead the mind to perfect health, that is, the knowledge of truth. Such a healing guide, he declares, has been given to man; and, after having told us that " he is called Jesus *, after having enumerated the many fabulous instructors which have presided over youth, and shewn their defects, he boasts that we have one of a very superior rank ; " for our Pædagogue is the holy God Jesus; the Word is the leader and conductor of all mankind; the merciful God himself

παύσομαι πότε προσκυνῶν. Κἂν γιλάσῃ, δάκρυσον αὐτὸν ὅτι μάινἷαι. Homil. 55.—Matth. cap. xvi.—Chrysostom lived late in the fourth century.

* Καλεἶται δὲ 'Ιησῦς. Pædagogi, lib. i. cap. vii. p. 15.

himself is our Pædagogue *: he is God, the Word, the Pædagogue †;" and "this Pædagogue is the Creator of the world and of man ‡."

" The Lord's portion is his people, Jacob is the lot of his inheritance. He found him in a desart land, in the waste howling wilderness: he led him about, he instructed him, he kept him as the apple of his eye. As an eagle stirreth up her nest, fluttereth over her young, spreadeth abroad her wings; so the Lord alone did lead him, and there was no strange God:" and yet Clement says that this conducting God was Jesus Christ, to whom the entire song of Moses, Deut. xxxii. (of which the quoted passage makes a part) is addressed. With Justin Martyr and Irenæus he agrees in acknowledging Christ the God who spoke, and covenanted with Abraham, Gen. xvii; who appeared to Jacob in a vision, and promised to be his conductor, Gen. xxviii. 15; who wrestled also with Jacob, but refused to tell his name, Gen. xxxii. 19; for, says this father, " he reserved his new name for a new and an infant people; and the Lord God was then nameless, not having been yet made Man §." He declares him, tho'
clothed

---

* Ὁ δὲ ἡμέτερ۞ Παιδαγωγὸς ἅγι۞ Θεὸς Ἰησοῦς, ὁ πάσης ἀνθρωπότητ۞ καθηγεμὼν λόγ۞, αὐτ۞ ὁ φιλάνθρωπ۞ Θεὸς ἐστι Παιδαγωγός. Pædagogi, lib. i. cap. vii. p. 15.

† Οὗτ۞ ἔστιν, ὁ Θεὸς, ὁ Λόγ۞, ὁ Παιδαγωγός. Ejusd. lib. et. cap. p. 16.

‡ Οὗτ۞ ὁ Παιδαγωγὸς ὁ τοῦ κόσμου, κ̀ τοῦ ἀνθρώπου δημιουργός. Lib. iii. cap. xii. p. 90.

§ Ἐτήρει γὰρ τὸ ὄνομα τὸ καινὸν τῷ λαῷ νέῳ, τῷ νηπίῳ. Ἔτι δὲ κ̀ ἀνονόμαστ۞ ἦν ὁ Θεὸς ὁ κύριος, μεδέπω γεγενημένος ἄνθρωπος. Lib. i. cap. vii. p. 16.

clothed in flesh, to be God uncontaminated in the fashion of man ‖;" that the Word, which was God in the Father, descending from the right hand of the Father, is yet God in the fashion of man: he is our likeness, and yet unpolluted *." Hosanna, which the multitude and children in the temple cried to the Son of David, he explains to be " light, and glory, and praise, with supplication to the Lord †." And from himself, on naming the incarnation, and reciting from Isa. ix. 6, that " unto us a Child is born, and that he shall be the mighty God," he exclaims, " O the great God, O the perfect Child; the Son in the Father, and the Father in the Son ‡." But this is not all; for, in the conclusion of his Pædagogue, he prefers a formal prayer, and pays the due tribute of praise and thanksgiving to the one true God, the Father, the Son, and the Holy Ghost, saying, " We will implore the WORD: be merciful to thy children, O Pædagogue, O guiding Father, O Lord, the Son and Father both one," " grant that, night and day, even to the day of consummation, we may, with praises, return thanks, and laud the only Father and Son, the Son and the Father, the Son, the Pædagogue, and Teacher, together with the Holy Ghost, in all things One, in whom are all things, through whom, One, are all things, through whom is eternity, whose members we all are, whose is the

‖ Θεὸς ἐν ἀνθρώπου σχήματι ἄχραντ۞. Pædagogi, lib. i. cap. i. p. 1.

* Λόγ۞ Θεὸς ὁ ἐν τῷ Πατρὶ, ὁ ἐκ δεξιῶν τῦ Πατρὸς σὺν καὶ τῷ σχήματι Θεὸς. ᾿Ουτ۞ ἡμῶν εἰκὼν ἡ ἀκηλίδωτ۞. Ibidem.

† Φῶς καὶ δόξα καὶ αἶν۞ μεθ᾽ ἱκετηρίας τῷ κυρίῳ. Lib. i. cap. v. p. 4.

‡ ῏Ω τῦ μεγάλυ Θεῦ. ῏Ω τῦ τελείυ Παιδίυ. Υἱὸς ἐν Πατρὶ, καὶ Πατὴρ ἐν υἱῷ. Lib. i. cap. v. p. 7.

the glory and eternity. To him who is in all things good, in all things fair, in all things wife, in all things juft, be glory, both now and for evermore. Amen *."

The prayer of the Pfalmift, "Remember us that we are but duft, the Father paraphrafes, "Have compaffion towards us, for, having fuffered, thou haft thyfelf experienced the weaknefs of the flefh †." He anfwers fuch as object the infliction of forrow to the hatred of God, that this is impoffible; for God faw that all his creation was good, and therefore could not hate it; that there exifted nothing but by his appointment, and that what he hated, he would not appoint. "If the WORD hateth any thing, he willeth it not to be: nothing therefore exifts which is hated by God, neither by the Word, for *both are one*, God; for *(the apoftle)* fays, In the beginning *the Word was in God*, and the Word was God ‡." On which I would have it obferved that Clement, rather alluding to, than directly quoting

---

* Τῷ λογῷ προσευξόμεθα, ἵλαθι τοῖς σοῖς, Παιδαγωγὲ, Παιδίοις, Παῖηρ ἡνιοχε, υἱε καὶ Παῖηρ, ἐν αμφω, κύριε". Πάρασχε νύκτωρ μεθ' ἡμέραν, εἰς τὴν τελείαν ἡμέραν, ἀινέιίας ἐυχαριςεῖν, ἀινεῖν τῷ μόνῳ Παἱρί καὶ υἱῷ, υἱῷ καὶ Παἱρί, Παιδαγωγῷ καὶ διδασκάλῳ ἱω, σὺν καὶ τῷ ἁγίῳ Πνεύμαῖι, πάνία τῷ ἑνί: ἐν ᾧ τὰ πάνία: δι' ὃν, τὰ πανία, ἐν: δι' ὃν τὸ ἀεί: ᾦ μέλη πάνίες: ᾧ δόξα, αἰῶνες: πάνία τῷ ἀγαθῷ, πάνία τῷ κάλῳ, πάνία τῷ σοφῷ, τῷ δικαίῳ τὰ πάνία, ᾧ ἡ δόξα καὶ νῦν καὶ εἰς τὰς αἰῶνας. 'Αμήν. Pædagogi, lib. iii. cap. ult. p. 90.

† Συμπάθησον ἡμῖν, ὅτι τὴν ἀσθένειαν τῆς σαρκὸς ἀυτοπαθῶς ἐπείρασας. Lib. i. cap. viii. p. 17.

‡ "Ει τὶ ἄρα μισεῖ ὁ λόγ⊙-, βάλεῖαι αὐτὸ μὴ εἶναι. 'Ουδὲν ἄρα μισεῖίαι ὑπο τῦ Θεῦ, ἀλλ' ὑδὲ ὑπο τῦ λόγυ, "ΕΝ ΓΑ'Ρ 'ΑΜΦΩ, Ὁ ΘΕΟ'Σ. "Οῖι εἶπεν, ἐν ἀρχῆ ὁ λόγ⊙- ἦν ἐν τῷ Θεῷ: καὶ Θεὸς ἦν ὁ λόγ⊙-. Ibidem.

quoting the language of St. John, fhews evidently the fenfe which he afcribed to the words of the evangelift. When our Lord himfelf declared, I and my Father are one, John x. 30, he, in like manner, maintained his pofition againft the Jews, who charged him with making himfelf God, by referring to the teftimony of his own works, " that ye may know and believe that the Father is in me, and I in him, ver. 38: on which " they again fought to take him," confidering thefe words as an acknowledgement of their charge, and an acquiefcence in their interpretation of his former affertion.

But, againft the accepted fenfe of this declaration, "I and my Father are one," it has been objected that, in the original Greek, the word *one* is neuter, ἓν not εἷς in the mafculine gender, as if the fubftantive (underftood) with which it fhould agree were Θεὸς, God; and the fentence has been accordingly declared to fignify, "I and my Father are one thing," not " one God."

Now, as I do verily believe Clement, the Athenian, to have underftood the Greek language, at leaft, as well as any modern Englifh Unitarian, to this mifinterpretation I oppofe the fenfe in which that venerable writer, and competent judge, accepted the teftimony borne by our Lord to his own unity with the Father; for, referring to our Saviour's affertion, and ufing the very fame neuter word ἓν, he annexes to it ὁ Θεὸς, God, not indeed as the fubftantive with which ἓν agrees, or by which its gender is governed, but as the fum of the unity of the Father and the Son: that character and circumftance, in refpect of which they are one. And his propofition (which I have turned very literally) amounts exactly to that great article of our faith, which I have

fo

so frequently stated, that *Jesus Christ is one with the Father, God.* The unity of the Godhead is not the subject of the speaker, and consequently not the point contended for; but the unity of a plurality of persons in that Godhead is the object of the assertion, which therefore requires to be expressed as our Lord has expressed it; not by εἷς, which, if Θεός were the substantive understood, would have shifted the subject, and maintained the unity of the Godhead, but by the neuter ἕν, which attests the unity of Jesus Christ with the Father in that Godhead. State the two positions, and see whether I am not well warranted in what I say:

Firſt, " I and my Father are,—one God;
Second, I and my Father are one,—God."

It is not yet as Father or Son that they are one, for here they are distinct persons, but in a neuter character, as God. This is the meaning of the assertion as it stands, whereas a unity of person between the Father and Son would result from saying, I and my Father are one, (masculine) *unus:* but the Father is not the Son, neither is the Son the Father. In this manner of understanding and explaining our Lord's assertion Tertullian perfectly agrees; for, in language not to be turned into literal English, he says that " these three, the Father, the Son, and the Holy Ghost, are one, *(neuter, not masculine)* in like manner as our Lord has said, I and the Father are one, *(neuter)* having regard only to the unity of substance, not to the singularness of the number" when united, either as one God, or one person *. Novatian has been already quoted *(p.* 31, *above)* declaring that, " from a consciousness

nefs

---

* Qui tres *(sc. Pater, Filius & Paracletus)* UNUM sunt NON UNUS, quomodo dictum est Ego & Pater UNUM sumus: ad substantiæ unitatem non ad numeri figularitatem. Tertulliani adv. Praxean, lib. cap. 25.

ness of his Godhead, Christ uttered these words, I and my Father are one." "And if Christ were only a man, what is that which he says, " I and my Father are one?" for how are the Father and I one, if Christ be not God and the Son; who seeing that he is a Son also, is therefore called one, *(neuter)*;" the personal distinction which subsists on account of this character, requiring a word that shall sum up the persons in the one Godhead, not a word which should contend for an idea then foreign from the speaker's intention, the unity of God, much less an idea incongruous with the truth, an unity of person. From this declaration, the distinct personality of the Father and the Son appears to me as strongly asserted as their united Godhead; for tho' it attests the unity, it is a unity within itself, in some respect admitting of distinction; it is, according to the quaint phrase of Clement, "a Trinity indivisibly divisible, in whom dwelleth the universally superintendant power of God *."

Though the belief which the fathers entertained concerning the divinity of our Lord and Saviour Jesus Christ be the main object of this enquiry, I endeavour to render the work more serviceable than a meer confutation of Mr. Lindsey's position could possibly make it. As opportunity offers, I take the sense of these early Christians on controverted passages of scripture, occasionally vindicate our almost wonderfully excellent translation of the sacred writings, and rescue even the original from the most disingenuous perversion. Mr. Lindsey's assertion, that it is *absolutely necessary* the less learned should be told that the fathers of the three first cen-

---

* Τριάς, μιᾶ᾽ ὧν ἡ παντεπίσκοπ⊙- τῦ Θεῦ δυνάμις, ἀμερῶς μερίστ. Stromat. lib. iii. p. 182.

centuries were Unitarians, has made me esteem it absolutely necessary to obviate the consequences of such a declaration; for, if a knowledge of the primitive faith be of such vast importance, it is essential to the true information of the less learned, that they shall not be left to the bare assurance of any Unitarian for it. It is for the benefit of such as are persuaded by the first part of this position (that the faith of the fathers is of so high authority) that I thus copiously bring to view the testimonies which they have themselves borne to it. For the benefit of those who, with myself, rely singly upon the word of God, I have endeavoured to develope and lay open to my fellow-creatures the true intent of that infallible testimony, upon which alone we can establish a fruitful faith in our Redeemer. If, in the discussion of any text, I shall be found guilty of errour, the nature of such an enquiry imposes very narrow limits on the ill effects that might follow from it. The less learned are excluded by an unknown language from the labyrinth, in which there subsists no danger to him who is furnished with a clue. Let this, however, plead for my pardon with the honest reader. If I have erred, I am not conscious of it; and I have taken a great deal of pains to obtain information. I know there are men, under whose malevolence I shall be brought when I am most right; nay, where they most plainly see me to be right: of such I only desire that they will proceed to lay their want of candour before the public. The froth of a torrent is always proportioned to the impediment that obstructs its course. Those who only read the angry productions of Unitarians may, perhaps, impute their rage to obstructions which they could not surmount; and thus shall their invective become my panegyric.

The charge which I have already stated was brought against the text last discussed, and accompanied by an infulting challenge to me to vindicate it if I could, together with an affurance that it has been urged a thoufand times, but remains unobviated ftill. In the former part of this affurance Novatian agrees, for he fays that Hereticks have always urged it, but that victory over them is eafy. He argues pretty much, as I have ftated above, that εἷς *unus* muft have agreed with either ἐγω or Πατηρ, which would have been contrary to the fact, as the Father is not the Son, neither the Son the Father, but that ἐν *unum* introduced a new term, in refpect of which they are both one. For my part, I think the victory is very eafy; and that, had not the objection been heretofore refuted as often as brought, I have myfelf now fufficiently obviated it. And yet I ftill expect, fince it has happened already a thoufand times, in the words of the adage, to fee the dog return to his vomit; but I will endeavour to drive him off, and put it beyond his power.

Part of the 11th, 22d, and 24th verfes of the 17th chapter of St. John's gofpel has been brought in proof that the declaration, " I and my Father are one," is very fully explained by our Saviour when he makes this prayer, " Holy Father, keep, through thine own name, thofe whom thou haft given me, that they may be one, as we are ; that they may all be one, as thou, Father, art in me, and I in thee; that they alfo may be one in us, that the world may know that thou haft fent me;— that they may be one, even as we are one;—that they may behold my glory which thou haft given me."

The word *one*, in each of thefe fentences, is neuter, which is confidered as the conclufive circumftance in behalf of Unitarianifm; but, on being weighed, this will appear an argument on the oppofite fide of the queftion, which Unitarians may not find it eafy to fubvert.

vert. I have already said that, when predicated of a number, it refers them all to some one point in which they all agree. There is nothing so like concurrence as concurrence. May not our Lord, therefore, be understood to illustrate the Unity which he desires to constitute among the disciples; and again, between them and himself, by saying, Let them be one in a certain respect, even as we are one in another respect: let them be one witness, even as we are one God? Had the word *one* indeed been masculine, it would have rendered the passage unintelligible, for it must have agreed with the name of some one of the individuals prayed for; nothing else is even pretended; these were the apostles; and it would rather have been an extraordinary request to the Father so to keep Peter, Matthew, James, and John that they should all together be only one Peter, Matthew, James, or John, even as you and I are one (ἕν) Father or one Son. It is not so revealed. The pronoun *one* is in both cases neuter, and that term, in respect of which plurality is united, is in both cases understood. In the one case it is Godhead, or, as Clement states it, ὁ Θεὸς; in the other it is testimony. In support of this interpretation I desire only to have the whole 17th chapter of St. John's gospel read over with attention. Our Saviour, in two or three instances, uses illustrations similar to that suggested above: he says, " They are not of the world, even as I am not of the world:" an assertion which Unitarians themselves will not contend for in its strictly literal acceptation. Though he came from above, and was incarnate of a virgin, and became man in order to his advent into a world that was made by him, and which, nevertheless, received him not; yet, as he had separated from the world men born in it, as all the rest of the children of Adam are, he very aptly exemplifies their separation from the world by his

own

own divine diſtinction from it. That neither they nor he were of the world is circumſtance ſufficient to warrant a compariſon, altho' the ſeveral reſpects in which they were not of the world bear no reſemblance. By reading the whole chapter, the character in which our Saviour prayed, and the purpoſe of his prayer, will be ſeen. " Thou haſt given him *(thy Son)* power over all fleſh, that he ſhould give eternal life to as many as thou haſt given him;" is our Redeemer's own declaration, in which he aſſerts his manhood, and the gracious purpoſe for which he aſſumed it; and even declares that the power of giving eternal life had been conferred upon him; which we very well know muſt be ſpoken only of his human nature; by the ſacrifice and reaſſumption of which we have been made heirs of immortality. Such was the benign end of his power over all fleſh; his hour was at hand, and he was now about to exert that power; but, as a teſtimony was neceſſary to a right faith in the benefits he conferred, he prefers a prayer to his Father, that he will glorify him as of old, and that he will ſanctify with truth his choſen witneſſes, whom he had ſent into the world, that the world might believe thro' their word. The teſtimony of our Saviour's glory is the end; the unity of evidence is therefore the unity deſired; the concurrence of God in this is demanded, for " the witneſs of God is greater than the witneſs of man." And what now ſo natural as a petition that, as the Father is in the Son, and the Son in the Father, even ſo the apoſtles may be, together with the Father and the Son, [who are one, God] one, witneſs, whereby the world ſhall know the Son to be the true God and eternal life; but, in the fleſh, ſent from God to gather together in one, all that are ſcattered abroad, by the aſſumption of our carnal nature, and by its crucifixion and reſurrection, which were now juſt at hand, to unite all to God. To this purpoſe

pose we find, after our Saviour's ascension into heaven, that "the Lord gave testimony unto the word of his grace, spoken boldly by his apostles, and granted signs and wonders to be done by their hands," Acts xiv. 3. That "God bore them witness by signs and miracles," Heb. ii. 4; that "the apostles were labourers together with God," 1 Cor. iii. 9. As a testimony, therefore, of Jesus Christ they were all together one; and by this *unity of evidence* it is that "we all come in the unity of the faith, and of the knowledge of the Son of God," Ephes. iv. 13.

The context, when enquired into, hardly ever fails to vindicate the little divided and subdivided extracts which Unitarians force into their service. In the present case I have called it, I trust not in vain, to the rescue of three half-texts, in which the similitude of a detached phrase is made use of as an argument against that very truth which it was written to confirm. That the apostles are one with the Father and Son, has some resemblance to an argument on the side of Unitarianism, and seems to take away from the weight of the assertion in controversy; but when it comes to be considered that the pronoun *one* is neuter, and that they are therefore one in respect to some circumstance; when the scripture is looked into, and that circumstance found to be *a testimony*, in which all were to be concurrent as *one*; the unity of the Father and the Son remains unaffected by being called into the comparison. The passage in which it is attested remains for a separate enquiry, and must be referred to its own context for an explanation of that character, in which the Father and Son are *one*. This the reader will find in John x. to which I refer him, and now return to the venerable Father who has so largely assisted me in the foregoing discussion.

I

I have now produced his own declarations, that "God and Man are, one Christ," and that "the Father and Son are one, God," and, what necessarily implies the unity of the filial with the paternal Godhead, I have even produced his attestation, that "the only-begotten Son is THE ONLY God *," *see p.* 137 *above*. I have produced a prayer preferred by him to our Redeemer; and, in addition to this, shall now exhibit that picture of St. John which this venerable writer has presented to our view; and in which we behold the beloved disciple of our Lord fallen on his knees, and with prayers imploring our Saviour to pardon and restore, by repentance, one whom the apostle had himself converted to Christianity, but who had lapsed into a vitious and dissolute course of life †. To these supplications, preferred and recorded, I have added an explicit doxology to the whole Trinity, of which this writer farther speaks, saying, "We have a treasure in earthen vessels, on all sides fortified by the power of God the Father, the blood of God the Son ‡, and the dew of the Holy Ghost §. Unless, therefore, Mr. Lindsey consent

* Ὁμογενὴς υἱὸς Θεὸς μόνος. Clement. quis dives salvabitur? cap. xxxvii.

† Ὡς ἄφεσιν αὐτῷ παρὰ τῦ σωτῆρος εὑρῆται. Δεόμενος, γονυπετῶν. Ejusdem lib, cap. xlii.

‡ Refer this expression to the note on Acts xx. 28, p. 157 above. In similar language Tertullian also writes, saying, "We are not our own, being purchased with a price: and with what a price! with the blood of God." Non sumus nostri, sed pretio empti: Et quali pretio? sanguine Dei. Tert. ad. Uxor. lib. ii. cap. iii.

§ Θησαυρὸν—δυνάμει Θεῦ Πατρὸς, κỳ αἵματι Θεῦ παιδὸς, κỳ δρόσῳ πνεύματος ἁγίου περιτετειχισμένον. Ejusdem libri, cap. xxxiv.

The little treatise from which these extracts have been taken is entitled Τίς ὁ Σωζόμενος Πλέσιος; It is a valuable work, and composed with more order and method than any other of the writings of Clement of Alexandria.——I omitted the title of this Tract in p. 143 by mistake.

consent to adopt these prayers and praises into his own new liturgy, I shall pronounce his assertion abandoned so far as it relates to this father, and consider his refusal as a concession that Clement of Alexandria was not an Unitarian. But the following hymn, which is subjoined to the Pædagogue, was composed previous to the heresy of Paul of Samosata. This man refused to concur in the hymns which were sung by the church to Christ. Let Mr. Lindsey now shew wherein he differs from Paul by joining this eminent Christian in thus singing to Christ: " Gather together thy simple children holily to sing, and, without guile, to hymn with their innocent mouths Christ the leader of infants: O King of saints; O all-subduing Word of the most high Father; O thou alleviation of sorrows; O Jesus, thou eternally gracious Saviour of a mortal race; O Shepherd; O Fisher of men of every language that shall be saved, taking them from the destructive wave of a sea of evils with the bait of a life of blifs; lead us, O holy Shepherd of rational sheep, that, being filled with the dewy Spirit, we may sing together pure praises, hymns of truth to Christ the King; that, being a choir of peace, the children of Christ, a temperate people, we may, with simplicity, sing to him who is alike the mighty Child; who is alike the God of Peace *."

The

* Τὰς σὰς ἀφιλεῖς παῖδας ἄγειρον, αἰνεῖν ἁγίως, ὑμνεῖν ἀδόλως, ἀκάκοις ςόμασι, παίδων ἡγήτορα Χριςόν, Βασιλεῦ ἁγίων, λέγε πανδαμάτωρ Πατρὸς ὑψίςε, ςήριγμα πόνων, αἰωνοχαρὲς βροτέας γενέας σῶτηρ Ἰησοῦ, ποιμὴν παναγὲς ποίμνης, ἁλιεῦ μερόπων τῶν σωζομένων, πελάγες κακίας κύματ᾽ ἰχθρῶ γλυκερῇ ζωῇ δελεάζων, ἡγῦ προβάτων λογικῶν ποιμὴν, ἅγιε ἡγῦ. Ἐμπιπλαμένοι πνεύματι δροσερῷ αἴνες ἀφιλεῖς, ὕμνες ἀτρεκεῖς βασιλεῖ Χριςῷ μέλπωμεν ὁμῦ, μέλπωμεν ἁπλῶς παῖδα κραῖερὸν,

χορὸς

The works of Clement are replete with similar assertions. Those, however, which I have laid before my reader, are so exceedingly particular, that they require no farther corroboration to ascertain the faith of this venerable man. Perhaps I may be thought to have extracted more than enough to this purpose, when it is considered that Mr. Lindsey has himself relinquished this father, having charged him with corrupting the simplicity of the gospel by the mixture of Gentile philosophy. Apology, p. 158. But let us hear his own answer to the charge, and he defines that philosophy, which I allow he has termed the schoolmaster of the Greek, as the law was the schoolmaster of the Jew to Christ, to be the very same which Solomon has described under the name of Wisdom; he declares that he does not consider the philosophy of Plato, Epicurus, or Aristotle, as true wisdom; but that, selecting so much of what every sect has held to the promotion of justice and virtue, to this alone he ascribes the name, and this he pronounces truly divine. And is it not so? and being so, what fitter guide to the truths of the gospel can be conceived, than a mind habituated to the love of every virtue? what fitter guide to the knowledge of the love of God, who laid down his life for our sake, than the cultivation of benevolence, and the love of mankind? Is it denied that the most candid dispositions are the most susceptible of the impressions

χορὸς εἰρήνης, οἱ Χριστόγονοι, λαὸς σώφρων, ψάλωμεν ὁμῶ Θεὸν εἰρήνης.

I have forborn to print this according to the measure of Clement's verse, and have omitted some images which are presented to us in the profoundest Spirit of the Bathos: for instance, he calls Christ the heavenly Wing of a flock of sheep. His sanctity and faith are all that I wish to lay before my reader; and, to the proof of these, it is by no means necessary to exhibit him in the poetical character which he so very ill sustains.

preffions of truth; that the cultivation of fuch a philofophy is an irrefragable teftimony of candour; or, that the gofpel is truth? If not, wherein confifts the errour of Clement, who has declared philofophy, as defined by himfelf, to be the fchoolmafter to Chrift? The evangelift is chargeable with a fimilar fentiment; for, to a noblenefs and generofity of mind, he imputes the readinefs of the Bereans to receive the word of God.— From having received they proceeded to enquire, and upon enquiry " many of them believed."—

When Clement fpeaks of philofophy, he ufually fpecifies the exact idea which he means to convey by the term: in the prefent inftance, he has abfolutely excluded all fcholaftic diftinctions, and, upon a generous promotion of juftice and truth alone, confers the honour of conducting to Chrift. But the definition being omitted, the term *philofophy* was capable of a double meaning. God grant, therefore, that there were no double meaning in having omitted the definition.

But why is philofophy to come under Mr. Lindfey's cenfure; and why is Clement charged with having deduced his ruinous tenets from philofophy? Was not Clement an Unitarian? and is not philofophy alone fufficient to falvation? for the affirmative in both inftances has this gentleman moft ftrenuoufly contended. Let us therefore now, from a view of the whole together, fee how much is to be concluded from his confiftent ftate of facts. *A faving philofophy has betrayed to deftruction an Unitarian, becaufe it has afforded thofe arguments upon which this Unitarian was not an Unitarian.* See above, p. 94.

It feems then that Mr. Lindfey has difcovered a great affinity between this fufficient philofophy and the faith which

which he has renounced; but a later advocate of his cause finds philosophy only consistent with the renunciation of his faith. He sees nothing in it repugnant to the doctrine of "a divine commission to Christ Jesus the Son of JOSEPH and Mary." But where has this man learned the blasphemous doctrine?—has the tenet which we embrace been brought into "*the school of Christ*" from Egypt, Greece, or Judea? No. The inspired witnesses of our glorious Redeemer have themselves related his incarnation of *a Virgin by the Holy Ghost*. "To the authority of the scriptures," he concludes his work, "Any Christian may subscribe with safety."—I can hardly conceive how, so long as the gospels of St. Matthew and St. Luke remain in the canon.

In order to accommodate this writer, I should think it necessary to retrench the authority of those two evangelists, and to rescind the epistles of St. Paul, together with several passages in other parts, of what the church of England acknowledge to be the scripture, for they contain many facts not in the least accordant to his philosophy. "To more than the scripture, no Christian," "he says, "can be safe in his subscription." This I should conceive must extend likewise to all that the scripture contains, beyond what the subscriber believes. For the safety of this writer, therefore, in subscribing, it is quite necessary that the scripture shall be *liberally* criticised and amended. See above, p. 115.

But what a sentence has he pronounced against those who, for the sake of preferment, have subscribed the articles of our church without belief. The sole end and purpose of his work, is to prove that these "are more than the scripture." It is thus rendered incumbent upon all our Unitarian dignitaries to rise up against this sentence of condemnation, and shew that our articles, which

they

they have subscribed, do not contain more than the scripture; or, if they accede to the judgement pronounced by their own advocate, it is recommended to them to weigh salvation against " a *livelihood* * :" and if the latter do not continue to preponderate, it is hoped they will retire from a station which they cannot occupy *with safety*. But perhaps they do not consider themselves within the description. If they thus reconcile their own conduct with propriety, it is a species of propriety with which I am unacquainted, and with which falsehood and duplicity may be very reconcileable for any thing that I know to the contrary. Morality, separated from the basis of God's immutable word, becomes a meer Proteus, and derives a form from every caprice with which it may be combined. I can only say that the attestation of what appears a falsehood, for the sake of a temporary emolument, is not consistent with the morality of a *Christian*; or, in the language of Tertullian, NON FAS EST ULLI DE SUA RELIGIONE MENTIRI. Apol. adv. Gent. cap. xxii.

I have now brought to view the tenets of every father, and every Christian of the second century, who has transmitted an account of his own faith to us. They have severally been called upon to answer to the charge brought against them, and each has, in his own person, given an account of the tenets which he embraced concerning the one Godhead of the Father, Son, and Holy Ghost. Whether, therefore, those numerous

---

* The work referred to is entitled, Subscription; or, Historical Extracts. The passages may be found in the 139th, 169th, and 186th pages. This author is guilty of the most flagitious calumny. Upon what authority can he say that the bishops "know to be false what they acknowledge to be true," &c. If he has any grounds for such a charge, he should have stated them: he should have named particulars rather than have brought such a general accusation.

merous confeffions of the Godhead of our Redeemer, and of the Holy Ghoft, which they have made, and I have ftated, can be reconciled, either with Mr. Lindfey's affertion or doctrine, I fhall leave it with every unprejudiced reader to determine. For my own part, I conceive that there fubfifts an unfurmountable inconfiftency between them, and fhall therefore conclude this chapter, as I did the former, by affuming to the fupport of my doctrine the entire authority of that age, of which it treats; for it is evident now that Chriftians, for the firft two hundred years after Chrift, were *wholly Trinitarians.*

CHAP.

CHAP. III.

The Sentiments of the Fathers of the third Century, together with those of some other Christian People.

Christianity had now greatly extended her limits, and found proselytes in almost every region of the earth. The providence of God, deducing good out of the worst purposes of man, turned even " the abomination of desolation" to the promotion of his own truth. The arms of Rome were pressed into the service of the Almighty, and, under the command of the Lord of hosts, her proud, and, what she little thought, her subaltern ambition went forth only to render the world accessible to the gospel of peace. Like the Baptist, she was sent out as an instrument to prepare the way of the Lord, and to make his paths straight; by her means every valley was exalted, and every hill and mountain was brought low; the crooked was made straight, and the rough way was made smooth for the entrance of the gospel, that all flesh might see the salvation of God.

Unconscious, nevertheless, herself of the glorious office, her heart was hardened; and, like Pharaoh, she deferred to yield obedience to the faith 'till even her own persecution had multiplied the attestations of heaven. The very blood which she shed, with a view to suppress the gospel, was rendered contributary to its progress, and erected by God into a testimony of his truth.. " She was drunk with blood," but it was the
" blood

"blood of the martyrs of Jesus," which, under the immediate superintendence of heaven, triumphed over the frustrated infidelity of the oppressor, and brought over numerous proselytes to the religion of the gospel.

But all were not yet converted: the Jew still stumbled; the Greek still derided; and heresy, which kept pace with the advancement of truth, contributed an internal enemy to the religion of our Redeemer.

When thus extensively disseminated, and thus on every part assailed, we are not to wonder that Christianity should find so many adherents to sustain her cause, nor be offended with that air of controversy which pervades the works of those who stood up in her defence. For this, and for the enormous size to which some of their volumes have swelled, the complicated errours with which they were to contend may very well account. They never had permission to lay down their arms. The Jew, the Infidel, and the Heretick, created unremitted employment for their pens. They were engaged, not only to extend the radiance of the gospel into the realms of antient darkness, but to disperse those clouds which gathered round this source of light, and threatened to obscure, nay, to extinguish its native lustre.

I have heretofore been able to give my reader some idea of the scheme of every father, and to show the manner in which the extracts that I have stated, stood connected with the general design of the work from which I had drawn them. From the writers of the first century I have extracted a copious testimony; of the doctrines of those who wrote in the second I have made a brief summary; but, from the fathers of the third century, I shall content myself, and, I hope, my reader, by laying before him only a few explicit passages. It is impossible poffible that any thing which I could in reafon offer to the public, fhould bear the moft remote proportion to the works of thefe voluminous authors; I am therefore obliged to extract inverfely as the fathers have written, and fo can fcarcely now do more than lay detached affertions before my reader. But here I will venture to affert that there is an inconfiftency between thofe paffages which I fhall produce, as embraced by the church in this early period, and any doctrine of modern Unitarianifm. I declare, from my own knowledge, that the context favours the pofition as I ftate it; but if I have not credit for this, I relinquifh the affertion, and give liberty to Mr. Lindfey, or any of his adherents, to invent fuch a context as fhall reconcile thefe doctrines with his tenets. For inftance, how will he reconcile his own declaration, that the Son had a created commencement, with Origen's declaration, that " there never was duration when the Son was not; that, according to the flefh, indeed he was not, but, according to the fpirit, he was before all things; and time was not when he was not *?" He cannot do it; for, with Irenæus, " we fhew that the Son, eternally coexiftent with the father, did not then commence being, when he united his fubftance with the workmanfhip of his own hands, and became a man, obnoxious to fufferings: and thus we cut off all contradiction from thofe who argue that, if Chrift was then born, he did not exift before †."

* Nunquam eft quando Filius non fuit—fecundum carnem non erat prius; fecundum Spiritum verò erat ante & non erat quando non erat. Orig. Parif. Edit. tom i. p. 483, folio.—Clemens Alexandrinus has called the Son ἀναρχως γενομένω, *exifting or begotten without commencement.*

† Oftenfio manifefte quod in principio verbum exiftens apud Deum unitum fuo plafmati paffibilem hominem factum. Exclufa eft omnis contradictio dicentium, fi ergo tunc natus, non erat ante Chriftus. Oftendimus enim quia non tunc cæpit Filius Dei exiftens femper apud Patrem. Vide fupra, p. 104, 110, 121. Vide quoque, p. 17, 44, 86, &c.

The most eminent fathers of the third century are TERTULLIAN, ORIGEN, GREGORY OF NÆOCESAREA, and CYPRIAN BISHOP OF CARTHAGE. The commencement of the fourth is entitled to the names of LACTANTIUS, EUSEBIUS, and ATHANASIUS. Of these I shall speak but incidentally, for they survived the Council of Nice, in which the two latter took a leading part; but let it be likewise remembered that they lived before this famous council.

QUINTUS SEPTIMIUS FLORENS TERTULLIANUS was born at Carthage of Gentile parents, in whose principles he was educated; but from which, by the force of his great natural and well-cultivated understanding, he became a convert to Christianity. The second century has the honour both of his birth and conversion; but the greater part of his writings which have come down to us were composed in the beginning of the third, for which reason I chuse to refer his name to this age. He has most vigorously defended Christianity against both Gentiles, Jews, and Hereticks, and yet this champion of truth was, in the end, deceived himself by an impostor, named Montanus, whose austerity of manners deluded many Christians, and, among others, persuaded even this great man that he was the promised comforter; by which, however, he did not mean to affirm that he was the third person of the Trinity, but, interpreting the promise of our Lord as referring to one who should come and explain his word more largely to mankind, he gave himself out to be this predicted *Paraclete*. Our author, who was at this time Presbyter of Carthage, attached himself to this extraordinary person, and accordingly incurred the censure of the church, by which he was excommunicated. Henceforward we know but little of the circumstances of his life. All that is related of

him

him is, that he held separate meetings with the rest of the followers of Montanus, and died in a very advanced age. He seems to have been a man of a rigid and severe temper, and to have become a convert to Montanus merely on account of his similar austerity; for the chief purpose of his writings, composed after his adherence to that impostor, is to reproach the too great levity of those, whose communion he had abandoned: with their tenets he does not seem to have instituted any quarrel. But, to avoid confusion on this head, I shall confine myself to such of his works as were written before his perversion to the errours of Montanus, and while he was considered as one of the most able defenders that ever sustained the cause of true Christianity.

I have already produced a few declarations of his faith, one particularly in the 104th page above, where I have quoted his assertion, that, in the Lord's prayer, "the Son is invoked in the Father." In his dissuasion from marriage between Christians and Gentiles, he maintains the same doctrine, and, esteeming it one of the principal inconveniencies incident to such an union, that there is no participation of worship, breaks out into the following interrogatories: "What discourse can there be concerning God? what invocation of Christ? how shall faith be sustained by reading the scriptures to each other? where is the refreshment of the Spirit *?" Whereas, on the other hand, he considers similar confidence in the salvation of Christ as the closest bond of union; for man and wife, pursuing his dictates, are always in the performance of some humane

* Quæ Dei mentio? quæ Christi invocatio? ubi fomenta fidei de scripturam interlectione? ubi Spiritus refrigerium? Tertulliani ad Uxorem, lib. ii. cap. vi.

mane and benevolent action, by which they become more eftimable in the eyes of each other, and take pleafure in being joint labourers to do his commandments. They are for ever chearful, not only from the approbation of their own confciences feparately, but from the certainty of reciprocal approbation. Their mutual congratulations are not filent, " but pfalms and hymns are heard from both, and their only conteft is, who fhall fing beft to their God. Chrift beholding fuch concert, and, liftening, rejoices, and fends them his peace*." In his book againft the Jews, he employs many of the fame arguments that I have already produced from Juftin Martyr to prove the divinity of our Saviour; and, comparing the extent of Chrift's kingdom with that of the Romans, he fays that their empire has bounds to it, " but the kingdom and the name of Chrift are extended without limits: he is every where believed in; he is worfhiped in all nations; he reigns every where; he is every where adored; he is in all places equally offered to the acceptance of all; with him there is no refpect of perfons; he is to all alike a King and a Judge; he is to all alike their God and Lord †." Which latter " appellation of Lord" this father declares in another place " to be the furname *(cognomen)* of God ‡." In his treatife on repentance, he exhorts to

mu-

* Sonant inter duos pfalmi & hymni, & mutuo provocant quis melius Deo fuo canet. Talia Chriftus videns & audiens gaudet. His pacem fuam mittit. Tertul. ad Uxor. lib. ii. cap. ix.

† Chrifti autem regnum & nomen ubique porrigitur, ubique creditur, ab omnibus gentibus fupra enumeratis colitur, ubique regnat, ubique adoratur, omnibus ubique tribuitur æqualiter; non regis apud illum major gratia, non barbari alicujus imperiofi lætitia, non dignitatum aut natalium cujufquam difcreta merita, omnibus æqualis, omnibus Rex, omnibus Judex, omnibus Deus & Dominus eft. Tertul. adverf. Judæos, lib. cap. vii.

‡ Auguftus imperii formator ne Dominum quidem dici fe volebat. Et hoc enim Dei eft cognomen. Apologeticus adv. Gentes, cap. xxxviii.

mutual confession; declares that it may be beneficially made to those who will rather lament our infirmities than publish or deride them, that it may be made among friends, and at home; for "that even two together make the church; that Christ himself *(who is present)* makes the church; and when therefore you prostrate yourself at the knees of your brethren, you deal with Christ; you effectually implore Christ §." But, as he proceeds to inculcate the persuasive powers of repentance, in calling down pardon on the penitent, fearful that he may encourage offence by shewing that there subsists such a refuge from its consequences, he corrects himself, and puts up a prayer directly to "Christ the Lord, that none may so interpret what he says, as to conceive a way opened to crimes, because there is a way open to repentance; that none may consider the redundance of heavenly mercy as a sanction for the indulgence of headlong lusts, nor, proportioning his evils to the goodness of God, pursue forgiveness with reiterated offence ||." I have already said that Tertullian, in general, establishes Christianity against the Jews with nearly the same arguments that Justin Martyr employed against them. Like him he argues from the prophecy in the Old, to its completion set forth in the New Testament. Some small difference, however, there subsists in the conduct of their several works, and passages of scripture have been applied to our Lord by each,

§ In uno & altero ecclesia est, ecclesia vero Christus. Ergo cum te ad fratrum genua protendis, Christum contrectas, Christum exoras. De Pænitentia, lib. cap. x.

|| CHRISTE DOMINE——absit ut aliquis ita interpretetur, quasi ro sibi etiam nunc pateat ad delinquendum, quia patet ad pœnitendum; & redundantia clementiæ cœlestis, libidinem faciat humanæ temeritatis. Nemo idcirco deterior fit, quia Deus melior est, toties delinquende, quoties ignoscitur. Ejusdem lib. cap. vii.

each, which the other has pretermitted *. Tertullian says that the prophecy in the 72d pſalm was fulfilled by the gifts made to our infant Saviour, and by the honour paid to him at Bethlehem by the wiſe men, "who, when they knew him, honoured him with gifts, and, believing in Chriſt, on their knees adored him as their God and King †." And ſuch is the concurrence here between the language of the father and the evangeliſt, that I chuſe to advert to the latter, as bearing in his relation of this tranſaction a very explicit teſtimony to the Godhead of our Redeemer; for the wiſe men, "who fell down and worſhipped the young child ‡," were altogether, in the inſtance, under the conduct of heaven, which, by an extraordinary appearance, directed them firſt to Jeruſalem, and afterwards to the houſe where he was laid with his mother. They went out with a purpoſe to obey the inſidious commands of Herod, but heaven again interfered, and God warned them not to return to Jeruſalem. Is it now probable that God ſhould become their guide only to error, and that he who made them the inſtrument of protecting the Infant, ſhould alſo, in the ſame action, make them the very firſt examples of miſconception concerning him? No; and it is even evident that they had preached the divinity of our Lord to Herod before they offered up their own gifts and adoration to him; for Herod covered his deſtructive intentions under the maſk of concurrence, and employed them to find the Infant,

that

* Tertullian agrees with Juſtin in ſaying that it was Chriſt who ſpoke from the burning buſh and to the patriarchs; that he pronounced judgement on our firſt parents, &c. &c.

† Qui cum illum cognoviſſent, & muneribus honoraſſent, & genû poſito honoraſſent quaſi Deum & Regem, ſub teſtimonio indicis & ducis ſtellæ credentes videlicet in Chriſto. Tertul. adv. Judæos, lib. cap. ix.

‡ Καὶ πισόντες προσεκύνησαν αὐτῳ. Matth. ii. 11.

that he might "come and worship him also [*]." Of the Gentiles who were adopted by Christ, in whose flesh the partition wall that kept the Jews select, and divided from the rest of the children of the first Adam, was taken away, these wise men were the very first who claimed the privileges extended to mankind at large; they were taken under the immediate direction of God, and made our leaders; the first who, by the spirit of adoption, called upon Christ as their God and Father; and shall we say that God intended to propose an ill example to us, whose first fruits they were? I can never conceive it, or believe that the manifestation of Christ to the Gentiles was made by the God of truth, in such a manner as instantaneously to plunge them into error, and conduct them to the idolatrous worship of a creature. With them we find Tertullian concurrent, and, with them, let us also concur, and unite in the adoration of "Christ our God and King;" for, "behold all nations henceforward emerging from the gulph of human ignorance to the Lord God the the Creator, and to God his Christ [†]." Yea! "the nations which have not known him, even on this day invoke Christ; and the people now run together to Christ, of whom they have been heretofore ignorant [‡]."

This father closes a comment on the Lord's prayer, which he says, "the Son has taught us [§]," with some
expres-

[*] Ὅπως κᾀγὼ ἐλθὼν προσκυνήσω αὐτῷ. Matth. ii. 8.

[†] Aspice universas nationes de voragine erroris humani exinde emergentes ad Dominum Deum creatorem, & ad Deum Christum ejus. Tertul. adverſ. Judæos, cap xii.

[‡] Christum enim hodie invocant Nationes, quæ cum non sciebant, & populi hodie ad Christum confugiunt, quem retrò ignorabant. Ejuſd. lib. cap. xiv.

[§] Filius docuit, De Orat. lib, cap, ix.

expreſſions of admiration at its comprehenſive conciſeneſs; "but what wonder," he corrects himſelf, and ſays, "God alone could inſtruct us how he would himſelf be addreſſed in prayer *;" and in like manner Origen has told us, "Chriſt is God; and he who adores him, ſhould adore him in ſpirit and in truth. Let us therefore pray of the Lord that we may be a building, founded upon a rock, which no ſtorm ſhall have power to overthrow, thro' our Lord Jeſus Chriſt, whoſe is the glory and dominion for ever and ever. Amen †." Here then we have the joint teſtimony of Ter-

* Quid mirum? Deus ſolus docere potuit, ut ſe vellet orari. De Orat. lib. cap. ix.

† Chriſtus eſt Deus: & qui adorat eum, in ſpiritu & veritate oportet adorare.—Oremus igitur Dominum ut ſimus ædificium, quod tempeſtas nulla ſubvertat, fundatum ſupra petram, per Dominum noſtrum Jeſum Chriſtum, cui eſt gloria & imperium in ſecula ſeculorum. Amen. Origen. homil. xxvi. in Luc. cap. iii.

This Doxology ends with extending our Saviour's glory to eternity; appoſite to which Tertullian, who is the preſent ſubject, chides the Chriſtians for attending at the theatres in Carthage, where they give applauſes with mouths that had uttered *amen to Chriſt*; and declares it a pollution to uſe ſuch ſalutations as were then cuſtomarily addreſſed to magiſtrates upon their entrance, and in which they were hailed with wiſhes for their eternal life, or denominated eternal. For Chriſtians to aſcribe ſuch attributes to men, he ſays, is altogether a profanation, or "to aſcribe eternity to any other beſides Chriſt, who is God," εἰς αἰῶνας alii omnino dicere niſi Deo Chriſto. Tertul. de Spectaculis, lib. cap. xxv. That theſe words εἰς αἰῶνα; ſignify eternity, the ſenſe of antiquity demonſtrates; for, when Chriſtianity at length comprehended the imperial throne, the Imperours diſallowed of the addreſs as blaſphemous, and ſubſtituted for them the word πολυχρόνιον, which ſignifies a long, but a limited time. If the former ſignify no more, wherein do they differ?——Who is the "Creator, who is bleſſed for ever?" Τὸν κτισάντα, ὅς ἐςι ἐυλογητὸς εἰς τὰς αἰῶνας; Rom. i. 25. Shall Chriſt be acknowledged the Creator here, for the purpoſe of maintaining that theſe words ſignify a limited period? or ſhall they be admitted to ſignify eternity, becauſe connected with the Father? Take it either way. If the firſt be conceded, reſt here, for all that is aſked for is granted; if the latter, turn back to the 28th page above, and apply the conceſſion.

Tertullian and Origen, that our Lord and Saviour was the object of worship in the third century; and "think ye that ye can bear a different love toward the Father and the Son? As the Father, love also the Lord Jesus Christ; love the Father in the Son, the Son in the Father, with all your heart, and with all your soul, and with all your strength ‡."

In the second book of his refutation of Marcion's heresy, Tertullian shews the difference between a God without passions and a God torpid with apathy. The latter, he says, is taught by the philosophers, but the former by the Christians; that the philosophers admit God to be a Judge, and yet rescind his motives to judgement, his sense of justice; but, for our part, he adds, " Who believe that God sustained a character on earth, and assumed the debasement of a human form, being clothed in flesh, for the sake of man's salvation; we differ very widely from their opinion, who deny that God takes an interest in any thing §." The long-suffering of God, who bears with the unrighteousness of bad men, and sheds his light alike upon the just and the unjust, he says, is an example of a sort of patience too remote from us to admit of imitation. " But what was that instance which was transacted on earth, and so near as in a manner to be grasped by us? God suffers himself to be conceived in the womb of a mother;

---

‡ Putas diversam habere posse in Patre & Filio charitatem? simul dilige Dominum Christum, dilige Patrem in Filio, Filium in Patre, ex toto corde, & ex totâ animâ, & ex tota virtute. Origen. in Luc. cap. iii. homil. xxv. tom. ii. p. 151.

§ Qui credimus Deum etiam in terris egisse & humani habitûs humilitatem suscepisse, ex causâ humani salutis, longe sumus â sententia eorum qui nolunt Deum curare quidquam. Tertul. adverf. Marcionem, lib. ii. cap. xvi.

ther;" and, while on earth, fo humbled himfelf, and gave fo many proofs of his patience and refignation, that we may find, even in God himfelf, an example of patience, which it is poffible for us to follow *.

This affertion is furely applicable to Philipp. ii. 6, and may abet the doctrine which I have already laid down upon that paffage. Refer it therefore to p. 158, *above*, together with the following declaration made by the fame father: " So God made man, in the image of God created he him, that is, in the image of Chrift, for the Word is God, who, being in the form of God, thought it not robbery to be equal with God †"

In his defence of baptifm againft Quintilla, who contended for the taking away the ufe of water in that facrament, he likens the perfon to be baptized to the maimed and fick who waited for the defcent of the angel upon the pool of Bethefda, and the water itfelf ufed in baptifm, to the waters of that pool after they had been troubled and endowed with fanative powers. And as the angel prepared this water, he fays, for the cure of dif-

* Quid illa autem quæ inter homines palàm in terris quodammodo manu apprehenfa eft? nafci fe Deus in utero patitur matris. De Patientia, lib. cap. iii.

† Fecit hominem Deus, ad imaginem Dei fecit illum, fcilicet Chrifti, et fermo enim Deus, qui in effigie Dei, &c. Tertull. de Refurrectione Chrifti, lib. cap. vi.

The writer already quoted, p. 181 above, has carried matters a little farther than his predeceffors in infidelity. He has built upon their foundation, and, not admitting even a doubt of the interpretation which he puts upon Philip. ii. 6, with unparalleled modefty declares: " St. Paul affures us our Saviour never thought that *equality* belonged to him, or was what he had any title to affume." p. 169. Whether I have, or have not proved that St. Paul declares the very reverfe, my reader muft judge. But a little hefitation might have become a man in fpeaking on a point at the very leaft doubtful; but that would have been betraying the caufe.

diseases, so the water used in baptism is made ready for the washing away of offence; and being cleansed in it, we are prepared for the reception of the Holy Ghost, whose harbinger baptism is, making straight his way, as John by baptism prepared the way of the Lord in the wilderness. "But the washing away of offence is an acquisition made by faith, sealed and witnessed by the Father, Son, and Holy Ghost. For if every word shall be established by three witnesses, how much stronger is the ratification of our hope when three divine names are set to it, when we have the same to bear witness to our faith, who have promised and engaged for our salvation in consequence of it *." The Father, Son, and Holy Ghost, we here find three distinct witnesses. It is true that their one Godhead is not the necessary inference from this assertion, but, to their being three witnesses, it is essential that they be acknowledged three distinct persons.

St. John has declared that there is a record whereby eternal life, an entrance into the kingdom of heaven, and adoption to be the children of God, is ensured to all who believe on him who came by water and blood, and who have a spirit bearing witness to the fertility of their faith. And of this record, he proceeds to declare that " there are three that bear it in heaven, the Father, the Word, and the Holy Ghost, and these three are one," 1 John v. 7.

The

---

* Superventuro Spiritui Sancto vias dirigit ablutione delictorum, quam fides impetrat obsignata in Patre & Filio & Spiritu Sancto. Nam si in tribus testibus stabit omne verbum, quanto magis, dum habemus per benedictionem eosdem arbitros fidei, quos & sponsores salutis, sufficit ad fiduciam spei nostræ etiam numerus nominum divinorum. De Baptismo, lib. cap. vi.

The authenticity of this paſſage has been long conteſted, and the principal ground of doubt urged, is the ſilence of the early fathers, who have never produced it in ſupport of the unity of the three perſons in the one Godhead. But, to obviate this objection, I ſhould conceive it a ſufficient reaſon for their ſilence, to ſhew that the unity of the Godhead is not the primary object of the apoſtle's aſſertion; and if this appear, it will follow that the text may be authentic, though not quoted by the fathers to a purpoſe for which it was not written.

I urge, with the greateſt humility, my own idea on this ſubject. The warmeſt advocate of the truth cannot juſtly be offended at an interpretation that takes away an argument on which he had not ventured to lay any great weight before; and I even hope the Unitarian may be inclined to leave it in peaceable poſſeſſion of the place it now occupies, provided he find that it does not, in its firſt and obvious ſenſe, declare the doctrine on account of which he has ſo ſtrenuouſly contended for its excluſion.

Had not this work already very far exceeded my original intention, I ſhould call many cogent arguments in behalf of the doctrine I am about to propoſe. As it is, I ſhall content myſelf with little more than ſtating it; and, for ſome of thoſe reaſons which tend to lead me into this opinion, muſt refer the reader to what I have already offered on the 17th chapter of St. John's goſpel, in the 172d page above.

I have there argued from ſeveral high authorities, that when our Lord prayed that the apoſtles might be with himſelf and the Father *one*, his intention was that they might be one in teſtimony, one, witneſs; the word one

one being in the neuter gender, and by confequence introductory of a new term, in refpect of which the fubject number are one.

With regard to the paffage before us I entertain the fame opinion: *one* is written here alfo in the neuter gender. The office affigned to the Father, the Word, and the Holy Ghoft, in the preceding part of the verfe, is the bearing of record; their entire concurrence may, without force, therefore, be fuppofed the fubject of the conclufion; and thefe three, thus bearing one record, may be faid to be one, witnefs. One they are certainly pronounced to be, but in what is the queftion, for the word one is neuter, and confequently indefinite. The anfwer to this is more naturally collected from the context than fought for among truths however certain, if not fo immediately within the writer's contemplation; I therefore fuggeft, that agreement in teftimony or record is that term in refpect of which "thefe three are one." The Complutenfian edition, though the reading is not generally adopted, affords an argument in behalf of this doctrine, for it exhibits, "And thefe three agree in one." It is not neceffary that this fhould be genuine, in order to prove that teftimony is the point of unity. The text, as received by us, is fufficient to the purpofe, and if fo, lends an argument in defence of what I have already faid on the 17th chapter of St. John's gofpel.

If this be received, it will appear that the paffage extracted from Tertullian is effentially a quotation of St. John's text; for "the Word," written by the apoftle, it is true this writer has fubftituted "the Son;" but this makes no difference in the doctrine. That the Word is the Son no body can difpute. It follows therefore that the record of the Father, *the Son*, and
the

the Holy Ghoſt, is the fame as the record of the Father, *the Word*, and the Holy Ghoſt. And if Tertullian has quoted the paſſage, if he has only alluded to it, it may be juſtly inferred that the text is genuine, and that it has come from the inſpired pen of the apoſtle.

But Tertullian, it will be ſaid, has declared that the promiſes of God made to us in the ſacrament of baptiſm, are the object of that teſtimony in which theſe three concur; ſo St. John, I maintain it, has done; for, to concur in record of the object to which the Father, the Word, and the Holy Ghoſt bear witneſs in heaven, he calls in three more witneſſes in earth, "the ſpirit, the water, and the blood, and theſe three, he ſays, agree in one." In what do they agree? Without doubt in witneſſing the covenant of baptiſm. To nothing elſe than baptiſm can the teſtimony of the *water* bear reference, for by water we are baptized; it is the viſible inſtrument of that covenant, and hereby we are baptized into the death of Chriſt. His *blood*, therefore, by which, as by the blood of the Paſchal Lamb, we are marked for mercy*, is made alſo an atteſting witneſs; it is the blood of the new covenant, by the ſprinkling of which our ſpirit is ſanctified and made pure †: but the old covenant, which conſiſted in fleſhly ordinances, was atteſted by purifications of the fleſh. The new, on the contrary, is a covenant of grace, and accordingly requires the record of a pure and ſanctified ſpirit. The *ſpirit*, therefore, thus purified by the blood of our propitiation, is called upon to bear record to our entrance into, and adherence to the conditions of that covenant. And now as, upon the record of *the ſpirit*, or a conſcience purified to ſerve the
living

---

* 1 Cor. v. 7.   1 Peter i. 19.   Rev. v. 9.   Exod. xii. 13.
† See Heb. xiii. 12.   1 Peter i. 2.   2 Theſſ. ii. 13.

living God; of *the water* wherein we are wafhed from our iniquities; and of *the blood* of Chrift, into which we are baptized, and by which we are made clean, we are entitled to claim thofe benefits that God has been pleafed to annex to our repentance and faith thus attefted: or, as in the words of St. Paul to the fame effect, " We have boldnefs to enter into the holieft by the blood of Jefus, and to draw near in full affurance of faith, having our hearts fprinkled from an evil confcience, and our bodies wafhed with pure water," Heb. x. 20, 22; fo we have, as a ground of this affurance, the promifes of God, on which we may rely with the fulleft certainty, for he is faithful who promifed; and, of his having by covenant conftituted a claim to adoption and eternal life, in as many as prefent themfelves with a concurrent atteftation of " the fpirit, the water, and the blood," that they have become parties to, and fulfilled their part in, that contract, " there are three that bear record in heaven, the Father, the Word, and the Holy Ghoft, and thefe three are one."

To the Chriftian's contract with God, therefore, it is that St. John has enumerated the witneffes; and that unity which he afcribes to them, is a unity of teftimony, in which the three perfons ftand engaged, the Father, the Word, and the Holy Ghoft, for the performance of the promifes of God made to man in that contract. But, in his engagement to enter into a new and an everlafting covenant with man, God has himfelf declared by the mouth of Ezekiel, " Then will I fprinkle clean *water* upon you, and ye fhall be clean: a new *fpirit* will I put within you, and caufe you to keep my ftatutes, and to do them; and their fins and iniquities will I remember no more*." But, " without
fhed-

* Ezek. xxxvi. 25. See alfo 2 Cor. iii. 2, &c.

shedding of blood," says St. Paul, "there is no remission ‖‖." To give force, therefore, to the covenant, and to carry, as it were, into execution this merciful act of oblivion, the blood of Christ was shed to purge our consciences to serve the living God. To authenticate, therefore, the claim of man, we take to witness a *spirit* thus purified, and "with which the Spirit of God witnesseth*," "*the water* wherein we are made clean from our filthiness †," and by the sprinkling of which, as by an instrument, we enter into the contract, together with "*the blood* of the new covenant, which was shed for many for the remission of sins ‡," and into which we are baptized §. And, under the concurrent attestation of these three, we become entitled to the adoption, to be the children of God, being " born of *water*, and of the *spirit* ‖," " and by the *blood* of Christ cleansed from all unrighteousness **."

To every covenant entered into between God and man a witness was appointed. The bow was extended across the heavens as our security from future deluge: " And it shall be a token of the covenant, saith the Lord, betwixt me and you ††." Circumcision was ordained upon entering into compact with Abraham: And, " because of the circumcision of her son, Zipporah upbraided Moses with being unto her a bloody husband ‡‡." Blood was the ratification of the old covenant; for, when it was entered into, Moses sacrificed offerings unto the Lord, " and then took of the blood, and sprinkled it on the people, and said, Behold the blood of the covenant which the Lord hath made with you §§."—To the new

co-

‖‖ Heb. ix. 22.   Rom iii. 25.   * Rom. viii. 16.
† Ezek. xxxvi. 25.   ‡ Matth. xxvi. 28. Heb. ix. 20.
§ Rom. vi. 3.   ‖ John iii. 5, and xiii. 8.   ** 1 John i. 7.
†† Gen ix. 13.   ‡‡ Exod. iv. 26.   §§ Exod. xxiv. 8.

covenant of baptifm, it is therefore only analogous to his former dealings that God fhould ordain a teftimony. By blood frequently fhed for the remiffion of fins, the Jews obtained frequent and temporary forgiveneffes; and by carnal purifications they were cleanfed in the flefh, and enabled to join the congregation in the *tabernacle*. But now, to our eternal remiffion, the blood of Chrift once fhed is a fufficient facrifice. By him our entrance into *the holieft* is enfured; but to this it is not a flefhly purification, but a clean fpirit, a heart purged by his blood from an evil confcience, and engraven with the law of God, that is requifite. This law is fpiritual and not of ordinances. The cleannefs of the fpirit, therefore, and not of the flefh, is the qualification of the contractor with God in this covenant of grace. If "our confcience, therefore, excufe" us before God, it is evident that we have not fallen away from, but adhered to our repentance and profeffions of faith, and reliance upon the advocacy and propitiation of Chrift. And thus the fpirit, and the water, and the blood are witneffes before God, maintaining our right to adoption, to an entrance into his kingdom, and to that eternal life which is in his Son, and which is evidently the object of record fpoken of by St. John.

It is true that the apoftle never ufes the term baptifm throughout his epiftle; but to what elfe but baptifm can the water fo frequently mentioned by him be referred? If no other anfwer can be given, I fhould abide by baptifm, the inftrument of the fecond covenant. St. John declares that the record borne is, that God hath given us eternal life, and that we are the children of God, if we believe in his Son Jefus Chrift, who came by *water* and by *blood*. The fame conditions are annexed throughout the fcriptures to an entrance into the baptifmal covenant, wherein, by the

C c means

means of water, we are made partakers of the benefits of his blood-shedding, through faith in the sufficiency thereof. That the contract entered into by baptism, therefore, is the object of the record, I hope I have now made sufficiently evident.

Under this idea, the two controverted verses claim a place in the chapter, not as a meer parenthesis, the omission of which no way affects the tenour of the apostle's argument, but as very contributary to the doctrine which he is inculcating. If we receive the witness of men, he says, the witness of God is of higher credibility, and of his Son Jesus Christ, who has come to us by water and blood, he has borne witness, testifying that he has, in his Son, given to us eternal life. This testimony is our security, and therefore to be relied upon by all to whom Christ has come by water and by blood, and who, by hearing and yielding their faith and obedience, denote a spirit of truth. With such the new and everlasting covenant, whereof Christ is the mediator, is entered into; to them this record of eternal life is borne, and confirmed by more than human testimony; for, while on earth, there are three, that bear concurrent witness to our engagement, to confide in Christ and lead a life correspondent to his will, even the water, the blood, and the spirit; there are three that bear record in heaven to the promises of God made to us in the sacrament of baptism, the Father, the Word, and the Holy Ghost, and these three are one testimony, one in record of these promises thus ratified.

Thus I interpret the passage, which is (even on admission of its authenticity) not easily intelligible in the common acceptation: the assertion seems abrupt, and not introduced by the context. But of its authenticity

I

I now make no doubt, and therefore endeavour to understand what I believe the apoſtle has written. This interpretation is not hard nor forced, and makes a ſenſe very conſiſtent with his entire epiſtle. If I have erred, I rejoice that I am not likely to induce any ill conſequences by my error. The paſſage has been ſo much controverted, that it has ſcarce been relied on; I do not therefore take away from the evidence what has ever been conſidered as any conſiderable part of it. Let the paſſage quoted from Tertullian be again adverted to now, and the father will be found to ſpeak the ſame ſenſe that I have aſcribed to St. John, which contributes an argument of great weight in behalf of my ſuppoſition.

How far the ſacrament of baptiſm, ordained in the name of the Father, Son, and Holy Ghoſt, extends to prove the divinity of thoſe perſons in whoſe name it is adminiſtered, is a queſtion that does not directly come before me now. The paſſage which I have juſt quoted from Tertullian, may ſerve to ſhew what is more to my preſent purpoſe, that the primitive church yielded ſtrict obedience to the commandment of our aſcending Saviour: to this end a very competent profeſſor of divinity in the univerſity of Oxford has already produced it, together with many concurrent paſſages from the ſame and other early fathers. Mr. Lindſey has aſſerted that the neceſſity of entering into this covenant, in the manner preſcribed by our Lord himſelf, was firſt inſiſted upon by the Council of Nice. How much the apologiſt's ſtate of facts is to be relied upon, I refer my reader to Dr. Randolph's Vindication of the Worſhip of the Son and of the Holy Ghoſt, to learn. This reverend gentleman has confronted the practice and doctrine of the Antenicene church, tranſmitted by its principal paſtors themſelves, to Mr. Lindſey's aſſertion.

tion. For misconception or erroneous inference the underſtanding alone is reſponſible. The errours into which weakneſs of intellect, or even the darkening prejudice that waits upon the ambition of leading a ſect, may betray in points of doctrine, I forgive, but I cannot extend equal indulgence to a miſrepreſentation of plain hiſtorical facts: in theſe no doubts can ſuggeſt themſelves, and inveſtigation muſt terminate in certainty. Ignorance cannot be pleaded as an extenuation of the offence. In matters ſo open to enquiry, it is equally criminal to aſſert without, as in oppoſition to knowledge.

But if, after all, the reader ſhall judge that the 7th verſe of the 5th chapter of St. John's firſt epiſtle aſſerts the Trinity in Unity *of the Godhead*, and ſo leave it open to the aſſaults of the whole Unitarian tribe, he may nevertheleſs find its authenticity defenſible againſt them. Cyprian, Biſhop of Carthage, has to a certainty quoted the latter part of it. Inſtead of " the Word," ſpoken of by St. John in the beginning, it is true he has written " the Son ;" and hence it is made a queſtion whether his aſſertion be more than a comment of his own upon other paſſages which he has quoted from the ſcripture. But how are the words " it is written" to be diſpoſed of? They introduce the teſtimony of St. John, that " *theſe three are one*," and evince that Cyprian does not utter this ſentence from himſelf, but from the apoſtle. The paſſage occurs in his Tract on the Unity of the Church, and is to this effect: " The Lord ſaith, " *I and my Father are one* ;" and again, concerning the Father, the Son, and the Holy Ghoſt, it is written, " *theſe three are one* *."

Where

---

* Dicit Dominus: Ego & Pater unum ſumus. Et iterum de Patre, & Filio & Spiritu Sancto ſcriptum eſt: Et hi tres unum ſunt. Cypriani de Unitate Eccleſiæ Liber, p. 109. Edit. Oxon. per Joannem Ceſtrienſem. 1682, folio.

It

Where is it so written excepting by St. John? If any where else, antecedent to Cyprian's day, another unknown Chriftian is fubtracted from Mr. Lindfey's early Unitarians. Cyprian himfelf is within this gentleman's comprehenfive affertion, and fhall prefently appear more particularly to exculpate himfelf from the charge.

But a farther vindication of this paffage has been rendered unneceffary. The teftimonies by which it is fuftained have been collected, and fo ftated to the world by the Reverend Mr. Jofeph Fifher of Drax, in Yorkfhire, that I believe few who have perufed his valuable work remain in doubt concerning it. To have engaged in the caufe of truth has been happily productive of the moft agreeable confequences to me. Her enemies have done me the honour to confider me as her friend, and I have been highly favoured with Job's bleffing. Mine adverfary has indeed written a book, and fuch a book——but calumny alone has not been my portion, the friends of truth have alfo done me the fame honour, and I have been incidentally defended by an able combatant in her caufe. Let

It is not the teftimony which is borne by thefe three in heaven which comes within the contemplation of Cyprian, their unity alone is his fubject; but to this he could not pay exclufive attention, had he quoted the beginning of the verfe *verbatim*, for herein their atteftation is predicated of them. The Father, the Son or Word, and the Holy Ghoft, are the fubject of both propofitions: Meaning therefore only to authenticate the latter, in this alone the father has adhered to the language of the apoftle; but in this there is found a nominative cafe to the verb, which therefore precludes the neceffity of extracting accurately from the former in order to find one. But as this nominative cafe is compofed of two relative pronouns, their antecedents muft therefore be fet before the reader. Without bringing to view what was more than his fubject, he could not have quoted the commencement of the verfe. Chufing, therefore, with great judgement, to keep the reader's eye on the one object which he defires to fet before it, he ftates, in language that continued his own argument, the fubject of the affertion, and tells us that, *of the Father*, &c. it is written, thefe three are one.

Let the decifion of this queftion be what it may, it is beyond a doubt that Tertullian has teftified his own belief in the three perfons whom he has enumerated. That he believed alfo the one Godhead of this Trinity I now proceed to fhew.

In a Tract written againft the Gentiles, he fays, "We have learned that *Chrift* proceeded forth from God, and was begotten by procedure, and therefore that he is called the Son of God, and God, from the unity of fubftance †." Here the confubftantiality of the Son with the Father is afferted as exprefsly as in the Nicene creed, and our author exemplifies their identity of fubftance by the light of the fun, which fubfifts in every ray that it fheds forth; for they are extenfions of his fubftance ftretched out, but not feparated from him: fo he fays, "What goeth forth from God is God, and the Son of God, and both are one ‡," (I do not hefitate here to add) God. The word *one* is mafculine, and the context requires this for the fubftantive, by which its gender is determined. Taking up his own idea again, the father proceeds to call our Lord "a ray of God, which, darting down upon a certain virgin, and being in her womb fafhioned into flefh, was born a Man mixt with God *." And thefe two natures, divine and human, he defires us to keep diftinct, "becaufe it is manifeft that the divine nature

is

* Ifte igitur Dei radius, delapfus in virginem quandam & in utero ejus caro figurata nafcitur Homo Deo miftus. Apologeticus adverfus Gentes. cap. xxi.

† Hunc ex Deo prolatum didicimus, & prolatione generatum & idcirco Filium Dei, & Deum dictum ex unitate fubftantiæ. Apologeticus adverfus Gentes, cap. xxi.

‡ Sol erit in radio quia folis eft radius, nec feparatur fubftantia fed extenditur; quod de Deo profectum eft Deus eft, & Dei Filius & unus ambo. Ibidem.

is immortal, when it is also evident that it is the human which is mortal, and which is to be understood when *the apostle* declares him to have been dead; that is, inasmuch as he was flesh and Man, and the Son of man, and not as he was Spirit, and the Word, and the Son of God †." " For not in his divine, but in his human substance do we pronounce him to have been dead ‡." " And when you hear him exclaim in his sufferings, My God, my God, why hast thou forsaken me, this is the voice of the flesh and human soul, that is, of the Man; not of the Word, nor of the Spirit; that is, not of God §." " For the flesh is not God, but he who was born in the flesh is God. A double nature then we see, not confused, but united in one person, viz. God and the Man Jesus. But I speak of the Christ, and thus preserve the distinct functions of both substances. In him the Spirit performed his own operations; that is, wrought works and signs; and the flesh also in him sustained its natural sufferings ‖."

This early writer, speaking of the two first persons of the Trinity, declares that " they are not two Gods, but

† Quanquam cum duæ substantiæ censeantur in Christo Jesu divina & humana, constet autem immortalem esse divinam, cum mortalem quæ humana sit, apparet, quatenus eum mortuum dicat; id est quâ carnem & Hominem & Filium hominis, non quâ Spiritum & Sermonem & Dei Filium. Adversus Praxean lib. cap. xxix.

‡ Non enim ex divinâ sed ex humanâ substantiâ mortuum dicimus. Ejusd. lib. cap. xxx.

§ Sed hæc vox carnis & animæ, id est Hominis; non Sermonis nec Spiritûs, id est non Dei. Ibidem.

‖ Caro autem non Deus est; sed ille, qui in eâ natus est, Deus. Videmus duplicem statum non confusum sed conjunctum Deum & Hominem Jesum; de Christo autem disero. Et adeo salva est utriusque proprietas substantiæ, ut, & Spiritus res suas egerit in illo; i. e. virtutes & opera & signa: Et caro passiones suas functa est. Ejusd. lib. cap. xxvii.

but that as Father and Son they are two, not by separation or division of substance, but by disposition. The Son we pronounce to be undivided and unseparated from the Father *." But he takes a larger scope, and pronounces the very same thing concerning the inseparability of the three persons from each other: "For I do testify," says he, "that the Father, Son, and Holy Ghost are undivided one from another †." And far be it from us, he replies to Praxeas, that there should be any ground for your objection of two Gods or two Lords. "Two, indeed, as Father and Son, we define them to be, and, with the addition of the Holy Ghost, three. Two Gods, however, or two Lords, we never have named them with our mouths: not as if the Father were not God, and the Son God, and the Holy Ghost God, and each of them God ‡." For " I every where hold one substance in three cohering together §."

Having cited several texts of scripture, he desires his adversary particularly to advert to the 110th Psalm, (which our Lord also has applied to himself, and so ascer-

* Dii non duo, sed quâ Pater & Filius duo, non ex separatione substantiæ, sed ex dispositione, quum individuum & inseparatum Filium a Patre pronunciamus. Adversus Praxean, cap. xix.

† Inseparatos ab alterutro Patrem & Filium & Spiritum testor. Ejusd. lib. cap. ix.

‡ " Provocabo te" (inquit Praxeas) " ut hodie quoque ex auctoritate istarum scripturarum constanter duos Deos & duos Dominos prædices." (cui Tertullianus) Absit. Nos enim qui & tempora & causas scripturarum per Dei gratiam inspicimus, maxime paracleti non hominum discipuli, duos quidem definimus Patrem & Filium, & jam tres cum Spiritu Sancto ——Duos tamen Deos & duos Dominos nunquam ex ore proferimus, non quasi non & Pater Deus, & Filius Deus, & Spiritus Sanctus Deus, & Deus unusquisque. Ejusd. lib. cap. xiii.

§ Ceterùm ubique teneo unam substantiam in tribus cohærentibus. Ejusd. lib. cap. xii.

ascertained the propriety of Tertullian's application). For here he says, "The Holy Ghost speaks from the third person concerning the Father and the Son, The Lord said unto my Lord, &c. and these few, out of many passages," he proceeds, "may suffice; so manifestly, even in these few, is the distinction of the Trinity revealed. For it is here the Holy Ghost who speaks, the Father to whom the Holy Ghost speaks, and the Son of whom he speaks; and in like manner other things which are spoken now to the Father of the Son, now to the Son of the Father, now to the Holy Ghost, make an orderly disposition of each of the persons. If yet the number of the Trinity offend you, as not connected in simple Unity, I demand how a Being, simply one and singular, speaks plurally, Let US make man after OUR image, when he should have said, *I* will make man after *my* image, as being simply one and singular? But again, in the following instances, Behold Adam has become as one *us*, he deceives or sports when, being single, solitary, and singular, he speaks thus plurally. Now, whether did he speak to angels, as the Jews interpret, because they do not acknowledge the Son, or did he speak plurally to himself, because he was Father, Son, and Holy Ghost? Yea, for this reason he has delivered himself in the plural number, (let US, OUR, and to US) because that the Son was adherent to him, the second person, his Word; and the third person also, the Holy Ghost in the Word, with whom he made man, and to whom he made man like; *with the Son, who was, in a day then future, to put on man,* and with the Holy Ghost, who was thereafter to sanctify man, he spoke from the Unity of Trinity, as with assistants and cooperators *." The father

* Animadverte etiam Spiritum Sanctum loquentem ex tertiâ personâ de Patre & Filio, *Dixit Dominus Domino meo*—hæc pauca de multis—his ita-

father proceeds to bring more instances of the like nature as those produced, and at length argues that, as there is a God who has said, Let there be light, &c. and a God who made two great lights, you have evidently two, one speaking and the other making. "But how you ought to accept the terms one and another by the name of person, not of substance, to distinction, not to division, I have already professed †;" for, as I stated

que paucis tam manifeste distinctio Trinitatis exponitur. Est enim ipse qui pronunciat Spiritus, & Pater ad quem pronuntiat, & Filius de quo pronuntiat. Sic & caetera quæ nunc ad Patrem de Filio, vel ad Filium, nunc ad Filium de Patre, vel ad Patrem, nunc ad Spiritum pronuntiantur, unamquamque personam in suâ proprietate constituunt.

Si te adhuc numerus scandalizat Trinitatis quasi non connexæ in Unitate simplici, interrogo quomodo unicus & singularis pluraliter loquitur, " *Faciamus* hominem ad imaginem & similitudinem *nostram*," cum debuerit dixisse, " *Faciam* hominem ad imaginem & similitudinem *meam*," utpote unicus & singularis? sed & in sequentibus; " Ecce Adam factus est tanquam unus ex *nobis*," fallit aut ludit ut, cum unus, & solus, & singularis esset, numerosè loqueretur. Aut nunquid angelis loquebatur ut Judæi interpretantur, quia nec ipsi Filium agnoscunt, an quia ipse erat Pater, Filius, Spiritus, ideo pluralem se præstans, pluraliter sibi loquebatur? Immò, quia jam adhærebat illi Filius secunda persona, Sermo ipsius; & tertia, Spiritus in Sermone, ideò pluraliter pronuntiavit, *faciamus*, & *nostram*, & *nobis*. Cum quibus enim faciebat hominem, & quibus faciebat similem, Filio quidem qui erat induiturus hominem, Spiritû verò qui erat sanctificaturus hominem, quasi cum ministris & arbitris, ex Unitate Trinitatis loquebatur. Tertull. adv. Praxean, cap. xi. and xii.

Irenæus tells us the very same thing: " Man," he says, " was formed in the likeness of God, and moulded by his hands; that is, by the Son and Holy Ghost, to whom also he said, Let *us* make man, &c. Homo— per manus ejus plasmatus est, hoc est, per Filium & Spiritum, quibus & dixit, Faciamus, &c.—And again, he declares of the Son that he is the same who, in the beginning, formed Adam; with whom the Father spoke, saying, Let *us* make man after *our* image; and who, in the last times, manifested himself to men." Plasmavit Adam, idem cum quo & loquebatur Pater, Faciamus, &c. in novissimis temporibus se ipsum manifestans hominibus. Præfat. ad lib. iv. & lib. iv. cap. xxxvii. Irenæi.

† Habes duos, alium dicentem ut fiat, alium facientem. Alium autem quomodo accipere debeas, jam professus sum, personæ non substantiæ nomine, ad distinctionem, non ad divisionem. Ibidem, cap. xii.

stated before, "I every where hold but one substance in three cohering together."

In his answer to Praxeas he makes the following profession of his faith: "We believe in one God, but under this dispensation, that this one God has a Son, his Word, who came forth from him, by whom all things were made, and without whom nothing was made. We believe that he was sent by the Father to a virgin, and was born of her, Man and God, the Son of man and the Son of God, and denominated Jesus Christ; that he suffered, and was dead and buried, according to the scriptures; that he was raised again by the Father, and reassumed into heaven; that he sitteth at the right hand of the Father, whence he shall come to judge the quick and the dead; that, according to his promise, he sent forth from the Father, the Holy Ghost, the Comforter, the Sanctifier of the faith of those who believe in the Father, Son, and Holy Ghost [*]." But the tenet of Praxeas, to which the Father has opposed this creed, was, that there is but one person of the Father, Son, and Holy Ghost, "as if," says Tertullian, "while all are of one, that is, by unity of substance, one may not be all in the same manner, and the dispensation of God be nevertheless pre-

---

[*] Unicum quidem Deum credimus; sub hâc tamen dispensatione, quam οἰκονομίαν dicimus ut unici Dei sit & Filius Sermo ipsius, qui ex ipso processerat, per quem omnia facta sunt, & sine quo factum est nihil. Hunc missum â Patre in virginem, & ex eâ natum, Hominem & Deum, Filium hominis & Filium Dei, & cognominatum Jesum Christum. Hunc passum, hunc mortuum & sepultum secundum scripturas, resuscitatum a Patre, & in cœlos resumptum federe at dexteram Patris, venturum judicare vivos & mortuos. Qui exinde miserit secundum promissionem suam a Patre Spiritum Sanctum Paracletum, Sanctificatorem fidei eorum qui credunt in Patrem & Filium & Spiritum Sanctum. Tertull. adv. Praxean, liber, cap. ii.

preserved, which difpofes this Unity into Trinity, arranging the Father, and the Son, and the Holy Ghoft into three; three, however, not in dignity, but degree; not in fubftance, but in form; not in power, but in *fpecies*; but they are of one fubftance, and one dignity, and one power †." "How they fall into number without feparation," he tells us is the fubject of the treatife he is juft here entering upon: in this, however, I do not mean to purfue his fteps. I decline all enquiry into the modus. He declares that "there is one God, the Father, and befides him there is none other, which he who infers denies not the Son, but another God, for the Son is not another (God) from the Father ‡." But "the names of the Father are, the Omnipotent God; the Moft Higheft; the Lord of Virtues; the King of Ifrael; I am; for fo the fcriptures teach: but we aver that thefe names appertain alfo to the Son. All things, he fays himfelf, that the Father hath are mine: why therefore not his names? When you accordingly read thefe denominations, confider if the Son be not demonftrated by them to be, in his own right, God omnipotent; for he is the WORD of the omnipotent God, and hath received power over all

† Unicum Deum non aliâs putat credendum, quam fi ipfum eundemque & Patrem & Filium & Spiritum Sanctum dicat: quafi non fic quoque unus fit omnia, dum ex uno omnia per fubftantiæ fcilicet Unitatem; & nihilominus cuftodiatur οἰκονομίας facramentum, quæ Unitatem in Trinitatem difponit, tres dirigens Patrem & Filium & Spiritum Sanctum. Tres autem non ftatu, fed gradu; nec fubftantiâ, fed formâ; nec poteftate, fed fpecie; unius autem fubftantiæ, & unius ftatûs, & unius poteftatis; quia unus Deus ex quo & gradus ifti & formæ & fpecies, in nomine Patris & Filii & Spiritûs Sancti deputantur. Quommodo numerum fine divifione patiuntur procedentes retractatus demonftrabunt. Tertull. adv. Praxean, liber, cap. ii.

‡ Unus Deus Pater, & abfque eo alius non eft. Quod ipfe inferens non Filium negat, fed alium Deum. Cæterum alius a Patre Filius non eft. Ejufd. lib. cap. xviii.

all things. He is the Moſt Higheſt, for he is exalted at the right hand of God*." And in the end he ſhews that Chriſt is, I AM, from the 8th verſe of the 1ſt chapter of the Revelation, which he applies to the Son, declaring him to be the beginning and the ending, which is, and which was, and which is to come, the Almighty. Is this language applicable to the Son, and ſhall Mr. Lindſey hope to ſubvert his omnipotence, to abridge his eternity? Does this gentleman conceive that, when with deſperate hand he has expunged the 11th verſe from this chapter, he has obliterated every teſtimony to the ſame effect? I am only ſolicitous to arreſt his temerity in the inſtance, for the paſſage which he would retrench from the ſacred pages is repeated ſo frequently, that it is by no means neceſſary to the proof of our Redeemer's Godhead. The 18th verſe of the ſame chapter aſcertains the Being whom the 17th declares to be "the firſt and the laſt," and the concluſion of the 8th verſe of the 2d chapter appropriates the commencement of it to the ſame eternal Son. But theſe very circumſtances, cries Mr. Lindſey, which appropriate, limit the ſenſe of firſt and laſt, and ſhew that they cannot mean, when applied to Chriſt, what they mean when ſpoken by God in the Old Teſtament, by the mouth of Iſaiah xlvi. 6. But why not? becauſe, forſooth, he "was dead and is alive." "He liveth and was dead?" But is it not added by our Lord himſelf, "Behold I am alive for evermore. Amen?" Theſe words are ſuppreſſed in Mr.

---

* Nomen Patris: Deus Omnipotens; Altiſſimus; Dominus Virtutum; Rex Iſraelis; qui eſt; quatenus ita ſcriptura docent. Hæc dicimus & in Filium competiſſe. Omnia, inquit, Patris, mea ſunt. Cur non & nomina? Cum ergo legis Dominum omnipotentem, &c. vide ne per hæc Filius etiam demonſtratur ſuo jure Deus omnipotens, quâ Sermo Dei omnipotentis, quâque omnem accepit poteſtatem. Altiſſimus, quâ dextrâ Dei exaltatus, &c. Tertull. adv. Praxean, cap. xvii.

Mr. Lindfey's quotation; but they are not neceflary to the proof, however contributary to the overthrow of mifreprefentation. That Chrift is the firft and the laft, can bear no other fenfe than that in which it is ufually received; and the cutting off of that body which he took and yielded up to death as a facrifice and propitiation for the fins of the whole world, gave no interruption to that life which was before all worlds, and which can never come to a determination. But if Mr. Lindfey refufe the authority of Tertullian for the eftablifhment of the 11th verfe, wherein Chrift declares that, " I am alpha and omega," let him take what may perhaps have greater weight with him, the authority of Marcus and Colarbafus, two famous hereticks of the fecond century, who founded a fyftem upon this verfe alone, and declared that our Saviour uttered it for the fingular purpofe of fhewing the myftical powers of the letters of the Greek alphabet.

Tertullian, and indeed all the fathers, rely very much upon the 1ft verfe of St. John's gofpel, in which the evangelift declares that " the Word was God." Mr. Lindfey fhews evident marks of the greateft diftrefs at this direct affertion; but not being able to elude the force of it, he contends only with our tranflation, and defires that *the Wifdom* may be fubftituted for *the Word*. I am very indifferent what he fubftitutes, fo long as the original is unchanged, and while I have his own conceffion that " the λόγ⊙· is not a being inferior to God." For his manner of reafoning on this head, fee, who will, this gentleman's Sequel to his late Apology. I do not fufficiently comprehend his meaning to give it in my own language; and to give it in his, would be to trefpafs too largely on my reader's patience.

As

As some argument that the word λόγ⊙ does not mean exactly the same thing as Wisdom, it should be observed that the early Latin fathers have uniformly translated it by sermo, or verbum, which can bear no other English term than *the Word*.

But, to leave this as it may be, let us see how Mr. Lindsey's interpretation of John i. 1, &c. contributes to his position, that Jesus Christ did not pre-exist.

In the beginning was Wisdom, and Wisdom was with God, and Wisdom was God. Now I desire to know if this "Wisdom of God, which was God," resided in the Man Jesus? whether that Being, who consisted of the Man Jesus and this Wisdom of God, had not some part pre-existent to his birth of a virgin? whether he did not consist of a mortal and commenced nature, and a nature pre-existing even from all eternity? Vary therefore the translation of the word λόγ⊙ as you may, 'till the description and attributes of it are as much varied, they remain an unabated testimony of the Godhead of our Redeemer. Quæcunque ergo substantia Sermonis fuit, illam dico personam & illi nomen Filii vendico. Tertull. adv. Praxean, cap. vii.

But it is with peculiarly ill-fortune that Mr. Lindsey has chosen to substitute the term *Wisdom* for *the Word*; for, here making an appeal from revelation (by which alone we learn the latter) to his own misunderstood judicature of reason, she readily enters into the question, and at once pronounces, that if God be eternal, so is his Wisdom; that if the Son of God be compounded of man and the Wisdom of God, he must be eternal also, and coeternal with the Father, whose

Wifdom he is. Did the exiftence of God precede the Wifdom of God? was there a day in which God was not wife? It were blafphemy, as well as abfurdity, to anfwer in the affirmative. But if the Son then be the Wifdom of the Father, there is no difficulty in conceiving the Son not preceded by the Father; and thus the coeternity of the Son with the Father is folved and rendered conceivable, nay almoft intuitively entered into by the leaft cultivated underftanding.

As he begun, fo this gentleman goes on; for, not contented to have converted *the Word* into *the Wifdom*, in the Englifh tranflation, through a zeal for his own opinion, fomewhat too fanguine, he perfuades himfelf that, even in the original, it ftood fo; or, at the leaft, tranflates himfelf back again into Greek, and for λόγος would fubftitute σοφία. This, it is true, he does not directly profefs to do; but it is the beft apology I can make for the remainder of his paraphrafe, in which, inftead of *him*, he writes, and emphatically marks the relative *her*, which it is impoffible he could have done but with a view to a feminine antecedent. For "all things," he fays, "were made by *her*, and without *her* was not any thing made. In *her* was life." One might now have hoped an end to the perverfions of one paffage; but Mr. Lindfey's fertile imagination, moving on with bolder career, has fupplied a nobler metamorphofis than any which adorns the pages of Ovid. That antient poet had degraded the male fex, and converted Tirefias into a woman, but it remained to our modern theologift to reverfe the indignity; and accordingly, having firft pronounced Wifdom a female, we find him, in his parody of the 14th verfe, as peremptorily pronouncing that, *fhe* was made *man*;

and

and this too he has done in marked characters, left it should escape the most cursory observation *.

Mine,

* Mr. Lindsey has annexed to his last chapter "a list of passages quoted in his work, in which our English version is rectified." Among the passages which he has *rectified*, stands that which is taken notice of above. From this single specimen, the nature and method of the process might be collected; but I shall not suffer this matter to rest here, but produce some farther instances of his abilities. And when I have presented these to my reader, shall refer it to him to judge whether Mr. Lindsey and his Coadjutor have not rectified rather too highly; and whether, instead of the spirit which they profess to draw from the scriptures, they have not raised a downright alkohol, and left the scripture itself as a meer vapid residuum, incapable of yielding any nutriment to vulgar operators, and consequently improper to be set before the ordinary world. To drop this idle sport of words, I shall now produce the examples themselves. The first of the following columns contains the text as translated in our English version; the second, Mr. Lindsey's rectified translation of the same.

Over the former Mr. Lindsey has inscribed:

Instead of,

Elias was a man subject to like passions as we are, James v. 17.

Over the latter:

Read,

Elias was a man of like nature to us.

The Greek word in the original is ὁμοιοπαθὴς ἡμῖν. The terms of which this is compounded I need not set before the Greek reader, and the meer English one can receive no benefit from having them stated. Suffice it then to say, that it is impossible to turn this word into literal English, otherwise than as our version has done it.

Instead of,

Before Abraham was, I am, John viii. 58.

Read,

Before Abraham was, I am *he; that is, the Christ, God's anointed prophet.*

Supposing, in the first place, that Mr. Lindsey were right in his translation, and that *he* ought to have been added; upon what authority does he supply this copious antecedent for his supplemental relative? This is too much to admit of. First making new scripture, and then inferences from it, which could not follow, even had the word *he* been genuine. But the fact is, that there is no such pronoun in the Greek. And had such a relative been written, it must have referred to Abraham, which would have made our Lord speak absolute nonsense. Why then must it be understood? The same nonsense results. From this our version stands exempted; from this our blessed Saviour stands exempted; but Mr. Lindsey is justly chargeable with it. See Scriptural Confutation, p. 66.

Instead

Mine, however, it should have escaped; at least it should have escaped my criticism, and been passed by in

Instead of,	*Read,*
But, *unto* the Son, he saith, *Thy throne, O God,* is for ever and ever, Hebrews i. 8.	But, *concerning* the Son, he saith, *God is thy throne* for ever and ever.

The first change made here by Mr. Lindsey is of the word *unto,* for which he would substitute *concerning.* This, though in some measure introductory of the subsequent alteration, is not of so high importance. Πρὸς τὸν υἱον is the Greek, which is literally turned in our version; and the meer consideration that an address to a second person (for even Mr. Lindsey acknowledges the authenticity of *thy* and *thou*) follows immediately, might obtain some allowance for the preference given to the most obvious meaning. " To *which* of the angels said he," &c. appears in the 13th verse. Πρὸς τίνα is the Greek: and this, though of the same construction, remains undisputed. The margin of our Bible also turns πρός τὰς ἀγγέλους *unto* the angels, verse 7, and so takes away the authority of that text from Mr. Lindsey. Indeed he could have derived but little from it, for it is followed by an assertion concerning third, not second persons. But the more material change introduced by Mr. Lindsey occurs in the latter part of the verse, where, instead of suffering an address to our Lord by the appellation of God, he makes God the subject nominative of the whole assertion, and declares him to be a throne. That God and the Lamb possess one throne, we are told in the Revelation xxii. 3, 4; (see Script. Confut. p. 171.) and that Christ sits at the right hand of God, is an assertion made in almost every page of the New Testament. But, in support of his construction, Mr. Lindsey refers to 2 Samuel vii. 13, 16, 1 Chronicles xvii. 12, 14, Psalm lxxix. 4. I desire no stronger authority for our received construction than these very passages afford, and earnestly request that they may be turned to. I should quote them, but that they are in all hands, and that the fear of prolixity restrains me. To say that God is a throne, is a bold figure, and, unless authorized, cannot be admitted. " But it is authorized," says the Unitarian, " and ὁ Θεὸς in this very passage is the nominative case." I grant that, had I a preceding nominative case to express, these are the terms I must necessarily use; but if this is the vocative case also, and the usual vocative of the Psalmist in the Septuagint version, which is here quoted by St. Paul, I apprehend it will be some argument that, in the present instance, it is also written in the vocative case. But the Grammarian tells us that the article prefixed to one, and omitted before another nominative case, when the two are united by a substantive verb, determines the subject and predicate in the proposition; for that before which it is omitted is predicated of the other: so now let us admit ὁ Θεὸς the subject nominative, and

in merited contempt, were it not neceſſary to ſet before my reader this gentleman's newly adopted ſtile of interpretation,

and ὁ θρόνος is not a regular predicate. The very verſe of which this paſſage makes a part, affords an example to this rule, *The ſceptre* of thy kingdom is *a ſceptre* of righteouſneſs. The word ῥάβδος has the article prefixed to it where it is the ſubject, but it is omitted before the very ſame word when it comes after the verb, and is made the predicate in the propoſition.

Eternity or eternal exiſtence is the predicate in the paſſage before us, and is hereby aſcribed to the throne of God, which is evidently a ſubject term. But there appears in the ſentence, we are told, another term, carrying ſimilar marks of being the ſubject. One of them muſt be diſmiſſed from this ſtation. With ὁ θρόνος nothing can be done if ὁ Θεός be retained; but if ὁ θρόνος be made the ſubject, it is eaſy to diſpoſe of ὁ Θεός, provided only I can ſhew it to be the uſual vocative caſe made uſe of by the Pſalmiſt.

"Save me, O GOD," is the prayer with which David commences the 69th Pſalm, and he proceeds to ſay, "O GOD, thou knoweſt my fooliſhneſs," verſe 5, but "let not thoſe that ſeek thee be confounded for my ſake, O GOD of Iſrael." The Greek is here:

Σῶσόν με, Ὁ ΘΕΟ'Σ.

Ὁ ΘΕΟ'Σ, σὺ ἔγνως τὴν ἀφροσύνην μᾶ.

Μὴ ἐντραπείησαν ἐπ' ἐμὲ οἱ ζητοῦντές σε, Ὁ ΘΕΟ'Σ τοῦ Ἰσραήλ.

See alſo Pſalm lxvii. 3, 5, and lxviii. 7, 9, 28, &c. &c. &c.

But what am I about? proving that ὁ Θεός is the vocative caſe? There is no truth ſo ſimple but theſe men with whom I have to deal, relying upon the lazy acquieſcence of their readers, will bring it into queſtion, nay, flatly deny it: But I will hunt their little fallacies thro' every winding ſophiſm; I will drag them to light, though they lurk in the darkneſs of falſehood. It has already been advanced by my learned Remarker that *non* is the Latin for *and*. I doubt not I ſhall ſoon be put to the proof, that *Deus* is in Latin a vocative caſe. See p. 169 above.

But has the Son a throne? and is the throne of the Son eternal? is it for ever and ever? Who then is that ſubordinate, finite, determinable Being which Mr. Lindſey aſſerts the Son to be? I have here his own conceſſion that εἰς τὸν αἰῶνα τοῦ αἰῶνος ſignifies eternal duration, even for ever and ever. It accordingly ſubverts his interpretation of Iſaiah ix. 6. Matth. xxiv. 3, and xxviii. 20. Let Mr. Lindſey therefore now ſtand, not

only

terpretation, assumed since his boasted connexion with Mr. Jebb; by whom, he declares, the greatest part of the only against himself, but against his own fraternity. He acknowledges here what he denies elsewhere, and herein he contradicts the rest of his tribe. I will leave them to reconcile their own differences. It is enough for me to mark them.

Instead of,
Who shall declare his generation? for he was cut off, &c. Isa. liii. 8.

Read,
Who shall declare his generation? *(that is, the wicked generation of men amongst whom he lived)* for he was cut off, &c.

Indeed but it is not, and the assertion is most reprehensible. St. Paul has understood the prophet in the ordinary sense of the words, and expressly determined his meaning in Heb. vii. 3, wherein the generation of our Lord is compared to that of Melchizedek, which no man could declare. See also the manner in which Irenæus accepted this passage, p. 103 above.

Instead of,
Thy holy *Child* Jesus, Acts iv. 30.

Read,
Thy holy *Servant* Jesus.

In Hosea xi. 1, the word which we here translate Child stands in two antient Greek versions preserved by Origen. It is also the original signification of the term παις. Why then seek for a sense in which it is less frequently used? The *Son* of God is the usual appellation of our Lord; *Child* is only of the same amount, and, at the time of translating the Bible, was more frequently used in that sense than it is at present.

Instead of,
And *because* I tell you the truth, ye believe me not, John viii. 45.

Read,
And *although* I tell you the truth, ye believe me not.

—Concerning Judas, which was guide to them that took Jesus; *for* he was numbered with us, and had obtained part of this ministry, Acts i. 16, 17.

—Concerning Judas, which was guide to them that took Jesus; *although* he was numbered with us, and had obtained part of this ministry.

The word which our translation has rendered *because* and *for* in the two quoted texts. is ὅτι, and this Mr. Lindsey asserts, but does not prove, sometimes signifies *although*; perhaps it does, but I do not remember an instance. and I am sure Mr. Lindsey has not brought one to view. The first of the above verses makes part of a reproof, in which our Saviour tells the Jews that they are of their father the devil, "who abode not in the truth, *because* there is no truth in him." "Why do ye not understand my speech? even *because* ye cannot hear my word." Now I desire to know

the sheets of his last publication have been revised. The public prints have lately been filled with accounts of a chemical procefs, by which a child has been formed in France. From the laboratory of Mr. Jebb, England can exhibit to the world as great a wonder. Therein I have little doubt it is, that this miraculous transformation has been effected " after a numerous train of experiments." How much does Britain owe to this emulous affertor of her glory!

The Holy Ghoft is declared by Tertullian to be " The third divine Being or Perfon in the Godhead; the third Name of Majefty; the Proclaimer of the Monarchy of one God; but alfo, if any will receive the words of his new prophecy, the Revealer of that difpenfation (whereby the Trinity is derived from this Unity). He is alfo termed " the Guide to (or Bringer down of) all truth which is in the Father, and in the Son, and in the Holy Ghoft, according to

the

know what is the neceffary fenfe of the paffage before us? Was the truth which our Lord revealed a motive for their belief, who were incapable of hearing his word, who were the children of him, in whom "there is no truth?" But let us fubftitute *although* throughout for *becaufe*, and Mr. Lindfey's criticifm will require no other anfwer. Ὅτι is the Greek for it in every inftance. That the devil abode not in the truth, *although* there was no truth in him; and that the Jews did not underftand our Lord, *although* they could not hear his word. are facts and reafons which Mr. Lindfey may affert and affign, & credat Judæus.

The fecond inftance in which Mr. Lindfey makes this arbitrary alteration commences with an affertion, that " *the Holy Ghoft, by the mouth of David, fpoke before* concerning Judas," &c. (as ftated); but this circumftance is withdrawn from fight: had it appeared, the abfurdity glares too ftrongly to be paffed by. The prophecy of David, referred to (Pfalm xli. 9.) could only have been fulfilled by one numbered with the difciples, and who had eaten bread together with our Lord, whom he betrayed.

The examples from the Old Teftament come under the fame predicament, but they do not belong here to my vindication, as the Greek in which ὅτι appears is itfelf only a tranflation.

the Chriſtian covenant *." "The Son," he ſays, "I deduce from no other ſource than the ſubſtance of the Father; the Holy Ghoſt from no other ſource than the Father by the Son †;" giving to the Holy Ghoſt the third rank, for "he is the third from the Father and the Son ‡." And "of theſe three coherent perſons," he declares, "that, as our Lord has ſaid, I and the Father are one, even ſo theſe three are one §." For "the WORD was always in the Father, as he faith, I am in the Father. The WORD was with God, and was never ſeparated from the Father, nor another *(God)* from the Father, becauſe I and the Father are one. This aſſertion is the guardian of the Unity, in which we declare the Son to be extended, or put forth by, but not ſeparated from the Father. For, as the Holy Ghoſt teacheth, God extended or put forth his WORD as a root puts forth the ſtem, as a fountain the river, as the ſun a ray; for theſe ſeveral ſpecies are the extenſions of the ſubſtances from which they proceed; nor ſhould I ſcruple to call any of them a ſon, for every commencement is a parent, and every thing that has its origin therein is a progeny; but much more the WORD of GOD, who has, even without a figure, received the name of THE SON. But as the ſtem is not ſundered from the root, nor the river from the fountain, nor the ray from the ſun, even ſo the Word

is

---

* Spiritum Sanctum, tertium Numen Divinitatis, & tertium Nomen Majeſtatis; unius Prædicatorem Monarchiæ, ſed & œconomiæ interpretatorem, ſi quis ſermonis novæ prophetiæ ejus admiſerit; & Deductorem omnis veritatis quæ eſt in Patre, & Filio, & Spiritu Sancto ſecundum Chriſtianum ſacramentum. Adverſus Praxean, cap. xxx.

† Filium non aliundè deduco, ſed de ſubſtantiâ Patris;—Spiritum non aliundè puto quam a Patre per Filium. Ejuſd. lib. cap. iv.

‡ Tertius enim eſt Spiritus a Deo & Filio. Ejuſd. lib. cap. viii.

§ Vide ſupra, p. 169.

is not divided from God. And therefore, according to the manner of this example, I profess that I call God and his Word, the Father and his Son, two. For as the root and stem are two things, but conjoined; as the fountain and river are specifically two things, but not divided; and as the sun and ray are to appearance two things, but cohering together; it is necessary that whatsoever proceeds shall be second to that from which it proceeds, but not that it shall be therefore separate. But where there is a second, there there are two; and where a third is, there there are three; but the Holy Ghost is a third from God and the Son, as the fruit from the stem is a third from the root, a branch from the river a third from the fountain, and a gleam from the ray a third from the sun. There is yet no alienation of the effluence made from the radical source. So the Trinity, running down from the Father by well-compacted and connected degrees, in no wise opposes or militates against the monarchy of God, while at the same time it supports the state of the dispensation, by which, out of the Unity, this Trinity is derived *." For so I am always warranted

---

* Sermo & in Patre semper, sicut dicit, *Ego in Patre*, Johan. xiv. 10. Et apud Deum semper, sicut scriptum est, *Et Sermo erat apud Deum*, Johan. i. 1. Et nunquam separatus a Patre, aut alius a Patre; quia, *Ego & Pater unum sumus*, John x. 30. Hæc erit *probola veritatis*, custos Unitatis, quâ prolatum, dicimus Filium â Patre, sed non separatum. Protulit enim Deus Sermonem, quemadmodum etiam paracletus docet, sicut radix fruticem, & fons fluvium, & sol radium. Nam & istæ species probolæ sunt earum substantiarum ex quibus prodeunt. Nec dubitaverim filium dicere & radicis, fruticem; & fontis, fluvium; & solis, radium; quia omnis origo Parens est; & omne, quod ex origine profertur, progenies est: multo magis Sermo Dei, qui etiam propriè nomen Filii accepit. Nec frutex tamen a radice, nec fluvius â fonte, nec radix a sole discernitur, sicut nec a Deo Sermo. Igitur secundum horum exemplorum formam, profiteor me duos dicere, Deum & Sermonem ejus, Patrem & Filium ipsius. Nam & radix & frutex duæ res sunt, sed conjunctæ. Et fons & flumen duæ species sunt, sed indivisa. Et sol & radius duæ formæ sunt.

ranted to translate the word οἰκονομία, as the author in whom it now occurs has himself given his own definition of it †.

It is a common subject of declamatory complaint among Unitarians, that the Jews and even the Gentiles are excluded from conformity with the Christian church, on account of the doctrine of the Trinity. The truths of Christianity, it was foretold, should be to the Jew a stumbling-block, and to the Greek foolishness. Had all, therefore, immediately conformed upon

---

sunt, sed cohærentes. Omne quod prodit ex aliquo, secundum sit ejus, necesse est, de quo prodit; non ideo tamen est separatum. Sucundus autem ubi est duo sunt. Et tertius ubi est, tres sunt. Tertius autem est Spiritus a Deo & Filio, sicut tertius a radice fructus ex frutice. Et tertius a fonte rivus ex flumine. Et tertius a sole apex ex radio. Nihil tamen a matrice alienatur, â quâ proprietates ducit. Ita Trinitas, per consertos & connexos gradus a Patre decurrens, & monarchiæ nihil obstrepit & οἰκονομίας statum protegit. Tertullian. adverf. Praxean, lib. cap. viii.

I have selected this passage, not for the sake of our author's illustration, as rendering the subject in the least degree more conceivable by our faculties, but because he has so very explicitly declared his belief in the consubstantiality of the three persons, and also attested that, " the Holy Ghost, proceeding from the Father and the Son," was a tenet in the beginning of the third century. The word *probola* in the first instance I have not translated; I chose rather to sink the absurdities of his adversary from whom he takes up the phrase. It means something of the same nature as the word emissio of the Gnostics, with which Irenæus has already been produced in contest. Such language frequently encumbers the style of the fathers, and renders them extremely difficult to turn into English. Add to this, that Tertullian was an African, and not equally skilled in the elegancies of the Latin tongue as his countryman Terence had been. There is nevertheless an air of stern dignity in what he writes, that engages the attention, and makes it for the most part not disagreeable to labour for his meaning. An infinite deal of good sense, joined to as much sanguine sincerity, seem to form the character of the man. To the latter we must ascribe his strange revolt and adherence to à sanctified plausible impostor.

† Vide supra, p. 135 and p. 212.

upon the promulgation of the gospel, universal assent would have argued to the reverse of what it is usually thought to support, and been an irrefragable evidence of falsehood. But if this doctrine were the ground of Jewish opposition, what withheld the concurrence of the Jew during the first three centuries, when "all the fathers and other Christian people were generally Unitarians?" Did the Jew alone find a Trinity among the Christians, of which they were themselves ignorant? Unquestionably they did, if Mr. Lindsey's position be true, and that by the Trinity alone the Jew is excluded. But that the Christians were also in the secret, Tertullian lets us know, and informs us that Mr. Lindsey is right in declaring the Trinity the grand point of difference between the followers of the law and of the gospel; for he tells us that "it is an article of the Jewish faith, so to believe in one God as not to reckon the Son to him, and after the Son the Holy Ghost; and what difference," he demands, "does there subsist between us excepting this? What is the office of the gospel? what the substance of the New Testament, which establisheth the law and the prophets until John; if not, that from thence these three, the Father, the Son, and the Holy Ghost, are to be believed to be one God ‡?"

But uniformity is so much the object of Mr. Lindsey's heart, that he cares not much in what doctrines men unite, provided only the Trinity and Godhead of

our

---

‡ Judaicæ fidei ista res, sic unum Deum credere ut Filium adnumerare ei nolis, *(Praxean alloquitur)*, et post Filium, Spiritum. Quid enim erit inter nos & illos, nisi differentia ista? Quod opus evangelii, quæ est substantia Novi Testamenti, statuens legem & prophetas usque ad Johannem, si non exinde Pater & Filius & Spiritus tres crediti unum Deum sistunt? Tertull. adv. Praxean, cap. xxxi.

our Saviour be excluded. He does not find the Jew of opinion that the New Teſtament is in all points the ſame as the Old; and ſo, rather than perſuade the Jew that there is a ſuperiority in the ſubſequent revelation, by which the law was ſet aſide, he thinks it better to compound matters, and fruſtrate the providence of God, "who took away the firſt that he might eſtabliſh the ſecond." And inſtead of inviting the Jew to embrace the unpolluted truth, would taint and corrupt her, or trick out a ſubſtitute, who with eaſy compliance ſhall conſult his taſte; and rather than not poſſeſs, bribe him by a conformity with whatever he requires: but the Jew requires that the goſpel ſhall be the ſame as the law; and be it ſo, ſays Mr. Lindſey, rather than that the Jew and I ſhould differ. Since he refuſes to be a Chriſtian, why, I will go over to him and become a Jew myſelf.—In effect he has done ſo. But why this rage for uniformity? Is it conſiſtent with his deſertion of every Chriſtian ſociety yet formed? He abandons a church that ſubſiſts, for no other reaſon than that it contains within it that common bond of union, without which no ſociety can ſubſiſt; a government by laws agreed upon by its own members, or rather bye-laws made under and with due reference to the great incorporating charter, the goſpel: and having gone out from her, connects himſelf with all thoſe who have heretofore profeſſed enmity againſt her. He lays ſtrait ſiege, and ſummons the fortreſs, commanding us to pull down every barrier that now entrenches us to their excluſion, and to unite ourſelves with thoſe who are without. How can that be? with whom are we to unite? Men who diſclaim all ſociety. For ſuch, I will maintain, are they who would take away all authority of legiſlature from a ſociety. Without it no ſociety can ſubſiſt. But our Lord has commanded us to aſſociate; in other terms, he has appointed a church.

Is

Is the church then of so very different a nature from every other association of mankind, that, in this alone, concurrence and compliance will spontaneously arise? Do men universally agree in their interpretation of the scriptures, that all shall associate under the gospel only? or do all who call themselves Christians promulgate the gospel to all? Experience shews the necessity of laws, even for the purpose of making the great law known. And were we to pause here, because that all who read deduced the same articles of belief from the gospel, yet even to this it is necessary that we act as a society, and hold up the scripture as the common point of concurrence to all who will associate.

But however desirable universal agreement may be, is the scripture interpreted alike by all? If not, the acceptance of the gospel alone is too vague, of too extensive comprehension to admit of this as the only point of association. Experience has instructed here again, and shewed us that some mode of interpretation must be agreed upon in order to form a society; for with the Protestant of the church of England it is not possible to unite the Papist: they must for ever differ. Is the Christian church therefore dissolved? No; nor is it possible that, if all agreed in doctrine, all could form one church. To form a church is nevertheless the duty of all who look up to Christ as their head; but when Christ commanded us to form a church, he did not prohibit the only means by which that church could, in the ordinary course of nature, subsist. He commanded us to associate, but did not forbid the means of maintaining our association. Unless there be then within ourselves an executive power to put his laws into execution, a legislature subordinate to his great statute, which is our charter, we must necessarily fall asunder; that is, we must, from a defect incident to our obedience, fall into a direct difobedience of the commandment which we make an effort to obey. Has Chrift himfelf fowed this feed of fin? I cannot believe it, and therefore conclude that, when our Lord has teftified his will that we fhould become a fociety, he has alfo implied his defire that we fhould ufe the ordinary means of rendering a permanent obedience to his command, and maintaining that affociated ftate which he has appointed.

But far be it from me to fay that, becaufe it is our duty to affociate and to require conformity of all who defire to profefs themfelves members of our fociety; far be it from me, I fay, for this reafon, to require that men fhall enter into that fociety of which I am a member. To infift upon this is to violate the right of private judgement; and fo long as there is a diverfity of opinions among Chriftians, and focieties formed refpectively profeffing thefe diverfe tenets, let every man be free to chufe his mates: but to affociate is his duty, and that once performed, neceffity will oblige him to eftablifh rules for the prefervation of his fociety; to fix upon certain exclufive circumftances that fhall defcribe, nay, define his fociety, and without a conformity to which, no man can be faid to have enrolled himfelf a member. I fpeak upon a fuppofition that I addrefs myfelf only to Chriftians, for Chriftians only are under an impreffion of this duty of forming themfelves into a church. Such as difclaim the fcriptures, difclaim the commandments contained in them. But when I renounce the right of forcing men to affociate with me, I maintain the right of fo defcribing my own fociety, that the defcription fhall exclude all who do not come within it. I may reduce to writing that defcription; and before I admit to any emoluments altogether in my own difpofal, may require an atteftation

of

of conformity with the sentiments therein set down, and, upon compliance or refusal, may give or retain what it is altogether in my own power either to impart or withhold. This attestation given, assures me of a concurrence in sentiment with me, and induces my bounty; refused, it only leaves the party where he had been before, and I, by withholding, exercise only my own undisputed right. I inflict no injury whatsoever.

But the society is desirous of promulgating its tenets for its enlargement, or, for the confirmation of its members, of having them enforced; for, carrying these purposes into execution, the utmost circumspection becomes requisite in the choice of teachers. And before a man be appointed to the office of an instructor, it is absolutely necessary that the society shall be apprized of his concurrence in sentiment with themselves. He may otherwise deceive them, and frustrate the end of his appointment. I desire to know if Mr. Lindsey would resign his rostrum to Dr. Randolph? Most certainly he would not; it would pervert the principles of his auditors. Would he depute a person, altogether unknown, to the office of instructing in his synagogue? Most certainly he would not; he might sow tares among Mr. Lindsey's good seed. Mr. Lindsey would know the principles of his deputy before he appointed him, and reject the candidate who refused to explain.

Of what greater crime does Mr. Lindsey accuse the church of England, which is but a religious association of the same individuals; who, in a civil association, form the state? As a church, opinions and doctrines belong to them; as a state, they are possessed of property and power: as a church, they seek to promulgate

gate and fix their own tenets; as a state, they annex those emoluments which are absolutely in their disposal to the promulgation of those tenets. But the society is too great to admit of an universal personal knowledge of every individual who is willing to assume the function of an instructor; and therefore, for the purpose of introducing him to the acquaintance of those who have the power of appointing him, he is required to give an attestation of his principles, and to certify his concurrence with the society from whom he seeks an appointment, together with the emoluments annexed to a due discharge of the office desired. Herein no greater authority is exerted than Mr. Lindsey himself would exert even in his private capacity. The means of coming at a knowledge of the person to be entrusted, it is true, are different; but the reason is, that the same could not answer in both cases.

The establishment of a church is the legal annexation of certain emoluments to the clerical function in that church exclusively. But to exclude from these appropriated advantages is not to oppress. The description to which they are annexed is very definitive. If men will have them, let them come within the description; but if, for the sake of those emoluments, any man shall set his hand to an assurance that he concurs, at his own peril be the deed. If, having, for such a sordid freight, made shipwreck of a good conscience, he drag about a wretched existence, let him not charge his miseries to those who required to know whom they were about to trust. They only have a right to complain who have been betrayed by an attested falsehood; and as the case actually stands, matters should be reversed. The nation has been defrauded by a number of men who have, under false pretences, obtained that livelihood which was by law appropriated

to

to the maintenance of such as promoted doctrines which they now impugn. The grievance is not theirs but the nation's; and parliament, instead of receiving an humble petition to quiet their consciences, should appear at the Feathers before them as suitors for the redress of grievances, and restoration of all those temporalities which they hold in prejudice of honester men. Had subscription been rendered a requisite after possession had been given without it, and had a refusal to subscribe been followed by the resumption of what had been conferred without such conditions, rights vested were then disturbed, and ex post facto terms were justly complained of as a severe imposition; but whoever has subscribed that he believes what he has had opportunity of enquiring into, and yet neglected, and in his heart knows that he does not believe, deserves not only to incur a forfeiture of such advantages as his fraud had procured for him, but literally merits an additional punishment. The infliction here would not be oppression. The conditions were open to his previous consideration, and upon that faith which he has violated, he has obtained advantages. Shall he profit by his wrong? shall fraud be admitted as a plea for indulgence? Let them quiet, let them satisfy their own consciences, let them relinquish the emoluments of falsehood and be at ease. Mr. Lindsey and Mr. Jebb have shewn them the means of shaking off the burden, and Mr. Jebb declares that he is restored to that serenity of mind, to which he had been long a stranger. I sincerely rejoice that he is so, but it was hardly kind in Mr. Jebb to give into my hands an argument so very powerful against his former associates. I urge it, again and again, that Mr. Jebb has unburdened his conscience and is happy. And the confutation of this argument I expect to receive from those to whom I direct it at Carlisle, Cleveland, Black-Nottly, and the Feathers.

To the honest dissenter, who has never subscribed, I do not direct it; with him I hold no quarrel, but, on the contrary, wish from my heart that our legislature would extend a toleration as large as would be consistent with the liberal spirit of our church. Let no legal provision, however, be made for him; keep that exclusively our own; even the dissenter will find his advantage in it. To constitute a legal claim favours of establishment.

Let it be observed that, in all I have said upon this subject now, I have held in my own mind a distinction which should ever be preserved; for there are not two subjects of enquiry more distinct than the establishment of a church, and the verity of the religion to be established. To the former only I have confined myself in this digression; the latter is the main subject of the work; and it is with great delight and gratitude that I see the providence of God, whilst he has led us to establish a church, with his own right hand plant the truth within it. To guard and cultivate this is the main duty of our existence here. It is the tree of life, whereof we may very safely pronounce that they have not gathered, who, by falsehood, obtain an entrance into the enclosure. At the same time I cannot say that there subsists a similar reason for their exclusion from tasting the fruit thereof, as occasioned a prohibition to our common progenitor. It does not in the least appear that they have ever tasted of the fruit of the tree of knowledge.

But, cry these men, it is not the truth which is professed in the church of England, God is therein believed to be incomprehensible and his nature inscrutable; whereas the scriptures contain no such difficult doctrine, all things are there laid plain and level to the under-

understanding, and such as no man can dissent from. If so, then I ask how it has happened that Lord Bolingbroke could not accede to them? It was not our establishment that excluded him, it was upon an examination of the inspired word itself that he dissented: he found a Trinity revealed, and therefore rejected revelation. Is not this their own process? Deism was his creed, and it is theirs. But it is our articles that exclude the Mahometan and the Jew, and not the unpolluted gospel. What! did the Mufti ever peruse our articles? what Jew Rabbi has taken them under his consideration? They may indeed have looked into the sacred word itself. Some among them probably have done so. They have there found a Trinity revealed, and therefore rejected revelation. A Trinity then they acknowledge to be the exclusion of the Jew and of the Greek. If therefore the Trinity be that ground of predicted derision to the one, and that peculiar article of the Christian profession over which the other stumbles, it is allowed by these its adversaries to be " the Wisdom of God, and the power of God unto salvation." I speak upon a supposition that they do not dispute the scripture premises in the instance, for such are the terms in which St. Paul proceeds to describe the grand obstacle to Jewish and Heathen conversion. Is the Trinity that obstacle? To the Trinity then, I do assert, it is that the residue of the apostle's assertion is applicable. See Rom. i. 16. 1 Cor. i. 18, 23, 24.

But Christianity is not of that comprehensive nature of which Unitarians want religion to be. The truth therefore is, that they want another religion which is not Christianity; and since the Jew, the Turk, and the Heathen Infidel cannot accede to the religion of the gospel, they are determined to reject such inflexible doctrines, and fabricate a religion of a more complying temper. To Christianity, as it stands founded, they see that Mahomet will not come; they see that it is in vain to cry, "Come ye, and let us go up to the mountain of the Lord," Isaiah ii. 3. They would therefore reverse the antient proverb, and oblige the mountain to come to Mahomet.

Nor is the name of Mahomet idly introduced, nor is it without a proof that the Unitarian has expresly ranked himself under his bloody crescent. Has "God raised your Mahomet to defend the faith with *the sword*, as a scourge on the *idolizing* Christians?" Yes, and that too " in conjunction with the Unitarian brethren, who have in all ages been exercised with their pens to defend the faith of one supreme God without personalities." Such is the language of Unitarians themselves. They bring down the sword of Mahomet upon the worshippers of the Son and Holy Ghost, I might indeed add of the Father also, for "whosoever denieth the Son, the same hath not the Father," 1 John ii. 23. And in their proposal of an alliance with all good Mussulmans to this great end, they assert that they do it " for the vindication of your law-maker's glory." And as a motive to the east to wage this holy war, and no doubt make reprisals upon this western world for the crusades of former days, they declare an intention "to lay down in what articles *we, the Unitarian Christians* (of all others) do solely concur with *you Mahometans*, to which we draw nigher in these important points than all other Protestant or Papal Christians. With *our* additional arguments to *yours*; to prove that both *we* and *you* have unavoidable grounds from scripture and reason to dissent from *other Christians* in such verities." They pronounce themselves " *your fellow-champions* for these truths,"

truths," and acknowledge Mahomet, for whose glory they are so very zealous, to have been " a preacher of the gospel." It is true this language has not been used by any existing Unitarian, but Mr. Lindsey has trumpeted forth the panegyrick of those who did use it, which is in a manner acceding to and subscribing it himself.

The reader's curiosity is probably raised at assertions so very extraordinary, at an acknowledgement of the prophet of the Mussulman so very explicit. When satisfied, surprize will succeed. The extracts given are drawn from an address actually presented, A. D. 1682, by the Unitarians " to his illustrious excellency *Ameth Ben Ameth*, embassador of the mighty Emperor of Fez and Morocco to Charles II, King of Great Britain *." Mr. Firmin, one of Mr. Lindsey's great authorities, was then living, and a leading man among this sect. Fearful lest the whole Christian church should *paganize*, he was desirous of constituting Unitarian assemblies for divine worship, distinct from the assemblies of any other denomination of Christians †. The temper

---

* Mr. Leslie, formerly chancellor of the cathedral of Connor in Ireland, in his " Socinian Controversie discussed, in six dialogues, &c." has preserved and transmitted this singular testimony of Unitarian Mahometanism entire. To him, therefore, I refer the reader for further information. And to such as are desirous of examining the state of the present controversy in the last century, I earnestly recommend the perusal of this work. Mr. Leslie's masterly pen had overturned, and for a season kept down the pernicious doctrines which again raise up their heads. He so effectually subverted them, that his own work ceased to be consulted. Like a skilful physician he restored the constitution, so as to have rendered his medicine no longer necessary; and thus a work has fallen into oblivion, merely because of its excellence. The Complaint has however now returned, and should again make us have recourse to the means of a second recovery.

† See Apology, p. 197.

of such assemblies may be very well understood from this specimen of the doctrines embraced by *the fraternity*, and we may fairly conclude that they were not designed to have been held distinct from the assemblies of the followers of Mahomet. To these, therefore, it is that Mr. Lindsey throws open the gates of the church, but against us who receive the gospel without the commentary of the Alcoran, he would shut his mosque; and, as a stronger security for our exclusion, give us perhaps to understand that "God has raised up Mahomet to defend the faith *with the sword*, as a scourge on idolizing Christians."

I have throughout, because I think meer words but a trifling ground of difference, admitted Mr. Lindsey and his sect to call themselves Unitarians. But as it seems to throw a charge of polytheism upon all who differ from them, I now deny their exclusive right to this denomination: we also are Unitarians who worship the Father, the Son, and the Holy Ghost in the unity of the one Godhead. We believe "the Father and the Son to be God, and both to be one;" we believe " the Holy Ghost to be God;" and though proceeding not separated, Spirit of Spirit, God of God, a third in degree numerically, but not in dignity ‡. I have professed already that the Father is the only one God*, and now declare that " I profess Christ to be the only God, according to the apostle's assertion; that of the Jews, as concerning the flesh, Christ came, WHO IS OVER ALL GOD BLESSED FOR EVER †."

But

‡ De Spiritu Spiritus, & de Deo Deus, modulo alternum numerum gradu non statu fecit, & a matrice non recessit, sed excessit. Tertull. Apologet. cap. xxi. Vide supra, p. 206 and 208.

* Vide supra, p. 211, & propè passim.

† Solum autem Christum potero Deum dicere, sicut idem apostolus, ex
quibus

[237]

But this is not all, for I do not mean to reſt contented with a joint poſſeſſion of this title, I demand the entire reſignation of it to us excluſively. Nothing leſs than the abſolute renunciation will ſatify me. Shall they who concur with the Jew, " who crucified the Lord of glory," and with the Muſſulman, to whom the name of our Redeemer is an abomination, make pretenſions to the title of Chriſtians? ſhall they pretend that they worſhip the Father, and are therefore Unitarians? Our Lord himſelf ſhall put them down, who ſays, " He that hateth me, hateth my Father alſo," John xv. 23.

I have drawn from Tertullian ſo ample a profeſſion of his faith in the one Godhead of the Father, Son, and

quibus Chriſtus inquit, Deus ſuper omnia benedictus in ævum omne. Tertull. adv. Praxean, cap. xiii.

Refer this paſſage to p. 31, wherein the authorities upon which our tranſlation of Romans ix. 5, is ſupported, are ſtated. In p. 109 there is a quotation of this verſe with the context of Origen: this alſo carry back, together with the following from Euſebius.—In the year 303, a city of the Chriſtians in Phrygia was deſtroyed under Dioclefian. The Soldiers ſurrounded it, and caſting in fire, conſumed the town and " burned all the inhabitants, with their children and wives, while they were calling upon Chriſt the God over all." Κατέφλεξαν αὐτὰς, ἅμα νηπίοις κỳ γυναιξὶ, τὸν ἐπὶ πάντων Θεὸν Χριςὸν ἐπιβοωμένας. Euſebii Eccl. Hiſt. lib. viii. cap. xi.—After the numerous authorities already produced in proof of the genuineneſs of this text, theſe may be thought unneceſſary; but I choſe to remind my reader that Origen has made uſe of it, and grounded the divinity of our Lord upon it, becauſe Mr. Lindſey has been pleaſed to aſſert that " Origen calls it raſhneſs (which, as Dr. Clarke obſerves, he would not have done if he had thought it to be the doctrine of St. Paul) to ſuppoſe Chriſt to be the God over all." Sequel to Apol. p. 204. Concerning Euſebius alſo, he has made a ſimilar aſſertion, but, as uſual, without referring to the author ſpoken of. The beſt anſwer I can give, is an example to the contrary, taken from each of the miſrepreſented fathers themſelves.—Refer this paſſage alſo to p. 176 and 137 above, where Chriſt is acknowledged by Clemens Alexandrinus, as here by Tertullian, to be " the only God."

and Holy Ghoſt, that no doubt can poſſibly remain now that this firſt of the Latin fathers was not an Unitarian. He has not only acknowledged the Unity of three perſons, but has actually combined them under the one denomination of *the Trinity :* the belief of Tertullian in the Trinity is therefore in no wiſe problematical. Clemens Alexandrinus has alſo been ſeen to have employed this term. From which circumſtances I would deduce, not the faith of theſe fathers only, but that farther, tho' leſs important concluſion, that the word *trinity* was in general uſe in their day. Theſe two writers, tho' younger men and ſurvivors of Theophilus of Antioch, were actually in part cotemporaries with that father. (See p. 125 above). To him it does not appear that either of them has ever adverted; from him therefore it ſeems highly improbable that either of them derived the term; and conſequently it is highly improbable that Theophilus, although he certainly be the earlieſt writer who has tranſmitted it to us, was himſelf the original inventor of the word *trinity* *. We find it uſed within a very brief ſpace of time by the three diſtant churches of Syria, Egypt, and Carthage; and let it even be admitted that it was then of recent invention, of thus much we are certain, that it was conſidered by the whole church as an apt and ſignificant expreſſion, for it was univerſally adopted

* The objection to this term *trinity*, that *it was invented to explain the doctrine*, is among the other logical accuracies of my Remarker. I ſhould have humbly thought that the doctrine was rather explanatory of the term. I deſire to know what doctrines are *explained* by the terms decad, myriad, ogdoad, biduum, and triduum? I will not accept of an explanation of theſe terms for my anſwer. A reduction to the conſtituent units which are combined, and the ſum of which is expreſſed by an aggregate noun, may give the meaning of that noun. No, ſays my Remarker, that very noun of number is invented to explain the conſtituent units.—On this principle alone I deſire of him to anſwer my queſtion. (See Remarks on Script. Conf. preface, p. 13.)

ed as soon as formed, and, by all the succeeding writers, whose works have descended to us, applied to a doctrine explicitly inculcated by all their predecessors.

As I have already showed that some passages from the fathers have been either misrepresented or falsely translated by Mr. Lindsey, I shall close this enquiry into the faith of Tertullian, by rescuing that venerable writer also from similar ill treatment. In the 87th page of the Sequel to his Apology, Mr. Lindsey has given the following translation of the passage, which appears in the note : " Again and again we avow—— that we worship God through Christ. Suppose him a man, *if you please*. It is by him and through him that we have been brought to know and worship God. As we may reply to the Jews that they have been taught to worship God by or through the man Moses *."

In

---

* Dicimus & palam dicimus, & *vobis torquentibus lacerati & cruenti vociferamur:* Deum colimus per Christum. Illum hominem putate, per eum & in eo se cognosci vult Deus & coli. Ut *autem* Judæis respondeamus & ipsi Deum per hominem Moysen colere didicerunt. Tertull. Apol. adv. Gent. cap. xxi.——Thus far Mr. Lindsey, but with the omission of those words which are printed here in italicks, and with a change of the meaning throughout, for I have compared him with three editions. Tertullian goes on thus: " Ut Græcis occurram Orpheus Pieriæ, Musæus Athenis, &c. initiationibus homines obligaverunt. Ut ad vos quoque, dominatores gentium, adspiciam, homo fuit Pompilius Numa, qui Romanos operosissimis superstitionibus oneravit. Licuerit & Christo commentari divinitatem rem propriam ; non qui rupices & adhuc feros homines multitudine tot numinum demerendorum attonitos efficiendo ad humanitatem temperaret quod Numa; sed qui jam expolitos & ipsâ urbanitate deceptos in agnitionem veritatis ocularet. Quærite ergo si vera est ista divinitas Christi.——The original of the whole chapter, which is here abridged, would be too long to transcribe. The brief extracts which I have made here, and in p. 206 above, sufficiently answer my purpose, which is to shew that Tertullian gives no countenance whatsoever to Mr. Lindsey's doctrine, but on the contrary opposes it with even an angry vehemence.

In the firſt place, it is obvious that the tranſlation is not juſt. It is not ſaid in the original, that " by him and through him we have been brought to know and worſhip God," (which is here aſcribed to the Father, that it may ſquare with what is afterwards ſaid of Moſes) but " that it is the will of God to be known and worſhipped through him and in him." In the ſecond place, it is obvious that Mr. Lindſey was aware of this inaccuracy, and that, contrary to cuſtom, he has conſulted the context which he has wilfully violated; for the little addition which he has made to the word "*ſuppoſe him a man*," is an internal proof that he rightly underſtood his author. In the very chapter whence this paſſage is taken, Tertullian has laid it down as a fundamental article of the Chriſtian faith, that the Chriſt is both God and man. *(See the aſſertion quoted above, p.* 206.) But of this, he ſays, the Jews are ignorant; for that, believing in but one appearance of Chriſt, they underſtand not that advent which has been already fulfilled *in the humility of the faſhion of a man*, but look only to his ſecond coming, in which he ſhall appear *in the ſublimity of his exerted Godhead*. But yet it has followed, that while they conſidered him only as a Man, they were obliged to account for his power by conſidering him as a Magician; and becauſe of the many miracles which he performed *(and which the father recounts)* they dragged him to death upon the croſs, from whence he aroſe and aſcended into heaven, of which we have much better evidence than your Proculuſes can give of the Apotheoſis of Romulus; for Chriſt himſelf, after his reſurrection, appointed his witneſſes, and ſent them forth to preach throughout the whole world. Pilate too, in his conſcience convinced of Chriſtianity, related all thoſe things to Tiberius; and the diſciples, ſcattered through the world, obeyed the command of God their maſter, and chearfully ſuffering

fering many things from the perfecuting Jews for the confidence of the truth, have at length, under the ferocious cruelty of Nero, fowed the Chriftian blood at Rome: here then the father, moved at the recollection of this dreadful carnage, makes a challenge to meet both Jew and Gentile, each on his own ground. His religion he declares he will not abjure, nor by denial transfer his worfhip from its proper object, "For we again and again avow it; gafhed and reeking we fhout it in the ears of our tormentors, that we worfhip God through Chrift: admit him a man; it is the will of God to be known and worfhipped through him and in him; but that we may reply to the Jews, even they learned to worfhip God by (or from) a man, Mofes. That I may meet the Greeks, Orpheus, Melampus, and others, who were but men, initiated them in their religion; and that I may now advert to you, O ye lords of the Gentiles, Numa Pompilius, who loaded the Romans with the moft burdenfome fuperftitions, was but a man alfo. Let it then be permitted to Chrift to difcourfe of that Godhead which is his own; to Chrift, who does not like Numa humanize the favage by the falfe terrour of numerous abfurd deities, but opens the eyes of fuch as are already polifhed, and lays the truth before thofe who have been deceived, even by their own refinements. Enquire ye therefore into the truth of Chrift's divinity." So that we find here the manhood of Chrift admitted by the father, for the fingle end of obviating fuch objections to him (as author of a religion) as were grounded upon that manhood, and to fhew that neither Jew nor Greek had a right to object a human teacher (fuppofing him no more) to the Chriftians, having themfelves received their refpective religions from inftructors who did not lay claim to any fuperior character.

But who has denied that Christ was a man? do we? or if we profess his perfect manhood, are we therefore Unitarians and deniers of his Godhead? I am so little afraid of the charge, that I do profess myself to believe that he not only was, but that he is at this hour a Man; I believe that he was not only the sacrifice and propitiation for my sins, but that, till my suit is obtained, he is my sacerdotal advocate; that he is an High Priest over the house of God so long as there remains a single votary to lay his hand upon the altar, and, with reliance upon the sufficiency of his blood, to plead the merits of his Redeemer as a compensation for his own transgressions. Our own exalted poet has made the Father address the Son in terms to which I am willing to subscribe; they are grounded on the language of the scripture; St. Paul, in his epistle to the Philippians, ii. 5, 6, 7, 8, has authorized the use of them.

—————————————— " because in thee
" Love hath abounded more than glory abounds,
" Therefore thy humiliation shall exalt
" With thee thy manhood also to this throne;
" Here shalt thou sit incarnate, here shalt reign
" Both God and Man, Son both of God and Man."
PARADISE LOST, b. iii. v. 314.

And that he is the one, in no respect controverts his being the other; and reason does not "decide with mathematical and intuitive certainty, that the Athanasian doctrine is not true," Remarks, p. 76. Right reason knows her own province; she knows herself; and when she looks for a conclusion, she seeks for it from proper premises. " Rash confidence leads to a reliance on ourselves, but the fear of infirmity warns us to take refuge in the help of God; it even influenced the Lord himself " to go a little farther, and to fall on his face and pray, Mat. xxvi. 39.

39. He therefore began to be forrowful, according to his human nature, which was fubject to fuch paſſions, but not according to his divine excellence, which is far removed from every fuch paſſion. And thefe things we fay concerning Jefus that you ſhould not, like fome herefies, think him to have been *(only)* a man, but that God had aſſumed the perfect nature of the human body, in which he could have a fellow-feeling of our infirmities, inafmuch as he was himfelf encompaſſed by the infirmities natural to the human body *."

The early fathers, when they fpoke of Chriſt's human nature, ufually brought to recollection his Godhead, as they fay themfelves, through fear of mifleading

---

* "Incauta confidentia ad jactantiam ducit, timor autem infirmitatis ad auxilium Dei confugere adhortatur, ficut & Dominum ipfum paululum progredi, & cadere in faciem, & orare. Ergo cœpit quidem triſtari fecundùm humanam naturam quæ talibus paſſionibus fubdita eſt, non autem fecundum divinam virtutem quæ ab hujufmodi paſſione longe remota eſt. Et hæc dicimus de Jefu, ut non arbitreris, ficut quædam hærefes, hominem eum fuiſſe, fed Deum veram humani corporis fufcepiſſe naturam, qui poterat compati infirmitatibus noſtris, quoniam & ipfe circundatus erat infirmâ naturâ humani corporis." Origen. tom. ii. p. 115. C. In Mattheum Tractatus 35. Parifiis, 1574, fol. a Gilberto Genebrando.—There is a remarkable paſſage in this Tractate, in which the writer fays, that Peter denied his Maſter thro' too much reliance upon his own ſtrength, whereas he might have been fupported if, when our Lord faid, " This night ye ſhall all be offended becaufe of me," Matth. xxvi. 31, he had addreſſed a prayer to Chriſt, and faid, "If all are offended becaufe of thee, be thou in me that I be not offended; and efpecially grant me this grace, that, in the time when all thy difciples ſhall fuffer offence, I may not fall into a denial of thee." Et fi omnes fcandilazati fuerint in te, efto in me, ut non ego fcandalizer; & dona mihi præcipuè gratiam hanc, ut in tempore cum omnes difcipuli tui fuerint fcandalum paſſi, ego in denegationem non cadam. Ibid. p. 114. The doctrine of prayer to our Saviour is fufficiently laid down here to mark Origen's idea of it, and to ſhew that, if ever he entertained the oppofite tenet, as Mr. Lindfey declares, he did not uniformly entertain it, and confequently that his authority can avail the Unitarian but little.—But of this more hereafter.

ing the world into an idea that he was only man. But the antient Jew and the modern Unitarian alike fupprefs every teftimony which the Chriftian cautioufly bore to the divinity of our Lord, and "the vulgar are now taught to know Chrift as fome ordinary man, on whom the Jews had pronounced judgement, that they may the more eafily be brought to think us the worfhippers of a man. We are not, however, yet afhamed of Chrift, nay, we even delight in contempt and condemnation for his name's fake, neither do we entertain any other conception of God *."

The eventful life and peculiar character of ORIGENES ADAMANTIUS, Prefbyter of Alexandria, would afford a copious fubject to the biographer. A few felected circumftances may be fufficient for my purpofe, which is only to fhew that the author, whofe faith is enquired into, is a fit fubject of enquiry, and that he comes altogether within the limits of Mr. Lindfey's defcription. When we read, we are naturally defirous of knowing who the writer is, and how efteemed. This I have all along ftated, and, to the extracts which I have drawn from each of the fathers, have, for my reader's fatisfaction, prefixed fome brief account of the father from whom I have drawn them.

ORIGEN was born at Alexandria, A. D. 185. At the age of feventeen years he had the misfortune to lofe his father, who chearfully laid down his life in maintenance of that religion, in the true principles of
which

---

* Sed & vulgus jam fcit Chriftum ut aliquem hominum, qualem Judæi judicaverunt, quo facilius quis nos hominis cultores exiftimaverit. Verum neque de Chrifto erubefcimus, quum fub nomine ejus deputari & damnari juvat neque de Deo aliter prefumimus. Tertul. Apol. adv. Gentes, cap. xxi.

which he had brought up his son. We are told of this venerable martyr that he was indefatigable in the business of his son's education. In his very infancy he instructed him in the religion of the gospel, and obeyed " the commandment of God, given to our fathers, that they should make known his laws to their children; that the generation to come might know them, even the children that should be born, who should arise and declare them to their children, that they might set their hope in God," Pfalm lxxviii. 5 *.

The

* The discharge of this duty, imposed by God himself, is what Mr. Lindsey and his fraternity esteem a criminal act in such as acquit themselves of it. To controvert the express commandments of God is altogether consistent with a contradiction given to the revelation of God; and such as determine to make their own little intellect the criterion of what he reveals and enjoins, are very likely both contumaciously to contradict and disobey him. But to have learned in infancy, is to have come under the influence of prejudices; and when arrived at man's estate, the only proof we can give of having a mind free from these prejudices, is to reject whatever we have learned. What! though true? No matter whether true or false. An attachment to truth, if it had been early instilled, is *mean and superstitious*. By the abdication of early principles alone our honesty can become approved. To adhere to them upon examination has a very suspicious appearance. And tho' truth were the first to make an impression on our infant minds, the only mark of liberality and freedom of spirit is to reject her in manhood, and take the opposite falsehood as her substitute. This is the sum total of Mr. Lindsey's doctrine on this subject, but by him delivered in language which I confess I did not expect to see him employ. That something like it should flow from the ribbald pen of my Remarker never surprized me. It was consistent with the whole of his work. But a certain dull decency, which had pervaded Mr. Lindsey's former pages, promised that his censure should at least be liberal. I am not however deterred from repeating the substance of what I said before. The doctrines which I maintain, I learned very early; and I again bless God for having consigned me to parents who, in dutiful obedience to his commands, instructed me in his word. Had I been the son of Mr. Lindsey, I might indeed have had an opportunity of proving my candour by the subsequent rejection of every tenet my infancy should have imbibed from him; but do I prove it less by an adherence to what I have learned? I adhere to, as had I found them false, I should

have

The good effects of this happy commencement attended Origen through life. In one respect alone we find him depart from the counsels of this competent instructor. An understanding almost premature had given Leonidas an opportunity of seeing that his son too much consulted imagination in his manner of interpreting the holy scriptures. Against this he warned him, and desired him to rest contented with the plain and obvious meaning of the words*. It had been happy for Origen had he attended to this sensible admonition; for whatever errours, or even seeming self-contradictions, he has fallen into, appear to have had their source in a passion for refinement. He finds an allegory couched in the simplest assertion, and his fancy sometimes erects a superstructure upon such a foundation, as his own judgement, if consulted, must have pronounced altogether inadequate to the burden which he has imposed.

A writer of this cast, it is evident, must have created much opposition and even enmity to himself. No doctrine could absolutely claim the authority of his concurrence; for, let him maintain a position, there was yet something to be found in the extensive compass of his writings which seemed, or was capable of being wrested till it seemed to favour the contrary opinion. By such a circumstance

---

have rejected, the lessons of my youth. Among them there was one which has occasioned my continuance in the rest; this is, never to take any thing implicitly, nor without strict examination. It is due to this that I have first read and next refuted Mr. Lindsey; it is due to this that I have referred his quotations to the authors quoted, and throughout detected misrepresentation, and even found assertions ascribed to writers the very reverse of which have proceeded from their own pens.

* In one instance, indeed, Origen too scrupulously adhered to the letter of the scripture. He lived, however, to repent and censure his practical comment on Matthew xix. 12.

cumſtance his authority is unqueſtionably diminiſhed; and for this reaſon I ſhall the leſs copiouſly adduce it.

And yet it is ſufficiently obvious, upon the whole, what doctrine preponderates: he has himſelf confeſſed and apologized for ſuch aſſertions as were capable of miſrepreſentation: he even declares that Hereticks had interpolated his volumes. The nature of thoſe aſſertions for which he apologizes, and of the interpolation of which he complains, demonſtrate what the doctrine is which he renounces. But, throughout his works, there does not once appear a ſingle retractation of thoſe numerous profeſſions which he has made of his faith in our Saviour's Godhead, and of the one ſubſtance of the three perſons in the divine Unity: I ſay, therefore, it is ſufficiently obvious, upon the whole, what the doctrine is which he retains. Beſides this, he is explicit on one ſide of the queſtion; whereas, upon the other, it is not without the greateſt violence of miſrepreſentation that he can be brought to ſay any thing that even ſeems to favour it. He has likewiſe had the good fortune to find an apologiſt in Pamphilus, who was himſelf a martyr, and who has vindicated the memory and writings of Origen from that calumny, which we cannot wonder ſhould attend upon ſuch a writer.——But of Pamphilus hereafter.

As a man, Origen ſeems to have poſſeſſed the moſt amiable diſpoſition, and to have been in practice truly a Chriſtian. During the confinement of Leonidas, previous to his martyrdom, this worthy young man threw himſelf into the priſon where he lay detained; and here, not only abetted his father's reſolution to meet his approaching end with courage and conſtancy, but, by the moſt explicit avowal of his own faith in Jeſus Chriſt, even ſought to provoke the mur-

derers

derers of his parent to bestow, what he esteemed an equally glorious triumph, upon himself: from this pursuit, however, he was with much difficulty dissuaded. The life of Origen was of the greatest consequence to a family, just about to be deprived of a father. He was the eldest of seven sons, and on him the rest depended for their support. These considerations were strongly urged by a tender mother, and under their influence the amiable youth complied with his mother's intreaties. Fearful, however, least Leonidas might feel their force, and redeem his life by apostacy, he wrote and fortified him by the following caution, which has been preserved to us by Eusebius: "Beware, my father, that you relinquish not your faith for our sake *."

So very eminent was Origen for his understanding and improvement in Christian knowledge, that, at the early age of eighteen years, he was appointed to the instruction of Catechumens, at Alexandria; and so very ably did he discharge this important trust, that multitudes, who received their knowledge of the gospel from his mouth, were not only baptized with water, but, as he expresses it himself, sustained "a baptism by fire" for the sake of their Redeemer.

It is nevertheless recorded of him, that he was not at all times ready to undergo this baptism himself. But this charge, resting upon a fact which is in the highest degree improbable, becomes itself so very much so, that, with the best writers on the subject, I am of opinion it ought to be set aside; and the more so, when it is considered that, under Decius, in the year 250, he sustained the most cruel torture without the smallest

con-

* Ἔπεχε μὴ δὲ ἡμᾶς ἄλλο τὶ φρονήσῃς. Euseb. Eccles. Hist. lib. vi. cap. ii. p. 258.

conceffion. Not to take away life, was the order to the executioner; and the reafon affigned, becaufe there muft be an end of torment. He furvived this cruelty about four years, and, A. D. 254, died a natural death at the age of feventy years.

As a writer he is beyond all conception voluminous. Not lefs than fix thoufand treatifes are faid to have proceeded from his inexhauftible pen; of thefe a confiderable portion have efcaped the wreck of time. His ftyle is, very various, in general diffufive and verbofe, yet, when engaged in controverfy, and kept to his point by an adverfary, fufficiently clofe and fententious. There is one circumftance, however, which greatly reconciles us to his wire-drawn pages; throughout the whole, his own excellent character is very confpicuous. It is true he has attenuated and fpread out every idea to a furprizing thinnefs and extent. They are yet in themfelves highly eftimable, and ductility is the criterion of gold.

I have already produced many paffages from this father. The adoration of our Lord is recommended by him in page 192 above; in the 141ft page he has avowed his belief in the one fubftance of the three perfons in the Unity of the Godhead; and in page 161, 185, has borne his teftimony to the united Godhead and Manhood in the perfon of our Saviour.

In regard to the firft of thefe particulars, if Origen has any where delivered a contrary doctrine, I will leave it to Mr. Lindfey to reconcile it with what is already ftated on this head, and to fhew how a precept not to pray to Chrift is in any wife confiftent with the following declaration; a declaration connected with an extract made by Mr. Lindfey himfelf, and which might have let this gentleman fee that, when Origen fays,

"The

"The honour we pay to Jefus is appointed by God, namely, that all men fhould honour the Son as they honour the Father," Apol. p. 8, the writer does not mean to inculcate the oppofite doctrine, namely, that all men fhould honour the Son in a degree inferior to, and confequently different from that in which they honour the Father.

Celfus, an heathen philofopher, had written an invective againft Chriftianity; and to this Origen returned an anfwer, which is defervedly preferred to any other of his writings. Celfus has objected to the Chriftians the worfhip of our Lord, adding, "If they worfhipped only one God, and no other, then fhould they have fome reafon to object polytheifm to others; but now they pay the moft exalted honours, which are due to God alone, to this Upftart of to-day, and think they fin not againft God, becaufe it is his Minifter who is worfhipped." "But to this," fays Origen, "it is eafily replied; for if Celfus underftood that declaration of our Lord, "I and my Father are one," John x. 30, or that claufe in his prayer, "Even as we are one," John xvii. 21, he would not have conceived that we worfhip any other befides God, the Lord of the univerfe; for he fays, "The Father is in me, and I am in the Father," John x. 38. But if, from not reconciling feeming inconfiftencies, any fhall object that, by acknowledging the unity of the Father and the Son, we betake ourfelves to thofe who deny that the Father and the Son are two perfons; let him aid his conception how *the Father and I are one*, by reflecting upon the affertion, that "in the multitude there was but one heart and one mind," Acts iv. 32. As we have ftated it, then we worfhip one God, the Father and the Son; and we remain poffeffed of our objection to polytheifts:

wo

we do not pay thofe honours, which are due to God alone, to an upftart of to-day, nor to one who has not heretofore exifted, for we believe him who has faid, "Before Abraham was, I am *, John viii. 58; who has alfo faid, " I am the truth," John xiv. 6. " We adore then the Father of truth and the Son who is truth as one; who in perfon is two, but in confent of mind and identity of will, one †."

" But Celfus affirms that, if we fing hymns to the fun and to Minerva, we worfhip the great God. But we know to the contrary; for we fing hymns to God alone, who is over all, and to his only begotten Son, God the Word; and with us the fun, the moon, the ftars, and

---

* Refer this to the note, p. 217 above. That Origen confidered this verfe as a declaration of our Lord's preexiftent ftate is evident. Origen underftood Greek as well as Mr. Lindfey, and better than my Remarker.

† Ἐι μὲν δὴ μηδένα ἄλλον ἐθεράπευον ἥτοι πλὴν ἕνα Θεὸν, &c. a Celfo, cui refpondet Origenes: Λεκτέον δὲ κỳ πρὸς τῦτο, ὅτι, ἵνασπερ γενόηκεν ὁ Κέλσ⊙ τὸ, ἐγὼ κỳ ὁ Παλὴρ ἕν ἐσμεν. Καὶ τὸ ἐν ἐυχῆ εἰρημένον, ὑπο τῦ υἱῦ τῷ Θεῷ ἐν τῷ, ὡς ἐγὼ κỳ σὺ ἕν ἐσμεν, ἐκ ἄν, ᾤηθο ἡμᾶς, κỳ ἄλλον θεραπεύειν παρὰ τὸν ἐπὶ πᾶσι Θεόν. Ὁ γὰρ Παλὴρ, φησὶν, ἐν ἐμοὶ, κἀγὼ ἐν τῷ Παρὶ. Ἐι δὲ τίς ἐκ τύτων περισπασθήσεται, μὴ πῆ ἀνεμοπλύμεν πρὸς τὰς ἀναιρῦνλας δύο ἔιναι ὑποςάσεις, Παλέρα κỳ ὑιόν: ἐπιρησάτω τῷ, ἣν δὲ πάνλων τῶν πιςευσάνλων ἡ καρδία κỳ ἡ ψυχὴ μία, ἵνα θεωρήση τὸ, ἐγὼ κỳ ὁ Παλὴρ ἕν ἐσμεν. Ἕνα ἓν Θεὸν, ὡς ἀποδίδωκαμεν, τὸν Παλέρα κỳ τὸν ὑιὸν θεραπεύομεν. Καὶ μένει ἡμῖν ὁ πρὸς τὰς ἄλλας ἀτενὴς λόγ⊙. Καὶ ὁ τὸν ἐναγχός γε φανέλα, ὡς πρότερον ἐκ ὄνλα ὑπερθρησκεύομεν: αὐτῷ γὰρ πειθόμεθα τῷ ἐιπόνλι, πρὶν Ἀβραὰμ γενέσθαι ἐγὼ ἐιμι· κỳ λέγονλι, ἐγὼ ἐιμι ἡ ἀλήθεια· θρησκεύομεν ἆν τὸν Παλέρα τῆς ἀληθείας, κỳ τὸν υἱὸν τὴν ἀλήθειαν, ὄνλα δύο τῇ ὑποςάσει πράγμαλα· ἓν δὲ τῇ ὁμονοίᾳ κỳ τῇ συμφωνίᾳ, κỳ τῇ ταυτότητι τῦ βουλήμαλ⊙. Origen. contra Celfum, lib. viii. p. 285. Edit. Cantab. Spencer, 1658, 4to.

and all the heavenly hoft unite their voices, and fing praifes to God and his Only-begotten ‡." From God, who is light, the fun, and every luminary of heaven, derives his fplendor. " Now, as the worfhippers of the fun, the moon, and the ftars, do not adore a fpark of fire, or a candle's blaze upon earth, feeing the incomparable fuperiority of thofe objects which they efteem worthy of adoration; fo thofe who underftand that God is light; thofe who admit that " the Son of God is the true light, which lighteth every man that cometh into the world," John i. 9; thofe who receive that faying, " I am the light of the world," John viii. 12, muft, by parity of reafoning, contemplate the fun, the moon, and the ftars, when compared to the God of true light, who is light, as little fparks of fire, and by confequence they muft withhold their adoration from them *."

In one of his homilies on the Old Teftament, this father, fhewing the fuperiority of the gofpel to the law, declares

‡ Ἡμεῖς δὲ τὸ ἐναντίον ἐσμεν. Ὑμνεῖς γὰρ εἰς μόνον τὸν ἐπὶ πᾶσι λεγόμεν Θεὸν, κ̓ τὸν μονογενῆ αὐτῦ, Θεὸν λόγον. Καὶ ὑμνῶμεν γε Θεὸν, κ̓ τὸν μονογενῆ αὐτῦ, ὡς κ̓ ἥλιος, κ̓ σελήνη, κ̓ ἄςρα, κ̓ πᾶσα ἡ ἐρανία ςρατία. Origen contra Celfum, p. 422.

* Καὶ ὥσπερ οἱ, διὰ τὸ φῶς αἰσθητὸν κ̓ ἐράνιον εἶναι, προσκυνεῦτες ἥλιον, κ̓ σελήνην, κ̓ ἄςρα, ἐκ ἂν προσκυνήσαιεν σπινθῆρα πυρὸς, ἢ λύχνον ἐπὶ γῆς, ὁρῶντες τὴν ἀσύγκριτον ὑπεροχὴν τῶν νομιζομένων ἀξίων προσκυνεῖσθαι παρὰ τὸ τῶν σπινθήρων κ̓ τῶν λύχνων φῶς. Οὕτως οἱ νοήσαντες, πῶς ὁ Θεὸς φῶς ἐςι: καταλαβόντες δὲ, πῶς ὁ υἱὸς τῦ Θεῦ φῶς ἀληθινόν ἐςιν, ὁ φωτίζει πάντα ἄνθρωπον ἐρχόμενον εἰς τὸν κόσμον· Συνιέντες δὲ κ̓, πῶς ἑτός· φησι τὸ, ἐγὼ εἰμι τὸ φῶς τῦ κόσμε. Οὐκ ἂν ἐυλόγως προσκυνήσαιεν τὸν ὡσανεὶ βραχὺν σπινθῆρα, ὡς πρὸς φῶς τὸν Θεὸν ἀληθινὸν φῶτος, ἐν ἡλίῳ, κ̓ σελήνῃ, κ̓ ἄςροις. Origen contra Celfum, p. 258.

declares that the latter ought not to be accepted in a literal fenfe, for that it is not poffible God fhould have pleafure in fuch diftributions of the facrifice as are appointed in Leviticus vii. or that his favour could ever depend upon the ufe of ovens or frying-pans. "But not fo," he adds, "have the children of the church learned Chrift, not fo have they been inftructed in him by the apoftles, that they fhould entertain fuch low and derogatory notions of the Lord of Majefty. Let us then, according to the fpiritual difcernment which the Spirit giveth to the church, rather fee what is that facrifice which is baked in the oven, and what the true interpretation of the oven itfelf. But where fhall I have fuch accefs to the holy fcripture as may teach me what is that oven? I will implore my Lord Jefus that, feeking, he may make me to find; that, knocking, he may open to me, Matth. vii. 7; and that I may difcover what that oven is, wherein I fhall bake the facrifice which God may accept *." He then proceeds to allegorize the whole ordinance, and declares that the oven is the heart of man, that obedience fhall be his facrifice, &c. I have produced this paffage, (and I might produce thoufands to the fame effect) only becaufe it exhibits the writer at prayer to Chrift.

Thus

* "Sed non ita ecclefiæ pueri Chriftum didicerunt, nec ita in eum per apoftolos eruditi funt, ut de Domino majeftatis aliquid tam humile & tam vile fufcipiant. Quin potius fecundum fpiritalem fenfum, quem Spiritus donat ecclefiæ, videamus quod fit iftud facrificium, quod coquatur in clibano, vel quis ifte clibanus intelligi debeat. Sed ubi inveniam modo ad fubitum fcripturam divinam, quæ me doceat quis fit clibanus? Dominum meum Jefum invocare oportet, ut quærentem me faciat invenire, & pulfanti aperiat, ut inveniam in fcripturis clibanum ubi poffim coquere facrificium meum ut fufcipiat illud Deus."——Cor ergo eft hominis clibanus, &c. Origen in Levit vii. hom v. p. 78.

Thus have I sufficiently proved the tenet of Origen, with respect to the adoration of our Lord; a tenet to which his practice bears the most copious testimony; for considerably more than one hundred homilies conclude with doxologies to the Son or to the Holy Ghost. "Let us then assist ourselves, that we become not unworthy to have our understanding thus enlarged, but that our mind, being first rendered an holy place, may be fitted for the reception of the holy mysteries, by the grace of the Holy Ghost, by whom whatever is holy is sanctified: to him be glory and power for ever and ever. Amen *." " This wisdom shall make known the mystery which was hidden in times past, but now is made manifest by the scriptures of the prophets, and the appearance of our Lord and Saviour Jesus Christ; to whom be glory through all ages. Amen †."

But if to be a proper object of religious worship, infer to the omnipotent Godhead of that object; so, on the other hand, an acknowledgement of that Godhead must infer to the propriety of the worship. And when such high expressions of our Redeemer's nature occur perpetually in the works of Origen, I cannot
see

---

* " Demus operam quomodo & nos hoc tanto & tam sublimi intellectu non efficiamur indigni, sed ut anima nostra prius fiat locus sanctus, & in loco sancto capiamus sancta mysteria, per gratiam Spiritûs Sancti, ex quo sanctificatur omne quod sanctum est. Ipsi gloria & imperium in secula seculorum. Amen." Origen, p. 106. M. vol. I.

† Ἀυτη δὲ ἡ σοφια ἡμῖν ἐνυποςηθήσεται τρανῶς, κ̣ ἀποκάλυψιν ἐμποιήσει μυστηρίῳ χρόνοις αἰωνίοις σεσιγημένῳ, φανερωθέντος δὲ νῦν διά τε γραφῶν προφητικῶν, κ̣ τῆς ἐπιφανίας τȣ κυρίȣ κ̣ σωτῆρος ἡμῶν Ἰησȣ Χριστȣ, ᾧ ἡ δόξα εἰς τάς συμπάσας αἰῶνας. Ἀμήν. Origen. Philocalia, cap. i. p. 6.

see why it should be doubted that this father esteemed our Lord the proper object of his adoration.

He tells us that " Christ has a two-fold dominion over every creature. By the first kind, as Creator of all things, and bearing sway over the universe, he has all things subject to him in right of his majesty, and by the necessity of power; by means of which he not only rules the good and holy intelligences, but the wicked and rebellious, and such beings as the holy scripture denominates evil spirits. For this cause, therefore, he is called the Possessor of the universe and the Almighty, according to what John in the Apocalypse reveals, saying, these things saith he, " which is, and which was, and which is to come, the Almighty." Revel. i. 8 *. This the father proceeds to say is one mode of the power by which Christ rules all things, " For what can resist the nod of the universal King, the Prince of all things, of God himself, the Word †." But the second species of his sovereignty is not by coercion, but invitation and persuasion; not by exerted power, but by compassion and lenity.

Here-

---

* Duobus ex modis constat in omnem creaturam Christi dominatio. Uno, per quem ut Creator omnium & potestatem gerens universorum, vi majestatis & potentiæ necessitate habet cætera subjecta, per quem modum non solum bonis & sanctis mentibus & spiritibus dominatur, verum & nequam & refugis & his quos scriptura divina malignos angelos appellavit. Idcirco igitur & Omnitenens & Omnipotens dicitur, secundum quod Joannes designat in Apocalypsi dicens, Hæc dicit qui est, & qui erat, & qui venturus est, Omnipotens. Apoc. cap. i. v. 8. Hic ergo unus est modus quo Christus omnibus dominatur. Origen. in Epist. ad Romanos, cap. xiv. lib. ix.

† Τί γὰρ ᾗ ἔμελλε τῷ παμβασιλέως, ᾗ πανηγμόν᾽, ᾗ αὐτῷ Θεῷ λόγῳ, ἐνήσεισθαι τῷ νεύματι. Eusebii Eccles. Hist. lib. z. p. 469. Edit. Cantab. Reading, 1720, folio.

Here then we see Christ confessed to be the omnipotent Creator of the universe; we find that Origen, as well as all the nations of the earth, together with Eusebius, who has recorded their concurrent faith, "acknowledged Jesus Christ our Saviour to be not a vulgar King over men, but the true Son of the God of all nature; and that with justice he adored him as being God himself *." For to Celsus, who objected to the Christians the adoration of a Man who had a mortal body, and an opinion that this Man was God, he answers, " Let those who bring the accusation know that he, whom we think and believe to be from the beginning God, and the Son of God, is the Self-word, the Self-wisdom, and the Self-truth †." " We believe him to be the Son of God and God the Word ‡."

On

---

* Ἰησῦν Χριςὸν τὸν ἡμῶν Σωτῆρα,—ὐχ οἷα κοινὸν ἐξ ἀνθρώπων βασιλέα γενόμενον ὁμολογεῖσθαι, αλλ' διὰ τῦ καθόλυ Θεῦ παῖδα γνήσιον, καὶ ΑΥΤΟΘΕΟΝ προσκυνεῖσθαι, καὶ εἰκότως. p. 468.—19. Euseb. Eccles. Hist. lib. x.

The term αὐτοθεὸν here is of the highest import. It may be translated Self-God; that is, God from his own nature, and without any other original than himself. He is yet a Son, but who shall declare his generation?—The following passage from Origen contains some terms of similar composition.

† Ὅμως δὲ ἴσωσαν οἱ ἐγκαλῦντες, ὅτι ὃν μὲν νομίζομεν καὶ πεπείσμεθα ἀρχῆθεν εἶναι Θεὸν κ̑ υἱὸν Θεῦ, ὕτος ὁ αὐτολόγο- ἐστι, κ̑ ἡ αὐτοσοφία, κ̑ ἡ αὐτοαλήθεια. Τὸ δὲ θνητὸν αὐτῦ σῶμα, κ̑ τὴν ἀνθρωπίνην ἐν αὐτῷ ψυχὴν, τῇ πρὸς ἐκεῖνο ὐ μόνον κοινωνίᾳ, ἀλλὰ κ̑ ἑνώσει κ̑ ἀνακράσει, τὰ μέγιστά φαμὲν προσειληφέναι, κ̑ τῆς ἐκείνυ θειότητ۞ κεκοινωνηκότα εἰς Θεὸν μεταβεβηκέναι. Origen. contra Celsum, lib. iii. p. 135.

‡ Ὃν πεπείσμεθα εἶναι υἱὸν Θεῦ, λόγον Θεὸν. Ejusd. lib. viii. p. 428.

On the declaration made by our Lord, that the disciples shall be brought to judgement for the testimony of his name, and that in the last day he will himself reject the workers of iniquity, Matth. x. 18, and vii. 22, 23, Origen observes that it is easy to deny the truth of these predictions before they are fulfilled; but when facts, thus authoritatively foretold, fall out according to the prophecy, " it becomes manifest that God, having truly been made man, delivered the doctrine of salvation to men *."

Here the united Godhead and Manhood of our blessed Redeemer are asserted by this early father in terms as explicit as those ascribed to Athanasius, and in which our Church makes profession of her faith; but the doctrine, cries Mr. Lindsey, is "absurd and unintelligible." Such, precisely, is the opinion of the heathen Celsus, who, in the fictitious character of a Jew, complains that the believers upon Christ made it a charge against the Jews, that they did not believe on Jesus as upon God; but to this complaint we have already made answer, says Origen, and " testified wherein we conceive him to be God, and wherein we profess that he is Man †." " Who, though in the beginning he was with God, yet, for the sake of those who are shackled by the flesh, and are therefore fleshly, was himself made flesh, that he might be comprehended by those who could not by any other means look upon him,

---

* Ὅτε δὲ ἐκβέβηκε τὰ μετὰ τοσαύτης ἐξουσίας εἰρημένα, ἐμφαίνει Θεὸν, ἀληθῶς ἐνανθρωπήσαντα, σωτήρια δόγματα τοῖς ἀνθρώποις παραδεδωκέναι. Origen. Philocalia, cap. i. p. 2. Edit. Cantab. Spencer, 1658, 4to.

† Δεικνύντες ἅμα, πῶς μὲν Θεὸν αὐτὸν νοοῦμεν, κατὰ τί δὲ ἄνθρωπον λέγομεν. Origen contra Celsum, lib. ii. p. 61.

him, inasmuch as he was the Word, and was with God, and was God," John i. 1, 14. And now, speaking in a body, and promulgating himself as flesh, he invites to him such as are fleshly, that he may first make them to be conformed with the Word which was made flesh, and thenceforward advance them to a capacity of conceiving him as he was before he was made flesh; that they, being profited by his instruction in the flesh, may grow up to an acknowledgement that, " tho' we have known Christ after the flesh, yet now henceforth know we him no more," 2 Corinth. v. 16, for God the Word is not to be comprehended. But, as we have said, the Son, being incomprehensible inasmuch as he is God the Word, by whom all things were made, dwelt among us *." This passage, like a Cheval-de-Frise, stretches out a point against Mr. Lindsey in whatever direction he approaches it. Does he declare that the Word, spoken of by St. John in his first chapter, is not the Son? This passage affirms that
the

* Ὅστις ἐν ἀρχῇ πρὸς τὸν Θεὸν ὤν, διὰ τὲς κολληθείσας τῇ σαρκὶ ᾗ γενομένες ὑπὲρ σάρξ, ἐγένετο σάρξ, ἵνα χωρηθῇ ὑπὸ τῶν μὴ δυναμένων αὐτὸν βλέπειν, καθὸ λόγος ἦν, ᾗ πρὸς Θεὸν ἦν, ᾗ Θεὸς ἦν. Καὶ σωματικῶς γε λαλόμενος, ᾗ ὡς σὰρξ ἐπαγγελλόμενος, ἐφ' ἑαυτὸν καλεῖ τὰς ὑλίας σάρκας, ἵν' αὐτὰς ποιήσῃ πρῶτον μορφωθῆναι κατὰ λόγον, τὸν γενόμενον σάρκα. Καὶ μετὰ τοῦτο αὐτὰς ἀναβιβάσῃ ἐπὶ τὸ ἰδεῖν αὐτὸν, ὅπερ ἦν πρὶν γένηται σάρξ. Ὅστε αὐτὰς ὠφεληθείσας, ᾗ ἀναβάσας ἀπὸ τῆς κατὰ σάρκα εἰσαγωγῆς, εἰπεῖν τὸ, Ει ᾗ Χριστὸν ποτε κατὰ σάρκα ἐγνώκαμεν, ἀλλὰ νῦν ἐκ ἔτι γινώσκομεν——δυσθεώρητος γὰρ ὁ Θεὸς, λόγος——ᾗ ὁ υἱὸς δυσθεώρητος ὤν, ἅτε λόγος Θεὸς, δι' ὅ τὰ πάντα ἐγένετο, ᾗ ἐσκήνωσεν ἐν ἡμῖν. Origen contra Celsum, lib. vi. p. 322.

For a passage in many respects parallel to this, see above, p. 159. Compare them both with the assertion of St. Barnabas, p. 15, and of Irenæus, p. 113.

the Word is the Son. Does he declare or concur with my Remarker in declaring that σωματικῶς, in Col. ii. 9, does not fignify *in a human body*, but *in an aggregate fum*. This paffage afcertains the meaning of the word σωματικῶς, and determines its fignification to be *in a human body*, or, as it is tranflated in our Bible, *bodily*. And by an extract which fhall prefently appear, the word πληρώμα being oppofed to κενότης, is afcertained to mean the fulnefs of that ftate in which our Lord had pre-exifted, and of which he emptied himfelf when he condefcended to be made Man : for "Jefus Chrift, when he was rich, became poor. For this reafon, therefore, he chofe for a mother, of whom he fhould be born, a poor woman, and for the place of his nativity, a poor town †." Here, too Mr. Lindfey's affertion that our blefled Saviour is no more than his own fellow-creature, may meet its obftruction, and appear perhaps to fall fomewhat fhort of a declaration which maintains that he is God; and yet this gentleman has ventured to plead the perfect agreement between himfelf and Origen in behalf of his own tenets. How far they differ now, is fufficiently obvious with refpect to the two natures fubfifting in the one Chrift, " who thought it not robbery to be equal with God ; that is, who confidered it not as any acceffion to his dignity, that he is indeed equal with God, and one with the Father *." " And thefe things we fay without feparating the Son of God from Jefus ; for, according to the difpenfation, the

foul

---

† Chriftus Jefus cum dives effet pauper factus eft, ideo ergo & matrem de quâ nafceretur, elegit pauperem, & patriam pauperem, de quâ dicitur, & tu Bethlehem, &c.—in Levit. cap. xii. 13. homil. viii, ex Erafmi verfione, p. 163.

* Nec rapinam duxit effe fe æqualem Deo, hoc eft, non fibi magni aliquid deputat quod ipfe quidem æqualis Deo, & unum cum Patre eft. Orig. in Romanos, â Wetfteinio citat. in Philip. ii. 6, 7, 8.

foul and the body of Jesus were made one with the Word of God ‡." With which "we believe that the mortal body and human foul, which are in him, not only hold communion, but are combined in unity *." The Man, on account of his humility and death, having received all power over things in heaven, inasmuch as they belong to the Only-begotten, that, being by absorption taken into his Godhead, and become one with him, he might with him enjoy a common sovereignty †."

These passages, together with the following, bear an evident relation to Philippians ii. 6, 7, 8, and may, if my reader think any farther vindication of that text necessary, be referred to, p. 161 above. "The WORD of God, condescending to us, and being, during his existence among men, humbled with respect to his own proper dignity, is said to have departed from this world unto the Father, John xiii. 1, that we may see him perfect, being returned to his own fulness, from that emptied state wherein he had made himself of no reputation §." But our author is arguing here that

God,

‡ Ταῦτα φάμεν, ἃ χωρίζαντες τὸν υἱὸν τῆ Θεῷ ἀπὸ τῆ Ἰησῦ· ἐν γὰρ μιᾷ τὴν οἰκονομίαν γεγένηται πρὸς τὸν λόγον τῆ Θεῷ ἡ ψυχὴ κὴ τὸ σῶμα τῆ Ἰησῦ. Origen contra Celsum, lib. ii. p. 64.

* See above for the Greek, p. 256.

† Διὰ τὸ τεταπεινωκέναι ἑαυτὸν, κὴ γινόμενον ὑπήκοον μέχρι θανάτου—λαβόντ⊕· τῆ κατὰ τὸν σωτῆρα ἀνθρώπων τὴν ἐξουσίαν τῶν ἐν οὐρανῷ ὅσον ἐπὶ τῶν ἐνυπαρχόντων τῷ μονογενεῖ, ἵνα αὐτῷ κοινωνῇ, ἀνακιρνάμεν⊕· ἐκείνῃ τῇ θεότητι, κὴ ἐνούμεν⊕· αὐτῷ. Orig. de Orat. partis secundae, sect. xv. p. 84. Edit. Oxon. 1686, 12mo.

§ Ὁ λόγ⊕· τῆ Θεῷ ἡμῖν συγκαταβαίνων, καὶ ὡς πρὸς τὴν ἰδίαν ἀξίαν, ὅτε παρὰ ἀνθρώποις ἐςι, ταπεινουμέν⊕·, μεταβαίνειν λέγεται

God, by defcent or afcent, does not change place; for that, filling all things, no local manifeftation of his prefence can argue to his abfence from any other part of his own infinity. But this ubiquity he afcribes to the Son alfo; "for if the God of the univerfe," he fays, " fhould defcend into Jefus for the falvation of man; if the WORD, which in the beginning was with God, the WORD, which was himfelf God, fhould come to us, he relinquifhes not his throne, fo as that any place fhall be without his prefence, or any other place be now filled, which had before been unoccupied by him. It is confequently in nowife neceffary to the defcent of Chrift, or the prefence of God among men, that his exalted throne on high fhall therefore be abdicated *."—Is ubiquity then an attribute of any being who is not God fupreme? and is not " the Son therefore God fupreme, who, looking from on high, is not abridged of his univerfal profpect by motion from place to place; who is at every time in every place, and never circumfcribed by any: all mind, all light paternal, all eye, beholding all things, hear-

ing

λέγεται ἐκ τῦ κόσμου τέτε πρὸς τὸν Πατέρα, ὅπως καὶ ἡμεῖς ἐκεῖθι τέλειον αὐτὸν θεασώμεθα, ἀπὸ τῆς παρ' ἡμῖν κενότητ©-, ἣν ἐκένωσεν ἑαυτὸν, ἐστι τὸ ἴδιον πλήρωμα παλινδρομῦντα. Orig. de Oratione, partis fecundæ, cap. xii. p. 70. Edit. Oxon. 1686, 12mo.

* Κἂν ὁ Θεὸς τοίνυν τῶν ὅλων τῇ ἑαυτῦ δυνάμει συγκαταβαίνει τῷ Ἰησῦ εἰς τὸν ἀνθρώπων βίον, κἂν ὁ ἐν ἀρχῇ πρὸς τὸν Θεὸν λόγ©-, Θεὸς κ᾽ αὐτ©- ὤν, ἔρχηται πρὸς ἡμᾶς. Οὐκ ἐξέδρ©- γίνεται, ἐδὲ καταλίπωσι τὴν ἑαυτῦ ἕδραν: ὡς τίνα μὲν τόπον κενὸν αὐτῦ εἶναι, ἕτερον δὲ πλήρη, ὃ πρότερον αὐτὸν ἰχοντα— ᾗ χρεία ἂν εἰς τὴν τῦ Χριςῦ κάθοδον, ἢ εἰς τὴν πρὸς ἀνθρώπως ἐπιστροφὴν τῦ Θεῦ, καταλίπεσθαι ἕδραν μείζονα. Origen adv. Celfum, p. 164. Edit. Cantab. Spencer, 1658, 4to.

ing all things, and knowing all things †?" And shall this omniscient, omnipresent, almighty, and eternal Creator of the universe,

Who, from the heaven of heavens, his high abode,
Girt with omnipotence, with radiance crowned,
Of majesty divine,

looks down upon his boundless empire, and beholds the magnificent fabrick of his own creation,

In prospect from his throne, how good, how fair,
Answering his great idea;

shall this "Filial power," I say, be dragged from "the imperial throne of Godhead," and degraded to the state of an inferior, created, circumscribed, and even a corruptible mortal being?

Yes, that he shall, cries Mr. Lindsey, and that too upon the authority of the very writer whom you have now quoted yourself; for " Milton, though, he undoubtedly shewed himself uniformly orthodox in his first writings, with respect to the Trinity and the Godhead of Christ, in his *Paradise Lost*, appears entirely to have gone over to the Arian sentiment.—In his *Paradise Regained* a nearer contemplation of Christ's character in the evangelists seems to have led our great author very naturally to *what is called* Socinianism." Sequel to Apol. p. 407. This

† Ὀυ γὰρ ἐξίσαται ποτὲ τῆς αὑτῦ περιωπῆς ὁ υἱὸς τῦ Θεῦ, ἐ μεριζόμεν⊙-, ἐκ ἀπολεμνόμεν⊙-, ἐ μιταβαίνων ἐκ τόπου εἰς τόπον, παντάχῦ δὲ ὢν πάντοτε, ϗ μηδαμῇ περιεχόμεν⊙-, ὅλ⊙- νῦς, ὅλ⊙- φῶς παtρῷ⊙-, ὅλ⊙- ὀφθαλμ⊙-, πάντα ὁρῶν, πάντα ἀκέων, εἰδὼς πάντα. Clement. Alexandr. Stromatôn, lib. vii. p. 299. This passage throws light of John v. 13.

This latter charge is preferred in very indefinite terms. But as the fame have been made ufe of by the author of *Familiar Illuftrations*, who declares that his little book contains " the effence of *what is called* Socinianifm," I fhall fuppofe that Mr. Lindfey means exactly what this gentleman has more particularly defcribed; and, to avoid prolixity, am contented to reft the decifion of this queftion upon a fingle article.

This author then lays it down as an article of *what is called* Socinianifm, that Chrift did not exift previous to his carnal nativity in this world. Now, if it appear that Milton, in his *Paradife Regained*, acknowledges the pre-exiftence of our Lord, it will neceffarily follow, that a nearer contemplation of Chrift's character in the evangelifts, was not productive of that change of fentiment which Mr. Lindfey lays to the charge of our great poet. I might here afk and infift upon much more, but I am fatisfied with refutation.

The angels, who miniftered to our Lord after his temptation and triumph,

" Sing heavenly anthems of his victory,"

and, calling former victory to view, victory obtained over Satan and his rebellious hoft, previous to the material creation, to our incarnate Saviour himfelf declare, that

————————Him long of yore
Thou didft debel, and down from heaven caft,
With all his army—now thou haft avenged
Supplanted Adam, &c. &c.
             Par. Reg. book iv. v. 604.
                                    Here

Here then is angelic worship addressed to Jesus Christ, his pre-existence acknowledged, and to his arm is ascribed that conquest over "the infernal serpent, which, in his *Paradise Lost*, has been by the same poet ascribed to

"————————the almighty power."

PAR. LOST, book I. v. 44.

Is this the language of Socinianism? Where now is that transition from orthodoxy, so naturally the consequence of a nearer contemplation of Christ's character in the evangelists *?

As

* As by one man sin entered into the world, and death by sin, and as in Adam all die, even so in Christ shall all be made alive; for since by man came death, by Man came also the resurrection of the dead, 1 Corinth. xv. 21; and as by one man's disobedience many were made sinners, so by the obedience of One many shall be made righteous, Rom. v. 19.

These few verses comprehend the entire subject of Milton's two noble poems; for the Paradise Regained, properly considered, is no more than a sequel to the Paradise Lost. The fall of man, and the origin of sin and death, make the subject of the Paradise Lost; our restoration and victory over sin and death, that of the Paradise Regained. But we fell under temptation which we did not resist, and from one common ancestor derived that corruption which his lapse introduced into our nature. One common Father then to all mankind restores us by the resistance of temptation, and by his firm obedience, fully tried, redeems us from death and sin, over whom he has obtained a victory, which is imputed to us if we resort to and confess him. It was Satan that tempted and seduced the first man, who was earthly; but it is Satan that is foiled in all his wiles, defeated and repulsed by "the second Man, who is the Lord from heaven." It was by man we fell: it is a greater Man who must restore us, and resume the blissful seat.—Now I desire to know in what other character than that of a man could Milton, consistently with the simplicity of his plan, have considered our Saviour?—In Paradise Lost, book iii. v. 294, he puts into the mouth of the Father an assurance to the "Filial Godhead" that, on his assumption of humanity,

—————————— so Man as is most just
Shall satisfy for man ——————————

As to the remaining pofition, that "Milton had, in his *Paradife Loft*, entirely gone over to the Arian fentiment," it is a meer *gratis dictum*; and the only paffage quoted on the occafion, is one upon which Mr. Lindfey declares he will not rely, becaufe it fpeaks to the contrary. This is a perfectly new method of fupporting an affertion; and it remains to be explained why Milton is not to be believed when he fpeaks concerning his own faith. In the mean while, however, I fhall venture to rely upon this paffage, as an argument in evidence of Milton's orthodoxy at the time of writing his *Paradife Loft*. It ftands in context with the verfes quoted p. 242 above, and which I have already obferved were grounded upon the affertion made by St. Paul to the Philippians.

Thus then does our truly Chriftian poet exhibit the Father addreffing the Son on the fubject of man's future redemption:

Nor fhalt thou, by defcending to affume
Man's nature, leffen or degrade thy own,
Becaufe thou haft, tho' throned in higheft blifs
Equal to God, and equally enjoying
God-like fruition, quitted all to fave, &c.
                        PAR. LOST. book iii. v. 306.

From this we may learn that Milton thought it not robbery in our bleffed Redeemer to be "equal to God;" that he confidered him here on earth as having humbly affumed "man's nature;" and that hereby he did not look upon the Godhead as degraded, even though, to the perfection of manhood, it was neceffary that he fhould be born, and rife from infancy, through youth, to maturity. That "youthful meditations" therefore fhould employ that youth, affords no argument againſt the undegraded, undiminiſhed Godhead of the Meſſiah †. "The Word was made fleſh;" and in this fleſh, which he took that he might become our facrifice and propitiation, and which he reaſſumed, that, by a participation with us, he might be our eternal advocate, our Redeemer was born, grew in wiſdom and ſtature, died, was buried, arofe from the dead and afcended into heaven: his Godhead was neverthelefs exempt from all infirmity and ſufferings. He was man, and " having aſſumed humanity, he aſſumed all its properties, that he might be acknowledged to have taken fleſh not in appearance only, but in reality. In this character it is that he prays "the cup of his paſſion may pafs from him, nevertheleſs not according to his own will, but the will of the Father," Matth. xxvi. 39. For, of every faithful man, it is characteriſtic, firſt, as he is fleſh, to fuffer pain with reluctance, efpecially pain that is mortal; and fecondly, inafmuch as he is faithful, to acquieſce in the will of God, even where it oppoſes his own will, left he ſhould feem more to relinquiſh hope, on account of his own weakneſs, than to indulge it from a confident reliance upon the ſtrength of God *." As man then, to

the

† This is faid in reply to an objection made by Mr. Lindfey to Dr. Newton's Comment on Paradiſe Regained, book i. verfe 101: "How finely and confiftenly does Milton here imagine the *youthful meditations* of our Saviour," is the remark of the learned Prelate, on which Mr. Lindfey adds, "*God can never become a child or a youth*. But early prejudice hinders us from feeing the groffeft contradictions in our own fentiments." Which is it, in candour or penetration that Mr. Lindfey confiders himfelf fo highly fuperior to Dr. Newton?

* Sufcipiens enim naturam carnis humanæ omnes proprietatis implevit, ut non in phantafiâ habuiſſe carnem exiſtimaretur ſed in veritate: fecundum quod in hoc loco orat calicem paſſionis tranfire, fi fe, fed non ficut vult ipfe, fed ficut vult Pater. Quoniam proprium eſt omnis hominis fidelis

the perfection of whose nature infirmity is essential, we here find antiquity declare that our Lord feared, deprecated, and yet sustained his afflictions; that, "by anticipating the office of the executioner, he voluntarily yielded up the Ghost, together with the WORD *." Thus then he even dies. What follows: Is he therefore not God? No, cry these men, for God cannot die. Peevish objection! Do we say he can? They know we do not. But let Lactantius answer them: "By the Spirit, Jesus Christ was the Son of God, and by the flesh, the Son of man; that is, CHRIST WAS BOTH GOD AND MAN. He is God, for Isaiah has declared, "They shall fall down unto thee, they shall make supplication unto thee, saying, Surely God is in thee, and there is none else, there is no God. Verily thou art a God that hidest thyself, O God of Israel, the Saviour, Isaiah xlv. 14 †."—Let Origen also rebuke their petulance:

fidelis primum quidem nolle pati aliquid doloris, maximè quod ducit usque ad mortem, quia homo est carnalis; si autem sic voluerit Deus, acquiescere etiam contra voluntatem suam, quia fidelis est, ne plus videatur in se desperare quam in Deum sperare." Orig. Tractatus in Matth. xxxv. tom II. p. 115.

This passage stands in context with that quoted in the 243d page: which see. See also p. 174, to which refer it.

* Spiritum cum VERBO sponte dimisit, prævento carnificis officio. Tertull. Apologet. adv. Gentes, cap. xxi.

† The life of LUCIUS COELIUS LACTANTIUS FIRMIANUS was continued into the fourth century. He is rather an elegant writer, having principally addicted himself to the study of Rhetorick.—The passage translated above is thus introduced: The author assures us that Christ was born of the Father, first without a mother, and afterwards of a woman without a father, that it might be truly said of him that he was without father and without mother: for in each nativity he was without one of them. Per Spiritum factus est Filius Dei, & hominis per carnem, id est, & Deus & Homo. He then applies the prophecies which I have stated, and declares that the 44th Psalm is addressed to the Son. Lucii Coelii Lactantii de verâ Religione & Sapientiâ, lib. iv. cap.

lance: " We do not fay that Chrift was a meer man, but confefs him to be both God and Man. We confefs him to be equally God and Man *." And that, " fulfilling the prophecies, he has evidently appeared, both according to his Godhead and according to his Manhood †." " For the Word of God, clothed in the flefh of Mary, came forth into the world; and in him was one fubftance which was feen, another which was underftood. His flefhly form was obvious to the eyes of all; but to the few only, and thofe a chofen few, was the knowledge of his Godhead imparted ‡."

For

cap. xiii. de *Jefu Deo & Homine*, deque eo teftimonia prophetarum.—The very title of this chapter affords an argument in proof of the writer's fentiments, and yet Mr. Lindfey lays claim to his concurrence with him. If Lactantius actually concur with Mr. Lindfey, under what neceffity did he lie to give an erroneous tranflation of his words?—I will not here tranfcribe the mifreprefented paffage throughout; I only afk of Mr. Lindfey, by what authority he ventured to turn the words " patriâ fcilicet virtute & majeftate *pollentem*," which fignify *pofitively*, " mighty in his Father's power and majefty," by a *comparative* term, which makes our Saviour only the moft excellent of the angels? " And although he afterwards created innumerable other fpirits by him, whom we call angels, yet this his Firft-born alone has he honoured with the name of God, as *excelling moft* in his Father's majefty and power." Preface to the Sequel to Mr. Lindfey's Apology, p. 20.—I accept of fuch a conduct as a conceffion of the author, and, upon Mr. Lindfey's acknowledgement, pronounce Lactantius not to have been an Unitarian.

* Chriftum non purum hominem dicimus, fed Deum & Hominem confitemur.—Deum pariter atque Hominem fateamur. Orig. Hom. viii. in Jofh. tom I. p. 185.

† Secundum Deitatem & fecundum Humanitatem Chriftus prophetatus evidenter appareat. Orig. Hom. xxii. in Numer. tom. 1. p. 153.

‡ Verbum Dei ex Mariæ carne veftitum proceffit in hunc mundum, & aliud quidem erat quod videbatur in eo, aliud quod intelligebatur. Carnis namque afpectus in eo patebat omnibus, paucis vero & electis dabatur Divinitatis agnitio. Orig. Hom. i. in Levit. tom I. p. 64.

For " Chrift is the Word of God, but the Word was made flefh," John i. 14. In Chrift, therefore, there is one fubftance from above, another affumed of the human nature and the virgin's womb. Chrift fuffers, but it is in the flefh: he became obedient to death, but it was as he is flefh. Neverthelefs the Word, which is Chrift as concerning the Spirit, remained in incorruption. *See above, p. 159.* He is therefore not only our Sacrifice, but alfo, as concerning the Spirit, he is our Prieft *." And through him " our foul is efcaped as a bird out of the fnare of the fowler: the fnare is broken and we are efcaped," Pf. cxxiv. 7. But who has broken the fnares, fave he who alone could not be holden of them? For tho' he was under the dominion of death, yet was obedience his own voluntary act. He died, but not as we do, who yield under the neceffity of fin; for he alone it is who was " free among the dead," Pf. lxxxiv. 4. And becaufe he was free among the dead, having vanquifhed him who had the power of death, he took away the bondage to death, Heb. ii. 14, Rom. viii. 15, and not only raifed himfelf from the

dead,

---

* Chriftus Verbum Dei eft; fed Verbum caro factum eft. Unum igitur in Chrifto de fuperioribus eft; alterum ex humana natura & virginali utero fufceptum. Patitur ergo Chriftus, fed in carne; & pertulit mortem, fed caro. Verbum vero in incorruptione permanfit, quod fecundum Spiritum Chriftus. Ideo ipfe & Hoftia eft & Pontifex fecundum Spiritum. Orig. Hom. ix. in Genefin. tom. I. p. 18.

The argument of the father here is the typical agreement both of Ifaac, who returned from the altar unhurt, and of the ram which was facrificed upon it, with Chrift at once both Prieft and Victim. In which latter character he fays that John addreffed him, faying, " Behold the Lamb of God, which taketh away the fins of the world," John i. 36. Gen. xxii. 13.

Anima autem hominis eft quæ conturbatur & triftis eft ufque ad mortem, non Verbum quod erat a principio apud Deum; quod nunquam mæret, nunquam turbatum eft, nunquam dixit, heu mihi. Neque enim Verbum fuftinet, fed homo qui iftos patitur affectus, ut fæpe expofuimus. Orig. Hom. xi. in Jerem. tom. I. p. 381.

dead, but with himself raised up also those who were held in death †."

But, with regard to Milton, Mr. Lindsey proceeds to bring farther, but similar proofs of his Socinianism, and says that, in one of his later writings, we find him thus delivering his sentiments:—" The hottest disputes among Protestants are about things not absolutely necessary to salvation.—The Arian and Socinian are charged to dispute against the Trinity: they affirm to believe the Father, Son, and Holy Ghost, according to scripture, and the apostolic creed. As for the terms trinity, triniunity, coëssentiality, triperfonality, and the like, they reject them as scholastic notions, not to be found in scripture, which, by a general Protestant maxim, is plain and perspicuous abundantly to explain its own meaning in the propereft words belonging to so high a matter, and so necessary to be known: *a mystery indeed in their sophistic subtilties, but in scripture a plain doctrine.*"

Here

† Quis autem contrivit laqueos, nisi ille qui solus in eis teneri non potuit? quamvis & ipse in morte fuit, voluntarie, & non ut nos necessitate pedcati. Solus est enim qui fuit inter mortuos liber. Et quia liber inter mortuos fuit, idcirco devicto eo qui habuit mortis imperium, abstraxit captivitatem quæ tenebatur in mortem. Et non solum seipsum resuscitavit a mortuis, sed & eos qui tenebantur in morte simul excitavit. Orig. Homil. iii. in Cantic. Canticorum, tom. I. p. 345.

On the prophecy of Jacob, which concludes, " Who shall rouse him up?" Gen. xlix. 9, this father affords a comment similar to the passage now quoted: " But the prophet says, " Who shall rouse him up?" thus interrogatively, because he is said sometimes to have been raised by the Father, Gal. i. 1. And he has also declared that, after three days, he will himself raise up the temple of his body." Quod vero ait, quis suscitabit eum? idcirco quia nunc a Patre dicitur suscitatus, nunc etiam ipse templum corporis sui post triduum suscitare se dicit; & merito in hoc quasi percontantis designatur affectus. Orig. Hom. xvii. in Num. tom I. p. 151.

Here Mr. Lindsey closes his extract: but to his own conscience I put the question, whether Milton here closes the sense? and whether he did not himself know that this great author proceeds without intermission in the following terms? "Their other opinions are of less moment: they dispute the satisfaction of Christ, or rather the word satisfaction, as not scriptural, but they acknowledge him both God and their Saviour *." If then they make this acknowledgement, it is evident that the Godhead of our Saviour is not one of those things about which Protestants engage in disputes among themselves, and consequently that it is not one of those things which Milton pronounces " not absolutely necessary to salvation." They dispute concerning scholastic terms, he says, which some reject because not found in the scripture, according to which, though they do not use the word *trinity*, they yet affirm to believe the Father, Son, and Holy Ghost. And as to " *their sophistic subtilties*," which Mr. Lindsey so emphatically prints in Italic characters, they will be found to be the subtilties of the Arian and Socinian, who have made into a mystery this high matter, so necessary to be known, and which is in scripture a plain doctrine †.

This

* The work from which this extract is taken, is entitled " Of true Religion, Heresie, Schism, Toleration, and what best Means may be used against the Growth of POPERY." It is a noble tract, and in every respect worthy of its great and liberal author.——A summary of the contents might contribute to my argument; but it is very brief, and I had rather the whole were adverted to.

† It hurts me exceedingly to relinquish the good opinion I had heretofore entertained of Mr. Lindsey's veracity; but where his deviation from truth tends evidently to mislead the reader, I am not at liberty to let it pass undetected. In the present instance, the evidence is easily accessible, and he accordingly stands convicted upon the fullest proof. But he may sometimes have made assertions of a similar nature, the reality of which
cannot

This charge, however seemingly paradoxical, may be, and indeed is, strictly true; for, although the Arian and Socinian exclaim against mystery, it is upon this very ground that they object to the plain and necessary truths contained in the scriptures.—" When you confess one God," says Origen, " and in the same confession assert that the Father, and the Son, and the Holy Ghost are one God, how perplexed, how difficult, how inextricable does this seem to the faithless! Again; when you say that the Lord of glory has been crucified, 1 Cor. ii. 8, and that it is the Son of man who has descended from heaven, John iii. 13, how perplexed! cries he who hears, but hears without faith, how difficult is this! The error is their own; do thou nevertheless remain stedfast, nor entertain

a

cannot be so readily investigated. He may have said that one gentleman of the name of Haynes had given assurance to another gentleman of the name of Baron, that Sir Isaac Newton denied, nay, derided, the incarnation of our Lord.—But he actually has said so. How then is such a charge to be refuted? All means of enquiring into a fact of this nature are rescinded. Is Sir Isaac Newton therefore to labour on for ever under the weight of this burdensome calumny? No, not another hour. The answer is obvious and sufficient. The accusation stands upon the very same testimony which has been already borne against the respected name of Milton: its validity has been already discussed; it has been already superseded. We are therefore at liberty to deny the assertion, and consider the whole together as only an exercise of *Arian or Socinian subtilty*.

If Mr. Lindsey should chuse to corroborate this third-hand testimony of Mr. Haynes, by citing Mr. Whiston also to give evidence against Sir Isaac Newton; I refer the reader to a letter written by Mr. Whiston himself to the Earl of Nottingham, dated July 10, 1719, " concerning the eternity of the Son of God and of the Holy Spirit." He will there find that, out of a considerable number of extracts from the fathers, scarce a single passage is justly represented, or truly and honestly translated, by that writer. This I should conceive a sufficient ground of objection to Mr. Whiston's testimony.—Lord Nottingham wrote an answer to this epistle, in which he has with great penetration detected, and with equal perspicuity exposed, the frauds of his adversary.

a doubt concerning this belief, knowing that God hath shewn to thee this way of faith *." This way of faith then it is that the Arian and Socinian would tangle and perplex. Not seeing what the plain truths of scripture really are, they convert them into what they are not, and then upbraid us with doctrines which we do not profess. "Had these disciples, like *modern tritheists,*" says Mr. Lindsey, (or somebody that he quotes, I care not who) " praised and blessed GOD *the Father*, GOD *the Son,* and GOD *the Holy Ghost*, the worshippers in the temple would have stoned them.' (Sequel to Apology, p. 30). I do verily believe they would, for so they actually did by our Lord himself, when, according to their own account, " he made himself to be God, John x. 33." So likewise they actually did by Stephen when " he called upon the Lord Jesus to receive his spirit," Acts vii. 59. Of the Jews, five times did Paul receive forty stripes, save one; thrice, as a minister of Christ, was he beaten with rods, and once was he stoned, 2 Cor. xi. 24. And Origen apprehends " that they will stone him also, as a blasphemer, for glorifying the Lord Jesus Christ †."—The glory of our Redeemer is the object of Jewish persecution, and consequently every exercise,

nay,

---

* Cum confitearis unum Deum, eademque confessione Patrem, & Filium, & Spiritum Sanctum asseris unum Deum, quam tortuosum, quam difficile, quam inextricabile videtur hoc esse infidelibus! Tu deinde cum dicis Dominum majestatis crucifixum, & Filium hominis esse qui descendit de cœlo, quam tortuosa hæc videntur & quam difficilia! qui audit, si non cum fide audiat, dicit; quia errant ipsi. Sed tu fixus esto, nec dubites de hujusmodi fide, sciens quia Deus tibi ostendit hanc fidei viam. Orig. in Exodum, Homil. vi. tom. I. p. 44.

† Nec vero quasi blasphemantem me lapidetis dum velim glorificare Dominum meum Jesum Christum. Orig. Homil. iii. in Isaiam, tom. I. p. 352.

nay, every inftrument of Jewifh perfecution may be confidered as bearing teftimony to his glory. With gratitude, therefore, I acknowledge Mr. Lindfey's contribution of a new witnefs to the Godhead of Jefus Chrift; for while, with threats of Jewifh perfecution, he enjoins us to hold our peace, and defift from " faying hofanna to the Son of David," he has literally made " even the ftones cry out," Luke xix. 40, (fee p. 166). —And does Mr. Lindfey at length fpeak out and profefs himfelf a Jew? or would he perfuade us that the Jewifh and Chriftian religions are under the fame difpenfation? This he can never effect, " for the Jews do not believe in Chrift †." — But is there not a little Socinian fubtilty here? Are we really *tritheifts*? or is tritheifm pretended by us to be the plain doctrine of the fcriptures? This is precifely the conduct objected to thefe men by Milton. The Trinitarian doctrine which we embrace, they charge to us as tritheifm, which it is not; and thus do they fubtilly fophifticate the fenfe of the fcripture, which alone we admit of as our rule of faith in this or in any other article of our religion. " There are fome indeed who make profeffion of the Father, Son, and Holy Ghoft, but not in fincerity, and according to truth: fuch are all heretics who profefs, but, being without faith, fophifticate the profeffion of, the Father, Son, and Holy Ghoft. For they either falfely divide the Son from the Father, by declaring the Father to be of one nature, and the Son of another; or elfe they falfely make confufion by thinking God a compound of three natures, or only a trinal name. But he who makes a good confeffion, afcribes to Father, Son, and Holy Ghoft their refpective peculiars, yet neverthelefs profeffes that,

among

† Chrifto Judæi non crediderunt. Orig. in Rom. cap. x.

among them, there subsists no diversity of nature or of substance ‡."

In his Homily upon the Decalogue, Origen asserts that the second commandment strictly prohibits not only the reality, but even the external appearance of devotion towards idols: " Thou shalt not bow down to them, nor worship them." "Now we must know that a resolution to obey this commandment, and to renounce all other gods and lords, and to adhere to, or acknowledge but one God and Lord, is a declaration of irreconcileable war upon all others. When, therefore, we come to the grace of baptism, renouncing all other gods and lords, we acknowledge one God alone, the Father, Son, and Holy Ghost †." And " this faith in the Father, the Son, and the Holy Ghost, we hold together with all who are assembled to the

---

‡ Sunt enim nonnulli qui annunciant quidem & prædicant de Patre, & Filio, & Spritu Sancto, non syncere, non integre: ut sunt omnes hæretici, qui Patrem quidem & Filium, & Spiritum Sanctum annunciant, sed non bene, non fideliter annunciant. Aut enim male separant Filium a Patre, ut alterius naturæ Patrem, alterius Filium dicant: aut male confundunt, ut ex tribus compositum Deum, vel trinæ tantummodo appellationis in eo esse vocabulum putent. Qui autem bene annunciant bona, proprietates quidem Patri, & Filio, & Spiritui Sancto suas cuique dabit, nihil autem diversitatis esse confitebitur in naturâ vel substantiâ. Qui ergo ita annunciant evangelium, non solum bona annunciant, sed bene & integre annunciant bona. Orig. in Epist. ad Roman. cap. x. lib. viii. tom. II. p. 383.

† Cum decreveris præcepti ejus servare mandatum, & omnes cæteros deos & dominos repudiare, & præter unum Deum & Dominum neminem habere vel deum vel dominum, hoc est bellum sine fœdere denunciasse omnibus cæteris. Cum ergo venimus ad gratiam baptismi, universis aliis diis & dominis renunciantes, solum confitemur Deum Patrem, & Filium, & Spiritum Sanctum. Orig. Homil. viii. in Exod. xx. tom. I. p. 52.

the church of God *," and "who follow their Lord and Creator Jesus Christ †." "It is therefore our part, who abjure the adoration of the creature, and worship and adore only the Father, and the Son, and the Holy Ghost, even as we err not in our religion, so likewise to offend not in our actions and our conversation ‡;" "but with such diligence to order our actions, with such diligence to order our conversation, that we may be thought worthy of the notice of God, that he may deign to take cognizance of us; that we may be thought worthy of the notice of his Son Jesus Christ, and of the notice of the Holy Ghost; that, being acknowledged by the Trinity, we may deserve fully, honestly, and perfectly to acknowledge the mystery of the Trinity by the revelation of Jesus Christ; to whom be glory and power for ever and ever. Amen.§"

Here again we have an instance of glory being ascribed to our Lord, to whom Origen farther addresses the

---

* Credo fidem Patris, Filii, & Spiritûs Sancti, in quam credunt omnes qui sociantur ecclesiæ Dei. Orig. Hom. v. in Levitic. tom. I. p. 77.

† Sequentur Dominum & Creatorem suum Christum Jesum. Origen, Homil. ii. in Exod. tom. I. p. 37.

‡ Nos autem qui nullam creaturam, sed Patrem & Filium & Spiritum Sanctum colimus & adoramus, sicut non erramus in cultu ita nec in actibus quidem & in conversatione peccemus. Orig. lib. i. cap. i. in Rom. tom II. p. 302.

§ Nos vero operam demus tales effici actus nostros, talem conversationem nostram, ut digni habeamus notitiâ Dei, ut nos scire dignetur, ut digni habeamur notitiâ Filii ejus Jesû Christi, & notitiâ Spiritûs Sancti; ut agniti a Trinitate, & nos sacramentum Trinitatis plene & integre & perfecte mereamur agnoscere, revelante nobis Domino nostro Jesu Christo, cui est gloria & imperium, in secula seculorum. Amen. Orig. Hom iv. in Genes. cap. xvii. tom I. p. 32.

the following prayer, bearing an obvious reference to John xiii. 5, &c. "Come, I beseech thee, O Lord Jesus, thou Son of David, and wash the feet of thy servants, and purge away the filth of thy sons and daughters. Wash the feet of our minds, that, casting off our old garments, we may imitate and follow thee ‡."

As Mr. Lindsey has himself allowed "religious worship, and the address of prayer to Christ, to be the principal argument for his divinity," it is not unreasonable to infer, that Origen, thus complying with "those plain declarations of scripture which enjoin prayer to Christ, intended thereby to ascribe the proper honour of divinity to him." Apol. p. 135. We may farther conclude from this direct petition to our Saviour, that, to Origen's understanding, the scriptures clearly appeared to authorise, nay, to command "the *invocation* of Jesus Christ our Lord," 1 Cor. i. 2. To Mr. Lindsey's, however, they seem to have prohibited all intercourse with him. The sense, therefore, in which Origen, an early Greek writer, accepted those injunctions, I shall here oppose to that interpretation which has been lately put upon them by Mr. Lindsey and other English Unitarians.

Mr. Lindsey declares (he says after Dr. Clarke and Dr. Hammond, but even their critical authority must sink under the weight of Origen) that this phrase of *calling upon Christ* (ἐπικαλύμεν⊕·) never occurs in scripture,

so

‡ Veni, precor, Domine Jesu Fili David, exue vestimenta quæ tu Domine induisti propter me, & accingere propter me, & mitte aquam in pelvim, & lava pedes servorum tuorum, & dilue sordes filiorum & filiarum tuarum. Lava pedes animæ nostræ, ut nos te imitantes & sectantes exuamus nos vetera vestimenta. Orig. Homil. viii. in Judic. tom. I. p. 219.

so as to imply directly *invoking him*, except in Acts vii. 59. And, laying it down as a general rule that it signifies, having the name of another called upon the subject spoken of, he alledges that, in 1 Cor. i. 2, inftead of, "with all who call upon the name of Jesus Chrift our Lord," it should be tranflated, "with all them that are called by the name of our Lord Jesus Chrift." See Apol. p. 132, and Script. Confut. p. 79 and 102.

It is only the reputation of Dr. Clarke and Dr. Hammond that can preferve such an affertion from contempt; and were not the ftrength of their authority placed beneath the obfervation, I should leave it to fall by its own weaknefs. The remark, fo far as it affects 1 Cor. i. 2, muft go upon a fuppofition that ἐπικαλεμένε here, and in every other paflage in which it occurs, (one only excepted) is a paffive participle, or, I rather think, the participle of a fubftantive verb. But if this were fo, it muft have been followed by the furname itfelf, put in the fame cafe with the fubject on which it is called, and with which it is brought into appofition; or, if followed by an accufative cafe, not appofite, a prepofition muft intervene to govern it, and the furname, which is impofed thereupon, whether expreffed or implied, be made the fubject of the propofition, as in the epiftle of St. James ii. 7, τὸ καλὸν ὄνομα τὸ ἐπικληθὲν ἐφ' ὑμᾶς. But if the verb ἐπικαλέομαι, or any of its tenfes, be immediately followed by an accufative cafe, evidently governed by it, it muft then clearly have an active or tranfitive fignification, and be rendered into Englifh by the like tenfe of the verb "*to invoke or call upon*;" fo likewife the participles ἐπικαλέμενω, &c. followed by an accufative cafe, muft fignify "*invoking or calling upon*," unlefs they be themfelves in the accufative cafe, and agree with fome antecedent accufative, of which they

they assert that which follows them, and predicate it the surname of the antecedent subject: and in such cases they may admit of the sense of *surnamed*, as in the following instance, εἰσῆλθε δὲ ὁ Σατανᾶς εἰς Ἰούδαν τὸν ἐπικαλέμενον Ἰσκαριώτην, Luke xxii. 3. But, in such circumstances, the surname is not governed by the participle, but agrees with and stands in apposition to the subject, of which it is thus substantively declared *to be* an addition. I need hardly add that, when transitive, the verb ἐπικαλέομαι and its participles are of the middle voice.

This brief rule seems to me to carry a full and sufficient answer to every objection which Mr. Lindsey has brought, or indeed is likely ever to bring, against the common acceptation of that verse, the sense of which he has been pleased to controvert.—In order that the subject spoken of may have the name of another called upon it, belief in that other cannot possibly be a requisite qualification, because the subject is passive; whereas, on the other hand, to invocation belief is absolutely and indispensably necessary; for how shall we invoke or call upon him whom we have not believed? Rom. x. 14. Invocation is obviously here the commandment of the apostle.—St. Paul desires Timothy to follow righteousness, faith, &c. μετὰ τῶν ἐπικαλεμένων τὸν κύριον ἐκ καθαρᾶς καρδίας, 2 Tim. ii. 22. Can the word here signify any thing but invoking or calling upon? To have a surname (in which the subject is meerly passive) from a pure heart is really rank nonsense; so that, in this passage, it cannot possibly be the meaning of the participle ἐπικαλεμένων.—The words, " whosoever shall call upon the name of the Lord shall be saved" or " delivered," were prophetically written by Joel ii. 32, and are evidently referred to by St. Paul, Rom. x. 13, and by him introduced with the word
"*for*,"

"*for*," as a cause already subsisting (the prophecy affording a sufficient establishment and assurance of it) for what he had said just before concerning the riches of the Lord unto all who shall call upon him *. Now, in whatever sense the prophet Joel uses this term, St. Paul also uses it in the same; and the Lord spoken of by the prophet, is the same that is spoken of by the apostle: so that here a dilemma meets Mr. Lindsey's assertion, and he is at liberty to chuse whether "*the Lord*" be put for God the Father or for our Lord Jesus Christ. If, for God the Father, he does not argue against the invocation which may be intended by the words "*call upon*;" but if, following St. Paul, he allows it to be put for our Saviour, and that the prophets therefore call him "*the Lord*," why must the word shift its meaning upon the new application? An hypothesis falls to the ground. Say rather with honesty that the divinity of our Lord Jesus Christ must be acceded to upon the authority of the Old Testament also. But "we desire to shew that the God revealed under the law and the gospel is the same God, the same God of old, to day and for ever. Amen. But there are some who, in their opinion, divide the Godhead of antient revelation from that which is now proclaimed to be in Christ. We yet know but one God in past and present time; one Christ, now and heretofore; and in like manner one Holy Ghost, together with the Father and the

---

* "For the same Lord over all is rich unto all that call upon him; for whosoever shall call upon the name of the Lord shall be saved. How shall they call on him in whom they have not believed?" Rom. x. 13. Thus in the original: ὁ γὰρ αὐτὸς κύριος πάντων πλουτῶν εἰς πάντας τοὺς ἐπικαλουμένους αὐτόν. Πᾶς γὰρ, ὃς ἂν ἐπικαλέσηται τὸ ὄνομα κυρίου σωθήσεται. And, omitting the word γὰρ, which the apostle introduces only to shew that he refers to a prophecy, the passage in Joel is exactly the same in the Septuagint version.

the Son eternal †." "Though not comprehending, yet confessing the Father and the Son, we do not separate the Father from the Son, nor the Son from the Father, while the Jews continue only to receive the Father, and, separating Christ from God the Creator, his Father, do not receive Christ, who is his Word and his Wisdom *." And is it to the Levite that we are now to resort for instruction? is it in the abrogated temple that we are now to seek for the gospel of Jesus Christ? No, "for the Jews have not believed in Christ, and therefore do not call upon him whom they have not believed, (Rom. x. 14). But in the beginning of St. Paul's first epistle to the Corinthians, where he says, "with all who, in every place, call upon the name of Jesus Christ our Lord, both theirs and ours," (1 Corinth. i. 2.) he pronounces Jesus Christ, whose name is there called upon, to be God. If therefore Enos, and Moses, and Aaron, and Samuel, called upon the Lord, and he heard them, without question they called upon the Lord Jesus Christ. And if to
call

† Hæc autem nos qui ecclesiastici sumus magis debemus advertere, qui volumus eundem Deum esse legis & evangelii, ipsum Deum & antiquitus & nunc & in omnia secula seculorum. Amen. Sunt quidem qui opinione suâ veterem divinitatem ab eâ quæ in Christo annuntiatur dividant. Nos unum novimus Deum & in præterito & in presente, unum Christum & nunc & modo, similiter & unum Spiritum Sanctum cum Patre &·Filio sempiternum. Origen, Homil. vi. in Jeremiam, tom. I. p. 372.

* Qui ergo separant Christum a Creatore Deo Patre suo hæretici, & Judæi, qui solum Patrem recipiunt, & Verbum & sapientiam ejus Christum non recipiunt, non faciunt ex duobus decimis unum panem. Nos autem mensuræ quidem ipsius, id est substantiæ nomen vel rationem comprehendere aut invenire non possumus: confitentes tamen Patrem & Filium unum facimus panem ex duabus decimis: non ut panis unus ex unâ decimâ fiat, & alius ex alia, ut sint ipsæ duæ decimæ una massa, & unus panis. Quomodo duæ decimæ una massa fit? quia non separo Filium a Patre, nec Patrem a Filio. Orig. Homil. xiii. in Levitic, tom. I. p. 105. Levit. vii.

N n

call upon the name of the Lord, and to adore God, be one and the fame thing; as Chrift is called upon, fo is Chrift adored; and as we addrefs our prayers to God the Father, fo likewife we addrefs them to the Lord Jefus Chrift; as we prefer our petitions to the Father, fo likewife we prefer them to the Son; and as we render our thankfgiving to God, fo likewife we render thankfgiving to our Saviour. For the holy fcripture teaches that one honour fhall be afcribed to both, when it fays that "all men fhould honour the Son even as they honour the Father, John v. 23 *. See above, p. 250.

The

* Chrifto enim Judæi non crediderunt, ideo "nec invocant eum cui non crediderunt," (πῶς ἓν ἐπικαλέσονlαι ἰις ὃν ὰκ ἐπιϛεύσαν;) Sed & in principio epiftolæ quem ad Corinthios fcribit, ubi dicit; "Cum omnibus qui invocant nomen Domini Jefu Chrifti, &c." (σὺν πάσι τοῖς ἐπικαλυμένοις τὸ ὄνομα τῦ κυρίυ ἡμῶν Ἰησῦ Χριϛῦ.) Eum, cujus nomen invocatur, Deum, Jefum Chriftum efle pronuntiant. Si ergo Enos (ὗτος ἤλπισεν ἐπικαλεῖσθαι τὸ ὄνομα τῦ κυρίυ τῦ Θεῦ. Gen. iv. 26.) Et Mofes, & Aaron, & Samuel invocabant Dominum & ipfe exaudiebat eos (Μωυσῆς κỳ Ἀαρὼν ἐν τοῖς ἱερεῦσιν αὐlῦ, κỳ Σαμυὴλ ἐν τοῖς ἐπικαλυμένοις τὸ ὄνομα αὐlῦ. Ἐπεκαλῦνlο τὸν κύριον, κỳ αὐlὸς ἰισήκυεν. Pfalm. xcix. 6.) Sine dubio Chriftum Jefum invocabant: Et fi invocare Domini nomen & adorare Deum unum atque idem eft; ficut invocatur Chriftus, & adorandus eft Chriftus; & ficut offerimus Deo Patri primo omnium orationes, ita & Domino Jefu Chrifto; & ficut offerimus poftulationes Patri, ita offerimus poftulationes Filio; & ficut offerimus gratiarum actiones Deo, ita gratias offerimus Salvatori. Unum namque utrique honorem deferendum, id eft, Deo Patri & Filio, divinus docet fermo cum dicit, ut honorificent Filium ficut honorificant Patrem, Johan. v. 23. Origen, lib. viii. in Roman. tom. II. p. 382.

It were an idle objection to fay here that my quotation is in Latin, whereas Origen wrote in Greek, and therefore that *invoco*, the fubject here, might not have been ἐπικαλέομαι in the Original. The texts, on which the father has made this comment, appear, and put the real fact out of all farther queftion.—He tells us himfelf too that he ufed the Septuagint verfion of the Old Teftament.—Nos Septuaginta interpretum fcripta per omnia cuftodimus. Origen, Hom. i. in Cantic. Canticorum, tom. I. p. 320.

The fenfe of antiquity is now ftated. To call upon, or invoke by prayer and adoration, is by Origen pronounced an acknowledgement of his Godhead, who is thus adored. And fhall modern criticifm ftand up againft the authority of this Greek father, who has thus explicitly attefted, that whofoever has, even in the Old Teftament, called upon the Lord, has called upon the Lord Jefus Chrift ?

But it is not denied, fays Mr. Lindfey, refcinding his former tenet, that, " in the Septuagint, ἐπικαλέομαι τὸ ὀνομα κυρίυ, is very often ufed, and always fignifies to call upon, or invoke by prayer and adoration, *the Lord, the God of Ifrael.*" Sequel to Apology, p. 56. Who that God of Ifrael is, the fathers have all concurred to fhew *. But that is not now the queftion. If the acknowledged fignification of ἐπικαλέομαι be *to invoke*, and if invocation be a teftimony of Godhead, the Godhead of Chrift muft be acknowledged upon this fingle conceffion relative to the meaning of the word. But the Godhead of Chrift is not to be admitted upon any terms: and whether the premifes can or cannot be eftablifhed, is a matter of little importance, for no change can take place in an hypothefis; and therefore, though every pretended ground of denial be taken away, the divinity of Chrift muft ftill be denied. Has not reafon intuitively decided againft the doctrine ? Remarks, p. 78. What then can demonftration do but argue ad abfurdum ? The conclufion alone muft be made the criterion of the premifes, and the teftimony of fcripture itfelf, the acknowledged revelation of God, be adjudged a falfehood, when brought into competition with thofe innate communications which he has been pleafed to imprefs on our nature.—But has fuch

* See page 190, 80, &c.

a communication been really made? has the human intellect been stamped with such an impreſſion of a God, as may with any adequacy repreſent the mode of his exiſtence? What grounds ſubſiſt on which we may form ſuch a ſubſtantial hypotheſis as ſhall not inſtantly vaniſh, when beamed upon by the light of his radiant Word?—" When I ſpeak of the omnipotence of God, of his inviſibility and eternity, I chuſe a lofty theme; when I ſpeak of the coëternity of his only begotten Son, and thoſe myſteries which concern him, I take a lofty theme; I take a lofty theme when I ſpeak of the majeſty of the Holy Ghoſt. Theſe alone afford an elevated ſubject of diſcourſe; and after theſe three, ſpeak thou of nothing in an elevated ſtrain, for all things are low and abject when compared to the glorious height of this Trinity *." But of theſe high matters it is not reaſon which has imparted any information. Right reaſon, whoſe dignity conſiſts in ſelf-knowledge, herſelf comprehended, and, as it were, inſulated within the all-ſurrounding infinity of that Being, who extends beyond comprehenſion, in modeſt ſilence yields attention to the uninterrupted words of her Creator. She ſees " the thick darkneſs which God has made his ſecret place," and, conſcious of her own inability to penetrate " the clouds which are round about him," with "the earth that ſhook and the heavens which drop at the preſence of God," " trembling, removed, afar off, ſhe enquires," " and hears him anſwer her by a voice;" ſhe is

" an-

---

* Quando de omnipotentiâ Dei loquor, de inviſibilitate & ſempiternitate ejus, excelſa loquor. Quando de unigeniti ejus coëternitate cæteriſque ejus myſteriis pronuncio, excelſa loquor. Quando de Sancti Spiritûs magnificentiâ diſſero, excelſa loquor. In his tantum nobis conceditur loqui excelſa. Poſt hæc tria jam nihil loquaris excelſum. Omnia enim humilia ſunt & dejecta. quantum ad Trinitatis hujus celſitudinem ſpectat. Nolite ergo multiplicare loqui excelſa niſi de Patre & Filio & Spiritu Sancto. Origen. lib. i. in Reges, tom. I. p. 225.

"answered in the secret place of thunder;" she hearkens to the voice of God; and when he speaks, she accedes, she believes. " The thick cloud now passes away, and brightness is before him. The heavens declare his righteousness, and all the people see his glory." " The cloud is taken up from his sanctuary," and reason is thenceforward enabled to proceed. The truth of God alone she assumes for her premises, and what unbiassed investigation must necessarily deduce from his word, she establishes as the conclusion: his attestation is to her conclusive. " In the scriptures then she finds and acquiesces in the testimony of his appointed witnesses, who have declared " that there is one God, who created and disposed all things, and who, out of nothing, gave existence to the universe; who was the God of all just men from the first creation of the world; the God of Adam, Enoch, Noah, Shem, Abraham, Isaac, Jacob, and the twelve patriarchs; the God of Moses and of the prophets. And that this God, as he had before promised by his prophets, did in the latter times send our Lord Jesus Christ*; first to call Israel, but secondly to call the Gentiles, because of the infidelity of the people Israel. That this just and good God, the Father of our Lord Jesus Christ, who is the God of the apostles, alike the God of the Old and
New

---

* " Think it not a disgrace to his nature," says Origen, " if the Son be sent by the Father. For, that you may acknowledge the Unity of the Godhead in the Trinity, Christ alone, according to Isaiah in a particular instance, forgiveth sins, and yet it is certain that sins are forgiven by the Trinity."

Nec putes naturæ contumeliam, si Filius a Patre mittitur. Denique ut Unitatem Deitatis in Trinitate cognoscas, solus Christus in præsenti lectione (scilicet, " ecce abstuli iniquitates tuas & peccata tua circummundavi. *Isaiah:)* nunc peccata dimittit, & tamen certum est a Trinitate peccata dimitti. Origen. Homil. iii. in Isaiam, tom. I. p. 350.

New Testament, himself gave the law, the prophets, and the gospel. These witnesses have also declared, that Jesus Christ who came, was himself begotten of the Father before every creature; that, after having, in the creation of all things, ministered to the Father, for " by him were all things made," (John i. 3.) in the latter times making himself of no reputation, he was made man; that, when he was God, he became incarnate; that, because he is God, the manhood has obtained eternity; that he assumed a body like to our body, in this alone different, that it was born of a virgin by the Holy Ghost; and that this Jesus Christ was born, and suffered in reality, not in appearance only, and truly died the common death of all, for he truly rose from the dead; and having, after his resurrection, conversed with his disciples, he was taken up into heaven. These witnesses have also declared that the Holy Ghost is joined with the Father and the Son in honour and dignity *." " By the gospel it is revealed

---

* Species vero eorum quæ per prædicationem apostolicam manifestè traduntur istæ sunt. Primo quod unus Deus est qui omnia creavit atque composuit, quique ex nullis fecit esse universa, Deus a primâ creaturâ & conditione mundi omnium justorum; Deus Adam, Abel, Seth, Enos, Enoch, Noë, Sem, Abraham, Isaac, Jacob, duodecem patriarcharum, Moyses & prophetarum. Et quod hic Deus in novissimis diebus, sicut per prophetas suas ante promiserat, misit Dominum nostrum Jesum Christum, primo quidem vocaturum Israël, secundo verò etiam Gentes post perfidiam populi Israël. Hic Deus justus & bonus Pater Domini Jesu Christi, legem & prophetas & evangelia ipse dedit, qui & apostolorum Deus est, & Veteris & Novi Testamenti. Tum deinde quia Jesus Christus ipse qui venit, ante omnem creaturam natus ex Patre est. Qui cum in omnium conditione Patri ministrasset, per ipsum enim omnia facta sunt, novissimis temporibus seipsum exinaniens homo factus est, incarnatus est cum Deus esset, & homo mansit quòd Deus erat. Corpus assumpsit nostro corpori simile, eo solo differens quòd natum ex virgine de Spiritu Sancto est. Et quoniam hic Jesus Christus natus & passus est; verè enim a mortuis resurrexit & post resurrectionem conversatus cum discipulis suis assumptus est. Tum deinde, honore ac dignitate Patri ac Filio sociatum,

tradi-

vealed that all things were made by the Son, and that without him nothing was made," John i. 3. Let him then who reads underſtand from this, that the name of *the Almighty* is not more antient in God than the name of *the Father*; for by the Son the Father is almighty; for through Wiſdom, which is Chriſt, God holds the univerſal dominion, not only by authority, as he is Lord, who can enforce his will, but by the ſpontaneous duty of thoſe who are ſubject to him. However, that you may confeſs that the Father and the Son poſſeſs one and the ſame omnipotence, as the Son is one with the Father, the ſame God and Lord, hear John in the Revelation teſtify, " Theſe things ſayeth he, which is, and which was, and which is to come, the Almighty," Rev. i. 4. But who is to come, the Almighty, beſides Chriſt? So now, as none ſhould be offended that the Father is God, and that the Saviour is God; ſo none ſhould take offence, when the Father is almighty, that it is alſo ſaid, the Son is almighty *."

" Of

tradiderunt Spiritum Sanctum. Orig. Proœmium Libri peri archôn ſeri de Principiis, tom. I. p. 420.

This paſſage may be referred to p. 144 above, in which Phil. ii. 6, 7, 8; is diſcuſſed, as may the following : " What ſhall I ſay of him who, for the love which he bore to us, made himſelf of no reputation, and, when he was equal with God, looked not on his own things, but on the things which are ours. He therefore humbled himſelf." Semetipſum exinanivit propter charitatem qvam habebat erga nos, & non quæſivit quæ ſua ſunt, cum eſſet æqualis Deo, ſed quæſivit quæ noſtra ſunt, & propter hoc evacuavit ſe. Origen. Homil. vii. in Levit. tom. I. p. 85.

* Per evangelium docetur quia omnia per ipſum facta ſunt & ſine ipſo factum eſt nihil; & intelligat ex hoc, quia non poteſt antiquius eſſe in Deo Omnipotentis appellatio quam Patris; per Filium enim omnipotens eſt Pater. Per Sapientiam enim, quæ eſt Chriſtus, tenet Deus omnipotentatum, non ſolum Dominantis autoritate, verum etiam ſubjectorum ſpontaneo famulatu. Ut autem unam & eandem omnipotentiam Patris ac Filii cognoſcas, ſicut unus atque idem eſt cum Patre Deus & Dominus, audi hoc modo Joannem in Apocalypſi dicentem, " hæc dicit Dominus

Deus

"Of the Holy Ghost also I conceive that such is his sanctity, that he cannot be sanctified, inasmuch as no alien sanctification may accrue to him from without, nor any, of which he was not before possessed, accede to him who is always holy, and whose sanctity never had a commencement. In like manner we must think of the Father and the Son, for the substance of the Trinity alone is of its own nature holy, and not by sanctification from without : for truly it is God alone who is always holy*." "The true faith then, from which every falsehood and fallacy is banished, acknowledges one sole God in a holy and consubstantial Trinity;" and therefore "I believe that there is one God, the Creator and Maker of all things ; and that the Word, which came forth from him, is God also, of one substance with the Father, eternal ; and that, in these latter times, he took manhood of Mary ; that he was crucified and arose again from the dead. I believe also in the Holy Ghost, who is eternal." "Of the Father I
believe

Deus qui est, & qui erat, & qui venturus est, Omnipotens. Qui enim venturus est omnipotens, quis est alius nisi Christus ? Et sicut nemo debet offendi cum Deus sit Pater, quod etiam Salvator est Deus ; ita & cum omnipotens Deus Pater, etiam nullus debet offendi quod etiam Filius omnipotens dicitur. Hoc modo namque verum erit illud quod ipse dicit ad Patrem, " quia omnia mea tua sunt, & omnia tua mea sunt, & glorificatus sum in eis," Joan. xvii. 10. Si vero omnia quæ Patris sunt Christi sunt, inter omnia vero quæ sunt Patris est etiam omnipotens, (vide supra, p. 213) sine dubio etiam unigenitus Filius debet esse omnipotens ut omnia quæ habet Pater etiam Filius habeat Et glorificatus sum, inquit, in eis. "In nomine enim Jesu, &c." Philip. ii. 9., Origen. peri archôn, tom. I. p. 425.

* Puto ergo quod Sanctus Spiritus ita sanctus sit ut non sit sanctificatus. Non enim ei extrinsecus & aliunde accessit sanctificatio, quæ ante non fuerat, sed semper fuit sanctus, nec initium sanctitas ejus accepit. Similique modo de Patre & Filio intelligendum est. Sola enim Trinitatis substantia est, quæ non extrinsecus acceptâ sanctificatione, sed sui naturâ sit sancta.—Vere autem & semper sanctus solus est Deus. Orig. Hom. xi. in Numer. tom. I. p. 134.

believe that with him no alien substance sits enthroned, and that he hath no assessor besides the Son and Holy Ghost: for this blessed Trinity is of one substance and inseparable *. "Moreover I believe that, as there is but one fountain of Godhead in this Trinity, none is afore or after other, none is greater or less than another †." But, to the comprehension of these deep things of God, the human intellect, I acknowledge, is altogether inadequate, neither has it entered into the heart of man to conceive them. To yield ourselves obedient to the faith, however, is our indispensable duty, and to believe, because the Word of God is our surety. "Let us therefore believe, so far as we are able, and call upon him to help our unbelief." "Let us acknowledge our own insufficiency, and with prostrate supplications implore the Word, which is the only begotten Son of God, that, pouring himself by his grace into our understandings, he will condescend to illumine what is dark, to lay open the things which are environed, and to disclose the things which are secret ‡;" " that he will render our hearts fit dwelling places for the abode of the Father, Son, and Holy Ghost

* Ἕνα Θεὸν κỳ κτίστην κỳ δημίεργον τῶν ἁπάντων εἶναι πεπίστευκα, κỳ τὸν ἐξ αὐτῆ Θεὸν λόγον, ὁμοέσιον, ἀεὶ ὄντα, κỳ ἐπ' ἐσχάτων καιρῶν ἀνθρωπον ἐκ Μαρίας ἀναλαβόντα, κỳ τοῦτον σαυρωθέντα, κỳ ἀναστάντα ἐκ νεκρῶν. Πιστεύω δὲ κỳ τῷ ἁγίῳ Πνεύματι, τῷ ἀεὶ ὄντι. Origen contra Marcionistas, sect. i.

Ἕνα κỳ μόνον Θεὸν ὑποδεικνύσα (πίστις) ἐν ἁγίᾳ κỳ ὁμοουσίῳ τριάδι·—ᾧ (τῷ Πατρὶ) ἐκ ὕλη σύνδρομος, ἔχ ἕτερόν τι, πλὴν τῆ υἱῆ, κỳ τῆ ἁγίᾳ Πνεύματι. Ὁμοούσιος γὰρ, κỳ ἀχώριστος ἡ μακαρία τρίας. Ibidem, sub fin.

† Porro autem nihil in Trinitate majus minusve dicendum est, quum unius Divinitatis fons, nihil in his anterius posteriusve intelligi potest. Orig. peri archôn, lib. i. cap. iii. tom. I. p. 427, & lib. ii. cap. ii.

‡ Certus sum humano ingenio vel sermone explicari non posse; nisi ipsum Verbum ac sapientiam, & justitiam qui est unigenitus Filius Dei,

prostrati

Ghoſt *;" and " that our Lord Jeſus may himſelf be our guide, and grant us to receive his heavenly kingdom. To him be glory for ever and ever. Amen †."

With this creed, this prayer, and this doxology to our Lord and Saviour Jeſus Chriſt, I ſhall cloſe my enquiry into the faith of Origen: and, unleſs Mr. Lindſey avow his concurrence with all that I have here laid before the public, I muſt neceſſarily conclude that *Origen was not an Unitarian.*

But here Mr. Lindſey may put me to the ſame teſt, and declare that he will not acknowledge Origen to have been a *Trinitarian*, unleſs I ſhall accede to every extract which he can oppoſe to mine. Let him, however, not forget that I am now poſſeſſed of that advantageous ſtation which Sceptics and Unitarians uſually ſeize. He has for once incautiouſly advanced an affirmative. Let him maintain it. He may be ſurprized at the novel neceſſity of beſtirring himſelf.—I have advanced nothing. I have not ſaid that Origen was a Trinitarian. I am at my eaſe; and my indolent negative reduces him to his proofs.

But come, I ſcorn and I relinquiſh the mean ſuperiority.—I admit that Origen has ſaid, as Mr. Lindſey has

proſtrati ac ſupplices deprecemur, qui per gratiam ſuam ſenſibus ſe noſ-' tris infundens, obſcura illuminare, clauſa patefacere, pandereque dignetur arcana; ſi tamen inveniamur eam dignè vel petere, vel quærere, vel pulſare, ut vel petentes accipere mereamur, vel quærentes invenire, vel pulſantibus jubeatur aperiri. Orig. peri archôn, lib. ii. cap. ix. tom. I. p. 445.

* Verum hæc & verè in ſcripturis dicuntur, in anima hominis Patrem, & Filium, & Spiritum Sanctum commorari. Origen, Hom. iii. in Jeremiam, tom. I. p. 370.

† Introducat nos illuc Dominus noſter Jeſus & percipere regnum ſuum cœleſte concedat. Ipſi gloria in æterna ſecula ſeculorum, Amen. Orig. Hom. vii. in Numer. tom. I. p. 124.

has stated, (Apol. p. 142) that we are not to pray to Christ; but, to this single precept, I here confront not only the numerous recommendations of that father, but his uninterrupted practice of religious worship to our Lord *."—But rather than contend alone, where I may avail myself of so good an ally, let me here call in the assistance of his antient and almost cotemporary apologist Pamphilus.—It is true that Pamphilus has not directly taken this passage under his consideration, but he

* As these run altogether counter to this one passage, I should have conceived that it must be understood with some qualification, had I been even deprived of an opportunity of consulting the original; but I have consulted the original, and there find that this singular charge occurs in the midst of a multitude of critical refinements upon the proper and catechretical application of prayer. He distinguishes between Christ, as he is God and Man, and as he is, in the latter character, our Priest. As Priest and Man, therefore, he says we are not to worship him, but, through him, to transmit our prayers to God. "We worship one God and his one Son, who is his Word and his Image," says the same father to Celsus, in context with the passage quoted, p. 252 above, " offering up our supplication and doxologies with our utmost strength. To the God of the universe we address our prayers, through his only begotten Son, to whom we prefer them, beseeching him, who is the propitiation for our sins, that, *as our High Priest*, he will deign to offer our supplications, sacrifices, and intercessions to God over all." The extracts in p. 260 above are drawn from the work in which this prohibition appears.—But the justification of Origen is not my object. I have already said enough in his behalf. An imagination, without sufficient restraint from judgement, and which seldom lost sight of an idea, till, by division and subdivision, he has rendered it too minute for the sight of his reader, has certainly betrayed him into some extravagancies. But he tells us himself that many of his writings were only exercises of his fancy, and had not been intended for public inspection. It were therefore an unjust severity to this good man's memory, to make him responsible even for the errours into which he actually did fall; how much more unjust then to impute, as a crime, the interpolations of his heretical enemies, who endeavoured to ruin the credit of his name, or, not finding this an easy task, to assume its weight to the establishment of their own tenets.—Rufinus, Presbyter of Aquileia, in the fourth century, has also maintained the cause of Origen, and written a little Tract expressly upon the interpolations made by Heretics in the writings of that father.—See also Cave's Life of Origen.

[292]

he has made it so evident that the sentiments of Origen were inconsistent with the prohibition, that, if we do not conclude it an insertion made after the days of Pamphilus, nay of Rufinus, we must of necessity acknowledge that it has been cancelled by its own author; repealed, as it were, and rendered utterly null and void by the force of his innumerable assertions to the contrary.

PAMPHILUS, Presbyter of Cesarea, was himself an eminent martyr, having suffered with great constancy under Diocletian, A. D. 303, for the religion of the gospel. This excellent man, for such Eusebius describes him, saw with admiration and reverence the true character of Origen, and with proportionable resentment declares that " a sort of insanity has gone abroad, and that many, while they possess his vast volumes replete with utility and instruction, because they yet contain a few scattered expressions, at which only the weak, or rather the malevolent, can take offence, omit and neglect all those passages which even themselves acknowledge adapted to edification and instruction. In contradiction to their duty, they refuse the advantages which it is in their power to derive from him, but with indefatigable diligence glean and lay up only such things as may afford matter for calumny and misrepresentation *." They lay heresies

---

* In alios vero novi furoris morbus & inauditæ cladis incessit infania: cum tam multa volumina referta totius utilitatis & instructionis habeantur, & satis rara & perpauca fortè loca sint in quibus vel imperitiores quique, vel (quod verius) malevoli posse sibi videantur offendi : omnia quidem illa quæ & catholica & ad ædificationem animæ, atque sententiæ instructionem etiam ipsi apta fatentur, omittunt & negligunt, nec aliquid inde, unde possunt & debent, proficere volunt: ea vera sola quæ ad calumniam proficiunt, summo studio edifcunt. Pamphili Apologia pro Origine, cum operibus Originis a Genebrardo, Parisiis edit. Rufino interprete, tom. I. p. 479.

fies to the charge of Origen, who retorts the accufation, and tells them that " he is the Heretic who entertains falfe doctrines concerning our Lord Jefus Chrift, whether he agree with thofe who fay that he is the Son of Jofeph and Mary, *(fee p. 180 above)* or with thofe who deny him to be the Firft-born, the God of every creature, (Colof. i. 15) the Word, the Wifdom, which is the beginning of the ways of God, before his works of old; fet up from everlafting, from the beginning, or ever the earth was, and brought forth before the mountains were fettled :" fuch alfo he pronounces heretics " who affert that Chrift is only a man *." For Origen, fays Pamphilus, held that " the Son was begotten of the Father, and that he is of one fubftance with the Father, but different and diftinct from created fubftance †; that the only begotten God, our Saviour, alone was generated of the Father, and is his Son by nature, not adoption, born, as it were, of the mind of the Father itfelf. For the divine nature, that is, the nature of the unbegotten Father, is not divifible, that we fhould conceive the Son brought forth by divifion or diminution of his fubftance ‡." " The only begotten Son alone is the Son of

---

* Hæreticus habendus eft, qui de Domino noftro Jefu Chrifto falfi aliquid fenferit, five fecundum eos, qui dicunt eum ex Jofeph & Mariâ natum, ficut funt Ebionitæ & Valentiniani, five fecundum eos qui Primogenitum eum negant, & totius creaturæ Deum. & Verbum & Sapientiam quæ eft initium viarum Dei, antequam aliquid fieret, ante fecula fundatam, atque ante omnes colles generatam. Prov viii. 24, 25, fed hominem eum folum dicentes. Origenis verba ex Pamph. Apologia pro Orig. p. 481.

† Ex Deo Patre natus eft Filius, & unius eft cum Patre fubftantiæ; alienus vero a fubftantiâ creaturarum. Ibidem, p. 486.

‡ Unigenitus ergo Deus Salvator nofter folus a Patre generatus, naturâ & non adoptione Filius eft, natus autem ex ipsâ Patris mente. Non enim divifibilis eft divina natura, id eft, ingeniti Patris, ut putemus vel divifione, vel imminutione fubftantiæ ejus Filium effe progenitum. Ibidem, p. 487.

of the Father by nature. "The only one true God, therefore, hath immortality, dwelling in the light which no man can approach," 1 Tim. vi. 16: *the one true God*, fays the apoftle, left we fhould conceive the name of the true God applicable to many. So alfo they "who receive the fpirit of adoption of fons, by which they cry Abba, Father," Rom. viii. 15, Gal. iv. 5, are indeed the fons of God, but not in like manner as the only begotten Son; for the only begotten Son is by nature the eternal and infeparable Son, while others have only, by receiving him, received power themfelves to become the fons of God, John i. 12. Wherefore, as great as is the difference between the true God, and thofe to whom it is declared, "I have faid ye are gods," even fo great is the difference between the true Son, and thofe who have heard, " ye are all exalted fons *." " From which declarations I conceive it abundantly and fufficiently proved now, that Origen confidered the Son to be born of the very fubftance of God; that is, that he is confubftantial, or of the fame identical fubftance with the Father; that he is not a creature, neither by adoption a Son, but by nature, and generated of the Father himfelf †."

I

---

* Unigenitus Filius Salvator nofter, qui folus ex Patre natus eft, folus naturâ non adoptione Filius eft. Unus ergo verus Deus folus habet immortalitatem, lucem habitat inacceffibilem. Unus, ait, verus Deus, ne fcilicet multis veri Dei nomen convenire credamus. Ita ergo & hi qui accipiunt fpiritum adoptionis filiorum in quo clamant Abba Pater, filii quidem Dei funt, fed non ficut unigenitus Filius. Unigenitus enim natura Filius, & femper & infeparabiliter Filius eft. Cæteri vero, pro eo quòd fufciperunt in fe Filium Dei, poteftatem habent filii Dei fieri, non tamen ex nativitate ut unigenitus Filius. Propter quod quantam differentiam verus Deus habet ad eos quibus dicitur, "Ego dixi, dii eftis;" tantam differentiam habet verus Filius ad eos qui audiunt "filii excelfi omnes." Origen. Verb. ex Pamph. Apol. p. 486.

† Satis manifefte, ut opinor, & valde evidenter oftenfum eft, quod Filium Dei de ipsâ Dei fubftantiâ natum dixerit (Origenes), id eft, ὁμοούσιος, quod

I had formerly laid it down that "he muſt be a perverſe interpreter who could underſtand the words of St. Paul to Timothy (1 Tim. vi. 16) in any other ſenſe than that of a declaration of our Saviour's exalted glory," (Script. Confut. p. 134) and I do not find myſelf at preſent much inclined to retract the opinion; though I lament that there ſhould ſubſiſt any perſon to whom the title is in its utmoſt ſeverity applicable: but ſuch a perverſe interpreter has appeared; and my Remarker, with the renunciation of Chriſt, renouncing every degree of Chriſtian moderation, has, in terms of the moſt virulent obloquy, reproached me for the application of this ſublime doxology to our Lord Jeſus Chriſt: "the King of kings and Lord of lords," Rev. xix. 16. I ſhall not enter into a diſcuſſion of the paſſage here, nor analyze the ſentence to prove from its ſtructure that our Lord and Saviour is the bleſſed and only Potentate named by the apoſtle. It was not from the ſtructure of the ſentence that I formerly drew this inference. The context at large ſuggeſted, and ſtill ſupports, the application. That Origen drew the ſame inference, and, from the general tenour of St. Paul's charge to Timothy, conſidered our Lord as that Being "who only hath immortality, dwelling in the light which no man can approach unto," is to me a ſufficient indemnification, and affords an ample proof that I have not, through ignorance of the Greek language, miſinterpreted the apoſtle. "For the ſake of ſuch as have put on the new man, who is created after God," ſays the ſame father, "has he, who was in the form of God, made himſelf of no reputation," that he might not "dwell only in the light which no man can approach unto,"

quod eſt, ejuſdem cum Patre ſubſtantiæ; & non eſſe creaturam, neque per adoptionem, ſed naturâ Filium verum, & ex ipſo Patre generatum. Pamph. ipſius Verba de Orig. in Apol. p. 486.

unto," and remain only in the form of God, but the Word was made flesh *." For unless " the anointed Son of God, when he was in the form of God, had made himself of no reputation, rendering " his name as ointment poured forth," and emptying himself of that fulness wherein he had before existed, had poured forth the ointment, that is, the fulness of the divine Spirit, none could have been able to receive him in " the fulness of the Godhead †." For the Father and the

---

* Μύρον ἐκκενωθὲν ὄνομα σȣ. Διὰ τȣτο νεάνιδες ἠγαπησαν σε. C. Cant. i. 3. Hæ autem (adolescentulæ) sunt isti novum hom nem induentes, qui secundum Deum creatus est. Propter istas ergo adolescentulas, & in augmentis vitæ & profectibus positas "exinanivit se ille qui erat in formâ Dei," ut fieret unguentum exinanitum nomen ejus; ut non jam inaccessam lucem tantummodo hab taret, 1 Tim. vi. 16, & " in forma Dei" permaneret; Philipp. ii. 6 7, 8, sed Verbum caro fieret; Joann. i. 14; quo possent istæ adolescentulæ non solum diligere sed & trahere eum ad se. Origen. Homil. i. in Cantic. Canticorum, tom. I. p. 318.

† " Unigenitus Dei Filius cum in forma Dei esset exinanivit seipsum & formam servi accepit," Philipp. ii. 6, 7, 8, exinanivit autem de plenitudine sine dubio in quâ erat, illi ergo qui dicunt, quia " de plenitudine ejus nos omnes accepimus, (ἐκ τȣ πληρώματ©-, &c.) ipsi sunt adolescentulæ quæ de eâ plenitudine, ex quâ se ille exinanivit & factum est unguentum exinanitum nomen ejus, percipientes, dicunt " post te in odorem unguentorum tuorum curremus." (C. Cantic. i. 4, secuhdum Septuaginta) Nisi enim exinanisset unguentum, hoc est, plenitudinem divini Spiritûs, & humiliasset se usque ad formam servi, capere eum nullus in illâ " Divinitatis plenitudine" potuisset, Coloss. ii. 9. Ibidem, p. 320.

That I may avoid any return to the consideration of this text, I shall add the following passages to the note.

The Lord is the Wisdom and Power of God, in whom dwelleth the fulness of the Godhead bodily: for we know Jesus Christ to be God."— Dominus qui est Sapientia, qui est Virtus Dei, in quo plenitudo Divinitatis in habitat corporaliter. Jesum Christum scimus Deum. Origen. Homil. i. in Jerem. tom. I. p. 361.

" The grace of the Holy Spirit was not given to Christ as to the prophets, but the substantial fulness of the Word himself of God dwelt in him: as the apostle says, " In whom dwelleth the fulness of the God-

head

the Son are infeparable and indivifible. In effence and fubftance they are one, " in whom dwelleth the fulnefs

head bodily," Coloff. ii. 9.—Non gratia Spiritûs ficut prophetis, ei data eft, fed ipfius Verbi Dei in eo fubftantialis inerat plenitudo; ficut & apoftolus dicit: "in quo habitat omnis plenitudo Divinitatis corporaliter." Origen. peri archôn, lib. ii. cap. vi. tom. I. p. 441.

Having fo very frequently had occafion to advert to Philipp. ii. 6, 7, 8, I have forborne to ufe many ftrong affertions made by Origen, merely becaufe that paffage is contained in them. This father confidered it as an explicit teftimony borne to the Godhead of Jefus Chrift, and has accordingly above an hundred times produced it as the ground of his own belief in that *fine quâ non* of the Chriftian faith.—In proof of what I advance, I fhall here annex a few farther inftances, and fo take my final leave of a fubject which, I fear, has but too frequently returned upon my reader. Its own importance, and the zealous mifreprefentation of Unitarians, muft be my excufe. For whenever it has returned, it has brought with it a proof of the fenfe in which antiquity received it.

" God is faid to defcend, whenever he deigns to extend his providential care to human frailty. But this muft be underftood in a more fpecial manner concerning our Lord and Saviour, " who thought it not robbery to be equal with God, but made himfelf of no reputation, taking upon him the form of a fervant." He defcended therefore. For no man hath afcended into heaven but he that came down from heaven, even the Son of man, which is in heaven, John iii. 13. The Lord defcended therefore to this end, not only to extend his care, but even to carry the burden of our infirmities, Ifaiah liii. 4, Matth. viii. 17; for "he took upon him the form of a fervant;" and he who is by nature invifible, inafmuch as he is equal with the Father, affumed a vifible figure, and " was found in fafhion as a man."—Defcendere dicitur Deus, quando curam humanæ fragilitatis habere dignatur. Quod fpecialius de Domino ac Salvatore fentiendum eft, qui non rapinam arbitratus eft effe fe æqualem Deo, fed, &c. defcendit ergo: neque alius afcendit in cœlum, &c. Joann. iii. 13. Defcendit ergo Dominus non folum curare, fed & portare quæ noftra funt; formam namque fervi accepit, & cum ipfe invifibilis fit naturæ, utpote æqualis Patri, habitum tamen vifibilem fufcepit, & repertus eft habitu ut homo. Orig. Homil. iv. in Genef. cap. xvi. tom. I. p. 12.

The Son of God, emptying himfelf of his equality with the Father, and fhewing to us the way of knowledge, becomes the exprefs fimilitude of his fubftance, that we, who could not look upon the glory of his wonderful light, when eradiating from the immenfity of his Godhead,

fulness of the Godhead." "And there never was time when the Son was not. But when we speak thus,

seeing that he is made the cognizable or comprehensible brightness of his glory, may, by the view of this brightness, thro' habit become capable of looking on the divine light." *See above, p.* 16, 113, 158.——Exinaniens se Filius æqualitate Patris, & viam nobis cognitionis ostendens, figura expressa substantiæ ejus efficitur: Ut qui in magnitudine Deitatis suæ positam gloriam miræ lucis non poteramus aspicere, per hoc, quod nobilis splendor efficitur, intuendæ lucis divinæ viam per splendoris capiamus aspectum. Orig. peri archôn, lib. i. tom. I. p. 424.

"We stand wrapt in astonishment that that nature, which is over all, rendering himself of no reputation, should, from the state of his majesty, be made man, and converse among men."——Cum summâ admiratione obstupescimus quod eminens omnium ista natura exinaniens se de statu majestatis suæ homo factus sit, & inter homines conversatus. Orig. peri archôn, lib. ii. cap. vi. p. 441.

"Christ, though he committed no sin, yet was he made sin for us, 2 Corinth. v. 21; who, while he was yet in the form of God, submits to be in the form of a servant; though he was immortal, dies; though impassible, suffers; though invisible, is seen; and because that death and every other frailty is introduced into our flesh by reason of sin, he was himself made in the likeness of men; and being found in fashion as a man, without doubt, suffering for our sins and bearing our infirmities, he offered his spotless flesh as an immaculate sacrifice to God."—"Christus peccatum quidem non fecit, peccatum tamen pro nobis factum est." Dum qui erat in formâ Dei, in forma servi esse dignatur; dum qui immortalis est moritur, & impassibilis patitur, & invisibilis videtur, & quia nobis hominibus vel mors vel aliqua omnis fragilitas in carne ex peccati conditione superducta est; ipse etiam qui in similitudinem hominum factus est, & habitu repertus ut homo, sine dubio, pro peccato quod ex nobis susceperat, quia peccata nostra portavit, vitulum immaculatum (Levit. i. 3,) hoc est, carnem incontaminatam obtulit hostiam Deo. Orig. Homil. iii. in Levit. tom. I. p. 68.

"When he was God, for our sake he was made man, and humbled himself even unto death, wherefore he is highly exalted."—"But the Word, which was in the beginning with God, being himself God, cannot admit of exaltation; but the exaltation which was conferred, was conferred upon the Son of man who glorified God by his death; and was this, that he should no longer be another and distinct from, but one and the same with, the Word."—"For the glory which accrued to him on account of the suffering of death for all men, was not ascribed to the

Only-

thus, we muſt be heard with indulgence. Such language refers to time, the exiſtence of that Being whoſe duration relates to eternity. For whatever is ſaid of the Father, the Son, and the Holy Ghoſt, muſt be underſtood to extend above and beyond all time, all ages, and even all eternity; for this Trinity alone extends beyond not only what can be meaſured by time, but whatever our limited intellect can conceive of eternity. To the exiſtence of every being, the Trinity alone excepted, time may be and is commenſurate;"

Only-begotten, whoſe nature is incapable of death, neither to the wiſdom, ſanctity, or other divine attributes of Jeſus, but it is aſcribed to the Man who was the Son of man, ' made of the ſeed of David according to the fleſh," Rom. i. 3. Wherefore he ſaith himſelf, " Now is *the Son of man* glorified," John xiii. 31. And thus it is, as I conceive, that " God hath highly exalted him" who became obedient unto death, even the death upon the croſs."— Qui propter nos, cum Deus eſſet, homo factus eſt, & humiliavit ſe uſque ad mortem, extollitur & effertur. (Orig. Homil. iii. in Judic. tom 1. p. 212.)—Illud Verbum, quod erat in principio apud Deum Deus, non recipit exaltari; cæterum exaltatio Filii hominis, ſibi facta glorificanti Deum per ſuam ipſius mortem, hæc fuit, ut non amplius ipſe aliud eſſet a Verbo, ſed idem cum ipſo.—Gloria contingens ob mortem pro hominibus non pertinebat ad Unigenitum, qui natura mori aptus non erat, neque ad ſapientiam, & pietatem & quæcunque alia eſſe dicuntur in Jeſu diviniora; ſed ad Hominem qui erat etiam Filius hominis, " genitus ex ſemine David ſecundum carnem." Quocirca quidem dixit, " Nunc glorificatus Filius hominis." Nunc etiam opinor Deus exaltavit factum obedientem uſque ad mortem, mortem autem crucis. Origen. in Evang. Joann. tom. II. p. 271.

" Let not my reader conceive that I pauſe here thro' want of additional matter; I might encreaſe it tenfold; but I flatter myſelf that I have laid before him at leaſt enough to prove my point; and this muſt be acknowledged by any who ſhall object that I have been ſuperfluous, that is, have done more than enough. I have taken the pains to examine nearly all the paſſages in the fathers of the firſt three centuries which refer to this text, and now declare, upon the whole, that I have not the ſmalleſt doubt remaining upon my mind that it is juſtly tranſlated in our Engliſh Bible, and that the interpretation which I have myſelf given above is in every reſpect ſtrictly right.

furate*;" Space may be and is commenfurate, but to fpace and circumfcription the Son muft not be referred. The Godhead of the Son fills up infinity: "For by the Son were all things created that are in heaven, and that are in earth, vifible and invifible, whether they be thrones, or dominions, or principalities, or powers: all things were created by him and for him. And he is before all things, and by him all things confift," Coloff. i. 16, 17. See above, p. 261.

I

* Quomodo ergo poteft dici, quia fuit aliquando quando non fuit Filius?—re & fubftantia unum funt in quibus plenitudo Divinitatis.—Hoc autem ipfum quod dicimus, quia nunquam fuit quando non fuit, cum veri!! audiendum eft. Nam & hæc ipfa nomina temporalis vocabuli fignificantiam gerunt, id eft quando vel nunquam. Supra omne autem tempus, & fupra omnia fecula, & fupra omnem æternitatem intelligenda funt ea quæ de Patre & Filio & Spiritu Sancto dicuntur. Hæc enim fola Trinitas eft quæ omnem fenfum intelligentiæ non folum temporalis verum etiam æternalis excedit. Cætera vero, quæ funt extra Trinitatem, in feculis & in temporibus metienda funt. Hunc igitur Filium Dei, fecundum quod Verbum eft Deus quod in principio apud Deum, Joann. i. 1. Nemo convenienter putabit in loco aliquo contineri.—Abfurdum namque eft dicere, quia in Petro quidem & in Paulo erat Chriftus, Galat. ii. 20, & in Michaele archangelo & in Gabriele non erat. Ex quo manifefte deprehenditur quia divinitas Filii Dei non in loco aliquo concludebatur, alioquin in ipfo tantum fuiffet, & in alio non fuiffet; fed fecundum incorporeæ naturæ majeftatem, cum a nullo loco concludatur, in nullo rurfum deeffe intelligitur.—His igitur nobis de æternitatis ratione breviter repetitis, confequens eft illud etiam breviter admonere, quod " per Filium creata dicuntur omnia quæ in cœlis funt & quæ in terra, vifibilia & invifibilia, five throni, five dominationes, five principatus, five poteftates, omnia per ipfum & in ipfo creata funt, & ipfe eft ante omnes & omnia illi conftant qui eft caput," Coloff. i. 16. Quibus confona etiam Joannes in Evangelio dicit quia omnia, &c. Joann. i. 3.

Poft hæc admonebimus de adventu corporali & incarnatione unigeniti Filii Dei. De quo ita fentiendum eft, ut neque aliquid divinitatis in Chrifto defuiffe credatur, & nulla penitus a paterna fubftantia, quæ ubique eft, facta putetur effe divifio. Origen. peri archôn, lib. iv. Anacephalæofis, tom. I. p. 473.

Juftin Martyr has ufed the following fimilar language concerning our Saviour, Ὁ δὲ υἱὸς ἐκεῖνο, ὁ μόνος λεγόμενος κυρίως υἱὸς, ὁ Λόγος πρὸ τῶν ποιημάτων, καὶ συνὼν, καὶ γενωμένος. Apol. 1. p. 44.

" I have laid thefe paſſages together that I may at once obviate the numerous Unitarian criticiſms which have paſſed upon Coloſſ. i. 15, 16, and ii. 9. I do not indeed expect that my Remarker will defift from miſinterpretation, becauſe I have confronted the authority of Origen to his objections. The public, however, for the benefit of which I have laid myſelf under the preſent burden, will probably decide in favour of a Greek father againſt an Engliſh grammatiſt. My "reputation as a ſcholar" I have very little at heart, and therefore ſtand unaffected by the groſs inſults of this rude man. Let him now turn his obtuſe artillery on Origen; for, though probably not "drawn into them by the Engliſh tranſlation," that venerable father has afforded me his concurrence in my "innumerable blunders."

I have now made it manifeſt that, to Pamphilus, Origen did not appear to be an Unitarian: but let us ſay that Pamphilus was miſtaken; I may yet of a certainty aſſume the authority of this Antenicene martyr himſelf to my ſide of the queſtion, and accordingly now declare that Pamphilus was not an Unitarian.

But I have ſo little doubt concerning the Trinitarian tenets of Origen, that I will no longer heſitate to make the ſame deciſion concerning him. If a doubt could poſſibly remain becauſe of that ſingle paſſage which Mr. Lindſey has appealed to, let it vaniſh before the multitudinous contradictions which this ſolitary precept has received from Origen himſelf. Let us not concur with "that maxim which is common to all Heretics, who, if a few expreſſions oppoſite to the general tenour can be found, invariably maintain the leſs againſt the more."

more *." Has Origen acknowledged that the Son is omnipotent, eternal, omnipresent, omniscient; from the Father and the Holy Ghost indivisible in Godhead; and, together with the Father and the Holy Ghost, coëqual, coëternal, and confubstantial? has Origen confessed, with zeal confessed that he knew our Lord Jesus Christ to be God, and yet forbid the adoration of our Lord Jesus Christ? Be it so. Let us admit the fact, and grant that the prohibition has genuinely flowed from his pen, yet will I not allow the authority of Origen's concurrence to that man who shall one moment hesitate to concur with Origen in the following prayers: "That we may be a fruitful and not a dry tree, and that the ax which is threatened in the gospel may not be laid to our root, let us beseech the Lord Jesus Christ with his Father; to whom be glory and power for ever and ever. Amen †." And "that, standing in the temple and embracing the Son of God, we may become worthy of pardon and amendment of life, let us implore the almighty God, let us implore the infant Jesus, whom we desire to address and hold in our arms; to whom be glory and power for ever and ever. Amen ‡."

GRE-

---

* Proprium hoc est omnium hæreticorum; nam quia pauca sunt quæ in sylva inveniri possunt, pauca adversus plura defendunt. Tertull. adv. Praxean, cap. ii. p. 505.

† Ut germinans lignum & non siccum efficiamur, ut nunquam ad radices nostras ponatur securis quæ in evangelio prædicatur, attentius Jesum Christum Dominum cum Patre suo precemur, cui est gloria & imperium in secula seculorum. Amen. Origen. Homil. xii. in Ezechiel, tom. I. p. 415.

‡ Nos stantes in templo & tenentes Dei Filium, amplexantesque eum, digni remissione, & profectione ad meliora simus, oremus omnipotentem Deum, oremus & ipsum parvulum Jesum, quem alloqui & tenere desideramus in brachiis: cui est gloria in secula seculorum. Amen. Origen. ad fin. Homil. xv. in Lucam. tom II. p. 143.

GREGORY THAUMATURGUS, a native and afterwards Bishop of the city of Neocæsarea in Cappadocia, on the death of his father, who was a Gentile, became a convert to Christianity. He placed himself under the tuition of Origen, on whom he has bestowed the highest encomiums. He was very eminent for his piety and the sedulous discharge of his episcopal duties. The relation of those miracles which are ascribed to this father forms no part of my plan. It is enough for me to state the time in which he flourished, and that, having absconded during the Decian massacre, he died a natural death, A. D. 264.

He has left behind him a brief summary of the Christian religion, which is so explicit, that I shall content myself with this single work, and make no farther extracts from the writings of this father.—By this creed alone it is sufficiently determined that Gregory of Neocæsarea was not an Unitarian:

"There is one God the Father of the living WORD, the substantial Wisdom and Might, the eternal Image (of the Father); perfect, the Begetter of him who is perfect; the Father of the only begotten Son.—There is one Lord, One of One, God of God; the Image and Form of the Godhead; the effectual WORD; the circumferent Wisdom by which all things consist; the creative Power by which all things were made; the true Son of the true Father; invisible of him who is invisible; incorruptible of him who is incorruptible; immortal of him who is immortal; and eternal of him who is eternal.—There is one Holy Ghost, having his subsistence of God, and appearing manifest to men through

If any farther vindication be thought necessary, see the London edition of Origen. de Oratione, 1728, cum notis subjunctis ab editore Gulielmo Reading, A. M. 4to.——See also the Life of Origen by Dr. Care.

through the Son; perfect life, the image of the perfect Son; the cause of life to those who live; the holy fountain, sanctity itself, and author of sanctification; in whom God the Father, who is over all and in all, is made manifest, and God the Son who is through all. —And these are a perfect TRINITY, which neither in glory, eternity, or dominion is divided or separated from itself *."

The wide-wasting arm of a capricious tyrant had now stained the face of the whole Roman territory with Christian blood. Spreading desolation and terror, he aimed at nothing less than the total obliteration of the gospel. An effect, however, unlooked for awaited his disappointed measures; and, to use a phrase not un-

* Εἰς Θεὸς Πατὴρ λόγου ζῶντος, σοφίας ὑφεςώσης καὶ δυνάμεως, καὶ χαρακτῆρος ἀϊδίου· τέλειος, τελείου γενέτωρ· Πατὴρ υἱοῦ μονογενοῦς.—Εἷς κύριος, μόνος ἐκ μόνου, Θεὸς ἐκ Θεοῦ· χαρακτὴρ καὶ εἰκὼν Θεότητος, λόγος ἐνεργός, σοφία τῆς τῶν ὅλων συστάσεως περιεκτικὴ· καὶ δύναμις τῆς ὅλης κτίσεως ποιητικὴ, υἱὸς ἀληθινὸς ἀληθινοῦ Πατρός· ἀόρατος ἀοράτου, καὶ ἄφθαρτος ἀφθάρτου, καὶ ἀθάνατος ἀθανάτου, καὶ ἀΐδιος ἀϊδίου.—Καὶ ἕν Πνεῦμα ἅγιον, ἐκ Θεοῦ τὴν ὕπαρξιν ἔχον, καὶ δι᾽ υἱοῦ πεφηνός, δηλαδὴ τοῖς ἀνθρώποις· εἰκὼν τοῦ υἱοῦ τελείου τελεία ζωή, ζώντων αἰτία· πηγὴ ἁγία, ἁγιότης, ἁγιασμοῦ χορηγός· ἐν ᾧ φανερεῖται Θεὸς ὁ Πατὴρ, ὁ ἐπὶ πάντων, καὶ ἐν πᾶσι, καὶ Θεὸς ὁ υἱὸς, ὁ διὰ πάντων.— Τριὰς τελεία, δόξῃ, καὶ ἀϊδιότητι, καὶ βασιλείᾳ, μὴ μεριζομένη, μηδ᾽ ἀπαλλοτριουμένη.

Dr. Cave has printed this creed in his life of Gregory Thaumaturgus, which I only mention here that I may guard against such doubts as naturally attend upon facts connected with miraculous circumstances. The authentic transmiss from Gregory to us may very reasonably be admitted, when the revelation from heaven to Gregory may perhaps be as reasonably rejected. There subsists no such intimate connection between them, that the fall of either position must necessarily involve that of the other.

uncommon with the writers of antiquity, the blood of the faints became the feed of the church. Like falt, which, though in reality it fertilize the foil, was yet erroneoufly fowed by the antients upon the ruins of a fubverted citadel, as emblematic or productive of fterility, this "falt of the earth" was profufely diffeminated by the hand of Pagan intolerance; but God preferving to it its natural favour, caufed it to invigorate an abundant increafe. The Gentile ARNOBIUS beheld, but inftead of regarding the ingenious torments which were inflicted for the extirpation of chriftianity as an object of terror, he contemplated the fortitude with which they were fuftained, and, perfuaded that this was derived from no ordinary fource, determined to enquire into the principles of a religion adapted to infpire it. He accordingly applied himfelf to an examination of the Chriftian tenets, and the authority upon which they were entertained. Enquiry was followed by. conviction, and conviction by an immediate engagement in the afflicted caufe. The heavieft burden which could be impofed upon a tranfitory life, when weighed againft the far more exceeding and eternal weight of glory, appeared, in his eyes, now no more than the light affliction of a moment, 2 Cor. iv. 17. Taking therefore, for an example of patience, the martyrs who had fuffered for the name of our Redeemer, in bold defiance of Diocletian, and the ruthlefs zeal of Pagan fuperftition, he embraced, and refolutely defended, the perfecuted doctrine of our Lord and Saviour Jefus Chrift *.

Q q · In

* For a few out of the multitudinous murders perpetrated by the authority of Diocletian, fee Nicephcri Hift. Eccl. lib. vii. cap. vi.—Eufebii Hift. Eccl. lib. vi i. cap. xi.—Lactantii de Morte Perfec.— Sulpicii Severi, lib. ii. p. 98.—See alfo the entire firft book of the author under confideration. The fubject is horrid, or I might refer to the numerous defcriptions which record the devices employed by th's detefted tyrant for aggravating the pains of death. They occur but too frequently, and with

In the firſt book of his Tract *againſt the Gentiles*, he enumerates the various motives which they had aſſigned for the perſecution of chriſtianity. He ſtates their objections as delivered by themſelves, and to each annexes his own reply. But as a jealouſy for their gods was the maſter-ſpring of Pagan animoſity, inſtead of entering into a formal defence of his own cauſe, he prefers recrimination, and objects to the vanity of theirs. He ridicules the abſurdity of thoſe tenets, for the maintenance of which they embraced theſe ſanguinary meaſures; and, though he does in ſome degree advert to the ſuperior excellency of the goſpel, yet his main purpoſe is to reprove the intolerance of polytheiſm, rather than to vindicate the innocence of chriſtianity.

From this circumſtance, it appears that no copious profeſſion of his faith is to be expected. The following incidental paſſage, however, affords one ſufficiently explicit:

He contends that " the gods of Rome have no reaſon to be offended at the worſhip of Chriſt, becauſe of his human birth and ignominious death upon the croſs. They have no reaſon to be offended, that he was acknowledged to be now alive, believed to be God, and adored with daily ſupplications. In the prejudice of what God is Chriſt worſhipped ? When multitudes, which you honour as deities yourſelves, have had an infamous origin, purſued a criminal courſe of life, and come to an untimely end, why ſhould your ears be wounded at hearing that Chriſt is worſhipped and received by us as God ? " But you worſhip a man,"

is

too many marks of authenticity and truth, in the *antient* hiſtories of the declining Roman empire.

is the burden of your accusation: suppose it true, yet (even on your own principles) he ought by us to be confessed our God, on account of the many liberal gifts which have proceeded from him. But, seeing that he is really and indisputably GOD, do you expect from us a denial that he is the object of our most zealous adoration, the acknowledged head of our body? What! cries the angry bigot, this Christ God! God, we answer, he is, and God of the internal faculties. And shall he be deemed a mortal being? shall he, at the voice of whose power disease and infirmity withdrew, be considered as but one of our generation? shall he, at whose bidding the seas and winds were rebuked, at whose command the long-departed spirit returned to the body, at whose call the dead came forth from their graves, and who, on the third day, burst the bands of death himself; shall he be considered as but one of our generation?—Nor yet by secondary means, or the observance of ceremonials, did Christ perform these works. Those mighty wonders which he wrought, he effected by the mere power of his own name.—He is the high God, sent forth by the Omnipotent, the God by whom we are preserved, and who causeth us to dwell in safety *." See above, p. 240 and 256.

This

* Sed non (inquit) idcirco dii vobis infesti sunt, quòd omnipotentem colatis Deum; sed quòd hominem natum, & (quod personis infame est vili us) crucis supplicio interemptum, & Deum fuisse contenditis, & superesse adhuc creditis, & quotidianis supplicationibus aderatis. Si vo is jucundum est, amici, ed sserate quinam sunt hi dii, qui a nobis Chr stum coli, suam credant ad injuriam pertinere. Janus Janiculi conditor? Diana & Apollo, circumlati per fugas matris, atque in insulis errantibus vix tuti? Thebanus, aut Tyrius Hercules, hic in finibus epultus Hispaniæ, Flammis alter conc ematus Ætnæ s? Venus intestini decoris publicatrix, &c. &c. &c.? Hinc ergo Christum coli, & a nob s a cipi, & existimari pro numine vulneratis accipiunt auribus?—Natum hominem colimus! quid enim? vos hominem nullum colitis natu..? non un m & alium? non innumeros alios? quinimmo non omnes, quos jam temp is
habetis

This single passage so fully demonstrates the faith of its author, that farther argument is unnecessary to prove that Arnobius was not an Unitarian.

"To the name of CYPRIAN, Bishop of Carthage, the world has lately been introduced. How far his character and conduct have been justly delineated, it is not my province to enquire. I am contented that a fervent zeal to unite, shall still be construed into an artful ambition to rule the church of Christ; that the strenuous effort to check the growth of error, shall still be

habetis vestris, mortalium sustulistis ex numero, & coelo syderibusque donatis?—Nihilo minus tamen nati hominis objectatis cultum; res agitis satis injustas, ut id in nobis constituatis esse damnabile, quod & ipsi vos jactitatis; & quae vobis licere permittitis, consimiliter aliis licitum esse nolitis.—Natum hominem colitis! etiam si esset id verum, (locis ut in superioribus dictum est) tamen pro multis, & tam liberalibus donis quae ab eo profecta in nobis sunt, Deus dici appellarique deberet. Cum vero Deus sit re certâ, & sine ullius rei dubitationis ambiguo, inficiaturos arbitramini nos esse, quàm maxime illum a nobis coli, & praesidem nostri corporis nuncupari? Ergone, inquiet aliquis furens, iratus, & percitus, Deus ille est Christus? Deus, respondebimus, & interiorum potentiarum Deus.—Ergo ille mortalis, aut unus fuit e nobis, cujus imperium, cujus vocem, popularibus & quotidianis verbis missam, Valetudines, morbi, febres, atque alia corporum cruciamenta fugiebant?—Unus fuit e nobis, qui redire in corpora jamdudum animas praecipiebat effiatas? prodire ab aggeribus conditos?—Atqui constitit Christum sine ullis adminiculis rerum, sine ullius ritûs observatione, vel lege omnia illa, quae fecit, nominis sui possibilitate fecisse.—Deus ille sublimis fuit, Deus radice ab intimâ, Deus ab incognitis regnis, & ab omnium principe Deus SOSPITATOR est missus. Arnob. adv. Gentes, lib. i.

This last title Arnobius gives to our Lord, in opposition to Jupiter, to whom it had been ascribed by the Gentiles, and from whom he now transfers it to its proper owner. I have omitted to translate or transcribe the very numerous instances of our Saviour's miracles, and of Pagan deities, which our author has produced as examples of the divine power of one, and the wretched absurdity of the other. They were altogether unnecessary to my purpose. He has indeed multiplied them to a degree that seems as if, even in his own time, they must have been superfluous.

be conſtrued into the claim or exerciſe of an uſurped prerogative. I have no immediate motive to deny, that the utmoſt felicity of human life is conſtituted by the mitigation of exile, and the ſafety of a chriſtian biſhop judiciouſly exemplified in the proſcription, the baniſhment, and the murder of Cyprian. The tenets, not the virtues, of the early Chriſtians, form the ſubject of the preſent enquiry; and, to the aſcertainment of the former, the vindication of the latter is by no means neceſſary. Let perſecution continue to enjoy the advocacy of a new-found apologiſt, and, aſſuming the ſymbols of juſtice, inflict a merited puniſhment on the guilt of chriſtianity, I am not now concerned to repel the blow; I have not undertaken to exculpate the members, but to inveſtigate and promulge the doctrine of the primitive church.

The eſtabliſhment of dates, however, is within my province, and therefore it is neceſſary that the merit of killing Cyprian, ſince meritorious we are taught to conceive it, ſhould be reſumed from Decius, to whom it has been erroneouſly aſcribed, and reſtored to its proper owner the emperor Valerian. But where that humility with which this martyr profeſſed the hope of eternal glory to be his ſole motive for preferring death to the abjuration of his faith in Chriſt, is repreſented as mere affectation, there I acquieſce; nay, I muſt accede; for, upon ſetting aſide the teſtimony of every antient record, it appears, upon the ſtronger evidence of modern ſuggeſtion, (and who can reſiſt it?) that he was inſtigated to extend his neck to the ſtroke of a common executioner by that far more adequate principle, the moſt aſpiring temporal ambition [*]. This

[*] See Mr. Gibbon's Hiſtory of the Decline and Fall of the Roman Empire, vol. I. p. 546.——Vide Cypriani Opera propè paſſim, præſertim ad Demetrianum lib. p. 193.

This "prieſt of God and of Chriſt," as PONTIUS, his martyrologiſt, uſing the language of St. John, has termed him †, having either abſented himſelf through the apprehenſions of falling a victim to the zealous ſuperſtition of Decius, or being compelled to abſence under a judgment of exile, was, for a conſiderable time, reduced to the hard neceſſity of adminiſtering his paſtoral function by letter. The diſtracted ſtate of a perſecuted church required a ſteady exertion of his authority. The confirmation of the timid, the reſtitution of the lapſed, and the ſuppreſſion of ſome innovations, which his preſence would probably have prevented, required his ſtricteſt attention: and both the language and argument which he has made uſe of to theſe ſeveral purpoſes, evince his fears that they might not prove effectual. He ſaw, from a diſtance, that diviſion was introduced among thoſe who were committed to his charge, and that, forgetting their abſent paſtor, many were drawn aſide to follow other leaders: deſirous, therefore, that the whole body, fitly joined together, ſhould again be compacted in the unity of the faith, he transfuſed the ardour of his mind into his writings, and endeavoured to render his animated page a ſerviceable repreſentative of himſelf.

It is ſcarce neceſſary, therefore, to add, that he is a voluminous writer, and that he has made frequent and ample profeſſions of his faith. From his primitive pages, however, I ſhall content myſelf with making but a few concluſive extracts, having already adduced the authority of Cyprian to the eſtabliſhment of many texts

---

† Dei & Chriſti pontifex. Pontii de vitâ Cypriani, p. 5, & poſtea, p. 9, Dei & Chriſti princeps.—See Rev. xx. 6, and v. 10. This Pontius was a Deacon at Carthage, and, according to his own account, enjoyed the intimacy of Cyprian.

texts which the unitarian fcepticifm of the eighteenth century has been pleafed to conteft §.

In a treatife written againſt the Jews, he formally undertakes the proof of our Lord's divinity. To this end, he draws together a great number of paſſages from the fcriptures ‖. Our Saviour's aſſertion in the apocalypfe, that " I am alpha and omega", he quotes in terms exactly correfponding with thofe which we receive as the genuine production of the apoſtle's pen *. He produces the addrefs of Thomas, on being fatisfied of his Maſter's identity, as an atteſtation of that apoſtle's belief that Jefus Chriſt was " his Lord and his God †." And, efteeming it an incontrovertible argument of our Redeemer's godhead, he relies upon that teſtimony which is borne by the almighty Father himfelf to the glory of the afcending Son, " Thy throne, O God, is for ever and ever," &c. Pfalm xlv. 8. Heb. i. 8. ‡ Nay, but, cries the Unitarian, does it appear too from Cyprian's Latin verfion of this text, that the name of God is written vocatively? I admit that it does not; but it does from the argumentation of a Jew, who told Origen, that becaufe God was here addreſſed by name,

Chriſt

§ See above, p. 31, 122, 158, 204.

‖ Pfalm xxv. 4—xlvi. 10—lxviii. 4. Ifaiah xxxv. 3—xl. 3—xlv. 4— lxiii. 9. Baruc. iii. 35. Hofea xi. 9. Zechar. x. 11. Matth. i. 23. Luc. i. 67—ii. 10. Joann. i. 1, &c. &c. Rom. ix. 5. Vide Cyprian. adv. Judæos, lib. ii. cap. vi. & fequent. Vide fupra, p. 31.

* Aroc. i. 8—xxi. 6—xxii. 13. Ibid. Origen has alfo declared this text to have been fpoken by our Lord Jefus Chriſt. This is a very antient proof of its authenticity. Origen. prefatio ad lib. in Evang. Joann. tom. II. p. 161. See above, p. 214.

† John xx. 28.—See Script. Confut. p. 75.

‡ Thronus tuus, Deus, in fecula feculorum. Cyp. adv. Judæos, lib. ii. cap. vi.—See Script. Confut. p. 155. And above fee p. 88, 106, 218.

Chrift is therefore not the object of the Pfalmift's doxology ‡. For nothing more than the verbal conftruction of the fentence do I defire the authority of this Jew. By him who was efteemed a wife man among the Hebrews, and who therefore probably underftood the royal prophet's original language, it is admitted that the perfon glorified is denominated God, though it be denied that Chrift is that perfon. But it is admitted by the Unitarian, that Chrift is the perfon glorified, though it be denied that he is denominated God. I have an undoubted right to avail my caufe of every argument which its adverfaries contribute; and now accordingly, againft the antient, I eftablifh the conceffion of the modern Unitarian; and *Chrift is therefore the being glorified*; whilft, carrying this forward, againft the modern I equally eftablifh the affertions of the antient Jew, and therefore *Jefus Chrift is denominated* God. Thus, collecting and laying together fuch portions as are admitted feverally by the members of this fraternity, the parts, though deficient, as feparately conceded, are yet, when united, found perfectly to correfpond with the doctrine of the fcriptures; and thus, by their own admiffion, this text, ftanding exempt from farther controverfy, remains a proof of the godhead of our Redeemer, of his feat on that throne, wherein he fhall reign for ever, of his fceptre in that kingdom

---

‡ Confidera quòd Deum alloquens propheta, cujus fedes eft in feculum feculi, & virga directionis virga regni ejus, hunc Deum ait unctum a Deo qui fit ipfius Deus, unctum autem præ participibus fuis, hic dilexit juftitiam & habuit iniquitatem in odio. Pf. 45, 6, 7. Heb. i. 8, 9. His verbis memini me urgere vehementer Judæum, qui fapiens habebatur apud fuos; cumque non poffet fe explicare, ficut decebat Judæum, aiebat ad univerfitatis Deum dictum effe illud, "fedes tua, Deus, in feculum feculi, &c." ad Chriftum vero illud "dilexifti juftitiam & habuifti odio iniquitatem, &c." Origen. contra Celfum, tom. II. p. 426.

kingdom, of which THERE SHALL BE NO END; Luke i. 33 *.

But St. Paul says, that "when they which are Chrift's fhall, at his coming, rife from the dead, THEN (cometh) THE END †; when he fhall have delivered up the kingdom to God, even the Father, and when all things fhall be fubdued unto him, then fhall the Son alfo himfelf be fubject unto him that put all things under him; that God may be all in all," 1 Cor. xv. 24, &c. From which pofition the Unitarian, erroneoufly conceiving this kingdom and the divinity by us afcribed to our Saviour to be fynonimous terms, infers and infolently urges the groundlefs inference, that he has found a period appointed to the filial godhead; and hoping to eftablifh his own opinions upon the fubverfion of confiftency in the revelation of God, with this affertion of St. Paul confronts the teftimony of the evangelift, and from confufion, which I think he is right in confidering as the only bafis of his tenets, concludes that " *Chrift fhall not reign for ever, and that of his kingdom there fhall be an end.*"

Before I enter into an enquiry what may be the intention of St. Paul in the paffage before us, it may not be amifs to premife, that, as among all men who admit the authority of the fcriptures, it muft be agreed that the fcriptures are the uniform dictate of one fpirit, fo it muft neceffarily be agreed, that the apoftle has not here advanced a pofition diametrically oppofite to

R r that

* Τῆς βασιλείας αὐτοῦ οὐκ ἔσται ΤΈΛΟΣ. Luke i. 33.

† Εἶτα τὸ ΤΈΛΟΣ, ὅταν παραδῷ τὴν βασιλείαν τῷ Θεῷ ϰ Πατρί, &c. 1 Cor. xv. 24.

that of the beloved affociate of his own miniftry, Coloff. iv. 14, 2 Tim. iv. 11.

And now, as it neceffarily follows that, if a future period be appointed for the fubjection of the Son, there is an interval of time in which the Son is not ſubject; that, if a future period be appointed for the furrender of our Redeemer's kingdom, there is an interval of time in which the Father is not in poffeffion of this kingdom; that, if the univerfality of the Father's godhead depend upon a future contingency, there is an interval of time in which the Father is not univerfal: and as I dare not, in the general fenfe of the terms, affert that the Son is not fubject from the hour of his having affumed our inferior nature; that he holds the godhead in temporary derogation from the Father's glory; or that God is not eternally all in all, for the purpofe of reconciling the fcripture of truth, both with itfelf, and with the eternal univerfality of the godhead, I firſt abjure the imputed interpretation, and confequently deny that the kingdom which Chriſt fhall deliver up is the unalienable godhead already compleat in the Father. The terms, therefore, which relate to the kingdom, taken even according to the Unitarian acceptation, do not affect a dignity to which they do not relate.

The fentiment alfo promulgated by the Unitarian as his own tenet, I equally abjure; and as I believe the drefs and cloathing which the facred writer gives to the fubject to be its true and proper predicate, fo, when Chriſt is introduced in fcripture, not only fitting on a throne, but exercifing regal dominion, I believe the *reality* of his kingly ftate. I believe his kingdom to be everlafting, and yet fuch as may perfectly confiſt with the eternal glory of the Father. It were furely fuperfluous

to

to argue againſt that fantaſtical, not to ſay blaſphemous, doctrine, that the revelation dictated by "the Spirit ſent to guide us into all truth," is made in language accommodated to erroneous prejudice, and conſequently calculated only to the eſtabliſhment of antient falſehood. It carries within itſelf its ſufficient confutation. I ſhall therefore only oppoſe it here with a peremptory negative. See Sequel to Apol. p. 269, &c.

But we learn from the holy ſcriptures, that to the Man Jeſus a kingdom has been given; that, the fulneſs of the godhead dwelling in him *bodily*, he is made the head of all principality and power, Coloſſ. ii. 9; that this Jeſus whom the Jews ſlew and hanged on a tree, him hath God exalted with his right hand to be a Prince and a Saviour, Acts v. 31, conſtituting the ſame Jeſus whom they had crucified both Lord and Chriſt, Acts ii. 36. We alſo learn that the glorious King, from whom we ſhall receive our final ſentence, is no other than the Son of Man, Matth. xxv. 34, Acts x. 42—xvii. 31.

Having thus ſeen our bleſſed Redeemer ſeated on the throne of his glory, and worſhipped by every knee in heaven and in earth, Phil. ii. 10, the purpoſe for which theſe high and ſtupendous honours have been conferred upon this Man remains to be enquired into; and this we find to be briefly, that "God, not having appointed us to wrath, but to obtain ſalvation by our Lord Jeſus Chriſt, who died for us that we ſhould live together with him," 1 Theſſ. v. 9, 10, has, for the ſuffering of death, crowned with glory and honour Jeſus the Son of Man, that, by the grace of God, he ſhould taſte death for every man, Heb. ii. 9, and that he might give repentance and forgiveneſs of ſins, Acts v. 31.

The kingdom of our gracious Redeemer we find alſo to have been predicted, and that the apoſtle declares all things ſubdued to him in conformity with the prophecy of the Pſalmiſt, that he muſt reign till God ſhall have put all enemies under his feet, Pſal. cx. 1, 1 Cor. xv. 25.

Thus then we have found, not only the ſure word of prophecy, but the motive and purpoſe of our Saviour's exaltation to the kingdom which he ſhall hereafter deliver up; and if now we can find him alſo appointed to any other office from the ſame motive, to the ſame purpoſe, and with reference to the ſame prophecy, the nature of that kingdom, which is the ſubject of the apoſtle's poſition, may perhaps appear. It may perhaps appear that it is a kingdom ſo conſtituted, that the Son may deliver it up to the Father without the diminution of the Filial, or the augmentation of the Paternal, glory.

That the Captain of our ſalvation, being made perfect through ſufferings, was therefore called of God an High Prieſt after the order of Melchizedec, we are expreſsly told by St. Paul, Heb. v. 8, 9, 10. We ſee him alſo made in all things like his brethren, that he might be a merciful and faithful High Prieſt in things pertaining to God, and this too in conjunction with terms which confer the moſt glorious dignity upon his ſacerdotal character, Heb. ii. 9, 14, 17. That King, by whoſe ſentence we ſhall all be finally determined, we have ſeen to be the Son of Man; but it is becauſe he is the Son of Man that he hath received authority to execute judgment, John v. 27. Thus do we find the apoſtolic ſpirit laboriouſly inſiſting upon the human nature of our Redeemer, as the ſubject of every aſſertion by which he is ſaid to have received an appointment; and every appointment, whether it be termed

royal,

royal, pontifical, judicial, or executive, which he has received on this account, we are evidently told has been conferred upon him merely with relation to us. The motive, therefore, to our Lord's appointment, both to the kingdom which he is to deliver up, and to the priesthood, being the same, even his participation of our carnal nature, the identity of his regal dignity and priesthood, is the natural inference. But if this be deemed too large a deduction from a single point of agreement, that they agree in the first article proposed, is all I shall yet insist upon, desiring only that this concurrence may be carried forward in aid of farther argument.

And this their agreement with respect to the purpose of the institution will contribute; for as our blessed Saviour is both King, Priest, and Judge from one motive; namely, because he is the Son of Man who has sustained, and can therefore have a feeling of, our infirmities, Heb. iv. 15; so we are instructed—that, as his royalty is conferred for the purpose of giving repentance and forgiveness of sins, the end of his priesthood also is to make reconciliation for the sins of the people; for in that he himself hath suffered, being tempted, he is able to succour them that are tempted, Heb. ii. 17, 18.

But if both be found to correspond with one and the same prediction, and are by the apostles alike inferred from the same prophecy, no farther doubt can be reasonably entertained of the identity of this sovereignty, and the priesthood of Jesus Christ. In the passage before us then, in the first chapter of St. Paul's epistle to the Ephesians, and in the declaration of St. Peter to a mixt multitude at Jerusalem, Acts ii. 34, we are told that God hath raised this Jesus from the dead,

made

made him Lord, and set him far above all principality, and power, and might, and dominion, in completion of the psalmist's prophecy, which says, "Thou madest him to have dominion over the works of thine hands; thou hast put all things under his feet," Psalm viii. 6; and which again addresses him, saying, "Sit thou at my right hand until I make thine enemies thy footstool", Psalm cx. 1. But not only St. Paul deduces the doctrine of our Saviour's priesthood from the same predictions in his epistle to the Hebrews, but the royal prophet himself has declared the subjection of all things under the feet of our great Mediator, "the Prince of our Peace," Isaiah ix. 6, Eph. ii. 14, to be a circumstance descriptive of a priesthood after the order of Melchizedec, King of Salem, which is, King of Peace, Priest of the Most High God, Psalm cx, Heb. i. 13—x. 12. And now, as the law was held under the Levitical priesthood, Heb. vii. 11, so we may, from the tenure of a better covenant under the mediation of our glorified Advocate, conceive the priesthood which, through the introduction of a better hope by which we draw nigh to God, has superseded the carnal ordinance, to be the first state of that kingdom, in the consummation of which we shall be put into the substantial enjoyment of the things hoped for, Heb. xi. 1, and, having been reconciled, be brought nigh to the throne of grace, and by the Captain of our salvation delivered up to God, even the Father.

Having thus demonstrated that the sovereignty of our Lord is that relative character which he now bears, and shall eternally bear to us, whom he has not been ashamed to call brethren, Heb. ii. 11, and which has been conferred upon that nature which he possesses in common with those for whom he ever liveth to make intercession, Heb. vii. 25, it necessarily follows that we

are

are the subjects which constitute his kingdom, and therefore that, as our salvation is to be, in the end, the fruit of his victory, Heb. v. 9, this kingdom is, in the interval of time, capable of increase, even till it ascend to final consummation; for as there now subsist enemies which for the present bear rule, but shall hereafter be subdued under his feet; till the period of their subjugation it is evident that he bears but a divided sway within this kingdom: the first office, therefore, that is appointed to the Son of man, in discharge of his royal power, is the extension of its present limits. He has already abolished distinctions among men, with relation to God, by his incarnation; and by his assumption of our carnal nature, the Gentile and the Alien are naturalized and become of the commonwealth of Israel. The world, thus rendered equal and united within itself, required yet the means of reconciliation with God. He, therefore, whose flesh had before gathered together those who were scattered abroad, and made one fraternity of all men, and yet, by continuing to participate of that flesh, for a while permitted man to remain divided from God, as the representative of our nature has already laid down his flesh, that so the enmity which subsisted before by the flesh, might, by the cutting off of this prepared body, be abolished, and we, by the crucifixion of our carnal Man, should thence be enabled to do thy will, O God. Thus are we reconciled to God by the abolition of the enmity which the cross had destroyed. We are first, all men, as well the Alien as the Jew, collected together in the temple; and the partition wall being broken down, one sacrifice is then offered up for all alike; the vail is now rent, and we may therefore enter into the holiest, being reconciled to God by the death of his Son, Eph. ii. But now is Christ risen from the dead, and become the first fruits of them that slept, 1 Cor. xv. 20. If therefore,

when

when we were enemies, we were reconciled to God by the death of his Son, how much more, being reconciled, shall we be saved by his life?" Rom. v. 10. To accomplish this infinitely merciful End is his present occupation, the exercise of his present function. He has already died, and, as our propitiation, has once offered his own immaculate body; but having raised this up from the darkness of the grave, and taken it with him into heaven, he stands forth our High Priest over the house of God, Heb. x, 12, 21, pleading the merits, and, by his intercession, rendering effectual the blood, of that one sufficient sacrifice which was given for our redemption, henceforth expecting till his enemies be made his footstool, Heb. x. 13. But this Mediator, 1 Tim. ii. 5, of the New Testament has at length accomplished the End of his advocacy, and obtained reconciliation for us. The enmity which had before subsisted is repressed, and sin being deposed, all they which are Christ's are made subject to the reign of righteousness and grace, Rom. v. The priesthood must therefore of necessity cease here. On the determination of either correlative, the relation is by consequence determined. But Man has obtained his suit, and is now no longer a client. The Advocate is henceforward unnecessary; the mediatorial kingdom of the Son is therefore no more; the sacrifice is accepted, and the Priest retires from the altar.

But, in the twinkling of an eye, the Son of Man is seen coming in the clouds of heaven with power and great glory. The trumpet sounds, and, from one end of heaven to the other, the elect are gathered together before the throne of his glory. To these THE KING is now heard to say, " Come, ye blessed of my Father, inherit a kingdom prepared for you," 1 Cor. xv. 52, Matth. xxiv. 30—xxv. 31, 34.

The

[321]

The decisive word is gone forth; the final sentence is pronounced, by which eternity is administered. The judicial royalty, therefore, of our most merciful Father is now also determined. Execution alone awaits the published judgment. At this point of time, therefore, the executive supremacy of our Lord receives its commencement, and accordingly the Captain of our salvation, who had called on us to come and inherit the kingdom which he had been heretofore occupied in preparing for our reception, leads us forth from the tribunal of reconciled justice, and becomes himself the conductor of many sons into glory, Heb. ii. 10.

Thus has our corruptible put on incorruption, our mortal, immortality; and that saying which is written is brought to pass: Death is swallowed up in victory, 1 Cor. xv. 54. We, that are Christ's are made alive, and being changed, by our Lord Jesus Christ, our vile body, that it may be fashioned like unto his glorious body, according to the working whereby he is able even to subdue all things unto himself, Philip. iii. 20, 21. Now indeed, I admit it, "cometh the End:" but of what? of the kingdom which has just attained to its predestined universality? No: but of strife and conflict; of all hostile rule, authority, and power; of the principality of sin which had reigned unto death, Rom. v. 21. Now indeed cometh the End, the glorious End; to the attainment of which our gracious Redeemer had taken, laid down, reassumed, and exalted into heaven, our carnal nature *. By him who

S s   hath

* Although "the End" unquestionably signifies "the determination of the subject," yet it as frequently indicates "the purpose to which any institution is made, means employed;" or, in the more comprehensive
                                             language

hath flain the enmity, that he might reconcile us to God by his crofs, " we have received the atonement;" and having through him obtained an accefs unto the Father, we are made of " the houfehold of God;" we are by him conducted " in one body," and delivered up to God, even the Father. This Man himfelf, who, for the fuffering of death, and accomplifhment of this great End of divine mercy, has been crowned with glory and honour, being now the chief corner-ftone, we are fitly framed and builded together, conftituting an holy temple in the Lord, an habitation of God through the Spirit, Eph. ii. We are turned from darknefs to light, from the power of Satan to God, being fanctified and having received forgivenefs, Acts xxvi. 18. Henceforward the reign of fin unto death being fuperfeded, God takes under himfelf the emancipated kingdom of our Lord; he

---

language of Cicero, " illud, cujus causâ aliquid facimus, finem appellatimus." Cic. de Fin. When, therefore, we read " then *(cometh)* the End," why are we, with the Unitarian, of neceffity to underftand it to mean " the end or determination of our Saviour's kingdom," and not rather " the end and purpofe for which our Lord employed the means of his own incarnation and fubfequent engagement in our behalf?" The recommencement of our life, in confequence of *his* refurrection, τὸ ΤΈΛΟΣ τῆς πίςεως ὑμῶν, σωτηρίαν ψυχῶν, 1 Peter i. 9, is the doctrine which the apoftle here inculcates, and to which this brief affertion appears therefore more naturally referable. And it feems to me, that we may with equal propriety affert, " then cometh the determination of the commandment when we love one another," as declare the kingdom of Chrift determined when "the End *(cometh)*," εἶτα τὸ ΤΈΛΟΣ, 1 Cor. xv. 24. Τὸ δὲ ΤΕΛΟΣ τῆς παραγγελίας ἐςιν ἀγαπη ἐκ καθαρᾶς καρδίας, 1 Tim. i. 5. In what fenfe is Chrift affirmed to be " the End of the law," but as the law was fulfilled in Chrift? ΤΕΛΟΣ γαρ νομᾶ Χριςὸς, Rom. x. 4. And how is " love the end of the commandment," but as love fulfilleth the commandment? πληρωμα ἂν νόμε ἡ ἀγαπη, Rom. xiii. 10. " For all the law is fulfilled in one word, even in this, thou fhalt love thy neighbour as thyfelf," Gal. v. 14, James ii. 8.

he receives our subjection to the reign of grace unto eternal life, Rom. v. 21.*; he takes us for his people, declares himself to be our God; and the rivals of his universal power being subdued under the feet of our Conductor to his throne, he no longer holds an empire divided with sin and death; their authority is put

* "God be thanked," says St. Paul, "that ye were the servants of sin; but ye have obeyed from the heart that form of doctrine whereto ye were delivered," Rom. vi. 17. Delivered to what, and from what? Not to the form of doctrine surely, (for this, besides the evident nonsense of the assertion, is written accusatively with a preposition) but from the service of sin to the obedience of that righteousness which is specified in the doctrine, and according to which they have become the servants of God, verse 16, 18, 22. Coloss. i. 13, &c. Eph. ii. 2, &c. Rom. i. 24. Here there subsists more than a verbal concurrence. Some similitude in the subject matter may instruct us how to understand in what manner the kingdom shall be delivered up to God. Our deliverance from the bondage of sin is stated here also, and the reign of righteousness and grace is put in direct opposition, and declared to be founded on the ruins of her subverted authority. In order to our subjection to this sway, the alienation of our Saviour's kingdom is not declared a necessary step, nor is he included in those hostile powers which he shall himself put down, any more than the Father who is manifestly excepted. That we should come under the dominion of God, was the very end of our Saviour's participation of our nature. To this, as coheirs, we are now delivered up, together with him who leads us into glory, and who still retains the preëminence, ἐν πᾶσιν αὐτὸς πρωτεύων, Coloss. i. 18. Why then should his resignation be thought to follow? But let us pass on to a comparison of the same apostle's language in these two passages: Εἶτα τὸ τέλος, ὅταν ΠΑΡΑΔΩ̃ τὴν βασιλείαν τῷ Θεῷ ᾗ Πατρὶ, 1 Cor. xv. 24. Χάρις δὲ τῷ Θεῷ ὅτι ἦτε δοῦλοι τῆς ἁμαρτίας, ὑπηκούσατε δὲ ἐκ καρδίας εἰς ὃν ΠΑΡΑΔΟΘΗΤΕ τύπον διδαχῆς, Rom. vi. 17. Lay them both together now, and it turns out that, having been released from a service, THE END of which is death, τὸ γὰρ ΤΕΛΟΣ ἐκείνων θανάτου, Rom. vi. 21, we are for ever emancipated and delivered up to an obedience, THE END of which is eternal life, τὸ δὲ ΤΕΛΟΣ ζωὴν αἰώνιον, Rom. vi. 22. This is THE END which the sufferings and merits of our Redeemer have compassed for us; this the eventual reconciliation and delivering up of his everlasting kingdom, 2 Pet. i. 11, to God, even the Father.

put down; it is abjured by the ranfomed inheritance of Chrift; and henceforward, with refpect to reftored mankind, God alone is all in all," Heb. ix.

I have proved now to my own, and, I hope, to my reader's fatisfaction, that the kingdom which Chrift fhall reconcile, and, in the End, deliver up to God, is that kingdom, to the poffeffion, improvement, and completion of which his manhood has been exalted. This cannot, indeed, admit of doubt, when it is confidered that thofe fufferings which his human nature alone could undergo, are affigned as the reafon for his promotion. " He became obedient unto death, wherefore God alfo hath highly exalted him." To this end Chrift both died, and rofe, and revived, that he might be Lord, both of the dead and living," Rom. xiv. 9, Philip. ii. 9, 2 Cor. v. 15. See above, p. 298, the note.

But it may perhaps be faid that the apoftle has here revealed the *future* fubjection of the Son, together with that of the kingdom which he fhall hereafter deliver up to God; and that if his human nature be really the fubject of this pofition, an abfurdity refults; for that the fubjection of his human nature having commenced in the moment of his incarnation, the commencement of that fubjection could not be dated from any future period, and therefore that his human nature is not the fubject of the apoftle's prefent pofition.

That Chrift having, as a Son, learned and rendered obedience, is therefore, in his individual capacity, fubject to God, is a point which I at once concede. Over him Sin had never extended her dominion; and the cords of that ftinglefs tyrant Death being caft from him, this one Man has unqueftionably, from the

very

very commencement of his carnal exiſtence, found it his chief delight to yield ſubjection, and to do the will of his Father. Some aggregate character muſt therefore be explored, in which the ſubjection of our King to the dominion of God alone has not yet attained to its perfection; but in which, when the End cometh, and that he ſhall have put down all rule, authority, and power, the Son may with propriety be affirmed firſt to enter into a ſtate of ſubjection to him who had ſubdued all things under him for that great and magnificent purpoſe, that God may be all in all *.

That aſſembly of the elect which ſhall, in the End, be convened under Chriſt, and which is here denominated the Kingdom, is frequently ſignified in the ſcriptures by the name of the Church. But whether we denominate it the kingdom or the church of Chriſt, it is obvious that, within the precincts of either term, the great Regent or Head is himſelf comprehended. Now, while other powers bore rule or exerciſed authority within that juriſdiction, in which it was his province to tread down thoſe enemies which perverted our allegiance to, and retarded our reconciliation with, God, Chriſt could not, in the plenitude of the appellation, be termed the King or Head; for though he was indeed appointed to the ſubjugation of the adverſary, yet ſo long as the banner of him who hath the power of death was diſplayed and reſorted to, the finiſhed ſtate of our Lord's ſupremacy was deferred, Heb. ii. 14; and conſequently, however perfect the Head himſelf, ſeparately

---

* The ſtructure of the text requires this interpretation, both in our verſion, and in the original Greek. It is not therefore to be concluded hence, "that the Son is ſubject, that God may be all in all;" but that " all things were put under the Son, that God may be all in all."

rately confidered, muft be acknowledged to have at all times been, " the church, which is his body," not being yet wafhed from every fpot or blemifh, precludes the poffibility of his rendering fubjection to God in the fulnefs of that aggregate character which is not yet acquired, but in which we fhall hereafter find him combined with and united to it.

For, to affume the apoftolic metaphor, if by this junction alone Chrift himfelf, in the End, become a part (though principal) in the affembly of thofe which are his own, till THE BODY has grown up to the meafure of the ftature of the fulnefs of Chrift, and by that increafe, to which he has himfelf adminiftered, has reached up to, and fitly joined itfelf in proportionate union with, THE HEAD, Eph. iv. the Head and Body could not be ftrictly faid to have adhered fo as to conftitute " a perfect Man," nor, confequently, the circumftances affecting or characterizing the one be, with propriety, predicated of the other inclufively. But " God the Father of glory *hath now put all things under his feet*[*], and given him to be the head over all things to the church, which is his body; the fulnefs of him which filleth all in all," Eph. i. 22. Their appofite union is therefore now formed, and Chrift is therefore now part and parcel of that church whereof he is the head, of that kingdom whereof he is the king. Now, firft that coherence between Chrift and the Church has taken effect, by which, when the circumftances of the Body are fpoken of, the affertion fhall be underftood to extend to and comprehend the Head, with which it has thus become one, and without which his fulnefs was incomplete. "For as the

Body

---

[*] This reference to the fame prophecy proves the fubject to be the fame.

Body is one, and hath many members, and all the members of that one Body, being many, are one Body; so also is Chrift," 1 Cor. xii. 12, Rom. xii. 5.

But, to the perfection of the Head, the perfect vigour of the Body is effential; to the vigour of the Body, the health and perfect freedom of every limb. But now, if we, for a feafon, have rendered ourfelves, who ought at all times to be members of Chrift, members of unrighteoufnefs, till the fubjugation of fin, how fhall we be fo united to his Body, that we fhall become active limbs, deriving our increafe and vigour from him who is the Head? Eph. iv. 15, 16: And how indeed, till the End cometh, when he fhall, by putting down all power and authority, have removed thofe impediments which in the interval control our functions, fhall the Head of that Body, whofe limbs are bound up in thraldom to iniquity, and have yielded themfelves members to unrighteoufnefs, be itfelf affirmed to enjoy a ftate of exemption from reftraint, and to have entered into that fubjection which alone is perfect freedom? 1 Cor. vii. 22, Rom. vi. 22. Firft he fhall fubdue the enemy, and, breaking his chains afunder, untie the limbs that were bound to fin. The Members thus emancipated, the Body thus invigorated and made free, the Head, to which we are then united, and from which "we derive encreafe," performing its proper offices, in union with an healthy Body, which, thus ftrengthened and cleanfed, it delivers up to God, even the Father, now firft enters into a fpecies of fubjection hitherto untried, and, together with that church of fouls, of which he is " the great Bifhop;" that kingdom, of which he is the mighty King, the Son himfelf, having attained to his fulnefs, becomes fubject to him who had for this

very

very end subdued all things under him, that he might be the Head of the church.—That the several relations, or, rather, degrees of one relation, which the crucified and glorified Son of Man bears to us, form the subject of the apostle's discussion in the passage before us, is an indisputable point. The perfection of that relation he tells us is at length attained to. The union of Christ and the church is now first instituted. Till every member was in subjection, the undivided Whole could not be justly considered as in subjection. While we were obedient to sin, our Head could not, with this reference, be considered as subject to grace; and consequently the subjection of the Son can only now be said to have had a commencement, when that aggregate character, in which he stands combined with us, has first attained to its perfection, when that union is effected by which the Head and Body are brought into coherence, 1 Cor. xii. 26, 27.

Let me still have permission to accompany the apostle in his close pursuit of this figure.—So long as we stood out and resisted, the Son could not lead us to the throne of grace, nor commence his own subjection in this connected capacity; but having at length enfranchised and reconciled us, he delivers up, not his supremacy, but his purchase, to the reign of righteousness, being himself incorporated with us. He does not alienate the kingdom which his blood and warfare had redeemed from the adversary; nor, withdrawing the Head, deliver up only the truncated Body to God, even the Father. He enters himself into the same subjection which is " not a bondage to fear," but a state in which " the Son has made us indeed free," John viii. 32. For the wages of sin which, with the service, we have refused, he obtains

for

for us that fubftitute which grace had through him appointed for the fubjects of righteoufnefs, even the free gift of God, which is eternal life. But having thus acquired for his people a participation of his own immortality, it does not appear that, fruftrated of the end for which he died and revived, he ceafes to participate of our now glorified nature, or, under God, to prefide over thofe children whom God had given him, Heb. ii. 13. "The Son abideth for ever," John viii. 31, 1 Theff. iv. 17, and "we are the members of his body, of his flefh, and of his bones," Eph. v. 30. And now, as " Chrift is the Head of every man," and thus the church is a Body to him, fo Chrift and the church, confolidated together, form a Body, of which God is the Head. Thus then it is that the Son fhall, when the End cometh, be fubject to him who had given him the victory for our exaltation; and thus confidered in his union with the church, it is juftly and intelligibly affirmed that "the Head of Chrift is God," 1 Cor. xi. 3, Eph. v. 23.

Thus do I chufe, though at the unavoidable expence of brevity, by the ufe of fcripture language to combine my argument and the proofs that fupport it; and thus, though at the expence of variety, do I chufe to adhere to that fingle metaphor which annexes authority to elucidation. On almoft every return to the fubject, the apoftle adduces, and frequently in its minuteft circumftances applies, the union of the human head and body to illuftrate the future union of Chrift and the church. And the ante-Nicene Origen, treading in his fteps, has authorized the ufe which I have here made of the allufion: for he afferts that "Chrift as Head cannot be declared fubject till every limb is fubject; and that the mode of fpeech is the fame with that by which we deny the health of a man in general, who in any particular member of his body is out of order *."

Collecting now the several parts of the foregoing argument, the whole may be summed up into the following paraphrase of the passage under enquiry.

As

---

* Si aliquod membrum corporis doleamus, quamvis reliqua omnia membra nostra sana sint, tamen quia dolore unius membri totus homo affligitur, non dicimus quia sani sumus, sed quia male habemus. Verbi causâ, dicimus "ille non est sanus." Quare? Quia pedes dolet, aut renes, aut stomachum. Et nemo dicit, quia " sanus est, si stomachum dolet," sed, " non est sanus quia stomachum dolet."—Apostolus dicit quia corpus Christi sumus & membra ex parte, Eph. v. 30, 32. Unusquisque nostrûm membra ex parte est, si aliquis ex nobis, ergo, qui membra ejus dicimur ægrotat & aliquo peccati morbo laborat, i. e. si alicujus peccati macula inuritur & non subjectus Deo, recte ille nondum dicitur esse subjectus, cujus sint membra illi, qui non sunt subjecti Deo. Cum autem omnes eos, qui corpus suum dicuntur ac membra, sanos habuerit, ut in nullo inobedientiæ laboraverint morbo, sanis omnibus membris, Deoque subjectis, merito se dicit esse subjectum illi, cujus, nos, membra Deo in omnibus obedimus. Origen. Hom. ii. in Psal. xxxvi. tom. I. p. 278.

Hilary, Bishop of Poictiers, in the middle of the fourth century, most solemnly avers, that, from the scriptures alone, he had deduced the very same doctrine concerning the one substance of the Father and Son, which had been approved of by the council of Nice; and this too before he had ever read or heard of the creed published by that synod. Something like the satisfaction, which this venerable father must have felt on finding that his sentiments had the concurrence of so wise a body, I now feel on finding my own manner of understanding the passage before us authorized by the concurrence of Origen: for, long before I knew that he had adverted to it, I had, from my own observation on the argument of St. Paul, supplied the interpretation which I have given above.

I shall here annex the testimony of Hilary. His ignorance of the Nicene faith may almost rank him with the ante-Nicene writers.

Testor Dominum cœli atque terræ, me, cum neutrum audissem, semper tamen utrumque sensisse, quod per ὁμοιούσιον ὁμοούσιον oporteret intelligi, id est, nihil simile sibi (sc. Patri) secundum naturam esse posse, nisi quod esset ex eadem natura. Regeneratus pridem & in episcopatu aliquantisper manens fidem Nicænam nunquam (nisi exulaturus) audivi. Sed mihi ὁμοούσιν & ὁμοιούσιν intelligentiam evangelia & apostoli intimaverunt. Hilarii de Synodis adversus Arrianos Liber, sub fin.

As by this Man came the resurrection of the dead, then cometh the attainment of that End for which he took manhood, when they which are his are made alive; then cometh the attainment of that End for which his manhood was exalted above all principality and power, to the regal functions of a Mediator and a Judge, when every inimical power is put under his feet, and Death himself swallowed up in victory; for then the kingdom, the administration of which had heretofore been of a militant nature, being perfectly delivered from the invasion of sin, and adapted to the dominion of God, shall have been brought nigh, and delivered up, to that God, to whose sole dominion it has thus been adapted. But this kingdom is the fulness of the Son. To his relative perfection, therefore, it is necessary that this shall be compleat. But it now is compleat. And now the great Finisher of our faith, having accomplished every end of his incarnation, may be affirmed first to have become perfect through sufferings; now first to have learned the full lesson of his own obedience. When, therefore, the Son of Man shall have presented to God a kingdom rescued from the bondage of corruption into the glorious liberty of the children of God; a kingdom no longer carnal, but set free, and made subject to the law of God; and to which, being reconciled by himself, God alone shall be all in all; then shall the Son himself be perfectly subject to the same law; for every obstruction which impeded his fulness is broken down, the promises of God are fulfilled to him, his expectations are answered, his enemies are subdued and made his footstool, and no farther difficulty remains to be superseded; the times of restitution of all things are arrived; that perfection which his sufferings and mediation had purchased accrues to him; we are now raised together with Christ; together with Christ we are exalted to sit in heavenly places;

places; his blood has cleanſed us, and we are put into an eternal fellowſhip with the Son; for ever with the Lord, where he is, being perfect in one, Chriſt himſelf in us, and God in Chriſt, we ſhall behold the glory which God has given to him who died and roſe for our adoption, and who, inaſmuch as he has made us the children of the reſurrection, and therefore the children of God, has not been aſhamed himſelf to call us brethren. See Rom. viii. 7, 21. Eph. i. 23—ii. 5. John xvii. 23, 24. 1 Theſſ. iv. 14, 17. Heb. ii. 10, 14, 15, 17—v. 8, 9, 10—x. 12, 13, 14. Coloſſ. i. 12. Acts iii. 21. Luke xx. 36.

And now, what has St. Paul delivered derogatory from the godhead of our Redeemer? That the kingdom is formed upon our reſurrection ſufficiently teſtifies that we are the ſubjects which form the kingdom of that Man, by whom came the reſurrection. That his MANHOOD is therefore the recipient of that kingdom which relates to us, and for the perfection of which every other power had been ſubdued to him, that the authority of God alone might prevail, is a neceſſary concluſion. And how far, I ſay, are we now authorized by the apoſtle to infer againſt the omnipotence of his godhead? He delivers up (however underſtood) a kingdom to which he had been exalted for ſufferings. And what then? Why then, cries the Unitarian, he is not God. I own I do not ſee the juſtice of the inference: for while I ſay that he is God, and therefore omnipotent, I yet acknowledge that he is Man, and therefore capable of an appointment to a peculiar kingdom. The relation in which the carnal nature of our Lord ſtands to us, forms the ſubject of the apoſtle's diſcourſe. To this he has with undeviating ſtrictneſs confined himſelf; and throughout we only find the "Son of Man glorified," John xiii. 31, Matth. xvi.

27—

27—xix. 28. Mark viii. 38, Luke xxii. 29, 30. At the very utmoſt, therefore, unleſs a negative be the logical inference from ſilence with reſpect to a matter foreign from the purpoſe of an argument, the purchaſed and appointed kingdom of our Saviour's manhood alone is ſurrendered.

But if terms of transfer thus annihilate, I deſire to know how the kingdom of the Father ſhall be ſecured from diminution when he ſhall have "tranſlated us into the kingdom of his dear Son," Coloſſ. i. 12, 13. For my own part, I do not conceive it poſſible for any thing to be withdrawn from under the hand of the Almighty, and muſt leave it for the Unitarian to carry forward againſt the Paternal authority that argument which he eſteems concluſive againſt the Filial ſceptre, or demand that, if he acknowledge the Father's dominion undiminiſhed by a transfer to that of the Son, he will acknowledge the dominion of the Son undiminiſhed, by his having delivered up his kingdom to the Father.

And this perhaps he may find to be the caſe, when, looking into a more particular detail of the diſpenſations of heaven ſubſequent to the final judgment of mankind, he ſhall behold the Lord God almighty and the Lamb conſtitute one temple for the worſhippers in his future kingdom; the glory of God lighten the new reſidence of thoſe who are written in the book of life, and the Lamb the light thereof, Rev. xxi. 23: And when ſeeing the throne of God, and the Lamb, who is the Lord of lords and King of kings, ſeated in the midſt of the throne, Rev. vii. 15, 17—xix. 16—xxii. 1, 4, he ſhall be called upon to recognize his own aſſertion, that "to ſit upon the throne is the moſt certain and irrefragable character of the one ſupreme God." Sequel to Apol. p. 37 and 39.

Our

Our gracious Redeemer's participation and consequent feeling of our infirmities had for its primary or immediate object our reconciliation with his carnal nature, which was therefore effected in the instant of his incarnation; and thus his flesh had placed a step, by which alone it was possible that an offending race could pass to God; for his manhood, with which we had been thus previously associated, being taken into God, by its double relation becomes a Mediator between both, and at length effects that reconciliation which was the final object of all that he had undertaken and undergone for us. He had offered his immaculate body as our one propitiatory sacrifice, and, dying for us while we were yet in our sins, became a curse for us; thus at once satisfying the indispensible demands of infinite justice, and by his blood cleansing us from all impurity which had rendered us unfit to stand before the perfect eyes of God. But corruption is abolished, and now shall Christ present us unto himself a glorious church, without blemish, spot, or wrinkle, Awake then thou that sleepest; arise from the dead, and Christ shall give thee light, Eph. v. 14, 27; for captivity is captive, mortality is swallowed up of life, and Christ filleth all things; his stature is perfected, and we are now the compleat fulness of him who filleth all in all, Eph. i. 23—iv. 13; "the everlasting kingdom of our Lord and Saviour Jesus Christ is come; we are now renewed, and Christ is all, and in all," Coloss. iii. 11. See also 2 Cor. v. 4, 21. Galat. iii. 13. For "Christ," says Cyprian, "is our God, who put on man, that, as a Mediator between both, he might become the Conductor of man to the Father*." "He is *our* God; that

---

* Deus noster, hic Christus est, qui Mediator duorum, hominem induit quem perducat ad Patrem. Cypriani de Vanitate Idolorum, p. 15. See above, p. 121, 122, 206.

that is, he is not the God of all, but only of the faithful and such as believe. He is the God who shall not keep silence when he shall be manifested in his second coming; for then shall he, who came before in obscure humility, appear manifest in power *." Psalm l. 3.

When the neglected objects of Pagan superstition were avenged by their zealous votaries, and the alternative of excessive torment or apostacy was proposed to the worshippers of Christ, however we may lament their timidity, we cannot reasonably wonder that, out of the prodigious numbers whose constancy was brought to the trial, some of inferior fortitude should take refuge at the Gentile altar, and, renouncing the Lord who bought them, should scatter incense before the imperial idol. The sad severity of their fate excited compassion in the cotemporary Christians, who, after the allowance of a reasonable time, in which they might have leisure to review and bewail their lapse, again received them into the bosom of the church. This interval of repentance, however, was by many considered in the light of a grievous burden. Impatient of delay, therefore, they importunately solicited the immediate restoration of such as had thus apostatized. But with this demand Cyprian uniformly refused to comply, urging " that the loss of salvation was the immediate consequence of a doctrine that would dispense with prayer to God, or prevent that man who had denied Christ from deprecating the wrath of him whom he had denied;"

---

* Hic est Deus *noster*, id est, non omnium, sed fidelium & credentium. Deus, qui cum in secundo adventu manifestus venerit non silebit: nam, cum in humilitate prius fuerit occultus, veniet in potestate manifestus. Cypr. de Bono Patientiæ.

nied †;" "for that in the gospel the Lord himself has declared, Whosoever shall deny me, him will I also deny, Matth. x. 33. And again, ye have poured out drink-offerings and made sacrifice to images, and shall not my indignation be kindled? saith the Lord, Isaiah lvii. 6. Such, therefore, as require the immediate restitution of those who have sacrificed to idols, intercede that the pardon of God, who has borne testimony to his own anger, may not be implored; that Christ, who has declared his resolution to deny that man who denieth him, may not be appeased with prayers and satisfactory repentance *." "I beseech you therefore to acquiesce in my counsel, who daily pour forth the unintermitted prayer to the Lord, and desire that, by the mercy of the Lord, ye may be recalled to the church ‡." "What! am I therefore become your enemy because I tell you the truth? If I had sought to conciliate men, I had not then been the servant of Christ. If, however, I shall fail to persuade others to please Christ, I shall yet of a certainty perform my own part, and, by keeping his commandments,

---

† Ad ruinam salutis inducitur, ut non rogetur Deus, nec qui negavit Christum quem negaverat deprecetur. Cyprian. Epist. xliii. p. 82.

* Dominus in evangelio dicit; qui me negaverit, negabo illum. Et alio loco indignatio & ira divina non tacet, dicens: Illis fudistis libamina, & illis imposuistis sacrificia: super haec non indignabor? dicit Dominus. Et intercedunt ne rogetur Deus, qui indignari se ipse testatur. Intercedunt ne exoretur pres bus & satisfactionibus Christus, qui negantem se negare profitetur. Cyprian. Epist. lix. p. 154.

I have intentionally avoided the detail of any farther circumstances concerning the restitution of penitent apostates than such as immediately relate to my own subject.

‡ Quaeso vos, acquiescite consiliis nostris, qui pro vobis quotidie continuas Domino preces tundimus, qui vos ad ecclesiam revocari per Domini clementiam cupimus. Cyprian. Epist. xliii. p. 84.

ments, pleafe Chrift, my Lord and my God *." "For us, and for our offences, did he endure, and watch, and pray; how much the more incumbent is it, therefore, upon us to be earneft in fupplications, and prayers, and entreaties; firft to the Lord himfelf, and then, thro' him, to make fatisfaction to God the Father †?" "If therefore ye will begin the work of repentance, and make full fatisfaction to God and his Chrift, whom I ferve, and to whom, whether in perfecution or in tranquillity, with pure and immaculate lips I offer up the facrifice of adoration; then may we enjoy your communion with us ‡;" "then may we offer up unceafing thanks to God the Father almighty, and to his Chrift our Lord, God, and Saviour, for his divine protection of the church §;" "then, in our facrifices and prayers, fhall we not ceafe to give thanks to God the Father, and to Chrift his Son, our Lord; we fhall not ceafe to afk and to pray, that he, who is himfelf perfect, and can bring to

per-

---

* Inimicus factus vobis fum, verum dicens vobis? Gal. iv. 16. Si hominibus placerem Chrifti fervus non effem, Gal. i. 10. Si quibufdam fuadere non poffumus ut eos Chrifto placere faciamus, nos certè, quod noftrum eft, Chrifto Domino & Deo noftro, præcepta ejus fervando, placeamus. Cyprian. Epift. iv. p. 10.

† Quod fi pro nobis ac pro delictis noftris ille & laborabat & vigilabat & precabatur, quanto nos magis infiftere precibus & orare, & primo ipfum Dominum rogare, tum deinde per ipfum Deo Patri fatisfacere debemus. Cyprian. Epift. xi. p. 25.

‡ Si pænitentiam temeritatis tuæ agere cæperis; fi Deo & Chrifto ejus, quibus fervio, & quibus puro atque immaculato ore facrificia, & in perfecutione pariter & in pace indefinenter offero, pleniffime fatisfeceris; communicationis tuæ poterimus habere rationem. Cyprian. Epift. lxvi. p. 169.

§ Et egiffe nos & agere, frater chariffime, maximas gratias fine ceffatione, profitemur Deo Patri omnipotenti, & Chrifto ejus Domino & Deo noftro Salvatori, quòd fic ecclefia divinitùs protegatur. Cyp. Epift. li. p. 94.

perfection, may preserve and perfect you to the attainment of a glorious crown *."

Such is the clear and decisive language in which this eminent martyr avows his own uninterrupted practice, and inculcates the adoration of our blessed Lord. He grounds the doctrine on the scriptures, in which he asserts, and by numerous extracts proves his assertion, that it is expressly commanded. From these, for more were unnecessary, I shall select but one, and that chiefly on account of the father's remarkable manner of quoting it. St. John, he says, about to render worship to an angel, is rebuked and told not to do it, but to " worship the Lord Jesus †," Rev. xix. 10—xxii. 9. This,

* Vicarias pro nobis ad vos literas mittimus, repræsentantes vobis per epiftolam gaudium noftrum, fida obfequia caritatis expromimus; hic quoque in facrificiis atque in orationibus noftris non ceffante, Deo Patri, & Chrifto Filio ejus Domino noftro gratias agere & orare pariter ac petere ut qui perfectus eft atque perficiens, cuftodiat & perficiat in vobis confeffionis veftræ gloriofam coronam. Cyprian. Epift. lxi. p 145.

I freely confefs that this paffage is not addreffed by Cyprian to any who had denied Chrift in the time of perfecution. Were its application of any importance whatfoever I fhould not have adduced it here. The phrafeology inculcates the worfhip of our Lord independent of any circumftances with which it is connected, and to this end alone I ufe it.

† In apocalypfi, angelus Joanni volenti adorare fe refiftit, & dicit, vide ne feceris, &c. Jefum Dominum adora. Cyprian. de Bono Patientiæ, fub fin.——Neither Wetftein nor Mill take notice of this reading.

My Remarker, arguing from the behaviour of St. John, rather than the rebuke of the angel, his made a moft extraordinary ufe of the apoftle's error; for he thence deduces the propriety of rendering worfhip to the creature, and concludes, that the adoration of the angel was not idolatry; for "it is not poffible," he fays, "that he, whofe long extended life had been fpent in propagating the knowledge of the one true God, and of the honour due to him alone, to whom fo extraordinary illuminations of the Holy Spirit had been vouchfafed for the very purpofe of breaking down the ftrong holds of idolatry, fhould clofe the fcene of his life and preaching with an overt act utterly repugnant to all ideas of true religion." Addenda to Remarks, p. 8, 9. But I now defire to learn whether

This, I grant, is not a literal verfion of the Greek as it has defcended to us; and I even doubt whether Cyprian

whether the apoftle died in the act of worfhipping the angel? whether he relinquifhed his evangelical occupation, but with life; or clofed the fcene of his life till he had recorded and reprobated his own tranfgreffion; till, fubfequent to his errour he had raifed his warning voice, and bequeathed to us a caution againft the identical inference which is now perverfely drawn from his mifconduct?

"But can no reafon," proceeds the idolater, "be given why the angel rejected the offer of St John, but that he thought it finful for the one to give, or the other to receive, the offered worfhip? Yes. The angel himfelf gives a moft fatsfactory one: *See thou do it not; for I am thy fellow-fervant, and of thy brethren the prophets.* He who gave commiffion to me has given thee the fame alfo; and thus we are upon a level, being made joint and equal minifters of the fame glorious difpenfation. *Worfhip God,* therefore, who has made thee a chofen veffel to himfelf, to whofe good pleafure the great honour of this appointment, which fets thee in the rank of angels, is folely due." Addenda to Remarks, p. 8, 9. Of this the whole amount is, that the angel was not too low to be an object of general worfhip, but that St. John was by a particular commiffion exalted, and made too high to prefer it. This, however, need not, hinder the Remarker from adoring the angel himfelf; for it does not appear that any fuch extraordinary commiffion has elevated or exempted him from worfhipping the creature, rather than the Creator. The whole Romifh calender is open to his adoration. Nay, if fuch a reafon be fatisfactory, and that all with whom we are not upon a level are entitled to worfhip, I hardly know what the Being is to which this man muft not efteem it an incumbent duty to bow the knee.

Why did Peter, who was "fet in the rank of angels," refufe the worfhip of Cornelius, who was certainly his inferior? and why did Paul, when called Mercurius, refer the Gentiles to the true God, and not rather arrogate their adoration to his own real dignity, as being the fellow-fervant of angels? Acts x. 25—xiv. 14.

"But it is only an inferior kind of worfhip that is authorized by this example."—That is more than the paffage warrants us to fay. The worfhip which the angel transferred from himfelf to God is the very fame worfhip which St. John offered to the angel. Ἔπισον ΠΡΟΣΚΥΝΗ-ΣΑΙ αὐτῷ, ϗ λέγει μοι, ὅρα μή. Τῷ Θεῷ ΠΡΟΣΚΥΝΗΣΟΝ.

The refources of the Unitarian fraternity deferve obfervation. Wherever the facred records feem to degrade our Redeemer to a rank below omnipotence,

prian intended it for more than a paraphrafe. But be that as it may, the fentiment of the father himfelf is equally clear from either fuppofition. If he has tranflated, it proves that, in fome very early copy, the paffage was thus read; and if he has only fupplied a comment, his inference from the doctrine is evident; That God, therefore, whom the apoftle was commanded to worfhip, was by Cyprian underftood to be no other than our Lord Jefus Chrift.

His frequent thankfgivings to our Saviour evince the belief of this excellent man, that Chrift was his Benefactor and Defender; his prayers, that the ears of our Lord were ftill open, and his power adequate to the accomplifhment of his defires. This latter tenet he has exprefsly avowed in a work dictated by the very

fpirit

potence, or to elevate other beings to a level with our Lord, then the infallibility of the apoftolic character is inftantly proclaimed. But let the language of fcripture glorify his omnipotence, and declare him to be "God bleffed for ever," we are then called upon to "confider that the facred penmen were left to themfelves." Sequel to Apol. p. 472. Now, as an anfwer to thefe evafive fophifms, I urge, firft, that the conduct of the apoftles, though probably in general the moft exemplary, was yet not neceffarily exempt from error; whereas, in the fecond place, as minifters of the New Teftament, their fufficiency was of God. When they preached, it was not they, but the grace of God that was with them, 1 Cor. xv. 10. 2 Cor. iii. 5. Their writings, therefore, are the only unerring rule. From thefe alone we are enabled to draw the infallible teftimony of Chrift. But thefe record their conduct. They do fo; but with it the reprehenfion which prohibits imitation. If St. Peter erred; for our learning his error was corrected and recorded. Paul has warned him who ftandeth to take heed left he fall; and even while the miniftry of reconciliation was confided with him, this great apoftle was urgent in prayer left he might himfelf become a caft-away. In the prefent inftance, St. John is feen to proftrate himfelf before an angel. But was this done for our edification? No:—that was the object of his writings; and accordingly this infpired man has himfelf tranfmitted the hiftory of his own tranfgreffion, and annexed that rebuke with which it was received, and which fhall to all fucceeding ages denote its criminality.

spirit of our benevolent religion; for, recommending mutual good offices among Christians, he says, with an allusion to Matth. xxv. 35, 36, "Unless you think that he who feedeth Christ is himself not fed by Christ, or that earthly things are wanting to that man to whom heavenly things are given," "let us give to Christ an earthly clothing, sure to receive an heavenly garment *." "Divide your revenues with the Lord your God; your fruits participate with Christ; make Christ a partaker of your earthly possessions, that he may make you a coheir of his heavenly kingdom †." "Let us, therefore, with our utmost diligence hasten to succour the afflicted, that we may thus, by a ready obedience, conciliate Christ, our Judge, our Lord, and our God ‡."

The testimony of Cyprian, that our Lord was both God and Man, has already been produced. Indeed, from a profession that he was truly God, it must necessarily be inferred that he believed in the two natures of Christ; for, notwithstanding that he raised his own body from the grave, according to the power which

---

* Nisi si putas quia qui Christum pascit, a Christo ipse non pascitur, aut eis terrena deerunt, quibus cœlestia & divina tribuuntur;—demus Christo vestimenta terrena, indumenta cœlestia recepturi. Cypriani de Opere & Eleemosynis, p. 202, 203.

† Reditus tuos divide cum Domino Deo tuo: fructus tuos partire cum Christo: fac tibi possessionum terrestrium Christum participem, ut ille te sibi faciat regnorum cœlestium coheredem. Ejusd. Operis, p. 202.

‡ Quibus possumus viribus elaborare, & velociter gerere, ut Christum Judicem & Dominum & Deum nostrum promereamur obsequiis nostris. Cyprian. Epist. lxii. p. 146.

This is urged in favour of many Christians who were in captivity, and from which Cyprian was desirous of procuring their release.

which he declares himself that he poſſeſſed, John x. 18 §, all muſt allow the crucified Jeſus to have been truly Man. That he was only Man, however, he declares to be the ſentiment of the Jews, who deduced the tenet from the humility of his fleſh and body, and yet were driven to the neceſſity of aſcribing magical powers to him, in order to account for his miracles *; whereas, had they believed and reſted in the truth, they would have known that, "the Holy Ghoſt coöperating, he took fleſh of a virgin, and thus became God mixed with Man †." In like manner Mr. Lindſey, contending on the ſide of Celſus in oppoſition to Origen, of Trypho in oppoſition to Juſtin Martyr, abets the ſentiment of this Hebrew, and pronounces Chriſt " to have been but a Man like ourſelves," Seq. to Apol. p. 397, &c. Nay, upon our diſſent from this Jewiſh creed, he even ſtamps the name of impiety: and ſuch preciſely was the objection of the ſynagogue to the worſhip of Chriſt. They pronounced it an hereſy: " but after the way which they call hereſy," ſays Paul, " ſo worſhip I the God of my fathers, believing all things which are written in the law and the prophets," Acts xxiv. 14.

And that Chriſt was the God whom the law revealed to our fathers, and whoſe humble advent in our nature was foretold by the prophets, the venerable man, whoſe
faith

§ Crucifixus prævento carnificis officio, Spiritum ſponte dimiſit, & die tertio rurſuſ à mortuis ſponte ſurrexit. Cypr. de Vanit. Idol. p. 16. Vide ſupra, p. 113, 267, 270.

* Judæi qui illum crediderunt hominem tantum de humilitate carnis & corporis; exiſtimabant magum de licentia poteſtatis. Cypriani de Vanitate Iddlorum, p. 16.

† Hic in virginem illabitur; carnem, Spiritu Sancto coöperante, induitur. Deus cum homine miſcetur. Ejuſd. Oper. p. 15. Vide ſupra, p. 206, 335.

faith is the subject of enquiry, has largely declared ‡. He asserts that " the name of Christ is preached as necessary to the remission of sins, not as if the Son alone were to be adhered to without, or in contradistinction to, the Father, but for the information of the Jews, (who boasted that they had the Father) that the Father would profit them nothing unless they believed likewise in the Son whom he had sent; for they who knew God the Creator should also know Christ the Son, that they might not flatter and congratulate themselves on the Father alone without the knowledge of the Son *." For, to adduce the authority of another early writer, " he who thinks that he worships the Father, inasmuch as he worships not the Son, so likewise he omits to worship the Father; but he who comprehends the Son, and assumes his name, together with the Son, worships the Father also †". (See above p. 287).

I need not insist upon the unity of the Son with the Father alone, as this is necessarily implied in a proof of his unity with the Father and the Holy Ghost; and to this

‡ For a reference to the texts, by which he maintains the latter position, see above, p. 311. For the maintenance of the former he quotes Gen. xxii. 11—xxxi. 13—xxxv. 1. Exod. xiii. 31—xiv. 19—xxiii. 20. Cyprian. adverf. Judæos, lib. ii. cap. v. See above, p. 281.

* Quod enim in evangeliis & in apostolorum epistolis Jesû Christi nomen insinuatur ad remissionem peccatorum, non ita est quasi aut sine Patre aut contra Patrem prodesse cuiquam solus Filius possit. Sed ut Judæis qui jactitabant se Patrem habere ostenderetur quòd ni il eis Pater profuturus esset, nisi in Filium crederunt quem ille misisset. Nam qui Deum Creatorem sciebant Filium quoque Christum scire debebant, ne sibi blandirentur & plauderent de solo Patre sine Filii ejus agnitione. Cyprian. Epist. lxxiii ad Jubaianum, p. 205.

† Qui solum Patrem se colere putat, sicut Filium non colit, ita ne Patrem quidem. Qui autem Filium suscipit & nomen ejus gerit, is vero cum Filio simul & Patrem colit. Lactantii, lib. iv. de verâ Sapientiâ, cap. xxix.—Vide supra, p. 267.

this Cyprian has born his explicit teſtimony; for, arguing againſt the validity of baptiſm adminiſtered by hereticks, and the neceſſity of baptizing ſuch as renounced their error, and were defirous of being admitted into the *one* catholic church, he argues, that " if any can receive baptiſm from hereticks, he may alſo receive forgiveneſs of ſins. But if he has obtained forgiveneſs of ſins, he is alſo ſanctified, and made the temple of God. I demand now, of what God? If I ſhall be anſwered, of the Creator, I reply, that he cannot be his temple who has not believed in him; if of Chriſt, neither can he be made the temple of Chriſt, who denies that Chriſt is God; if of the Holy Ghoſt, inaſmuch as THESE THREE ARE ONE, how can the Holy Ghoſt be in amity with him who is the enemy of either the Father or the Son *?" " On what grounds then can any man aſſert

---

*.Si baptizari quis apud hæreticos potuit; utique & remiſſam peccatorum conſequi potuit. Si peccatorum remiſſam conſequutus eſt, & ſanctificatus eſt, & templum Dei factus eſt; quæro cujus Dei? fi Creatoris, non potuit qui in eum non credidit? fi Chriſti, nec hujus fieri templum qui negat Deum Chriſtum; fi Spiritūs Sancti, CUM TRES UNUM SINT, quomodo Spiritus Sanctus placatus eſſe ei poteſt, qui aut Patris aut Filii inimicus eſt? Cyprian. Epiſt. lxxiii: p. 203.

This ſeems to allude to 1 John v. 7. See above, p. 204.

Cyprian here indiſputably indicates the Father by the title of " the Creator." He, neverthelefs, afcribes the creation to the Son in another part of his works, which proves that he does not here alcribe it to the Father excluſively. Animating the victims of heathen outrage to ſuſtain their faith with fortitude, he ſays, " In perſecution the earth is ſhut out, but heaven is opened; antichriſt threatens, but Chriſt defends; death invades, but immortality enſues. And how great is the glory, for a moment to ſhut the eyes by which men and the world are ſeen, and inſtantly to open them to the view of God and Chriſt." " If we endure reproaches in this world, if flight, if torments, THE MAKER AND LORD OF THE WORLD experienced heavier ſorrows, and apprized us of future perſecution, ſaying, If the world hate you, ye know that it hated me, &c. John xv. 18. Whatſoever our Lord and God taught, that he did, that the diſciple may be without excuſe, who learns, but does not alſo carry into practice." Let us then have reſpect to the recompence of the reward, and ſuffer

with

assert that a Gentile, howsoever baptized, not only without, but even in opposition to the church, can receive remission of sins, when Christ himself commands the nations to be baptized in the full and united Trinity * ?" For, in giving command to the apostles to go and to teach all nations, baptizing them in the name of the Father, and of the Son, and of the Holy Ghost, Matth. xxviii. 19, " he signifies the Trinity into a covenant with which the nations should be baptized †." " If we, therefore, are the priests of God and of Christ, I do not perceive whom we should follow in preference to God and Christ, who in the gospel has expressly said, " I am the light of the world," John viii. 12, and who has expressly commanded

with the patience of hope; " for, oh! how great is the glory, how vast the joy, to behold your God! to be exalted to the enjoyment of salvation and eternal light with Christ your Lord and God."—" Clauduntur persecutionibus terræ, sed patet cœlum: minatur antichristus, sed Christus tuetur: mors infertur, sed immortalitas sequitur: occiso mundus eripitur, sed restituto paradisus, exhibetur: vita temporalis extinguitur, sed æterna reparatur. Quanta est dignitas—claudere in momento oculos quibus homines videbantur & mundus, & aperire eosdem statim ut Deus videatur & Christus." " Si contumelias in hoc mundo, si fugam, si tormenta toleramus, graviora expertus est MUNDI FACTOR ET DOMINUS, qui & admonet dicens; si seculum, &c. Joann. xv. 18. DOMINUS ET DEUS NOSTER quicquid docuit & fecit, ut discipulus excusatus esse non possit, qui discit & non facit." " Quæ erit gloria, & quanta lætitia, admitti ut Deum videas; honorari, ut cum Christo Domino & Deo tuo salutis & lucis æternæ gaudium capias." Cyprian. de Exhortat. Martyrii, p. 183. Epist. lviii. p. 123, 125.

* Quomodo ergo quidam dicunt foris extra ecclesiam, imo & contra ecclesiam, modo in nomine Jesu Christi ubicunque & quomodocunque Gentilem baptizatum, remissionem peccatorum consequi posse; quando ipse Christus gentes baptizari jubeat in plena & adunata Trinitate. Cyprian. Epist. lxxiii. p. 206.

† Ite, docete, &c. Matth. xxviii. 19, insinuat Trinitatem cujus sacramento gentes baptizarentur. Cyprian. Epist. lxxiii. p. 205.

manded us to baptize in thefe three names * :" for
" baptifm is a fymbol or confeffion of. the Trinity †;"
and confequently, in the adminiftration of this facrament,
no one of the three names fhould be omitted. The name
of the Son, therefore, when ufed without that of the
Father, is unprofitable; and in like manner the name
of the Father, exclufive of the Son's, is ufed without advantage ‡. " In fhort, we may compendioufly affert,
that they who hold not the Father to be true Lord,
cannot hold the truth of the Son and of the Holy
Ghoft §;" " nor, with a full and fincere knowledge of
God the Father, and of Chrift, and of the Holy Ghoft,
march forth from the tents of holinefs to war againft
the

* Si facerdotes Dei & Chrifti fumus, Rev. xx. 6, non invenio quem magis fequi, quam Deum & Chriftum debeamus; quando ipfe in evangelio maxime dicat, Ego fum lumen mundi, Joann. viii. 12, & ipfe dixit, ite ergo, docete omnes gentes, tingentes eos, &c. Matth. xxviii. 19. Cyprian. Epift. lxiii. p. 157.

† Symbolum Trinitatis.—This appellation is given by FIRMILIANUS, Bifhop of Cæfarea in Cappadocia, the pupil of Origen, the cotemporary and correfpondent of Cyprian. His epiftle, whence this and fome few farther extracts are taken, is printed among thofe of Cyprian as the lxxv. Epift. p. 223.—This eminent bifhop convened a council at Iconium, in which the doctrine of Cyprian concerning baptifm was confirmed.

CORNELIUS likewife, the cotemporary Bifhop of Rome, on the reformation of fome refractory perfons, declares to Cyprian, " I greatly rejoice, and return thanks to the Almighty God and Chrift our Lord, for that they have, on knowing their errour, of their own accord, come back to the Church from which they had ftrayed." " Tantâ lætitiâ adfecti fumus, et Deo omnipotenti et Chrifto Domino noftro gratias egimus, cum ii, cognito fuo errore, ad Ecclefiam unde exierant fimplici voluntate venerunt." Cypr. Epift. xlix. p. 92.—He recommends fimilar gratitude to Cyprian, " Deo omnipotenti et Chrifto Domino noftro gratias ageres." Ejufd. Epift p. 93.—" Nor are we ignorant," he likewife fays, " that there is one God, one Chrift the Lord, whom we have confeffed, and one Holy Ghoft." " Nec ignoramus unum Deum effe, unum Chriftum effe Dominum, quem confeffi fumus, unum Spiritum Sanctum." Ibid.

‡ Vide fupra, p. 343.

§ Satis eft breviter illud in compendio dicere: eos qui non teneant verum Dominum Patrem, tenere non poffe, nec Filii, nec Spiritus Sancti veritatem. Firmiliani Epift. ad Cypr. inter Cypr. Epift lxxv. p. 220.

the devil ‖." Let us then unite together, and render ourſelves members of that *one* body which Chriſt has inſtituted, and, calling upon the Trinity, even upon the names of the Father, and of the Son, and of the Holy Ghoſt, let us ſeek for grace by that *one* baptiſm, the adminiſtration of which he has veſted ſolely in the church. Let us reſt aſſured that our concord and brotherly love, and the preſenting of ourſelves as a people united, concerning the unity of the Father, Son, and Holy Ghoſt, is an acceptable ſacrifice to God *; and accordingly, by rendering obedience to him, whom by baptiſm we have put on, Galat. iii. 27, let us labour with our utmoſt ſtrength, and with our utmoſt ſpeed haſten, to conciliate " Chriſt, our Judge, our Lord, and our God †," who will comply with the prayers of thoſe that confeſs him ‡, and who, looking into the purpoſes of the faithful mind, will deal out the reward of glory in proportion to the degree of our attachment to him. §

That,

‖ Ad debellandum diabolum, de divinis caſtris, cum plenâ & ſincerâ Dei Patris & Chriſti & Spiritûs Sancti cognitione, procedere. Cyprian. Epiſt. lxxiii. p. 208.

* " Qui baptizatus ſit, gratiam conſequi potuerit, invocatâ Trinitate nominum Patris & Filii & Spiritûs Sancti."—" Sacrificium Deo majus eſt pax noſtra, & fraterna concordia, & de unitate Patris, & Filii & Spiritûs Sancti adunata. Firmiliani Epiſt. lxxv. p. 221, & Cypr. de Orat. Dom. p. 149.

† Quibus poſſumus viribus elaborare *(debemus)* & velociter gerere, ut Chriſtum Judicem & Dominum & Deum promereamur obſequiis noſtris: cum, quotquot in Chriſto baptizati eſtis, &c. Galat. iii. 27. Cyprian. Epiſt. lxxii. p. 146.

‡ Credo enim Chriſtum, martyribus ſuis petentibus indulturum. Cᴇʟᴇʀɪɴɪ Epiſtola ad Lucianum Confeſſorem inter Cypr. Epiſt. xxi. p. 45. —Celerinus alſo was a confeſſor. Euſeb. Eccl. Hiſt. lib. vi, cap. xliii.

§ Hanc cogitationem noſtram Deus videat, hoc propoſitum mentis & fidei

That, previous to the Council of Nice, there lived a Perſon of the name of HIPPOLYTUS, who drew his pen in the cauſe of Chriſtianity, is certain: but the preciſe time in which he flouriſhed, the eccleſiaſtical

fidei Dominus Chriſtus aſpiciat, daturus eis gloriæ fuæ ampliora præmia, quorum circa ſe fuerint deſideria majora. Cypr. de Mortalitate, ad fin.

A. D. 256 a council was convened at Carthage, at which, beſides a numerous body of the church, ſeventy-eight African biſhops gave their attendance. From this great ſynod the doctrine of Cyprian concerning baptiſm received its confirmation. The Biſhops ſeverally delivered, and for the moſt part in one ſhort ſentence, each compriſed his opinion. "Chriſt, our Lord and God," ſay they, "going to the Father, commended to us (the church) his ſpouſe; and whether ſhall we preſerve her unſeduced and inviolate, or betray her innocence and chaſtity to the adulterer?" "Inſtructing the apoſtles with his own mouth, our God and Lord Jeſus Chriſt has fully perfected our faith, and the grace of baptiſm, and the rule of law to the church, ſaying, "Go and teach all nations, baptizing them in the name of the Father, and of the Son, and of the Holy Ghoſt," Matth. xxviii. 19. Falſe, therefore, is the baptiſm of heretics, from whoſe mouth proceeds, not life, but poiſon; not the grace of heaven, but a blaſphemy of the Trinity." "But upon a rock, and not upon hereſy, has Jeſus Chriſt, our Lord and God, the Son of the Father and Creator, founded his church." "And it cannot enter into doubt, that human preſumption is weak, when compared with the adorable and fearful majeſty of our Lord Jeſus Chriſt." "Since, therefore, we evidently know that heretics have not the Father, nor the Son, nor the Holy Ghoſt," "it is alſo evident that heretics, that is, the enemies of Chriſt, do not make the full and entire confeſſion which is neceſſary to this ſacrament."

VENANTIUS *a Teniſâ.*

Chriſtus Dominus & Deus noſter ad Patrem proficiſcens ſponſam ſuam nobis commendavit. Utrumne eam incorruptam & inviolatam cuſtodiemus, an integritatem ejus & caſtitatem mæchis & corruptoribus prodemus? Cypriani Concil. Carthagin. p. 238.

Venantius was a *confeſſor*; that is, a Chriſtian who had undergone, and yet ſurvived, the judgement of a Pagan tribunal, without ſwerving from his profeſſion of Chriſt. Among the many devices framed by " *the mild genius of Rome and Polytheiſm.*" the preſervation of life for the protraction of torment was not one of the leaſt remarkable. Lactantius declares that the diligence uſed to this end was as great as if their ſolicitude ſprung from affection. The faith of Venantius is evident here, and that he was one of thoſe " who with a glorious voice confeſſed his God;" and from the 86th epiſtle of Cyprian, it is equally certain that thoſe men who were

con-

[349]

ftical function which he discharged, and even the place of his residence, are points by no means decided. He is supposed, and I think upon very good grounds, to have been an Arabian Bishop, and to have suffered martyr-

condemned to the mines, and to whom he directs it, were sufferers for the same confession, that they were under condemnation as "martyrs of God the Father almighty, and of Jesus Christ our Lord, God, and Saviour, from whom they hoped for eternal salvation, and by whom, even in the midst of their toil and bondage, they were refreshed and cherished." Qui gloriosa voce Deum confessi. Cyprian. Epist. v. p. 10. Martyribus Dei Patris omnipotentis & Jesû Christi Domini & Dei conservatoris nostri.—In metallis non fovetur lecto & culcitris corpus, sed refrigerio & solatio Christi fovetur—quæ exultantia in metallo corde regnante scire Christum secum esse præsentem! Epist. lxxxvi. p. 231, 233. See above, p. 249.

EUCHRATIUS *a Thenis*.

Fidem nostram, & baptismatis gratiam, & legis ecclesiasticæ regulam, DEUS & Dominus noster Jesus Christus, suo ore apostolos docens, perimplevit, dicens, "Ite & docete, &c." Matth. xxviii. 19. Falsum ergo hæreticorum baptisma, de quorum ore virus, non vita, nec gratia coelestis, sed blasphemia Trinitatis exprimitur. Cypr. Concil. Carthagin. p. 235.

FORTUNATUS *a Thuchabori*.

Jesus Christus Dominus & DEUS noster, Dei Patris & Creatoris Filius, super Petram ædificavit ecclesiam suam, & non super hæresin. Ejusdem lib. p. 233.

FELIX *ab Uthinâ*.

Nemini dubium est non in tantum posse humanam præsumptionem, quantum DOMINI NOSTRI JESU CHRISTI ADORANDAM ET VENERABILEM MAJESTATEM. Ejusd. lib. p. 335.

MONNULUS *a Girbâ*.

Cum ergo manifeste sciamus hæreticos non habere, nec Patrem, nec Filium, nec Spiritum Sanctum. Ejusd. lib. p. 232.

LUCIUS *a Castro Galbæ*.

Ergo manifestum sit hæreticos, id est, hostes Christi, non integram sacramenti confessionem habere. Ejusd. lib. p. 232.

A council held at Arles, A. D. 317, gives the same opinion, and declares, "Si quis ab hæresi venerit, interrogent eum symbolum, & si perviderint eum in Patre, & Filio, & Spiritu Sancto baptizatum esse, manus ei tantum imponantur."

See above, p. 203.

Origen, as well as Eusebius, has denominated Christ ΑΥΤΟΘΕΟΣ, and explained the term by adding, hoc est, PER SE DEUS. Orig. in Joann. Evang. tom. II. p. 173. See above, p. 256.

martyrdom in the year 230. But be this as it may, an antient monument has preserved the titles of several works afcribed to him, and we are poffeffed of fome tracts which correfpond with thefe titles; they are not, however, of unqueftionable authority: my extracts therefore from the unauthenticated pages fhall be very brief; and even thefe fhall be fuch as are leaft liable to difpute, having been cited by antient Authors, who undoubtedly read the genuine productions of this Writer, or already adduced by moderns to the maintenance of the argument which I now fupport, and confequently bearing the marks of a favourable Judgement from thofe learned men who have efteemed them of weight in this important caufe.

" Coming forth into the world," he tells us, " that Jefus Chrift appeared both God and Man: His Manhood," he fays, " is eafily comprehended from the feveral imbecillities which characterized the feveral fufferings which afflicted him. But his Godhead may be eafily difcerned from the adoration of Angels, the numerous miracles which he performed, and the powers which he imparted to his Difciples;" and indeed " you have feen it revealed, that as concerning the Flefh, he is of David, but according to the Spirit, of God.—— Whence it is demonftrated that he is at once both God and Man." *

To

See above, p. 26.

* Hippolyti Epifcopi & Martyris Arabum metropolis in memoria Hærefum. Hic procedens in mundum Deus & Homo apparuit; et Hominem quidem ejus facile eft intelligere, cum efurit, & fatigatur, & laborat, & fitit, & formidat, & fugit, orat, contriftatur, & fuper cervical dormit, & calicem refpuit paffionis, & anxius fudat, & ab angelo confortatur, & a Juda traditur, & contumeliam patitur, a Caiapha & ab Herode defpicitur, a Pilato flagellatur, & a militibus illuditur, & a Judæis ligno configitur, & ad Patrem clamans commendat Spiritum, & inclinato capite Spiritum tradit, Latus lancea perforatur, involutus in Sindone ponitur in fepulchro & a patre die tertia fufcitatur, Divinitatem vero ejus videre rurfus clarum eft,

To the Son he afcribes the fame Divine Nature, and the fame attributes as to the Father, to wit, "Exiftence without commencement, and without having been made, Infinity, Eternity, and Incomprehenfibility."* And in his Homily on Antichrift, he introduces the Saints in the final Judgement thus addreffing Chrift the Lord: "O thou who art terrible, when faw we thee naked and cloathed thee? O thou who art immortal, when faw we thee a ftranger and took thee in? O thou who art merciful, when faw we thee fick, or in prifon, and came unto thee? For thou art eternal; thou art with the Father uncommenced, with the Holy Ghoft coeternal; thou art he who out of nothing haft made all things." † This worfhip, however, in a work entitled *of one God in three Perfons, &c.* "he avers, does not comprehend a Plurality of Gods; for that while he acknowledges

eft, quando laudatur ab angelis, & hoc a paftoribus infpicitur, & expectatur a Simeone, & ab Anna teftimonium perhibetur, & quæritur a magis, & ab ftella defignatur, & aqua in nuptiis operatur vinum, & increpat mare violentia commotum ventorum, & ambulat fuper mare & cæcum ex nativitate videre facit, & mortuum Lazarum quatriduanum refufcitat, & varias facit virtutes, datque difcipulis poteftatem.

Ejufdem. Vidifti quod fecundum carnem quidem ejus eft. ex David narrat, quod vero fecundum Spiritum ex Deo: quapropter probatum eft eundum & Deum & Hominem. Gelafius Ep fc. Rom. A. D. 492, ad Epifc. Illyr. Epift. 2da, Bibliothera P. P. apud Sonnium Paris. Fol. Tom. v. p. 478.

* Apud Anaftafium Bibliothecarium in collectaneis, Fragm. 60, p. 228. Filio eandem prorfus naturam divinam addicit (Hippolytus) quæ in patre eft, eafdemque Proprietates; nempe ἀναρχίαν, ἀγεννησίαν, ἀπειρίαν, ἀϊδιότητα, ἀκαταληψίαν. *Imprincipalitatem, infactionem, fempiternitatem, incomprebenfibilitatem*, ut verè licet Barbarè vertit Anaftafius. Senfit itaque Hippolytus, Filium effe perinde ac Patrem ἀνάρχον κỳ ἀΐδιον, initii expertem & æternum.—Bulli Defenfio Fidei Nicenæ. Sect. 3, cap. 8.

† In eo (libro de Antichrifto) Hippolytus in extremo Judicio (Sanctos) introducit Chriftum Dominum ita alloquentes. Φοβερὶ, πότε σε ἴδομει, &c. ἀθάνατε, πότε σε, &c? φιλάνθρωπε, πότε σε, &c. ut Mat. 25. 38, 39. Σὺ ἦ ὁ ἀεὶ ὤν· σὺ ἦ ὁ συνάναρχο- τῷ Πατρὶ κỳ συναΐδιο- τῷ Πνεύματι. σὺ ἦ ὁ ἐκ μὴ ὄντων τὰ πάντα ποιήσας. Ib.

knowledges the Godhead of the Word, according to John i. 1. he does not yet herein profess two Gods, but one God and two Persons." *

Prudentius has recorded the martyrdom of one named HIPPOLYTUS, an Italian Presbyter, who suffering a death of exquisite torture at Rome, followed the example of St. Stephen, and recommended " his soul to Christ." † Notwithstanding that some have confounded them, I have not a doubt that these are two distinct Persons of the same denomination. ‡

Besides

---

* "Ει δε ην ὁ λογος προς τον Θεον, Θεος ὤν, τι ἐν φήσειαν τις δύο λέγειν Θεός; δύο μὲν ἐκ ἐρῶ Θεὸς, ἀλλ' ἢ ἕνα, πρόσωπα δὲ δύο. Adv. Noetum.

† — Tu rape Christe Animam. Prudentii peri Stephanôn. Hym. xi. No. 105. See above, p. 135.

‡ As dubious writings cannot be applied to prove any Doctrine of Faith, and as I find no other writers whose works are not very questionable, I wave the use of many Tracts which appear in the Bibliotheca Patrum. Bishop Bull has, however, stamped a value on some passages ascribed to METHODIUS, Bishop of Tyre, who suffered martyrdom under Diocletian, A. D. 302. Photius also, Bishop of Constantinople, A. D. 860, has preserved a considerable fragment from this Author.

This Father speaks of our Lord's Eternity and Assumption of our nature, and avers, that " the Son, when he was God himself, chose to put on human Flesh ;" and that " the Man Christ was full of the pure and perfect Godhead."

Μήτε αὖ προϋπαρξαντα τέλ⊙ ἐσχηκέναι, ἀλλὰ εἶναι ἀεὶ τὸν ἄϋλον—πρὸ τῆς ἐνανθρωπήσεως τῦ Χριςῦ. Phot. Bibliothec. Genev. 1611, Fol. p. 959.

Eo consilio elegit humanam carnem, Deus ipse cum esset, induere, ut velut in tabulâ divinum exemplar vitæ propositum intuentes Pictoris in exprimendo fidelitatem imitaremur--Christum Hominem merâ Divinitate & perfectâ plenum & Deum in homine quodammodo inclusum.—Meth. Orat. 1 & 2. Bibliothec. P.P. Tom. iii. p. 678, 681, a Bull. citat. p. 167.

HERMIAS

Besides the many Christian Writers who have been already produced in evidence of their own Faith, there were several others whose works have perished: For the preservation of a few fragments, however, which evince their religious sentiments, we are obliged to the subsequent Writers of the Church. To these we are likewise indebted for having committed to writing the Doctrines which were orally promulged by a few eminent Preachers of the Gospel; and also for having transmitted the testimony borne by an army of Martyrs, which

HERMIAS and MINUTIUS FELIX have both rather exposed and derided the weakness of idolatry than declared the Doctrines of the Gospel; from these two writers, therefore, I can deduce nothing decisive. ACHELAUS, in his dispute with a Manichæan, is not more explicit on the tenet under enquiry. ———

Origen, it is true, has quoted the RECOGNITIONS ascribed to Clemens Romanus; but Epiphanius, about the year 370, sets their authority quite aside: for he declares them adulterated throughout by the Ebionites. Dr. Mosheim goes farther, and thinks, that not only the recognitions, but the Constitutions and Clementina are falsely attributed to S. Clement.— Were they indisputably the work of that Apostolic Father, it were superfluous to adduce them in proof of that Faith which he has been already heard to profess. Such passages, however, as have escaped heretical corruption, are certainly of the Ante-Nicene Ages of the Church, and the following Professions, Prayers, and Praises seem not to have been interpolated by the pen of one who entertained mean and derogatory conceptions of the character and dignity of our Redeemer, whose Eternity he acknowledges, and whom he thus addresses: " O God, the only begotten, Son of the mighty Father, rebuke thou the spirits of iniquity, and deliver the works of thine own hands, from the influence of every spirit at enmity with thee: wherefore, to thee be glory, honour, and adoration, and through thee to the Father in the Holy Ghost, for ever and ever, Amen." " We confess that Christ is not a meer man, but God the Word and Man, the Mediator between God and Men, the Priest of the Father:" "That the Lord God, who appeared to us in the flesh," " was pleased, on our account, to be born of a Woman; that he appeared in life, in his baptism demonstrating, that he who was manifested was God and Man;—that for us he suffered, O Father, by thy permission, and that being dead he was raised again by thy power:" " Gather us, therefore, together into the kingdom of heaven in Jesus Christ our Lord, with whom, to thee, and the Holy Ghost, be honour and glory:" " To thee

which the fanguinary rage of Pagan zeal had arrayed, and which fuftained a warfare in defence of the Divinity of their Lord. As thefe witneffes do not directly fpeak for themfelves, I have deferred calling on them till after many others whom they had preceded in point of time: That they wrote, or otherwife teftified their Faith in Jefus Chrift, within the period under enquiry, is enough to afcertain. The more minute obfervation of order feems to me a fuperfluous and unneceffary attention.

EUSEBIUS,

thee be glory, praife, majefly, worfhip, and adoration, and to thy Child Jefus Chrift our Lord, and God, and King, and to the Holy Ghoft, now and for evermore, Amen."
Chriftus qui ab initio & femper erat. *Recognit.* Lib. i.—Unigenitum Verbum Deum, Regem & Dominum omnis intellectivæ & fenfitivæ naturæ, qui eft ante omnia, per quem omnia.—Unigenite DEUS magni Patris Fili, increpa Spiritus nequam, & libera opera manuum tuarum ab alieni Spiritûs vexatione, quoniam tibi gloria, honor, & adoratio, & per te tuo Patri in Sancto Spiritu in fecula, Amen.— Chriftum non confitemur purum hominem, fed Deum Verbum & Hominem, mediatorem Dei & Hominum, pontificem Patris.—Deus Dominus qui apparuit nobis in carne—propter nos nafci voluit ex muliere, apparuit in vitâ, demonftrans fe in Baptifmo quod Deus & Homo erat qui apparuit; pro nobis paffus eft tuâ permiffione, et mortuus tua potentia fufcitatus.—Nos omnes congrega in regnum cœlorum in Chrifto Jefu Domino noftro, cum quo tibi gloria, honor, cultus, & Sancto Spiritui in fecula, Amen.—Tibi gloria, laus, majeftas, cultus, & adoratio, & puero tuo Jefu Chrifto Domino noftro, & Deo, & Regi, & Sancto Spiritui nunc & femper & in fecula feculorum, Amen.——*Conflitutionum S. Apoftolorum*, Lib. viii. c. 16, 8, Lib. vi. c. 14. Lib. vii. c. 27, 36. Lib. viii. c. 22, 23.——

The Harmony of the four Gofpels afcribed to AMMONIUS of Alexandria, the Mafter of Origen, commences thus: " In the beginning was the Word, by whom all things were created, or by which all things were founded; in the end he has now been made flefh, and that by a new mode of birth, having been born of the Virgin Mary."

In principio erat Verbum per quod condita funt omnia, in fine tandem temporum caro factum, idque novo nafcendi modo, ex Virgine Maria.— Bibliotheca Patrum, Tom. ii. p. 105.——

VICTORINUS, Bifhop of Pitabion in Pannonia, A. D. 270, wrote a comment on the Apocalypfe: We are poffeffed of a work bearing this title,

which

[355]

* EUSEBIUS, who, in the fourth century, wrote the History of the Christian Church, and who commences his own work with an earnest prayer to the Father, and to the Word his Son, who had been manifested to us*, has recorded, that the Apostle THADDÆUS (Matth. x. 3.) attested to Agbarus, King of Edessa, that " our Lord God, Jesus Christ, fulfilled the will of his Father; and having fulfilled it ascended up to his Father †. And that having, by miracles, con-

which is attributed to him; it is, however, but of disputable authority. The writer says, " we profess that Christ, the Son of God, was begotten of the Father before all ages, and was a spiritual Being; that he was made Man, and that having overcome Death, he was received up by the Father into Heaven with his body; that he poured forth the Holy Ghost, as his gift and a pledge of immortality."

Dicimus & hujus Filium Christum ante originem seculi spiritualem apud Patrem genitum, hominem factum, & morte devictâ in cœlos cum corpore a Patre receptum, effudisse Spiritum Sanctum donum & pignus immortalitatis. Bibliothec. P.P.——

I know of no other writer that has any tolerable pretensions to authenticity: The claims of ANATOLIUS appear unsupported, nor do those of " COMMODIANUS, the beggar of Jesus Christ," seem better founded.

* Τὸν τῷ Λόγῳ Πατέρα Θεὸν, κ͵ τὸν δηλέμενον αὑτὸν Ἰησᾶν Χριςὸν τὸν Σωτῆρα κ͵ Κύριον ἡμῶν τὸν ἐράνιον τῷ Θεῷ Λόγον, βοηθὸν ἡμῖν κ͵ συνεργὸν τῆς καλὰ τὴν διήγησιν ἀληθείας ΕΠΙ-ΚΑΛΗΣΑΜΕΝΟΙ. Euseb. Eccl. Hist. Lib. i. cap. v. p. 16. Vide supra, p. 278.

Αὑτὸν ΓΕΡΑΙΡΟΜΕΝ μὴ φωναῖς μόνον, ἀλλὰ κ͵ πάσῃ διαθέσει ψυχῆς. Euseb. Hist. Ecclef. Lib. i. cap. iii. p. 14. Eusebius also declares, that " the only begotten Son, the Word of God, reigns together with his Father, from uncommenced to endless and indeterminable ages. Ὁ μὲν γε τῷ Θεῷ μονογενὴς Λόγος, τῷ αὑτῷ Πατρὶ συμ-βασιλεύων ἐξ ἀνάρχων αἰώνων εἰς ἀπείρυς κ͵ ἀτελευτήτυς αἰῶνας. Euseb. Orat. de Laud. Constant. p. 719. Refer this to p. 28 and 192 above, and let it stand a permanent confutation of all the Unitarian sophistry on the subject there discussed.

† Ὁ Κύριος ἡμῶν κ͵ Θεός Ἰησᾶς ὁ Χριςὸς τὸ θέλημα τῷ Πατρὸς αὑτῷ πεπλήρωκε, κ͵ πληρώσας, ἀνελήφθη πρὸς τὸν ἐκτῷ Πατέρα. Euseb. Ecclef. Hist. Lib. i. Sec. i. cap. xiii. p. 40.——Edit. Cantab. à Reading, Fol. 1720. I have nothing to say to the story, but as it is related by Eusebius.

convinced the people of Edeſſa, "he brought them to the worſhip of the power of Chriſt." ‡

HEGESIPPUS, the earlieſt Eccleſiaſtical Hiſtorian, in his narrative of St. James's martyrdom, quoted by Euſebius, relates that, "upon the teſtimony of that Apoſtle, the people cried Hoſanna, and glorified the Son of David." *

MELITO, Biſhop of Sardis in Aſia, towards the cloſe of the ſecond century, is quoted in the Alexandrian Chronicle, (Olymp. 236.) as having declared that the Chriſtians do not adore inſenſible ſtones; but that they worſhip one God alone, who is before all things, and in all things, and Jeſus Chriſt, who is God and the Word before all ages †. And "who is he," ſays GAIUS, A. D. 220, "that knows not the writings of Melito, which declare Chriſt to be both God and Man? §

THEOGNOSTUS, an Ante-Nicene Writer, much applauded by Athanaſius, has maintained, and endeavoured to illuſtrate, the conſubſtantiality of the Father and Son, in a manner ſo very ſimilar to that uſed by Tertullian, in

‡ Ἔπι σίβας ἀγαγὼν τῆς τῦ Χριςῦ δυνάμεως. Lib. ii. c. i. Sec. i, p. 45.

* Πόλλων πληροφορηθέντων κỳ δοξαζόντων, ἐπὶ τῇ μαρτυρίᾳ τῦ Ἰακώβυ, κỳ λεγόντων ὡς ἀνὰ τῷ Ὑίῳ Δαβὶδ. Euſeb. Hiſt. Ec. Lib. ii. cap. xxiii. p. 79.

† Du Pin. Eccleſ Hiſt. Vol. I. p. 55.

§ Τὰ γὰρ Εἰρηναίῳ τε κỳ Μελίτων۞ κỳ τῶν λοιπῶν τίς ἀγνοεῖ βιβλία, Θεὸν κỳ ἀνθρωπον καταγγέλλοντα τὸν Χριςὸν.——Euſeb. Eccl. Hiſt. Lib. v. cap. xxviii. p. 252.

in support of the indivisible unity of the three Persons in the Godhead, that instead of superfluously translating the words of this Father, I refer the reader to p. 223 above. §

The Emperor CONSTANTINE, in his Oration to the Church, published by Eusebius, has quoted an Acrostic from the Erythræan SIBYL, which asserts, that " the Faithful and Infidel shall behold the most high God clothed in flesh ;" and concludes with a declaration, that " it is God our Saviour the immortal King who has suffered for us." *

But it is said that the Sibylline Oracles are a forgery. I grant it: but how does this affect the present argument?

§ Θέογνως⊙ μὲν ἀνὴρ λόγι⊙ ἃ παρηήσαῖο τὸ ἐκ τῆς 'ΟΥΣΙΑΣ ἐιπεῖν· γράφων γὰρ περὶ υἱοῦ ἐν τῷ δευτέρῳ τῶν ὑποτυπώσεων ὅλως εἴρηκεν· ἐκ ἐξωθεν τὶς ἐστιν ἐφευρεθεῖσα ἡ τὲ Υἱᾶ ἐσία, ἐδὲ ἐκ μὴ ὄντων ἐπεισήχθη· ἀλλὰ ἐκ τῆς τῷ Παῖρος ἐσίας ἐφυ· ὡς τῷ φῶτος, τὸ ἀπαύγασμα· ὡς ὑδατ⊙ ἀτμίς· ὅτε γὰρ τὸ ἀπαύγασμα, ὅτε ἡ ἀτμὶς, αὐτὸ τὸ ὕδωρ ἐστὶν, ἢ αὐτὸς ὁ ἥλι⊙. ὅτε ἀλλότριον· ἀλλὰ ἀπόρροια τῆς τῷ Παῖρος ἐσίας· ἃ μερισμὸν ὑπομείνασας τῆς τῷ Παῖρος ἐσίας· ὡς γὰρ μένων ὁ ἥλι⊙ ὁ αὐτὸς ἃ μειᾶται ταῖς ἐκχυομέναις ὑπ' αὐτῷ αὐγαῖς, οὕτως οὐδὲ ἡ ἐσία τῷ Παῖρος ἀλλοίωσιν ὑπέμεινεν, εἰκόνα ἑαυτῆς ἔχεσα τὸν Υἱόν.—
Athanasii Synod. Nicænæ contra Heræsim Arianorum Decret. p. 421, Ex Officina Commeliniana, 1600, Fol.

* Ὀψόνται Θεὸν —— πιστοὶ κ̀ ἀπιστοι
Ὕψιστον —— —— ,
Σαρκοφόρον —— —— .
Οὑτὸς ὁ —— Θεὸς ἡμῶν
Σωτὴρ, ἀθάνατ⊙ βασιλεὺς ὁ πάθων ἐνεχ' ἡμῶν.
Euseb. Constantini Oratio ad Sanctorum Cœtum, p. 701.

The initials of this Acrostic are, Ιησους χρειςτ⊙ Θεῦ Υἱ⊙ Σωτὴς ςαυρ⊙.

ment? Let us say, that they were fabricated with a view to promote the Christian cause; it is not then to another cause that the Sibyl is feigned to have given her sanction. Her authority is most certainly called upon to maintain the sentiments of the person, or perhaps conspiracy, which believed it might have weight with the Pagan world. Rome, though she disregarded the prophecy of the Jew, revered the predictions of the Sibyl; to these then she was referred, and an artful fiction had adapted these to the narrative of the Gospel: but how that narrative was understood by a Christian writer, previous to the days of Justin Martyr, (for Justin too has quoted the Sibyl) is a point easily determined. The supposititious prophecy is made to quadrate with the event, which was, therefore, unquestionably understood to be, that he who had taken upon him our nature, and died for our offences, was no other than the almighty and immortal God.

St. Basil assures us that JULIUS AFRICANUS, a writer of the highest reputation, early in the third century, has declared that, " not ignorant of the grace of faith, we give thanks to him who bestowed upon our fathers the Saviour of all men, our Lord Jesus Christ, to whom, with the Holy Ghost, be glory and majesty for ever." *
The same doxology he says was used by Gregory Thaumaturgus, (see p. 303 above) by Firmilianus, (see p. 346 above) and by MELETIUS, a name cited by Athanasius, and spoken of by Eusebius with the greatest respect. †

BASIL

* Τῆς πίστεως ἐκ ἀγνοοῦντες τὴν χάριν εὐχαριστοῦμεν τῷ παρασχομένῳ τοῖς ἰδίοις ἡμῶν πατράσι, τὸν τῶν ὅλων Σωτῆρα κỳ Κύριον ἡμῶν Ἰησοῦν Χριστὸν, ᾧ ἡ δόξα κỳ ἡ μεγαλωσύνη ζὺν ἁγίῳ Πνεύματι εἰς τοὺς αἰῶνας. Jul. African. a Basilio citat. in libro suo de Spiritu Sancto, cap. xxix. p. 219. Edit. Fol. apud Sonnium, Paris, 1518.
† Ibid.——Euseb. Lib. vii. cap. ult.

BASIL was himself Bishop of Cæsarea in Cappadocia, A. D. 369; he avers that "the people repeat that *antient or primitive* saying, We ascribe glory, or, Glory be to the Father, and to the Son, and to the Holy Ghost.* And for a testimony borne to the divinity of the Holy Ghost, he immediately refers to the dying Hymn of the Martyr ATHENOGENES. †

DIONYSIUS, Bishop of Alexandria, A. D. 247, having been accused of saying, that the Son was a creature, exculpates himself from the charge before a council convened by Dionysius, Bishop of Rome, and peremptorily asserts, that " he does not declare the Son to have been made; but that, on the contrary, he confesses him to be of one substance with the Father ‡. And in language similar to that of Julius Africanus, who has been just now cited, he calls on us " who have received the form and ordinance from our predecessors to join our voices to theirs, and offer up our thanksgivings. To God, therefore, the Father, and to the Son, our Lord Jesus Christ, together with the Holy Ghost, be glory and power for ever and ever, Amen." §—It follows

* Λάος 'ΑΡΧΑΊΑΝ ἀφίησι τὴν φωνὴν, 'ΑΙΝΟ͂ΥΜΕΝ Πατέρα, κỳ Ὑιὸν, κỳ ἅγιὸν Πνεῦμα Θεε͂. Ejusd. lib. p. 220.

† Ibid.— Basil has not preserved any passage from this Hymn, nor does he recount any particulars of the Author: That his martyrdom by fire, and his Hymn, were subjects very generally known, is evident from the manner in which the Father has adverted to them.

‡ Μήτε γὰρ ποιητὸν εἰρηκέναι τὸν Ὑιὸν; ἀλλὰ κỳ 'ΟΜΟΟΎΣΙΟΝ αὐτὸν ὁμολογεῖν διεβεβαιώσατο. Athanasii Synod. Nicæn. contra Hæresin Arian. Decret. p. 421.

§ Ἡμεῖς, παρὰ τῶν πρὸ ἡμῶν πρισβυτέρων τύπον κỳ κανόνα παρειληφότες, ὁμοφώνως αὐτοῖς προσευχαριστοῦντες—τῷ δὲ Θεῷ Πατρὶ, κỳ Ὑιῷ τῷ Κυρίῳ ἡμῶν Ἰησοῦ Χριστῷ ζὺν τῷ ἁγίῳ Πνεύματι, δόξα κỳ κράτος εἰς τὰς αἰῶνας αἰώνων, Ἀμήν. Dionys. Alexandr. a Basil. citat. in libro de Sp. Sanct. cap. xxix. p. 218.

Ruffinus,

lows alfo, from this narrative, that the Church, before which the imputed Unitarianifm of Dionyfius was confidered as erroneous, was not itfelf an Unitarian Church.

Athanafius has extracted and preferved the following paffage from a letter written by DIONYSIUS, Bifhop of Rome, in the name of the COUNCIL, before whom the Bifhop of Alexandria had been accufed of Herefy: "It is neceffary that the Divine Word fhall be one with the God of the univerfe, and that the Holy Ghoft fhould adhere and refide in God; it is likewife neceffary that the Holy Trinity fhould converge into unity, and, as it were, draw to a point or fummit, which is the Almighty God of the univerfe." *

HOSIUS, a Spanifh Bifhop, at whofe inftance the Council of Nice was convened †, in an epiftle quoted by Athanafius, declares, " I do not concur with the Arians, but altogether anathematize and abjure their Herefy." ‡ What occafioned this categorical renunciation

Rufinus, in his Apology for Origen, (fee above, p. 291.) has declared that " Dionyfius has ftrenuoufly defended the Unity and Equality of the Trinity." In quamplurimis Unitatem & Æqualitatem Trinitatis defendit.—Inter Orig. Oper. Tom. i. p. 494.

* Ἡνῶσθαι γὰρ ἀνάγκη τῷ Θεῷ τῶν ὅλων τὸν Θεῖον λογον· ἐμφιλοχωρεῖν δὲ τῷ Θεῷ, κỳ ἐνδιαιτᾶσθαι δεῖ τὸ ἄγιον Πνεῦμα· ἤδη κỳ τὴν Θείαν τριάδα εἰς ἕνα ὥσπερ εἰς κορυφήν τινα, τὸν Θεὸν τῶν ὅλων τὸν παντοκράτορα λέγω, συγκεφαλαιοῦσθαί τι κỳ συνάγεσθαι πᾶσα ἀνάγκη. Athanaf. Synod. Nic. contra Her. Arian. Decret. p. 421.

† Sulpicius Severus Sacr. Hift. Lib. ii. p. 108. Edit. Elzev. 1656.

‡ Ἐγὼ ὅτε Ἀρειανοῖς συγκατίθεμαι: ἄλλα δὲ τὴν αἵρεσιν αὐτῶν ἀναθεματίζω. Athanaf. Epift. ad folit. Vit. agent. p. 651.

tion of the Unitarian Herefy, does not appear from the Father who has preferved it. An early Ecclefiaftical Hiftorian, however, has furnifhed ground for a conjecture, that this venerable Bifhop has thus vehemently condemned the Arian Tenets, in refutation of an opinion entertained by fome, that he had lapfed from his original faith and embraced them: If this idea be juft, Hofius appears in his own defence, and has himfelf rejected the report as a calumny. * I do not rely on this.

Jofephus has afcribed the deftruction of Jerufalem to the cruelty of the Jews in putting St. James to death: "But why," fays Origen, " is it not more reafonable to fay, that it was effected on account of Jefus Chrift, to whofe Godhead fo many churches of men, who have been purged from all the dregs of evil, bear witnefs?" †

Of the truth of this affertion, I have already produced fome proofs; for the tenets of the Phrygian church, fee above, p. 237, the note; and for a paffage from Eufebius of the fame import as this from Origen, fee p. 256. We have alfo the teftimony of Sulpicius Severus, that the primitive CHURCH OF JERUSALEM believed our Lord to be God. ‡

The

* Sulp. Sev. p. 108.

† Πῶς ὀχὶ εὐλογώτερον διὰ Ἰησῦν τὸν Χριστὸν τῦτο φάσκειν γεγονέναι; ἃ τῆς Θειότητ©· μάρτυρες αἱ τοσαῦται μεταβαλόντων ἀπὸ τῆς χύσεως τῶν κακῶν ἐκκλησίαι, κὶ ἠρημένων τῦ δημιεργῦ κὶ παντ' ἀναφερόντων ἐπι τὴν πρὸς ἐκεῖνον ἀρέσκειαν. Origen. contra Celfum, p. 36.

‡ Tum (fc. imperante Hadriano, A. D. 120.) pene omnes CHRISTUM DEUM fub legis obfervatione credebant. Sulp. Sev. Hift. Sacr. Lib. ii. p. 99. Edit Elzev.—Eufebius concurs: for he tells us, Ἑβραίων τὴν γνῶσιν τῦ Χριστῦ γνησίως καταδέξασθαι. Hift. Eccl. Lib. iv. c. v.

The CHURCHES of LYONS and VIENNA, in an Epiftle very generally directed, commence the narrative of their fufferings under L. Verus, A. D. 168, with a prayer for " peace, grace, and glory from God the Father, and Chrift Jefus our Lord."* I fhall, as much as poffible, avoid engaging in the melancholy tale; the very few words which fell from the dying lips of fuch martyrs as " Chrift was pleafed fhould be taken hence in the very act of confeffion," † or fuch expreffions as betray the religious fentiments of the antient Churches in Gaul, I fhall lay before my reader; and, few as they are, I truft they are fufficient to difcredit, nay abfolutely to difprove the imputation of Unitarianifm.

" Nothing," fay the writers, " is terrible where the love of the Father is; nothing is grievous where fubfifts the glory of Chrift;" ‡ whofe immeafurable compaffion and long-fuffering were difplayed in the martyrdom of Pothinus, who, though bent with the decrepitude of ninety years, " retained yet life fufficient for the triumph of Chrift," and in the recall of fome who had, through apprehenfion of death, fallen into a temporary apoftacy; for in the return of thefe Chrift was glorified before the Gentiles, who had, in their fall, confidered them-

* Οἱ ἐν Βιέννῃ κỳ Λυγδούνῳ τῆς Γαλλίας παροικοῦντες δέλοι Χριςῦ τοῖς ἀδελφοῖς εἰρήνη, κỳ χάρις, κỳ δόξα ἀπὸ Θεῦ Πατρὸς, κỳ Χριςῦ Ἰησῦ τῦ Κυρίυ ἡμῶν. Eufeb. Hift. Eccl. Lib. v. cap. i. p. 198.

† Οὓς ἐν τῇ ὁμολογίᾳ Χριςὸς ἠξίωσεν ἀναληφθῆναι. Ejufd. Lib. cap. ii. p. 211.

‡ Μηδὲν φοβερὸν ὅπυ Πατρὸς ἀγάπη, μὴ δὲ ἀλγεινὸν ὅπυ Χριςῦ δόξα. Ejufd. Lib. cap. i. p. 203.

themselves triumphant over his name; * an assertion in concurrence with which we are told by Gaius, that Natalis, after his perversion to the Heresy of Theodotus, was miraculously recovered to the truth; " for our most merciful God and Lord Jesus Christ was not willing that he, who was a witness of his own sufferings, should perish without the church." †

It is difficult to decide which is the most wonderful, the inventive cruelty of the persecutor, or the persevering constancy of a young woman named BLANDINA, who, after she had sustained torments hardly conceivable, at length expired on the horns of a bull. She was, however, say the martyrologists, rendered in a manner insensible to the torments inflicted by her murderer, by means of the hope through which she seemed even to possess the object of her faith, and by that communion which (by prayer) she had so intimately entered into with Christ. ‡ I intentionally omit such prayers or assertions as are addressed to, or spoken of, *the Lord*,

Z z 2 without

---

* Τὸ ἀμίτρητον ἔλεος ἀνεφαίνετο Χριστοῦ—τηρουμένης δὲ τῆς ψυχῆς
ἐν αὐτῷ, ἵνα δι' αὐτῆς Χριστὸς θριαμβεύσῃ.—'Εδοξάζετο δὲ μεγάλως
ὁ Χριστὸς ἐπὶ τοῖς πρότερον ἀρνησαμένοις, τότε, παρὰ τὴν τῶν
ἐθνῶν ὑπόνοιαν, ὁμολογοῦσι. P. 207.

† Ευσπλαγχ© Θεός καὶ Κύρι© ἡμῶν 'Ιησᾶς Χριστὸς ἐκ ἐθέλει
ἔξω ἐκκλησίας γινόμενον ἀπολέσθαι μάρτυρα τῶν ἰδίων παθῶν.—
Euseb. Hist. Eccl. Lib. v. cap. xxviii. p. 253.

Natalis had been a Confessour, that is, one who had resolutely sustained, and yet survived, the tortures inflicted with a view to compel apostacy; such were frequently termed Martyrs, or Witnesses of Christ's sufferings, which is the meaning of the term in this passage. Let us reject the miracle, the narrative is sufficient for me, it was made in the third century.

‡ Μὴ δὲ αἴσθησιν ἔτι τῶν συμβαινόντων ἔχουσα (Βλανδῖνα ὑπὲρ τῆς Χριστοῦ δόξης πάθων) διὰ τὴν ἐλπίδα κ͵ ἰσχὺν τῶν πεπιστευμένων, καὶ ὁμιλίαν πρὸς Χριστόν. P. 209. Ruffinus warrants my translation.

without farther specification; tho' in my own mind convinced, that it was " by our Saviour these martyrs are said to have been fortified or strengthened both in body and mind." Tho' convinced that it is " to our Saviour that their prayers in imitation of St. Stephen were addressed," yet, as the term by which he is signified is said to be of equivocal interpretation, I have thought proper not to adduce the passages which contain them : For the same reason, though satisfied myself, I have omitted to call the words of a very considerable number of martyrs into evidence of their faith. * They have spoken of the Lord in terms of the utmost veneration, and we are even told, that in themselves they displayed the tokens of *our Saviour's* divine and unspeakable power. †

PHILEAS, Bishop of Thmuis in Egypt, who suffered martyrdom under Maximin, has recorded some of the astonishing cruelties with which Christianity was oppressed by the *Genius of Polytheism*; and, in an Epistle from Alexandria, describes the sufferers " as cheerfully fixing their mental eyes upon him who is God over all, and giving a welcome reception to death for the maintenance of their faith, to which they had firmly adhered, from a conviction that our Lord Jesus Christ had taken Manhood for our sake, that he might abolish sin, and prepare the way for such as seek eternal life." ‡

ALPHÆUS

* For instance, Potamiæna, who unquestionab'y suffered for the faith of Christ, ὑπὲρ τῆς εἰς Χριστὸν πίστεως. Euseb. Lib. vi. cap. v. p. 263. but called upon *the Lord* for his grace, παρακεκληκέναι χάριν αὐτῷ τὸν Κύριον. Ibid.

† Τῆς δὲ τοῦ ζωῆς ἡμῶν Θείας ὡς ἀληθῶς καὶ ἀπορρήτου δυνάμεως ἐφάνη δι' ἑαυτῶν τὰ τεκμήρια παρεστήσαντο.——Euseb. Hist. Eccl. Lib. viii. cap. xii. p. 393.

‡ Μάρτυρες, τὸ τῆς Ψυχῆς ὄμμα πρὸς τὸν ἐπὶ πάντων Θεὸν νηφαλέως τείναντες, κỳ τὸν ἐπ' εὐσεβείᾳ θάνατον ἐν τῷ λαβόντες, ἀσπασίως

ALPHÆUS and ZACCHÆUS having, in the persecution under Maximin in Paleſtine, endured the moſt excruciating torments, were at length beheaded for perſiſting in their belief and confeſſion of one God alone, and one Chriſt Jeſus their King.* PORPHYRIUS died, " invoking Jeſus the Son of God to be his aſſiſtant :" † And in the Thebaid, or ſouthward part of Ægypt, Euſebius *on his own knowledge* aſſerts, that " PHILOROMUS ſet every worldly advantage at nought, in compariſon of true piety and faith in our Saviour and Lord Jeſus Chriſt." ‡ " At Tyre he was alſo a witneſs to the teſtimony borne by many martyrs to the divine Power of our Saviour Jeſus Chriſt," ‖ under whoſe banner many choſe to enliſt as the ſoldiers of his Kingdom, in preference to ſecular glory and the proſperity of this world. §

In

ἀπρὶξ τῆς κλήσεως εἴχοντο· τὸν μὲν Κύριον ἡμῶν Ἰησῦν Χριςὸν εὑρόντες ἐνανθρωπήσαντα δἰ ἡμᾶς, ἵνα πᾶσαν μὲν ἁμαρτίαν ἐκκόψη, ἐφόδια δὲ τῆς εἰς τὴν αἰώνιον ζωὴν εἰσόδε ἡμῖν καταθῆται· ὁ γὰρ ἁρπαγμὸν ἡγήσατο, &c. Phil. ii. 5, 6, 7. Euſeb. Hiſt. Eccl. Lib. viii. cap. x. p. 388.

* Μόνον ἕνα Θεὸν καὶ μόνον Χριςὸν βασίλεα Ἰησῦν ὁμολογήσαντες. Euſeb. de Martyribus Palæſtinæ, cap. i. cum Hiſt. Eccl. p. 409.

† Τὸν Υἱὸν τῦ Θεῦ Ἰησῦν βοηθὸν ΈΠΙΒΟΏΜΕΝΟΣ. Ejuſd. Lib. p. 431.

‡ Πάντα γε μὴν δεύτερα θέμενοι τῆς ἀληθοῦς εὐσεβείας, καὶ τῆς εἰς τὸν ζωῆρα καὶ Κύριον ἡμῶν Ἰησῦν Χριςὸν πίςεως· διὸ Φιλόρωμ⊕ ἦν. Euſeb. Hiſt. Ec. Lib. viii. cap. ix. p. 386.

‖ Οἷς γινομένοις καὶ αὐτοὶ παρῆμεν, ὁπηνίκα τῦ μαρτυρεμένε ζωτῆρ⊕ ἡμῶν αὐτῦ δὴ Ἰησῦ Χριςῦ τὴν θείαν δύναμιν ἐπιπαρῦσαν, ἐναργῶς τε αὐτὴν τοῖς μάρτυσιν ἐπιδεικνῦσαν ἱςορήσαμεν. Ejuſd. Lib. cap. vii.

§ Πλεῖςοι ὅσοι τῆς Χριςῦ βασιλείας ςρατιῶται, τὴν εἰς αὐτὸν ὁμολογίαν μὴ μελλήσαντες, τῆς δοκέσης δόξης καὶ εὐπραξίας ἧς εἶχον, διαμφιλόγως προτίμησαν. Ejuſd. Lib. cap. iv.

The

[366]

In the year 276, the eastern Bishops, convened in a synod at ANTIOCH, condemned the tenets of Paul of Samosata, concerning the Doctrine of the Trinity as heretical and impious. To that council, though to the Pagan Gallio, who " cared for none of these things," they might have seemed *nice and subtle*, the errors of this most wonderfully immoral man appeared obvious and important. " To the denial of his God and Lord, and apostacy from that faith which he had originally professed, they naturally ascribed the violation of his engagements ;" to his impiety, the uncontrolled indulgence of every inordinate appetite ; * for his heresy alone it is true they excommunicated and deposed him from the Episcopacy of Antioch, for beyond this species of criminality their jurisdiction extended not; so that Mr. Gibbon

The ten Persecutions, or rather the one uninterrupted persecution, which raged from the first carnage by Nero to the accession of Constantine, has contributed a prodigious number of testimonies of the same nature with those adduced above : I shall, however, rest here. The Martyrologists, after the Nicene Council, may be said to have misrepresented facts in order to abet their cause ; or may possibly have adorned their subject by the fiction of words which were never pronounced ; or what is more certain, there have descended to our times but very few writings of this nature which are free from the suspicion of having been adulterated. From Eusebius alone I have therefore deduced this species of evidence; the time in which he lived, and the virtues which adorned his life, exempt his veracity from the slightest doubt. I have by no means selected all the instances recorded by him, they would be unnecessary : See however p. 199—393—433, in which the martyrdom of Vettius Epagathus, Lucian, and Julian are related, &c. &c.—See also his other writings.

* Ἀνεβάλλετο παρακρεσθεὶς (Φιρμιλιανὸς) ὑπ' αὐτῶ τῶ καὶ τὸν Θεὸν τὸν ἑαυτῶ καὶ Κύριον ἀρνουμένω, καὶ τὴν πίστιν ἣν καὶ αὐτὸς πρότερον εἶχε μὴ φυλαξαντω.——Μέχρι γε Ταρσῶν ἧκεν, ὅτε τῆς ἀρνησίθεω αὐτῶ (Παύλω) κακίας πεῖραν εἰληφώς (ὁ Φιρμιλιανὸς) &c.—Ὅσα δὲ ἀποσάς τῶ κανόνων ἐπὶ κιβδήλα καὶ νόθα διδάγματα μετελήλυθεν, οὐδὲν δεῖ τῶ ἔξω ὄντα τὰν πράξεις κρίνειν. Epistola a Synodo Antiocheno apud Euseb. Hist. Ec. Lib. vii. c. xxx.

bon may perhaps be right in saying that, "if Paul had preserved the purity of the orthodox faith, his reign over the capital of Syria would have ended only with his life.*. But Mr. Gibbon is certainly not right in ascribing the *possible* continuance of this reign to the indifference with which the church regarded the manners of its several members. The eastern Bishops were incompetent to sit in judgement on the morals of Paul of Samosata; before their respectable convocation his tenets alone were cognizable; to the proof of these indeed we may collect, from their general epistle, that they admitted the impurity of his unchristian life to appear in evidence; and from the terms of manly reprehension with which they have stigmatized his voluptuous sensuality, his ambitious pursuit of temporal dignity, and that avarice which prompted him to every act of extortion and violence, we may very fairly infer, that they wanted not the will but the power to chastise those enormities which so justly kindled their zeal and indignation. His suspension from the Episcopal function was all they were authorized to adjudge, and even this they were restrained by the hand of Zenobia from carrying into immediate execution. Aurelian, however, when he had subdued that Princess, " by a determination founded on the general principles of equity and reason," gave sanction to " a sentence pronounced in violation of the rights of the clergy and people." † And accordingly Paul, the flatterer and favourite of Zenobia, was degraded from the see of Antioch by the same victorious arm which had pulled his queen and protectress herself from the throne, and consigned her minister, the excellent Longinus, to the stroke of an executioner.

That

* See Mr. Gibbon's History of the Decline and Fall of the Roman Empire, Vol. I. p. 562.

† Ibid. p. 562 and 563.

That in the courſe of an argument maintaining the conſubſtantiality of the Son with the Father, we are told by Hilary, that eighty Biſhops, who had conſtituted this or a prior council convened on the ſame occaſion at Antioch, had rejected *the word* conſubſtantial, or ὁμοϝέσιο·, I allow: But does not Hilary profeſs, that he would himſelf have concurred in their judgement, provided the ſenſe in which Paul received the term were its real ſignification? Does he not affirm that it had a very different meaning, in which the church accepted it, and which this violent ſchiſmatick endeavoured to pervert?* Now, truly, I know of no better reaſon for the omiſſion or change of a phraſe, than that its ſenſe can be eaſily miſunderſtood and wreſted to ill purpoſes; nor, from the conduct of this ſynod, or of Paul himſelf, can I deduce any other inference, than that the language from which he hoped to derive preſcription to his hereſy was the antient and eſtabliſhed language of the Chriſtian church; that having been heretofore underſtood in its obvious ſenſe, it had remained unſuſpected; but that, in conſideration of this man's duplicity, it was found neceſſary to ſubſtitute the definition for the term; for none can deny, that if our Lord be profeſſed " from all eternity to be in ſubſtance

---

* ——Patres noſtri, cum Paulus Samoſateus hæreticus pronunciatus eſt, ętiam ὁμούσιον repudiaverunt; quia per hanc unius eſſentiæ nuncupationem, ſolitarium atque unicum ſibi eſſe Patrem & Filium prædicabat negata perſonarum proprietate.——Quis, ſecundum Samoſateum, in Chriſto renatus, & Filium confeſſus ac Patrem, quòd Chriſtus in ſe ſibi & Pater & Filius ſit, confitebitur? Par itaque in condemnandis impietatibus hæreticorum noſtra ſententia eſt; & hanc ὁμοούσιν intelligentiam non modo reſpuit ſed & odit.——Male ὁμοούσιον Samoſateus con'eſſus eſt, ſed nunquid melius Ariani negaverunt? Octoginta Epiſcopi olim reſpuerunt, ſed trecenti decem & octo nuper (Nicæna Synodus) receperunt——illi contra hæreticum improbaverunt; nunquid & iſti non adverſum hæreticum probaverunt? *Hilarius de Synodis adverſus Arianos Liber*, p. 243.——See above, p. 330.——Athanaſius delivers preciſely the ſame judgement.

stance and in person God,"* he is necessarily professed to be in its plain and unsophisticated meaning ὁμοούσιΘ-, or consubstantial with the Father.

Thus far we have the sense of the council of Antioch, that Christ is God; that he is both God and Man the members of this synod have likewise asserted; that, " taking flesh, he was made man; and that the body which he had taken of a virgin, having received the entire fulness of the Godhead bodily, is immutably united to the Godhead and taken into God, for which reason Jesus Christ is at once both God and Man." " God he is acknowledged to be by the whole church, who emptied himself from a state of equality with God; but man of the seed of David, as concerning the flesh, Phil. ii. 6, 7, 8. Rom. i. 3 ;" † and in proof of this tenet, they proceed to quote Rom. ix. 5, in the identical terms in which that text has been transmitted to our times.

A a a   Eusebius,

---

* Σοφίαν, καὶ λόγον, καὶ δύναμιν Θεῦ πρὸ αἰώνων ὄντα, ἃ προσ-νώσει, ἀλλ' 'ΟΥΣΙΑ ΚΑΙ' 'ΥΠΟΣΤ'ΑΣΕΙ ΘΕΟ'Ν, Θεῦ 'Υιὸν ἐν τε παλαιᾷ καὶ νέᾳ διαθήκῃ ἐγνωκότες ὁμολογῦμεν και, κηρύσ-σομέν.——Ex Epistola Episcoporum Synod. Antiochen. apud Labbæi Concil. Vol. I. p. 481.

† Σαρκοθέντα ἐνηνθρωπηκέναι, διόπερ καὶ τὸ ἐκ τῆς παρθίνυ σῶμα χωρῆσαν πᾶν τὸ πλήρωμα τῆς θεότητΘ- σωματικῶς της θεότητι ἀτρέπτως ἡνῶσαι, καὶ τεθεοποιῆσαι· ὃ χάριν ὁ αὐτὸς Θεός καὶ ἀνθρωπΘ- Ἰησῦς Χριστός ——'Εν τῇ ἐκκλησία πάσῃ πεπίσ-τευῖαι Θεός μὲν κενώσας ἑαυτὸν ἀπὸ τῦ εἶναι ἴσα Θεῷ, ἀνθρωπΘ- δὲ ἐκ σπερμάτΘ- Δαβιδ τὸ κατὰ σάρκα. Ibidem.
There is extant an EPISTLE TO PAUL OF SAMOSATA, which has been ascribed to Dionysius of Alexandria; the Author is disputed by many who acknowledge the antiquity of the work; if the latter be allowed, I am indifferent as to the former. The following testimony to the divinity

of

Eusebius, in his Ecclesiastical History, quotes the following remarkable passage from a writer whom he does not name, but whom his excellent annotator Valesius calls GAIUS *, and whose work he tells us was entitled the Little Labyrinth. " This Author," he relates, " proving the Novelty of that Heresy, which says that Christ the Saviour is a meer man, in contradiction to the leaders of the Sect of Artemon, (now revived by Paul of Samosata) who boasted of its antiquity, having adduced many arguments to discountenance their blasphemous lye, gives the following relation word for word : They affirm, says he, that all the first teachers, and even the apostles, received and taught the very same doctrine which they propagate themselves; and that the truth of preaching, or of those things which they now preached, was preserved till the days of Victor the thirteenth Bishop of Rome from Peter † : but that from the time of his successor Zephyrinus the truth was adulterated and deformed; and, perhaps, their assertion might obtain credit, were it not that in the first place the

of our Lord appears in it. The coeternal Word which was in the Father— being equal with God, assumed, for our sake, a passive nature, emptying and humbling himself, as it is written, (Phil. ii. 6, 7, 8.) to death, even the death of the cross.

Ὁ ὢν ἐν τῷ Πατρὶ ΣΥΝΑΪΔΙΟΣ ΛΟΓΟΣ, ἐν αὐτῷ πρόσωπον, ἀοράτ^Θ. Θεός.——Τὸ παθ^Θ. ὑπὲρ ἡμῶν κατεδέξατο, κενώσας ἑαυτὸν καὶ ταπεινώσας ἕως θανάτῃ, θανάτῃ δὲ ςαύρῃ, ἴσα Θεῷ ὑπάρχων, ὡς γέγραπται. Dionysii Epist. ad Paul. Samosat. inter Labb. Concil. vol. I. p. 854.

Eusebius, however, says, that " when THE WORD condescended to become Man, his Divinity was not impaired by it, but he was every where present, filling all things, and ruling all things, ἀδὲ ἀποπεσὼν τῆς θεότητ^Θ. Demonst. Evang. p. 169. Jortin's Rem. on Eccl. Hist.

* Eusebius himself mentions Gaius or Caius, (for so his name may be translated) as writing in the time of Zephyrinus.

† Victor filled the Episcopal Chair of Rome from A. D. 196 to 219; Zephyrinus from 219 to 224.

the Scriptures of God directly crush and overwhelm it; besides that there are extant the writings of some of the brethren antecedent to Victor's time, which they published in defence of the truth against the Gentiles, and against the Heresies which then subsisted. I speak of Justin and MILTIADES, and Tatian and Clement, and many others, by every one of whom Christ is declared to be God *. Nay, Who is he that is ignorant of the writings of Irenæus and Melito, &c. which testify that Christ is both God and Man? The Songs and Psalms of the Brethren also composed by the Faithful, in the very commencement of Christianity, hymn forth Christ the Word of God, and ascribe Divinity to him. Seeing then that the sentiments of the Church have been so many years professedly declared, How does it agree with the Truth, to assert that the Apostles and Fathers have preached according to the assertion of these sectaries? How indeed do they not blush to utter such falsehoood concerning Victor, as they must in their own consciences know that Victor excommunicated Theodotus, the author and father of this God-denying apostacy, the first who said that Christ was a meer man? For if Victor concurred with them, and entertained the same tenets which their blasphemy prescribes, How then should it happen *that he cast out* from the Church Theodotus the Inventor of the Heresy?" †

* Miltiades flourished about the year 180. One undecisive fragment preserved by Eusebius, lib. v. c. 17. excepted, we are not in possession of any part of his writings; and must therefore rest the history of his tenets upon the testimony of Gaius. He wrote against the Montanists. See above, p. 186.

† Τὴν γὰρ τοι δεδηλωμένην αἵρεσιν ψιλὸν ἄνθρωπον γενέσθαι τὸν Σωτῆρα φάσκουσαν, ὁ προπολλῷ νεωτερισθεῖσαν διευθύνων ἐπειδὴ σεμνύνειν αὐτὴν ὡς ἂν ἀρχαίαν οἱ ταύτης ἔθελον εἰσηγηταί· πολλὰ κỳ ἄλλα εἰς ἔλεγχον αὐτῶν τῆς βλασφήμου ψευδηγορίας παραθεὶς ὁ λόγος, ταῦτα κατὰ λέξιν ἱστορεῖ· φασὶ γὰρ τὰς Ἀποστόλας παρειληφέναι

And now let me assume this mode of argument, and, addressing myself *ad hominem*, demand of our modern God-denying Apostates how they can, without blushes, utter such falshood as they have promulged concerning the opinion of ALEXANDER BISHOP OF ALEXANDRIA, which they have declared to have been indisputably Unitarian, as they have even acknowledged that Alexander was the first " who began the contest with Arius;" nay, as they must have known from the same authority, whence they have derived any knowledge whatsoever concerning Alexander, that he called a council (but not " of war," as Dr. Jortin has affectedly called it) consisting of near an hundred Bishops, and deposed, excommunicated, and anathematized Arius, and such as adhered to his tenets. If Alexander concurred with these, and entertained the same tenets which their blasphemy

ληφέναι τε κỳ δεδιδαχέναι ταῦλα, ἃ νῦν ὖτοι λέγυσι· κỳ τελήρησθαι τὴν ἀλήθειαν τῷ κηρύγμαῖ⊙ μέχρι τῶν βίκλορ⊙ χρόνων ὃς ἦν τρισκαιδέκαλ⊙· ἀπὸ Πέτρυ ἐν Ῥώμη ἐπίσκοπ⊙· ἀπὸ δὲ τῷ διαδόχῳ αὐτῇ Ζεφυρίνε παρακεχαράχθαι τὴν ἀλήθειαν· ἦν δ' ἂν τυχὸν πιθανὸν τὸ λεγόμενον, εἰ μὴ πρῶτον μὲν ἀντέπιπλον αὐτοῖς αἱ θεῖαι γραφαί· κỳ ἀδελφῶν δὲ τίνων ἐςὶ γράμμαλα πρεσβύτερα τῶν βίκλορ⊙ χρόνων, ἃ ἐκεῖνοι πρὸς τὰ ἔθνη ὑπὲρ τῆς ἀληθείας, κỳ πρὸς τὰς τότε αἱρέσεις ἔγραψαν· λέγω δὲ Ἰυςίνε κỳ Μιλτιάδος κỳ Ταλιανῦ κỳ Κλήμενλ⊙ κỳ ἑτέρων πλειόνων, ἐν οἷς ἅπασι ΘΕΟΛΟΓΕΙΤΑΙ Ὁ ΧΡΙΣΤΟ῀Σ. Τὰ γὰρ Εἰρηναίε τε κỳ Μιλίτων⊙ κỳ τῶν λοιπῶν τὶς ἀγνοεῖ βιβλία, Θεὸν κỳ ἀνθρώπον καλαγγέλλονλα τὸν Χριςὸν· Ψαλμοὶ δὲ ὅσοι κỳ ᾠδαὶ ἀδελφῶν ἀπαρχῆς ὑπὸ πιςῶν γραφεῖσαι, τὸν λογὸν τῷ Θεῷ τὸν Χριςὸν ὑμνῦσι θεολογῦνλες· πῶς ἂν ἐκ τοσύτων ἐτῶν καλαγελλομένε τῷ ἐκκλησιαςικῷ φρονήμαλ⊙, ἐνδέχελαι τῆς μέχρι βίκλορ⊙ ἕλως ὡς ὗτοι λέγυσι κεκηρύχέναι. πῶς δὲ ἐκ ἀιδῦνλαι ταῦλα βίκλορ⊙· καλαψεύδεσθαι, ἀκριβῶς εἰδότες, ὅτι βίκλωρ τὸν σκιλέα Θεόδολον τὸν ἀρχηγὸν κỳ παλέρα ταύλης τῆς ἀρνησιθέυ ἀποςασίας, ἀπεκύρυξε τῆς κοινωνίας, πρῶτον ἐπινύλα ψιλὸν ἄνθρωπον τὸν Χριςὸν· εἰ γὰρ βίκλωρ καθ' αὐτὰς ἐφρόνει ὡς ἡ τύτων διδάσκει βλασφημία, πῶς ἂν ἀπέβαλλε Θεόδολον τὸν τῆς αἱρέσεως ταύλης εὑρελήν. Euseb. Hist. Eccl. Lib. v. c. xxviii. p. 252.

phemy prefcribed, How then fhould it have happened that he caft out from the Church Arius the inventor, or rather the renovator, of the Herefy ? *

But let Alexander himfelf come forward, and we find, that in a brief recital of the tenets of Arius and his affociates, he informs the Bifhop of Conftantinople, that "they deny the Godhead of our Saviour, and teach that he is only equal with all other men;" "that they refcind fuch paffages of the Scripture as reveal his Godhead and his ineffable glory with the Father from the beginning;" "and with infidelity affert, that there was time when the Son was not; and that not having been from the beginning he was made in time: Nay, that whenfoever the period of his creation might have been, he was made in the nature of every man: For they aver, that God made all things out of nothing, herein comprehending the Son of God himfelf †." The Writer then makes profeffion of his own faith, and affirms, that he had ufed his utmoft endeavours to perfuade Arius to return to the truth, to the eftablifhment of which he had produced many fcriptural proofs; and among others, had, from St. John's Gofpel i. 18, inferred, that the Father and Son were two things infeparable

* Addenda to Remarks on a Scriptural Confutation, p. 21.—Jortin's Remarks on Ecclefiaftical Hiftory, vol. III. p. 181, Octavo, London, Whifton, 1767.

† Τὴν Θεότητα τῦ Σωτῆρ۞ ἡμῶν ἀρνέμενοι κὴ τοῖς πᾶσιν ἴσον ἔιναι κηρύσσοντες.—Τῆς ἀρχῆθεν Θεότητ۞ αὐτῦ κὴ παρὰ τῷ Πατρὶ δόξης ἀλέκτῃ τὰς λόγους ἀποςρεφόμενοι.—Διὰ δὴ κὴ ὑδὲν μελλήσας, ἀγαπητοὶ, δηλῶσαι ὑμῖν τὴν τῶν τοιύτων ἀπιςίαν ἐμαυτὸν διένησα, λεγόντων ὅτι ἦν ποτὲ ὅτε ἐκ ἦν ὁ Ὑιὸς τῦ Θεῦ, κὴ γέγονεν ὕςερον ὁ πρότερον μὴ ὑπάρχων, τοιῦτ۞, ὅτε κὴ ποτὲ γέγονεν, ὅιος κὴ πᾶς ἔιναι πέφυκεν ἀνθρωπ۞, πάντα γὰρ φασὶν, ὁ Θεὸς ἐξ ἐκ ὄντων ἐποίησε, (υναναλαμβάνοντες τῇ τῶν ἀπάντων λογικῶν τε κὴ ἀλόγων κτίσει κὴ τὸν Ὑιὸν τῦ Θεῦ.

separable one from the other." * But that finding his efforts vain, and that Arius, &c. persisted in their heresy, he had at length convened a council at Alexandria, " by whose universal suffrage we have excluded these men from communion with a Church which worships the Godhead of Christ." †

And now was the doctrine of the Alexandrian Church, of the Alexandrian Council, or of Alexander himself, indisputably Unitarian? I ask a question, Does Mr. Lindsey adopt it?

If a similar test be proposed to me, and it be asked, Whether I adopt Alexander's assertion, that the Son is of a middle nature between the unbegotten Father and the things which were created by him out of nothing? ‡ I answer, that the question is unfairly stated; for that Alexander has not any where advanced this assertion, and that the translation, by which it has been attributed to him, is false and defective. But let us for argument's sake, during one moment, admit that the Son is of a middle nature between things created out of nothing and God: Now I desire to know, as this middle nature must be conceded not to have been created out of nothing, out of what self-existing substance it was created? What substance is self-existent, but the substance of God himself? If there subsist no other, that nature which was not created out of nothing was created out of

* In Joan. i. 18. ΆΛΛ'ΗΛΩΝ ΆΧ'ΩΡΙΣΤΑ πράγματα δύο, τὸν Πατέρα κỳ τὸν Ὑιὸν, ὄνα αὐτὸν ἐν τοῖς κολποῖς· τῦ Πατρὸς ἐνόμασεν (Ἰωάννης.)

† Ἡμεῖς μὲν ὖν παμψηφεὶ τῆς προσκυνήσης Χριστῦ τὴν Θεότητα ἐκκλησίας ἐξηλάσαμεν. Alexandri Alexandrini Epist. ad Alexandrum Constantinopolitanum, apud Theodoretum, Hist. Eccl. Lib. i, c. iv.

‡ Addenda to Remarks on Script. Conf. p. 24.

of this self-exiftent fubftance: But is the fubftance of God divifible, that he who is created out of it fhall be another from God? If not, this middle nature is, by confubftantiality, one with that felf-exiftence, is in fhort one with the Father, God.—But does not the word Creation lofe propriety when it is attributed to a Being whofe fubftance is felf-exiftent? If fo, and it cannot be denied, we muft admit that the Son is altogether increate.

But confeffing that the Son, though of one fubftance with the Father, is yet not the Father; we are therefore compelled to fay, that in one Godhead (for fuch is that felf-exiftent fubftance) there are two diftinct *uncreated* perfons. That the Son, however, tho' uncreated, is " of the Father," we acknowledge; for this derivation the Scripture has given us an expreffion which, tho' we cannot comprehend with any precifion, we are under a neceffity of ufing; and therefore we fay, that he is begotten of the Father: But " in the beginning was the Word;" " by him the world was made;" " and without him was not any thing made that was made," John i. We, therefore, profefs, that he was " begotten of the Father before all worlds;" and herein alone we admit, and herein alone Alexander has made ufe of, the terms firft and fecond with relation to the perfons of the Godhead, that *the Father is unbegotten, and that the Son is begotten of the Father:* For in no other refpect can degrees fubfift. From eternity and infinity, whether pofitively afcribed to the Deity, or figuratively combined with the feveral attributes of the Divine Nature, every idea of comparifon is precluded. Herein alone fuperiority and inferiority are terms that can find no place. Notwithftanding which——

——This

—— This middle nature, as it is called, is by the logic of the eighteenth century, placed in a moſt extraordinary relation; for on the one hand, tho' exiſting, he is referred to nothing; and on the other, tho' circumſcribed, he is referred to infinity.

And was this really the doctrine of the primitive ages? No, and when Alexander wrote μακρὸν ἂν ἔιη μἑταξὺ Πατρὸς ἀγεννήτυ κỳ τῶν κτισθέντων ὑπ' αὐτῦ ἐξ ἐκ ὄντων—ἂν μεσιτεύυσα φύσις μονογενής, δἰ ἧς τὰ ὅλα ἐξ ἐκ ὄντων ἐποίησεν ὁ Πατὴρ τῦ Θεῦ λόγη, ἡ ἐξ αὐτῦ τῦ ὄντ۞ Πατρὸς γεγεννηται*, he never meant to be underſtood, that the Son was of a middle nature between nothing and infinity; but, in concurrence with the apoſtolic aſſertion to ſay, that by him God made the worlds, Heb. i. 2. Δἰ ἇ κỳ τὰς αἰώνας ἐποίησεν.

By φύσις, he does not mean *Nature* in ſuch a ſenſe as ſhall diſcriminate between the parental and filial ſubſtance: for he tells us himſelf, that they are of one ſubſtance, but that in perſon they are two, and this, in the very ſame epiſtle, he expreſſes by the very ſame term, ἐδὲ τὰς τῇ ὑποςάσει δύο φύσεις μίαν εἶναι. Alexander is ſurely the beſt commentator on his own language; but were any other requiſite, Photius, in his account of the writings of PIERIUS, catechiſt of Alexandria, in the cloſe of the third century, has aſſured us, that " this writer had entertained juſt and pious ſentiments concerning the Father and the Son, excepting only that he calls them two ſubſtances and two natures (ἐσίας κỳ φύσεις;) but in this, he proceeds, it is evident FROM THE CONTEXT, that he uſes the name of ſubſtance or nature in the ſenſe of *perſon*, and not in that ſenſe in

which

---

* Alexander apud Theodoretum, Hiſt. Eccl. Lib. i. c. iv. p. 17.

which it is accepted by the adherents to Arius:"* And had not the venerable Bifhop himfelf, by the fortunate repetition of the controverted term fully explained the fenfe in which he employed it, this atteftation of Photius, concerning his cotemporary and fellow-citizen, muft have abfolutely afcertained it.

Μονογενης is an epithet which feems to perfonify the term to which it is annexed.

Μεσιτευσα is not an adjective, but an active participle intimating the voluntary agency of the only begotten in the creation of all things out of nothing; or the part of mediator, which this μεσιτης Θεα κ̓ ἀνθρωπων, 1 Tim. ii. 5. may have taken between God and his creature; in this great work (ὧι) the Son ἐμεσιτευσεν, as in Heb. vi. 17. we are told that God ἐμεσιτευσεν ὁρκω· and be it farther remarked, that Alexander has called *the Word* by the exprefs name of *God*.

The whole paffage then requires the following tranflation: " Wide is the diftance between the unbegotten Father and the things which out of nothing were created by him, between which and the Father ftands forth as a mediator (whether in creation or in any other office) the perfon of the only begotten; by which the Father of God the Word made all things, and which was begotten

* Ἀλλὰ περὶ μὲν Πατρὸς κ̓ Υἱοῦ, εὐσεβῶς πρεσβεύει· πλὴν ἀσίας δύο, κ̓ φύσεις δύο λέγει: τῷ τῆς ἀσίας κ̓ φύσεως ὀνόματι ὡς δῆλον ἐκ τε τῶν ἐπομένων κ̓ προτιθεμένων τε χωρίῳ, ἀπὸ τῆς ὑποστάσεως, κ̓ ἐχ ὡς Ἀρειῳ προσανακείμενοι, χρώμενο. Pierius apud Photium, p. 300.

Photius proceeds to fay, that the doctrine of P'erius, with refpect to the Holy Ghoft, was not found for that he has faid the glory of the Holy Ghoft is inferiour to the glory of the Father and of the Son, ὑποτηκέναι αὐτὸ τῆς τῇ Πνεύματο Πατρὸς κ̓ Υἱῷ ἀποφάσκει δόξης. Ibid. The context is loft, and Photius is filent concerning it.

gotten by the felf-exiftent Father himfelf:" And what is there here with which I cannot concur? I anfwer, that I do concur, and fhould have been efteemed orthodox in the diocefe of Alexander: for by the Son I acknowledge, that " all things were created that are in heaven and in earth; that all things were created by him and for him; and that by him all things confift." Colof. i. 16, 17. *

But it has been alledged, that every expreffion in the original language of St. Paul's Epiftle to the Coloffians, chap. i. ver. 16, 17, feems to be decifive of the Son's inferiority, by exhibiting him as the Father's minifter. In maintenance of this pofition the following mutilated fentences are felected from thofe verfes, Ἐν αὐτῷ ἐκτίσθη τὰ πάντα—Τὰ πάντα δι' αὐτοῦ ἔκτισται—Τὰ πάντα ἐν αὐτῷ συνέστηκε; and thefe have been rendered, *by his miniftration all things were created—all things have been created by his miniftration—by him*, that is, *by his miniftration, all things*
confift;

* How unfairly, how rafhly do Unitarians deal! they endeavour to impeach the authority of the Smyrnæan Epiftle (p. 53 above) and the integrity of Dr. Randolph in adducing it, by an affertion, which, by the way, is not true, that it refts only upon the credit of a vifion: yet now having found (but where I neither know, nor care) a legend which they erroneoufly imagine abets their own doctrine, we are gravely referred to it as a teftimony borne by God himfelf to the truth of their tenets. Tho' it evidently appears now that Alexander entertained opinions diametrically oppofite to Unitarianifm, I do not defire to retain, nay, on the contrary, I moft willingly refign the concurrence of a monkifh vifion; the juftice of Alexander's fentiments remains unaffected by the conceffion. I refign the vifionary bafis upon which it is falfely pretended the Smyrnæan Epiftle ftands; the authenticity of the Smyrnæan Epiftle remains unaffected by the conceffion.—Let Pionius and Pachomius go fleep and dream together, we have not the fmalleft occafion for affiftance from either of them.—— Suppofe that I fhould now affume the miraculous recall of Natalis (p. 363) from Unitarianifm to the acknowledgement of our Lord's Divinity, as an argument in behalf of my own caufe, would it be allowed to me? And yet let me fay, that it refts upon no contemptible authority. I, notwithftanding, wave the miracle, and have only related it becaufe the narrative was written within the time inveftigated.

consist; and for this the reason assigned is, that ἐν and διὰ mean, ordinarily at least, the agency of a minister, a person employed under the control of a first mover. *

Now as I have contended for it, that our Saviour was the subject of St. Paul's doctrine at Athens, Unitarians must withdraw their opposition to this tenet, or else maintaining that the Father alone is spoken of, admit that ἘΝ αὐτῷ ζῶμεν, κỳ κινέμεθα, κỳ ἐσμεν, Acts xvii. 28. And I apprehend they will hardly contradict an assertion concerning the Father, Ὅτι ἐξ αὐτȣ, κỳ ΔΙ' αὐτȣ κỳ ἘΙΣ αὐτὸν τὰ πάντα, Rom. xi. 36. or affirm that our Lord ΔΙ' ȣ τὰ πάντα, κỳ ἡμεῖς ΔΙ' αὐτȣ, 1 Cor. viii. 6. is the subject of the Apostle's position, Πιςὸς ὁ Θεὸς ΔΙ' ȣ ἐκλήθητε, &c. 1 Cor. i. 9. Under the control of what first mover now is the Almighty Father employed?

But τὰ πάντα δι αὐτȣ ἐκλίςαι.—I ask the Writer, with whom I contend, is that the whole of the sentence, and whether he did not himself know that the words δι αὐτȣ are immediately followed by κỳ ἘΙΣ αὐτὸν? If he answer that he knew it not, let him find protection behind his ignorance from any heavier charge than that of incompetency; but if he were, on the contrary, aware of the Apostle's whole assertion, he must in that case have known, that some expressions in the original were not decisive of the Son's inferiority: for " the glory of Jesus," says St. Barnabas, " is hereby established, in as much as that all things were created *by* him and *for* him," ἔχεις κỳ ἐν τυλῷ τὴν δόξαν τȣ Ἰησȣ, ὅτι ἘΝ αὐτῷ πάντα, κỳ ἘΙΣ αὐτὸν. Barnabæ Epist. Cathol. †

Mr.

*. Remarks on Scriptural Confutation, p. 96.

† The Antiochene Council, mentioned above, say upon this passage of the Apostle, " Πάντα δι αὐτȣ κỳ εἰς αὐτὸν "—Οὕτω δὲ, ὡς ἀληθῶς ἐν ⊙

Mr. Lindfey's accufation of Unitarianifm againft all chriftian people extending no farther than " till the council of Nice," here alfo my enquiry into the tenets of the primitive Church fhall find a termination. By that famous council, which was convened at Nice, a city of Bythynia, A. D. 325, and which, I truft, I have now redeemed from the infinuated charge of innovation, the opinions of Arius were abfolutely condemned, and the very doctrines, which are at this day received by the Church of England, were ratified and promulged to the chriftian world. How far thofe doctrines which were then promulged, and which are now embraced by the Church of England, accord with the gofpel of Jefus Chrift, and the faith of Ante-Nicene antiquity, it has been my Office to enquire and to communicate; and thus have I made it appear, not by a *fingle* exception only, that Mr. Lindfey's *general* pofition is falfe, but by the teftimony of every Chriftian writer of the firft three centuries, that, without a fingle exception, the contradictory of his pofition is true. I have made it appear beyond a contradiction, that the glorious company of the Apoftles, the goodly fellowfhip of the Prophets, the noble army of Martyrs, and the holy Church throughout all the world, have praifed and acknowledged the Father of an infinite Majefty, his honourable,

υἱὸς καὶ ἐνεργῶν, ὡς Λόγε ἅμα καὶ Θεῦ, δι' ὃ ὁ Πατὴρ πάντα πεποίηκεν, ἐχ' ὡς ὀργάνε, ἐδ' ὡς δι' ἐπιςήμης ἀνυποςάτυ.— Labb. vol. i. p. 841.

And Eufebius obferves, that " all things owe their exiftence and their perfections to THE WORD, and TO THE HOLY SPIRIT; that THE WORD called the Angels into being; and that THE HOLY GHOST at the fame time illuminated and fanctified them." Ἀγγέλων γῦν τὴν μὲν εἰς τὸ εἶναι πάροδον ὁ δημιεργὸς Λόγος ὁ ποιητὴς τῶν ὅλων παρεῖχετο· τὸν ἁγιασμὸν δὲ αὐτοῖς τὸ Πνεῦμα ἅγιον ζυνεισέφερεν. Comment. in Pfalm. p. 125.—See Jortin's Remarks on Ecclefiaftical Hiftory, vol. II. p. 258.

nourable, true, and only Son, also the Holy Ghost the Comforter. But to all these quotations, by which Antiquity has made profession of its own faith in the divinity of the three persons in the unity of the godhead, there is one ready answer which I expect to receive. It is, that in the very same writings whence I have made these extracts, there may occur many passages in which the authors have not professed so much. But suppose that I should even grant this true, to what does it amount? To no more than that, the entire faith of a Christian being compounded of many articles, the separate profession of each article is not the aggregate profession of the whole. But is a partial acknowledgement a total abjuration? nay, does absolute silence on a subject constitute a denial of its truth? With its parts the whole can never be inconsistent; and yet a declaration, that any one of these parts is the whole, is absolutely void of truth; for such a position denies the existence of the remaining parts; and this denial is false. Thus the divinity of Christ is by no means inconsistent with his manhood, his priesthood, his appointed jurisdiction, or any other character in which he is held forth to us; whereas a declaration, that any one or more of these inferiour characters constitute the whole of Christ's nature, is a denial of his divinity. No single instance of such an exclusive declaration occurs in the scriptures, nor the writings of the early fathers, to contradict the frequent assurances they afford us of his godhead. The limitation, therefore, contended for by the Unitarian must be pronounced of a more modern date: And if Christ be truly God, it amounts to a denial of Christ; a denial, against which the full severity of almighty justice is proclaimed.

But the conduct of Mr. Lindsey himself precludes the possibility of a concession, that such passages as do

not

not speak the whole afford the smallest argument against the force of such as do. He has relinquished our church because she has spoken the whole, which he could not have done if partial assertions afforded a total repeal; for a repeal of this nature he must have found in our obnoxious liturgy, and might thence have argued, that the church of England is a Unitarian church. The general confession is addressed only to the Father; the remission which follows it is addressed to the Father only, through Jesus Christ our Lord; the prayer for the clergy and people acknowledges his inferiority, and denominates this Son of Man our Mediator and Advocate.—I need not here state the frequent acknowledgements of the one identical godhead of Father, Son, and Holy Ghost, which appear throughout our liturgy. Mr. Lindsey's apostacy has sufficiently testified that they remain in ample force and vigour, notwithstanding those partial assertions in which the doctrine is not thus fully declared.

But, a marked inconsistency subsisting between the passages here drawn from the primitive writers, and the dogmas of this gentleman, he has not, therefore, written any thing in the least degree bearing a resemblance to these passages; whereas, no such inconsistency subsisting between these extracts, and the remaining works of the early fathers, men as well informed in the doctrines of Christianity, and equally capable of discerning the agreement or disagreement of two propositions, have not scrupled to insert these passages in the body of their several writings. But let me close with Mr. Lindsey himself on this ground.——Of you therefore, Sir, I now enquire whether *you* accede to the positions stated above from the fathers; whether, consistently with your own tenets, *you* think that you could have written them yourself; or whether you abide by that

desperate

desperate assertion which in effect subscribes to whatever doctrines may have flowed from their pens? If not, it pains me to hurt you with an assurance that, you are not a Christian such as the fathers were; that the fathers were not Unitarians, such as you are; and consequently, that your position concerning them, whether you be erroneously or intentionally guilty, is, at the very best, a gross misrepresentation. You have conferred upon the fathers of the church a degree of importance beyond their pretensions, and even proclaimed it ABSOLUTELY NECESSARY that the less learned should be told they were Unitarians. The consequence you look for, therefore, is certainly their acquiescence in those tenets which, they are *thus* instructed by you, were held by the primitive Christians. But, upon this assertion, *the less learned* were your intended proselytes. You call upon the blind to follow the step that misleads them: The blind alone cannot detect you. They alone who are precluded by ignorance from enquiry, are assured that, *upon enquiry,* they will find your allegation to be *undeniably true.*— I have now proceeded to make that enquiry, and, instead of demanding the assent of any man, even the most ignorant, to a general assertion concerning what I have read, or saying that your testimony concerning the fathers is *undeniably false*, I have called upon those fathers to answer for themselves; and, without the intentional exception of a single writer, whose works are received as genuine, and who has delivered his sentiments on this subject, have produced each individual to be the professour of his own faith,*—By translations which I conceive

---

* I know of no other writers, or fragments of writers, than those I have already stated to the reader, and shall be obliged by any information. That MALCHION, and some others, wrote against Artemon, Theodotus, and Paul of Samosata, is some proof that they opposed Unitarianism; but of their writings nothing remains to put this out of doubt.——

conceive to be strictly literal, or paraphrases which I conceive to be strictly just to the sense of the author, I have rendered them intelligible to the less learned; and for the more easy correction of any errors into which I may unconsciously have fallen, have annexed the original language, or if this has perished, the antient version of the several writers.—I do not desire the one Godhead of the Father, the Son, and of the Holy Ghost to be inferred from the assertions of the fathers; for, though I esteem their verdict a proof of the sense in which they accepted the evidence of the gospel, and therefore

It had been superfluous to have adduced evidence that ATHANASIUS abets a cause, which Unitarians have from his name denominated *Athanasian*.—I do not pretend that this Bishop of Alexandria was the composer of the creed, which is usually ascribed to him; but thus much I can from my own knowledge aver, that every article of that creed is repeatedly to be found in his writings. I have myself extracted them,—this I mention, in order to protect his name from the treatment bestowed upon that of his immediate predecessour Alexander; for as Alexander's vehement opposition to Arius could not prevent the charge of adherence to Arius, I could not tell but the council of Nice, and that principal member of this great convocation, Athanasius, who condemned Arius, might be charged with an entire concurrence in sentiment with the object of their condemnation; and that we should next be modestly assured ' the Nicene Fathers themselves were Unitarians." Addend. to Rem. p. 22.—Could a Papist derive strength to his cause from the temporary concurrence of Chillingworth? If not, I refuse to allow it to the Arian. In what did Chillingworth settle in the end?

The authority of Apollo, though probably of the same stamp with that of the Sybil, (p. 357) is, however, valuable, as it has given occasion to Lactantius to make a verbal criticism, which is applicable to Rom. ix. 5, and which therefore refer to p. 26, 169, above.

The words of the oracle are $\Theta\nu\eta\tau\grave{o}\varsigma\;\ddot{\eta}\nu\;\kappa\alpha\tau\grave{\alpha}\;\sigma\acute{\alpha}\rho\kappa\alpha$, on which the Father observes, that when it is said *he is mortal as concerning the flesh*, which we also affirm, it follows, and this too we profess, that he was God as concerning the Spirit; why else should it be said " as concerning the flesh," " when that he is mortal" would have been sufficient? Cum fatetur secundum carnem fuisse mortalem, quod etiam nos prædicamus, consequens est ut secundum Spiritum Deus fuerit, quod nos affirmamus. Quid enim fuerit necesse carnis facere mentionem cum satis esset dicere fuisse mortalem. Lactant: Lib. iv. c. 14. De âvera sapientia.

therefore unqueftionably of much confequence, all I require is, that men fhall, firft, not think it *abfolutely neceffary* to know what tenets they held, as the very fame evidence remains open to their own enquiry; and fecondly, that, if any man be fo weak as to think their tenets an *infallible* rule for his, he may learn that there did not, among the fathers of the firft three centuries, fubfift a fingle Unitarian: and this, not from my unfupported affertion, but from the copious and conclufive profeffions of the Ante-Nicene fathers themfelves.

C c c   CHAP.

CHAP. IV.

Collateral Evidence of the Sentiments of the Chriſtians of the firſt three Centuries.

FROM the reproaches or deriſion of the Jew, the Heretick, and the Gentile, it is eaſy to aſcertain the common point which has proved to the one a ſtumbling block, and to the other fooliſhneſs.——In the fields of controverſy, it is lawful to array againſt an adverſary the arguments which he has himſelf involuntarily contributed, or the conceſſions which preclude his reply: I ſhall therefore now proceed to turn upon the enemies of truth, the arms which have been ſupplied to us by their antient allies; and accordingly, without farther preface, ſhall lay before my reader the teſtimony which has been contributed to the antiquity of our faith by the few early writers, &c. who, without embracing, have in any concluſive manner adverted to the religion of the goſpel. " Et firmum eſt genus probationis," ſays Tertullian, " quod etiam ab adverſariis ſumitur, etiam ut veritas ab ipſis inimicis veritatis probetur."

The relation made to Tiberius by PONTIUS PILATE, as recorded by Euſebius, concludes with an aſſurance that " Chriſt was already believed by many to be God." *

Euſebius

---

* Ἤδη Θεὸς εἶναι παρὰ τοῖς πολλοῖς ἐπεπιςεύετο. Euſeb. Hiſt. Eccl. lib. i. cap. ii. p. 47.

Eusebius has called upon Tertullian to vouch the narrative whence I have extracted this passage; to Tertullian alone I shall therefore confine myself in the following considerations: for, upon the state of facts presented to us by that Father, and which I set before my reader in the note*, Le Fevre has most conclusively said *Hem!* and Mr. Gibbon has been pleased to favour us with a copious paraphrase of the significant interjection.

"We

---

* Ut de origine aliquid retractamus ejusmodi legum. Vetus erat decretum ne qui Deus ab Imperatore consecraretur, nisi a senatu probaretur: Ut. M. Æmilius de Deo suo Alburno. Facit & hoc ad causam nostram, quòd apud vos de humano arbitratu divinitas pensitatur. Nisi homini Deus placuerit, Deus non erit. Homo jam Deo propitius esse debebit. Tiberius ergo, cujus tempore nomen Christianum in seculum introivit, annuntiatum sibi ex Syria-Palæstina quæ illic veritatem ipsius divinitatis revelaverat, detulit ad senatum cum prærogativa suffragii sui. Senatus, quia non ipse probaverat, resuit. Cæsar in sententia mansit, comminatus periculum accusatoribus Christianorum.—CONSULITE COMMENTARIOS VESTROS, illic reperietis primum Neronem in hanc sectam, tum maxime Romæ orientem, Cæsariano Gladio ferocuisse, &c. &c. Tertull. Apologet. cap. v.

Ad doctrinam vero ejus quia revincebantur magistri, primoresque Judæorum, ita exasperabantur, maxime quòd ad eum ingens multitudo deflecteret, ut postremo oblatum Pontio Pilato Syriam tunc ex parte Romana procuranti, violentia suffragiorum in crucem Jesum dedi sibi extorserint. Prædixerat & ipse ita facturos. Parum hoc, si non et Prophetæ retro etiam.

Tamen suffixus multa mortis illius propria ostendit insignia, nam spiritum cum verbo sponte dimisit, prævento carnificis officio. Eodem momento diei, medium orbem signante sole, subducta est. Deliquium utique putaverunt qui id quoque super Christo prædicatum non scierunt: et tamen eum mundi casum relatum in ARCHIVIS VESTRIS HABETIS. Tunc Judæi retractum & sepulchro conditum magna etiam militari manu custodiæ diligentia circumsederunt, ne, quia prædixerat tertio die resurrecturum, sua morte, discipuli furto amoliti cadaver jactarent suspectis. Sed ecce die tertia, concussa repente terra, & mole evoluta quæ obstruxerat sepulchrum, & custodia pavore disjecta, nullis apparentibus discipulis, nihil in sepulchro repertum est, præterquam exuviæ sepulti. Nihilominus tamen primores, quorum intererat & scelus divulgare, & populi vectigalem & famularem ad fidem vocare, surreptum a discipulis jactitaverunt. Nam nec ille se in vulgus eduxit ne impii errore liberarentur, ut et fides non

mediocri

"We are required by Tertullian," says this Gentleman, "to believe,

I. That Pontius Pilate informed the Emperor of the unjuſt ſentence of death which he had pronounced againſt an innocent, and, as it appeared, a divine perſon, and that, without acquiring the merit, he expoſed himſelf to the danger of martyrdom;

II. That

mediocri Præmio deſtinata difficultate conſtaret. Cum diſcipulis autem quibuſdam apud Galilæam Judææ regionem ad quadraginta dies egit, docens eos quæ docerent. Dehinc, ordinatis eis ad officium prædicandi per orbem, circumfusâ nube in cœlum eſt receptus, multo verius quam apud vos aſſeverare de Romulo Proculi ſolent.

Ea omnia ſuper Chriſto Pilatus, & ipſe pro ſua conſcientia Chriſtianus, Cæſari tunc Tiberio nuntiavit, ſed et Cæſares credidiſſent ſuper Chriſto ſi aut Cæſares non eſſent ſeculo neceſſarii, aut ſi et Chriſtiani potuiſſent eſſe Cæſares. Tertull, Apologet. cap. xxi.

In ENGLISH thus:

That we may treat ſomewhat of the original of ſuch laws. There was an antient decree that no god ſhould be conſecrated by an Emperor, unleſs he were approved of by the ſenate; as in the caſe of M. Æmilius concerning his god Alburnus. And it makes for our cauſe, that among you Godhead is diſpenſed according to human arbitrement. Unleſs God pleaſe man, he ſhall not be God. It is Man then that ſhould be propitious to God. Tiberius, therefore, in whoſe time the name of Chriſt entered into the world, together with the prerogative of his own vote, referred to the ſenate the account that was given to him from Paleſtine in Syria, which therein revealed the truth of his Divinity The ſenate, becauſe the ſenate diſapproved, rejected (Chriſt.) Cæſar continued in the ſame ſentiment, threatening danger to the accuſers of the Chriſtians — Conſult your *commentaries*, you will *therein* find that Nero was the firſt ferociouſly to wield the Cæſarian ſword againſt this ſect, &c. &c. &c.

The rulers and elders of the Jews were ſo highly exaſperated becauſe of the multitude which inclined to him, that in the end, with tumultuous voices, they extorted from Pontius Pilate, the Roman Deputy of Syria, his conſent that Jeſus, who ſtood arraigned before him, ſhould be delivered up to them for crucifixion: Theſe things he predicted himſelf; yet that were but of ſmall account, if the Prophets, who had preceded his coming, had not foretold them alſo. But even when he was nailed to the croſs, he ſhewed many ſigns peculiar to his death: for, anticipating the

executioner,

II. That Tiberius, who avowed his contempt for all religion, immediately conceived the design of placing the Jewish Messiah among the Gods of Rome;

III. That his servile senate ventured to disobey the commands of their master;

IV. That Tiberius, instead of resenting their refusal, contented himself with protecting the Christians from the severity of the laws many years, before such laws were enacted, or before the Church had assumed any distinct name or existence;

V. And

executioner, he, with the Word, spontaneously gave up the ghost. In the same moment, even when the sun occupied his noon-tide station, the day was withdrawn; they who were ignorant of the Prophecies which referred this darkness also to Christ, conceived it an eclipse; and yet, in your own ARCHIVES, you possess a relation of this defection of nature. The Jews then surrounded his body, when taken down and laid in the sepulchre, with a military guard, lest, because he had foretold his resurrection on the third day after his death, his disciples might steal him away, and deceive the people. But, behold! on the third day the earth being suddenly shaken, the stone rolled away from the mouth of the sepulchre, the guard appalled with terrour, and no disciple at hand, nothing was found in the tomb except the appurtenances of an interred body: Nevertheless the elders, who were interested to publish a falsehood, and to recall the people to their allegiance, gave out that he was stolen away by his disciples: For he did not exhibit himself in public, left the impious should be delivered from their errour; and also that Faith, by having a difficulty to surmount, might become proportioned to no mean reward. With some disciples, however, he passed forty days at Galilee, a region of Judea, teaching them the things which they should teach; and thence, when they were ordained to the office of preaching through the world, he was taken up in a cloud to heaven : Much more truly than your Proculuses are used to assert concerning Romulus. All things concerning Christ did Pilate, who was himself in conscience convinced of Christianity, relate to Tiberius, who was at that time Emperor; and the Cæsars would have believed on Christ, either if Cæsars were not necessary to the Age; or if Cæsars could have been Christians; (or perhaps this last sentence should be translated, "if Christians could have been Cæsars;" the impossibility of which might have been the sentiment of the rigid Tertullian, who lived long before Christianity comprehended the imperial purple.)

V. And laftly, That the memory of this extraordinary tranfaction was preferved in the moft publick and authentick records, which efcaped the knowledge of the Hiftorians of Greece and Rome, and were only vifible to the eyes of an African Chriftian, who compofed his Apology one hundred and fixty years after the death of Tiberius." See Mr. Gibbon's Hiftory of the Decline and Fall of the Roman Empire, vol. I. p. 556.

I. In anfwer to the firft of thefe objections, thus formidably arrayed againft the veracity of Tertullian, let it be remembered that Pontius Pilate, when he permitted the fentence of crucifixion, pronounced, not by himfelf but by the Jews, to be carried into execution againft our Saviour, wafhed his own hands of the blood of that juft Perfon, and appealed to the multitude to teftify his innocence. When thus defirous of extenuating the crime of an enforced acquiefcence, and of ftanding juftified before thofe who were fubject to his authority, why are we, in contradiction to every fpecies of probability, to fuppofe that he brought an overcharged accufation againft himfelf, and exaggerated his guilt before one whofe authority was paramount to his own ? That, having fuffered the Jews to take upon themfelves and their children the blood of our Saviour; and in the inftant providently laid the foundation of his defence againft a time when the extraordinary events then tranfacted fhould come under the imperial cognizance, he now in the day of danger waived the advantage of a nation's teftimony to his reluctant concurrence, and loading his narrative with opprobrious epithets, fubftituted himfelf as the fingle criminal, refumed the guilt from thofe who had even folicited the exclufive imputation, and felected the Emperor Tiberius as the perfon with whom to depofit the act of refumption ? — The fuppofition I readily grant is an abfurdity, but it is

not

not Tertullian's. And from the emphatical language in which that Father reprefents the neceffity under which the governour of Paleftine lay to deliver up our Lord to the clamour of the Jewifh Elders, although he has not fpecified a fingle fyllable of Pilate's Epiftle to the Emperor, it may be more reafonably collected, that (if any thing) we are required to believe that Pilate informed the Emperor of the irrefiftible importunity of the Jewifh Elders, and that, by inhancing the merit of his own reluctance, he took effectual care to fecure himfelf from the danger of imperial refentment.

II. With refpect to the fecond objection brought by our Hiftorian, I will admit the Emperor's avowed contempt for religion, that the Jewifh nation was under the heavy difpleafure of Tiberius, and that Jefus Chrift was the Meffiah of this obnoxious nation: But is there no deference due to the teftimony of an antient and uncontradicted tranfmifs; fhall an hypothetic inference from a general character ftand and obtain credit in oppofition to direct, particular, and unimpeached evidence; and did the impiety of Tiberius admit of no interruption? Two inftances are furely recorded in which he appears to have been influenced by a tranfient veneration for the Gods of his country; for Suetonius affirms that he dedicated a Temple to Concord, and another to Caftor and Pollux. *

But

* Sueton. Tiber. cap. xx.—Let us fay that the whole ftory of a voice calling upon Thamnus, the commander of a Roman veffel, and giving him commiffion to proclaim the death of Pan, when he fhould reach Palodes, is a fiction of Æmilianus, who related it as a fact, to which he had been himfelf a witnefs; we have yet the authority of Plutarch for a narrative within the ordinary limits of nature, which is, that on the affair becoming a general topic at Rome, Tiberius called Thamnus before him, examined into the matter, and believed the mariner's teftimony, infomuch as afterwards to become exceedingly inquifitive into the hiftory and genealogy of Pan.

But did Pontius Pilate denominate our Lord, *the Jewish Messiah*, that Tiberius, who hated the Jews, might have a still farther objection to surmount? Tho' I give no credit to the Epistle which has been by later writers ascribed to Pontius Pilate, I must yet conclude, that when that Governor transmitted an account of our Saviour's resurrection to Rome, he accompanied it with a recital of the circumstances of his crucifixion; and therefore that the Emperor's aversion to the Jews could have had no operation against the apotheosis of a person rejected by that people, against whom they had actually proceeded to extremities, and of whom it is highly improbable he had ever heard under the title of *their Messiah*; a title which to him, without a comment, must have been absolutely unintelligible; and I am not aware that any commentary on the Law and the Prophets has ever been ascribed to Pontius Pilate.

III. That the senate of Rome has exhibited a terrible example how easily a lapse may be made from a state of consummate freedom to a state of the most abject servility, and that Tiberius had become the absolute master of this degenerate legislature, are points that must be conceded. It is, notwithstanding, true that at a period when this tyrant had, by his astonishing ferocity, rendered himself even the most formidable, the senate, in a particular instance, refused to comply with his desire: He therefore pronounced himself contemned, and even sought refuge from their imaginary indignation, by a precipitate flight to his natural fortress at Caprea. *

IV. But

* Sueton. Tiber. cap. lxxiii. Dio Cassius has also related a circumstance somewhat similar. When the Emperor had forbid any kind of respect to be paid to the memory of Livia, the senate, notwithstanding, voted to have an arch erected to her honour: That he stopped the execution of this structure is true, but it was under false pretences of œconomy; for he did not dare to infringe the decree openly—but the whole of his conduct, on the present occasion, might, perhaps, be accounted for by the caprice of the man.

IV. But the Emperor did not always thus resent their disobedience to his commands; for on the contrary, which may apply to the fourth objection, " He did not so much as utter a complaint at some decrees which were passed in opposition to his will." He acquiesced when, on a division in the senate-house, the majority stood against him, when even his own presence and conspicuous vote were unable to procure the concurrence of a single senator. * Why then should he not now have acquiesced in their refusal to place *the Jewish Messiah* among the Gods of Rome? Was an avowed *zeal* for religion too among the qualifications of Tiberius, that his indignation must have been particularly excited here?—It was the uninterrupted practice of this Emperor to lay all matters, however great or unimportant, before the senate †; and in the senate alone, by an antient law alluded to here by Tertullian ‡, the power of enrolling Gods was vested; Tiberius being therefore now apprized of the extraordinary event which had just taken place in Syria, it was but consonant with his usual custom that he should refer the account at large to the senate; and, though perfectly indifferent with regard to the event, submit it to the decision of their peculiar authority, whether the person whom it concerned should be placed among the Gods of Rome. To his having forwarded the proposal with his own vote, and then acquiesced in the opposition of the senate, the case which I have already stated from Suetonius is exactly in point. But does Tertullian affirm that the Emperor had *commanded* the Deification of Jesus Christ? No,

D d d not

* Sueton. Tib. cap. xxxi.

† Ejusd. lib. cap. xxx. Dio Cass. LVII. p. 606,

‡ One of the laws of the Twelve Tables runs thus: " Separatim nemo habessit Deos, ueve nuvos, sed ne adveaas, nisi publicè ascitos privatim coluato."

not once; but it was neceſſary to exaggerate his atteſtation, that the prodigy of ſenatorial diſobedience might obſtruct our faith in what this miſrepreſented Father has in reality atteſted.

The remainder of this objection is founded on a farther fiction of the Hiſtorian's own; for Tertullian has neither named *a law enacted againſt the Chriſtians*, nor has he called the primitive Diſciples of Jeſus Chriſt by the appellation of *a Church*. That " Tiberius threatened danger to the accuſers of the Chriſtians", is the whole of that writer's aſſertion, and the intention of this widely paraphraſed poſition appears ſufficiently obvious: That the immediate hearers of our Lord, whom he ſent out to diſſeminate the Goſpel, were *Chriſtians*, whether as yet ſo denominated or not, is a fact, the denial of which can only amount to a diſingenuous cavil; that the firſt Chriſtians were accuſed of blaſphemy againſt the law, and therefore were perſecuted by the Jews, who had crucified their Maſter himſelf, is a point alſo indiſputable; and we have the beſt hiſtorick authority to believe that Tiberius, towards the cloſe of his reign, treated the Jews with the utmoſt rigour. This oppreſſive conduct of the Emperor towards the accuſers of the Chriſtians has been variouſly accounted for, according to the reſpective perſuaſions of the various authors who have recorded it; that their ſuperſtitious adherence to their own ritual had excited his indignation, is the reaſon aſſigned for it by the Heathen Suetonius [*]. Joſephus, who was himſelf a Jew, attributes it to a breach of truſt perpetrated by a few individuals of his own nation [†]: And why may not the Chriſtian Tertullian aſcribe it to a deſire of protecting a ſpecified ſociety, whoſe only crime was ſtated to have been a blaſphemy againſt that very law which is, on all hands, agreed to have been

obnoxious

[*] Suet. Tib. cap. xxxvi.   [†] Joſephi Antiquit. Jud. 18—5.

obnoxious to Tiberius? From the language of this Father, it is an inference far more reasonable than many drawn by our Historian, and yet an inference on which I by no means rely, that a rescript, denouncing vengeance against the murderers of Jesus Christ, unless they desisted from the persecution of his followers, was returned by Tiberius in consequence of the information which he had received from Pontius Pilate. The Jewish persecution alone was under the consideration of Tertullian; for he tells us himself, that "Nero was the first to wield the *Cæsarian* sword against the Christians." All consideration of Roman laws enacted against the *Church*, is consequently foreign to the subject before us, and, I should conclude, had been originally introduced only to incumber our faith with articles not proposed by antiquity: Let it therefore be remembered, that the obstacle is created by the Historian himself; and if the reader find it still to impede his progress, let him learn, that though no law of the empire had, in this early period, specified the Christian by name, there yet subsisted, from antient times, a voluminous code of statutes, under any one of which, as coming within the description, Christianity must have been adjudged an offence, the professors of Christianity must have been convicted and treated as criminals. In religion novelty alone incurred the censure of the Roman law, and novelty is an offence of a nature not usually created, and the heinousness of which is not for the most part highly aggravated by the progress of time.

V. As the passage from Tertullian is before my reader, it is obvious that the Historian's final objection is also levelled against a misrepresentation of his own; for, if any credit be due to the authority of Mr. Gibbon himself, the Writer, over whom he brandishes his indignant pen, has NOT affirmed, "that the memory of this extraordinary tranfaction was preferved in the moft public and authentic records;" nor does he arrogate to himfelf any exclufive knowledge of the contents of the imperial archives.

If, however, the words *confulite commentarios veſtros*, which are incontrovertibly appropriated by the adverb *illic* to the fubfequent narrative, muft yet be torn away from their proper context, referred to the paffage under confideration, and then tranflated *confult your moſt public and authentic records*; even fo there appears no violent tranfgreffion of the limits of probability. Within a Roman province, configned to the government of Pontius Pilate, an affair of unqueftionably fome importance, calling it no more than a tumultuary execution, had taken place; to tranfmit an account of this to Rome, appears, therefore, no more than a duty of office, and the official inftrument in which it was communicated, we may reafonably conclude to have been of a nature fit to be depofited and preferved among the records of the empire. That thefe were only vifible to the eyes of an African Chriftian, is an inference, I fuppofe, from the filence of other writers; but does it follow, or do we look for the teftimonies of Jefus Chrift among the infidel hiftorians of Greece and Rome? Nay! is Mr. Gibbon himfelf the man to drag them from their concealment? The credulity of fcepticifm is furely fatisfied with premifes on which faith, the perpetual object of our author's hiftoric irony, would find and acknowledge herfelf unable to found any conclufion. That Tacitus, however, who wrote for the inftruction of the Gentile reader, has dated the period of our Saviour's crucifixion by the government of Pontius Pilate, affords fome ground for a prefumption that this great Hiftorian had accefs to, and obtained the information he has imparted, among the archives of the empire.

empire. But Suetonius has more directly affirmed that the individual Emperor, whose conduct is now controverted, recorded every event of his life; he has even assured us that his *Commentarii* were extant for some length of time after his death; for "these, he says, and these alone, constituted the study of Domitian,"* who set the conduct of Tiberius before his eyes as a rule for his own government, and would, perhaps, have followed him even in this solitary act of mercy, had not the reign of Nero intervened, which furnishing a precedent for the destruction of the Christians also, excited a still higher spirit of emulation, and taught him to obliterate the single page in which the example of Tiberius had pointed out an object of forbearance. It is, therefore, evident that the *Commentarii* of that Emperor had NOT escaped the knowledge of the Historians of Rome, and that they were not visible ONLY to the eyes of an African Christian, who composed his Apology one hundred and sixty years after the death of Tiberius.

But this, I may be told, is only combating an interpretation of my own; for it is not among these *Commentarii* that Mr. Gibbon charges Tertullian with having affirmed "that the memory of this extraordinary transaction was preserved." *Relatum in ARCHIVIS vestris habetis* is certainly the assertion against which the Historian has taken exception, and against which the force of his final objection is directly levelled; for nothing can be more withdrawn from controversy, than that this passage has in clear and explicit terms referred the Gentiles to their " most public and authentic records."—And is the meaning of this passage really thus determined, and does Mr. Gibbon himself thus acknowledge its clear exemption from every species of ambiguity?

* Sueton. cap. xx.

guity? This is indeed my own opinion, and therefore I readily accept of the conceffion. But let us hear the Hiftorian himfelf: " When Tertullian affures the Pagans that the mention of this prodigy (the darknefs which accompanied our Saviour's paffion) is found in ARCANIS (not ARCHIVIS) *veftris*, he probably appeals to the Sibylline verfes, which relate it exactly in the words of the Gofpel." *Note* 194 *on chap.* xv. *of Mr. Gibbon's Hiftory of the Decline and Fall of the Roman Empire.*

The candid critic, where various readings equally authorized are offered to his choice, will felect and uniformly abide by that which appears the beft adapted to the general fenfe of the writer under his confideration. To Mr. Gibbon alone it belongs, without decifion, to retain every variety, and, viewing the paffage in its feveral diftinct relations, occafionally to receive into the text that reading which he efteems the leaft correfpondent with the purpofe, or the moft likely to fubvert the reputation of an antient author, with whofe credit or confiftency he perceives the eftablifhment of his own novel hypothefis to be altogether incompatible. That the imperial archives fhould contain a record of an extraordinary tranfaction in a province of the empire, does not appear to me in the leaft degree an improbability: to Mr. Gibbon, however, it feems " a difficulty fufficient to perplex the fceptical mind." For this reafon, therefore, though on another occafion, where he deemed another reading more contributary to his argument, he has fubftituted *arcanis*, and annexed a far fetched interpretation, in the prefent inftance he adopts into the text that reading which, in his opinion, imputes a falfehood to Tertullian, and not only acquiefces in the term ufually accepted, but contends for it, that the genuine language of the Father is ARCHIVIS.

That

That one or the other of thefe two paffages is the ground-work of Mr. Gibbon's objection, I do not entertain a fingle doubt, becaufe, that in the compafs of Tertullian's writings, I cannot find another that in any refpect whatfoever relates to the information given by Pilate to the Emperor. If, however, I be in an errour, it is the Hiftorian himfelf who is to blame for having reprehenfibly omitted fuch a reference to his authority as might ferve to facilitate enquiry, and affift in the removal of fuch perplexities as may involve the fceptical mind with regard to reprefentations that reft only upon the veracity of our author himfelf: with him, therefore, in that cafe it remains to fhew that he is not guilty of an abfolute fiction; whereas, if our enquiry muft, as I apprehend, terminate here, the reader is now competent to form a judgement between the integrity of Tertullian and that of a writer, who has defcended to the little artifices already ftated for the purpofe of defeating the evidence of antiquity, and building his Pagan hypothefis upon the fubftituted foundations of his own conjecture.

However ferviceable the purfuit might prove, it is not my bufinefs to follow Mr. Gibbon any farther. To the eftablifhment of a paffage quoted above from Eufebius, I have thought it neceffary to vindicate the authority of Tertullian, becaufe to this Eufebius has, in fome meafure, appealed for the truth of his own narrative. Mr. Gibbon had endeavoured to encumber the fimple tale with a thoufand circumftances that did not belong to it, and, by inferences which did not follow, to perfuade his reader that the antient Father had ftated facts, refutable by their leading directly to abfurdity. The confideration of thefe I efteemed to be within my province; and now truft I have made it clear, that the additional circumftances are a fiction, and the inconfequent inferences abfurdities no longer

to

to be imputed to Tertullian, but which may very well serve to inftruct the reader what degree of confidence he may venture to repofe upon the teftimony of the Hiftorian himfelf.

"SEVERUS ALEXANDER defigned to build a temple to Chrift, and to receive him among the Gods: which is reported alfo to have been the intention of HADRIAN, who commanded temples without idols to be erected in every city: But *he* * was reftrained from his purpofe by thofe who, on confulting the Gods, reported that, if he proceeded, all men would become Chriftians, and that every other temple would be deferted." † Such is the narrative of ÆLIUS LAMPRIDIUS, who was himfelf a Pagan; and hence refults an Heathen teftimony, that the Chriftian Churches were edifices raifed for the worfhip of Chrift. Could the Arufpices elfe have concluded, that all Chriftians would refort to a temple in which Chrift was received as a God; or could Hadrian have

* I think, with Dr. Jortin, that Alexander is the name referred to here.

† Chrifto templum facere voluit, (Severus Alexander) eumque inter Deos recipere. Quod et Hadrianus cogitaffe fertur, qui templa in omnibus civitatibus fine fimulachris jufferat fieri : (quæ hodie idcirco quia non habent numina, dicuntur Hadriani, quæ ille ad hoc paraffe dicebatur:) fed prohibitus eft ab his, qui confulentes facra, repererant omnes Chriftianos futuros, fi id optato eveniffet, & templa reliqua deferenda. Ælii Lampridii Alexander Severus, p. 272. Edit. Paris. Roberti Steph. 1544, 8vo.

Of thefe two facts the firft is pofitively afferted, and muft ftand upon the authority of the Hiftorian : the fecond is only faid to have been an inference from circumftances that are ftated, and therefore may admit of doubt. There is nothing in the character of either Alexander or Hadrian to contradict or even to render the narrative improbable. The *Syrian* Alexander was an object of contempt to Julian, who always depreciated the friends of Chriftianity; and the fpeculative Hadrian had, on the utter fubverfion of the Jews, yet reftored the Chriftians of Jerufalem from a tedious exile which they had fuftained at Pella.—But let me not anticipate the Sceptic.

have so greatly mistaken the unsculptured object of the Christian's adoration?

Certain as our Saviour's exclusion from exclusive Godhead must always have been, when brought before the jurisdiction of a Pagan Pontiff, yet we may see that his character was a subject more than once referred to the discussion of the deities of the empire: for, upon the answer returned to some persons who had consulted an oracle concerning the nature of our Lord, PORPHYRY, a very eminent Platonic Philosopher of the third century, has put the following interpretation: " The oracle," says he, " has pronounced him (a Man) of consummate piety, and declared that his soul, which the Christians weakly worship, has passed through death to immortality." *

And a very prudent and well-weighed piece of celestial management we must allow this answer to have been, when we consider that the Gods had nothing less than their own dignity at stake, with which, by the assistance of a few philosophic eyes, they plainly saw that the admission of our Saviour into Heaven was altogether incompatible; indeed, according to Porphyry, they

* Ἐυσεβέστατον ἄρα ἔφη αὐτὸν· κ͂ τὴν Ψυχὴν αὐτε, καθάπερ κ͂ τῶν ἄλλων, μέλα θάνατον ἀπαθαναλισθῆναι, ἣν ΣΕΒΕΙΝ ἀνοήλως τὰς Χρισιανὰς. Porphyrii apud Euseb. Demonstrat. Evangelic. lib. iii. cap. vi. p. 134. Edit. Paris. apud Sonnium, 1628, fo io.

Though a negative, to the divinity of our Saviour was the natural answer for an oracle to give, it was not probably the answer always expected by those who went to enquire. " Their strict and decent adherence to the religion by law established, gave to Dionysius of Halicarnassius, the highest opinion of the Roman people; but nothing more excited his wonder than the cautious attention with which they received any proposal of change or innovation; for here the measure was referred to the Gods whom they had heretofore acknowledged, and ratified only upon the divine approbation."

they might have acquired this wifdom by their earthly experience: "For is it now a wonder," exclaims the Sage, " that difeafe has fo many years poffeffed a city which is no longer the refidence of Æfculapius and the other deities? For, fince Jefus began to be honoured, no man has been fenfible of the general and beneficial fuperintendence of the Gods."* It is a frequent complaint with the early apologifts for our religion, that every calamity which befell the Gentiles, was fuperftitioufly charged to the account of Chriftianity, and accordingly made a ground of perfecution. Here we have an inftance of the very charge complained of; but is it not melancholy to hear this cry of Havoc come from the mouth of a Philofopher? The fentence of Conftantine, who condemned his writings againft Chriftianity to the flames, was more probably induced by this and fimilar incentives to perfecution, than by any danger which he apprehended to the caufe of the Gofpel, from the force of this philofopher's polytheiftical reafonings.

Philoftratus has written the life of Apollonius Tyanæus, an extraordinary perfon who had lived under Nero, and to whom he has afcribed the performance of many miracles. HIEROCLES abridged this work, and, in a piece entitled Philalethes, drew the fubject of it into competition with our Saviour, and concludes with faying, " Thefe things I have recorded as a ground of comparifon between the gravity of our accurate judgement and the levity of the Chriftians: For, at a time when we do not confider Apollonius,

* Νυνὶ δὲ θαυμάζουσιν, εἰ τοσούτων ἐτῶν καθείληφε τὴν πόλιν ἡ νόσος, Ἀσκληπιε̃ μὲν ἐπιδημίας κỳ τῶν ἄλλων Θεῶν μηχεῖ οὔσης· Ἰησοῦ γὰρ ΤΙΜΩΜΕ'ΝΟΥ, ἐδεμιᾶς τὶς Θεῶν δημοσίας ὠφελείας ᾔσθετο. Porphryii ap. Eufeb. Præparat. Evangelic. lib. v. cap. i. p. 179. Edit. ejufd. ac Demonftrat.

Ionius, who has performed the actions (here recounted) to be God, but a Man favoured by the Gods, they, on the contrary, becaufe of a few miracles, proclaim this Jefus to be God." * In like manner Julian the Apoftate expreffes his contempt for the weaknefs of the Chriftian intellect, which could efteem the reftoration of feet to the lame, and eyes to the blind, and other matters of this nature, performed by Jefus Chrift in Bethefda and Bethany, as works of any confiderable importance. †

CELSUS lived in the fecond century, fo that when we hear him object to the Chriftians, their adoration of our Saviour's Godhead, we are not to conceive that he is only making a reply to the affertions of Origen; in fact he is fpeaking to the worfhippers of a prior age; and againft thefe it is that he objects " an acknowledgement that Chrift is God." ‡ Numerous extracts have been already made from Origen's Anfwer to this writer,

E e e 2   from

* Τίνος ἂν ἕνεκα ἐμνήσθην· ἵνα ἐξῇ συγκρίνειν τὴν ἡμετέραν ἀκριβῆ κὶ βεβαίαν ἐφ' ἑκάςῳ κρίσιν, κὶ τὴν τῶν Χριςιανῶν κουφότητα: εἴπερ ἡμεῖς μὲν τὸν τοιαῦτα πεποιηκότα ἢ Θεὸν, ἀλλὰ Θεοῖς κεχαρισμένον ἄνδρα ἡγούμεθα· οἱ δὲ δι' ὀλίγας τεραλείας τινὰς τὸν Ἰησοῦν Θεὸν ἀναγορεύουσι. Hierocles, apud Eufeb. contra Hieroc. p. 512. cum Demonftrat. Evangel.

† Ὁ Ἰησοῦς, ἐργαζομένος παρ' ὃν ἔζη χρόνον ἔργον ἐδὲν ἀκοῆς ἄξιον, εἰ μὴ τις οἴεται τὰς κυλλὰς κὶ τυφλὰς ἰᾶσθαι, κὶ δαιμονιῶντα; ἐξορκίζειν, ἐν Βηθσαϊδᾷ κὶ ἐν Βηθανίᾳ ταῖς κώμαις, τῶν μεγίςων ἔργων εἶναι. Julian. apud Cyrillum, lib. vi.

‡ Καὶ ὡς φάτε Θεὸς ὤν ——
Ἐγκαλεῖ ἡμῖν (ὁ Κελσὸς) περὶ τῦ Ἰησοῦ ὅτι ἐκ θνητᾶ σώματος ὄντα Θεὸν νομίζομεν, κὶ ἐν τούτῳ ὅσια δρᾶν δοκοῦμεν. Celfi, apud Orig. contra Celfum, lib. iii. p. 135.

Οἰόμενος

from many of which the grounds of the Philosopher's aversion from Christianity may be farther collected.— *See above, p.* 256, *&c.*

Let it also be inferred from the character of a Jew, which Celsus sometimes assumed, that he considered the Jewish objections to Christianity to be of the same nature.—That Trypho looked upon the Godhead of the crucified Jesus as a doctrine replete with folly, does not argue that he did not allow it to be the tenet of the Christian; on the contrary, he charges it against Justin Martyr, with vehemence and acrimony *.—According to Eusebius, Philo, a Jew of Alexandria, in the time of Caligula, has corroborated the testimony of the Younger Pliny, given above in page 59, and to his we may annex the concurrent evidence of Lucian, the subject of a future article, who avers that the Christians rose to midnight hymn-singing †. Of the compositions which were at that time chaunted, but very few have descended to our days; a specimen, however, is set before the reader in page 177 above; of this kind, I have no doubt, was the hymn recorded to have been sung by the dying Athenogenes, page 359; and we may, not unreasonably, suppose that Prudentius, whose Poems are still extant, formed his style upon the model of his predecessours, and so from the imitation infer to the genius of the original. *See p.* 139, 371, *above*.

As

'Οιόμεν☉· τὸ καταγινόμενον κ͗ κολαζόμενον ζῶμα τῦ Ἰησῦ, κ͗ ὃ τὴν ἐν αὐτῶ Θεότητα, Θεὸν ἡμᾶς λέγειν: κ͗ ὅτι καθευρέθω κ͗ ἐκολάζετο Θεὸν νενομίσθαι (λέγει ὁ Κέλσ☉·) " ὅτι τὸν δὲ σὸν Θεὸν παριόντα καταγενοντες κ͗ κολάζοντες," &c. Ejusd. lib. viii. p. 405.

* See above, p. 86, &c. See also p. 512.

† Ἐπὶ παννύχοις ὑμνῳδίαις ἐπαγρυπνοῦντες. Luciani Philopat.

As the Orator LIBANIUS flourished some time after the Nicene Council, and it may therefore admit of doubt, whether his testimony, similar to that of Celsus, concerning the Christians, have a retrospect to days of which he was not a personal witness, I content myself with the following brief assertion preserved by Socrates, the Ecclesiastical Historian, who relates that Libanius, in the Funeral Oration of Julian the Apostate, "with derision affirms that the Christians make that (Man) of Palestine both God and the Son of God." *

The same objection lying against the evidence of that young prototype of our James the first, the pedantick JULIAN himself, I have thought it sufficient to say, after Dr. Jortin, that " this Emperor, who rejected Christ, did not reject the notion of a Λόγος, [or THE WORD, John i. 1.] his Λόγος was the Sun whom he accounted to be the visible image of the invisible God." † And this may at least serve to shew that, even by the enemies of Christ, the term Λόγος was not restricted in its signification to an impersonal attribute or ἐπιςήμη ἀνυποςάτΘ. *See above, p. 216 and 379, the last note.*

" And this verily," says AMELIUS, " was the Word, by whom, being eternal, were made the things that were made, (which is also the sentiment of Heraclitus) and whom the Barbarian, *(St. John who was an Hebrew)* placing him in the rank and dignity of a Principle, has

held

* Ἐπειδὴ δὲ κͅ ὁ ζοφιςὴς ΛιβάνιΘ ἐπιχλευάζων, τὸν ἐκ Παλαιςίνης, φησιν, ἄνθρωπον Θεὸν τε κͅ Θεῦ παῖδα ποιῦσιν.——— Socratis Hist. Eccl. lib. iii. cap. xxiii.

† Jortin's Remarks on Ecclesiastical History, vol. II. p. 41. London, Whiston, 1767, 8vo.

held to be with God, and to be God, by whom all things were made, and in whom whatever liveth, pofsesseth life and exiftence; to have *descended to bodies*, and putting on flesh, to have assumed the form of man; to have subsequently manifested the majesty of his nature, and returning to have resumed his Godhead, and to be God, such as he was before his descent into a body, into flesh, and into man." *

Julian has borne the same testimony to the doctrine preached by St. John, who alone, he says, of all the

Evan-

* Ἀμήλιος· αὐτὰ δὴ ταῦτα πρὸς ῥῆμα γράφων ἐπιμαρτυρεῖ, "Καὶ οὗτος ἄρα ἦν ὁ λόγος, καθ᾽ ὃν ἀεὶ ὄντα τὰ γινόμενα ἐγίνετο, ὡς ἂν καὶ ὁ Ἡράκλειτος ἀξιώσειε, καὶ νὴ Δί᾽ ὃν ὁ βάρβαρος ἀξιοῖ ἐν τῇ τῆς ἀρχῆς τάξει τε καὶ ἀξίᾳ καθεστηκότα πρὸς Θεὸν εἶναι, καὶ Θεὸν εἶναι, δι᾽ οὗ πάνθ᾽ ἁπλῶς γεγενῆσθαι, ἐν ᾧ τὸ γενόμενον ζῶν, καὶ ζωὴν, καὶ ὃν πεφυκέναι, καὶ εἰς τὰ σώματα πίπτειν, καὶ σάρκα ἐνδυσάμενον, φαντάζεσθαι ἀνθρώπον, μετὰ καὶ τῇ τηνικαῦτα δεικνύειν τῆς φύσεως τὸ μεγαλεῖον, ἀμέλει καὶ ἀναλυθέντα πάλιν ἀποθεοῦσθαι, καὶ Θεὸν εἶναι, οἷος ἦν πρὸ τοῦ εἰς τὸ σῶμα, καὶ τὴν σάρκα, καὶ τὸν ἄνθρωπον καταχθῆναι." Euseb. Præparat. Evangel. lib. ii cap. xix, p. 540.

On this passage I have two observations to make; the first is, that Amelius having been a Platonick Philosopher, the cotemporary and friend of Plotinus, Porphyry, and Longinus, might in his ardour to maintain their favourite doctrine of principles or ἀρχαι, have mistaken the assertion of St. John. We have already seen the language of the Evangelist ἐν ἀρχῇ, &c. John i. 1. considered, by Theophilus, as equivalent to διὰ τῆς ἀρχῆς, &c. and heard our Saviour denominated ἀρχὴ in p. 129, above; may we not, therefore, suppose that the τάξις καὶ ἀξία τῆς ἀρχῆς, in which St. John is said to have placed the word, is no more than the interpretation put by Amelius upon the assertion of the Apostle, ἐν ἀρχῇ ἦν ὁ λόγος. From this, if assented to, I will leave the reader to draw his own inferences.

The second observation respects the words εἰς τὰ σώματα πίπτειν· which, to avoid farther controversy, I have translated very literally: I am, notwithstanding, of opinion that their true meaning is congruous with the tenets of another Barbarian, who has told us, that our Saviour

" took

Evangelists, has denominated our Saviour God, and appealed to the witness of John Baptist, that "it is Christ whom we should believe to be God the Word." It is rather ludicrous to hear Mr. Lindsey charge this avowed apostate with being too orthodox, and with not having dealt candidly by the Unitarians in his acknowledgment that the weight of St. John's testimony is against them. *See Sequel to the Apology,* p. 198.

LUCIAN, in his History of the Death of Peregrinus, affirms that " the Christians adore that Man who was crucified in Palæstine :"* " That they altogether abjure the Gods of Greece, but worship that crucified impostor of theirs, and regulate their lives according to laws prescribed by him." † Of their amiably simple manners he then proceeds to give a description, which, if with regard to religious tenets there had ever yet subsisted a medium between contempt and concurrence, might

"took upon him the form of a servant." The plural ζώματα, which, exclusive of the peculiarity of the whole sentence, I should conceive more than enough to express our Lord's assumption of one body, was a common name of contempt given to the herd of slaves. To the humble rank of a servant therefore I apprehend it is that the Philosopher has said, the Word had descended. To have taken the form of Man, might very reasonably be considered as a precipitate descent from a state of omnipotence to a condition which, if comparison were possible, we must surely look upon as a state of the most profound humility and servile abasement.

St. Ignatius has declared " Jesus Christ to be the ETERNAL WORD," Ἐις ἐςὶν Θεὸς ὁ φανερώσας ἑαυτὸν διὰ Ἰησοῦ Χριστοῦ τοῦ Υἱοῦ αὐτοῦ, ὅς ἐςὶν αὐτοῦ ΛΟΓΟΣ ΑΙΔΙΟΣ. Ignat. Epist. ad Magnesios.

* Ἐκεῖνον ἔτι ΣΕΒΟΥΣΙΝ ἄνθρωπον, τὸν ἐν τῇ Παλαιςίνῃ ἀνασκολοπισθέντα. Luciani de Morte Pergrini.

† Θεοὺς μὲν τοὺς Ἑλληνικοὺς ἀπαρνήσωνται, τὸν δὲ ἀνεσκολοπισμένον ἐκεῖνον σοφιςὴν αὐτὸν ΠΡΟΣΚΥΝΩΣΙ, καὶ κατὰ τοὺς ἐκείνου νόμους βιῶσι. Ibid.

might reasonably have exempted the legislator who had
enjoined them from the opprobrious appellation.

Of this quotation Lucian is the undisputed author;
whereas the Dialogue whence the following more remarkable passages are extracted, is not so universally ascribed
to his pen. A particular description of St. Paul's person, and an allusion to a victory not specified, but
which commentators have been pleased to confer upon
Trajan, have induced an opinion, that it is the work of
a prior writer; an opinion, however, with which I do
not altogether concur.—For the reality of a fact asserted
by Lucian, whose purposes were usually just as well answered by fiction, I do not see that there subsists any necessity; and therefore I conceive the victory alluded to
here may possibly be no more than a fiction: and as to the
person of St. Paul, that active apostle had in so many
places attracted the observation of multitudes, that we
may conceive tradition fully possessed of it at least for one
century after his death. Within this period flourished
Lucian, himself a native of Syria, and for a considerable
time a resident in the Christian metropolis of Antioch,
where " Paul was separated to the work that he afterwards fulfilled;" where " the disciples of Jesus were
first called Christians;" and where, in the days of Lucian himself, Theophilus presided over the Church.*
It is true that Lucian had quitted Antioch before the accession of Theophilus to the episcopal function; we may
yet suppose him to have obtained his knowledge of the
doctrine which he derides from the predecessors of that
Bishop, and their numerous contemporary adherents.
Let not my reader conceive that I am here laying a
claim, I am in reality making a concession; for if I
shall be thought to err in ascribing this little work to
Lucian

* See above, p. 125.

Lucian who died A. D. 171, the confequence is the eftablifhment of an earlier date, which alone ftands in competition with the author to whom I would afcribe it, and which is yet more contributary to my purpofe.

The title of the Dialogue is Philopatris, or *the Lover of his Country*, a title with which the fubject-matter holds but very little correfpondence; for, though, on account of a national fuccefs, there *do* occur fome few expreffions of pleafure, and gratitude to the God who was unknown at Athens, from which it is obvious how St. Paul was underftood by the Gentiles †, the main purpofe of the author is to deride the religion of the Gofpel; to this end he has felected the ridicule of Ariftophanes for his model; that Poet, eminently fkilled in the art of comic exaggeration, has prefented Socrates to our view, delivering fome very ludicrous doctrines in his fchool: but in the eyes of our author the doctrine of the Trinity in Unity appeared as great an abfurdity as it does to-day in thofe of Mr. Lindfey, or of any other modern Unitarian: the fubject, in his eftimation, was fitted to his hand; he did not, therefore, think it neceffary to exercife his invention in any fportive mifreprefentation of the real matter of fact; but at once introduces a Chriftian, to whom he gives the name of *Triephon*, as chiding an Heathen for fwearing by Jupiter, and thence immediately proceeding to inftruct

---

† Ἡμεῖς δὲ τὸν ἐν Ἀθήναις ἀγνώςὸν ἐφευρόντες, κỳ προσκυνήσαντες, χεῖρας εἰς ἐράνον ἐκτείναντες, τούτῳ εὐχαριστήσομεν. Luciani Philopat.—Remember that this is the language of *Triephon*.

Origen, to the fame effect, has faid, that " when Paul walked forth among the altars and idols of the Athenians, and there found an infcription To THE UNKNOWN GOD; even from this word he took occafion to enter upon the publication of Chrift." Sed et cum perambulaffet (Paulus) aras & idola Atheniénfium, ubi invenit fcriptum IGNOTO DEO, et ex hoc verbo fumpfit Chrifti prædicationis exordium; et am ibi, ar,s Gentilium luftrans, in fanctis pofitus erat, quia fancta cogitabat. Origen. Homil. 17. in Levitic. tom. i. p. 103.

inſtruct him in the place of Jove and the other Pagan Deities, to ſubſtitute " the mighty, immortal, heavenly God who reigneth on high; the Son of the Father; the Spirit proceeding from the Father; one of three, and three of one. Account theſe Jupiter, think this your God." To which he receives the following anſwer from Critias: " You teach me to reckon and make an oath a problem; like Nicomachus you deal in numbers. I underſtand you not: One three? Three one? Do you not ſpeak of the *ogdoads and triacads* of Pythagoras? †

Here

† ΤΡΙΕΦΩΝ. Ὑψιμέδοντα Θεὸν, μέγαν, ἄμβροτον, ἐρανίωνα, Ὑιὸν Πατρὸς, Πνεῦμα ἐκ Πατρὸς πορευόμενον, Ἐν ἐκ τριῶν, κ̣ ἐξ ἑνὸς τρία.

Ταῦτα νομίζε Ζῆνα, τὸν δὲ ἡγοῦ Θεόν.

ΚΡΙΤΙΑΣ. Ἀριθμεῖν με διδάσκεις, κ̣ ὅρκ@ ἡ ἀριθμητική· κ̣ γὰρ ἀριθμεῖς ὡς Νικόμαχ@· ὁ Γερασηνός· ἐκ οἶδα γὰρ τί λέγεις· Ἐν τρία, τρία ἕν! μὴ τὴν τετρακτὺν φῂς τὴν Πυθαγόρου, ἢ τὴν ὀγδοάδα, κ̣ τριακάδα. Luciani Philopatris.

Critias, in a ſubſequent part of the Dialogue, ſays, Ν ἢ τὸν Ὑιὸν ἐκ Πατρὸς ὦ τοῦτο γενήσεται. ΤΡΙΕΦ. λέγε, παρὰ τε πνεύματος, δυνάμιν, τῶ λόγω λάβων. Ibid.

If the following verſe be now extant in the works of Euripides, it has eluded my ſearch, but both Athenagoras and Clemens Alexandrinus have quoted and aſcribed it to that Poet.

" Ταῦτα νομίζε Ζῆνα, τὸν δὲ ἡγοῦ Θεόν."

That Lucian's expreſſion is derived from this Iambic, cannot admit of a doubt; but in the change which he has made in the firſt word, he has difpenſed with the quantity of the original verſe; whence, tho' I know I ſhall ſubject myſelf to the charge of refinement, I am bold to infer that our Author intended to ſignify, by the plural ταῦτα, the trinal number which is ſummed up into unity, the τρία which are ἕν. This, I grant, adds nothing to the proof of my point, that the ſubject of Lucian's ridicule ſubſiſted previous to the Epiſcopacy of Theophilus, when it incurred his deriſion, for that is indiſputable; but, which is the only uſe I deſire to make of the obſervation, it accounts for the change introduced into the language of Euripides.

[411]

Here not only the doctrine of the Trinity in Unity is attested in language that cannot admit of controversy, but the very term "Trinity" is seen to derive a plenary exemption from the charge of barbarity and novelty; for had Critias proceeded to apply his objection to the arithmetical doctrines of Triephon, he must, in order to mark the likeness which they bore to those of Pythagoras, have necessarily formed the word Τρίας, *(Triad)* for with this, and with this alone, the terms Ὀγδοὰς and Τριακὰς *(Ogdoad and Triacad)* possess a common mode of derivation;*—and to corroborate this remark, let it be farther observed, "that the name, by which our author has thought fit to characterize a Christian, whom he has also represented as the immediate disciple of St. Paul, is ΤΡΙΈΦΩΝ, a name which, being strictly and literally interpreted, signifies no less than " A PREACHER OF THE TRINITY."

———

The DOCETÆ or PHANTOMISTS were so far convinced of the Godhead of our Redeemer, that they held his Manhood to be no more than an apparition; they could not conceive it possible that the purity of God should unite with the corruptible nature of man, and not imbibe some stain or blemish from the disproportionate union. Mr. Lindsey, who seems aware of the necessary inference from their tenet, contends for it that they considered our Lord

---

* As it is not easy to give a Latin formation to the Words *Ogdoad* and *Triacad* (which mean, the one *a combination of eight*, the other *a combination of thirty*) the analogy between these terms and the word *Trinity*, can be rendered obvious to an English reader, only by giving a Greek formation to the latter. The idea then that is conveyed by the word *Trinity*, which is a derivative from the Latin denomination, is, on this principle, expressed by the Greek derivative TRIAD: " And surely," says Hilary, " a name can have no criminality which corresponds with a religious meaning." " Nomen nihil habet criminis quod sensum non perturbat religionis." Hilar. de Synodis, lib. contra Arianos. *See above, p.* 356.

Lord only as an emanation; but is not this trifling? For, even upon his own state of their doctrines, our Saviour must have been such an emanation as precluded all impurity; such an emanation as must have pre-existed in a state superior to that which it now seemed to have assumed. That Being to whom the Phantomists denied the possibility of contamination, must have enjoyed a previous incontaminate existence; and how far such an emanation from God can, even upon the Gnostic Principle, that Christ is an emitted Being from a progenitor, be considered as separate and another in Godhead, I refer my reader to Irenæus to learn: some part of the arguments with which that Father has subdued this frantic heresy, I have quoted above, in page 101.*

If the following assertion do not obviate Mr. Lindsey's interpretation of the heresy of the Phantomists, it does more, for it contributes an additional testimony to the general belief of our Saviour's Godhead, as Novatian assures us that "there were some hereticks who conceived Christ to be so truly God, that, denying his Manhood, they believed him to be God alone." †

As I have made only a few detached extracts from the refutation of Praxeas by Tertullian, I intentionally reserved, till now, a state of the tenets of that
heretick;

* See Lindsey's Apology, p. 155, and Script. Confut. p. 204.
The Gnostics are usually termed Philosophizing Christians; I think them rather to have been Christianizing Philosophers, if such a title may be ascribed to men who appear only to have raved, not thought: for the Gospel seems rather to have been a superinduction than the basis of their doctrines.

† Alii quoque hæretici usque adeo eum Deum esse, ut quidam illum, subtracto homine, tantummodo putaverint Deum. Novat. cap. xvii.

heretick; but so far was Praxeas from denying the Godhead of our Saviour, that he held him to be, not a compound of the Word or second Person of the Trinity, and Man, but to be the Father himself united to the human nature of Christ, and with him sustaining all the sorrows which our Lord underwent for our redemption. The unity of the Father and the Son, he maintained in the strictest sense; for he did not admit of their personal distinction, but held that the Father was actually present himself, and united to the Christ. Allow the fact, and let Unitarians themselves decide whether this heresy does not proceed upon the admission of our Saviour's Godhead. This Praxeas saw too well attested to admit of a denial; the unity of God too he saw to be incontrovertible: But Praxeas was a Philosopher, and could not see how a Trinity should consist with this Unity. But, says Tertullian, "the Devil, for the establishment of errour, usually admits of some truth, as a foundation to go upon; and here he contends for the unity of God, merely to make an heresy out of that Unity: he has put the Holy Ghost to flight, and crucified the Father." According to Praxeas then, their own ally, Jesus Christ is not only God, but even the impersonal God of the Unitarians.

The followers of Praxeas, who started up about the middle of the second century, were termed *monarchians*, because of their exclusion of the Son and Holy Ghost from the Godhead, which, confounding the persons, together with the incarnate imbecility of our Lord, they vested in the Father only: and a name thus given for distinction's sake, is an evident demonstration that they were considered as embracing a doctrine rejected by the Christian Church. The same sect, because of the tenet already stated, that the Father was crucified in

union

union with the manhood of our Saviour, was likewise denominated *Patropaffians*. * —*See above, p.* 211.

Even hereticks, who denied the Godhead of our Saviour, denied it in terms of controversy: they denied it as if it had been somewhere affirmed. Of these heretics, "who were all Unitarians, and much resembled those now called Socinians," Mr. Lindsey has brought forward the testimony of Epiphanius, "who tells us that they were wont to say to other Christians, " Well, Sirs, are we to have one God or three Gods?" † Tritheism is the objection made here, and what one might conclude to have been their ground of dissent: but they held that a Trinity was subversive of the Unity of God; it was a belief in the Trinity therefore, which they held to be tritheism.—See for the concurrence of Athanasius, page 134 above.

It is some felicity to the doctrine which we profess, that every argument made use of by its most strenuous adversaries, spend their force without reaching the intended mark: they always strike at some substituted mis-

---

* Tertullian has written a refutation of the heresy of Praxeas, which he, who doubts my assertions above, may easily turn to; it were too long for this place to extract the several passages on which I have stated the doctrines of that heretick. In the course of the work he opposes the monarchical idea of Praxeas, by saying, that the true monarchy of God is by no means impeded by his tripersonality: " For how is it that God should seem to suffer division or dispersion in the Son and Holy Ghost, who possess the second and third place, and are partakers or joint possessors of the substance of the Father?" " the superinduction of a rival power of its own condition or proper state, is the only subversion of the monarchy, that is, when another God is brought in against the Creator."

† Τί ἂν ἤτωμεν, ὦ οὗτοι; ἵνα Θεὸν ἔχωμεν ἢ τρεῖς Θεούς· Epiphan. Hæref. 62. Sequel to Apol. p. 142.

misrepresentation which, when it falls, they endeavour to impose upon their followers for the reality. See p. 270.

Still, however, the truth stands erect upon her own firm basis, unaffected by the sophistry or subtilty of men, whom Mr. Lindsey, with pride, adopts into the fraternity of Unitarians: But does Mr. Lindsey recollect, that when he thus eagerly assumes the concurrence of Noëtus, Sabellius, Praxeas, &c. he relinquishes his original claim to all the Christians of the first three centuries; or does he mean to associate Tertullian, Origen, and the other Fathers, with men whose communion they so warmly abjured, and whose heretical innovations they so effectually refuted? The absurdity of such an endeavour must surely appear too manifest. I therefore conceive that his prudence alone remains for our approbation, and that having experienced the impossibility of procuring any assistance to his cause from "the Christian people of the first three centuries," he now provides himself with an alliance of a very opposite character, makes good his party, and secures a retreat, among *the heretics*; but, be it so, I am amply satisfied with that portion, which, on such a division of forces, falls to our side of the question, and am contented to add Mr. Lindsey's own concession to the multitudinous proofs that warrant me to assume the concurrence of the whole primitive Church: With him, therefore, I shall leave the office of calling upon any farther heretical evidence*, reserving still to myself the power of asking

a

---

* I do not recollect any other Pagan writers who have spoken of the Christian tenets within the first three centuries. Both Tacitus and Suetonius name the sect with the disgust natural to the votaries of the Pantheon, but not in terms from which any thing particular with respect to their belief in our Saviour's Godhead can be collected. As Nerva certainly rescinded the bloody edicts of Domitian against the Christians, I suspect that the Christians are meant by Dio Cassius in his assertion concerning Nerva,

a few cross questions, by which, when in maintenance of his own plaint, he shall have produced the sharpest invectives and keenest raillery of his witnesses, I may, perhaps, be able to convert their testimony into an irrefragable establishment of the very point which he would thus, by the exaggeration of their ridicule, or misrepresentation of their contumely, aggravate into an absurdity; and so subvert.

The

Nerva, whose pardon to those who had been condemned for impiety to the Gods, he records in the commencement of that Emperor's life.

Themistius lived too long after the Council of Nice to make his testimony, provided it were even more particular, of any great value.

Zosimus is liable to the same objection, and, besides this, has betrayed such consummate ignorance of his subject in the course of his narrative, that were he in other respects a competent witness, we could not venture to rely upon his assertion. He professes enmity to the Christian cause, but this could not affect his evidence, his invective would have been equally valid and conclusive with his panegyrick. See above, p. 307.

Josephus has given a very particular account of our Saviour, but not in language applicable to the present enquiry, I should otherwise have undertaken its defence against a doubt suggested that it is only a forgery. See above, p. 312.

Of heretical evidence I have stated that which appeared to me the most important; if, however, it be thought requisite to enquire any farther, I refer the reader to the history of numerous heresies by Epiphanius. I think them, however, but little to the purpose. See above, p. 104, 366.

I cannot take my leave of this subject without vindicating myself from the charge of having, at every turn, in the Scriptural Confutation of Mr. Lindsey's Apology, had the name of Heretick in my mouth: I really do not recollect having once used the word throughout that volume; I have no such pleasure in bestowing opprobrious appellations as should tempt me to turn out of my way to inflict them. I do not believe that even in this book I shall be found to have affixed a name of reproach to any man, excepting in the moment of having caught him in the fact which suggests it: For instance, where my Remarker justifies the worship of angels, I call him there, but no where else, an idolater, and where he is the advocate of two Gods, I there, and there alone, call him Polytheist; but the fact being then recent, and the man taken, as it were, with the manor, the term is in the instant accounted for, and justified by the present witness to the propriety of its application.

The whole body of Christian men constitute the tribunal, and consequently every individual sits as a judge in that court, before which I have, thus, first, stated the evidence of the scriptures, and subsequently exhibited the verdict which primitive antiquity returned upon that evidence; upon this verdict, thus founded, it only remains that judgement be awarded, and as I see no reason for delay, I accordingly now demand it. Had I not myself appeared so long as an advocate, I should commence with a delivery of my own sentence; nay, as it is, having had no other end than unadulterated truth in view, and having very diligently sought for this, I shall not hesitate to pronounce that Unitarians, guilty of errour in having laid it, must for ever hereafter relinquish their claim to a prescriptive sanction from the Christians of the first three centuries.—And upon the whole, I affirm my own sincere belief in the ONE GOD-HEAD OF THE FATHER, AND OF THE SON, AND OF THE HOLY GHOST.

Before I lay aside my pen it may be necessary to say a few words in my own behalf; and first, though I can safely declare myself unconscious of any misrepresentation, yet it is very possible that, in the multitude of extracts which I have stated, I may have lapsed into some errours; that I may have mistaken, and consequently misrepresented, some passages from the numerous difficult writers with whom I have had to deal. If this be really the case, and that I shall be detected, I have little doubt that something worse than "blunders" will be imputed to me, and that an exaggerated imposture will be laid to the charge of my intention. Now, to this I obviate, not only a denial of the intention, but an ample and entire concession of every passage that may be thus challenged. With a view to this possibility I have

multiplied

multiplied extracts, and am so very certain that when every exceptionable affertion is subducted, enough will yet remain to juftify my inference from the whole, that I fhall perfift in requiring the affent of my reader upon the refidue which continues unaffected : Like the Sibyl I fhall abide by my firft demand, on every reduction of the volume fhall return, and, without abatement, challenge for the mutilated remnant, the undiminifhed value, for nothing lefs than the full and entire attainment of which I now make an offer of the whole to the public. *Rode Caper vitem*, &c.

An earneft and fincere wifh to advance the eternal interefts of mankind might, as it prompts, fo very well alleviate the arduous occupation of eftablifhing that bafis of univerfal good-will, the gofpel of Jefus Chrift, were it not that a kind of warfare, incident to the nature of controverfy, unhappily neceffitates a feeming fufpenfion of that very charity whofe true foundations are thè object of vindication. To redeem the word of God from the mifreprefentations of an adverfary, and thus to erafe the foundations of errour, engage the advocate of truth in a fpecies of perfonal conflict. From the detected fallacy or degraded fophifm with which the object of his defence had been affailed, a general fufpicion againft the intellect or integrity of a writer, who had either wilfully or erroneoufly employed them, is a natural inference ; to deduce it, is contributary to the caufe which he would maintain; and, in the moment of detection, to mark the man as an object of derifion or queftionable veracity, is no more than an act of juftice by which the public fhall be difabufed, and the repetition of fuch fraudulent meafures rendered for the future not only ineffectual but inconvenient. So far however, and fo far only as his controverfial character is concerned, do I defire to affect the credit of any man; and if in the courfe

of

of this work I have uttered a cenfure that may feem capable of being carried, even by remote inference, beyond this point, I do hereby make what reparation I can, I difavow the intention and refcind the excefs.

But in fome inftances, exafperated perhaps by the appearances of defective integrity in an opponent, I may have fpoken with too much acrimony, and not feeling now the unwarrantable impulfes of either indignation or contempt, I fear that fome paffages may have been written under their undue dictate; here then let me be the firft to reprehend my own offence, and, fo far as a demand of forgivenefs may atone for the injury, let me thus anticipate and allay refentment; to this end therefore, of every perfon thus injured, I earneftly and even with humility requeft their pardon.

Let me however be underftood, and not fubject myfelf to the charge of timidity by this petition. In the courfe of controverfy many facts are alledged, and many arguments adduced in maintenance of either fide of the litigated queftion: Errour with refpect to the one, and mifconception with regard to the other, may naturally induce falfehood and fophifm; to thefe, prejudice, or even zeal, may give the appearances of truth and deduction in the eyes of that party whofe caufe they advance, while his adverfary, poffibly unwilling to fee the juftice of a better argument, is quick-fighted in the purfuit and difcovery of thefe defects. When detected, they are imputed to an intention to deceive, and the perfon who has ufed them is confidered as difhoneft and fallacious, while perhaps he was only guilty of too great credulity, or was unable to develope the falfehood couched in a fpecious fophifm. If therefore error or fophifm have been unknowingly advanced to a place in argument, and that I have inferred from thefe to the prepense guilt of my opponent, it is here and here alone that I am desirous of compensating for the injustice of my misinterpretation. But if, on the contrary, a falsehood has been wilfully stated, or a sophism intentionally advanced as a ground of deduction, I abide by whatever my utmost disgust at such a conduct may have suggested; and, as in case I have done an injury I have desired forgiveness, so I refuse to receive it from him who feels in his own breast that I have uttered no more than the truth. By the man of integrity I am certain that it will be liberally extended; conscious criminality may be vindictive and withhold it; any farther attack upon me therefore, on this account, I shall consider as a plea of guilt; and whatever I am now disposed to wish no more than an hasty misrepresentation of my own, I do hereby confirm as true of the convicted culprit, who, to use the language of the historian, "si irascitur de se ipse dictum fatebitur."

And now, having performed my part towards a reconciliation with all men, and to the utmost of my power endeavoured to compensate for that asperity which is unavoidably incident to the nature of disputation, particularly when the subject is of all others the most interesting, let me have leave to withdraw from a controversy, the immediate end of which were attained to in vain, if the means employed for its accomplishment were calculated only to frustrate the more remote but ultimate purpose for which we are required to hold the mystery of faith; for of this, however exempt from errour, if held exclusive of a pure conscience and the love which is in Christ Jesus, if urged with all the deep suggestions, but without the meekness of wisdom, we should be found only to have made a lamentable shipwreck; we should thus come under the curse of wrath denounced against the unrighteousness of men to whom

the

the truth has been made known, and feel at length the flaunting luxuriance of our unfruitful foliage shrink and wither away before the voice that blasted the barren fig-tree.

But let us not, while we thus extol the excellence of Charity, conceive this virtue possessed of any religious existence whatsoever in a state of separation from Faith; for as Faith without Charity is but the truth in unrighteousness, so that Charity which does not stand upon the pillar and ground of Faith can never assume to itself the merit of obedience, for this plain and evident reason, that it was never referred to a divine command.——By the means of that Faith, through which alone we are adopted to be the children of God, it is, that our fraternal charities are made to bear any relation to him; and thus by an injunction, dictated by nothing less than the infinite Love himself, do we find our good-will towards man exalted in its nature, and elevated into an acceptible act of glorification to God on high.

To these combined virtues, enjoined under the new covenant, and consequently enjoined with promise, Hope, though their natural result, is, by a law, calculated not to introduce but to abolish sin, erected also into a virtue, and given to be their inseparable associate. To her is assigned the felicitating office to point out, and direct the eye of Charity to that reward which is prepared for the righteous from the beginning of the world: And thus, uniting the past, the present, and the future, does the same voice, which has denounced death against the sorrow of the world, 2 Cor. vii. 10. and for the attainment of everlasting felicity rendered it an indispensible duty for us to be happy even here, make this life a little epitome of that eternal NOW in which all time, no longer progressive, shall stand at

once

once before us, command us with a grateful retrospect to our adoption, and the sacrifice by which it has been effected, to look upon all, who with ourselves acknowledge his paternal relation, as our own brethren, the children of one common father, and, under the influence of this persuasion, exercising ourselves for the present in obedience to his royal law, with chearful confidence to look forward to that day in which he will himself conduct many sons into glory.

Thus to " Faith, Hope, and Charity," hath God, as it were, in emblem of his own trinal unity, dispensed one common essence; " these three" hath God himself thus joined together, and so intimately united, as to render the association of all essential to the existence of each, the subduction of any one necessarily destructive to the existence of all. To maintain this important union, therefore, against the efforts of men, who, rescinding the reference to a divine command and promise, and thus exclusively vesting in a moral life the sum of all religious duty, would ruinously deprive Charity of the conduct of Faith, " without which it is impossible for us to please God" *, and snatch from her the invigorating society of Hope, " provided for us only by the gospel;" † to persuade mankind, instead of the supposititious suggestions of a misunderstood faculty, the proud imaginations and unstable dictate of the unassisted human intellect, to reassume the infallible word of the omniscient Giver of all wisdom, as the only firm foundation of any knowledge that it is possible for us to acquire concerning his otherwise inaccessible nature; and bringing into captivity every thought to the obedience of Jesus Christ," from Religion alone to seek for the uniform and immutable principle of every social virtue; from her to derive " righteousness to our sacrifice," and in consequence of

the

* Hebrews xi. 6. † Heb. xi. 39, 40.

the " record of God borne to the value of our obedience," to look for a reward fuitable to the majefty of an omnipotent legiflator—Such is the end to the attainment of which I have thus laborioufly adduced, not the feeble fuggeftions of man's wifdom, but the unerring teftimony of the God of truth fpeaking by prophets and apoftles, together with the fentiments of every antient writer who has delivered an opinion concerning the true intent and fignification of that teftimony; by the univerfally concurrent voice of whom, and God is in the voice, we are inftructed on brotherly love to ground our charity, and on that Faith alone, by which being empowered to become the children of God, we have received the Spirit of adoption, our brotherly love [*]; to make this the bond of our Chriftian fociety, thus truly rendered the fellowfhip and communion of the Spirit; on this, as on a rock that may not be fhaken, to build ourfelves up "a temple to the Holy Ghoft;" " holding faft the confidence and the rejoicing of hope unto the end to grow up an holy temple in the Lord, the houfe of Chrift," by his grace, and the confolation that is in him, to rife a temple of the living God;" and, even in this life, through the hope by which we fhall finally receive falvation, enjoying a foretafte of our eternal reward, to receive that God, who is Love, as an inmate of the building, in which he has promifed to dwell, if fitly framed together as an habitation of God through the Spirit [†].

[*] Romans viii. 15.—Galat. iv. 5, 6.
[†] Eph. ii. 21, 22.—Heb. iii. 6.—1 Corinth. vi. 19.—2 Corinth. vi. 16.—xiii. 5, 14.—Rom. viii. 24.—1 John iv. 8, 16.—Philip. ii. 1.

F I N I S.

INDEX

TO THE

Several TEXTS *of* SCRIPTURE *adduced in argument, or otherwise referred to.*

Genesis.			1 Chronicles.		
Ch.	V.	Page	Ch.	V.	
i	1	129	xvii	12	218
—	26	15, 88, 209	—	14	218
—	27	194			
iii	22	88	Ezra.		
iv	26	282	iii	2	91
ix	13	200	—	9	91
xvii	—	165			
xviii	—	87	Psalms.		
xxii	11	343	ii	—	82
—	13	269	viii	6	318
xxviii	15	165	xix	—	88
xxxi	13	343	xxiv	—	84
xxxii	19	165	xxv	4	311
xxxv	1	343	xxxii	2	13
xlix	9	270	xxxiv	32	163
			xliv	—	84, 267
Exodus.			xlv	6	88, 106, 218, 311
iii	2	82, 86, 112, 190	—	7	88, 106, 218, 311
—	14	80	—	8	88, 106, 218, 311
—	15	81	xlvi	10	311
iv	26	200	xlvii	—	86
vii	1	107	l	3	335
xii	13	198	lxviii	4	311
xiii	31	343	lxxii	—	82, 190
xiv	19	343	lxxviii	5	245
xxiii	20	343	lxxix	4	218
xxiv	8	200	lxxxiv	4	269
			xcvi	5	107
Leviticus.			xcix	—	82, 86
i	3	298	—	6	282
vii	—	253	c	3	108
xxvi	12	49	cx	—	82, 208, 318
				1	106, 316, 318
Deuteronomy.			cxviii	22	82
x	16	81	cxxiv	7	269
—	17	81			
xxxii	—	165	Proverbs.		
			viii	—	87
Joshua.			—	24	293
v	14	82	—	25	293
2 Samuel.			Solomon's Song		
vii	13	218	i	3	296
—	16	218		4	296

II h h   Isaiah

Isaiah.			Matthew.		
Ch.	V.	Page	Ch.	V.	Page
i	2	294	vii	7	253
ii	3	234	—	22	257
vii	14	120	—	23	257
—	15	120	viii	17	297
ix	6	166, 219, 318	x	3	355
xxviii	16	82	—	18	257
xxxv	3	311	—	33	336
xl	3	311	xi	27	80
xlii	17	107	xvi	27	332
xliv	9	107	xix	28	333
xlv	4	311	xx	12	153
—	14	267	xxii	24	107
xlvi	6	213	xxiv	3	27, 219
liii	4	297	—	30	320
—	8	102, 220	xxv	31	320
liv	3	81	—	34	315, 320
lvii	6	356	—	35	341
lxiii	—	81	—	36	341
—	9	311	xxvi	28	200
lxv	1	81	—	31	243
—	2	81	—	39	242, 266
—	3	81	xxviii	19	345, 348
			—	20	219

Ezekiel.			Mark.		
xxxvi	25	199	viii	38	333

Hosea.			Luke.		
xi	1	220	i	33	313
—	9	311	—	67	311
			ii	10	311

Joel.					
ii	32	279	vi	34	153
			xix	40	274

Zechariah.			xx	36	332
vi	13	82	xxii	3	279
x	11	311	—	29	333
xii	10	89	—	30	333

Malachi.			John.		
i	—	91	i	1	156, 194, 214, 222, 258, 261, 300, 311
Wisdom of Solomon.			—	2	156
i	7	108	—	3	156, 286, 300
			—	9	252
			—	10	311
Baruch.			—	11	311
iii	35	113	—	12	294
			—	14	44, 216, 258, 266, 269, 296
Matthew.			—	18	157, 373
i	23	311	—	36	269
ii	8	190	iii	5	200
—	11	190	—	13	272, 297
vi	13	28			

John

INDEX.

John.				Acts.		
Ch.	V.	Page		Ch.	V.	Page
v	18	152, 154		xvii	28	379
—	23	250, 282		—	31	315
—	27	316		xx	28	65, 157, 176
viii	12	252, 345		xxiv	14	342
—	15	81		xxvi	18	322
—	31	329				
—	32	323		Romans.		
—	45	220		i	3	299, 369
—	58	213, 217, 251		—	16	233
x	18	342		—	24	323
—	30	{104, 168, 170, 204, 222, 250}		—	25	192
				iii	25	200
—	33	273		v	—	320
—	38	168, 250		—	10	320
xi	25	139		—	19	264
xiii	1	260		—	21	321, 323
—	3	157		vi	3	20
—	5	277		—	16	323
—	8	200		—	17	323
—	31	299, 332		—	18	323
xiv	6	251		—	21	323
—	10	222		—	22	323, 327
xv	18	344		viii	7	332
—	23	237		—	15	269, 294, 423
xvii	3	133		—	16	200
—	10	288		—	21	332
—	11	172		—	24	23
—	21	250				{23, 26, 30, 108,
—	22	172		ix	5	119, 237, 311,
—	23	332				369, 348}
—	24	172, 332		x	4	322
xx	28	32, 311		—	13	279
				—	14	279, 281
Acts.				xi	36	379
i	16	220		xii	5	327
—	17	220		xiii	10	322
ii	34	317		xiv	9	324
—	36	315		—	10	52
iii	15	129		—	11	52
—	21	332		—	12	52
iv	30	220		xvi	14	16
—	32	250				
v	31	315		1 Corinthians.		
vii	59	273, 278		i	1	277, 281
viii	10	105		—	2	277, 281
x	25	339		—	9	379
—	42	315		—	18	233
xi	17	153		—	23	233
—	24	14		—	24	87, 233
xiv	3	175		ii	8	272
—	14	339		—	10	37
xvii	—	66		iii	9	175
—	11	179		v	7	198

1 Corinthians.

1 Corinthians.		
Ch.	V.	Page
vi	19	423
vii	22	327
viii	4	107
viii	5	107
—	6	107, 379
xi	3	329
xii	12	327
—	26	328
—	27	328
xv	3	114
—	9	114
—	10	340
—	20	319
—	21	264
—	24, &c.	313, 322, 323
—	25	316
—	52	320
—	54	321

2 Corinthians.		
iii	2	199
—	5	340
—	17	45
iv	17	305
v	4	334
—	10	52, 98
—	11	52, 98
—	15	324
—	16	258
—	21	298, 334
vi	16	49, 423
vii	10	421
viii	9	12
xi	24	273
xiii	5	423
—	14	423

Galatians.		
i	1	270
—	10	337
ii	20	300
iii	13	334
—	27	347
iv	5	294, 423
—	6	423
—	16	336
v	14	322

Ephesians.		
i	—	317
—	22	326
—	23	332, 334
ii	—	319, 322

Ephesians.		
Ch.	V.	Page
ii	2	323
—	5	332
—	14, &c.	318
—	21	423
—	22	423
iv	—	326
—	13	175, 334
—	15	327
—	16	327
v	14	334
—	23	329
—	27	334
—	30	329, 330
—	32	330

Philippians.		
ii	1	423
ii	6	9, 113, 119, 144, 156, 166, 194,
—	7	42, 259, 260, 287, 296, &c.
—	8	365, 369, 370
—	9	288, 324
—	10	52, 315
iii	20	321
—	21	321
iv	3	7

Colossians.		
i	12	332, 333
—	13	323, 330
—	15	293
—	16	300, 378
—	17	300, 378
—	18	323
ii	9	259, 296, 315
iii	4	139
—	11	334
iv	14	314

1 Thessalonians		
iv	14	332
—	17	329, 332
v	9	315
—	10	315

2 Thessalonians		
ii	4	113
—	13	198

1 Timothy.		
i	5	322
ii	5	320, 377

1 Timothy.

INDEX.

1 Timothy.		
Ch.	V.	Page
iii	15	157
—	16	65
vi	16	294, 295

2 Timothy.		
ii	22	279
iv	11	314

Hebrews.		
i	2	27, 376
i	8	88, 106, 218, 311
—	13	318
ii	4	175
—	9	315, 316
—	10	321, 332
—	11	318
—	13	329
—	14	269, 316, 325, 332
—	15	332
—	17	316, 317, 332
—	18	317
iii	6	423
iv	15	317
v	8	316, 332
—	9	316, 319, 332
—	10	316, 332
vi	17	377
vii	3	220
—	11	318
—	25	318
ix	—	324
—	20	200
—	22	200
x	12	318, 320, 332
—	13	320, 332
—	14	332
—	20	199
—	21	320
—	22	199
xi	1	318
—	6	422
—	39	422
—	40	422
xiii	12	198

James.		
ii	7	278
—	8	322
v	17	217

1 Peter.		
Ch.	V.	Page
i	2	198
—	9	322
—	19	198
ii	24	52

2 Peter.		
i	11	323

1 John.		
i	7	200
ii	23	234
iii	1	157
—	2	157
—	16	115
iv	8	115, 116, 423
—	16	423
—	12	115
v	7	195, 204, 344
—	20	130

Revelation.		
—	4	287
—	8	213, 255, 311
—	11	214
—	17	213
—	18	27, 213
ii	8	51, 213
—	9	51
—	10	53
iii	14	129
v	9	198
—	10	310
vii	15	333
—	17	333
xix	10	338
—	16	295, 333
xx	6	310, 345
xxi	6	311
—	16	153
—	18	153
—	23	333
xxii	1	333
—	3	218
—	4	218, 333
—	9	338
—	13	311

INDEX OF WRITERS, &c.

The first column contains their names;—the second, the time in which they flourished;—the third, the pages in which the faith of each respectively forms the subject;—the last, the pages in which any incidental quotations are made.—Such as are in Italic are not Christians.—Those marked with an asterism are quoted from some other writer, by whom the passage, &c. has been preserved.

Writers' Names.	A. D.	Subject.	Incidental Quotations.
Ælius Lampridius	293	400	
* Alexander, of Alexandria	320	372—379	
* Alphæus	300	365	
Ammonius	200	354	
Arnobius	303	304—308	
Athanasius	325	— —	357, 359, 368
Athenagoras	177	62—67	
* Athenogenes		359	
Ausonius	392	— —	64
* *Amelius*	280	405—406	
Barnabas	50	14—16	279
Basil	369	— —	358, 359
Celerinus	256	347 —	
* *Celsus*	170	403 —	256, &c.
Chrysostomus, Joannes	400	— —	163
* Church of Jerusalem	120	361 —	
* —— of Phrygia	303	237 —	
—— of Lyons and Vienna	168	362—364	
Clemens Alexandrinus	195	143—181	138, 185, 262
Clemens Romanus	100	7—14	353
Constantine the Emperor	325	357 —	
Cornelius Romanus	255	346 —	
Council of Antioch	276	366—369	379
—— of Arles	317	349 —	
—— of Carthage	256	348—349	
Cyprian	258	308—347	31, 72, 122, 158, 204
Cyrillus	348	— —	403
Dionysius Alexandrinus	247	359 —	
——— Romanus	247	360 —	

Epiphanius

INDEX of WRITERS, &c.

Writers' Names	A. D.	Subject.	Incidental Quotations.
Epiphanius	347	— —	76, 414
Epistle to Paul of Samosata	276	370 —	
Euchratius	256	349 —	
Eusebius	330		
——— Ecclesiastical History	—	— —	⎧ 56, 100, 237, 248 ⎨ 255, 256, 362, 380 ⎩ 386
——— Demonstratio Evangelica	—	— —	401, 403
——— Præparatio Evangelica	—	— —	402, 406
——— Commentaria in Psalmos	—	— —	380
——— Contra Hieroclem	—	— —	402
Fælix	256	349 —	
Firmicus Maternus	343	— —	84
Firmilianus	256	346 —	358
Forunatus	256	349 —	
* Gaius	225	370—371	356, 363
Gregorius Thaumaturgus	264	303—304	358
* Hegesippus	150	356 —	
Hermas	70	16—18	
* Hierocles	300	402 —	
Hilarius	354	— —	330, 368, 411
Hippolytus	230	348—352	
* Hosius	325	360—361	
Ignatius	116	19—47	90, 113, 158, 407
——— his Martyrdom	116	47—50	
Irenæus	180	99—125	30, 185, 210
* Julian	363	405 —	407
* Julius Africanus	220	358 —	
Justin Martyr	164	67—98	106, 300
Lactantius	318	— —	268, 343, 384
* Libanius	363	405 —	
Lucian	171	407—411	404
Lucius	256	349 —	
* Meletius	—	358 —	
* Melito	190	356 —	
Methodius	300	352 —	
* Miltiades	180	371 —	
Monulus	256	349 —	
Novatian	200	— —	31, 138, 169, 412
Origen	254	244—292	⎧ 108, 140, 141, 159, ⎪ 160, 161, 185, 192, ⎨ 193, 243, 296, 298, ⎪ 312, 330, 349, 361, ⎩ 403, 404, 409
Pamphilus	303	292—302	
* Phileas	300	364 —	
* Philoromus	300	365 —	

* Pierius

INDEX of WRITERS, &c.

Writers' Names.	A. D.	Subject.	Incidental Quotations.
* Pierius	290	376	
* Pliny	100	—	56
Polycarp	147	50—53	
———— his Martyrdom	147	53—57	
* Pontius Pilate	33	386—400	
* Porphyrius	303	365	
* Porphyry, the Philosopher	280	401—402	
Prudentius	398	—	135, 352
* Praxeas	170	413	
Smyrnean Epistle	—	—	{ See Polycarp his Martyrdom
Socrates	406	—	405
* Sibylla Erythræa	—	357	
Sulpicius Severus	420	—	360, 361
Tatian	177	98—99	
Tertullian	212	186 244	{ 31, 104, 122, 135, 158, 169, 176, 181, 267, 302, 387, 413
* Thaddæus	33	355	
Theodoret	400	—	374, 376
* Theognostus	—	356	
Theophilus Antiochenus	182	125—143	
Venantius	256	348	
Vienna and Lyons	—	—	See Church
Victorinus	270	354	
* Zacchæus	300	365	

INDEX

INDEX
TO
ATTRIBUTES and EPITHETS, &c.

Ascribed to our LORD JESUS CHRIST *by the Members of the primitive Church, and inserted in the present Volume.*

A

Adunans per se hominem Deo 104, 121, 122
Aequalis Patri — 297, 298
——— Deo, 259, 287, 297
Aeternus — 111, 185, 300
Alienus a substantia Creaturæ 293, 295
Alius a Patre, non qua Deus, sed qua Pater & Filius — 208, 212
——— persona non substantia — 210
Altissimus — 213
Amans humanum genus — 122
Ante omnia, per quem omnia 354
Antiquior omni Creatura, 17
Audiens Psalmos & Hymnos canentium — 187

C

Carnis humanæ naturam suscipiens — 266, 342
Caro factum ex virgine, Verbum 354
Christus, conjunctus Deus & Homo Jesus — 207
——— ante originem secli genitus apud Patrem spiritualis 354
Carnem indutus — 342
Clemens — 336
Coëternus cum Patre — 284
Coëxistens Patri semper, 104, 185
Comprehensibilis factus (incomprehensibilis) — 113

Conclusus nullo loco — 300
Conculcans Diabolum — 50
Conjunctus Deus & Homo, 122, 207
Consiliarius mirabilis — 111
Conservator noster — 348
Conspiciens secreta cordis — 32
Corpus ex virgine nostro simile assumens — 286
Creator omnium — 255, 276
Creaturæ totius Deus — 293
Creatura, non, & ejusdem cum Patre substantiæ, 295
Crucifigens peccatum & ejus inventorem — 48

D

Daturus præmia se desiderantibus 384
Deitas — 298
DEUS—*passim*
——— Altissimus — 213
——— ex unitate substantiæ, 206
——— fortis — 85, 111
——— idem cum Patre & unus 287
——— interiorum potentiarum 308
——— manifestus potestate venturus, — 335
——— non alius a Patre — 212, 223
——— omnibus — 188
——— omnipotens — 84, 113 255, 287, 288
——— perennis, ex Deo, 135
——— radice ab intima — 308
——— salvator — 337

l i i   DEUS

INDEX to Attributes, &c.

DEUS fermo — 194
——— Solus — 137, 236
——— fufpitator potens — 308
——— fublimis — 308
——— fuo jure omnipotens — 213
——— fuper omnia — 31, 32, 109, 237
——— totius creaturæ, — 293
——— vivorum — 112
——— Verbum — 354
——— verus — 137, 139, 294
——— unus — 139
——— a Patre non alius, 223
——— ab omnium principe, 308
——— unus cum Patre — 112, 259
——— unus atque idem cum Patre — 31, 287
——— unus, ambo Pater & Filius — 206
——— unus, uterque Pater & Filius — 109
——— unus, Pater, Filius, & Spiritus Sanctus, 225, 273, 375
——— unigenitus — 293
Deus & Homo, 85, 121, 123, 211, 244, 267, 268, 286, 350, 351, 354
——————— conjunctus, mittus 122, 206, 207, 342
——— Homo factus, 121, 299
——— incarnatus — 286
——— in carne natus — 207
——— in terris agens — 193
——— in homine quodammodo inclufus — 352
——— veram humani corporis naturam fufcipiens — 243, 266
——— humani habitûs humilitatem fufcipiens ex caufa humanæ falutis — 193
——— nafci in utero matris fe patiens — 194
——— Dominus qui apparuit nobis in carne — 354
——— Verbum & homo — 354
Deo æqualis — 259, 287, 297

Diftinctus a Patre, non divifus— 210
Dives, pauper factus — 259
Divifus a paternâ fubftantia, non 300
Divinitas — 32, 139, 268, 281, 296, 300, 339, 350
Divinitatis non aliquid Chrifto deeft — 300
Dominatur fpiritibus & omni creaturæ — 255
Dominus, 107, *& paffim*
——— amans humanum genus 122
——— fortis — 85
——— intellectivæ & fenfitivæ naturæ — 354
——— majeftatis, 253, 273
——— miferecors — 122
——— mundi, & factor, 345
——— orbis terrarum, 15, 17
——— piiffimus — 122
——— potens in prælio, 85
——— fanctus — 111
——— fuper omnes — 109
——— unus — 107
——— unus & idem cum Patre — 287
——— virtutum — 213

E

Ego sum — 213
Ejufdem fubftantiæ cum Patre— 295
Eminens omnium natura — 298
Exinaniens fcipfum de plenitudine divinitatis — 296
Exiftens femper apud Patrem— 185

F

Factor mundi — 111, 211, 345
Factus homo, (Deus) 121, 299, 355
Filius Dei, 49—*& prope paffim*
——— a Patre individuus — 208
——— ——— infeparatus, 208, 280
——— ——— prolatus non feparatus — 223

Filius

INDEX to Attributes, &c. 435

Filius antiquior omni creaturâ — 17
—— coëternus cum Patre, 284
—— coëxistens Patri semper — 104, 185
—— de substantia Patris, 222, 295
—— Deus ex unitate substantiæ 206
—— et Pater, unus ambo, Deus 206
—— et Pater, duo, non dii, sed quâ Pater & Filius, 208
—— et Pater & Spiritus Sanctus, tres, non dii, sed quâ Pater, Filius, & Spiritus Sanctus — 208
—— et Pater et Spiritus unus Deus, 225, 273, 275
—— existens semper apud Parem — 185
—— ex ipso Patre generatus — 295
—— Hominis, et Filius Dei — 211
—— Hominis per Carnem, Dei per Spiritum — 267
—— Dei qua Spiritus & Sermo 207
—— Hominis qua caro & Homo 207
—— —— per mortem exaltatus & idem cum verbo 299
—— Homo factus — 355, 298
—— a Patre, sed non separatus 223
—— In Patre — 193
—— in Patre invocatus — 104
—— inseparabiliter — 294
—— omnipotens — 288
—— receptus a Patre cum corpore in cœlos — 355
—— Naturâ non Adoptione, 293, 294, 295
—— Per Spiritum — 267
—— sanctus semper, non aliunde sanctificatus — 288
—— semper — 185, 294
—— unigenitus, 48, 294, 300, 354

Filius incarnatus adventu corporali — 300
—— unius cum Patre substantiæ 293
Fortis in prælio — 85, 111

G
Generatione inenarrabili — 103
—— —— nova — 123
Generis humani Pater — 104
Gerens potestatem universorum 255
Gloriæ Rex — 85
Gloriâ inenarabili venisse potens 113

H
Habitum visibilem suscipiens, invisibilis utpote æqualis Patri — 297
Hominis & Dei Filius — 211
Homo Deo mistus — 22, 206
—— et Deus — 121, 123, 211, 267, 268, 286
Homo et Deus conjunctus — 122, 207
—— factus, Deus — 111, 121, 297, 298
—— indecorus — 111
—— natus ex virgine — 211
—— pariter et Deus — 85, 268
—— vivens & perfectus — 123
—— merâ et perfectâ divinitate plenus — 252
—— non verbum, patiens affectus tristitiæ ad mortem, 269
Humani habitûs humilitatem suscipiens, Deus — 193

I
Idem ac Pater Deus — 31
—— cum Patre Deus & Dominus — 287
Immortalis — 298
Impassibilis — 113, 298
In hominibus & angelis — 300
Incarnatum Verbum — 111
Incarnatus cum Deus esset, 286
Incomprehensibilis — 113
Incorporeâ naturâ — 300

436 INDEX to Attributes, &c.

Individuus a paternâ fubſtantiâ 300
——— a Patre — 208, 300
Induliturus martyribus — 347
Infictus — 351
Inſeparatus a Patre, 208 (281)
Inviſibilis — 113, 297, 298
Judex noſter — 341
——— omnibus, 104, 188, 190
——— univerſorum, 104, 111, 211
Juſtitia Dei — 289

L
Loco nullo concluſus — 300

M
Majeſtate adorandâ & venerabili 348
Majeſtate naturæ incorporeæ, 300
Majeſtatis Dominus, 253, 273
Mediator Dei & Hominum, ad utroſque domeſticitatem habens — 122
Mediator duorum Dei & hominum, ex eo quod Deus eſt hominem induens— 334, 354
Mera divinitate plenus, Deus in homine incluſus — 352
Miſerecors Dominus — 122
Mortalis pro nobis, immortalis 207, 298
Mundi factor & Dominus — 111 345

N
Naturâ duplici — 269
Naturâ & fubſtantiâ nihil habenti diverſitatis, Pater, Filius, & Spiritus Sanctus — 275
——— incorporeâ — 300
——— non adoptione, Filius — 293, 294, 295
Natus ante omnem creaturam, ex Patre — 286
——— de fubſtantia Patris abſque diviſione vel imminutione vel feparatione fubſtantiæ divinæ ——— 293, 294

Nomine magno & immenſo, 17
Non alius a Patre Deus — 212, 223
Nullo loco concluſus — 300
——— abſens — 300
Numen — 307
Numen Chriſti — 84
——— ſalutare — 85
——— venerandum — 85
Nunc & modo — 281
Nunquam fuit quando Filius non fuit — 185, 300

O
Omnibus Deus & Dominus, 188
——— Judex — 188, 190
——— Rex — 188, 190
Omni creaturâ antiquior — 17
Omnipotens Deus, 84, 213, 255, 287, 288
Omnipotentia Patris & Filii una & eadem — 287
Omnitenens Deus — 255
Omnium Creator — 255, 276
Orbis Dominus, fuſtinens pati pro animâ noſtrâ — 15
Orbis a nomine ejus magno fuitentatus — 17

P
Pariter Homo & Deus — 86, 268
Paſſibilis factus, impaſſibilis — 113, 298
——— Homo factum verbum 185
Pater generis humani — 104
Patri æqualis — 297
Pauper factus, dives — 259
Peccata dimittens, 32, 121, 285
Perennis Deus ex Deo — 135
Perfectus & vivens homo — 128
Per quem omnia — 354
Per ſe hominem adunans Deo — 104, 121, 122
Perſonæ non fubſtantiæ nomine diſtinctus a Patre 210
Perſona Trinitatis ſecunda, 211
Piiſſimus Dominus — 122
Petentibus indulturus — 347
Pontifex — 269, 354
Potens in Prælio Dominus — 85
Poteſta ·

INDEX to Attributes, &c.

Poteſtatem gerens univerſorum 255
Poteſtate manifeſtus adventurus 335
Præmia daturus quibus ſui deſiderium — 348
Præſens martyribus — 349
Prolatus a Patre non ſeparatus — 206, 223
Primogenitus — 293

Q

Qui ab initio & ſemper erat, 254

R

Rex — 190, 353
Rex æternus — 111, 188
—— gloriæ — 85
—— intellectivæ & ſenſitivæ naturæ — 354
—— omnibus, & ubique regnans 188, 190
—— & Deus — 190
—— ſupercæleſtis — 48, 290

S

Salvator — 104, 228, 288, 293, 294, 297
———— Deus — 288, 337
Salutare numen — 85
Sanctus ſemper — 288
Sapientia Dei, 281, 287, 289, 296
Seipſum a mortuis reſuſcitans — 270, 342
Semper exiſtens Patri — 104, 185
Sempiternus cum Patre & Spiritu Sancto — 281, 351
Separatus a Patre nunquam —— 223, 281
Sermo 2da Perſona Trinitatis — 210
Sermo Dei — 135, 194, 207, 211, 222, 223
—— in Patre ſemper — 223
—— Deus — 194
—— perſona & Filius — 215, 223
Solatio fovens martyres in metallis — 349

Solus Deus — 137, 236, 194
Spiritualis genitus ante originem ſech — 355
Spiritus — 122, 207
Sponte ſurgens a mortuis — 342
Statu duplici, Deus, & Homo — 207
Subſtantiâ Deus — 121
———— Divinâ & Humanâ — 207
———— de ipſâ Dei, Filius — 294
Subſtantiæ unius cum Patre — 206, 222, 275, 293, 295
Supercæleſtis Rex — 48
Super omnia Deus — 30, 31, 32, 109, 137, 237
Supra omnem æternitatem, 300
Surgens ſponte a mortuis — 342
Suſcipiens veram humani corporis naturam, 243, 266
———— humilitatem humani habitûs — 193
Suſtinens pati pro anima noſtrâ, Orbis Dominus — 15

T

Thronus ei in ſecula ſeculorum 311
Totius Creaturæ Deus — 293
Tuetur Chriſtus — 345

U

Ubique adoratus & cultus, 188
Ubique præſens — 300
—— regnans — 188
Unigenitus — 48, 111, 113, 141, 284, 288, 289, 224, 296, 299, 300, 354
———— non mori aptus, ſed homo genitus ex femine David, 296
Unius cum Patre ſubſtantiæ, 293
Univerſorum gerens Poteſtatem, 255
———— Judex — 111
Unum re & ſubſtantia, Pater & Filius, 32, 104, 169, 204, 259, 293

Unus

Unus ambo, Pater & Filius, 206
Unus cum Patre — 259
Unus Deus — 139
—— Pater, Filius & Spiritus Sanctus — 273
Unus & idem cum Patre Deus — 31, 287
Unus, uterque Pater & Filius, Deus — 109

V
Venerandum numen — 85
Veniens de cœlo — 32
Venturus falvator & judex, 105
Verbum Dei—*passim*
—— —— caro factum, 31, 269
—— ex Mariæ carne vestitum 298

Verbum homo — 298
—— incarnatum — 111
—— non sustinens, sed homo 269
—— non recipiens exaltari — 299
—— passibilis homo factum — 185
—— per quod omnia — 354
—— in fine caro factum ex Virgine — 354
Verus Deus — 137, 139, 294
Virtus Dei — 296
Visibilis factus, invisibilis — 113, 297, 298
Vita æterna — 139
Vivens & perfectus Homo — 123
Vivorum Deus cum Patre — 112

INDEX

INDEX
TO
ATTRIBUTES and EPITHETS, &c.

Ascribed to our LORD JESUS CHRIST *by the Members of the primitive Church, and inserted in the present Volume.*

A

Α Καὶ Ω — 214, 311
Ἄγγελος — 82
Ἀγένητος — 22, 351
Ἅγιος — 165, 177
Ἀεὶ ὤν — 289, 351, 352
Ἀθάνατος — 44, 304, 351
―――― βασιλεύς — 357
―――― θεός — 159
―――― εἰς θνητὸν ἐρχόμενος σῶμα — 160
―――― ἐν παθητῷ σώματι — 44
―――― καὶ θνητός — 160
―――― ὁ παθὼν ἐνεχ' ἡμῶν, 357
Ἀΐδιος — 304, 351, 407
Αἴτιος ἁπάντων ἀγαθῶν ἡμῖν, 144
Αἰωνίας, εἰς ἀπείρας κ᾽ ἀτελευτήτας — 355
Αἰώνιος, 44, 54, 57, 82, 86
Αἰώνων
―――― ἐξ ἀνάρχων — 355
―――― πρὸ — 44, 86, 369
Αἰωνοχαρὴς — 177
Ἀκατάληπτος — 351
Ἀκηλίδωτος (ἐν σχήματι ἀνθρώπου) 166
Ἄκμων πάντα — 262
Ἀληθινὴ ζωὴ — 22
Ἀληθινὸν ἡμῶν ζῆν — 90
Ἀληθινὸς — 304
Ἀλήθεια — 251
Ἀληθῶς ὢν κ᾽ ἐνεργῶν — 380

Ἁμαρτίαν πᾶσαν κοπιῶν, ἐναν-θρωπήσας δι' ἡμᾶς, 365
Ἄμφω, θεὸς κ᾽ ἄνθρωπος, 144, 162
Ἄναρχος — 351
Ἀνάρχως γενόμενος — 185
Ἀνεπιθυμήτως ἐξ ἀρχῆς — 138
Ἀνερχόμενος εἰς οὐρανὸν, 82, 86
Ἀνὴρ—κ᾽ θεὸς — 162
Ἀνθρωπίνως φανερούμενος, θεός, 23
Ἄνθρωπον ἐκ Μαρίας ἀναλαβὼν, 289
Ἄνθρωπος, 79, 82, 88, 89, 93, 97, 138, 162, 257, 356, & prope passim
―――― γενόμενος, 79, 95, 106
―――― διὰ τῆς παρθένου, 97, 360
―――― τὸ κατὰ σάρκα ἐκ σπέρματος Δαβὶδ θεῷ ἴσα 369
Ἄνθρωπος δημιουργὸς, κ᾽ κόσμου, 165
Ἄνωθεν—θεὸς — 88
Ἀόρατος — 21, 304, 370
Ἀπαθὴς — 21, 22, 44
Ἀπαράδεκτος κακίας — 159
Ἄπειρος — 351
Ἀπόρροια τῆς τε πατρὸς οὐσίας, 357
Ἀπολεμνούμενος, ἐκ — 262

Ἀρχὴ

INDEX to Attributes, &c.

Ἀρχη — 129
Ἀρχηθεν θεος 256
——— υἱος θευ — 256
Ἀρχιερευς αἰωνι☉ — 54
Ἀρχιςραηγ☉ — 82
Ἀσωματ☉, ἐν ζωματι 44
Αὐτοαληθεια — 256
Αὐτοδικαιοσυνη — 256
Αὐτοθε☉ — 256, 349
Αὐτολογ☉ — 256
Αὐτοσοφια — 256
Ἀφθαρτ☉ — 304
Ἀχραντ☉ θεος ἐν σχηματι ἀνθρωπυ — 166
Ἀχρον☉ — 21
Ἀχωριςτος ἀπο πατρος κ᾽ πνευματος ἁγιε, 289, 374
Ἀψηλαφητ☉ — 21

B
Βασιλευς, 54, 90, 125, 177, 357, 365
——— αἰωνι☉ — 56, 82
——— ἀθανατ☉ — 357
——— μονος — 365
Βασιλευων εἰς τυς αἰωνας, 57
Βοηθ☉ — 13, 355, 365

Γ
Γεννητος (κ᾽ ἀγεννητ☉) 22, 351
Γνησι☉ τυ θευ παις — 256

Δ
Δημιυργ☉ — 380
Δημιυργ☉ τυ κοσμυ κ᾽ ἀνθρωπυ 165
Δι ἡμας ἀνθρωπος γενομενος, θεος — 79, 138
——— ἐνανθρωπησας, ἁμαρτιαν πασαν κοπτων, θεος
——— ἐπι παντων — 365
——— ὁρατος, ἀορατος, 21
——— παθητος, ἀπαθης — 21

Δι ἡμας, ὑπομεινων παντα, ἀψηλαφητος — 21
Δια παντων — 304
Διδασκαλ☉ — 56, 79, 167
Δοξα τυ γεννητ☉ — 87
Δοξα — 362
Δυναμεν☉ ἐν κομπω ἐλθειν, 8
Δυναμεων κυριος — 83
Δυναμις, 356, 364, 365, 369
Δυναμις ποιητικη — 304
——— τυ γεννητ☉ — 87
Δυο τη ὑποςασει πραγματα, ὁ πατηρ κ᾽ ὁ υἱος — 251
Δυσθεωρητ☉—ὁ θεος, λογος, 258

E
ΕΓΩ ΕΙΜΙ — 251
Ἑδραν ἑαυτε ὐ καταλειπων, προς ἡμας ἐρχομενος — 261
Εἰδων παντα — 262
Εἰκων θεοτητ☉ — 304
——— πατρος — 357
Εἰς θεος ὁ πατηρ κ᾽ ὁ υἱος, 251
Εἰς κυριος — 304
Εἰς μονος — 138, 176
Εἰς ὁ πατηρ κ᾽ ὁ υἱος, 63, 251
Εἰς τω πατρι, πνευματικως, 21
Εἰς αὐτον παντα κ᾽ ἐν αὐτω (ἐν ω ἡ δοξα αὐτη) — 379
Ἐκυσιως καταβας — 161
Ἐλεος ἀμετρητον — 363
Ἐν ἀμφω, ὁ θεος, ὁ πατηρ κ᾽ ὁ υἱος — 167
Ἐν θανατω ζωη ἀληθινη — 22
— πατρι, υἱος — 106
Ἐνανθρωπησας — ὁ θεος, 257, 352, 365, 369
Ἐν σχηματι ἀνθρωπυ θεος ἀχραντ☉ — 166
————— ἀκηλιδωτ☉ — 166
Ἐν ἀνθρωπυ μορφη θεος — 99
— ἀνθρωπω θεος — 22
— φθορα ζωη — 44, 90
Ἐνεργος — 304

Ἐνεργω

INDEX to Attributes, &c. 441

Ἐνεργων — 380
Ἐπὶ πάντων Θεὸς 237, 251
Ἐπιστήμη ἀνυπόστατος, ἡ, 380
Εὐσπλαγχ⸐ Θεὸς κỳ κυριος, 363

Z

Ζην ἀληθινὸν ἡμῶν — 90
Ζωη ἀληθινη ἐν Θανάτῳ — 22
— ἐν φθορᾷ — 44, 90
Ζωην εἰς ἀΐδιον παραπεμπομεν⸐, 144
Ζων Θεὸς — 162
Ζων λογος — 304
Ζωντων κριτης, κỳ νεκρων — 52

H

Ἡγητωρ παιδων — 177
Ἡνωμεν⸐ τῷ πατρὶ, πνευματικῶς, 23, 360

Θ

Θειος λογος — 160
Θεοτης — 159, 256, 361
Θνητὸς δι' ἡμας, ἀθάνατος, 160
ΘΕΟΣ — *passim*
—— Ὁ — 20, 22, 46, 47, 79, 87, 91, 92, 125, 157, 159, 160, 162, 163, 165, 167, 261 366, 369
—— ἁγιος — 165
—— ἀεὶ ὤν — 289
—— ἀθάνατ⸐ — 159, 160
—— ἄνωθεν — 88
—— ἀόρατος — 370
—— ἀρχηθεν — 256 (373)
—— αὐτοθεος — 256, 349
—— αὐτος, λογος — 255
—— δυσθεωρητος — 258
—— εἰς μονος — 138, 176
—— ἐπι παντων, 237, 251, 365
—— εὐσπλαγχος — 363
—— ζων — 162
—— θιξ, τε — 92

ΘΕΟΣ —— υἱος — 93
—— ἰσχυρος — 90
—— λογος, 159, 160, 252, 255, 256, 258, 289, 261, 352
—— μεγαλος — 166
—— μηδαπω ἄνθρωπος — 165
—— μονος, ὁ, παντων ἀνθρωπων, 162
—— Ὁμοούσιος (τῳ πατρι) 289
—— Οὐσίᾳ κỳ ὑποστασει, 369
—— παις — 176
—— παμβασιλευς — 255
—— πανηγεμων — 255
—— προ αἰωνων — 86
——— ἐστια κỳ ὑποστασει ὤν, 369
—— προσκυνητος, 88, 90, 93, 106
—— προσκυνουμενος — 162
—— Ζωης — 357
—— υἱος — 356, 304, &c.
—— υἱος κỳ ὁ πατηρ, εἰς, 63, 251
——— ἐν ἀμφω, ὁ, 167
—— ὑποστασει κỳ ἐστια — 369
—— ὑψιστος — 357
—— φιλάνθρωπος — 165
—— φιλοικτιρμων — 156
—— φυσεως — 160

—— ἀληθως ἐνανθρωπησας — 257, 369
—— ἀνθρωπινως φανερομενος, 23
—— ἀνθρωπος γινομενος, 95, 106
—— ἐν ἀνθρωπε μορφη. — 99
—— ἐν ἀνθρωπε σχηματι ἀρχαιος — 166
——— ἀκηλιδωτος, 166
—— ἐν ἀνθρωπῳ — 22
—— κỳ ἀνηρ — 162
—— κỳ ἄνθρωπος, 257, 356, 369, 372
—— ὁ μονος ἀμφω, 144, 162
—— κενωσας ἑαυτον, 156, 159, 261, 369, 370

Kkk   Θεὸς

442 INDEX to Attributes, &c.

ΘΕΟΣ Σαρκωθεις — 369
—— Σαρκοφορος — 21, 357
—— Σκηνωσας ἐν ἡμῖν — 258
Θεοσεβηλεον — 163
Θεοίης — 260, 370, 373, 374
Θεοίηίος χαρακίηρ — 304
—————— εἰκων — 304
—————— ἀπο της ἐκ ἀποπεσων 370
Θνηίος, καία Σαρκα — 384

I

Ἰασιν ποιησας ἀνθρωπος δί ἡμας γενομενος — 79
Ἰαίρος — 44
Ἰερευς — 82, 91
Ἰσα Θεῳ ὑπαρχων, 369, 370
Ἰσχυρος Θεος — 90

K

Καίαβας ἑκυσιως — 161
Καίακυλοθηλεον — 163
Κενωσας ἑαυίον Θεος, 156, 159, 261, 369, 370
Κοσμυ δημιεργος κ) ἀνθρωπυ, 165
Κραίερος (παις) — 177
Κριίης ζωνίων κ) νεκρων, 52, 125
Κυριος — passim
—— δυναμεων — 83
—— εἰς μονος — 138, 125
—— ὁ φιλανθρωπος — 138
—— των ὁλων κ) ζωίηρ, 358

Λ

Λιθος — 82
ΛΟΓΟΣ — passim
—— αἴδιος — 407
—— δημιεργος
—— δυσθεωρηίος — 258
—— ἐνεργος — 304
—— ἐνεργων — 380
—— ζων — 304
—— ἡνωμενος τω Θεω των ὁλων 360

ΛΟΓΟΣ Θεος, 252, 255, 256, 289, 352, 380
—— ἀθανᾶος — 159
—— φυσεως — 160
—— Θειος — 366
—— καθηγεμων — 165
—— μενων λογος, ἐδεν πασχει ὧν πασχει Σωμα — 159
—— μορφωθεις — 95, 99
—— ὀρανιος — 355
—— παθηθ· γενομεν⊙, 82
—— πανδαμαίως — 177
—— ποιηίης των ὁλων, 380
—— προ των ποιημάίων, 300
—— ζων τω παίρι ἐν ἀμφω, Θεος 167
—— Συναίδιος — 370

M

Μεγαλος Θεος — 166
Μεριζομενος, ἐ — 262, 357
Μεσιίευυσα φυσις — 370
Μίλαβαινων ἐκ τοπυ εἰς τοπον,ἐ 262, 355
Μη ποιηίος — 359
Μονογενης, 56, 252, 260, 304 355, 370, 376
Μονος ἀμφω Θεος κ) ἀνθρωπος, 144, 162
Μονος ἐκ μονυ — 304
Μονος Θεος — 138, 176
—— παίων ἀνθρωπων, 162
Μονος ὑιος κυριως λεγομενος 300
Μορφωθεις λογος — 95, 99

N

Νεκρων κ) ζωνίων κρίίης — 52
Νυς — 66
—— ὁλος 262

O

Ὁλος νυς — 262
—— ὀφθαλμος — 262
—— φως παίρωος — 262

Ουρ.

INDEX to Attributes, &c. 443

Ὁμογενὴς υἱὸς — 44, 176
Ὁμοούσιος (τῷ πατρὶ) 330, 359
Ὁμοούσιος—τῷ πατρὶ κ̀ πνεύματι ἁγίῳ — 289, 294
Ὁρατὸς δι' ἡμᾶς, ἀόρατος — 21
Ὁρῶν πάντα — 262
Οὐράνιος — 355
Οὐσία κ̀ ὑποστάσει θεὸς, 369
Οὐσίας ἐκ τῆς τοῦ πατρὸς, 357
Ὁ παθὼν ἕνεκ' ἡμῶν — 357
Ὀφθαλμὸς ὅλος — 262

Π
Παθητὸς δι' ἡμᾶς, ἀπαθὴς, 21, 22, 44, 82
Παιδαγωγὸς — 165, 167
Παιδίον τέλειον — 82, 166
Παίδων ἡγήτωρ — 177
Παῖς — 176, 177
—— ἀγαπητὸς — 54
—— γνήσιος τοῦ θεοῦ — 256
—— θεὸς — 176
—— κραταιὸς — 177
—— μονογενὴς — 56
Πάλιν παραγινόμενος, 82, 86, 88
Παμβασιλεὺς — 255
Πανδαμάτωρ — 177
Πανηγύρων — 255
Πάντα ἀκούων — 262
—— ἰδὼν — 262
—— ὁρῶν — 262
—— δι' αὐτοῦ ἐγένετο — 63
Πανταχοῦ — 262
—————— ζωήσιος 162
Παντὸς — 262
Πάντων ἀνθρώπων θεὸς μόνος, 162
Παραπέμπων εἰς ζωὴν αἰώνιον, 144
Πατρῷος φῶς ὅλος — 262
Περιεχόμενος μηδάμῃ — 262
Πνεῦμα — 45
Πνευματικὸς κ̀ σαρκικὸς — 22
Πνευματικῶς εἰς τῷ πατρὶ — 21
Ποιητὴς τῶν ὅλων — 380
Ποιήσας τὰ πάντα ἐκ μὴ ὄντων, 351

Ποιμὴν — 177
Πραγμάτεια δύο ὑποστάσει, πατὴρ κ̀ υἱός — 251
—————— ἀλλήλων ἀχώριστα, 374
Πρὸ αἰώνων
—————— θεὸς — 86
—————— παρὰ πατρὶ — 44
—————— υἱὸς μονογενὴς, 44
Πρὸ τῶν ποιημάτων λόγος, 300
Προσκυνητὸς, 86, 88, 90, 93, 106, 256
Προσκυνούμενος — 162
Προσομιλήσας Μωσεῖ ἐκ βάτου, ἐν ἰδέᾳ πυρός — 80
Προσφιλὴς — 13
Πρόσωπα δύο, εἷς θεὸς, ὁ θεὸς κ̀ ὁ λόγος — 352
Πρόσωπον ἐν αὐτῷ — 370
Προϋπάρξας — 352
Προϋπάρχων θεὸς — 86
Πρωτότοκος — 80

Σ
Σαρκικὸς κ̀ πνευματικὸς, 21, 22
Σαρκωθεὶς υἱὸς — 124, 369
—————— ὑπὲρ ἡμετέρας σωτηρίας 124
Σαρκοφόρος θεὸς — 21
Σὰρξ ἐγένετο — 258
Σκηνώσας ἐν ἡμῖν, θεὸς λόγος, 258
Σκῆπτρον μεγαλωσύνης θεοῦ — 8
Σοφία τοῦ γεννήσαντος, 66, 87, 369
Σοφίη περικλεινὴ — 304
Στήριγμα πόνων — 177
Συγκαταβαίνων ἡμῖν — 260
Συμβασιλεύων τῷ πατρὶ ἐξ ἀνάρχων αἰώνων, &c. — 355
Συμμέτοχος παθῶν ἡμετέρων, 79
Σύκαΐδιος τῷ πατρὶ κ̀ τῷ πνεύματι 351, 370
Συνανέχος τῷ πατρὶ κ̀ τῷ πνεύματι — 351
Συνεργὸς ἡμῖν — 355
Σύνθρονος τῷ πατρὶ κ̀ τῷ πνεύματι ἁγίῳ — 289

INDEX to Attributes, &c.

Σινων (παῖςι) — 300
Σωματικως ἑνωμενος θεότητι, 369
—— χωρησας πληρωμα θεο-
τητος, ζωματικως θεοποιησας,
369
Σωτηρ, 46, 52, 54, 125, 176,
177, 254, 256, 355,
358
Σωτηριος πανταχου — 162

T

Ταπεινωμενος — 260, 370
Τελειος — 166, 263, 304
Τελος μη ἐχων — 352

Υ

Υἱος—passim
—— του θευ—passim
—— ἀληθινος — 304
—— ἐν δευτερᾳ χωρᾳ — 80
—— ἐν παῖρι — 166
—— θεος — 256, 304
—— θευ θεος — 93
—— κὴ πατηρ,: ἐν ἀμφω, ὁ θεος,
63, 167
———— εἱς θεος — 251
—— κυριως — 300
—— ὁ μονος — 300
—— ὁμογενης — 176
—— προ αἰωνων μονογενης, 44
—— πρωτοτοκ. του θευ — 80

Ὑιος ἀνθρωπυ κὴ ὑιος θευ, 23
—— ζαρκωθεις — 124, 369
Ὑπερ ἡμων κενωσας ἑαυτον κὴ
ταπεινωσας ἑως θανατυ—
370
Ὑπερκαιρος — 21
Ὑποτασσει, δυο, πατηρ κὴ ὑιος—
251
—— θεος — 369
Ὑποταγεις τω πατρι, τα κατα ζαρ-
κα — 44
Ὑποπτωσεων δευτερος — 357

Φ

Φανερωμενος ἀνθρωπινως θεος, 23
Φιλανθρωπος κυριος θεος, 138,
165
Φιλοικτιρμων—ὁ θεος — 156
Φοβερος — 351
Φυσεως θεος — 160
Φυσις μεστιτευσα — 370
Φως ἀληθινον — 252
—— πατρωος ὁλος — 262

Χ

Χαρακτηρ ἀιδιον — 304
———— θεοτητος — 304

Ω

Ὠν ἀει — 285, 351, 352
—— ἀληθως — 380

INDEX

TO THE
TERMS of ADORATION and PRAISE

Addressed to our LORD JESUS CHRIST.

ADoro genu posito — 190
Adoro, 84, 114, 188, 190, 192, 276, 282, 307, 338, 349
—— Supplicationibus, 69, 307
Agnosco — 276
Adoratio nunc & semper, & in secula seculorum, 354

Carmina cano — 59
Colo, 188, 276, 308, 343
Confugio ad — 194
Contrecto — 189
Credo — 100, 361
Credo in — 190, 343
Confiteor, 268, 275, 281, 347
Cultus nunc & semper & in secula seculorum, 354

Deprecor — 49, 290, 336
—— prostratus — 290
—— supplex — 290
Diligo — 193, 296

Exoro — 189, 336

Genu posito adoro — 190
Genuflecto — 49
Glorifico — 50, 111, 273
Gratias ago, 49, 282, 338, 346
—— offero — 282
—— profiteor — 337
Gloria in æterna secula seculorum — 50, 192, 276, 290, 302, 354

Honorifico — 282
Honoro — 190
Honorem defero — 282

Honor nunc & semper & in æterna secula seculorum, 354
Imploro — 85
Invoco, 104, 187, 191, 282, 347, 253
Imperium in secula seculorum, 192, 276, 302

Laus nunc & semper & in secula seculorum, 354

Majestas nunc & semper & in secula seculorum, 354

Obsequiis promereor — 341, 347
Obsequor — 347
Orationes offero — 282, 338
Oro — 192, 302, 337, 338

Peto — 338, 347
Postulationes offero — 282
Placeo — 337
Precor — 64, 277, 302
Preces fundo — 336
Precibus insisto — 337
—— exoro — 336
Potentia in secula seculorum, 50

Rogo — 337

Sequor, 104, 187, 191, 282, 346
Satisfacio — 337
Suscipio — 343
Sacrificia offero — 337
Supplicationibus adoro, 307
Supplex deprecor — 290

Veneror — 349

INDEX

INDEX

TO THE
TERMS of ADORATION and PRAISE
Addressed to our LORD JESUS CHRIST.

ἈΓΑΠΑΩ — 46, 79, 125
Αἰνεω, 166, 167, 177, 359
*Αινῶ — 166

Γεραιρω — 355
Γονυπετεω — 176

Δεομαι — 176
Δοξαζω, 13, 20, 23, 53, 54, 56, 356, 363
Δυλευω — 52, 54
*Δοξα κỳ νυν κỳ εἰς ζυμπανίας αἰωνας, 13, 54, 56, 57, 166, 167, 254

Ἐϊχεω καρδιαν ἐνωπιον αὐτῦ — 162
Ἐλπιζω — 363
Ἐυρεπω — 8
Ἐξομολογεομαι — 124
Ἐπιβοαω — 237, 365
Ἐπικαλεομαι — 282, 355
Ἐυλαβεομαι — 52
Ἐυνοια — 56
Ἐυσεβω — 365
Ἐυχαριςεω — 167
Ἐυχομαι — 22, 90

Θεολογω — 372
Θεοσεβω — 163
Θεραπευω — 251
Θρησκευω — 251
*ΘρονὍ· αἰωνιὍ· — 57

Ἱκέτευω — 166

Καρδιαν ἐνωπιον αὐτῦ ἐϊχεω — 162
Κηρυσσω — 369
*Κραϊῶ· εἰς αἰωνας, 56, 359

Λαϊρευω — 52
Λιβανευω — 46

Μελπω — 177
*Μεγαλωσυνη εἰς αἰωνας — 56, 57, 358

Ὁμολογεομαι, 125, 256, 359, 363, 365, 369

Πιςευω, 46, 162, 289, 365, 369, 386
Προσευχομαι — 167
Προσκυνεω, 56, 79, 80, 86, 88, 90, 93, 106, 163, 256, 374, 407
Προσευχαριςεω — 359

Σεβω, 56, 80, 83, 356, 401, 407

Τιμαω — 56, 80, 402
*Τιμη, ἀπο γενεας εἰς γενεαν, 57

Ὑμνεω, 177, 252, 372, 404
Ὑπερθρησκευω — 251

Φοβεω — 52, 99, 163
*Φως κỳ ἱκέτηρια — 166

Ψαλλω — 178

INDEX

INDEX

TO

ATTRIBUTES and EPITHETS, &c.

Afcribed to the HOLY GHOST, *by the Members of the primitive Church, &c. &c.*

A

ADnumerandus Deo uni, tertia perfona — 225
Adorandus — 276
A Filio effufus — 355
A Patre per Filium — 222
——— & Filio infeparatus, 208
Arbiter fidei noftræ — 195
Augens hominem — 123
Aeternus — 299

B

Benignus — 135

C

Colendus — 276, 308
Continens omnia — 109

D

Deductor veritatis — 222
Deus, 105, 208, 275, 308, 344
——— ab utroque Patre & Filio miffus — 135
——— ab omnium principe, 308
——— de Deo — 236
——— omnia continens — 109
——— unus cum Patre & Filio, 169, 204, 225, 273
Dignitate fociatus Patri & Filio, 286
Divinitatis numen tertium, 222
Dominus — 112

E

Effufus a Filio — 355

F

Fidei arbiter — 195
——— in Patre, Filio, & Spiritu Sancto fanctificator, 211

G

Gloria Spiritui Sancto, Patri & Filio — 51
Glorificandus in fecula feculorum 50, 254, 276

H

Honore fociatus Patri & Filio— 286

I

Imperans in fecula feculorum — 254, 276
Infeparatus a Patre & Filio, 208

L

Loquens ex tertia perfona, 209

M

Magnificens — 284
Magnus — 284
Majeftatis nomen tertium, 222
Miffus ab utroque Patre & Filio, Deus — 135
Miffus nobis a Chrifto — 72

N

Natura fanctus non extrinfecus fanctificatus — 288
——— unus cum Patre & Filio, 275
Neque anterior pofteriorve, major aut minor Patre & Filio, 289
Nomen majeftatis tertium, 222
Nutriens hominem — 123

O

Omnia continens — 109

Paracletus

INDEX to Attributes, &c.

P
Paracletus, 142, 169, 210, 223
Perſona Trinitatis tertia — 140, 142, 209, 210
Perſonâ diſtinctus, ſubſtantiâ & naturâ unus cum Patre & Filio — 142

R
Refrigerans — 187

S
Sanctificator fidei eorum qui credunt in Patre, Filio, & Spiritu Sancto — 211
——— omnis quod ſanctum eſt — 254
Sanctus ſemper non aliunde — 288
Sempiternus cum Patre & Filio, 281
Sociatus Patri & Filio honore & dignitate — 286

Spiritus veritatis — 142
Spiritus de Spiritu — 136
Sponſor ſalutis noſtræ — 195
Subſtantiæ unius cum Patre & Filio — 142, 208
Supra omnem æternitatem, 300

T
Tertia Trinitatis Perſona, 140, 142, 209, 210
Tertium nomen majeſtatis, 222
——— numen divinitatis, 222
Tertius a Patre & Filio — 222, 224
——— quâ Perſona, non quâ Deus, 209, 210, 274

U
Unius cum Patre & Filio ſubſtantiæ — 142, 208
Unus cum Patre & Filio Deus — 169, 204, 225, 273, 344

INDEX

INDEX
TO
ATTRIBUTES and EPITHETS, &c.

Ascribed to the HOLY GHOST, *by the Members of the primitive Church, &c. &c.*

A

Ἁγιασμον ἀγγελοις συμφερον, 380
Ἁγιασμα χορηγος — 304
Ἁγιοτης — 304
Ἀδιακριτον — 45
Ἀει ὀν — 289
Αἰτια ζωῆων — 304
Ἀπορροια — 66

Δ

Δια προφητων κεκηρυχ⊙ ἐλευσιν Ἰησου Χριστου — 124
Δἰ ἰου πεφην⊙ — 304
Δοξαζομενον — 54, 56
Δροσερον — 176

Ε

Εἰκων του ὑιου τελειο — 304
Εἰς τω πατρι κ͗ τω ὑιω, 63, 64, 66, 167
Ἐν τρίτη ταξει — 80
Ἐμφιλοχωρον τω Θεω — 360
Ἐνδιαιτωμενον τω Θεω — 360

Ζ

Ζωη τελεια — 304
Ζωντων αἰτια — 304

Θ

Θεος — 63

Λ

Λαλησαν ἐν προφηταις — 128

Ο

Ὁμοουσιον τω πατρι κ͗ τω ὑιω, 289

Π

Πεφην⊙ δἰ ἰου — 304
Πηγη ἀγια — 304
Προκαταγγελον τα παντα — 128
Προσκυνουμενον — 80
Προσωπω ἀπ᾽ ἰδιω ἀποκρινομενον, 85
Προφητικον πνευμα — 80, 124, 128

Σ

Σεβομενον — 80
Σοφια — 129, 140
Συνθρονεις αὐτω κ͗ ὑιω ὑπαρχ⊙, 141
Συνθρονον τω πατρι κ͗ τω ὑιω, 289
Συναιδιον (τω πατρι κ͗ τω ὑιω) — 351
Συμφερον ἁγιασμον ἀγγελοις, 380

Τ

Τελεια ζωη — 304
Τιμωμενον — 80
Τριτον ταξει — 63, 80

Υ

Ὑιου τελειου εἰκων — 304
Ὑποταγεντες αὐτω ἀποστολοι, 44
Ὑπαρξιν ἐκ Θεου ἰχον — 305

Χ

Χορηγ⊙ ἀγιασμου — 304

INDEX

TO

ATTRIBUTES and EPITHETS

Addreſſed to the TRINITY *by the Members of the primitive Church, &c. &c.*

Trinitas Creator — 141
Trinitas adunata — 345
Trinitas ex unitate derivata, 135
—— monarchiæ nihil obſtrepens — 224
—— peccata dimittit, 285
—— ſupra omnia ſecula, 300
—— ſupra omne tempus, 300
—— ſupra omnem æternitatem — 300
Trinitatis natura, una, 109, 142, 275—Celſa — 284
—— ſubſtantia, una, & ſuper omnia, 109, 142, 169, 208, 212, 275
—— ſubſtantia ſola naturá ſancta — 288
—— unitas — 210, 212
In Trinitate nihil majus minuſve dicendum — 289
—— nihil anterius poſteriuſve, 289
—— unitas deitatis — 285
Pater, Filius, & Spiritus Sanctus, tres, non Dii tres, 208, 212
—— inſeparati ab alterutro, 208

Pater, Filius, & Spiritus Sanctus, tres, quà perſonæ, diſtincti, quarum unicuique ſua proprietas, 210, 275
—— diſtincti non diviſi, perſouæ non ſubſtantiæ nomine, 210
—— numerum ſine diviſione patientes — 212
—— nihil diverſitatis habentes naturæ vel ſubſtantiæ, 275
—— tres cohærentes & unam ſubſtantiam habentes, 208
—— æquales & unus — 360
—— tres, unum ſunt, 344, 347
—— unum, ad ſubſtantiæ unitatem — 169
—— tres unius ſubſtantiæ, poteſtatis & ſtatûs — 212
—— tres, crediti unus Deus — 225, 273, 204
—— unus & ſempiternus Deus, 281
—— ſolus Deus — 275
—— unicus Deus — 211, 212
—— in animâ hominis — 290

ΤΡΙΑΣ ἅγια — 289
Τριας ἀμέρως μεριϛη, 170
Τριας ἀχωριϛ⊙ — 289
—— ἐν ᾗ μον⊙· θεος — 289
—— θεια — 347
—— κορυφη τις τε πατρος, τε υιε, κϳ τε πνευματ⊙ ἁγιε
ὁ θεος παντοκρατωρ, 360
—— μακαρια — 289
—— μεθ᾽ ὧν τε θευ δυναμις, 170

Τριας μη μεριζομενη — 304
—— μη ἀπολλοιριϛμενη — 304
—— ὁμοουσιος — 289
—— τελεια, δοξα, αἰδιοτης, κϳ βασιλεια — 304
Πατηρ υιος, κϳ πνευμα ἁγιον κατα δυναμιν, ἐν — 66
—— ἐν — 167
—— ζωοφοροι — 289
ὁις ὑπεδιαγκαλες ἀποϛολοι, 44

INDEX

INDEX

TO THE

Several ARTICLES of the CHRISTIAN FAITH, professed by the Members of the Primitive CHURCH, extracted from their WRITINGS, and inserted in the present Volume.——The Order that of the Athanasian Creed.

THE CATHOLICK FAITH IS THIS, THAT WE WORSHIP ONE GOD IN TRINITY, AND TRINITY IN UNITY.

I.

ONE GOD IN TRINITY.

ONE sole God in a holy and consubstantial Trinity —— —— 288
One Godhead to the Trinity of Father, Son, and Holy Ghost —— —— 289
One God in three Persons —— —— 64, 351
One God alone, the Father, Son, and Holy Ghost —— —— —— 275, 299
God spoke (on the creation of man) from the Unity of the Trinity —— —— 108, 209
Unity of Father, Son, and Holy Ghost 347
Unity from itself deriving a Trinity —— 135, 223
Unity of God, an arrangement of Father, Son, and Holy Ghost into Trinity —— 212

II.

TRINITY IN UNITY.

A Trinity in Unity —— —— 360, 410
The Trinity, one God who alone is holy 288

A Trinity in which refides the power of God — 170
The Three Perfons, one God — 141, 344.
Father, Son, and Holy Ghoft, one God 63, 64, 66, 169, 208, 211, 225, 272, 304, 345, 347

III.

WORSHIP TO THE TRINITY.

To the Father, with the Son and the Holy Ghoft, are afcribed all honour, glory, power, praife, majefty, worfhip, and adoration, now and for ever and ever. — 50, 57, 166, 276, 354, 358, 359
To the Father, with the Son in the Holy Ghoft, is afcribed glory now and to all fucceeding ages — 54
Praife and thankfgiving addreffed to Father, Son, and Holy Ghoft, one — 79, 166
A prayer addreffed to the Father, who, with the Son, ruleth in the power of the Holy Ghoft — 112
Worfhip and adoration, addreffed not to the creature, but only to the Father, the Son, and the Holy Ghoft — 80, 276
An invocation to the Trinity of Father, Son, and Holy Ghoft — 347

NOT CONFOUNDING THE PERSONS; FOR THERE IS ONE PERSON OF THE FATHER; ANOTHER OF THE SON; AND ANOTHER OF THE HOLY GHOST.

IV.

DISTINCTION OF PERSONS.

Among thefe who are one God, there is a diftinction — 64

Diftinct

INDEX to the Articles, &c.

Diftinct perfonality of Father, Son, and Holy Ghoft	170, 211, 284, 303, 344
The Three Perfons accurately diftinguifhed	84
All terms of number, when applied to Father, Son, and Holy Ghoft, refer to their perfonal diftinction	210
Diftinct operations in the creation of man afcribed to the Father, Son, and Holy Ghoft	123
Refpective peculiars to Father, Son, and Holy Ghoft, though in nature and fubftance one	274, 368
Three, but not in dignity, fubftance, or power	212

V.

PERSON OF THE FATHER.

The Father the firft perfon of a Trinity, which is one God	209
The Father in perfon, another from the Son and Holy Ghoft	141
The Father, Son, and Holy Ghoft, three, which are one God	225
The Father one of three witneffes, the Father, the Son, and the Holy Ghoft	195
The Father diftinct from the Son and Holy Ghoft, not as God, but as the Father	208
Diftinct operations afcribed to Father, Son, and Holy Ghoft	128, 275
The terms *one and another* do not divide the fubftance of the Godhead, but diftinguifh the perfon of the Father from that of the Son	210, 212, 223
The Holy Ghoft fpeaks concerning the Son, either from his own perfon, or the perfon of the Father	84
The Holy Ghoft has diftinguifhed between the Father and Son	107, 108

Father

Father and Son two persons, though in Godhead one —— —— 250, 251, 352

VI.

PERSON OF THE SON.

The Son the second person of a Trinity, which is one God —— ——	209
The Son in the second place ——	80
The Son in person second to the Father	208, 250
The Son a distinct person from the Father	170, 225, 284, 288, 344
The Son and Father one God, two persons	352, 372
The Son to whom the Father addressed himself on the creation of man ——	208
The Holy Ghost has distinguished between the Father and the Son ——	84, 107, 209
The Son distinguished in person, though not divided in Godhead from the Father by the terms *one and another* ——	210, 212, 223, 250
The Son, though one with the Father in Godhead, yet not the Father ——	141
The WORD a person and the Son ——	215, 380, 405
Distinct operations ascribed to Father and Son —— —— ——	123, 175
The Son the second of three witnesses, Father, Son, and Holy Ghost ——	195

VII.

PERSON OF THE HOLY GHOST.

The Holy Ghost the third person in the Godhead —— —— ——	209, 221
The Holy Ghost a third from the Father and the Son —— ——	80, 223, 225
The Holy Ghost the third of three witnesses, Father, Son, and Holy Ghost	195

The

INDEX to the Articles, &c. 455

The Holy Ghost speaks in the third person concerning the Father and the Son	84, 209
Distinct operations of the Holy Ghost from those of the Father and the Son	123, 176, 309, 303, 342, 380
Father, Son, and Holy Ghost, three distinct persons	170, 225, 284, 288
The Holy Ghost another from the Father and the Son, with whom he is one God	141
Distinguished in person, but not divided in substance from the Father and the Son by the terms *one and another*	210, 212, 236
The Holy Ghost a third from the Father and the Son, with whom he is one indivisible substance	208

NOR DIVIDING THE SUBSTANCE: FOR THE GODHEAD OF THE FATHER, AND OF THE SON, AND OF THE HOLY GHOST, IS ALL ONE; THE GLORY EQUAL, THE MAJESTY COETERNAL. SUCH AS THE FATHER IS, SUCH IS THE SON, AND SUCH IS THE HOLY GHOST. THE FATHER IS GOD, THE SON IS GOD, AND THE HOLY GHOST IS GOD; AND YET THEY ARE NOT THREE GODS, BUT ONE GOD.

VIII.

THE GODHEAD OF THE FATHER, SON, AND HOLY GHOST, ONE AND INDIVISIBLE.

The Godhead one	112, 138, 221, 352, 360
The Substance of the Trinity one, inseparable and indivisible	169, 274, 288, 289, 304
The nature of God indivisible	293
A Trinity indivisible	170
One undivided substance of Father, Son, and Holy Ghost, three persons, and one God	208, 211, 272

The

The nature and one substance of a Trinity of Father, Son, and Holy Ghost, inferred from the Godhead of each, and the unity of the Godhead — 199, &c.
These three, Father, Son, and Holy Ghost, one in the unity of substance — 169, 211
The Spirit, the Son, and the Father, one 164
One God alone, Father, Son, and Holy Ghost — 275
Father, Son, and Holy Ghost, three, of one substance, one dignity, and one power — 212
The substance not divided, though the persons are distinguished by the terms *one and another* — 210
The substance and nature of the Trinity, of Father, Son, and Holy Ghost, but one — 141
To this Trinity of Father, Son, and Holy Ghost, but one fountain of Godhead — 141, 289

IX.

THE GLORY EQUAL, the MAJESTY COETERNAL.

In this Trinity none is afore or after other, none is greater or less than another. — 289
Father, Son, and Holy Ghost, three, of one dignity and power — 212
Father, Son, and Holy Ghost, one, whose is the glory and eternity — 166
A perfect Trinity, neither in glory, eternity, nor dominion divided from itself 304
The Holy Ghost joined with the Father and the Son in honour and dignity — 286
The Son and Holy Ghost assessors with the Father on his throne — 289
Father, Son, and Holy Ghost, coeternal and of omnipotent majesty — 284

THE

INDEX to the Articles, &c.

X.

THE FATHER, GOD.

The Godhead of the Father and his Attributes	*in almost every page.*

XI.

THE SON GOD, SUCH AS, AND OF ONE SUBSTANCE WITH THE FATHER.

God, *(so denominated without epithets)*	*in almost every page.*
The only God	137, 138, 176, 236, 294
God over all	26, 30, 32, 108, 237, 364
God supreme	261
The Almighty God	84, 113, 213, 255, 287, 288
God and Lord	93, 106, 108, 110
The true God	137, 139, 294
God on high	208
God most high	213
The God of all men	162
The God of every creature	293
The God of the internal faculties	308
I AM	213, 217, 251
The God who spoke with Moses and the patriarchs	80, 86, 112, 165
The adorable God	88, 90, 93
The merciful God	156, 165, 368
Forgiving sins and supporting by his grace	31, 54
The Creatour of angels	380
The Creatour of Man	210
The Creatour of the world	88, 104, 111, 121, 286, 354, 375

M m m The

INDEX to the Articles, &c.

The Maker and Lord of the world	276, 344, 353
The Lord of the whole earth, and Creatour of the Sun	215
Swaying the universe	255
The Lord of hosts and king of glory	83, 84
The Lord of majesty	253, 273, 348
The one Lord	107, 287
The Inſtructor of men and angels	79, 386
Of unſpeakable glory	113
Heavenly King	470
Immortal	44, 159, 207, 298, 303, 351
Immenſe	297
Inviſible	21, 22, 112, 203, 297, 298
Incorporeal	44, 300
Impalpable	21, 22, 112
Impaſſive	21, 22, 112, 298
Incomprehenſible	113, 258, 297
Infinite	300
Preſent at once to all infinity	261, 300
Previous to his incarnation, able to have come in ſplendour inſtead of the humility of a human body	8, 15, 113
Eternally pre-exiſtent to the creation	8, 15, 17, 86, 88, 104, 113, 129
Without commencement	185, 351
Eternal King	82, 110, 191
Eternal	21, 44, 54, 57, 82, 86, 289, 294, 300, 303, 304, 351, 355, 407
Eternally God in ſubſtance	369
Coeternal with the Father and the Holy Ghoſt	284, 351, 370
Coexiſting with the Father and the Holy Ghoſt	104, 185
Not inferiour to the Father	108

Equal

INDEX to the Articles, &c. 459

Equal with the Father	259, 287, 297, 298
Of one and the same omnipotence with the Father	287
Not another God from the Father	212, 223
With the Father one and the same God	30, 169, 187
One with the Father	27, 30, 32, 63, 104, 112, 206, 212, 223, 251
One with the Father and the Holy Ghost	63, 108
In nature and in substance not different from the Father and the Holy Ghost	275
Of one substance with the Father	121, 206, 212, 275, 288, 293, 294, 295, 300
In essence and substance one with the Father, and from him indivisible	297
Indivisible or inseparable from the Father	208, 281, 294, 300, 373
The divine word one with the Father of the universe	360
The Son ruling with the Father in the power of the Holy Ghost the only one God	112
Worshipped by prayer	49, 90, 167, 177, 237, 243, 253, 277, 289, 302, 336, 337, 338, 351, 353, 354, 355, 356
Worshipped by thanksgiving	49, 336, 338, 346
Worshipped by benediction	52, 53, 362
Worshipped by doxology	50, 54, 56, 166, 192, 252, 254, 276, 290, 302, 353, 354, 371

M m m 2   Worship

INDEX to the Articles, &c.

Worship professed, prescribed, and recorded	46, 59, 79, 80, 83, 85, 90, 104, 106, 114, 162, 187, 188, 189, 190, 191, 251, 256, 273, 282, 343, 347, 374, 401, 404, 407

XII.

THE HOLY GHOST, GOD, SUCH AS, AND OF ONE SUBSTANCE WITH THE FATHER AND THE SON.

God	63, 105, 109, 208, 275, 359, 359
God containing all things	108
Mighty and majestic	284
Eternal	288
Reigning for ever and ever	254, 276
Who spoke by the prophets	80, 124, 128
Perfect life	304
The cause of life in those who live	304
By nature and not acquisition holy	288
The sanctifier of whatever is holy	254
The sanctifier of angels	380
The sanctifier of their faith who believe in the Father, and in the Son, and in the Holy Ghost	211
Fountain of sanctity, and author of sanctification	304
With the Father and the Son, eternal	280, 289, 300, 351
From the Father and the Son, inseparable	111
In dignity not inferiour to the Father	45, 360
In dignity conjoined with Father and Son	236
In substance and nature one with the Father and the Son	286, 142, 275

Of one-substance with the Father and the Son — 63, 64, 66, 167, 208, 289
With the Father and the Son, one God — 137, 169, 204, 225, 273, 344,
The nourisher and increaser of man — 123
The bringer down and revealer of all truth — 224
Worship and adoration addressed to the Holy Ghost — 254, 289, 348, 80

XIII.

EACH BY HIMSELF GOD.

The Father is God
The Son is God
The Holy Ghost is God
And each of them is God — 105, 141, 208, 284

XIV.

THEY ARE NOT THREE GODS, BUT ONE GOD.

Father, Son, and Holy-Ghost not three Gods — 108, 208, 210, 212
Father, Son, and Holy Ghost one sole God — 108, 211, 225, 272, 275, 280,

See also N°. I, II, VIII, IX. — 285, 289

THE FATHER IS MADE OF NONE, NEITHER CREATED NOR BEGOTTEN. THE SON IS OF THE FATHER ALONE, NEITHER MADE NOR CREATED, BUT BEGOTTEN. THE HOLY GHOST IS OF THE FATHER AND THE SON, NEITHER MADE NOR CREATED, NOR BEGOTTEN, BUT PROCEEDING.

XV.

XV.

**THE FATHER NOT MADE NOR BEGOT-
TEN.**

Not created —— 276, & *passim.*
The unbegotten Father —— 79, 293, 377,
& *passim.*
Self-exiftent —— 276, & *passim.*

XVI.

**THE SON OF THE FATHER ALONE,
NOT MADE BUT BEGOTTEN.**

Not made —— 351, 373
Not a creature, but by nature eternally
generated of the Father himfelf —— 294
Begotten of the Father, and of one fub-
ftance with him, but different from cre-
ated fubftance —— 293, 376
Not created nor adopted, but by nature
the eternal and infeparable Son, and
generated of the Father himfelf —— 294
Not created, being with the Father and
the Holy Ghoft diftinguifhed from the
creature —— 276
Not made, but of one fubftance with the
Father —— 352, 359
The true Son of the God of all nature —— 256
The only begotten Son of God —— 44, 48, 113, &c.
Begotten of the Father of the univerfe —— 87
Born of the very fubftance of God —— 294
From no other fource than the fubftance
of the Father —— 108, 222

XVII.

**THE HOLY GHOST OF THE FATHER
AND THE SON, NOT MADE BUT PRO-
CEEDING.**

Not created, but with the Father and the
Son diftinguifhed from the creature 276

Having

INDEX to the Articles, &c.

Having his subsistence of God ——— 303
Proceeding, God of God, not separated — 236
Appearing manifest through the Son — 304
Poured forth by the Son ——— 355
From no other source than the Father, by the Son ——— ——— ——— 222

WE ARE ALSO INSTRUCTED THAT OUR LORD JESUS CHRIST IS PERFECT GOD AND PERFECT MAN; GOD OF THE SUBSTANCE OF HIS FATHER, BEGOTTEN BEFORE THE WORLDS; AND MAN OF THE SUBSTANCE OF HIS MOTHER BORN IN THE WORLD; AND THAT THE GODHEAD AND MANHOOD, WITHOUT CONFUSION, IN THE UNITY OF HIS PERSON CONSTITUTE ONE CHRIST.

XVIII.

PERFECT GODHEAD OF CHRIST.

The man Christ full of the pure and perfect Godhead ——— ——— 352

See also Nº XI, XXI, XXIII, &c. &c.

XIX.

GOD OF THE SUBSTANCE OF HIS FATHER.

God of the substance of the Father — 102, 121, 357
Son of God, and God from the unity of substance ——— ——— 206
The Son, from no other source than the substance of the Father ——— 222
Generated of the Father himself, and of the same identical substance ——— 294

The Son generated of the Father as one
  flame by another — — 97
Eternal image of the Father — 303
The WORD, God, of one substance with
  the Father — — 288
In essence and substance one with the Fa-
  ther — — — 297
Of one nature with the Father — 176, 274
The Son inseparable from the Father 64, 208, 281,
  294, 297, 374
The Father and Son one — — 103, 104
The WORD the Son of the Father, and
  came forth from him — — 211
The only begotten Son of the Father 42, 113, 299
The only begotten had a glorious genera-
  tion from the most high Father — 110
The Son not another God from the Fa-
  ther — — — 212
God begotten of the Father and of his
  substance — — 293
The true Son of the true Father, perfect
  of him who is perfect, &c. — 303
By the spirit the Son of God — 267
As concerning the spirit, of God — 350
God of God, one of one, eternal, perfect,
  and incorruptible Son of the eternal,
  perfect, and incorruptible Father — 22, 303
Of, but not beneath, the Father — 108

XX.

BEGOTTEN BEFORE THE WORLDS.

Our God Jesus Christ before ages the only
  begotten Son and WORD — — 44
Begotten of the Father before all ages 355, 386
The WORD begotten before all things 129
Begotten of the Father before every crea-
  ture — — — 211, 286
Pre-existent to all time as God — 185

The

INDEX to the Articles, &c. 465

The WORD and God before all ages.	356
Before the appointment of time	15
Did not then commence being when made man, but was the Son co-exiftent with the Father from the beginning	185
The Son more antient than the world, it being himfelf, the Son and the Holy Ghoft, to whom the Father applies the plural terms *we* and *us*, when fpeaking on the fubject of creation	15, 17, 88, 210
The only begotten Son reigns together with the Father from uncommenced to indeterminable ages	355
The only begotten Son eternal and from all eternity in fubftance God	294, 358

XXI.

PERFECT MANHOOD.

A man, born and fuffering in reality, not in appearance only	82, 286
The Son of God came in the flefh	15
God clothed in the flefh	21, 268, 357
The WORD made flefh	79, 100
Man in union with God	85
Man and the Son of Man	299
The WORD becoming man, and called Jefus Chrift	95
The incarnate WORD, a man defpifed and bowing down even to death	110
The body of Jefus united with the WORD	260
Of a twofold nature, God and the man Jefus	207
God put on Man	334, 364
God put on human flefh, and the man Chrift is full of the pure and perfect Godhead	352
God became incarnate, and making himfelf of no reputation was made man	285

N n n

Under the dominion of death	269
The blood of God the Son	157, 176
God in the fashion of a man our likeness	166
By nature invisible and equal with God, assumed flesh and the fashion of a man	297
God born in the form of a man	99, 297
The Maker of the world in latter times made man	111
God submitted to be born and to be made man	89, 106, 121, 257, 298, 355
Man and God, son of man and son of God	211, 253
The incomprehensible, invisible, and impassive WORD took upon him the comprehensible, visible, and infirm nature of man	112
The immortal God assumed a mortal body and an human soul	159
Mortal at once and immortal	160, 298
God assumed the perfect nature of the human body, together with the infirmities incident to it	243
Thou hast suffered, and thyself experienced the weakness of the flesh!	167

XXII.

MAN OF THE SUBSTANCE OF HIS MOTHER.

Made man of the Virgin Mary	44
Fashioned into flesh in the womb of a virgin, and born man	206
Of Mary, subject to sufferings	22
Born man of a Virgin	104, 110, 124
Incarnate of a virgin	122
Conceived in the womb of a mother	193
As concerning the flesh of the race of David	23, 30, 350
Born of a woman	353

Assumed

Assumed the human substance from the
  virgin's womb ——— ——— 269, 286
By the flesh the son of man — ——— 267
Clothed in the flesh of Mary, the WORD
  came forth into the world — ——— 268, 299
Assumed a body of the virgin by the Holy
  Ghost ——— ——— ——— 286
God the Son of God, taking flesh of a vir-
  gin, was born man the son of man — 211
Made flesh, being born of a Virgin Mary 354
Took manhood of Mary ——— ——— 288
Took flesh of a virgin, and thus, the Holy
  Ghost co-operating, became a man mixt
  with God ——— ——— ——— 342
Took a body of a virgin, in which the
  entire fulness of the Godhead dwells,
  and therefore both God and man ——— 369

XXIII.

GOD AND MAN ONE CHRIST, NOT BY
CONFUSION OF SUBSTANCE, BUT IN
UNITY OF PERSON.

The Christ the mighty God, and man
  formed in the womb ——— ——— 90

God and man ——— ——— { 88, 93, 138, 144, 156, 160, 162, 193, 206, 267, 342, 350, 353, 356, 369, 371

In himself united, God, and man born of
  a virgin ——— ——— 104, 122
The son of man and the son of God — 28, 267
This crucified person explicitly declared
  to be both man and the adorable God 93
Not a man only, but also God one with
  the Father ——— ——— ——— 30

N n n 2   Fleshly

INDEX to the Articles, &c.

Fleshly and spiritual, created and not created, of Mary and of God, subject to sufferings and then impassive, God in man ——— 22
Incorporeal in a body, exempt from sufferings in a body obnoxious to them, immortal in a mortal body, life in corruption ——— 44, 112, 297, 298
God and man united in his person ——— 122
Man in the flesh, in spirit one with the Father ——— 21
The Spirit of Christ antecedent to time, the flesh not ——— 185
Of two substances, one from above, another assumed of the virgin's womb ——— 269
Of two substances, one of Mary, seen, the other Godhead, revealed ——— 268
God of the substance of the Father, eternal, man of the substance of his mother 288
By the spirit the son of God, by the flesh the Son of man, the Christ, both God and man ——— 267, 350
The Christ a man full of the pure and perfect Godhead ——— 352
United his substance to the work of his own hands ——— 185
Not mere man, but God the WORD and man ——— 253
As flesh comprehensible, incomprehensible as God ——— 257
Both God and man, the manhood in which the fulness of the Godhead had dwelt bodily, being taken immutably into and united with the Godhead ——— 369
In the Christ the two natures of spirit and flesh preserve their distinct functions ——— 207
Mortal as concerning the flesh ——— 384
Obedient to the Father as concerning the flesh ——— 44

Of

INDEX to the Articles, &c. 469

Of a double nature, not confused, but
 united in his person, God and the man
 Jesus ——— 207
Christ died inasmuch as he was man and
 the son of man, not as he was Spirit and
 the WORD, for not his divine but his
 human nature was liable to sorrow 207
The flesh not God, but he who was born
 in the flesh ——— 207
Sorrowful in his human but not in his divine nature, which is exempt from paffions ——— 243
The manhood assumed by the WORD was
 born, and died, whilst the Godhead remained exempt from all infirmity and
 sufferings ——— 266
His manhood discriminated by imbecility,
 his Godhead by miracles and the adoration of angels 350
As concerning the flesh suffers, as the
 WORD, which is Christ as concerning
 the spirit, incorrupt ——— 269
The WORD speaking in a body, unchanged
 by his union with flesh, still preserves
 the substance of God, and remains exempt from the sufferings inflicted on
 the man ——— 159
The WORD which was God, receiving no
 pollution nor derogation from having
 taken flesh, is still God in the fashion
 of man, and though clothed in flesh,
 God uncontaminated 160, 165, 166,
The divinity of the WORD not impaired 357
 by the assumption of our passive nature 370
The man because of sufferings taken into
 the WORD, man and the WORD ——— 110
The manhood, on account of his death
 and sufferings, taken into and united
 with the Godhead in his person ——— 260
Eternity conferred upon his manhood because of its assumption into his Godhead ——— ——— ——— 286, 298

Exalted

INDEX to the Articles, &c.

Exalted and glorified becaufe of death in his manhood only, his Godhead, which is incapable of death, not admitting of any acceffion to his perfect glory —— 299
As man he may have a feeling of our infirmities, as God have mercy upon them 121

HE SUFFERED FOR OUR SALVATION, AROSE FROM THE DEAD, ASCENDED INTO HEAVEN, WHENCE HE SHALL RETURN TO JUDGE THE QUICK AND THE DEAD.

XXIV.

OUR SALVATION THE END OF HIS INCARNATION AND SUFFERINGS.

The Lord God born of woman on our account, and thus in himfelf uniting God and man, a mediator between both —— 353
United man and God in his perfon, that in confequence of the double relation he might become a proper mediator to reconcile man to God —— —— 121
Put on man, that as a mediator he might conduct man to God —— —— 334
The WORD taking manhood fubftituted for Adam, in whom we fell, as a perfect Father from whom we fhall again inherit what had been forfeited before —— 122
The Lord defcended to carry the burden of our infirmities, he who is by nature invifible affumed for our fake a vifible form —— —— —— 21, 297
The merciful Lord made man for our fake, and to the renewal of eternal life —— 22, 138
The tenderly merciful God defirous of man's falvation made himfelf of no reputation, but for our fake affumed the debafement of the human form —— 124, 156, 193

One

INDEX to the Articles, &c. 471

One phyſician both earthly and ſpiritual, made man and a partaker of our paſſions, that he might effect our cure	22, 79
Took manhood, and came in the fleſh, that he might aboliſh death and ſin	15, 364
Took manhood for the deſtruction of ſin and the ſalvation of his own work	121
The WORD united to a human body, to emancipate man and conquer death	85
For us made ſubject to ſufferings, and undergoing all things that we might be ſaved	21, 357
The Lord Jeſus, whoſe blood was given for us, ſuffered for our ſouls that we may live in him, for the ſalvation of all ſuch as ſhall be ſaved, the righteous for the ungodly	8, 15, 52, 56
For our ſake God, aſſuming a paſſive nature, made man, and humbling himſelf even to death	298, 370
For the redemption of mankind, and the love he bore to his creature, born a man and ſuffered death upon a croſs	94, 104
Chriſt ſuffering in our ſtead is our ſacrifice, and took away the bondage to death	113, 269
God born in the faſhion of a man, in our likeneſs ſuffering for our ſins and bearing our infirmities, offered his immaculate body a ſacrifice to God	298

AROSE, ASCENDED, AND SHALL RETURN TO JUDGE AND TO REWARD.

Aroſe for our ſake	113
Raiſed his own body from the grave	112, 342
Aroſe and was taken into heaven	286
Aſcended into heaven, and ſhall again appear on earth	86
Aſcended into heaven, again to return with glory	82

He

INDEX to the Articles, &c.

He shall come again, and they who have pierced him shall bewail —— ——	88
Arose, was assumed into heaven in the flesh, shall again return in glory ——	124
Arising from the dead, and being received up into glory, will come again the Saviour and Judge of all who shall be saved and judged —— ——	104
Raised, taken into heaven, sitteth at the right hand of the Father, whence he shall come again to judge the quick and the dead —— —— ——	211
We must all stand before the judgment-seat of Christ, and each render an account for himself —— —— ——	52
Christ the mighty God coming in the clouds, the Judge of all men ——	110, 188
Let us by obedience conciliate Christ our God and our Judge —— ——	341
Heaven is due from Christ to those who suffer for him, and awarded by him to those who love him —— ——	53, 124
He will deal out the reward of glory in proportion to the degree of our attachment to him ——	347
He will raise up all flesh, and every tongue shall confess to him; he will judge righteously, the wicked he will send into eternal fire, but the righteous he will of his grace invest with life incorruptible and with eternal glory ——	124

www.ingramcontent.com/pod-product-compliance
Lightning Source LLC
Chambersburg PA
CBHW051843300426
44117CB00006B/251